Windows® Administration Resource Kit:
# Productivity Solutions for IT Professionals

D1567932

*Dan Holme*

PUBLISHED BY
Microsoft Press
A Division of Microsoft Corporation
One Microsoft Way
Redmond, Washington 98052-6399

Library of Congress Control Number: 2007941090

Printed and bound in the United States of America.

1 2 3 4 5 6 7 8 9   QWT   3 2 1 0 9 8

Distributed in Canada by H.B. Fenn and Company Ltd.

A CIP catalogue record for this book is available from the British Library.

Microsoft Press books are available through booksellers and distributors worldwide. For further information about international editions, contact your local Microsoft Corporation office or contact Microsoft Press International directly at fax (425) 936-7329. Visit our Web site at www.microsoft.com/mspress. Send comments to rkinput@microsoft.com.

Microsoft, Microsoft Press, Active Directory, ActiveX, Excel, Expression, FrontPage, Groove, Internet Explorer, MSDN, MSN, Outlook, PowerPoint, SharePoint, SQL Server, Visio, Visual Basic, Visual Studio, Windows, Windows Media, Windows NT, Windows PowerShell, Windows Server, and Windows Vista are either registered trademarks or trademarks of Microsoft Corporation in the United States and/or other countries. Other product and company names mentioned herein may be the trademarks of their respective owners.

The example companies, organizations, products, domain names, e-mail addresses, logos, people, places, and events depicted herein are fictitious. No association with any real company, organization, product, domain name, e-mail address, logo, person, place, or event is intended or should be inferred.

**Acquisitions Editor:** Martin DelRe
**Developmental Editor:** Karen Szall
**Project Editor:** Melissa von Tschudi-Sutton
**Project Management:** Publishing.Com
**Compositor:** Curtis Philips
**Copy Editor:** Roger LeBlanc

Body Part No. X14-38533

**Technical Reviewer:** Rozanne Whalen; Technical Review services provided by Content Master, a member of CM Group, Ltd.
**Proofreader:** Teresa Barensfeld
**Indexer:** Potomac Indexing, LLC: Julie Kawabata & Seth Maislin
**Cover:** Design by Tom Draper Design; Illustration by Todd Daman

*This book is dedicated to my incredible clients,*
*who have provided a decade-plus of learning,*
*a lifetime of experiences, and a wealth of knowledge.*
*This book is to them, but it is also from them, through me,*
*to you, the community of Windows administrators.*

# About the Author

**Dan Holme** is a graduate of Yale University and the Thunderbird School of Global Management. He has spent over a decade as a consultant and trainer, delivering solutions to tens of thousands of IT professionals from the most prestigious organizations and corporations around the world. Dan's company, Intelliem, specializes in boosting the productivity of IT professionals and end users by creating advanced, customized solutions that integrate clients' specific design and configuration into productivity-focused tools, training, and knowledge management services.

Dan is also a contributing editor for *Windows IT Pro* magazine, a Microsoft MVP (Microsoft Office SharePoint Server), and the community lead of OfficeSharePointPro.com. From his base in beautiful Maui, Dan travels around the globe supporting customers and delivering Windows technologies training. Immediately following the release of this resource kit, he will be preparing for the Beijing Olympic Games as the Windows Technologies Consultant for NBC television, a role he also played in Torino in 2006.

# Acknowledgments

The book you hold in your hands has a long history shaped by the many wonderful people who've helped me along the way.

First, there are my clients—you slave-driving, insane, and awe-inspiring friends who trust me to guide you and your enterprise, and who share your expertise and experience with me. Without you, there'd be no body of knowledge, solutions, and experience from which to create this resource kit. Thank you for making my career one of constant learning. Thank you for your business and your faith in me. Thank you for providing me many opportunities of a lifetime.

Next, there are my colleagues—you über-crazy, über-guru guys and gals who blow me away with your brains and brawn. Jeremy, Don, Darren, Mark, Rhonda, Derek, Alan, Gil, Sean, Guido, Jim, Brian, Steve, Richard, Joel, Tom, and I'm *so* sorry if I missed someone. . . . Thanks for setting the bar so high and encouraging me to reach it!

Then, there are the incredible folks at Microsoft Press. Starting with Martin Del Re. You saw me presenting solutions-based content back in 2003 and said, "Someday we need to write this stuff down," and you stuck by me all the way. We made it! Karen Szall, I cashed in my entire bank of credits on this project, and I owe you the next one! Melissa von Tschudi-Sutton, you came on board this big train without ever having worked with me before, and you gracefully extracted more than 650 pages of content and dozens of scripts in a period of just 10 weeks. There aren't enough words to thank you, Melissa! And, of course, Curtis Philips, Rozanne Whalen, Roger LeBlanc, and Teresa Barensfeld—you tackled this new type of resource kit with amazing skill. This project was mammoth, and it could not have happened without each of you. I am so lucky to have worked with you!

Finally, and most importantly, to my friends and family: Lyman, Maddie, Mom and Dad, Bob and Joni, Stan and Marylyn, Julie, Joe, and the entire gang in Maui and Phoenix. Your patience and support and love have been the fuel in my fire. Thank you for cheering me on, picking me up, and waiting for me at the finish line. I owe you all a lot of quality time when this project is finished. You have taught me the meaning of ohana! Mahalo!

# Contents at a Glance

# Table of Contents

**What do you think of this book? We want to hear from you!**

Microsoft is interested in hearing your feedback so we can continually improve our books and learning
resources for you. To participate in a brief online survey, please visit:

**www.microsoft.com/learning/booksurvey/**

**What do you think of this book? We want to hear from you!**

Microsoft is interested in hearing your feedback so we can continually improve our books and learning resources for you. To participate in a brief online survey, please visit:

**www.microsoft.com/learning/booksurvey/**

# Introduction

Welcome to the *Windows Administration Resource Kit: Productivity Solutions for IT Professionals!*

The *Windows Administration Resource Kit* is a treasure trove of solutions designed to help you implement Microsoft Windows technologies to solve real business problems. Whereas most resource kits have focused on an individual product or feature and have drilled down deep to explore the internals of the technology, this resource kit takes an entirely different angle. In this resource kit, we look at how to align Windows technologies with your business objectives.

If this sounds like something that you'd normally have to hire a consultant to do, that's right! The impetus behind this book was the many years I've spent as a consultant and trainer helping clients overcome business and technical challenges. Many times I've presented solutions to clients and have been asked, "Is there a book about this stuff?" Well, now there is! I like to think of this as "Windows Consultant in a Box." Or in a book, I guess.

This book addresses dozens of the kinds of problems that I've seen fought by enterprises large and small. My goal is to help you work SMART. That's an acronym I coined at Intelliem. It means

- Secure
- Managed
- Agile
- Rapid
- Trustworthy

To get SMART, and to solve these problems, we need more than the internal details of a single technology. We need, instead, to do one or more of the following:

- Assemble several technologies, putting the pieces together in just the right way to achieve the desired outcome.
- Automate repetitive steps with scripts.
- Align technologies with business processes through workflows and provisioning.
- Integrate third-party utilities.
- Work around limitations of Windows' out-of-box features and administrative tools.

If those last two bullets surprised you, let me tell you they surprised me, too! I'm actually going to be able to share with you, in black and white, examples of scenarios that you simply cannot address without acknowledging, and then working around, limitations of Windows. If you appreciate this kind of candor from Microsoft, let the folks at Microsoft Press know!

I think that the approach we're taking in this resource kit is an extremely useful complement to the documentation and resources Microsoft provides about its technologies. It puts the technologies into the context of the real world!

Speaking of the real world, what good could these solutions be if they applied only to Windows Server 2008?

> **Important**   Most solutions in this resource kit are designed to apply in a real-world, mixed environment consisting of Windows XP SP2 or later, Windows Vista, Windows Server 2003 SP2 or later, and Windows Server 2008.

"Solutions" is what this resource kit is all about. Some solutions are simple. Some are quite complex. Some solutions build upon other solutions. Some stand alone. Many of the solutions consist of guidance—the kind of guidance you'd receive from a consultant, pointing you to best practices and helping you to align technology and business. Other solutions consist of scripts.

The scripts that I've provided on the companion media are not like the tools included with previous Windows resource kits. These are not executable utilities that perform one specific task. Most are meta-tools that perform provisioning and automation tasks. They're designed to teach you how to raise the level of your administrative productivity. To achieve that goal, I've written the vast majority of tools as scripts, in VBScript. So you'll be able to open, read, and customize the scripts! If you're not familiar with VBScript, you'll find that most scripts require only very simple configuration changes to work in your environment. If you're an experienced scripter, you'll be able to extend the tools to create solutions that are even more powerful and more customized to your requirements.

The scripts, and the solutions, don't end on the last page of this book. Another marked departure from previous Windows Resource Kits is the community site that I'm creating to support the resource kit: *www.intelliem.com/resourcekit*. There you'll find corrections, discussions, revisions, and entirely new solutions provided by the community of IT professionals who read this book.

You'll find out more about all of this in Solution Collection 1. Let me just finish this by saying "thank you" for all the work you do to support your organization with Windows technologies. I know it's not always easy—I'm in the trenches, too. I appreciate the time you'll take to read, interpret, customize, and implement the solutions I'm sharing with you. And I hope you'll share your knowledge and experience with other readers on the resource kit Web site. We're in it together, and I look forward to bringing the collective knowledge of the thousands of IT professionals I've worked with over the years together to help us do it smarter!

# Document Conventions

The following conventions are used in this book to highlight special features or usage.

## Reader Aids

The following reader aids are used throughout this book to point out useful details:

| Reader Aid | Meaning |
|---|---|
| Note | Underscores the importance of a specific concept, or highlights a special case that might not apply to every situation. |
| Important | Calls attention to essential information that should not be disregarded. |
| Caution | Highlights a problematic issue or a security concern. |
| Best Practice | Delivers advice for strategies and techniques that optimize the efficiency or security of the technology. |
| Guidance | Summarizes a discussion to provide the "bottom line." |

## Command-Line Examples

The following style conventions are used in documenting command-line examples throughout this book:

| Style | Meaning |
|---|---|
| **Bold font** | Used to indicate user input (characters that you type exactly as shown). |
| *Italic font* | Used to indicate variables for which you need to supply a specific value (for example *file_name* can refer to any valid file name). |
| Monospace font | Used for code samples and command-line output. |
| %SystemRoot% | Used for environment variables. |

# System Requirements

The scripts provided on the companion media have been fully tested against Windows Server 2008. Most are compatible with Windows Server 2003 SP2 or later, Windows XP SP2 or later, and Windows Vista, and where there are known limitations I have made notes in the resource kit text or in the script itself.

# Web-Based Content

In addition to the content that is included in the resource kit and on the companion media, additional bonus content is available at *http://www.intelliem.com/resourcekit*.

# Find Additional Content Online

As new or updated material becomes available that complements your book, it will be posted online on the Microsoft Press Online Developer Tools Web site. The type of material you might find includes updates to book content, articles, links to companion content, errata, sample chapters, and more. This Web site will be available soon at *www.microsoft.com/learning/books/online/developer* and will be updated periodically.

# Companion Media

The companion CD is loaded with useful tools and links to help you with your Windows Server 2008 installation. The CD includes:

- **Complete eBook**. An electronic version of *Windows Administration Resource Kit: Productivity Solutions for IT Professionals* in PDF format.

- **Scripts**. More than 75 sample scripts to help you automate system administration tasks.

- **Tools**. Many links to tools for IIS, PowerShell, System Center Data Operations, and more that you can put to use right away.

- **Product Information**. Links to information about the features and capabilities of Windows Server 2008 as well as product guides to help you optimize Windows administration in your enterprise.

- **Resources**. Links to whitepapers, guides, webcasts, newsgroups, and more to help you use and troubleshoot the features of Windows Server 2008.

- **Sample chapters**. Chapters from 15 Windows Server 2008 books that contain a wealth of information and provide a preview of other recently published titles.

# Using the Scripts

The use of each script is documented in the resource kit solution that presents the script. Most scripts are written in Visual Basic Scripting Edition (VBScript), so you can run them from the command prompt by typing **cscript** *script_name*.**vbs** followed by any parameters required by the script. Several scripts are batch files, which you can execute from the command prompt by typing the script's name and any parameters.

Finally, there are a number of HTML Applications (HTAs), which are scripts with a graphical user interface (GUI). You can run HTAs by double-clicking the HTA. You can also integrate most of the HTAs into the Active Directory Users and Computers snap-in using steps found in Solution 1-3 so that they can extend the functionality of your native administrative tools.

> **Important** It is extremely important that you treat scripts as samples only. Open each script in Notepad or in a script editor, read the script and its comments, make required configuration changes, and above all, *test the script* in a lab environment before using it in a production environment. Neither Microsoft nor Intelliem warrant or guarantee the script samples or tools.

That said, you'll generally find that with minor modification to the *Configuration Block* of a script, you'll have success in your lab. I've tried to make the scripts as readable and customizable as possible. Scripts will be updated on the resource kit Web site, *www.intelliem.com/resourcekit*. If you find bugs, or if you make useful changes to a script, please share your findings on the Web site.

Before you report a bug, make sure you've done the following:

- Read the entire solution that presents the script. Make sure you've performed all the steps outlined in the solution.

- Examine the configuration section of the script, which is usually labeled *Configuration Block*. I've included a sample configuration for a fictitious domain, *contoso.com*. Some scripts will not run until you change the configuration to match your environment.

- Double-check that you are running the script with permissions that can perform the task that is automated by the script. This task might require running the HTA or a command prompt with elevated credentials, particularly in Windows Vista and Windows Server 2008. Right-click the tool, or the Command Prompt icon in the Start Menu, and choose Run As Administrator.

- Test the script on other operating system platforms. Most scripts and HTAs will run on the operating systems listed earlier, but some scripts and HTAs have limitations. Some HTAs require Internet Explorer 7 and will not run on a system with Internet Explorer 6.

## Resource Kit Support Policy

Every effort has been made to ensure the accuracy of this book and the companion media content. Microsoft Press provides corrections to this book through the Web at the following location:

*http://www.microsoft.com/learning/support/search.asp*

Corrections will also be posted to the Resource Kit web site at *http://www.intelliem.com/resourcekit*. If you have comments, questions, or ideas regarding the book or companion media content, or if you have questions that are not answered by querying the Knowledge Base, please send them to Microsoft Press by using either of the following methods:

E-mail:

*rkinput@microsoft.com*

Postal mail:

Microsoft Press
Attn: *Windows Administration Resource Kit: Productivity Solutions for IT Professionals* editor
One Microsoft Way
Redmond, WA 98052-6399

Please note that product support is not offered through the preceding mail addresses. For product support information, please visit the Microsoft Help and Support Web site at the following address:

*http://support.microsoft.com*

Solution Collection 1

# Role-Based Management

Welcome to the first Solution Collection of the *Windows Administration Resource Kit: Productivity Solutions for IT Professionals.* In this collection, we'll try to achieve several goals concurrently.

First, I'll introduce a number of the concepts and tactics I'll use throughout the resource kit. By the end of the third solution, you'll have taken a journey from identifying a common administrative problem (in this case, reporting the full, nested group membership of a user), to creating a scripted solution, to building a graphical user interface (GUI) administrative tool, to integrating that GUI tool directly into the Active Directory Users and Computers snap-in.

The skills you learn on that journey will enable you to implement many other solutions in the resource kit. If you're experienced at writing VBScript, you'll pick up some great tips and approaches for applying your knowledge. If you're not an experienced scripter, you'll learn how to take the ready-to-use scripts and tools that are contained on the companion media that accompanies this book, make simple modifications to allow them to work in your enterprise, and put the solutions right to work without even needing to understand VBScript or other scripting languages.

This book is *not* designed as a scripting tutorial. In certain solutions, we'll be jumping right into *applying* scripting to solve problems. I'll point you to some great resources you can use to learn to script, but, again, you do *not* need to be a scripter to use and benefit from the solutions in the resource kit.

In fact, quite a few of the solutions in the resource kit are *not* script-centric. Later in this collection, you'll find solutions that enable you to manage users, computers, groups, security—just about everything—more effectively. These solutions, which focus on role-based management, involve disciplined management of groups in Active Directory and a lot of business-focused analysis and process. No scripts, per se, are involved in designing and implementing role-based management, though we'll introduce some in this and other Solution Collections that will leverage your role-based management model and give you superhero-like powers to manage your enterprise.

So by the end of this Solution Collection, you'll be well on your way to implementing role-based management in your enterprise. That is the second goal of this collection. I'll give you more details in the "Scenarios, Pain, and Solution" section, but suffice it to say that, in my experience with my clients, role-based management is one of the most valuable investments of time and thought that you can make as an IT professional.

## Scenarios, Pain, and Solution

If you were to study network administration, among the first lessons you would learn is this: "Don't manage your enterprise user by user. Manage with groups." And I hope that if you didn't study network administration and instead learned on the job, you also know that already!

Yet, there is a lot of wasted productivity, on the part of both IT professionals and end users, because of the management of users, groups, computers, security, configuration, application deployment, and other components of an IT enterprise. Perhaps some of the following scenarios sound familiar to you:

- When a new employee is hired at Contoso, Ltd., it takes several days for the user account to be provisioned. Furthermore, after the employee arrives at work, it can take days or even weeks before he or she has all the necessary applications and can access all the resources required for the job.

- When one user needs the same access to resources as a second user, there's no easy way to figure out what the second user can access.

- When a user moves to another location, the process of moving the user's data and settings to servers in the new location is not seamless.

- When an employee is moved to another site, department, or job, no one can be sure that he or she will get all the new applications and resources that are required. Quite often, the employee can continue to access resources that he or she no longer needs.

- When a user resigns or is terminated, it is difficult to be certain that all management related to that user—for example, permissions granted to that user—has been cleaned up.

■ It is difficult to analyze how many copies of a software application have been deployed, which makes license management a challenge.

■ When software is deployed to a user—for example, when Janice needs Visio—it follows her into the conference room. When she logs on to another computer, such as the one in the conference room, Visio gets installed, which should not happen—as Visio licensing is per machine, not per user.

■ It is difficult to track where a computer or a user is located: which office, which Active Directory site, and so on.

■ There are constant discussions about the Active Directory organizational unit (OU) design, and whether it should be based on office locations or object types.

■ When a user needs access to a resource for special reasons, the user is added directly to the access control list of the resource, violating the tenet of "Manage by groups." For example, if Janice in the Marketing department is an expert at writing Microsoft Office Excel macros and is recruited by the Accounting department to help create the Budget workbook for next year, she needs permissions to that workbook. The Accounting group has already been given permissions, but Janice is not in Accounting. The administrator does not want to add Janice to the Accounting group, but she needs that permission.... What happens? Typically, she is given permissions directly on the access control list (ACL). That solution might suffice for the one, Budget workbook. But what about the Sales Forecast workbook, the Operations Planning workbook, and all the other workbooks to which she needs "special" access? You can see why it gets out of hand.

■ Auditing a user's group memberships is difficult. If an administrator is asked, "To which groups does Janice belong?"—and wants the answer to include nested groups—it is impossible to figure that out, or at least it is a multistep process.

■ Auditing the security model is challenging. If an administrator is asked, "Who is able to read the plans for next year's budget?" or "What can Janice get to?," the answer is difficult or impossible to authoritatively deliver.

These illustrate just a few *pain points*—scenarios in which productivity is wasted, time or money is lost, security is inadequate, or other inefficiencies are experienced. These and other pain points can be addressed with role-based management. This Solution Collection will prepare you to eliminate all types of pain points. Some of them will be solved completely within this Solution Collection, while others will require additional solutions that are presented later in this resource kit.

**Note**   The goal of role-based management is to align your IT management model with your business process and requirements.

Role-based management allows you to define a user (that is, his or her *roles*, which is a term that will be clarified as we progress) and to automatically enable management of a user, including determining the following details:

- What the user can or cannot get to (resource access)

- What the user can or cannot do on systems (user rights)

- Applications that are made available to the user (software distribution)

- The user's Microsoft Windows environment, such as its interface configuration, the level of "lock down," mapped drives, and so on (user experience and configuration, including Group Policy)

- Management of the user's data (redirected folders and profiles)

- E-mail distribution lists to which the user belongs

Likewise, role-based management allows you to define a computer by its roles (for example, a desktop or laptop, conference room computer, shared workstation, public kiosk, database server, file server) and thereby automatically enable management of that computer, including determining the following details:

- What can or cannot be done on that computer (user rights)

- What can or cannot be accessed on or from that computer (resource access)

- Configuration and security (Group Policy)

- Special configuration for users on the computer (for example, loopback processing of Group Policy objects)

I hope some of the scenarios presented at the beginning of this section sounded familiar to you. They reflect the kinds of pain points I find at every client, large and small, that has not thoroughly implemented role-based management. Let me balance those scenarios with a scenario of what it might look like in an enterprise that has role-based management in place. The picture I paint in this scenario might help you to envision what role-based management really means.

Contoso, Ltd., recently implemented a role-based management model for its Windows enterprise. The company hired a fantastic consultant, Dan Holme. . . . Oops, sorry. . . . I got carried away there. . . . I digress.

Now, a tool called My Memberships is used to report the status of a user or computer at Contoso.

> **Note**   My Memberships.hta is in the Scripts folder of the companion media. It will be discussed in Solution 1-6.

Recently, James Fine was hired as an accountant in the Denver office. At the time his user account was provisioned (as explained in Solution 7-7 on page 526), it was defined in the following roles: Accounting and LOC_DEN. He was given a computer named DESKTOP432, which was assigned to the LOC_DEN role.

With those three changes, his complete status (as seen in the My Memberships screen shot in Figure 1-1) fully enabled him to perform his work as an accountant.

**Figure 1-1**   Management of James Fine, accountant in Denver

Notice all the other capabilities James inherits simply by being defined as a user assigned the Accounting role in Denver: he has access to several resources (including read access to the Budget resources), software, configurations such as the Accounting logon script and redirected folders to Denver servers, and e-mail lists. None of those capabilities are given to him directly. They're all part of what is called role-based management: the business logic that defines and supports what accountants in Denver require to do their jobs.

Six months later, James is promoted to manager of Finance. As such, his role is changed from Accounting to Finance Manager. However, business logic at Contoso indicates that finance managers are *also* accountants, so James still belongs to the Accounting role, but indirectly through a nested group membership. He is also moved to the site where he could do his job most effectively: Sydney. With those two changes, all the capabilities shown in Figure 1-2 become his.

Notice James can now *edit* the Budget, he has a new application (BudgetPro), he has his folders redirected to Sydney, and he belongs to a new e-mail distribution list.

James does so well that, two years later, he is promoted to Chief Financial Officer. As the CFO, his role is now defined as Executive and his office is moved to London, at the global headquarters. All of the other roles and capabilities shown in Figure 1-3 become his.

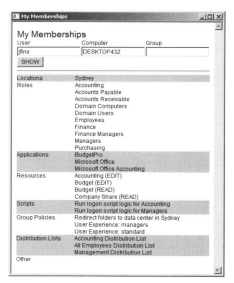

**Figure 1-2**   Management of James Fine, finance manager, Sydney

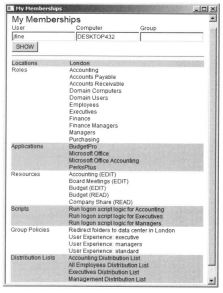

**Figure 1-3**   Management of James Fine, CFO/Executive, London

As an Executive, James gets a new application (PerksPlus), additional resource access (to Board Meeting folders), additional configurations, and e-mail distribution list membership. All with just two changes to his role definition: Executive and London. James is defined by only three direct roles: Finance Managers, Executives, and London. The remaining roles, and all capabilities, are inherited from those three roles.

And, to pick another pain point raised in earlier scenarios, look how easy it is for the IT department to report who can access a resource at a particular level, as shown in Figure 1-4.

**Figure 1-4**   Access Report

The tool shown in Figure 1-4, the Access Report, is also available to you on the companion media. It's called Members_AccessReport.hta, and it's located in the Scripts folder. It will be discussed in Solution 1-6.

This scenario illustrates how, after role-based management is in place, simply defining a user or computer by its roles fully enables the automatic provisioning and management of all that is required by the business for that user or computer to perform. The scenario is simple, to be sure, and I hope there are at least a few questions or comments in your head right now, such as the following ones:

- "OK, this sounds great, but how do you *do* it?" Well, that's the focus of this Solution Collection, and there will be a number of other solutions later in the book that build upon the foundation you establish here. I'll give you a few sneak peeks: It has a lot to do with sophisticated group management and equally sophisticated management of resources, applications, group policies, scripts, and more. But "sophisticated" does *not* mean "difficult." So read on!

- "My enterprise is more complicated...." That's what they all say. Trust me. I've seen this kind of thing work at very large organizations. It *does* work. This scenario is simplistic, but the concepts, skills, and tools you master will allow you to apply this solution in your organization.

■ "If this is all about groups, won't you end up with a *lot* of groups?" Yes! But after you really look at what's happening currently in your enterprise, you'll find that group management is much easier. Plus, I'll give you tools to make it all the more straightforward and automated. Trust me: It's *easier*!

■ "How many roles should a user belong to?" Well, that really depends on a number of factors, and we'll look at that later in this Solution Collection. But the bottom line is that a *typical* user will probably be defined by a small handful, maybe even up to a dozen, *direct* roles. Other roles can be inherited.

And there might be yet more questions or comments in your head. That's great! Read on and I'll try to address them all.

A couple of other notes bear mention before we dive into our first solutions.

## The 80/20 rule

There is a tried-and-true guideline that you can often solve 80 percent of the problem with 20 percent of the effort and, conversely, that solving the remaining 20 percent (that is, making the situation "perfect") takes 80 percent of the effort. I'm a big believer in attacking problems with the 80/20 rule in sight. If I can solve 80 percent of the pain I'm feeling, that will free up so much of my time that I can, by moving on to other challenges, provide far more value than trying to address every exception to the rule that gets me to the 100-percent-solved mark.

I believe that this is what productivity is all about. Freeing up that 80 percent of your effort so that you can get your head above water, look ahead, build and address strategies to add value to your enterprise, and lead a healthier, more fulfilling job life. Because this book will hopefully be read by billions of people (OK, I exaggerate, let's hope for lots and lots) in enterprises of every shape, size, location, and culture, the best we can do is try to solve 80 percent of everyone's problems! That would be a feat worth celebrating! Approach these solutions with the 80/20 rule in mind and you'll be amazed at the productivity gains you experience. There will probably be a few gaps here and there: opportunities for you to take a solution to that last step to work perfectly for your organization. Go for it!

## Scripts and tools on the companion media

The companion media that accompanies this book is loaded with extras. The resources on the companion media are for reference, as samples only. What that means is these tools are not supported by Microsoft, by me, or by anyone, really. You should absolutely evaluate, understand, *test* (!), and prepare a rollback plan for any tool you implement. You're on your own.

Now that our lawyers will be satisfied, we will of course *try* to make the tools as useful as possible. You will need to open them (most are scripts and HTML Applications, or HTAs, which you can open with Notepad) and make modifications as indicated to parameters such as company and domain names. No big deal. Then evaluate, understand, *test* (!), and prepare a rollback plan for any tool you implement. And enjoy!

The online community, mentioned in the section "The Windows Administration Resource Kit online community," will have any updates to scripts and tools, as well as discussions around each solution. It will be an invaluable resource. And, except where mentioned otherwise (in the book, in the tool's README file, in the tool's license agreement, or in the script or tool comments), you are welcome to change the tool and extend it to meet your needs. You will have to maintain copyright notices and comments. And we'd appreciate it if you post your creations on the community site to benefit everyone else in the community. If this all sounds vaguely open source, you're on the right track. We're all in this together: respect, create, and benefit.

## Microsoft and third-party tools

Throughout the resource kit, I'll also mention tools that can help you solve the problems we are tackling. Some of them can in fact get you that last 20 percent of the way to "perfection." There's no doubt that there are tools developed by Microsoft and other software developers that are a great asset to any Windows IT professional.

For example, Microsoft Identity Lifecycle Manager (ILM) and System Center Configuration Manager are two Microsoft server applications that can play a significant role in moving you toward role-based management. Such tools add enormous value and are likely to result in reduced total cost of ownership (TCO) for an enterprise. However, TCO and return on investment (ROI) calculations involve taking into account the *time* spent by IT professionals and end users: How much time is spent, how much time is saved, and what is that worth? I find most organizations completely incapable or unwilling to account properly for the sweat equity of their employees. Most organizations end up looking just at the hard-dollar costs and savings related to a purchase. Therefore, the ROI can't be accurately calculated to show the reduced TCO of the tool, and the tool doesn't get bought. It's a pity, but that attitude is all too common.

If you are lucky enough to work for an organization that has guidelines for how to account for human time, be sure to calculate not just how much money will be *saved* by rolling out a particular solution. That's the easy part. You also need to calculate how much additional value will be added to the bottom line when someone's time is taken away from something that is a drain on value and redirected to creative, strategic, or tactical thinking and work that creates *extra* value for the organization.

So this book aims to provide you with tools that you can implement for no hard cost and, hopefully, with optimally minimized time and effort. Where we can do it for free, we'll do it.

And when there's a great tool, outside of what is built into Windows Server 2008, Windows Server 2003, Windows Vista, or Windows XP, I'll point you to it—particularly when it's free.

Just know that neither I nor Microsoft, nor anyone remotely related to this resource kit, can vouch for whether a particular tool will provide value in your organization or will even work as promised. I can tell you when I've had a good experience with a tool in past projects at clients or that I've heard great things about a tool, but these are neither endorsements nor warranties of any kind. Do your research, test, and make the decision that's right for your enterprise.

---

### A lesson in the ROI of productivity

There have been several occasions in my career as a consultant in which my client provided numbers with which to calculate ROI including the amount of time saved by employees. Employee time will generally be worth something more than double an employee's wage, after taxes, benefits, and overhead are accounted for.

Each of these occasions taught me that, when you are lucky enough to have such numbers available, you will likely need to significantly understate your ROI calculations.

On one such occasion, we rolled out a solution that provided productivity guidance to information workers at an enterprise. The solution consisted primarily of very targeted training and an online self-help portal. Based on an analysis of the time savings produced by the solution, which was measured several times and was consistent with my experience at other customers, we determined that end users were saving 10 minutes per user per day. We assumed we were reaching a fraction of the workforce because not all employees would participate. The ROI with a mere 10 minutes per day of time saved was over 1000 percent. That's a *tenfold* ROI. Most public companies use an internal rate of return to evaluate their investments, and that rate of return is generally in the 10 to 20 percent range. A 1000 percent ROI was absurd (though supported). We presented the results to the CIO, and he and his team agreed that we needed to pitch the ROI in our project summary as somewhere just under 100 percent (a twofold ROI). Nobody would believe a 1000 percent ROI.

Even more amusing was the fact that this ROI reflected only recovered waste (the recovery of time wasted by performing tasks inefficiently) by employees. It did not account for the benefit to the company as that time was applied to value-generating activities. If you're lucky enough to be able to account for human time, and if your project reaches even a few employees in your enterprise, you will find pitching productivity projects the world's easiest sales job.

---

## The Windows Administration Resource Kit online community

We've assembled a great online resource for you, the readers of the *Windows Administration Resource Kit*. Just log on to *http://www.intelliem.com/resourcekit* and you'll find a community of IT professionals who are working to implement these and other fantastic solutions. If there are changes to the scripts or tools we provide in the book or on the companion media, or if we find (oops!) errors, we'll post them on the site. And you'll be able to discuss what works, what doesn't, and how to take solutions to the next step.

## Enough, already!

So I've prepared you for some of what you will experience throughout the resource kit. I've set you up with a basic understanding of the manageability problems that role-based management helps you to solve. I've pointed you to the companion media and to the online community, and I've said what the lawyers want me to say about the scripts in the book and tools I mention. Let's dive into the solutions in this collection! First, we will warm up our custom tool development skills, and then we'll apply them to role-based management.

# 1-1: Enumerate a User's (or Computer's) Group Memberships

## Solution overview

| | |
|---|---|
| **Type of solution** | Tool (Script) |
| **Features and tools** | Command-line commands, VBScript |
| **Solution summary** | Create a script to enumerate a user's (or computer's) group memberships. |
| **Benefits** | Answers the question, "What groups does ____ belong to?" Makes group memberships more visible than what is possible using the standard GUI toolset. |
| **Preview** | Figure 1-5 illustrates the output of a script that reports the group memberships of a user. |

**Figure 1-5**   Group membership report script

# Introduction

Our first solution exemplifies a common approach to problem solving in this book. We start with a problem known to most administrators and identify the limitations of the standard Windows administrative tools. We then look at extended tools that provide functionality to address the problem. Finally, we build a script that solves the problem entirely.

In the following solutions, we turn the script into an administrative tool with a GUI front end. Then we hook the tool into the standard Active Directory Users and Computers snap-in so that our new, problem-solving functionality is available to us from within a standard administrative tool. By following and applying these solutions, you'll get a preview of some of the unique approaches we will build upon throughout this book.

# Active Directory Users and Computers

There come moments in every administrator's life when she must report the groups to which a user belongs. You would think that, after over a decade in the business of creating GUI-based administrative tools for Windows networking, Microsoft's standard toolset (including the Active Directory Users and Computers snap-in) would provide this functionality. But it does not. You are, of course, able to open a user object's properties and see its direct memberships on the Member Of tab, shown in Figure 1-6. However, this list does not reveal the nested memberships of this user. For example, we cannot see that James is a member of Accounts Payable because the Accounting group is a member of the Accounts Payable group.

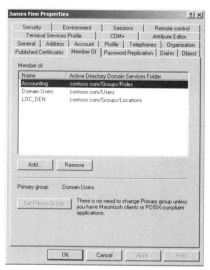

**Figure 1-6** Member Of tab of a user object's Properties dialog box

You can double-click any group in the Member Of list to open its properties and continue to "drill down" until you find a group that is not a member of any other one.

> **Note**  You can double-click any group in the Member Of list to open its properties.

This is a sloppy, slow way to discover the user's group memberships. If you're paid by the hour, this might be your preferred method. The rest of us need to find a better way.

## DS commands

Enter the DS commands. The DS commands are command prompt tools for accessing and manipulating Active Directory. We will leverage these commands in several solutions in this book. For this task, we will leverage dsget.exe, which allows you to get a property of an Active Directory object. The syntax we require is as follows:

```
dsget user UserDN -memberof -expand
```

The first parameter, *user*, indicates the class of object we are interested in "getting." The second parameter, *UserDN*, is the distinguished name of the object. The third parameter, *memberof*, is the property we want; and the fourth parameter—the magical one for us—tells *dsget* to expand the membership to include nested groups. So, to discover the memberships of our user, James Fine, we use this command:

```
dsget user "cn=James Fine,ou=employees,ou=people,dc=contoso,dc=com" -memberof -expand
```

It's no fun to have to type the entire distinguished name (DN) of a user, so we recruit another DS command to find the user: dsquery.exe searches Active Directory with the properties you provide, and it returns the distinguished name of matching objects. If we enter

```
dsquery user -samid jfine
```

we get the distinguished name of the user object with the *samid* (pre–Windows 2000 logon name) property that matches jfine, specifically:

```
cn=James Fine,ou=employees,ou=people,dc=contoso,dc=com
```

Because *dsquery* produces the distinguished name that *dsget* requires, we can "pipe" the results of *dsquery* to *dsget*, as shown next:

```
dsquery user -samid jfine | dsget user -memberof -expand
```

Notice the *dsget* command no longer includes a distinguished name. If you leave out the distinguished name of the object you want to get, *dsget* expects you to type in the distinguished name. Try it—type in the distinguished name of an object or objects, surrounded by quotes, and press Ctrl+C to indicate you are finished. You are using *StdIn*, the standard input stream, to provide the DN.

The pipe symbol ( | ) redirects the output generated by the *dsquery* command into the *StdIn* of the *dsget* command, saving you the need to type the DN. You need only type the pre–Windows 2000 logon name of the user.

There is still room for improvement in the output of our *dsquery* | *dsget* command: The groups are listed as distinguished names, which is not pretty. Let's modify our command to return just the names of the groups:

```
dsquery user -samid jfine | dsget user -memberof -expand | dsget group -samid
```

Notice we're piping the list of distinguished names provided by the first *dsget* command to a second *dsget* command. The second *dsget* command specifies that each distinguished name will be that of a group, and that we want to retrieve the *samid* property. Note that the actual name of the pre–Windows 2000 name property, according to the Active Directory schema, is *sAMAccountName*. DS commands, unfortunately, do not follow Microsoft's own standards, so *samid* is the switch used.

So the solution from the command line is a package of three commands:

```
dsquery user -samid UserSAMAccountName | dsget user -memberof -expand | dsget group -samid
```

If we want to find the group memberships of a computer, we simply substitute *computer* as the object class in our DS commands and query for the computer using its common name:

```
dsquery computer -name ComputerName | dsget computer -memberof -expand | dsget group -samid
```

## Creating a batch script

Now that we know the DS commands required to enumerate nested group membership, we can turn those commands into a simple, one-line script. Open Notepad and enter the following line:

```
dsquery user -samid %1 | dsget user -memberof -expand | dsget group -samid
```

Save the script as "User_MemberOf_Enum.bat". Be sure to surround the file name in quotes; otherwise, Notepad will add a .txt extension. I recommend you save the script to an easily accessible folder, such as a folder on the root of a disk volume.

Then at the command prompt, navigate to the folder where you saved the script, and run the script as follows:

```
User_MemberOf_Enum UserSAMAccountName
```

For example:

```
User_MemberOf_Enum jfine
```

The *%1* in the script inserts the first argument you provide after the command (the user's pre–Windows 2000 logon name or "SAM Account Name") into the correct location in the command sequence. We could make the script more elegant by assigning the first argument to a variable and then using the variable in the command sequence, as follows:

```
set userdn=%1
dsquery user -samid %userdn% | dsget user -memberof -expand | dsget group -samid
```

The first line assigns the argument to a variable named *userdn* (variable names can be any non-reserved word), and the variable is referred to by surrounding its name with percent signs (%) in the command sequence.

# Enumerating group membership with VBScript

VBScript is a powerful, flexible scripting language that enables a number of administrative solutions. This book is not designed to teach VBScript. If you want to learn scripting, I highly recommend *Microsoft Windows Administrator's Automation Toolkit* (Microsoft Press, 2005) or any other book written by its author, scripting guru Don Jones.

When scripts are presented and used in this book, you'll find, for the most part, that they are ready to use with minor modifications that do *not* require you to be a scripter to perform. Scripts will often be examined to a certain level of detail. If you aren't ready for that detail, skip that part of the discussion. You'll find the instructions for how to *use* the script easy to follow. So, for example, if you are not a scripter, you can skip the following discussion and jump to "Using ADObject_MemberOf_Enum.vbs" on page 25.

## Understanding ADObject_MemberOf_Enum.vbs

The following code creates a special type of array called a dictionary, and fills it with the group memberships of our user, James Fine:

```
' Create dictionary object to store group names
Set oMemberOfList = CreateObject("Scripting.Dictionary")
' Set comparison mode to case insensitive
oMemberOfList.CompareMode = vbTextCompare

Set oUser = GetObject("LDAP://cn=james fine,ou=employees,ou=people,dc=contoso,dc=com")
Call ADObject_MemberOf_Enum(oUser)

aMemberOfList = oMemberOfList.Keys
WScript.Echo "MEMBERSHIPS"
For Each sMemberOf In aMemberOfList
    WScript.Echo sMemberOf
Next

Sub ADObject_MemberOf_Enum(ByVal oObject)
    ' Enumerates MemberOf property of an object
    ' INPUTS:  oObject: object for which to enumerate MemberOf
    ' REQUIRES:  oMemberOfList dictionary object with global scope
```

```
    On Error Resume Next
    aMemberOf = oObject.GetEx("memberOf")
    If Err.Number <> 0 Then
        ' Assume error is because memberOf has no distinguished names
        Err.Clear
        On Error GoTo 0
        Exit Sub
    Else
        On Error GoTo 0
        For Each sMemberOf In aMemberOf
            Set oMemberOf = GetObject("LDAP://" & sMemberOf)
            sMemberOfSAM = oMemberOf.sAMAccountName
            If (oMemberOfList.Exists(sMemberOfSAM) = False) Then
                ' We have not seen this group yet
                ' Add it to the dictionary object
                oMemberOfList.Add sMemberOfSAM, True
                ' Enumerate this group's nested memberships
                Call ADObject_MemberOf_Enum(oMemberOf)
            End If
        Next
    End If

End Sub
```

The workhorse of this script is the subroutine called *ADObject_MemberOf_Enum*. The routine takes an Active Directory object (user, group, or computer) and examines its *MemberOf* property. If the *MemberOf* property is found, each group is examined to see whether it has already been added to the membership list. If not, it is added to the list and then the routine calls itself to examine the membership of the group. This iterative, nested process is called recursion, and it allows the routine to enumerate all memberships of the original object, including memberships resulting from nested groups.

The list of memberships produced by this script is almost, but not entirely, complete. Each user and computer object in Active Directory has a primary group membership: Users typically belong to Domain Users and computers to Domain Computers. This primary group affiliation is not stored in the *MemberOf* property, but rather in the *PrimaryGroupID* property. The *PrimaryGroupID* has to be translated to the actual group name. For example, *PrimaryGroupID* 514 corresponds to Domain Users.

The following chunk of code takes an Active Directory user or computer, represented by *oObject*, and adds the object's primary group to our membership list dictionary:

```
iPrimaryGroup = oObject.PrimaryGroupID
sPrimaryGroup = ""
Select Case iPrimaryGroup
    Case 513
        sPrimaryGroup = "Domain Users"
    Case 514
        sPrimaryGroup = "Domain Guests"
```

```
    Case 515
        sPrimaryGroup = "Domain Computers"
    Case 516
        sPrimaryGroup = "Domain Controllers"
End Select
If sPrimaryGroup > "" Then
    Call ADObject_MemberOf_Enum(sPrimaryGroup)
    oMemberOfList.Add sPrimaryGroup, True
End If
```

With these two important components in place, we can build the rest of the script. The script is named ADOBJECT_MEMBEROF_ENUM.vbs and, like all scripted solutions in this book, you can find it in the Scripts folder of the companion media accompanying this book. I will not always reprint the entire script in the book so that I have more pages to share more solutions. But in this case, I can use this script to illustrate how scripts will be built for this book, some of the conventions I'll use, and how you can apply the scripts in your enterprise.

**ADOBJECT_MEMBEROF_ENUM.vbs**
```
Option Explicit
Dim oMemberOfList
Dim aMemberOfList
Dim sMemberOf
Dim sDomainDN
Dim sArgument
Dim sObjectDN

' CONFIGURATION BLOCK
sDomainDN = "dc=contoso,dc=com"

If WScript.Arguments.Count <> 1 Then
    ' Wrong number of arguments passed
    WScript.Echo "USAGE: cscript //nologo <name of script> [DN | ADSPath | NAME]"
    WScript.Echo "where the object can be represented by a distinguished name,"
    WScript.Echo "ADSPath, pre-Windows 2000 logon name (user/group) or name (computer)"
    WScript.Quit(501)
    ' 501 is an Exit Code that I use indicate a generic error in scripts I write
End If

' Get Argument
sArgument = WScript.Arguments(0)
' Translate it to DN
sObjectDN = ADObject_DN_UCG(sArgument, sDomainDN)
If sObjectDN = "" Then
    WScript.Echo "ERROR--NOT FOUND: " & sArgument
    WScript.Quit (501)
End If

' Create dictionary object to store group names
Set oMemberOfList = CreateObject("Scripting.Dictionary")
' Set comparison mode to case insensitive
oMemberOfList.CompareMode = vbTextCompare
```

```
Call ADObject_MemberOf (sObjectDN)
aMemberOfList = oMemberOfList.Keys
aMemberOfList = Array_Sort(aMemberOfList)
WScript.Echo "MEMBERSHIPS"
For Each sMemberOf In aMemberOfList
    WScript.Echo sMemberOf
Next


' =======================
' FUNCTIONS FROM LIBRARY
' =======================
Function ADObject_DN_UCG(ByVal sObject, sSearchDN)
    ' Version 070706
    ' Takes any input (name, DN, or ADsPath) of a user, computer, or group,
    ' and returns the distinguished name of the object
    ' INPUTS:    sObject:   name, DN or ADsPath to a user, group, or computer
    '            sSearchDN: the DN within which to search (often, the DN of the domain,
    '                       e.g. dc=contoso, dc=com)
    ' RETURNS:   ADObject_DN_UCG: distinguished name (cn=...) of the object
    ' REQUIRES:  ADObject_Find_UCG routine

    Dim sObjectName, oObject, sObjectADsPath, sObjectDN

    If Len(sObject) = 0 Then
        sObjectDN = ""
    ElseIf Len(sObject) < 3 Then
        ' can't be a DN or an ADsPath - must be a name
        sObjectADsPath = ADObject_Find_UCG(sObject, sSearchDN)
        If sObjectADsPath <> "" Then sObjectDN = mid(sObjectADsPath,8)
    ElseIf LCase(Left(sObject,3)) = "cn=" Then
        ' is a DN - make sure it exists
        On Error Resume Next
        Set oObject = GetObject("LDAP://" & sObject)
        sObjectDN = oObject.distinguishedName
        If Err.Number <> 0 Then
            ' Error - couldn't find object
            sObjectDN = ""
            Err.Clear
        End If
        On Error GoTo 0
    ElseIf Len(sObject) < 8 Then
        ' can't be an ADsPath and isn't a DN, must be a name
        sObjectADsPath = ADObject_Find_UCG(sObject, sSearchDN)
        If sObjectADsPath <> "" Then sObjectDN = mid(sObjectADsPath,8)
    ElseIf Ucase(Left(sObject, 7)) = "LDAP://" Then
        ' is an ADsPath - make sure it exists
        ' first, make sure LDAP:// is upper case, to avoid error
        sObject = "LDAP://" & Mid(sObject, 8)
        On Error Resume Next
        Set oObject = GetObject(sObject)
        sObjectDN = oObject.distinguishedName
```

```
        If Err.Number <> 0 Then
            ' Error - couldn't find object
            sObjectDN = ""
            Err.Clear
        End If
        On Error GoTo 0
    Else
        ' must be a name
        sObjectADsPath = ADObject_Find_UCG(sObject, sSearchDN)
        If sObjectADsPath <> "" Then sObjectDN = mid(sObjectADsPath,8)
    End If

    ADObject_DN_UCG = sObjectDN

End Function

Function ADObject_Find_UCG(sObjectName, sSearchDN)
    ' VERSION 070706
    ' Returns the full ADsPath (LDAP://...) of a user, computer, or group
    ' Inputs:
    '     sObjectName: The unique identifier for the object class.  The script supports:
    '         User:     sAMAccountName (pre-Windows 2000 logon name)
    '         Group:    sAMAccountName (pre-Windows 2000 logon name)
    '         Computer: Name (translated by the script to the computer's sAMAccountName
    '                   by adding a $)
    '     sSearchDN:   the DN within which to search (often, the DN of the domain, e.g.
    '                  dc=contoso, dc=com)


    Dim oConnection
    Dim oRecordset
    Dim sLDAPObjectQuery
    Dim sLDAPIdentifierQuery
    Dim sLDAPQuery
    Dim sProperties
    Dim oADObject
    Dim aProperties
    Dim sProperty
    Dim sLDAPIdentifier
    Dim sSearchScope

    sLDAPIdentifier = "samAccountName"
    sProperties = "ADsPath"
    sSearchScope = "subtree"

    ' Open an ADO connection using null credentials
    Set oConnection = CreateObject("ADODB.Connection")
    oConnection.Provider = "ADsDSOObject"
    'On Error Resume Next
    oConnection.Open "", vbNullString, vbNullString
    If oConnection.State = 0 Then ' 0 = adStateClosed
        ' Error handling code: can't connect to AD
        ADObject_Find_UCG = ""
        Exit Function
    End If
```

```
    ' Build the LDAP Query
    sLDAPQuery = "<LDAP://" & sSearchDN & ">;"
    sLDAPQuery = sLDAPQuery & _
        "(|(samAccountName=" & sObjectName & ")" & _
        "(samAccountName=" & sObjectName & "$));" & _
        sProperties & ";" & sSearchScope

    ' Retrieve the result set, close the connection, and check to make
    ' sure we received at least one result
    Set oRecordset = oConnection.Execute (sLDAPQuery)
    If oRecordset.EOF and oRecordset.BOF Then
        ' Error handling code: no object found
        ADObject_Find_UCG = ""
        Exit Function
    End If

    ADObject_Find_UCG = oRecordset.Fields("ADsPath")
    oRecordset.Close
    oConnection.Close

End Function

Sub ADObject_MemberOf(ByVal sObjectDN)
    ' Version 070701
    ' Enumerates the group memberships of a user or computer
    ' INPUTS:    sObjectDN: the DN of the user or computer
    ' RETURNS:   oMemberOfList sorted with each group
    '            to which the user or computer belongs.
    ' REQUIRES:  ADObject_MemberOf_Enum function
    '            Array_Sort function
    '            oMemberOf List with global scope
    '            e.g.
    '            Set oMemberOfList = CreateObject("Scripting.Dictionary")
    '            oMemberOfList.CompareMode = vbTextCompare ' Case INsensitive

    Dim oObject
    Dim iPrimaryGroup
    Dim sPrimaryGroup
    Dim aMemberOf

    On Error Resume Next
    Set oObject = GetObject("LDAP://" & sObjectDN)
    If Err.Number<>0 Or oObject Is Nothing Then
        Err.Clear
        Exit Sub
    End If
    On Error GoTo 0

    If oObject.Class = "computer" Or oObject.Class = "user" Then
        iPrimaryGroup = oObject.PrimaryGroupID
        sPrimaryGroup = ""
        Select Case iPrimaryGroup
            Case 513
                sPrimaryGroup = "Domain Users"
```

```
            Case 514
                sPrimaryGroup = "Domain Guests"
            Case 515
                sPrimaryGroup = "Domain Computers"
            Case 516
                sPrimaryGroup = "Domain Controllers"
        End Select
        If sPrimaryGroup > "" Then
            Call ADObject_MemberOf_Enum(sPrimaryGroup)
            oMemberOfList.Add sPrimaryGroup, True
        End If
    End If

    On Error Resume Next
    aMemberOf = oObject.GetEx("memberOf")
    If Err.Number <> 0 Then
        ' Assume error is because memberOf has no distinguished names
        Err.Clear
        On Error GoTo 0
        Exit Sub
    Else
        On Error GoTo 0
        Call ADObject_MemberOf_Enum(oObject)
    End If

End Sub

Sub ADObject_MemberOf_Enum(ByVal oObject)
    ' Version 070701
    ' Enumerates MemberOf property of an object
    ' INPUTS:    oObject: object for which to enumerate MemberOf
    ' REQUIRES:  oMemberOfList dictionary object with global scope
    '            e.g.
    '            Set oMemberOfList = CreateObject("Scripting.Dictionary")
    '            oMemberOfList.CompareMode = vbTextCompare ' Case INsensitive

    Dim aMemberOf
    Dim sMemberOf
    Dim oMemberOf
    Dim sMemberOfSAM

    On Error Resume Next
    aMemberOf = oObject.GetEx("memberOf")
    If Err.Number <> 0 Then
        ' Assume error is because memberOf has no distinguished names
        Err.Clear
        On Error GoTo 0
        Exit Sub
    Else
        On Error GoTo 0
        For Each sMemberOf In aMemberOf
            Set oMemberOf = GetObject("LDAP://" & sMemberOf)
            sMemberOfSAM = oMemberOf.sAMAccountName
```

```
                If (oMemberOfList.Exists(sMemberOfSAM) = False) Then
                    ' We have not seen this group yet
                    ' Add it to the dictionary object
                    oMemberOfList.Add sMemberOfSAM, True
                    ' Enumerate this group's nested memberships
                    Call ADObject_MemberOf_Enum(oMemberOf)
                End If
            Next
        End If

End Sub

Function Array_Sort(ByVal aArray)
    ' VERSION 070701
    ' Sorts an array, very quickly, using .NET objects
    ' INPUTS:    aArray: an array (incl Dictionary object) requiring sort
    ' RETURNS:   Array_Sort: sorted
    ' REQUIRES:  .NET Framework 2.0

    Dim oNAL
    Dim nIdx

    Set oNAL = CreateObject("System.Collections.ArrayList")
    For nIdx = 0 To UBound(aArray)
        oNAL.Add aArray(nIdx)
    Next

    oNAL.Sort

    For nIdx = 0 To UBound(aArray)
        aArray(nIdx) = oNAL(nIdx)
    Next

    Array_Sort = aArray

End Function
```

To run the script, open a command prompt, navigate to the folder containing the script, and enter this command:

```
cscript.exe ADOBJECT_MEMBEROF_ENUM.vbs "name of user, computer, or group"
```

To make the script very flexible, I have coded it so that you can indicate the object you want to analyze using any of the following:

- The distinguished name (DN) of a user, computer, or group.
- The full LDAP path to the object (LDAP://CN=...), which has an "LDAP://" prefix followed by the DN of the object. This is called the ADsPath of the object.
- The pre–Windows 2000 logon name of a user: the user's *sAMAccountName* attribute.
- The pre–Windows 2000 logon name of a group: the group's *sAMAccountName* attribute.

- The name of a computer: the computer's *Name* attribute. A computer's *sAMAccountName* attribute is the computer's *Name* attribute with a dollar sign ($) appended, so the script can derive the *sAMAccountName* from the computer *Name*.

I've provided the option to enter a simple name as an argument for two reasons. First, a simple name is just that—simple—compared to typing a DN. Second, in the next solution, we will be launching the script not from a command line, but from within the Microsoft Management Console (MMC), with a specific user (or computer or group) selected. Depending on how we launch the script, a different form of the object's name will be passed to the script as an argument, so the script needs to be ready to receive several types of names.

Examples of commands to launch the script include the following:

```
cscript //nologo ADOBJECT_MEMBEROF_ENUM.vbs "cn=james
fine,ou=employees,ou=people,dc=contoso,dc=com"
```

or

```
cscript //nologo ADOBJECT_MEMBEROF_ENUM.vbs jfine
```

The *//nologo* switch suppresses the typical header from the *cscript* command. In the first example, the distinguished name of James Fine is passed as the argument to the script. In the second, his user name (the pre–Windows 2000 logon name) is passed. Quotes are necessary around the last argument if it includes spaces, as in the first example.

The script begins with the *Option Explicit* statement, which requires that you declare each variable by a *Dim* statement, like those on the following lines, prior to its use. It is a scripting best practice to use *Option Explicit* and declare variables, as it reduces the likelihood of errors resulting from typos in variable names. The scripts on the companion media will use *Option Explicit* and declarations, though I'll usually omit those statements when I reprint a script in the book so that we can focus on the functional aspects of the script.

If one of these names is passed to the script, it will look up the matching object in the domain specified by *DomainDN* in the script's *Configuration Block*.

> **Important**   Many of the scripts and tools provided in this resource kit have a configuration block, where you will make most or all the necessary customizations for your enterprise. Also, read the comments in the script, which will point out other customizations that might be required. Comments in a VBScript begin with an apostrophe ('), and comments in HTML are surrounded by two tags: <!-- at the beginning and --> at the end.

We hard-code the domain because the *sAMAccountName* attribute is guaranteed to be unique only within a single domain. A well-worn alternative to determine the DN of the domain is to connect to the *RootDSE* object and examine the default naming context, but that doesn't work in a forest with an empty forest root and a child domain with all the users and computers. So I prefer just to hard-code the domain name.

If you are a skilled scripter, you might want to use other ways to dynamically determine the correct value for *sDomainDN*. The script declares *sDomainDN* as a variable, rather than as a constant so that you can have flexibility in how you assign its value.

*WScript.Arguments( )* is the collection of arguments that you passed to the script from the command line. I use the collection's *Count* property to ensure you passed one and only one argument to the script. If not (meaning you either didn't specify an argument or you specified too many arguments), a usage reminder is displayed.

If an argument was passed to the script, it is assigned to the variable *sArgument*. The *Arguments* collection is zero based, so *WScript.Arguments(0)* is the first argument.

The script then uses two routines from our library to translate the argument to the DN of the selected object. The two routines are functions: *ADObject_DN_UCG* and *ADObject_Find_UCG*. These two functions, together, take a user, computer, or group name and return the distinguished name of the object in Active Directory. The name that the functions take can be a distinguished name (for example, CN= . . .), ADsPath (for example, LDAP://CN= . . .), or *sAMAccountName* (a pre–Windows 2000 Logon Name). If you provide a distinguished name or ADsPath, the routines confirm that the object exists and return its distinguished name. If you provide a *sAMAccountName*, the *ADObject_Find_UCG* function searches for a matching object within a search scope–typically, the entire domain–that is passed to the function as a distinguished name (for example, DC=contoso,DC=com).

The script calls the *ADObject_DN_UCG* function, which is responsible for translating any of the four types of names that could be used for the object into a DN. If the name that was passed was not a DN or ADsPath, the function calls *ADObject_Find_UCG*, which searches the specified scope (in this case, the entire domain) for a user, computer, or group with a name that matches the specified argument. Next, the script prepares the *oMemberOfList* dictionary object, which holds each group membership that is found for the user or computer. The code then calls the *ADObject_MemberOf* subroutine, which begins the process of enumerating group memberships. The code passes to the subroutine the object's distinguished name determined earlier in the code.

The subroutines populate the *oMemberOfList* dictionary with each group to which the object (user, computer, or group) belongs, including its primary group. I'll detail the subroutines in a moment. The resulting dictionary object's key field is copied into an array, *aMemberOfList*, which is then sorted by the *Array_Sort* function. The array is then displayed, one item at a time.

Two subroutines are responsible for populating *oMemberOfList*. The first, *ADObject_MemberOf*, creates a reference to the object and, if it is a user or computer, interprets its primary group. If the object has other memberships, the object is passed to *ADObject_MemberOf_Enum*, which, as described earlier in this solution, recursively examines group memberships, adding each, once, to the *oMemberOfList* dictionary. This script, like others in this book, includes light to moderate error trapping. When clients ask me what the difference is between scripting and coding, I often highlight the requirement that a script gets the job done, period. An application must be more robust, more flexible, more bulletproof, and more able to support a broader range of inputs. When scripting, you always make assumptions and concessions in the name of expediency and efficiency of code. You are certainly welcome to enhance the scripts' error handling, input validation, or other such characteristics.

### Using ADObject_MemberOf_Enum.vbs

The ADOBJECT_MEMBEROF_ENUM.vbs can be found in the Scripts folder of the companion media accompanying this book. To run the script, open a command prompt (cmd.exe) and enter the following command:

```
cscript //nologo ADOBJECT_MEMBEROF_ENUM.vbs "name of user, computer, or group "
```

You should carefully test this and all other scripts I present. Scripts are short, efficient solutions, not fully regression-tested applications. So be sure you understand a script, understand the modifications that you must or can make to it, and test the script fully in a lab prior to implementing it in production.

## Why VBScript?

As you might know, Windows Server 2008 supports Windows PowerShell as an interface for administration and automation. Windows PowerShell can also be downloaded from the Microsoft Web site and installed on Windows Vista, Windows XP, and Windows Server 2003.

However, we will be leveraging VBScript for most of the solutions in this book. The reason is that we want to create code that is as flexible and reusable as possible. The VBScript subroutines we wrote earlier, for example, could be easily incorporated into a logon script, into a Web page, or into an HTML Application (.hta). In fact, the next solution incorporates the code in a custom administrative GUI, written as an .hta file. In each of these scenarios, VBScript can run without worrying about whether Windows PowerShell is or is not installed. Even on Windows Server 2008, there is no guarantee that PowerShell is available because it has to be installed as a feature. Finally, PowerShell is a new product and does not provide a uniformly robust feature set. A lot of our solutions involve Active Directory, for example, for which PowerShell is not as rich as it is for other components, such as the Windows Management Instrumentation (WMI).

So for maximum flexibility, reuse, compatibility, and a rich feature set, VBScript will often, but not always, be our weapon of choice. You can be sure that future editions of this book will incorporate increasing amounts of PowerShell script, as PowerShell and Windows client and server technologies become increasingly integrated.

## Next steps

The ADObject_MemberOf_Enum.vbs script is a ready-to-use solution for enumerating group memberships of a user, computer, or group. But its functionality isn't that different from our *dsquery | dsget | dsget* command sequence, other than a sorted output. The real reasons why we've spent so much time on this script are, first, to introduce you to our approach to scripting in this book. Second, we will use this code to create a truly useful GUI-based administrative tool in the next two solutions. So don't stop reading yet!

## For more information

To learn more about VBScript, start with the incredible resources on the TechNet Script Center, at *http://www.microsoft.com/technet/scriptcenter/default.mspx*. I highly recommend the book *Microsoft Windows Administrator's Automation Toolkit* (Microsoft Press, 2005) or any of the other titles by scripting guru Don Jones. There are myriad resources for learning VBScript and finding sample code on the Internet. I suggest searching using keywords that indicate what you are trying to achieve with a script, and include the keyword "VBScript." For example, searching using the search term **vbscript group membership** will turn up a variety of other approaches to the problem we just solved. Certainly one of the most reputable and active sites is Don Jones's *www.ScriptingAnswers.com*.

## Solution summary

Windows' standard, GUI-based administration tools do not report the complete group memberships of a user or computer, as they do not expose nested group memberships. The *dsget [user | computer] -memberof -expand* command will enumerate all group memberships, as can VBScript, such as this solution's script, ADObject_MemberOf_Enum.vbs. But this solution is only "half-baked." The next two solutions build upon it to create a highly useful extension to the Active Directory Users and Computers snap-in.

# 1-2: Create a GUI Tool to Enumerate Group Memberships

## Solution overview

| | |
|---|---|
| **Type of solution** | HTML Application (HTA) |
| **Features and tools** | HTA, HTML, VBScript |
| **Solution summary** | Create a GUI tool to enumerate a user's (or computer's) group memberships, and learn how to turn scripts into administrative tools. |
| **Benefits** | Answer the question, "What groups does _____ belong to?" Make group memberships more visible than what is possible using the standard GUI toolset. |
| **Preview** | Figure 1-7 shows the Group Membership Report HTA in action, enumerating the memberships of a user whose pre–Windows 2000 logon name is jfine. |

Figure 1-7    The Group Membership Report HTA

# Introduction

Solution 1-1 presented a VBScript that enumerates, or lists, the group memberships of a user, computer, or group, including nested group memberships and the account's primary group. This solution takes that script to the next level, creating an administrative tool with a graphical user interface (GUI) by developing a simple Web page and an HTML Application, or HTA for short.

Web-based administrative tools are advantageous because they can be accessed from any system using standard Web browsers, such as Internet Explorer. You are able to update and manage the tool in one location, and you don't need to install components on clients. One challenge with Web-based tools, however, is that Internet Explorer places a number of security restrictions on the type of code that is allowed to execute. You can work around some of these restrictions by placing your administrative Web site in the Local Intranet security zone. Or you can code your administrative tools as ASP.NET pages, which run in the security context of the Web site's application pool, and which can execute a rich variety of code, server-side, delivering a rendered page to the client that requires little to no client-side script.

# HTML Applications

Alternatively, you can leverage HTML Applications (HTAs) as your administrative tools. HTAs are self-contained applications written with standard HTML, VBScript, and/or JavaScript code. The code of an HTA is identical to that of an HTML Web page except for one additional <HTA> tag. However, instead of running with Internet Explorer (iexplore.exe), they are executed using mshta.exe, which places far fewer security restrictions on the code that runs within the HTA.

Because HTAs are stand-alone applications, they can also be launched when network access is unavailable. They can be executed from the local disk of a system, from a USB key, or from optical media—you do not need a Web server to host them.

To code HTAs, you should be comfortable with a scripting language, such as VBScript, and with HTML. You can use HTML editors such as Microsoft Expression or FrontPage 2003 to help with the HTML. Script editors can make the VBScript easier. Although this book is not meant to be a tutorial in scripting, this solution will give you a jump start in the skills required to turn any script into an HTA.

If you are not a strong scripter, you will still be able to *use* the HTAs we develop. Each is found in the Scripts folder of the companion media. You will need to make modifications to the HTA, which can be done by opening the HTA in Notepad or any other text editor. Don't use Microsoft Office Word or another word processor that might change characters and formatting. Word, for example, might change quotes (") into curly quotes (" and "). You'll find comments embedded in each HTA or script that point out what you need to change to make the HTA work in your environment.

Even if you are not particularly strong with HTML or VBScript, I encourage you to read this solution with an eye on how a good script can be incorporated, fairly easily, into an HTA. Pay attention to how input controls, such as text boxes, can be used to provide parameters for the GUI tool instead of command-line arguments for the script.

## Create an HTA

In fact, it is fairly trivial to convert a well-written script into an HTA. The following discussion will give you a head start in mastering the steps required to do so.

### Write the functional code first

Before worrying about what your HTA—the "interface" for your administrative tool—looks like, get your script to work. All code should be in subroutines and functions that are self-contained, meaning that they take input from parameters passed to the routine or found on input controls (such as text boxes) on the HTA page, and return results to the calling code, or display results on the page. If a script has been written to accept arguments and to display results efficiently, this should be an easy task.

For example, our ADObject_MemberOf_Enum.vbs script is highly modular, with subroutines and functions doing the real work. The script's functionality is therefore almost ready to migrate to HTA-appropriate code. Only the code at the very beginning of the routine is not part of a subroutine or function. That code, minus the usage prompt, is shown here:

```
Option Explicit
Dim oMemberOfList
Dim aMemberOfList
Dim sMemberOf
Dim sDomainDN
```

```
Dim sArgument
Dim sObjectDN


' CONFIGURATION BLOCK
sDomainDN = "dc=contoso,dc=com"

' Get Argument
sArgument = WScript.Arguments(0)
' Translate it to DN
sObjectDN = ADObject_DN_UCG(sArgument, sDomainDN)
If sObjectDN = "" Then
WScript.Echo "ERROR--NOT FOUND: " & sArgument
WScript.Quit (501)
End If


' Create dictionary object to store group names
Set oMemberOfList = CreateObject("Scripting.Dictionary")
' Set comparison mode to case insensitive
oMemberOfList.CompareMode = vbTextCompare

Call ADObject_MemberOf (sObjectDN)
aMemberOfList = oMemberOfList.Keys
aMemberOfList = Array_Sort(aMemberOfList)
WScript.Echo "MEMBERSHIPS"
For Each sMemberOf In aMemberOfList
WScript.Echo sMemberOf
Next
```

This code controls the flow of the script. All we need to do is turn it into a subroutine by surrounding it with *Sub* and *End Sub* statements:

```
Option Explicit
Dim oMemberOfList
Dim sDomainDN
' CONFIGURATION BLOCK
sDomainDN = "dc=contoso,dc=com"

Sub MainRoutine()
    Dim aMemberOfList
    Dim sMemberOf
    Dim sArgument
    Dim sObjectDN
    ' Get Argument
    sArgument = WScript.Arguments(0)
    ' Translate it to DN
    sObjectDN = ADObject_DN_UCG(sArgument, sDomainDN)
    If sObjectDN = "" Then
        WScript.Echo "ERROR--NOT FOUND: " & sArgument
        WScript.Quit (501)
    End If

    ' Create dictionary object to store group names
    Set oMemberOfList = CreateObject("Scripting.Dictionary")
    ' Set comparison mode to case insensitive
    oMemberOfList.CompareMode = vbTextCompare
```

```
    Call ADObject_MemberOf (sObjectDN)
    aMemberOfList = oMemberOfList.Keys
    aMemberOfList = Array_Sort(aMemberOfList)
    WScript.Echo "MEMBERSHIPS"
    For Each sMemberOf In aMemberOfList
        WScript.Echo sMemberOf
    Next
End Sub
```

Notice that we declare the *oMemberOfList* and *sDomainDN* variables outside of the subroutine. That is because, for this particular code, we need variables of global scope that can therefore be shared between functions and subroutines.

## Creating a user interface: the HTML

Hopefully, you have an HTML editor, such as FrontPage 2003 or Microsoft Expression Web, to help create the HTML for your HTA. If not, you can use Notepad. Following are the important lines of code you require:

```
<html>
<head>
<title>My Administrative Tool</title>
<hta:application>

<script language="vbscript"> SCRIPT GOES HERE </script>
</head>
<body> USER INTERFACE HTML GOES HERE </body>
</html>
```

The *<title>* tag creates the text in the title bar of the browser. The HTML code that you place between the *<body>* opening and *</body>* closing tags creates the visible elements of the user interface. The functional code is placed between the *<script>* opening and *</script>* closing tags. These elements are shared with any Web-based administration tool.

To create an HTA, you must save the page with an .hta extension. Additionally, you add the *<hta:application>* tag, which enables the application to run under mshta.exe, exempt from the security restrictions typically placed on Web-based code.

You can certainly do much more than this, adding styles, metadata, and other tags to the page, but this is the bare-bones structure of an HTA. For more details about HTAs, see *http://msdn2.microsoft.com/en-us/library/ms536471.aspx*. There you will find an overview of HTAs and details about the powerful *<hta:application>* tag.

## Creating a user interface: inputs

Only a few lines of our script that process input will be necessary to migrate to HTA-appropriate code:

```
sArgument = WScript.Arguments(0)
sObjectDN = ADObject_DN_UCG(sArgument, sDomainDN)
```

This code assigns the first argument passed to the script to a variable called *sArgument*, then translates that argument into a distinguished name using the *ADObject_DN_UCG* function. In an HTA, such parameters, arguments, or inputs to code will be provided using input controls, such as text boxes, drop-down lists, list boxes, and check boxes. These controls will be part of the body of the page, inside the *<body>* tags.

For example, this line of code, after the opening *<body>* tag, will create a text box where we can enter the distinguished name of the user or computer whose group memberships we want to enumerate:

```
<input type="text" name="txtObjectDN" id="txtObjectDN" size="20">
```

The *<input>* tag's attributes create a text box, 20 characters wide, with a *name* and *id* of *"txtObjectDN"*. The *name* and *id* attributes should be set to the same value. The actual name doesn't matter, though you cannot use certain reserved words (such as *body*) and convention suggests you use a prefix to indicate the type of control (for example, *txt* for a text box).

The *name* and *id* of your input controls can then be used by your functional code to retrieve what the user entered into those controls. If we change this line of our script

```
sArgument = WScript.Arguments(0)
sObjectDN = ADObject_DN_UCG(sArgument, sDomainDN)
```

to

```
sObjectDN = ADObject_DN_UCG(txtObjectDN.value, sDomainDN)
```

we have now migrated the input portion of our script to the Web. When the code runs, the value that is entered into the text box will be passed to the *ADObject_DN_UCG* routine and translated into a distinguished name. Pretty easy, huh?

## Wiring up events

But what, exactly, causes the code to run? Unlike a stand-alone script, which executes the code when the script is opened, HTAs and Web pages are event driven. That means code runs only when a triggering event occurs. There are two ways to tie an event to the code that you want to run—a process called wiring up events.

The first option is to add an event handler attribute to the HTML tag:

```
<input type="text" name="txtObjectDN" id="txtObjectDN" size="20"  onchange="MainRoutine()"/>
```

Text boxes, and many other input controls, expose an event when the value of the control is changed. The *onchange* event handler attribute causes the client to execute the specified code when that happens.

Similarly, we can add a button to the page that, when clicked, executes the subroutine:

```
<input type="button" name="btnSubmit" id="btnSubmit" value="Go" onclick="MainRoutine()"/>
```

The second option is to name the subroutine to wire up the event handler automatically. Instead of naming our subroutine *MainRoutine()*, we could name it *txtObjectDN_onChange()*. The name is not case sensitive, but the name itself must be in the form *control ID_event*. If we have our button, but leave out the *onclick* attribute, we could name our subroutine *btnSubmit_onClick()*. By naming a subroutine with this format, the event will call the code automatically.

You can even use page-level events to trigger code. You will see in many of our HTAs an event handler attribute in the *<body>* tag, such as the following one:

```
<body onload="Initialize()">
```

When the page loads, the routine executes to perform initialization tasks, such as changing the window size or initializing variables.

## Creating a user interface: output

When you create an HTA, you will not be using *WScript.Echo* statements to provide output. In fact, *WScript.Echo* is not available for use, though *MsgBox* is: *MsgBox* is used to display an error message if the name entered in the text box is not valid.

For most output, however, you will typically change the HTML of the displayed page. For example, this script displays a message, "The page loaded" in an area (*div*) of the HTML page identified as *"MessageBox"*:

```
<html>
<head>


<script language="vbscript">
Sub DisplayMessage(sMessageHTML)
    MessageBox.innerHTML = sMessageHTML
End Sub
</script>

</head>

<body onload="DisplayMessage('<h1>The page loaded</h1>')">

Results:
<div id="MessageBox" name="MessageBox"> </div>

</body>
</html>
```

In the code just shown, the event that triggers the *DisplayMessage* subroutine is the page loading—the *onload* event handler attribute of the body tag.

To demonstrate another event, add the following line of code above the *</body>* closing tag:

```
<input type="button" name="btnTest" id="btnTest" onclick="DisplayMessage('<i>You just clicked
the button.</i>')" value="Click Me"/>
```

This line creates a button. The *name* and *id* attributes of the button are set to *btnTest*. The *onclick* event handler calls the *DisplayMessage* subroutine. And the button label, or *value*, is set to display "Click Me."

You will be using this type of technique to create output, so be sure that your script prepares output to be effectively displayed on the HTML page, without *WScript.Echo* statements. Our group membership enumeration script contains this code, which outputs the membership list:

```
WScript.Echo "MEMBERSHIPS"
For Each sMemberOf In aMemberOfList
   WScript.Echo sMemberOf
Next
```

We could alter the code to build the membership list, and then display it on a Web page, as such:

```
sMessageHTML = "MEMBERSHIPS"
For Each sMemberOf In aMemberOfList
   sMessageHTML = sMessageHTML & "<br/>" & sMemberOf
Next
Call DisplayMessage(sMessageHTML)
```

## The final HTA

After encapsulating our functional code within subroutines and functions, creating a user interface with input controls, wiring up events to trigger the code, and providing a mechanism for displaying the output, we're pretty close to a "perfect" HTA. It is named ADObject_ MemberOf_Enum.hta, and it can be found in the Scripts folder of the companion media.

You'll notice an additional element. We added a *<style>* tag to the *<head>* element of the page:

```
<style>
   body, tr, td, table, p, input {font-family: arial; font-size: 9pt;}
</style>
```

This will set the font to 9-point Arial for the HTA.

The final HTA code is shown next, although I've collapsed the five functions that are part of our function library so that the main elements and functionality of the HTA can be more easily evaluated:

```
ADObject_MemberOf_Enum.hta
<html>
<head>
<title>Group Membership Report</title>
<hta:application>
<script language="vbscript">
Option Explicit
Dim oMemberOfList
```

```
Dim sDomainDN
' CONFIGURATION BLOCK
sDomainDN = "dc=contoso,dc=com"

Sub MainRoutine()
    Dim aMemberOfList
    Dim sMemberOf
    Dim sResults
    Dim sObjectDN

    sObjectDN = ADObject_DN_UCG(txtObjectDN.value, sDomainDN)
    If sObjectDN = "" Then
        MsgBox "Could not find " & txtObjectDN.value
    End If

    ' Create dictionary object to store group names
    Set oMemberOfList = CreateObject("Scripting.Dictionary")
    ' Set comparison mode to case insensitive
    oMemberOfList.CompareMode = vbTextCompare

    Call ADObject_MemberOf (sObjectDN)
    aMemberOfList = oMemberOfList.Keys
    aMemberOfList = Array_Sort(aMemberOfList)
    sResults = "MEMBERSHIPS"
    For Each sMemberOf In aMemberOfList
        sResults = sResults & "<br/>" & sMemberOf
    Next

    divResults.innerHTML = sResults
End Sub
' =====================
' FUNCTIONS FROM LIBRARY
' =====================

Sub ADObject_MemberOf(ByVal sObjectDN)
Sub ADObject_MemberOf_Enum(ByVal oObject)
Function Array_Sort(ByVal aArray)
Function ADObject_DN_UCG(ByVal sObject, sSearchDN)
Function ADObject_Find_UCG(sObjectName, sSearchDN)

</script>

<style>
   body, tr, td, table, p, input {font-family: arial; font-size: 9pt;}
</style>

</head>
<body>
<input type="text" name="txtObjectDN" id="txtObjectDN" size="20"
onchange="MainRoutine()"/>
<h3>Group memberships</h3>
<div id="divResults" name="divResults"> </div>
</body>
</html>
```

Just double-click the HTA to run it! The text box uses an *OnChange* event to trigger the *MainRoutine*, so enter the name of a user, computer, or group and then press Tab to see the object's group memberships.

## For more information

To learn more about HTAs, start with the overview on MSDN, at *http://msdn2.microsoft.com/ en-us/library/ms536471.aspx*. Then peruse the TechNet Scripting Center's HTA site: *http:// www.microsoft.com/technet/scriptcenter/hubs/htas.mspx*.

## Solution summary

Create a custom, GUI-based administrative tool to enumerate group memberships by migrating the functional VBScript code developed in Solution 1-1 into an HTA. To create an HTA, ensure that all code is encapsulated in subroutines and functions. Create an HTML-based user interface and wire up events to execute the code. The code can display its results by injecting HTML into a *<div>* tag.

# 1-3: Extend Active Directory Users and Computers to Enumerate Group Memberships

## Solution overview

| | |
|---|---|
| **Type of solution** | Tool (HTA) |
| **Features and tools** | HTA, MMC snap-in task pads, Active Directory display specifiers |
| **Solution summary** | Extend the Active Directory Users and Computers snap-in so that you can right-click a user, computer, or group and produce a report of its group memberships, including nested groups. Learn how to integrate custom tools into MMC snap-ins. |
| **Benefits** | Answer the question, "What groups does _____ belong to?" Make group memberships more visible than what is possible using the standard GUI toolset. |
| **Preview** | There are two ways we can integrate our custom HTA into the Active Directory Users and Computers snap-in. When a user is selected, a task appears in the left margin of the MMC details pane. Alternatively, a command appears on the context menu. Typically, you will use just one of these two methods. Figure 1-8 illustrates both. |

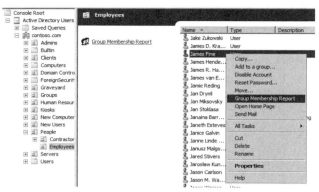

**Figure 1-8**   Integrating a custom tool with Active Directory Users and Computers

## Introduction

In Solutions 1-1 and 1-2, we developed a script that enumerated group memberships and turned that script into a stand-alone HTML Application (HTA) to provide a GUI front end. We're still left, however, with having to find and launch the HTA, and manually enter the user or computer name. Wouldn't it be nice to be able to simply select a user in an administrative tool such as Active Directory Users and Computers and, with one or two clicks, produce a group membership report for that user? That's what this solution will achieve.

But perhaps more important are the skills you will learn that enable the integration of our custom tool with a standard MMC snap-in. With these skills, you will be able to integrate any script, HTA, executable, third-party utility, or other tool into your MMC to produce a super-powerful suite of administrative tools.

## Arguments and HTAs

If we're going to launch our custom HTA and expect it to magically produce a group membership report for our selected user, we're going to need to pass the user name to the HTA, behind the scenes, in the form of an argument. And the HTA is going to need to be able to receive that argument and process it.

Unfortunately, HTAs do not have a particularly elegant way to do this. There is no *Arguments()* collection as there is in VBScript, for example. We have to jury-rig a solution.

Let's assume we were to try to launch our HTA from the command shell. We would use the following syntax:

```
mshta.exe "\\path-to-HTA\HTA-name.hta"
```

If we wanted to pass an argument, such as a user name, we would add that argument to the command:

```
mshta.exe "\\path-to-HTA\HTA-name.hta" "jfine"
```

As I mentioned earlier, the HTA cannot readily identify the argument "*jfine*". However, the HTA does know the command line with which it was launched. The command line is a property of the application itself, and the application is identified by the *id* attribute of the *<hta:application>* element. So, for example, consider an application that has the following *<hta:application>* element:

```
<hta:application
   id="oMyHTA">
```

In this case, the application is represented by an object, *oMyHTA*, and the command line can be accessed by getting the *oMyHTA.commandline* property, for example:

```
sHTACommandLine = oMyHTA.commandline
```

All we have to do, then, is evaluate the command line. The HTA will be called by name (for example, *[mshta.exe] "path\MyHTA.hta"*), so we can look for the .hta extension and assume anything after it is arguments. We then parse the remainder of the string, using the space character as a delimiter between arguments, and quotes as qualifiers that surround arguments including spaces—just like a normal command line.

If you examine the HTA_Arguments.snippet code on the companion media, you'll see two functions. The first function, *HTA_Arguments*, is called with the object reference of the HTA. It finds the command line, looks after the .hta extension to see whether there are any arguments, and then parses the remainder of the command line using the second function, *Text_Delimited_Parse( )*. This second function is a very useful function for parsing any delimited text, such as lines from a comma-delimited text file (.csv) or, in this case, space-delimited arguments where arguments that include a space are qualified (surrounded) by quotes. When these two functions have done their work, the array returned by *HTA_Arguments( )* includes any arguments that were passed on the command line to the HTA.

All we need to do, then, is call these functions when the HTA launches. The following code, inside the *<script>* tag of our HTA, will do the job:

```
Dim aArguments        ' we declare this outside of our subroutine
                      ' so that it has global scope and is available
                      ' to other code in the HTA
Sub Window_Onload     ' a routine with this name will run automatically
                      ' when the HTA launches
   aArguments = HTA_Arguments(oMyHTA)
   ' Modify oMyHTA in the above function call so that it matches
   ' the value of the "id" attribute of the <hta:application> element
End Sub
```

The *aArguments* array contains any arguments. Because it is declared with global scope, we can access *aArguments* in any other part of the code.

**Note**    This solution for receiving arguments in an HTA is highly *under*documented. You'll find it very helpful as you write HTAs.

For our ADObject_MemberOf_Enum.hta, we need to add an *id* attribute to the *<hta:application>* tag, such as:

```
<hta:application
   id="oMyHTA">
```

We can then add the following code within the *<script>* tags:

```
Dim aArguments
Sub Window_Onload
    aArguments = HTA_Arguments(oMyHTA)
    If uBound(aArguments) >= 0 Then
        ' An argument was passed to the HTA
        ' Prepopulate the text box and then run the main routine
        txtObjectDN.value = aArguments(0)
        Call MainRoutine()
    End If
End Sub
' include the HTA_Arguments.snippet which contains these two functions:
Function HTA_Arguments()
Function Text_Delimited_Parse()
```

This code launches when the HTA is opened, examines the command line to see whether any arguments were passed, and, if so, assumes the first argument (arrays are zero-based) is the name of the user or computer that we want to evaluate group memberships for. It pre-populates the text box on the page with that name and runs the code that reports group memberships.

The result is our final Group Membership Report HTA, named MemberOf_Report.hta. I snuck in one additional subroutine, which sizes and centers the HTA window, as well as an explanatory label and button in the HTML portion of the HTA. You can see that additional code by opening the HTA in Notepad or another HTA editor.

### Using the MemberOf_Report.hta

This command-line-ready version of the HTA is called MemberOf_Report.hta and is in the Scripts folder of the companion media. Launch it with the following command syntax:

```
path\MemberOf_Report.hta "name of user, computer, or group"
```

where the user, computer, or group name is a DN, ADsPath, or *sAMAccountName* of the object.

## Integrating a custom HTA with an MMC snap-in using tasks

Now comes the fun part! You've waited a long time, or you've waded through a lot of applied scripting, to get to this part. It will be worth the wait! By the time we're done, you will be able to select a user, computer, or group and, with one click, generate a membership report for that object.

We have an HTA that we can launch with a command line. That's step one—obtaining a tool that accepts arguments.

## Saving the HTA to an accessible location

The HTA (MemberOf_Report.hta from the Scripts folder of the companion media) needs to be accessible to all administrators who will use it. You can store it in a shared folder or distribute it to the local disks of administrative workstations.

If you save the HTA (or other scripts and tools) to a shared folder, you are likely to run into security restrictions that either prevent code from running or create prompts. I recommend distributing local copies of the tools, just as you do for the standard Microsoft Administrative Tools. However, if you want to save the tools in a shared location, the following paragraphs explain what you must do.

First, you need to be sure the server you have saved the HTA to is in your machine's Local Intranet security zone. In Internet Explorer, click Tools and then Internet Options, click the Security tab, select Local Intranet, and click Sites. Click Advanced (if that button is visible, which depends on the operating system you are on), and then enter the address **\\*server-name.company.com*. (Be sure to use the fully qualified domain name of the server.) Click Add, and the address you entered will be converted to the format file://*servername.company-name.com*. Click Close and OK.

If you run the HTA now, you will be prompted with an ADO Security Warning. To avoid this warning, customize the Local Intranet security zone settings to enable the Access Data Sources Across Domains setting. There are security implications to anything you do to loosen security, so spend some time looking at Internet resources to determine if that is what you want to do. Otherwise, you can live with clicking through the ADO Security Warning.

Some HTAs, including many of the most powerful HTAs we're providing on the companion media, will produce so many similar warnings that, if you don't loosen security, the tool will be painful to use. And, depending on the code that a tool executes, you might need to loosen other settings on the Local Intranet zone.

The alternative that I recommend is to ensure that the HTA is in a local path on each administrator's system (for example, C:\Program Files\\*Company*Tools\MemberOf_Report.hta). Create a folder, such as *Company*Tools, in the Program Files folder, and copy scripts, HTAs, and other tools into that location. This is the best way to avoid the most serious security limitations on HTAs and scripts.

 **Best Practices**   Distribute custom scripts and administrative tools as you would any other local application to the administrators' workstations.

## Creating a taskpad and shell task to launch the HTA

Now we're going to integrate our tool into our standard Windows administrative tools. Because this tool is related to users, computers, and groups, it makes sense to integrate it into the Active Directory Users and Computers snap-in. However, these steps work with just about any snap-in.

But you have to use the snap-in within a custom console—you can't do this with the Active Directory Users and Computers standard MMC console. The steps for creating a taskpad and task are summarized in the upcoming paragraphs. If you need more detailed steps, consult the Help function of mmc.exe.

First, you need to create a custom console with the Active Directory Users and Computers snap-in:

1. Click Start and choose the Run command (Windows XP), or click in the Search box (Windows Vista/Windows Server 2008), type **mmc.exe**, and then press Enter.

2. An empty MMC console appears. Choose File, choose Add/Remove Snap-In, and add the Active Directory Users and Computers snap-in.

3. Save the console by choosing File and then choosing Save. You should save it in the network share where the HTA is located, or in some other shared folder that is easily accessed by administrators.

Now you must create what is called a taskpad:

1. Expand the details pane of the console to an OU that contains users.

2. Right-click the OU, and choose New Taskpad View.

3. The New Taskpad View Wizard appears. Click Next.

4. On the Taskpad Style page, accept all defaults and click Next.

5. On the Taskpad Reuse page, select Selected Tree Item and click Next.

6. On the Name And Description page, accept or change the default name and description and click Next.

7. On the Completing page, be sure the check box is selected and click Finish.

You have actually finished creating the taskpad, and a second wizard launches to help you create the task on the taskpad:

1. The New Task Wizard appears. Click Next.

2. On the Command Type page, choose Shell Command and click Next.

3. In the Command box, type **mshta.exe**.

4. In the Parameters box, type "*Path to the HTA*\**MemberOf_Report.hta**" followed by a space. If you are saving the tool in a shared folder, use the fully qualified domain name of the server—for example: \\**server01.contoso.com\admintools\memberof_report.hta**.

5. With the cursor positioned after the space, click the arrow, which is a browse button.

6. Select Pre–Windows 2000 Logon Name.

   Choose Name to perform this task for computers, and choose Pre–Windows 2000 Logon Name for users and groups.

7. The Parameters box should look like this:

   ```
   "Path to the HTA\MemberOf_Report.hta" $COL<9>
   ```

   For a computer, it will look like this:

   ```
   "Path to the HTA\MemberOf_Report.hta" $COL<0>
   ```

8. In the Start In box, type "\\**path to the HTA**". If you are saving the tool in a shared folder, use the fully qualified domain name of the server—for example: "\\**server01.contoso.com\admintools**".

9. Click Next.

10. On the Name And Description page, in the Task Name box, type **Group Membership Report**. Optionally, enter a description, such as "Display sorted list of all group memberships, including nested groups and primary group."

11. Click Next.

12. On the Task Icon page, select an icon. There are several that evoke "group."

    If you click Custom Icon, you can browse to find an icon that is part of an executable, or from one of the icon libraries, such as C:\Windows\System32\Shell32.dll or, in Windows Vista and Windows Server 2003, C:\Windows\System32\Imageres.dll.

13. Click Next.

14. Click Finish.

Now there's one more *very* important step. This step is *so easy to forget* and *so confusing to solve if you forget it* that I recommend you *don't forget this step*! Any column referenced as a parameter for the task *must* be visible. Otherwise, the task won't appear when you select an object.

1. Click View and then click Add/Remove Columns.

2. Select Pre–Windows 2000 Logon Name, and click Add.

3. Click OK to close the Add/Remove Columns dialog box.

4. Save the console.

## Using the HTA

You've done it! Now, select any user in the OU and click the Group Membership Report link in the task list, which appears in the left margin of the details pane. Voilà! And if you think that's great, just wait until the next section, when we will add the command to the context menu that appears when you right-click a user.

Now wasn't that cool? Gets you thinking, doesn't it! And yes, we will integrate many other useful solutions into our standard Windows tools throughout this book.

And because you saved both the console and the HTA to a shared folder, and built the task using commands with parameters including a network path to the HTA, any administrator can now launch the custom MMC and use the custom HTA.

Repeat the steps shown for an OU with groups. Then repeat it one more time for an OU with computers, only this time use the Name column instead of the pre–Windows 2000 logon name column as the parameter. The Name column is already visible in the console, so you don't need to add it.

Amazing, huh?

So, to summarize this approach, we've created what is called a taskpad in our custom MMC console with the Active Directory Users and Computers snap-in. Our task is a shell task that executes a command, passing it a parameter that includes a column from the selected object. Our HTA interprets its command line and identifies the arguments.

### Removing a task or taskpad

To remove a task, right-click the OU that has the taskpad view, choose Edit Taskpad View, and then click the Tasks tab. Select the task and click Remove.

To remove an entire taskpad view and restore the OU to the standard view, right-click the OU that has the taskpad view and choose Delete Taskpad View.

### For more information

If you have any questions or problems related to the creation of taskpads and tasks, consult the Help menu of the Microsoft Management Console. Other solutions will go into more detail about taskpads and tasks, and we will have many more examples of custom solutions to integrate into our standard administrative tools. We'll also solve something you might have found annoying if you followed this solution: the Pre–Windows 2000 logon name column, which you added to the users OU, is visible in *every* OU, including computer OUs and even domain controller OUs. These and many other issues will be addressed.

## Integrating a custom HTA with an MMC snap-in using display specifiers

This approach will kick it up a notch, giving us the ability to right-click a user, computer, or group and generate the membership report. The MemberOf_Report.hta still needs to be accessible from a shared or local folder, but you won't need a custom MMC. You'll get the context menu command using *any* console (including the built-in consoles) that include the Active Directory Users and Computers snap-in.

> **Important**    Before attempting this approach, you need to know that display specifiers affect the entire forest. You might not have the appropriate delegations to do so, and, if you do, you should be sure you've tested changes in a lab environment before modifying the display specifiers in your production environment. The changes we will make here are not earth shaking but, like any change, should be tested and understood before rolled into production.

The Configuration partition of Active Directory includes a container called *DisplaySpecifiers* (for example, CN=DisplaySpecifiers,CN=Configuration,DC=contoso,DC=com), which you can view using ADSI Edit. ADSI Edit is available by default on Windows Server 2008. For Windows Server 2003, install the Support Tools by double-clicking the Suptools.msi file in the Support\Tools folder on the Windows Server 2003 CD-ROM. You can then run ADSI Edit by clicking Start, clicking Run, and entering **ADSIEdit.msc**. With ADSI Edit, you can open the Configuration container to see its contents, shown in Figure 1-9. You might need to right-click the root node of the ADSI Edit snap-in, choose Connect To, and in the Select A Well Known Naming Context box, choose Configuration.

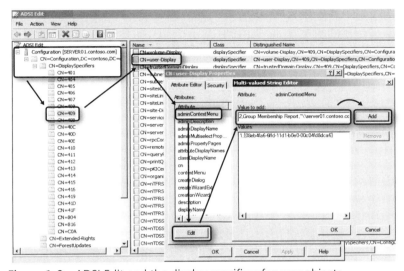

**Figure 1-9**   ADSI Edit and the display specifiers for user objects

The containers immediately below *DisplaySpecifiers* are language containers. 409 is English. To help identify which container you need for your language, see *http://msdn2.microsoft.com/en-us/library/ms776294.aspx*. Within the language container are objects representing each object class, such as *user-Display*.

If you open the properties of the *user-Display* object, an attribute called *AdminContextMenu* is responsible for displaying custom commands when you right-click a user in an administrative tool (for example, a snap-in). Other commands on the context menu (for example, Reset Password) are hard-wired into the snap-in itself. This attribute is multivalued. Each value you add takes three elements, separated by commas: the index number (the order in which the command appears), a user-friendly menu command that is displayed on the context menu, and the command to run when the menu command is selected. So, for example, if we add

```
2,Group Membership Report,"Path to HTA\MemberOf_Report.hta"
```

we will have customized the context menu for users.

> **Note**   If you've been following along, you might have found you received an Access Denied error when you tried to add the command. If that's the case, read on. We'll discuss this in just a moment.

You need to close Active Directory Users and Computers if it is open. The next time you open it, the new context menu command will be available. If you get security warnings, review the discussion in the previous section about adding the server to your Local Intranet security zone or saving the tool to your local disk.

> **Important**   The argument that is passed to the command using a custom context menu entry is the distinguished name of the selected object. Only one selected object is allowed—if you select multiple objects, only one will be passed. If you need more than that, you need to open Visual Studio and create your own MMC snap-in, which is of course way beyond the scope of this book.

## Using AdminContextMenu.hta

To make all of this easier, so that you don't have to dig into ADSIEdit and risk making mistakes, I've included an HTA (surprise!) to do the hard work for you. On the companion media, in the Scripts folder, you'll find AdminContextMenu.hta.

Open the HTA and fill in the following:

- **Language**   Select from the drop-down list. The HTA is coded to support a limited number of languages. You can extend the HTA to include more.
- **Object Class**   Select from the drop-down list. The HTA is coded to support a limited number of object classes. You can extend the HTA to include more.
- **Menu Command**   The text that appears on the context menu when you right-click an object of the selected object class in an administrative tool.
- **Command Line**   The command to launch when the menu command is chosen.

Then click Add To Administrator Context Menu. The change will be made for you. If you received an Access Denied error, I'll address that in the following paragraphs. Again, you need to close and reopen any instance of administrative tools before your change will be visible.

## Removing a custom command

If you need to remove a command, you need to use ADSI Edit. Open the Configuration container, and then browse to *DisplaySpecifiers* and the container for the language you modified (409 is English). Open the object class you changed, and select *AdminContextMenu*. Click Edit and remove the command.

## Display specifiers, delegation, and the forest

If you ran into Access Denied errors as you attempted to customize the context menu, or if you ever run into such errors, it's because the *DisplaySpecifiers* container is in the *Configuration* container, which is, by default, delegated to Enterprise Admins.

A number of my clients freak out if I suggest delegating any part of Active Directory outside of the domain partition. But it's *just a database*, and if lower level administrators need, for valid business reasons, to be able to modify another part of the database, such as *DisplaySpecifiers*, you should delegate them that capability!

This is one exception to the rule of delegation. The rule is to delegate at the container level. However, with display specifiers, I suggest you delegate each display specifier that you want a group to be able to modify. If, by some chance, you want a group to be able to change display specifiers for all objects, you should delegate the language container, or even the *DisplaySpecifiers* container. But I expect you'll be needing to delegate only the user, computer, group, and organizational unit display specifiers for one or two languages. Be granular. Then follow these steps to delegate:

1. Open the display specifier (for example, user-Display) within the appropriate language (such as CN=409 for English) in ADSI Edit.
2. Click the Security tab.
3. Click Add, and select the group to which you want to delegate the ability to modify display specifiers. I suggest having a capability management group named something like AD_DisplaySpecifiers_Modify.
4. Select the Allow Write check box and then click OK to save your changes.

## Managing changes to the context menu

Because display specifiers are in the Configuration container, they affect the entire forest. Any command you add to the *AdminContextMenu* attribute, for example, will be visible for every administrator who uses Active Directory Users and Computers in the entire forest. So modifications to display specifiers should be thoughtful, planned out, and tested so that you don't end up with a lengthy, messy context menu.

This can be a challenge in large, decentralized IT organizations. What if each IT organization wants different customizations to the context menu?

Here is the approach that I recommend in such scenarios. Create a "master" HTA that receives the argument (the distinguished name of the selected object) from Active Directory Users and Computers and then provides some form of menu or navigation with which to select the appropriate command. That command is then executed, and the distinguished name is passed on as an argument.

### For more information

For more information about display specifiers, see *http://msdn2.microsoft.com/en-us/library/ms675904.aspx*.

## Tasks or display specifiers

You've seen two ways to integrate our custom tool into the Active Directory Users and Computers snap-in: a custom task and a custom command in the context menu. Custom tasks can be created by anyone with the skills to customize an MMC console. They also give you the opportunity to choose which property of the selected object is passed to the command as an argument. But administrators must have the custom console to execute the custom task.

You can perform display specifier modifications once and immediately affect all instances of the native administrative tools, such as the Active Directory Users and Computers snap-in. But they require appropriate delegation of permissions, and you will likely want to keep the length of your context menu under control.

## Solution summary

We've taken our example of an administrative solution to its ultimate implementation. The script that enumerated group membership was integrated into a custom HTA. That HTA was extended to accept arguments from a command line. And the HTA was then integrated into our standard administrative tool, the Active Directory Users and Computers snap-in, using either a task on a taskpad or a custom context menu command created by modifying the display specifiers in Active Directory. Both the task and display specifier approach have advantages, and you might end up with a blend of solutions.

# 1-4: Understand Role-Based Management

## Solution overview

| | |
|---|---|
| **Type of solution** | Guidance |
| **Features and tools** | Active Directory groups |
| **Solution summary** | Understand the fundamentals of role-based management using Active Directory. |
| **Benefits** | Communicate effectively about role-based management. |

# Introduction

In "Scenarios, Pain, and Solution" on page 2, I laid out the challenges of an unmanaged environment and presented a vision of a well-managed environment. I highly recommend that you review that section. In this solution, I'll lay out the fundamentals of role-based management.

As I stated in "Scenarios, Pain, and Solution," the goal of role-based management is to enable an enterprise to define its users and computers by the roles they play, and through that role-based definition to enable, automatically, all required management. That means providing resource access, system privileges, software applications, user experience configuration such as mapped drives, user data and settings management, e-mail distribution lists, security and update configuration, and more—all based on roles.

The assumption is that in an organization, the enterprise is bigger than the individual: that it is the part the individual plays that really drives what that individual (user or computer) requires to achieve the organization's goals. So even in a small organization, defining roles that align with the business allows the one individual who plays certain roles today to be replaced by another individual, playing the same roles, who will be thereby managed identically.

Another goal of role-based management is to simplify reporting, auditing, and compliance. Questions such as, "What can Janice get to?" and "Who can edit the Budget resources?" need to be answered quickly, easily, and authoritatively.

From the highest level, role-based management is how you align your information technology to answer the basic questions, "*Who* can do *what* and *where*?" If you keep those three question words—*who*, *what*, and *where*—in mind, it will help you put the pieces of role-based management together.

We can simplify the job of the IT professional to this point: We connect users with the stuff they need. That stuff could be e-mail, files, printers, software applications, and so on. Conversely, we also need to ensure users are *not* connected to stuff they should not get to. But if we do the first job effectively, the second is achieved.

Because we assume that the organization is bigger than the individual, and because we've all learned the golden rule of administration, we know we need to manage with groups, not individual users (or computers). If you have three users who need read permission to a shared folder containing the budget, you would not add each user, individually, to the access control list (ACL) of the folder. At least I hope you wouldn't! Instead, you would create a group and grant the group read permission to the folder. Figure 1-10 represents this approach.

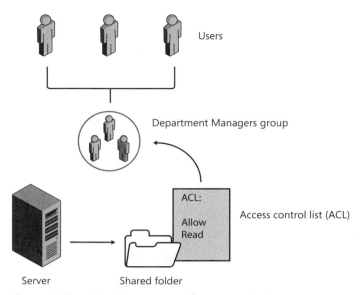

Figure 1-10    Assigning a group of users permission to a resource

# Role groups

Let's assume the users in our scenario share a common characteristic: They are all departmental managers.

The *who* component of our *who*, *what*, and *where* approach is, for the most part, our roles. We can create a role group called Department Managers and add those three users to it. Role groups define a collection of users or computers based on similarities that can include business units, geography, departments, function, seniority or status, teams, projects, or other business-related characteristics.

> **Important**    A role group defines a collection of users or computers based on business-related commonalities. It helps to define *who* a user or computer is.

## The problem with having *only* role groups

Most organizations have various degrees of understanding and implementation of role groups. It's pretty common to see groups like Sales, Marketing, Finance, or even Consultants in an organization's Active Directory.

Unfortunately, that is sometimes where it stops. If you have only role groups, and you've assigned your Department Managers permission to read the budget, what happens when you hire a consultant that, in order to perform the job you want done, also needs to be able to read the budget?

If you add the consultant to the ACL of the Budget folder, you've solved the immediate problem. But what about the next exception to the rule or the next user or group that also requires read access? And how, now, will you answer the reporting question, "Who can read the budget?" You will have to scan the ACL of the Budget folder for any security principal with Allow Read effective permissions. That's not easy. And what if Budget isn't just one folder, but is in folders on four different servers?

You can see, I hope, that having *only* role groups isn't enough, because roles do not map one-to-one with what you are trying to manage: in this case, read access to the Budget resources.

## Capability management groups

So let's continue that scenario. What would you do if you had shared folders on four different servers, all of which had to do with next year's budget? We'll call these four shared folders Budget Resources or Budget.

The best approach to managing resource access in this scenario is to create a single group that represents read access to the Budget resources. Let's call the group ACL_Budget_Read, (for reasons that we'll explain as this Solution Collection progresses). Give that group the Read permission to each of the folders on the four servers. Put the Department Managers group into that group. When the consultants need access, add Consultants to the ACL_Budget_Read group. And when another exception to the rule requires that a single user (who is neither a departmental manager nor a consultant) be given the Read permission to the folders, add that one user to the ACL_Budget_Read group. Voilà. You are managing read access to that collection of resources for the Budget. Figure 1-11 represents this model.

Now stop and think, in this simple scenario, what this means for reporting and auditing. If someone asks you, "Who can read the budget?", you will be able to answer. Simply look at the membership of the ACL_Budget_Read group. What would you have had to do otherwise? Look at the ACLs of the shared folders and evaluate who has read permissions, one folder at a time. This *is* a very simple scenario. The importance of managing access to a collection of resources grows logarithmically as you introduce more resources and more users—and thereby more complexity—into the environment.

What we just explained was the creation of a capability management group. A capability management group represents a single, granular management task. In this case, we are managing the capability to read a particular collection of resources (the Budget). This is the *what* component of our *who*, *what*, and *where* approach. If we add James to the ACL_Budget_Read group, *what* can he now do? Read the budget.

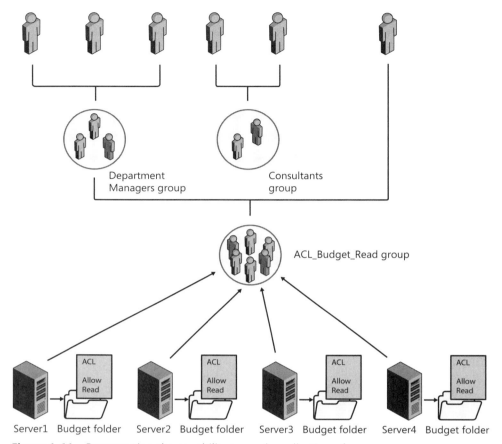

**Figure 1-11**    Representing the capability to read a collection of resources

Some of my clients like to call this kind of group a task group. That's a perfectly fine name in this scenario—we're managing who can perform a task: reading the budget. But I prefer "capability management group" because role-based management extends beyond files and folders to things like printing on special printers, being on a distribution list, or even getting an application such as Visio deployed to a desktop. So we're managing a user's capability to use Visio, her capability to print on the special printer, or even her capability to receive e-mail messages targeted to a particular distribution list.

The *where* component of our *who*, *what*, and *where* approach is called the scope of management, or SOM. Where can our users read files? The Budget folders.

> **Important**    Capability management groups represent a single, granular management task. They represent *what* a user can do and *where* they can do it.

A group called ACL_Budget_Read doesn't actually do anything until you've *implemented* its capability. In the case of a capability to read a set of folders, that means adding the ACL_Budget_Read group with Allow Read permissions to the ACLs of the four shared folders. Those four shared folders are the "scope of management" for this group, and you *implement the scope of management* using folder ACLs. I emphasize this again because when we look at other management tasks, you will *implement* the scope of management differently.

### The problem with having *only* capability management groups

Some organizations have managed to find themselves in a place where what they have is, in actuality if not in name, mostly or entirely capability management groups. One of my clients (which has an outsourced support organization, by the way) has groups that represent different types of access to different folders. That's what I would call "capability management" groups, though this client refers to them as if they are role groups: A user is assigned to Project Surfboard, so he can have access to the Project Surfboard folders. But users are placed *directly* into these groups. There is no layer of "roles." So whenever a user's role changes, his new manager has to, in effect, request all the individual capabilities that that user requires. Not that the user isn't any different than anyone else in that role—there just isn't a way to *represent* the role. Guess what? That process takes days or weeks, and typically requires several help desk calls along the lines of, "Oops, I forgot my new team member also requires access to x-y-z as well." Because the outsourced support organization is paid for each help desk ticket, this is a windfall for them! And a complete waste of money for the client.

Capability management groups, alone, are not enough. And look carefully at your organization. Chances are you have some role groups and some capability management groups, but there isn't an easy way to distinguish them. They're mixed up together and used incorrectly. So you're likely to be experiencing some of the pain I introduced at the beginning of this Solution Collection.

## Role groups are nested into capability management groups

Now that we have a role group, such as Department Managers or Consultants, and a capability management group, such as ACL_Budget_Read, we can nest the role group into the capability management group. That way, when we promote a new user to manage her department, we simply add that role to the user by adding the user to the Department Managers group—and, voilà, she can read the budget. Chances are Department Managers share other common resource access needs. They share an e-mail distribution group: The Department Managers group belongs to the LST_Department Managers distribution group. And they can all edit the company newsletter so that they can update their department's section of the newsletter. So the Department Managers group belongs to the ACL_Newsletter_Edit group. Another role, Communications, also belongs to the ACL_Newsletter_Edit group.

The Auditors role and the Finance Managers role both belong to the ACL_Finance_Audit group, which provides read access to all finance-related files in the enterprise. The CEO also belongs to the ACL_Finance_Audit group as part of the data visibility project so that the CEO feels comfortable signing off on financials.

 **Important**     Role groups nest into capability management groups.

Figure 1-12 represents the simple structure we've set out in the discussion so far.

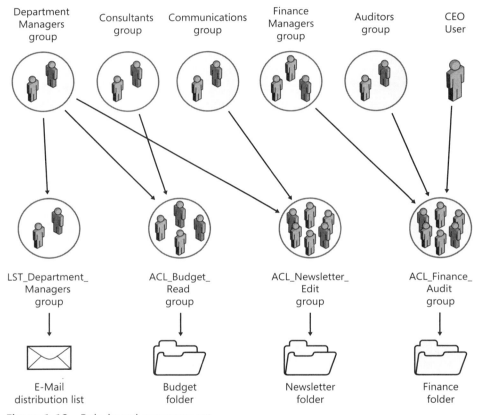

**Figure 1-12**   Role-based management

## Other nesting

As we saw in the previous paragraph and earlier in this discussion, it is perfectly fine for a single user to belong to a capability management group. That's how we manage the exceptions to the rule. What you want to watch out for is when you start having too many users belonging to a single capability management group. Treat that as an alert to examine *why* so many individual users are in a capability management group. My experience suggests that means they share a characteristic that would allow you to define them as a role. You then nest the role group, instead of the individual users, in the capability management group.

Also, it's very common to have role groups nest into other role groups. Take the IT organization for example. Let's assume there are two roles: Windows Engineers and Help Desk. Chances are you've assigned rights and resource access to the Help Desk staff to enable them to do their jobs. But the more experienced Windows Engineers are also frequently asked to reset a user's password and to perform basic support tasks. In other words, Windows Engineers should be everything the Help Desk is, plus some more. So the Windows Engineers role, instead of nesting into all the individual capability management groups, could nest into the Help Desk role and thereby inherit all the capabilities assigned to the Help Desk. Additionally, you would nest the Windows Engineers role directly into capabilities that are unique to that role. We will explore the role-based management of Active Directory, administrators, and support personnel in Solution Collection 5, "Active Directory Delegation and Administrative Lock Down."

It should be less common that capability management groups nest into other capability management groups. Although there might be valid scenarios for such a design, it's more likely that you're beginning to blur roles and capability management groups. You might need the roles that are in one capability management group to *also* have another capability. Nest the roles into the capability management group, and ensure that capability management groups have a one-to-one relationship with *what* you are trying to manage and *where* you are trying to manage it.

Finally, I've been focusing on users and groups. But computers are security principals as well. Imagine defining roles of computers such as, simply, "Denver computers," "conference room," "desktop," "laptop," "roaming salesforce laptops," "administrators' workstations," and so on. You can imagine using those roles to manage capabilities. The Denver computers role might allow the Denver site support team to be a member of the local Administrators group, while another location includes a different support team. The roaming salesforce laptops might be excluded from certain configurations that are not easy to maintain when the users rarely connect to the network. Sensitive corporate documents might be made unavailable to the conference room computers. These are just a few examples.

## Data, business logic, and presentation

A role-based management model requires three major components: data, business logic, and presentation. Data is the database, or store of information, regarding the model. Business logic is the representation of business requirements, organizational characteristics, workflows, processes, and policies. And presentation is how the model appears in tools, reports, and other user interfaces.

The goal of this book is to enable you to leverage Active Directory as a database. After all, it is one. And it's highly available in your enterprise. It's replicated (very efficiently). It's backed up. It's secured. And there are a number of tools with which to access and manage it. It pains me to see organizations that have significant Active Directory implementations that, after many years, still serve only the role of authentication—enabling users to log on. Make the most of it!

Business logic will be implemented primarily through the nesting of users and computers into role groups, the recursive nesting of role groups, and the nesting of role groups and occasional users or computers into capability management groups. That's your *logic layer*. Gathering and analyzing the data about your business to understand and model its business logic is, without doubt, the most difficult part of implementing role-based management. The technology is easy. The business is not.

Presentation—the visible aspect of the role-based management model—is a weak spot for Microsoft's native tools, such as the Active Directory Users and Computers snap-in. As we saw in Solutions 1-1 through 1-3, it actually takes quite a bit of creativity to be able to expose a user's full group memberships. And to manage group membership, there is only one tool—the Active Directory Users and Computers snap-in—which is not a tool you want to give to nontechnical users who might have business reasons to manage group memberships.

So throughout this resource kit, I'll present solutions to help you build sophisticated and effective role-based management by leveraging Active Directory as a data store, group management for business logic, and custom tools for presentation.

## Third-party tools

Microsoft and other vendors offer tools that can supplement or completely manage your enterprise in a role-based model. Server products such as Microsoft Identity Lifecycle Manager (ILM) and System Center Configuration Manager 2007 are phenomenal tools. Companies such as Sun Microsystems, Oracle, Quest, and others offer identity and role-management solutions.

Each of these tools offer components to manage the data, business logic, and presentation of role-based management. But in the end, most end up *implementing* the business logic back in Active Directory and on scopes of management such as folder ACLs. So if you're new to role-based management, I encourage you to *start* with Active Directory and the tools offered in this resource kit. Defining your business logic and requirements will be an involved and evolving task. When your requirements are such that implementing the infrastructure in Active Directory no longer makes sense, you'll be ready to make an intelligent choice for a new product to fill the gaps you've identified, and you'll have a business logic defined and ready to migrate.

## Solution summary

Role-based management provides a structure with which to align enterprise IT with business logic and requirements. By representing users and computers as role groups, and by representing capabilities and scopes of management as capability groups, you can reflect your business logic by nesting role groups in capability groups. Thereafter, simply adding, removing, or redefining a user's or computer's role will automatically configure the resources, applications, configuration, and other IT components that are required for that user or computer to perform the tasks related to its roles.

# 1-5: Implement Role-Based Access Control

## Solution overview

| | |
|---|---|
| **Type of solution** | Guidance and best practices |
| **Features and tools** | Active Directory group management |
| **Solution summary** | Implement role-based access control through disciplined and sophisticated group management. |
| **Benefits** | Automate the management of resource access based on user and computer roles and business requirements. |

## Introduction

Role-based access control, or RBAC, is role-based management applied to the security of resources: files, folders, printers, SharePoint lists and libraries, and so on. In this solution, we'll build an RBAC implementation for a resource collection and, in doing so, will gain skills that apply to other applications of role-based management.

In this solution, we'll flesh out the scenario presented in the previous solution by implementing access to the Budget resources. At Contoso, Ltd., the files related to next year's budget are in shared folders on servers in the department's primary site. Marketing, Sales, Manufacturing, and Research and Development each have servers with a share named Budget. Together, these make up what we will call a resource collection: a distributed set of files that will nonetheless be managed as a single resource. We'll implement the *who*, the *what*, and the *where* of role-based access control. Along the way, we'll lay out the best practices for role-based management.

A warning: what we do in this solution will seem quite labor intensive. That is for two reasons. First, as IT professionals we've become oblivious to the costs of managing resources without role-based management. We'll address the old and new ways of managing in a solution later in the chapter. Second, we have not yet built tools that allow us to automate and provision within our role-based management model. Those tools will be developed in this and later Solution Collections.

## Role groups

As defined in the previous solution, role groups define users and computers by using business-driven criteria such as business unit, function, department, team or project membership, location, or seniority. Typically, roles are very clear and easy to understand: James is an Accountant in Sydney; Janice is a Finance Manager in London and a member of the Special Project.

> **Important**    Roles and their members should be highly trusted.

Resource owners will manage resources by granting capabilities related to the resources for the roles you've defined. Therefore, roles and their members should be highly trusted. For example, William is the lead of the Special Project and, as such, has been given ownership of a shared folder and a SharePoint team site for the team. He will grant access to the Special Project group, and he will want to know that the membership of that group is accurate and trustworthy. Otherwise, he would be forced to grant access to individual users to his resources. By providing him a trustworthy definition of a role, we can offer a relief to a management burden.

> **Important**    Roles should, wherever possible, be driven by authoritative data sources.

If membership in a role is driven not by a human being, but rather by an authoritative data source, that role can be more highly trusted. Contoso, Ltd., has created a link between its human resources (HR) software and the roles it has defined in Active Directory. When Janice was promoted to Finance Manager, that was implemented first in the HR application. She was then automatically moved into the Finance Manager role in Active Directory based on the attributes of her HR record. Such database-driven role definitions enhance the trustworthiness of the role groups.

Such links can be made using sophisticated and not inexpensive identity management applications. Identity management (IdM) applications typically have interfaces for many different database applications and formats. Agents in the IdM application monitor changes in the source database, and, when a trigger occurs, the IdM application performs changes in other databases, such as Active Directory, based on the logic that has been entered into the application. So an IdM application could monitor a Job Title field in an HR database and, based on that title, synchronize a user's membership with a specific group in Active Directory.

Similar functionality can be built, instead of bought. I have several clients with extensive and elaborate home-grown applications that interface between financial, HR, and operational databases and, based on those data sources, make changes in Active Directory.

Another simple example is computer roles. Most organizations maintain some kind of computer inventory that is updated when a new system is purchased. At a bare minimum, such an inventory should be able to drive simple roles such as "desktop" versus "laptop," and, when the computer is provisioned to a user, that information can drive the location-based role of that computer.

> **Note**   Role groups are typically global security groups.

Role groups are typically global security groups, which can contain users and computers and other global groups, from the same domain only. You can add groups for the same domain as members of global security groups if your domain is at the Windows 2000 native or greater domain functional level. Global groups cannot contain any object from another domain. In multidomain forests, role groups can be implemented as universal groups when they need to include members from more than one domain.

In rare situations in which a role needs to include accounts from a trusted domain outside of the forest, the role needs to be a domain local group. Such a role group cannot nest in a global group, which prevents it from being useful for filtering Group Policy objects. But GPOs wouldn't be applying to users or computers in the trusted external domain anyway. Use domain local groups for role groups only as a rare exception.

> **Note**   Role groups contain users, computers, and other roles.

Role groups contain, primarily, users and computers. Typically, a role group has users *or* computers. But certain types of role groups, such as location role groups, contain both.

Contoso's LOC_SYD group, for example, represents users *and* computers in the Sydney site. It is used to manage several capabilities, including the capability to have the Sydney office's home page as the home page for Internet Explorer (implemented in a Group Policy object filtered to LOC_SYD), a set of network printers (implemented in the same GPO), and the capability to be supported by the local Sydney support team. (The Sydney Support role belongs to the local Administrators group through a Restricted Groups MemberOf policy.) The specifics of these GPO-related capabilities will be discussed in the Group Policy Solution Collection.

Role groups also, occasionally, contain other roles. For example, the Finance Managers and Marketing Managers role groups might nest into the Departmental Managers role group. Role group nesting creates business logic, indicating the relationship—the hierarchy and the associations—of an organization. Your organization chart will likely be reflected in the nesting of role groups in Active Directory.

> **Important**   Role groups should be contained in one or more dedicated OUs.

Because role groups are the foundation of role-based management, they need to be highly trusted and, wherever possible, driven by authoritative data sources. You can further this cause by separating role groups in Active Directory from groups with other purposes.

Contoso, Ltd., has an OU named Role Groups within its Groups OU, but it is separate from (a peer to) other OUs for Resource Access Groups, Application Groups, and other capability management groups.

Putting role groups in one or more dedicated OUs allows you to delegate (secure) the management of role group memberships. In most medium to large organizations, and in many smaller enterprises, it would not be appropriate for a Help Desk professional to change the role definition of a user (for example, to add James to the Finance Managers group). That task should be delegated to a trained, trusted and, hopefully, authoritative team or tool.

Contoso, in fact, has several role group OUs. In addition to the Role Groups OU, there is a Location Groups OU. This OU contains role groups related to a user's or computer's location (for example, the LOC_SYD group). This particular OU is, in fact, delegated to the Help Desk so that when a user is relocated, the Help Desk can move the user and his or her computer between location role groups. The Role Groups OU, which contains all other role definitions, is tightly controlled.

When you are fortunate enough to link role group memberships to authoritative data sources, you should further limit the possibility for human beings to interfere with the synchronization between the authoritative data source and the Active Directory groups. In this situation, create a separate OU—for example, Role Groups Authoritative—and delegate management of group membership *only* to the IdM application or tool that you have built. You might, of course, also delegate membership management to a very limited number of trusted individuals in the event that the IdM link is down and manual maintenance must be performed.

 **Important**    Role groups should strictly adhere to your naming convention.

## Group naming conventions

Naming conventions are *critical*. Did I mention they are *critical*? They are *critical* to effective role-based management. Let me preview some of the naming standards I'll be detailing later in the resource kit:

- Resource Access Groups: ACL_*Resource_Access Level*
- Software Deployment: APP_*Application*
- Administrators Groups (for example, Help Desk): ADM_*Description*
- Group Policy Filtering Groups: GPO_*GPO Name*
- Patch Management Groups (for example, the "update pilot" group): UPD_*Description*

You get the idea. Groups will have a prefix that denotes the group's purpose.

> **Important**    Group prefixes should denote the group's purpose.

Why prefixes? Because they achieve several goals. First, they make finding the right group much easier. Imagine if all the groups you should use to manage resource security started with *ACL_*. Whenever you add a group to an ACL, in the Security Properties or Advanced Security Settings dialog boxes, you click Add and you're presented with a dialog box where you can enter a partial group name and then select from a list of matching groups, as shown in Figure 1-13.

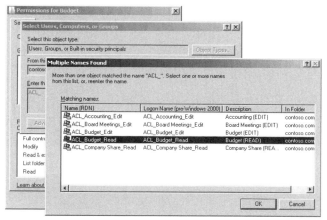

**Figure 1-13**    Selecting a group using the ACL_ prefix

The prefix acts as a way to narrow down your many groups to the type of group you really need for a particular task.

Using a prefix also helps you group your groups when you list them. In other words, all the resource security groups will appear together on a list of groups because they all begin with *ACL_*.

> **Important**    Use a consistent character, such as an underscore (_) to separate or *delimit* the parts of a group's name.

It is important to find a way to designate which part of the group name denotes its purpose—its description, its suffix, or other components of the name. I recommend using an underscore (_) as the delimiting character. That means you do *not* use an underscore as any part of the name itself—the underscore becomes reserved as a delimiter.

For example, in the upcoming paragraphs, I detail the recommendation to use *ACL_Resource Collection_Access Level* as the naming convention for capability groups for managing resource access. Note the underscore delimits (separates) the prefix (ACL) from the resource collection name (which uses spaces, not underscores) from the access level.

A naming convention such as this facilitates automation, provisioning, and *presentation* of your role-based management model. Remember Figures 1-1 to 1-3, in which we examined the life of James Fine as he progressed through his career at Contoso? Guess how his group memberships were categorized by that HTA? The prefix! Any group that began with ACL_ was listed as being in the Resource Access group section. And in the screen shots, you'll notice the access level is in parentheses. Guess how we did that? We took the second underscore delimiter and put everything after that in parentheses. The delimiter allowed us to easily recognize and break apart, or parse, the group names.

There are many more reasons for naming conventions. I could write a book just on naming conventions. Don't know if anyone would buy it. But I digress.

So, what should the naming convention be for role groups?

> **Important**   Roles of normal human beings should have *no prefix*.

Whoa! Didn't I just harp on the importance of prefixes? Yes, I did. But having *one* exception to a rule is a rule in itself, right? So here's the "exception" rule. A role group that represents normal human being users should have no prefix. Just a name. Finance Managers. Sales Team. Executives. Special Project.

The reason is that these role groups will be the most visible groups in your enterprise. When a nontechnical resource owner, such as William who leads the special project, is going to "see" a group to give it some kind of access, he will see the human role groups such as Special Project. So make those groups as easy, obvious, and simple as possible for your users.

Now other types of role groups should have prefixes. For example, I recommend using ADM_ as a prefix for the roles of administrators, such as ADM_Help Desk or ADM_Desktop Support.

> **Note**   Prefix administrative roles with a tag such as ADM_.

Administrators are different. They're special (in so many ways). And, typically, they're logging on with alternate credentials. At least I hope they are. Put those administrative secondary credentials in an ADM_ group, and assign capabilities (such as the ability to install Administrative Tools or the ability to reset a user's password) to the ADM_ role.

Computers are also different. I recommend denoting roles that will contain *only* computers with a prefix, such as COMP_.

> **Note**   Flag roles that contain only computers with a prefix such as COMP_.

So your conference room and training lab computer objects would be members of COMP_ Conference Room Systems and COMP_Training Lab Systems, respectively.

### Role groups summary

We've covered a lot of territory. Role groups are the foundation of your role-based management model. They should be trusted, and therefore separated and delegated carefully in Active Directory. Their membership should be driven by authoritative data sources whenever possible, whether by a commercial IdM application or by scripts and tools you build yourself to synchronize properties of authoritative databases such as HR and inventory with Active Directory groups.

Role groups will most often be global security groups and will contain users, computers, and other role groups. They should strictly follow your naming convention, which should entail name components separated by delimiters, and, in the case of role groups for normal human users, should be as simple, straightforward, and recognizable as possible.

### Role groups in our RBAC scenario

For our RBAC scenario, we need several role groups: Marketing, Marketing Managers, Sales, Sales Managers, Manufacturing, Manufacturing Managers, Research and Development, Research and Development Managers, Finance, Consultants, and Auditors. If you are testing this solution in a lab, create an OU called Role Groups in an OU called Groups and create a global security group for each of the roles mentioned earlier.

Business logic is accomplished by nesting role groups. Nest each Managers group into its department group. For example, make Marketing Managers a member of Marketing.

## Capability management groups

Capability management groups represent a granular management task. In RBAC, they represent access at a particular level (for example, Read, Edit, Full Control) to a collection of resources (one or more files in one or more shares on one or more servers).

### Group naming convention

> **Note**   Prefix resource access groups with an indicator such as ACL_ (for "access control list").

Naming conventions are critical (does that sound familiar?) for capability management groups. I recommend using the ACL_ prefix for RBAC capability management groups, though you might use another prefix such as RES_ (for "resource") or PERM_ (for "permission"). One reason I like ACL_ is that managing ACLs is one of the most common day-to-day tasks for IT professionals, so having all the right groups near the top of an A-to-Z sorted list is helpful.

> **Important** The group name should include a unique identifier for the resource collection.

The middle component of the group name should be a unique identifier for the resource collection. In our scenario, it's simple: Budget. But the complexities of your business requirements might require a more sophisticated convention for the resource collection piece of the group name.

> **Important** Append resource access groups with a suffix that indicates the access level.

In our scenario, we'll have groups such as ACL_Budget_Read and ACL_Budget_Edit. The delimiter, followed by the access level, will help to improve the presentation of our role-based management model. Figures 1-1 to 1-3 break apart a group name, using the delimiter. The ACL_ prefix is used to categorize the group. The access level suffix is put in parentheses after the resource collection's name.

> **Important** When creating a capability management group, include details about *what* it manages. You should certainly populate the *Description*, *Notes*, and *Manager* attributes.

A group's name should, if you're lucky, go a long way in helping someone understand what the group does. ACL_Budget_Read is pretty self-explanatory. But it's not enough. Use other properties of the group object, such as its *Description* attribute. One of my favorite RBAC implementations used the *Description* attribute to store the actual path to the shared folder or folders that the group managed. Because the *Description* is presented in the Active Directory Users and Computers snap-in as a column, it is highly visible and helpful.

The Notes field is also very helpful. Although it can't be viewed as a column in the Active Directory Users and Computers snap-in, it can be seen in the group's Properties dialog box and viewed using scripted or custom tools. (Tip: It is the *info* attribute.)

The *ManagedBy* attribute is also helpful. Link it to the user or group that is responsible for questions about the group or for the group's membership. If you want to set the *ManagedBy* attribute of one group to another *group*, you must open the first group's properties, click the Managed By tab, click Change, and then (here's the trick) click Object Types, select the Groups check box, and then click OK. Otherwise, when you enter a group's name, it will produce an error message because the dialog box is not including groups in its search by default.

The *ManagedBy* attribute can also be used to delegate actual permissions to manage group memberships. In the group's properties, on the Managed By page, select the check box labeled Manager Can Update Membership List. As the Managed By name is changed, the ACL will be changed as well.

> **Important**    Resource access groups should be domain local security groups.

Resource access groups should be created as domain local security groups. With the domain local scope, these groups can provide long-term flexibility. Perhaps today the only users who require access to the Budget resources are in our domain. But perhaps next year we'll have a major audit and need to create a trust to the auditor's domain. Their roles will be added to our capability management groups. And domain local groups can include objects from other domains.

There are two downsides to domain local security groups. The first is that they can scope management only within a single domain. Our ACL_Budget_Read group cannot, as a domain local security group, be given permissions to budget resources in a trusting domain, even in the same forest. In such situations, you use a universal security group, which can scope management across multiple domains in a forest, or you use a global group in the very rare situation where you need to scope management (for example, add the group directly to an ACL) in a trusting domain. Use domain local groups for resource access capability groups unless absolutely driven to do otherwise.

The second downside to domain local security groups is their impact on the user's token size. This issue will be detailed in Solution 1-7. If you run into token size problems, implement resource access capability management groups as global security groups. You won't be able to include roles or users from other domains, but chances are good you're in a single domain environment, anyway. Or if your enterprise is *that* large, you might be turning to other IdM solutions for RBAC.

> **Important**    Capability management groups should contain user or computer roles and, as exceptions, individual users or computers.

Capability management groups should contain, for the most part, role groups. That's role-based management, right? But there will always be exceptions. In the last solution, we proposed that the CEO required access to all financial documents as part of her need to oversee finances so that she could sign off on them for compliance and audit. So although she might not be part of a specific role that has been given a capability to read a certain resource collection, we would add her user account directly to the capability management group. Adding individual users or computers to capability management groups to meet their business requirements is perfectly acceptable. But, as suggested in the last solution, if you find a capability management group with *lots* of users or computers, it is probably an indicator that those users or computers share a business-driven characteristic that should be defined as a role.

> **Important** Collect resource access capability management groups in one or more dedicated OUs.

Separate capability management groups for resource access from other types of groups. There are likely to be a lot of resource access management groups, and you'll probably dedicate the management of the groups' memberships "down" in your organization, either to a help desk or to the actual owners of the resources. Having a single OU or OU branch within which resource access groups are contained facilitates effective delegation.

### Capability management groups summary

Capability management groups for resource access should be domain local security groups in one or more dedicated OUs, to facilitate delegation of the groups' memberships to support teams or to resource owners. They should contain primarily role groups (user and computer roles), but they'll often contain individual user or computer accounts that are exceptions to the rule, requiring access while not fitting nicely into one of the roles that already has that access. Names should include a prefix indicating the group's purpose for RBAC, such as ACL_, include a unique identifier for the resource collection, and end with a suffix that indicates the level of access.

### Capability management groups in our RBAC scenario

For our scenario, we need only two capability management groups: ACL_Budget_Read and ACL_Budget_Edit. If you are testing this solution in a lab, create an OU called Resource Access in the Groups OU. Create a domain local security group for each of those capabilities.

## Representing business requirements

Business requirements are represented by nesting role groups and, occasionally, individual users and computers into capability management groups. Simple enough!

In our scenario, add each of the four department role groups (Marketing, Sales, and so on) to the ACL_Budget_Read group. Also, add Auditors and a user account representing the CEO. Add the four Managers groups to the ACL_Budget_Edit group. Also add Consultants.

The key to RBAC is that this layer of the process should be 100 percent aligned with business requirements. There should be one or more roles that share a business requirement, and that requirement relates to a common capability for those roles. Nest the roles into the capability management groups and you've got it!

# Implementing capabilities

How you implement a capability for a scope of management varies depending on exactly *what* capability you are managing. What you do to give read access to the budget is quite different than what you do to deploy to those users the budget application.

In the case of RBAC, it's simple enough. Add the capability management groups to the ACLs of the folders that are part of the resource collection. Solutions in Solution Collection 2, "Managing Files, Folders, and Shares," go into detail about how you implement capabilities such as Read and Edit. Edit, particularly, is nowhere near as simple as most organizations think. If you think "Modify permission," you are setting yourself up for a denial of service scenario. So don't set this book down before you've read through that Solution Collection.

# Automating and provisioning

When I discuss RBAC with clients, we usually get to this point and they just can't contain themselves any longer and someone asks, "Isn't this a lot of work?" The answer is, "Yes!" but not where you think. The creation of groups, the population of all the properties, the enforcement of naming conventions, and the setting of ACLs are all tasks that can be easily provisioned and automated *after you have RBAC in place*. It's analyzing your business to determine roles; analyzing your enterprise to identify what capabilities you need to manage; and *understanding* what you need to build that is the tough part. But the payoff is really, *really* huge, as you'll see as we build solutions upon this foundation of RBAC and role-based management.

Imagine a day when RBAC is in place and you need to create folders for the next year's budget on four servers. You will pull up a tool, enter a name for the folder, select the four servers you want to provision the folder on, and indicate that you need to implement Edit and Read capabilities. The tool will then create the folder and the share on each server, create the two capability management groups (following your naming convention), and assign the eight ($2 \times 4$) sets of permissions that are required to implement the capabilities. All you then have to do is nest the handful of roles that require each capability into the appropriate group, and voilà. Such a tool will be yours by the end of Solution Collection 2.

# Solution summary

This solution laid out the requirements for implementing role groups, capability management groups, and business requirements, using an RBAC scenario. The concepts, guidance, and tasks outlined in this solution are useful in other role-based management scenarios as well. This solution will serve as a foundation for many powerful solutions in this and other Solution Collections.

# 1-6: Reporting and Auditing RBAC and Role-Based Management

## Solution overview

| | |
|---|---|
| Type of solution | Guidance and tools |
| Features and tools | Active Directory group management, HTAs, VBScript |
| Solution summary | Leverage your role-based management model to produce reports and to audit the integrity of the model. |
| Benefits | Easy answers to "What can James get to?" and "Who can edit the Budget?" The ability to monitor that your organization is actually following the guidelines of your role-based management. |
| Preview | Figure 1-14 shows two tools, My Memberships and Resource Access Report, which answer the questions posed above. |

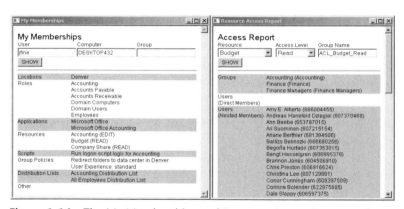

**Figure 1-14**    The My Memberships and Resource Access Report tools

## Introduction

This solution provides several important capabilities of role-based management related to reporting, auditing, and compliance. You can probably see from Figure 1-14 that the type of information you can glean by easily using role-based management is exactly the kind of information that we IT professionals are being asked to provide every day:

- An analysis of who a particular user is: the user's roles, what applications the user should have, the resources the user can access, what logon scripts run (and thereby what drives are mapped), what group policies apply, and the e-mail distribution lists to which the user belongs

- An analysis of a specific resource: who can get to it, and with what level of access

If you've been following this Solution Collection in order, which I recommend doing, you're already prepared and probably anticipating how these reports can be generated and integrated directly into Active Directory Users and Computers or other administrative snap-ins. They simply perform group membership enumeration. And they can be added, as tasks or as custom commands on the context menu, to your administrative tools.

As you read though this solution, pay attention to how the rules and discipline discussed in the previous solution allow us to build tools using skills learned in Solutions 1-1 through 1-3 to enable many of the benefits of role-based management discussed in Solution 1-4.

# My Memberships

The My Memberships tool, shown in Figure 1-3 and Figure 1-14, analyzes a user and reports how that user is being managed. When I show this tool to enterprise customers, they drool. What gives us the power to produce this information? Disciplined group naming standards. To make a long story very short, the tool simply enumerates the group membership of a user, as in Solution 1-2, and then performs reverse logic on group names.

For example, if a group name begins with ACL_, the code knows that the group is a Resource Access group, and therefore the group is displayed in that category. And to make the report all the more readable, rather than displaying the group name, the tool displays the group's description attribute. This happens because, of course, we've been disciplined about entering the group description for every group we created, or we have a provisioning tool such as the one presented in Solution Collection 2.

## Using My Memberships

My Memberships is in the Scripts folder of the companion media and is named My Memberships.hta. My Memberships is designed to be launched several ways. First, it can be opened just by double-clicking, in which case it evaluates the memberships of the currently logged-on user. Second, it can be launched from a command line, MMC taskpad task, or custom context menu command, in which case it will receive arguments specifying the user, computer, or group that should be evaluated.

After it's open, My Memberships displays information about the selected user, computer, or group. You can then modify any of the additional fields (User, Computer, or Group), and My Memberships will perform a cumulative analysis of memberships.

For example, if James Fine is logged on to Desktop 432, as shown in Figure 1-3 and 1-14, My Memberships displays the combined memberships of both the user and computer objects, providing insight into what is in effect for that user on that computer. You can enter a different computer name, such as the name of a computer in a conference room, and the tool displays what James would experience when logged on to that computer.

You can also evaluate a group's memberships to identify what groups the selected group is nested into, directly or indirectly. If you are evaluating a user or computer and you enter a group name in which the user or computer already exists, you won't see any new information, because the report already includes that group. However, you can perform "What If" analyses by adding the name of a group to which the user or computer does not already belong, and you'll see the effect of that addition.

Because the tool can be launched in so many different ways, you can easily integrate it into the Active Directory Users and Computers snap-in as detailed in Solution 1-3. If you use a task to launch My Memberships for a user, be sure to use the pre–Windows 2000 logon name as the parameter, which is *$COL<9>*. For a group, also use the pre–Windows 2000 logon name. For a computer, use the name *$COL<0>*. Remember to add the column to the details pane view as well, by choosing the Add/Remove Columns command from the View menu.

You can also launch My Memberships as a custom context menu command, using steps also detailed in Solution 1-3.

As we've done with other tools in this section, we'll take a short look at the code in the next section. If you're not a strong scripter, you should skim the section to learn what it takes to customize My Memberships to reflect your naming conventions.

## Understanding and customizing My Memberships

My Memberships is the most complex tool we've presented in this Solution Collection, but that doesn't mean you can't understand and customize it. Particularly if you've followed our recommendations and have implemented detailed and enforced group naming standards, you'll find it's pretty easy to adapt My Memberships.

As mentioned earlier, My Memberships is designed to be launched several ways, with several different types of arguments. When My Memberships first opens, *Window_Onload* is automatically executed and the HTA centers itself on the screen (the *CenterMe* subroutine) and identifies the name of the local computer and the currently logged-on user (the *Initialize* subroutine). The DN of the domain is derived from the currently logged-on user's DN.

The HTML portion of the HTA has text-box controls for a user name, computer name, and group name. *Windows_Onload* calls the *Prepopulate* subroutine, which examines the command line with which the HTA was launched to identify the argument (using our *HTA_Arguments* function). If no argument was passed, the currently logged-on user and computer name are entered into the text boxes.

If an argument was passed, it is used to find the selected object in Active Directory. The object's class determines which of the form's text boxes (user, computer, or group) is used to display the object's name.

My Memberships then runs the *MainRoutine* subroutine, which performs a group member-ship enumeration on the user, computer, and/or group entered in the form. *MainRoutine* is also called when you click the SHOW button on the form, or when you update any of the text boxes by entering new information and pressing Tab to move to the next field.

The code used to enumerate group memberships is the *ADObject_MemberOf* routine that was created in Solution 1-2. As the user, computer, and/or group are evaluated, the cumulative membership is tracked in a dictionary object, *oMemberOfList*. After all memberships have been enumerated, the list is transferred to an array, *aMemberOf*, and is sent to another subrou-tine, *ReportGroups*.

The *ReportGroups* subroutine is the workhorse of this tool, and it's the portion you'll need to customize for your enterprise. It creates string variables for each type of group (for example, Resource Access, Applications, Distribution Lists), analyzes each group in the membership array (*aMemberOf*), determines which type of group it is, and adds it to the appropriate group type string. This will be easier to see with an example.

Let's assume our user is ACL_Budget_Read. That membership will be enumerated by the *MainRoutine*'s call to *ADObject_MemberOf* and will be one element of the *aMemberOf* array that is passed to the *ReportGroups* subroutine.

*ReportGroups* declares a string variable, *sACL*, to store all group memberships related to resource access. The *For Each* statement loops through each group in *aMemberOf* and stores the current group in *sMemberOf*:

```
For Each sMemberOf In aMemberOf
```

The code finds that group in Active Directory and gets its *Description* attribute.

```
sGroupADsPath = ADObject_Find_UCG(sMemberOf, sDomainDN)
Set oGroup = GetObject(sGroupADsPath)
sDescription = oGroup.Get("Description")
```

Then the code looks to see whether there is a prefix, by checking to see if there is a delimiter (the underscore) in the group name, indicating a group type as described in Solution 1-5. This is where your naming standards and discipline start to pay off. If we find an underscore, we know it's a specific *type* of group.

```
aGroupName = Split(sMemberOf,"_")
If UBound(aGroupName) > 0 Then
```

The *Split* function creates an array (*aGroupName*) of items by splitting the group name (*sMemberOf*) wherever there's an underscore. If there are no underscores, the *UBound* func-tion returns −1 and the *Else* statement further down the code assumes that the group is a Role group.

If there is a prefix, we'll have the components of the group's name in the *aGroupName* array. The first element, *aGroupName(0)*, is the prefix. We look at it to identify the type of group. In our example of ACL_Budget_Read, the following code is executed:

```
sMemberOfPrefix = aGroupName(0)
Select Case UCASE(sMemberOfPrefix)
    Case "ACL"
          ' ACL (resource access) groups
          ' ACL_RESOURCE COLLECTION_ACCESS LEVEL
          ' sACL = sACL & aGroupName(1) & " (" & aGroupName(2) & ")" & sDelimiter
          sACL = sACL & sDescription & sDelimiter
```

We are now performing reverse engineering based on our group naming standard. In the case of a resource access group, we know the second component of the group name, *aGroup-Name(1)* or Budget in our example, is the name of the resource. We also know that the third component of the group name, *aGroupName(2)* or Read in our example, is the level of access. So we add that information to *sACL*, which you might remember is the string specifically dedicated to collecting our resource access groups. We make it look pretty by appending the resource, *aGroupName(1)*, and surrounding the access level, *aGroupName(2)*, with parentheses.

We also append a delimiter, the pipe symbol ( | ) by default, which is defined earlier in the code. That will become important in a moment.

As the *For Each* loop progresses, each of the groups in the membership array, *aMemberOf*, is processed in the same manner.

Several types of groups display the group's description field, rather than its name, because the description field is more detailed and user friendly. For example, our naming standard for groups that indicate a user or computer's location specifies a prefix, LOC_ followed by the three-letter airport code for the location, such as DEN for Denver, Colorado, USA. Instead of displaying DEN or LOC_DEN in the My Memberships report, the group's description field, "Denver, Colorado," is displayed.

To customize My Memberships for your organization, you simply need to have a section within the *Select Case* structure that identifies the type of group by its prefix (or whatever other logic you have in your naming standard), and adds that type of group to the string that is tracking that type of group, formatted in whatever manner you desire.

When the *For Each* loop is complete, the enumerated group membership (*aMemberOf*) has been split into the strings for each type of group. Remember that each string was built by adding information, such as a group name, followed by a delimiter (the pipe symbol). The next lines of code remove the pipe symbol after the last entry in each string, and then use that delimiter to split the string into an array, which then can be sorted. The sorted array is then rejoined into the string, again using the delimiter. The result is a string with *sorted* groups.

Finally, each string is added into a specific division (*<div>*) in the HTML of the page. The delimiter is replaced by line breaks (*<br/>*). If you are customizing the tool, you need to be sure that each type of group you are reporting is represented by a *<div>* in the HTML and is being inserted at the end of the *ReportGroups* subroutine.

Voilà! Because this tool needs to reflect your specific naming standards, you are likely to have to customize it quite a bit. You should be able to limit your customization to the *ReportGroups* subroutine and to the HTML *<divs>*.

# Access Report

The Access Report tool answers that all-important question, "Who can get to this folder?" It's unfortunate that we don't have tools built into Windows to provide such critical reporting, but luckily, with role-based management, we can now do just that.

The engine of the Access Report HTA is actually quite simple at its core. It enumerates the membership of a group, such as ACL_Budget_Read, reporting all members, direct and indirect. Solutions 1-1 and 1-2 provided scripts to enumerate a user's or computer's *MemberOf* attribute. This tool uses a subroutine, *Group_Members_Enum*, which is almost identical to our *ADObject_MemberOf* subroutine, except that it examines the *Member* property instead of the *MemberOf* property.

It is the HTML part of Access Report that is actually more complex. There is a text box, Group Name, where you can enter **ACL_Budget_Read**. But to make it more straightforward, we dynamically populate two drop-down lists by looking at group names with our resource access prefix (ACL_) and splitting the resource (Budget) and the access level (Read). Based on your selections in those two drop-down lists, we re-create the Group Name field. In most situations, you have to do minimal customization of this tool to get it to work in your role-based management model.

## Using Access Report

Members_AccessReport.hta is in the Scripts folder of the companion media. It can be opened by double-clicking the HTA, in which case you select the Resource and the Access Level (or enter the Group Name directly) and click Show. You can also launch the tool from a command line, MMC taskpad task, or custom context menu command.

To use a taskpad task, follow the instructions in Solution 1-3. Create a shell task for group objects and use the pre–Windows 2000 logon name as the parameter, which is *$COL<9>*. To create a custom context menu command, refer to the detailed steps in Solution 1-3.

## Understanding and customizing Access Report

When the tool opens, Windows_Onload executes and centers the window (the *CenterMe* subroutine) and identifies the currently logged-on user and computer (the *Initialize* subroutine).

It then calls *Sub Prepopulate*, which identifies whether an argument was passed and, if so, places the argument in the Group Name box.

To populate the drop-down lists, the HTA scans Active Directory for all group objects with a prefix that indicates the group is used to manage resource access. The tool assumes you use a naming standard such as ACL_Budget_Read, where a configurable prefix—such as ACL_—is followed by the name of the resource, a second underscore, and the access level. If your naming standard is different, you need to work with the tool so that it populates drop-down lists in a way that is appropriate for your enterprise.

Early in the script, the *Configuration Block* section sets the variable *sGroupsOUDN* to the distinguished name for the base of the search. You need to set *sGroupsOUDN* to match your Active Directory structure.

If you have a prefix that identifies groups used for resource access—such as ACL_—you're in luck. All you need to do is configure the *sPrefix_ACL* variable in the *Configuration Block* section of the HTA to match your prefix. If you don't have a prefix in your naming standard, you will have to do heavier revisions to the tool.

The *FillResources* routine uses the *All_Objects* subroutine to walk the tree from *sGroupsOUDN* looking for any group with a prefix matching *sPrefix_ACL*. It sorts the results and creates drop-down list items (called *<options>* in HTML) for each resource. No customization is necessary.

The search includes this object and all subcontainers. Hopefully, you have your resource access groups in a single OU or OU branch; however, if resource access groups are scattered throughout your domain, you can enter the DN of your domain as **sGroupsOUDN** and the entire domain will be searched.

This, by the way, is one weak link in this tool. If you are doing a very broad search, or if you have many objects, the tool might take a while to populate the drop-down lists. If this happens, the easiest solution is not to launch the tool on its own, but rather launch it from the command line, a taskpad task, or a context menu command with an argument specifying the group you want to analyze. If the HTA is called with an argument, it runs its report first, and *then* it populates the drop-down list, resulting in better performance.

The other solution is to create more efficient code to populate the drop-down lists, by performing an ADO search for group objects matching your prefix. The current code walks the Active Directory hierarchy from the base container specified by *sGroupsOUDN*. Check the community site for this book, *http://www.intelliem.com/resourcekit*. There will likely be enhancements made to this tool by the community.

After the Resources drop-down list is populated, a user can select a resource. When the Resources list is changed, the *cboResource_OnChange* event is wired up, which then looks through the list of groups that the tool created earlier and finds all groups with the same resource name. It then looks for the second underscore and generates the Access Level drop-down list.

When an access level is chosen from the drop-down list, the *cboAccess_OnChange* event is wired up, which populates the group field by appending the prefix (*sPrefix_ACL*) with the selected resource, an underscore, and the selected access level. In other words, the group name is derived by the choices made in the drop-down lists.

The tool then performs an enumeration of all members of the group. It separates members based on the type of object: users, computers, and other groups. And if the member is a user, the tool evaluates whether the user is a direct member of the selected group or an indirect (nested) member. That design choice was to help identify those exceptions to the rule that we discussed in Solution 1-4: users who are given access to a resource directly rather than via roles.

The code that is used to categorize members is very similar to the code that is used by My Memberships to categorize groups by type. This time, however, no customization is necessary: the object classes of user, group, and computer are all you need. Once the members have been categorized, they are displayed in appropriate divisions (*<div>*s) in the HTML.

What are we actually looking at here? Well, we are looking at two tools that produce valuable reports by leveraging a disciplined naming convention. Because we have a structured, well-thought-out naming conventions, we are able to look at any group name and identify exactly what the group is doing (My Memberships). And we can perform membership analysis on a single group (Access Report). Access Report leverages our naming convention in order to scan the database (Active Directory) and locate all groups that serve a specific function (resource access management).

## Auditing internal compliance of your role-based access control

There is one more important component of this solution. If you are using group membership enumerations such as My Memberships and Access Report as the basis of your role-based access control reports, you must be confident that nobody has gone outside the box of your guidelines. For example, if you are using Access Report to answer the question, "Who can read the budget?", you are assuming that the ACL_Budget_Read group is the only group with Allow:Read permission. I suggested in Solution 1-5 that you assign Allow:Read to the ACL_Budget_Read group, and a user who required read access would be added to that group, either via one of his or her roles or directly, as an exception to the rule. You must ensure that no other security principal (user, group, or computer) has been given Allow:Read permission on the ACL; otherwise, your report based on the membership of ACL_Budget_Read will not be accurate.

Luckily, this is where our disciplined naming standard once again comes to our rescue. To give ourselves the confidence that our model is working properly—that our data, business logic, and presentation layers discussed in Solution 1-4 are effective—we simply audit or scan the ACLs of our folders and look for any occurrence of a security principal that does *not* begin with ACL_, our chosen prefix! Of course, we also ignore well-known security principals such as System, Administrators, Users, and Everyone.

How do you dump the ACLs of a folder or file to achieve this type of audit? There are tools such as subinacl.exe (which you can download from the Microsoft Downloads Web site at *http://www.microsoft.com/downloads*), icacls.exe (native to Windows Server 2008 and Windows Vista), cacls.exe (native to Windows XP), and xcacls.vbs (which you can also download from the Microsoft Downloads Web site). Each of these tools provides the ability to report ACLs. However, they produce very verbose reports. For our purposes, we only need to ensure that there are no exceptions to the rules of our RBAC implementation—that there are no security principals on ACLs other than those that meet our guidelines.

## Using Folder ACL Report.vbs

I've therefore provided a script named Folder ACL Report.vbs on the companion media, in the Scripts folder. This tool is a wrapper around icacls.exe. It executes icacls, captures its output, and then filters each line so that only exceptions—unexpected permissions—will be reported.

To run Folder ACL Report, open a command prompt, access the folder in which the script is stored, and then use the following syntax:

```
cscript //nologo "Folder ACL Report.vbs" "path to folder" E|I
```

where you specify either *E* (or *explicit*) or *I* (or *inherited*) as the last argument to indicate that you want to report only explicit access control entries (ACEs) or to include inherited ACEs. By viewing only explicit ACEs, the report will be significantly shorter, allowing you to focus on what is different or what has changed beneath the specified folder. The script will, by default, report *all* permissions (including inherited) on the specified folder, since that information is important to understanding what is happening beneath that folder. The explicit or inherited filter is applied to files and folders below the specified folder.

You need to configure the filtering capability of the script. This is achieved by changing the following block of code in the script:

```
aTranslatePerms = Array(_
    "NT AUTHORITY\System", "" , _
    "BUILTIN\Administrators","", _
    "CREATOR OWNER:(OI)(CI)(IO)(F)","", _
    "CONTOSO\ACL_", "" )
```

The array *aTranslatePerms* contains *pairs* of items. It is used to change permissions as produced by icacls into another form for reporting. The first element of each pair is what *icacls* would produce. The second is what you want to report, and if you specify an empty string (two double quotes, ""), the script will report the permission only on the folder specified on the command line, not on any child files or folders. For example, the fourth line of the code block just shown tells the script to ignore occurrences of the permission that grant Creator

Owner full control. That permission will be reported only on the folder specified, not on any child files or folders.

You can use partial strings in the array. The second and third lines instruct the script to skip all permissions assigned to the System and Administrators identities. The last line is an important item for you to customize: It directs the script to ignore permissions assigned to groups in our domain that begin with ACL_, because those are compliant with our RBAC implementation.

Here is an example of the script in action:

```
c:\DEMOS>cscript //nologo "Folder ACL Report.vbs" "C:\data" e
FOLDER TREE FILTERED ACL REPORT
C:\data NT SERVICE\TrustedInstaller:(I)(F)
C:\data NT SERVICE\TrustedInstaller:(I)(CI)(IO)(F)
C:\data NT AUTHORITY\SYSTEM:(I)(F)
C:\data NT AUTHORITY\SYSTEM:(I)(OI)(CI)(IO)(F)
C:\data BUILTIN\Administrators:(I)(F)
C:\data BUILTIN\Administrators:(I)(OI)(CI)(IO)(F)
C:\data BUILTIN\Users:(I)(OI)(CI)(RX)
C:\data BUILTIN\Users:(I)(CI)(AD)
C:\data BUILTIN\Users:(I)(CI)(WD)
C:\data CREATOR OWNER:(I)(OI)(CI)(IO)(F)
C:\data\Budget  ACCOUNT UNKNOWN:(OI)(M)
C:\data\Budget  ACCOUNT UNKNOWN:(CI)(R)
C:\data\Budget  ACCOUNT UNKNOWN:(OI)(CI)(RX)
C:\data\Accounting\2007 CONTOSO\jfine:(OI)(CI)(M)
Successfully processed 9 files; Failed processing 0 files
```

The script was executed against the C:\Data folder. All permissions on that folder were reported. Again, you can use **icacls.exe /?** to learn what the permission reports mean, but these are the standard permissions for a Windows Server 2003 or Windows Server 2008 folder at the root of the disk volume. Below the root data folder, there were several other folders, but the script reported only four permissions that were unexpected. The Budget folder has three instances where a group had been assigned permissions and then the group was deleted, so we are left with an ACE associated with a security identifier (SID) that cannot be resolved in Active Directory. Additionally, the user named jfine was given explicit permission to modify the C:\Data\Accounting\2007 folder. This is not compliant with our RBAC model. His user account should be added to an appropriate resource access capability management group, such as ACL_Accounting 2007_Edit. We want to examine how, when, by whom, and why this permission was granted.

## Next steps for Folder ACL Report.vbs

Folder ACL Report.vbs is useful for spotting ACEs that are not given to a limited number of expected identities, such as System and Administrators, or to a group with our RBAC prefix, ACL_. The script should get you thinking about modifications you could make to enhance its power.

For example, in its current form, the script does not confirm that the permissions assigned to a group are expected. For example, it would not check to see that a group called ACL_Budget_Read was actually given the Read permission; nor would it highlight a problematic folder that had Modify permission granted to that "read" group.

There are reasons for this apparent gap. In a well-managed environment, folders are *provisioned* in an automatic fashion, as you'll see in Solution Collection 2. So we are confident, at Contoso, Ltd., that the _Read group was in fact given read permission because it is automated and logged. Additionally, NTFS auditing has been configured to watch for successful changes to NTFS permissions. So after the folder is provisioned, any modifications to the access control list are noticed in the security audit log.

However, we can also extend this script to examine the group name, using our naming convention, and identify that the access level of the group is "read." The script can determine that the permissions assigned to the group were in fact "read and execute" (RX) and *only* "read and execute." Join us at the online community, *http://www.intelliem.com/resourcekit*, and you'll likely find that someone has already posted just such a solution.

## Solution summary

This solution introduced three types of tools that leverage a role-based management model to provide critical reporting capabilities. Each tool relies on our strict adherence to a logical, structured naming standard for our groups.

My Memberships reports the management of a user by enumerating the user's group memberships and, based on the naming standard, categorizing and sorting the groups into a useful display. It even uses group description attributes in places to make the report very easy to understand.

Access Report (Members_AccessReport.hta) starts with a single group that is used to manage access at a particular level to a particular resource and enumerates up to identify all the users, computers, and other groups that belong to that group. Members are split into categories based on the object class and whether the member is a direct member or an indirect (nested) member. This tool leverages our naming standard—which specifies an ACL_ prefix followed by the name of the resource, another underscore, and the access level—as it scans Active Directory and dynamically builds a user-friendly set of drop-down lists with which to help us find just the right group.

The reports are based only on what our database, Active Directory, says is going on. To make sure the reports are accurate, we need to scan the *implementation* of our role-based management to ensure that rules were followed. The Folder ACL Report script is an example. It scans ACLs of a folder tree to identify ACEs that were given to security principals that do not match our RBAC group naming standard. This last tool is a demonstration, primarily, of the type of simple auditing you can perform to ensure that the rules are being followed. If you can ensure that rules are being followed, reports from the data layer—Active Directory—can be confidently presented as accurate.

# 1-7: Getting to Role-Based Management

## Solution overview

| | |
|---|---|
| **Type of solution** | Guidance |
| **Features and tools** | Registry, communication, process, leadership |
| **Solution summary** | Answer questions and provide guidance related to the business and technical challenges of moving to role-based management. |
| **Benefits** | Sell role-based management to your peers and to management. Answer common challenges to the validity and viability of role-based management. Avoid pitfalls and leverage guidance in your path towards role-based management. |

## Introduction

Role-based management, as presented in Solutions 1-4 through 1-6, is a powerful approach to aligning information technology with business strategy, organizational requirements, and job tasks. As I suggested in the introduction to this chapter, it is as close to a "no brainer" in IT as I can imagine. The ROI is huge, and unless you're paid by the hour or have a *very* small and static enterprise, you *need* role-based access control at a minimum and role-based management at a broader level.

## A review of role-based management

Solution 1-4 introduced the concepts of data, business logic, and presentation of role-based management. You need a database to maintain the information related to your model, business logic to drive the alignment of IT management with business requirements and workflows, and a set of tools to present the model in a fashion that is friendly to administrators and even to nontechnical resource owners. Additionally, you need to implement each capability you are trying to manage. For example, to use role-based access control to manage resource access, you need to assign permissions to files, folders, printers and other resources that can be secured with ACLs. The permissions need to reference groups in your RBAC implementation.

Throughout this resource kit, I'll be enhancing your understanding of that implementation component as it relates to various aspects of IT administration, including file and folder management, Group Policy, printers, application deployment, and more. We'll also continue to develop tools to facilitate the presentation layer: administration, management, and reporting of role-based management. The first such tools were introduced in Solution 1-6.

Solution 1-5 focused on the data and business logic layers. Although tools such as Microsoft Identity Lifecycle Manager (ILM), System Center Configuration Manager, and tools from other vendors provide alternatives, we focused on a database that you already have in your enterprise: Active Directory. This database is distributed across multiple servers (domain controllers); is highly efficient in its replication; is certainly a focus of your backup, recovery, and business continuity plans; is a known technology; and is relatively easy to work with. The business logic can be built using groups and group nesting within Active Directory. And all of this can be done with little or no hard costs.

## Reliance on groups and group management

In the end, our approach to role-based management relies very heavily on group management: sophisticated, nuanced, detailed, and disciplined group management. One benefit I've not mentioned until now is that, by relying on groups, you are setting yourself up for easy migration to more advanced management tools. Many systems management tools, including Microsoft System Center Configuration Manager 2007 and other non-Microsoft options, can use groups to define which users or computers receive certain applications or configuration. So if you've built your database and business logic in Active Directory, you can easily roll into more sophisticated tools.

Groups are easy to work with. Native tools, such as the Active Directory Users and Computers snap-in, enable management of group membership, and, as we've seen in this solution, it's not too tough to write custom tools to work with groups as well. The Solutions in Solution Collection 8, "Reimagining the Administration of Groups and Membership,"enable even more efficiency. When groups are used as a data container, used to track who belongs to roles, or used to track which capabilities are being managed, they provide easy visibility throughout your role-based management implementation, as you can simply enumerate the *Members* and *MemberOf* attributes of Active Directory as a kind of query against your data layer.

## "Scars" from group management days of yore

Unfortunately, groups have a tarnished past that has left scars on many IT professionals from their experiences in Windows administration. Back in the days of Windows NT 4.0 and earlier, groups had very limited nesting: Global groups could nest into local groups. That was it. The best practice was to nest users in global groups and global groups into local groups, and then assign permissions to a local group.

The problem was that local groups existed only in the security accounts manager (SAM) database of the server or workstation, not in the domain. So if your budget was distributed across four servers, you'd need four separate sets of local groups, one per server, if you followed the best practice. This best practice was quite painful in larger, complex organizations, many of which resorted to making all groups global groups. Because these groups couldn't nest inside of each other, this approach provided for no hierarchy whatsoever, so there was no opportunity to represent business logic in a group model. Moreover, there was a significant limitation to the number of accounts that could be supported in a single domain. So it all broke down rapidly.

All of this changed with the introduction of Active Directory. As soon as a domain was at the Windows 2000 domain functional level or higher, a new scope of group (domain local) was available throughout the domain, and nesting global groups into global groups, or domain local groups into domain local groups, became possible. Universal groups are also available for nesting. Computers can now be added easily to groups, and group scopes and types can be converted. Finally, there is no practical limit to the number of objects that can be supported in an Active Directory domain. So life is *much* better now.

However, many IT professionals carry scars that become clearly visible when you start talking about group management. Either they believe that they already know all there is to know about groups, or they recoil in pain thinking, incorrectly, of how difficult group management must still be. It can take a lot of work to get past those scars.

If this sounds funny to you, consider yourself lucky! I've worked with *many* clients where, as we charted out a role-based management strategy, we actually had to ban the words "global group" and "domain local group" from the discussion! Administrators often want to jump right into the technology, the *how*, skipping the more important questions of *why*, *what*, *when*, *where*, and *who*. And invariably they end up introducing what they feel are salient technical concerns without first envisioning the future, recognizing the pain points that can be solved, and understanding that it's not a one-page cheat sheet that will get them to the solution. Role-based management—its analysis, design, implementation, support, and troubleshooting—takes work. But it pays off!

## Discussing and selling role-based management

If you need to communicate the benefits of role-based management, I suggest you start by highlighting the pain points. Ask key stakeholders to answer these questions:

- What can <name a user> do and get to?
- If <name a user> loses his or her computer, what applications should be installed on a new computer?
- Who can make changes to <name a sensitive resource>?
- A new user is hired and needs the same access as <name a user>. What is that?

If your stakeholders can answer all of these questions, you already have a pretty well-managed environment. But chances are they can't, or you would not be reading this Solution Collection.

After the pain points are understood, demonstrate some of the tools from this Solution Collection in action. Have some samples already created in your environment that illustrate the power of role-based management.

Then start discussing how it is achieved. And, as you do so, do not use the terms "global group" or "domain local group." Instead, talk about "role groups" and "capability management groups." Focus on what the groups are doing, not how they are implemented. Only when everything else is understood do you need to even worry about which types of groups are global (role groups) and which are domain local (most capability management groups).

## "Won't there be a lot of groups?"

I've alluded several times in this Solution Collection to the fact that role-based management can result in a significant number of groups in Active Directory. That is likely to be the top concern that is raised in any discussion of this approach to role-based management.

Let's now address that concern. Yes, it will result in more groups. If implemented fully, you will have several groups for each resource: one for each access level. That, alone, will increase the number of groups in the directory service.

The key to addressing this concern is to remind yourself and your team what the alternatives are: multiple access control entries (ACEs) on access control lists (ACLs) on multiple folders in multiple shares on multiple servers, or multiple groups in a single, centralized, replicated, highly manageable database (Active Directory).

Remember the scenario in Solution 1-4 of resources related to a budget being spread across four different servers. How tough is it to manage those ACLs and to report who has access to the budget? Very! If we were applying Read, Edit, and Full Control capabilities for the budget, we'd have a minimum of 12 ACEs (three capabilities over four servers). Actually, it's more than that because Edit, if it's well implemented, requires several ACEs, as you'll learn in the next Solution Collection. To *manage* that resource, we have to work with each of those ACEs: adding or removing groups with those ACEs and, most painfully of all, scanning and analyzing the ACEs to produce audits and reports.

With role-based management in place, we still have just as many ACEs, but we no longer have to manage them. We have to manage only three groups: ACL_Budget_Read, ACL_Budget_Edit, and ACL_Budget_Full Control. We've actually *reduced* the number of points of management by 75 percent (12 ACEs to manage versus three groups to manage)!

My experience is that IT professionals are so used to working with ACLs and permissions that they ignore just how much time is spent (wasted) doing so. If you've done a good job of highlighting pain points in your enterprise, your team members will recognize the tradeoff you're making: trading the management of lots and lots of ACEs for the management of a few more groups. Totally worth it!

Now there are two other implications of maintaining more groups in Active Directory. The first is the need for tools with which to manage those groups. Luckily, even the Active Directory Users and Computers snap-in is easier for managing group membership than the ACL Editor is for managing permissions. But we need even better tools. We've developed several in this Solution Collection, and there are more yet to come in Solution Collection 8. The second implication relates to the size of a user's security token. We'll also address that in a later section of this solution. But assuming you design your role-based management model well, it will absolutely centralize and reduce the burden of management, thereby reducing your TCO.

# The road to role-based management

The road to role-based management is complex. Not from a technical perspective because it's just group management, but from a business perspective.

## Analyze your environment

The first step to take, after getting management buy-in for the effort, is to analyze your environment:

- **Identify the capabilities you are trying to manage.**   What are the resource collections that require access control? What applications are you trying to deploy and manage? What configuration—such as mapped drives, printers, and Group Policy—is being deployed? Keep in mind that in the context of role-based management, the term "capability" doesn't always mean something positive or enabling. For example, assume you are trying to keep users from applying personal desktop wallpaper to computers in conference rooms and other public areas. You are managing the capability to work on a restricted computer. Although "restriction" and "capability" seem contradictory in other contexts, they are two sides of the same coin in role-based management. You are giving *yourself* the ability to stop worrying about those computers, right? This exercise will generate your capability management groups.

- **Identify the exceptions you need to manage.**   This step is often overlooked but very important. Certain capabilities require exceptions. For example, you might be trying to manage the automatic deployment of security updates to all client computers in your domain, so that all computers get updates within 24 hours and reboot automatically to ensure the updates take effect. As soon as you set a rule, you're likely to find the exceptions to the rule. For example, there might be a computer that runs a lengthy data analysis algorithm that takes 48 hours to complete. If an update causes a reboot, the analysis fails. You should create a capability to be excluded from the "update and reboot" rule. This would be represented by a group, perhaps named UPD_Update Reboot Exceptions, and that group could be used to filter a Group Policy object with settings appropriate for those exceptions. So this exercise of identifying exceptions will also generate capability management groups to manage the exceptions.

- **Identify the roles associated with those capabilities.**   Look at which users and computers currently have the capabilities you've identified. You'll probably find some groups, some individual users, and perhaps some computers. Tease out the relationships that suggest role definitions. This activity will lead to your role groups.

- **Identify data sources.**   What data sources exist to facilitate the definition of roles? Your human resources database will certainly be a valuable store of information that can define user roles. Your computer inventory can help drive computer roles, such as roles for desktops versus laptops.

## Define your naming convention and processes

Use the guidance in this resource kit to design your role-based management model. Establish naming conventions and determine consistent processes with which roles and capabilities will be managed.

To summarize and reiterate what we've discussed regarding naming conventions, I recommend a naming convention that leverages prefixes to indicate the *type* of group, such as ACL for resource access and APP for application deployment groups. Use a delimiter, such as an underscore, to separate the key parts of the group's name—for example, ACL_2008 Budget_ Read or APP_Visio. The key parts you must delimit within the group's name are the prefix (ACL or APP) and the type of permissions you're assigning to the group (Read, in the budget example). Do *not* use the same delimiter elsewhere in the name. (Notice the space in the 2008 Budget group name.) That allows you to leverage delimiters to "break apart" a group name in custom scripts and tools.

The goal of your naming convention should be to have a logical standard that can be used in three ways. First, the convention should enable you to find groups quickly. We saw that it became easier to locate the correct resource access group when we assign a permission to a folder, when we can type ACL_, and then we can choose from a list of groups with that prefix. It reduces the chance that we will misuse a group of another type. Second, the convention should facilitate auditing. Solution 1-6 demonstrated how easy it was to scan a folder tree for any permission that was assigned to an object that did *not* begin with ACL_ as a way to ensure that other types of groups were not being misused. Third, group names should enable scripts to be written that can leverage the standard to break apart, reassemble, and understand the group's purpose.

Define how groups will be created. What fields must be filled in—such as Description and Notes—and what information should those fields contain? What is the correct group scope (here's where you can discuss global and domain local) for each type of group? How are groups to be nested? What tools and scripts should be used? Who should be allowed to create, modify, and manage the membership of various groups? What is the process for retiring and eventually deleting a group?

## Encourage or mandate discipline

Your next step should be to determine how to encourage or mandate disciplined adherence to the design and process. Leadership and detailed documentation can encourage discipline, but let me save you some time: You are likely to find your role-based management is *not* strictly followed. Microsoft's native tools require too many clicks and don't do any validation of input against your business requirements.

Therefore, you will be well served by creating tools that provision groups and automate their creation and management. If your tools enforce and apply your design, and if your administrators use your tools because you've made the tools efficient and available, you are much more likely to succeed.

If you have the opportunity to enforce discipline around role-based management, do it! This can be done by creating tools and then ensuring that the *only* way for administrators to manage groups is with your tools. This requires a bit of trickery that will be detailed in Solution Collection 8. In short, you must *remove the delegation* that allows administrators to manage groups. Yes—you prevent them from being able to create or modify groups in Active Directory. You code your tools to perform group management using alternate credentials. So a support person won't be able to change group membership directly in the Active Directory Users and Computers snap-in, but she can use your tool, which works under a special account (unknown to the support person) to make the changes in Active Directory on her behalf. Your tool *proxies* the activity for the administrator. Options for proxying—executing tasks with a hidden alternate credential—will be presented in Solution Collection 8.

### Create a transition plan

You will not roll out role-based management over a weekend. It will be a lengthy, evolving process. But you can take some steps to make migration significantly easier. The first is to create your new groups and to nest existing groups in them.

Let's say, for example, your analysis helped you identify four folders that have budget-related resources and three groups that had been assigned read permissions on each of those folders. Role-based management suggests that you should create a group named ACL_Budget_Read to manage the capability to read the budget. Create the group, and assign it Read permission on the folders. Nest the three groups in the ACL group. Moving forward, if another budget folder is created, assign read permission only to the ACL group. When you have time, you can remove the three legacy groups from budget ACLs.

In other words, start implementing the best practices and slowly, over time, clean up the remnants of legacy management methods.

## Token size

I hope I've sold you on the benefits of role-based management. It's a simple concept with a relatively simple roadmap to implementation. There's a lot of business analysis, leadership, and project management involved, but the technology is pretty straightforward. Hopefully, you agree that the ROI makes role-based management a no brainer.

I say "hopefully" because I'm going to close this Solution Collection with the only downside of our approach to role-based management—one that is the result of a limitation in Windows. It is a limitation that can be worked around in almost every scenario, but I've found it creates a dark cloud of gloom around an otherwise bright picture of a manageable future. So I want you to be excited enough about role-based management to work through this issue.

The issue is token size.

As you know, when a user "touches" a system—by logging on locally or over remote desktop, or by connecting to a resource such as a shared folder—the system generates what is referred to as a *token* that contains the security identifiers (SIDs) of the user and of all the groups to which the user belongs. It is possible that as you expand your role-based management, a user could belong to enough groups to "break" the token, and all kinds of strange things will happen. The solution is to make a change to the registry that expands the size of security tokens. But that change will, for all practical purposes, need to be made on every system in your enterprise—preferably through a change management tool such as Group Policy.

Similar problems can occur when group membership exceeds what is supported by the Kerberos Privilege Attribute Certificate (PAC) or in the request used to authenticate against an IIS application over HTTP.

A token or PAC contains SIDs for the user and the groups to which the user belongs. Those SIDs required 40 bytes of storage prior to Windows Server 2000 Service Pack 4 (SP4). The maximum token size was 8000 bytes under Windows 2000 through Service Pack 1. After overhead and user rights were accounted for, that meant a user could belong to 100 to 200 groups before the token would break. Service Pack 2 of Windows 2000 expanded the default token size to 12,000 bytes. Additionally, Service Pack 4 of Windows 2000 changed the way SIDs were stored in a token—so that domain local groups still required 40 bytes, but global and universal groups required only 8. The effect of those changes was that, through Windows Server 2003, a user could belong to 200 to 300 groups before the token would break.

> **Important**    When a user or computer belongs to more than 200 to 300 groups, the security token and other authentication mechanisms break down.

When I say "breaks down" or "breaks," what exactly does that mean? Well, as any consultant likes to say, "That depends." The symptoms of this problem are numerous. Windows applications, Web applications, the Windows operating system—you name it—all begin to experience problems. The manifestations of those problems are also diverse: access denied messages, problems with logon, even bizarre errors like Out Of Memory errors. You will experience general bizarreness like you've never seen before. Unfortunately, that makes identifying the root cause next to impossible. That's why it's critical that you account for this problem now, as you design the future of your Windows administration. If you read this book and forget about the token size issue, it will come back to haunt you in awful ways. Trust me. I've been there.

Let me set the first rumor straight. You will hear lots of "experts" claim that, if you belong to enough groups to break an authentication component such as a token, you will simply be unable to access anything. *Not true.* I've seen this happen in the real world. We had a user (at the top of the food chain) who belonged to just over 400 groups. That user could function perfectly well. The user just couldn't perform a few tasks that had been granted to groups that, it turns out, had just fallen out of his token. Think about the security implications of this: The token was just missing some of its memberships. Luckily, we got the equivalent of "Access Denied" messages when the user tried to do things. What if those missing memberships had been assigned Deny permissions? Kind of scary, huh? And this was on Windows Server 2003 domain controllers. Very scary.

Let me set the second rumor straight—the rumor that suggests the token size issue has been solved. It has not. Changes to the token size and the reduction in the number of bytes used by global group SIDs has helped a lot. Users can now belong to somewhere near 300 groups before problems are encountered. And that's a *lot* of groups. So you are less likely to experience limitations. But they will happen, some day, in some scenario, in any moderately complex role-based management enterprise.

## Increase *MaxTokenSize*

The solution to this issue begins with a registry modification to the *MaxTokenSize* value, which can be found in HKEY_LOCAL_MACHINE\System\CurrentControlSet\Lsa\Kerberos\Parameters. The value is a REG_DWORD type, and it can be set as high as 65536 decimal, or 0xFFFF hexadecimal. That size theoretically supports around 1600 domain local group memberships or 8000 global/universal group memberships. So, in a mixed group scope implementation, you're looking at a 3000- to 5000-group membership limit. That is a *huge* number of groups for a single user or computer.

Because tokens are generated locally, you need to make this change on every machine that would be "touched" by any user belonging to more than 200 to 300 groups. That means every domain controller, every server, and—who knows where those users might log on—every client. In other words, for a practical discussion you need to make the change to every system in your enterprise, *forestwide*. I highly suggest creating a custom Group Policy administrative template (.ADM or .ADMX) to deploy this change through a Group Policy object.

A change this significant and this widespread should be *thoroughly* tested. I also recommend that you do *not* raise the value to 0xFFFF immediately. Raise it slowly and thoughtfully, based on your estimate of what is actually required. I have seen this change made in the real world, and I've not yet seen it break anything. However, I remain highly cautious and prudent about testing.

I'll also assign some required reading as your role-based management model begins to head toward managing a user belonging to more than 200 groups.

 **Important**   Knowledge Base articles 263693 and 327825 are required reading.

Knowledge Base articles 263693 and 327825 also link to related articles. If you search the Internet for those two article numbers, you'll also find all kinds of other information regarding this issue. Finally, I suggest you obtain tokensz.exe from the Microsoft Download Web site at *http://www.microsoft.com/downloads*. Tokensz performs several tasks to help you understand concerns about token and PAC sizes and calculate the size.

Please just remember that, regardless of what is stated or implied on the Internet, including on Microsoft's site, the token size problem is real. It exists. Enterprises are less likely to encounter it than in earlier releases of Windows, but that means enterprises without role-based management. When you start leveraging groups for their power, you'll run into the problem. Change *MaxTokenSize* forestwide, in reasonable, tested increments.

Also remember that although *MaxTokenSize* resolves problems related to security tokens being overwhelmed by group membership, there are other limitations you might encounter, including the size of authentication headers sent over HTTP and authenticating Web applications. Custom applications that evaluate group membership might also have been written with assumptions of a limited number of group memberships for a single user. Keep an eagle eye out for problems.

I would like to pass on several other thoughts regarding this issue.

## Consider implementing groups as global (or universal) instead of domain local

You can work around the token size limitation by using more global or universal groups and fewer domain local groups. Global and universal groups take only 8 bytes in a security token, versus 40 for domain local groups. So you can squeeze a lot more global groups into the default 12-KB token. It is easy to convert a domain local group into a global group and vice versa. Just convert it to a universal group first. The main advantage of domain local groups is that they can contain users and global groups from other domains. Within a single, multi-domain forest, universal groups boast the same advantage. Between domains in separate forests, you need to stick with domain local groups, but only in scenarios in which capability management is being extended to users or roles in the external domain. Additionally, with the increased emphasis on forest isolation and Active Directory Federated Services (ADFS), there will be fewer trust relationships between domains in separate forests. When there is no trust relationship, there is no need, really, for domain local groups.

If this sounds to you like I'm hinting at an all-global group implementation of role-based management, you're right. In a single domain, with no trust relationships, this is very achievable. Global groups can nest within global groups. So you can support the business logic of role-based management with each group SID requiring only 8 bytes. We're right back to the days of yore of Windows NT 4.0, when all groups became global. But this time it's not painful. It's effective.

### Clean up your *sIDHistory* attributes

My second tip is that you need to ensure you've cleaned up your SID History. The *sIDHistory* attribute of a user, group, or computer tracks *previous* SIDs of that object if it had been migrated from another domain using tools such as the Active Directory Migration Tool (ADMT). Some enterprises that migrated to Active Directory from Windows NT 4.0, or that have consolidated domains for one reason or another, have been lackadaisical about cleaning up use of legacy SIDs so that they can clear objects' *sIDHistory*. SIDs in *sIDHistory* also take up space in the token. Finish your migration, if you migrated, now.

After you've cleaned up your *sIDHistory*, considered moving to an all-global group model, and maybe bumped up your *MaxTokenSize* a little bit, you should have plenty of room for your business logic layer to be supported effectively by the Active Directory directory service.

## Solution summary

Role-based management is an art and a science. Your leadership, effective project management, careful design, and communication will enable you to move role-based management forward in your enterprise. Chart a course that includes analysis, design, and implementation of tools and processes to encourage or enforce compliance with role-based management.

Be prepared to sell role-based management, emphasizing pain points that have become so commonplace that administrators tend to overlook them, and highlight the efficiencies that can be obtained through role-based management. Know how to address the question, "Won't there be a lot of groups?" by demonstrating the fact that the increased number of groups results in a *decreased* number of points of management. And plan for the transition, moving forward with best practices but supporting previous techniques until you have time to clean up the legacy.

Be aware that if a user (or computer) belongs to more than 200 to 300 groups, authentication components such as the security token will begin to fail and the symptoms of the failure are bizarre, have frightening implications (from a security perspective), and are virtually impossible to recognize. Before tokens begin to fail, you need to take action by increasing the *Max-TokenSize* registry value forestwide. In extremely large or complex role-based management implementations, you can consider using only global (and universal) groups to support the model. And you can use this issue as the impetus to clean up the *sIDHistory* of users, computers, and groups that you migrated from other domains.

I hate to close this Solution Collection with such a strong warning about such an important consideration, but it is something you need to be keenly aware of if you want role-based management to succeed. It won't affect you right away, so don't *panic* about it. Just be aware.

And, with that, you are armed to begin charting the course to a world in which your management of IT resources—users, groups, computers, resources, applications, configuration, and more—aligns with, supports, and is able to grow with your business' strategy, workflows, processes, and requirements. Role-based management is absolutely, positively worth the effort!

Solution Collection 2

# Managing Files, Folders, and Shares

Since the beginning of Microsoft Windows networking time, one of the key roles of Windows servers has been to provide a centralized location for users to share files. And 15 years later, you would think we, the information technology (IT) professional community, would have file servers figured out—and that Microsoft would have met all of our needs for file servers. But alas, fundamental gaps remain in the toolset with which we manage file servers, and potentially serious gaps in implementation lead to environments in which data is, at best, undermanaged and, at worst, exposed to security violations and denial-of-service or data-loss scenarios.

Solutions in this chapter will equip you to manage data on file servers more consistently and more securely with less effort. I'll address common questions about Windows file servers, shared folders, access control lists (ACLs), Access-based Enumeration (ABE), shadow copies, and more. We'll also look at exciting new features of Windows Server 2008, including changes to the capabilities of file owners.

# Scenarios, Pain, and Solution

Chances are that you have experience managing files and folders within shared folders on Windows servers. And I'll assume you understand components of security such as NTFS permissions, inheritance, and share permissions. "What could there possibly be left to learn about a Windows file server?" you might ask. Consider the following scenarios, and the common gaps in implementation of the file server role:

- The Finance department of Blue Yonder Airlines maintains a share that is used for employees in that department to collaborate on files, primarily Microsoft Office Excel worksheets. The network administrator secured the share with a permission that allows the users Modify permission on the root folder, which, of course, all subfolders inherit. Early Monday morning, before his coffee has kicked in, Mark Bebbington, a Finance manager for Blue Yonder Airlines, opens an Excel budget spreadsheet from the folder to prepare it for a presentation to the CEO. He then clicks the parent folder to look at its contents so that he can decide if he needs to change any other worksheet. He turns his eyes to Excel and the spreadsheet, where he sees a number that does not belong. He presses the Delete key. Not noticing that the Windows Explorer folder still has focus, and not paying attention to the message that pops up in front of his still-bleary eyes, he clicks a button and then realizes—too late—that he has just deleted the contents of the entire Finance share.

> **Important**    If you have ever given a *group* the Allow::Modify NTFS permission, you have set yourself up for just this kind of scenario: an accidental or intentional denial of service. Any user in the group can delete *all* items in the shared folder.

- Engineers at Trey Research require access to engineering documents. The network architecture and the nature of the engineering applications have led the IT organization to determine that a hub-and-spoke model is most appropriate. In this model, changes are made *only* to the master documents in the shared folder in the datacenter, and those changes are distributed to read-only replicas on servers in distributed geographical offices. Because the replication technology also replicates NTFS ACLs, the IT organization needs to determine how to enable modification of the documents in the hub share while preventing changes to the documents in the spoke shares.

- As part of its effort to decrease costs, increase responsiveness to customers, and improve user productivity, the IT department of Proseware, Inc., wants to enable users to recover accidentally deleted, modified, or overwritten documents without requiring a call to the help desk to restore items from tape backup.

■ Administrators of Litware, Inc., want to prevent nontechnical users, and nonapproved users, from changing permissions of files or folders, even if they created those files or folders.

■ The IT professionals at Contoso, Ltd., want to make it easier to locate data through a logical namespace that organizes folders the way users think about them, rather than presenting users with a server-based view of folder storage.

As we explore solutions for these and other scenarios, we'll address the following questions and needs:

■ What has changed with Windows Server 2008 file services?

■ How can you facilitate moving folders to a new server without having to "touch" every shortcut, mapped drive, and link that points to the original location?

■ How is quota management different in Windows Server 2008 than in Windows 2000 and Windows Server 2003?

■ Now that the NET SEND command is no longer available, how can you notify users connected to a server before taking the server offline?

■ What is the danger of moving files between two folders with different permissions?

■ How can a user be prevented from changing permissions on a file he or she created?

The components of solutions in this chapter will include the following:

■ NTFS files and folders and their permissions: access control entries, which are stored as part of the discretionary ACL (DACL) in the security descriptor of the file or folder

■ Shared folders, including their permissions and settings: the share name (including hidden shares), Server Message Block (SMB) ACLs on the share, the share description, and caching settings

■ Access-based Enumeration (ABE)

■ The Creator Owner entry in the security descriptor

■ The new Owner Rights identity

■ Group Policy

■ Quota management

■ Distributed File System (DFS) namespaces

■ Symbolic links and network places

■ Shadow copies of shared folders

■ Robocopy

# 2-1: Work Effectively with the ACL Editor User Interfaces

## Solution overview

| | |
|---|---|
| **Type of solution** | Guidance and tips |
| **Features and tools** | The ACL editor user interfaces: the Properties dialog box on the Security tab, Advanced Security Settings dialog box, and Permission Entry dialog box |
| **Solution summary** | Ensure that you are fully up to speed on the nuances of ACL editor user interfaces. |
| **Benefits** | Use ACL editor user interfaces more effectively. |

## Introduction

Security permissions are implemented as access control entries (ACEs) in the DACL within the security descriptor (SD) of a securable resource. The SD also contains the system ACL (SACL), which stores auditing entries.

An important feature of the NTFS file system is that it supports SDs for files and folders. The SD is, in fact, just one attribute of a file or folder, along with data attributes that contain the actual data of a file. All of these attributes make up what we think of as the file or folder on the NTFS volume.

The ACL is the basis for determining which users can access resources and at what level. The security token that is generated by the server's local security subsystem to represent the user upon his or her authentication contains the security identifiers (SIDs) not only of the user's account but also of all the groups of which that user is a member. When a user attempts to access a resource, the SIDs in the token are compared to the SIDs in the ACL, and access is calculated based on granular permissions that are allowed or denied.

In Windows 2000, ACLs determine access regardless of whether the resource is being accessed locally or over the network. Windows Server 2003 added the ability to specify different permissions based on local versus over-the-network access.

## The ACL editor

The ACL of a resource is exposed in the graphical user interface (GUI) by the ACL editor user interfaces. Following is a list of these interfaces:

- The Security tab of the resource's Properties dialog box
- The Advanced Security Settings dialog box
- The Permission Entry dialog box

Each of these interfaces is described in more detail in the following sections.

## The Security tab of the Properties dialog box

Right-click any resource, choose Properties, and select the Security tab. You will see a general overview of the SD on the Security tab, also called the Security Settings dialog box, which is shown in Figure 2-1.

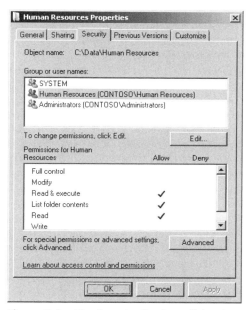

**Figure 2-1**   The Security Settings dialog box

On the Security tab of a securable object's Properties dialog box, permission templates appear in the lower half of the tab. These templates support typical access scenarios such as Read, Write, Modify, and Full Control. They represent a collection of the more granular permissions that can be explored on the Permissions tab of the Advanced Security Settings dialog box and in the Permission Entry dialog boxes. The type of permission template is indicated by the state of the check boxes next to the permission. A check mark in the box next to a permission template indicates that it is in force. Allow and Deny templates appear under the Allow and Deny columns, respectively. Templates selected with a disabled (gray) check box are inherited from a parent folder or volume, whereas check boxes that are selected and enabled (with a white background) are assigned explicitly to the selected file or folder.

Generally, these permission templates do not tell the full story. When there are ACEs for a security principal that do not fit nicely into the templates shown in the Security Settings dialog box, the template labeled "Special" at the bottom of the permissions list is selected. In this case, you must click Advanced to see more detail regarding the permissions in the ACL. However, it is recommended that you *always* click Advanced to view the details of the SD displayed on the Permissions tab of the Advanced Security Settings dialog box.

**Best Practices**    Always click the Advanced button on the Security tab of the Properties dialog box to view the details of the security descriptor displayed in the Advanced Security Settings dialog box.

**Note**    The Advanced button does not appear on the Security tab of the Properties dialog box of a volume accessed from the Share and Storage Management snap-in. You must go to the properties of the volume from Windows Explorer to access the Advanced Security Settings dialog box.

### The Permissions tab of the Advanced Security Settings dialog box

From the Security tab of the Properties dialog box, click the Advanced button to see more detailed information about the SD. This interface, called the Advanced Security Settings dialog box, shown in Figure 2-2, has tabs for permissions, auditing, ownership, and effective permissions.

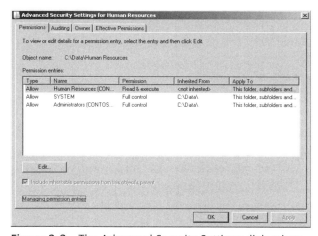

**Figure 2-2**    The Advanced Security Settings dialog box

The Permissions tab of the Advanced Security Settings dialog box has the following important features, some of which might not be familiar to you:

- In Windows Server 2008 and Windows Vista, each tab of the dialog box is in view mode. You must click the Edit button on a tab (which will be enabled only if your credentials enable you to make a change) to modify settings on that tab.

- Unlike the Security tab of the Properties dialog box, you can identify the source of inherited permissions: The Inherited From column indicates the parent folder or volume where the permissions are explicitly defined. Permissions assigned explicitly to the selected object show "<not inherited>" in the Inherited From column.

- The initial view of permission entries is in *canonical order*. This means the ACEs are listed in the order in which the local security subsystem analyzes them against the SIDs in the security token. The first match that is found—allow or deny—for the specific type of access that is being requested is used to determine whether that access is permitted. Therefore, the "more important" or "winning" permissions are at the top of the list. You can sort the list by clicking any column header, and therefore change the list from canonical order. However, when you close and reopen the Advanced Security Settings dialog box, you will again see the ACEs in canonical order.

**Best Practices**    Recognize the importance of the canonical listing of permissions in the default view of the Advanced Security Settings dialog box. Interpreting canonical order can facilitate an understanding of how permissions are applied to a user attempting to access the resource.

- Permission sets (ACEs) that cannot be summarized correctly in the Permission column display "Special" in the Permission column. Windows Server 2008 also shows "Special" in the Permission column if the selected object is a folder and the inheritance setting of the permission is not "This folder, subfolders and files."

We'll explore additional features and uses of the Advanced Security Settings dialog box later in this chapter.

## The Permission Entry dialog box

The permissions as listed on the Permissions tab of the Advanced Security Settings dialog box are certainly more informative than the Security tab of the Properties dialog box, but they're still not fully enumerated. To identify all the granular ACEs that make up a permission, you must view the ACEs in the Permission Entry dialog box.

**Best Practices**    Whenever a permission displays as "Special" in the Permission column of the Permissions tab of the Advanced Security Settings dialog box, or whenever you want a complete understanding of a particular permission, view the permission in the Permission Entry dialog box.

To access the Permission Entry dialog box, follow these steps:

1. If the Permissions tab of the Advanced Security Settings dialog box is in view mode (indicated by the presence of an Edit button but no Add or Remove buttons), click Edit.
2. Select a permission entry from the Permission entries list.
3. Click Edit. The Permission Entry dialog box, shown in Figure 2-3, appears.

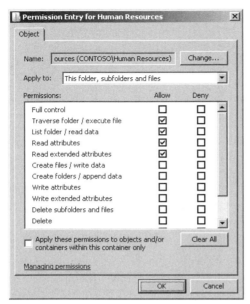

**Figure 2-3**    The Permission Entry dialog box

The permission that is displayed in the Permission Entry dialog box is broken down into the individual permissions (ACEs) that it comprises. Each permission's status is further broken down to Allow and Deny ACEs. If the ACE is inherited, the check box is disabled (grey). If it is explicit, the check box is enabled (white). Finally, the inheritance flags are displayed in the Apply To drop-down list. Inheritance will be discussed in later solutions in this Solutions Collection.

## Evaluating effective permissions

Whether a request for access to a file or folder is allowed or denied is determined by the local security subsystem, which evaluates the ACEs in the ACL in canonical order against the SIDs in the user's security token. The first ACE for the particular type of access (for example, read, write, or delete) that is applied to a SID found in the token decides whether the access request is allowed or denied. The *effective permissions* for a user are evaluated by the cumulative effect of allowed, denied, explicit, and inherited permissions applied to the user account and the groups in which those accounts are members.

To understand how the effective permissions are derived, we must look at the hierarchy of permission settings and their precedence on an ACL. Following are the golden rules of ACEs:

**File permissions override folder permissions.**    The only ACL that matters is the ACL for the object that is being accessed. When a user has only Read permission on a folder and when Full Control permissions are given to a child object (such as a file), the user will have Full Control over that object. The same is true in reverse. So when the user has Full

Control for a folder but only Read permission on the file, the user can read but not modify the file.

**ACEs have one of five possible states.**

❑  Not Specified: Neither the Allow nor Deny check box is selected.

❑  Explicit Allow: The Allow check box is selected.

❑  Inherited Allow: The Allow check box is gray and selected—which means the permission is inherited from the parent folder or volume.

❑  Explicit Deny: The Deny check box is selected.

❑  Inherited Deny: The Deny check box is gray and selected—which means the permission is inherited from the parent folder or volume.

**Allow permissions are cumulative.**   Whether you assign permissions to a user or to a group or groups to which a user belongs, all the permissions apply to the user. For example, when a user is individually given Read permissions to a file and is a member of a group that has Write permissions, the user has both Read and Write permissions. If that user is also a member of another group that has Full Control of the parent folder and inheritance is in use, the user has Full Control of the resource.

**Deny overrides Allow.**   A Deny permission takes precedence over an Allow permission—so even when a user is a member of seven groups that have Allow permissions to a resource specified, the user is denied access if one group is assigned a Deny permission. Remember, however, that access is evaluated per ACE. If a user has Allow permissions that give her Read and Write access, and a Deny Write permission, she is unable to change the file, but she can continue to read it.

**Explicit permissions override inherited permissions.**   A selected gray check box in the ACL editor indicates that permissions are being inherited from a parent folder or multiple parent folders. Although the default condition is that the permissions are cumulative between inherited permissions and explicit permissions (indicated by a white check box with a check mark in it), in the event the two settings contradict one another, the explicit permission overrides the inherited one. For example, suppose a user has an inherited Deny Read permission, but a group to which that user belongs has an explicit Allow Read permission. The Allow permission takes precedence and the user will be able to read the file.

**Access is often not determined by NTFS ACEs alone.**   ACEs on NTFS files and folders determine the maximum available access to the resource. However, resource access might be further modified by permissions that are applied by the service through which access is obtained. For example, shared folder permissions (SMB permissions) will, if more limited than effective NTFS permissions, further restrict access. Resources served through an IIS application can have access limited by more restrictive security settings on the Web site or virtual directory.

Evaluating effective permissions can be tricky. The Effective Permissions tab of the Advanced Security Settings dialog box, shown in Figure 2-4, can be helpful. To use it, select the user or group for which you want to evaluate effective permissions; a rough estimate of the security principal's effective permissions is displayed.

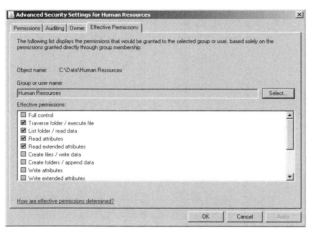

**Figure 2-4**    The Effective Permissions tab

However, this tool has its weaknesses. It does not account for the following:

- Whether the user accesses the file while logged on locally or via Remote Desktop, or remotely through a shared folder. These access modalities are represented by well-known SIDs such as Interactive, Network, or Remote Interactive User.

- Other well-known SIDs, including Restricted, Anonymous Logon, and Limited User.

You can learn more about the Effective Permissions tab, how it works, and what its weaknesses are by clicking the How Are Effective Permissions Determined? link. This will take you to the Access Control User Interface help file, then to the How Effective Permissions Are Determined topic.

**Best Practices**    Understand the limitations of the Effective Permissions tab.

In the end, it is difficult and time consuming to evaluate resource access at the level of individual ACLs. In Solutions Collection 1, "Role-Based Management," I presented a database-driven approach to managing an enterprise environment that used Active Directory groups to implement both the database and business logic components of role-based management (RBM). I suggested creating groups with names such as ACL_Budget_Read and ACL_Budget_Edit to establish a one-to-one relationship between a database object (the group) and a point of management (the ACLs on a collection of resources, such as the budget). Doing so provides a visible, easily managed approach to the security of distributed resources.

> **Best Practices**   Unless business requirements mandate otherwise, do not use well-known SIDs—such as Interactive, Network, Remote, Terminal Services User, Restricted, Anonymous Logon, or Limited User—to configure ACEs on a securable resource. Doing so makes the evaluation of effective permissions much more difficult. Instead, elevate the management of ACLs to a managed level by applying the concepts and tools of role-based access control I presented in Solutions Collection 1.

## Solution summary

The ACL editor user interfaces can be used to view or edit permissions on a securable resource, such as a file or folder. Although you might be very familiar with the Security tab of the Properties dialog box, the Advanced Security Settings dialog box, and the Permission Entry dialog box, it is worth ensuring that you know and follow these best practices:

- When viewing permissions, always click the Advanced button on the Security tab and evaluate permissions using the Advanced Security Settings dialog box. In most situations, the permissions templates on the Security tab will not provide a complete picture of the resource's ACL.

- Understand the importance of the canonical listing of permissions on the Advanced Security Settings dialog box. Permissions at the top of the list override permissions below them. Knowing that fact can facilitate the evaluation of effective permissions.

- When a permission displays "Special" in the Permission column of the Permissions tab of the Advanced Security Settings dialog box, view that permission in the Permission Entry dialog box to fully understand its ACEs and inheritance flags.

- Recognize that the results of the Effective Permissions tab are an *approximation* of effective permissions and that they ignore a number of special identities.

- To reduce the burden of security management, implement the concepts and tools of role-based access control presented in Solutions Collection 1.

## 2-2: Manage Folder Structure

### Solution overview

| | |
|---|---|
| **Type of solution** | Guidance |
| **Features and tools** | NTFS volumes |
| **Solution summary** | Maintain a wide and shallow folder structure, enabling the management of folder security using inheritance, with minimal levels of explicit ACLs. |
| **Benefits** | Increased manageability and security |

# Introduction

"Beauty is only skin deep," the saying goes. And life is beautiful when the scopes of management of security are only skin deep as well. Said another way, "Go wide, not deep."

Folders serve two purposes. A folder organizes content—files and subfolders—in a single container. And a folder, by maintaining an ACL with inheritable ACEs, establishes the scope of security for its contents.

Typically, file servers are characterized by multilevel hierarchies of folders. For example, a top-level folder named "Data" might have subfolders for each department. A departmental subfolder is further divided into projects and teams. Those folders contain many levels of subfolders.

# Create a folder structure that is wide rather than deep

Such deep folder structures are relatively harmless with regard to those folders' role of organizing content. However, if you are having to scope security by managing ACLs on folders more than a few levels down, you are likely to start feeling pain. The deeper you go to scope a particular level of access for a specific user or group, the more difficult security management becomes. You begin to deal with increasing numbers of exceptions to the rule, where "the rule" is a level of access scoped by ACLs on a parent folder, and you find yourself having to open up or lock down access on a subfolder. You might also find yourself with mutually exclusive access needs. For example, a user named Joe might need access to a folder four levels down when he should not be accessing files in the folder above it, only three levels down. Although such a requirement *can* be met using Traverse Folder permissions and rights, that doesn't mean it *should* be met that way.

Instead, it is a best practice to configure permissions on a high-level folder, for those permissions to be sufficient to describe security for all subfolders and files, and to allow ACL inheritance to apply those permissions down the tree.

 **Best Practices**    It is best practice to manage security with inheritance wherever possible so that permissions can be administered at a single point, higher in the folder hierarchy.

## A quick review of inheritance fundamentals

ACLs, like several other Windows components, are characterized by the concept of *inheritance*. With ACL inheritance, you can configure permissions of a container, such as a volume or folder, and those permissions propagate automatically to that container's contents.

When you assign permissions for a folder, most of those permissions are inheritable by default and will be passed down to all the objects in that folder. This inheritance happens because child objects are configured to allow inheritable permissions from the parent to propagate to the child ACLs by default. Therefore, an administrator needs to set permissions only once at the parent folder, and those permissions will propagate automatically to child files and folders.

## Managing inheritance

Inheritance is the combined effect of inheritance flags of ACEs of a parent volume or folder and a child file or folder that allows inheritance. Therefore, inheritance is configured at two points of management: a parent folder or volume, and a child file or folder. At the parent, inheritance flags of ACEs are configured using the Permission Entry dialog box, shown earlier in Figure 2-3.

Specifically, the Apply To drop-down list allows you to specify that a permission entry affects one of the following scenarios:

- This folder, subfolders and files (Default)
- This folder only
- This folder and subfolders (not files)
- This folder and files (but not subfolders)
- Subfolders and files only (but not this folder)
- Subfolders only (but not this folder or any files)
- Files only (in this folder only, not in subfolders)

Additionally, inheritance is affected by the Apply These Permissions To Objects And/Or Containers Within This Container Only check box. This option modifies the scope inheritance so that it applies only one level down, rather than applying to an entire branch of a folder tree.

Configuring whether a child file or folder allows inheritance is done in the object's Advanced Security Settings dialog box, on the Permissions tab. On Windows XP and Windows Server 2003 systems, shown in Figure 2-5, the inheritance option is labeled "Inherit from parent the permission entries that apply to child objects. Include these with entries explicitly defined here." On Windows Vista and Windows Server 2008 systems, shown earlier in Figure 2-2, the same inheritance option is labeled, "Include inheritable permissions from this object's parent."

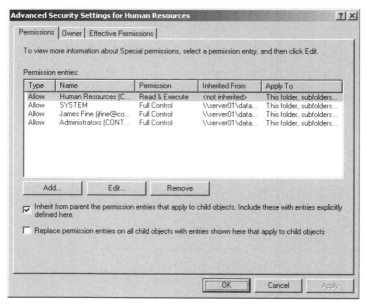

Figure 2-5   The Windows XP and Windows Server 2003 Advanced Security Settings dialog box

ACE inheritance is granular and dynamic. If a child object is configured to allow inheritance, any changes to inheritable permissions on the parent folder or volume propagates to the child without any user intervention. Inherited permissions do not remove permissions assigned explicitly to the child object. The fact that ACEs are propagated is an important concept: Adding, removing, or changing an inheritable ACE causes the NTFS file system to reconfigure ACLs on child objects that allow inheritance. This behavior leads to challenges we'll address elsewhere in this Solutions Collection. In a container with a large number of objects, this propagation can take some time.

**Important**   If you are experiencing an emergency situation in which access to resources must be quickly restricted, change permissions on the SMB share rather than NTFS permissions. SMB share permission changes take effect immediately for the entire share, whereas NTFS permission changes need to propagate to each object, which can take a significant amount of time.

## The impact of inheritance on folder hierarchy

Because it is best practice to manage security with inheritance wherever possible, it is also best practice to avoid, whenever possible, configuring explicit permissions on folders more than a few levels deep in the folder hierarchy. In an ideal world, only the first-level folders (the departmental folders) or maybe the second-level folders (the team or project folders) require explicit ACEs. It is unlikely this ideal will be achievable in every shared folder, but it is worth aiming for that goal.

Generally speaking, then, from an access control management standpoint, you should adhere to the following best practice.

> **Best Practices**    You will be best served with a folder structure that is wide rather than deep.

By having a larger number of folders at higher levels, you will be able to more effectively manage ACLs on those folders.

## Use DFS namespaces to present shared folders in a logical hierarchy

You might be concerned that by flattening and widening your folder structure, your users will have trouble navigating to locate resources they require. In Solution 2-15, "Distribute Files Across Servers," on page 151, we'll explore the following best practice in detail.

> **Best Practices**    Use the DFS Namespaces feature to present your shared folders to users in a hierarchy that reflects the logical organization of information in your enterprise, rather than forcing users to navigate the physical storage structure of servers and folders.

The DFS Namespaces feature enables you to abstract the physical structure of shared folders—the servers on which shared folders are hosted and the paths to those folders—and to present shared folders in a virtual namespace. That means you can have a physical structure of folders on your servers that provide for effective scopes of management for access to resources (that is, a wide folder structure rather than deep) and still expose those folders to users in what appears to be a deep, organized hierarchy. If you are familiar with data management concepts, you know that the management of the files and folders (the physical storage of your files and folders) is separated from the presentation of the folders to users (the logical organization of the folders in a DFS namespace).

As a pleasant side effect, NTFS volumes perform better when the directory structure is wide rather than deep. So not only will you be able to manage access more effectively, you'll also get a performance increase, albeit a small one.

## Solution summary

Create a folder structure that is wide rather than deep. Use high-level folders—preferably, first-level or second-level folders—to scope the management of access by applying an ACL with inheritable ACEs that will not need to be overridden, opened up, or locked down below. Present the shared folders to users in a DFS namespace that reflects the logical organization of content in your enterprise.

# 2-3: Manage Access to Root Data Folders

## Solution overview

| | |
|---|---|
| **Type of solution** | Guidance |
| **Features and tools** | NTFS volumes, Group Policy File System policy settings |
| **Solution summary** | Create consistent root data folders on each file server, and manage support teams' access to those root data folders using Group Policy to apply and maintain ACLs. |
| **Benefits** | Increased manageability and security |

## Introduction

Throughout this resource kit, I'll emphasize that consistency and manageability are fundamental building blocks of security. I'll also remind you to manage security on a least-privilege basis, giving users only the rights and permissions they require to perform their job. This solution provides a manageable way to achieve consistency and least privilege for root, or top-level, data folders on file servers.

## Create one or more consistent root data folders on each file server

File servers will be accessed remotely, not just by users as they connect to shared folders, but also by support personnel who need to perform tasks such as creating, removing, and securing folders.

Too often, I see a data volume on a file server with top-level folders acting as shares for users. But what happens if support people need to modify permissions on one of those top-level shared folders? They cannot. When you connect to a shared folder remotely, you cannot change its NTFS permissions. You can change permissions only on folders *within* the shared folder. To change the NTFS permissions of the shared folder, you must either use MMC snap-ins or open the folder's Properties dialog box with Windows Explorer. Typically, the latter approach is desirable. But that means the support people are either connecting to the server with Remote Desktop (which might not be desirable given the two-connection limit of Remote Desktop Protocol [RDP] used for remote administration) or connecting to the hidden administrative share of the server (which means they are in the Administrators group on the server, which means it's likely they have more rights than they really need). Personnel who support shared folders are not necessarily (or should not necessarily be) administrators of the server, so they will not always be able to connect to the server using its hidden drive share.

Therefore, you should create a folder on the server's data volume that will host shared folders, and you should secure that folder so that users and support personnel can perform tasks required for first-level folders within that root. We'll call such folders *root data folders*.

For example, if two servers will host shared folders for projects and teams on their E:\ drive, create a folder on each server named E:\Data. Support personnel require the ability to create a top-level folder for a new project or team: Assign the Create Folders ACE to an appropriate group. The Create Folders permission is shown in Figure 2-6.

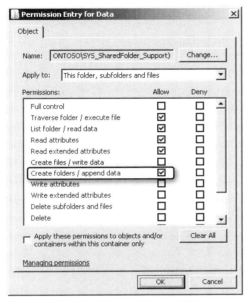

**Figure 2-6**   The Create Folders ACE

Create additional root data folders if one the types of data stored in shared folders mandates delegation to unique support teams. If three different IT support teams are responsible for administering subfolders, create three different root data folders with ACLs that enable the functionality required by each team.

Wherever possible, keep data volumes and root-level data folders consistent on file servers. This approach enables you to more effectively manage security on those folders.

## Use Group Policy to manage and enforce ACLs on root data folders

When root data folders are provisioned consistently, Group Policy can be leveraged to manage and enforce the ACLs on those folders. The following steps show how this is done:

1.  Create a Group Policy object (GPO) scoped to your file servers. Name the GPO according to your naming conventions—for example, GPO_File Server Configuration. For more information on scoping and naming GPOs, see Solutions Collection 10, "Implementing Change, Configuration, and Policies."

2.  Open the GPO in the Group Policy Management Editor (which is called the Group Policy Object Editor in Windows Server 2003).

3.   Navigate to Computer Configuration, Windows Settings, Security Settings, File System.

4.   Right-click File System and choose Add File.

Note that the Add File command allows you to manage files *or* folders.

5.   In the Folder box, type the path to the root data folder as it exists on the local volumes of the file server or servers that will be managed by the GPO—for example, E:\Data.

Note that you can type the path—the folder does not have to exist on the system from which you are editing the GPO.

6.   Click OK.

7.   The Database Security dialog box opens, as shown in Figure 2-7. This dialog box is equivalent to the Security tab of the Properties dialog box for a folder. Use it to configure the appropriate ACL for the specified root data folder. Be particularly careful to manage the inheritance flags of ACEs in this ACL. Detailed guidance and sample ACLs are provided later in this chapter.

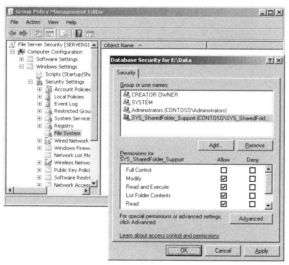

**Figure 2-7**   Group Policy configuration of folder security

8.   Click OK to close the Database Security dialog box.

9.   In the Add Object dialog box, select Configure This File Or Folder Then and select Propagate Inheritable Permissions To All Subfolders And Files. If, in fact, all subfolders and files should contain an ACL identical to that of the root data folder, select Replace Existing Permissions On All Subfolders And Files With Inheritable Permissions.

10.   Click OK.

The GPO will now enforce the specified ACL for any system that is within the scope of the ACL and contains a folder matching the specified path. Because File System policy settings are applied by the Security Configuration Engine (SCE) extension, those settings will be reapplied every 16 hours, by default, even if the GPO has not changed. Therefore, if an administrator modifies the folder's ACL directly on the server, the ACL will be reset to the specified configuration, on average, within eight hours.

## Solution summary

Create a root data folder—a top-level folder on the data volume of a file server—to support each unique top-level access requirement (for example, different support teams responsible for subfolders). Use File System Group Policy settings to configure and enforce the ACLs of root data folders.

# 2-4: Delegate the Management of Shared Folders

## Solution overview

| | |
|---|---|
| **Type of solution** | Guidance |
| **Features and tools** | Group Policy Restricted Groups policy settings |
| **Solution summary** | Where possible, dedicate the File Server role and manage the membership of the Administrators group using Restricted Groups policy settings. |
| **Benefits** | Managed delegation of the capability to create, delete, and modify shared folders |

## Introduction

Shared folders can be managed, by default, only by members of the server's Administrators group. It is not possible to specify that certain users can create shared folders in certain locations on the server: It is a system privilege.

## Dedicate servers that perform a file server role

If a server performs mixed roles, anyone who requires the ability to create shared folders will be an administrator, and therefore, they'll be able to affect other services on the server. For this reason, it is often necessary to dedicate servers that perform a file server role.

 **Best Practices**     Dedicate servers that perform a file server role.

# Manage the delegation of administration of shared folders

To delegate the management of shared folders, you must add a user to the Administrators group. The easiest way to manage this delegation is to use Restricted Groups settings in Group Policy to add a capability management group into the local Administrators group:

1. Create a group to centrally manage and represent the capability to administer shared folders. Name the group based on your naming conventions—for example, SYS_Shared Folder_Admins. For more information on capability management groups and naming conventions, see Solutions Collection 1.

2. Create a Group Policy object (GPO) scoped to your file servers. Name the GPO according to your naming conventions—for example, File Server Configuration. For more information on scoping and naming GPOs, see Solutions Collection 10.

3. Open the GPO in the Group Policy Management Editor (which is called the Group Policy Object Editor in Windows Server 2003).

4. Navigate to Computer Configuration, Windows Settings, Security Settings, Restricted Groups.

5. Right-click Restricted Groups and choose Add Group.

6. Click Browse and search for the group you created.

   Although you can type the group name (in the format *domain\groupname*), if you make a mistake the setting will not take effect correctly. Therefore, it is recommended that you search for and select the group. Click OK when you've selected the group.

7. Click OK to close the Add Group dialog box.

8. In the Properties dialog box for the group, click the Add button next to the This Group Is A Member Of section.

9. In the Group Membership dialog box, type **Administrators** and click OK. The result should look like Figure 2-8.

10. Click OK to close the Properties dialog box.

This GPO will now ensure that the selected group is a member of the local Administrators group on all servers within the scope of the GPO. It will not remove members from, or otherwise manage, membership of the Administrators group.

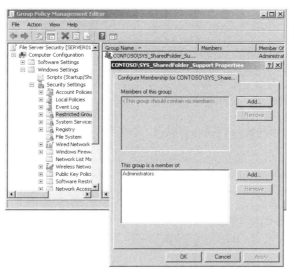

**Figure 2-8**   Group Policy Restricted Groups policy placing a group into the local Administrators group

> **Note**   If the local Administrators group should contain *only* the capability management group (SYS_Shared Folders_Administer), perform the procedure just described, but in step 6 type **Administrators**, and in step 8 click the Add button next to the Members Of This Group section and select the group—SYS_Shared Folders_Administer, for example. Doing so will result in the list of members being the complete and authoritative membership of the Administrators group. The server will remove any members of the Administrators group not provided for by the GPO.
>
> The tricky part about this approach to group management is that if more than one GPO attempts to specify group membership for a group with the Members Of This Group list, only the most authoritative GPO's setting will be applied.

It is unfortunate that Windows does not enable an enterprise to delegate the management of shared folders with a user right or ACL. The only supported method for allowing a user to create or manage shares is for that user's token to include the Administrators SID. Therefore, you must take either of the following courses of action:

- Accept the fact that support personnel who should be able to manage shared folders will be administrators of the file server. This means they have a number of avenues with which to access, modify, delete, or otherwise damage the integrity of the file server and all of its data.

- Provide a tool that provisions shares using alternative credentials. Such tools are described in Solutions Collection 8, "Reimagining the Administration of Groups and Membership." Given the security-sensitive nature of data on file servers, this approach is highly recommended.

## Solution summary

Create a group in Active Directory that represents and manages the capability to administer shared folders (for example, SYS_Shared Folders_Administer). Implement the capability by nesting that group in the local Administrators group of file servers using Restricted Group settings in a GPO scoped to file servers.

# 2-5: Determine Which Folders Should Be Shared

## Solution overview

| | |
|---|---|
| **Type of solution** | Guidance |
| **Features and tools** | Shared folders |
| **Solution summary** | Understand the design criteria that determine whether a folder should be shared and how many shares are required. |
| **Benefits** | Optimize the number of shared folders in your environment. |

## Introduction

There are best practices for determining whether and how to share a folder. The best practices, which will be laid out later in this solution, require consideration of the following settings:

- NTFS permissions. A folder should be configured with the correct permissions with NTFS ACLs prior to being made available as a shared folder.

- Share protocols. Windows Server 2008 enables you to share folders using SMB, the standard share protocol for Windows clients, and Network File System (NFS), which is used for compatibility with Unix and Linux clients. In this Solutions Collection, we'll examine only SMB shared folders.

- The name for the SMB shared folder.

- An optional description for the shared folder.

- A limit to the number of concurrent users that the shared folder will allow.

- SMB permissions, also known as *share permissions*.

- Caching settings that determine whether files and folders within the shared folder can be taken offline.

- Access-based Enumeration (ABE), which, if configured, hides the contents of a shared folder to which users do not have Read permission when accessing the shared folder remotely. ABE is available for download and installation on Windows Server 2003 Service Pack 1 (SP1) or later, and it is installed by default on Windows Server 2008. ABE is discussed in Solution 2-12, "Prevent Users from Seeing What They Cannot Access," on page 143.

■  Whether and how the shared folder will be presented in a DFS namespace. The DFS Namespaces role service is discussed in Solution 2-18, "Create an Effective, Delegated DFS Namespace," on page 163.

# Determine which folders should be shared

From a design perspective, the art and science of deciding what to share boils down to two key factors, which are discussed in the following sections.

## Presentation of information to users

Shared folders provide a unique connection to a collection of files and folders. The Universal Naming Convention (UNC) to the share is, of course, \\*servername*\*sharename*. Therefore, if you want to have separate entry points to a collection of Finance documents and a collection of Marketing documents, you can create a shared folder for each, such as \\*servername*\ finance and \\*servername*\marketing. If you organized the information in your enterprise in this manner, you could end up with a large number of shares. Unfortunately, this is exactly what most enterprises have done, and it is not the best practice.

Since the introduction of Windows 2000, Windows clients have the ability to connect below a share. Therefore, you could have a single root data folder shared as Departments$, within which folders exist for Finance and Marketing. UNCs can target \\*servername*\departments$\ finance and \\*servername*\departments$\marketing. If those UNCs are used to map a network drive to Marketing or Finance, or if the UNCs are used as targets for folders in a DFS namespace (discussed in Solution 2-18 on page 163), users will not be able to go up to the Departments folder from their own department. The dollar sign at the end of the share name, Departments$, prevents the share from appearing on network browse lists. Hidden shares are one way to discourage users from poking around the network. Of course, more important are the NTFS permissions you set on the Department folder itself.

The combination of client connections to subfolders of a shared folder and the implementation of the DFS Namespaces feature enables an enterprise to share only top-level data folders, rather than sharing each subfolder.

## Management of SMB settings

Shared folders also provide a scope of management for settings described earlier: user limits, SMB permissions, ABE, and caching settings. It is for these reasons that you might need to create additional shared folders. If, for example, two departments require different caching settings, those two departments must be in two separate shared folders in order to provide two unique scopes of management.

Interestingly, this does *not* mean they need to be in separate folders on the file system. In a scenario requiring Marketing users to be able to take files offline but restricting Sales users from doing the same, you could create a file system hierarchy with two folders: E:\Data\Sales and E:\Data\Marketing. You could, if you so chose, share each folder separately with appropriate caching settings. Alternately, you could share E:\Sales and Marketing as Sales$ with caching disabled and SMB permissions allowing only Sales users to connect to the share. The exact same folder could be shared a second time as Marketing$ with caching enabled and SMB permissions allowing only Marketing users to connect to the share. The properties of the SMB shared folder are enforcing caching settings, not properties of the NTFS folder.

## Solution summary

Create a shared folder for a top-level data folder. Create additional shared folders wherever a scope of management is required for SMB permissions, caching, connection limits, or ABE.

# 2-6: Implement Folder Access Permissions Based on Required Capabilities

## Solution overview

| | |
|---|---|
| **Type of solution** | Guidance, scripts |
| **Features and tools** | NTFS folders, ACLs, icacls |
| **Solution summary** | Support folder access scenarios by applying thoughtful, nuanced collections of NTFS permissions. |
| **Benefits** | Manageable, automated, and consistent application of least-privilege access to folders. |

## Introduction

Prior to creating a shared folder, you must ensure that the folder's NTFS permissions are configured correctly. NTFS ACLs should be the primary, if not the sole, method with which access levels are implemented.

Some organizations refer to a user having the "role" to access a folder at a particular level. I prefer to reserve the word *role* to describe a user or computer based on business-driven characteristics, such as location, department, team, or function. Several user roles (for example, departments) might each require the *capability* to read files in a folder. In keeping with the terminology set forth in Solutions Collection 1, we'll refer to access levels as *capabilities*—in this case, capabilities to access a file or folder at a particular level.

This solution examines specific access capabilities that might be desired and the ACLs that must be implemented to enable those capabilities. I'll describe how capabilities can be implemented in the user interface, and I'll use icacls.exe to apply the permissions. Icacls.exe is available on Windows Server 2003 SP2, Windows Vista, and Windows Server 2008. It replaces and enhances commands from previous versions of Windows, including cacls.exe, xcacls.exe, and xcacls.vbs.

> **Best Practices**    It is always a best practice to assign permissions to groups, not to individual users.

## Implement a Read capability

Read access is the simplest to implement. The Read permission template can be assigned on the Security tab of the Properties dialog box for a file or folder, as detailed by the following steps:

1. Open the Security tab of the Properties dialog box for a folder or file.

2. Click the Add button. If it is not visible on a Windows Vista or Windows Server 2008 system, click Edit and then click Add.

3. Select a security principal, preferably a group.

The default permissions that are applied include Read & Execute, Read, and, if the object is a folder, List Folder Contents. In the Advanced Security Settings dialog box, on the Permissions tab, the three permissions templates that are applied by default when you add a security principal to the ACL are listed simply as Read & Execute in the Permission column. The specific ACEs that make up this permission, which can be viewed in the Permission Entry dialog box, are as follows:

- Traverse folder/execute file

- List folder/read data

- Read attributes

- Read extended attributes

- Read permissions

> **Note**    You can learn more about what each permission provides by clicking the Managing Permissions link at the bottom of the Permission Entry dialog box.

These permissions make up an effective and secure Read capability.

To implement a Read capability using icacls.exe, use the following command:

```
icacls.exe <path to folder> /grant <security principal>:(CI)(OI)RX
```

Or use this to assign the read capability for a single file:

```
icacls.exe <path to file> /grant <security principal>:RX
```

For example, to implement a capability to read Team A's folder, use the following command:

```
icacls.exe "e:\data\team a" /grant "ACL_Team A_Read":(CI)(OI)RX
```

> **Note**    The parameters *(CI)* and *(OI)* implement the inheritance flags of a permission. *(CI)* means apply to this folder and subfolders. *(OI)* means apply to files in this folder and in sub-folders. To apply a permission one level deep, add the *(NP)* parameter, which means "no prop-agation." To configure a permission to apply to objects within this folder but not to the folder itself, use the parameter *(IO)*, or "inherit only." Because we are assuming that you are managing ACLs at a high-level folder for all of its files and subfolders, we'll be using *(CI)* and *(OI)* switches.

The default Read & Execute permission template—which includes the Read template and, if the object is a folder, the List Folder Contents template—allows users to open all file types. You can prevent users from opening and running executables by removing the Execute File per-mission entry. The easiest way to do this is to clear the Allow::Read & Execute check box, leav-ing only Allow::Read and, if the object is a folder, Allow::List Folder Contents.

This resulting ACL should be tested to ensure it does not overly restrict users and prevent them from opening file types they require for business reasons. With the File Server Resource Manager (FSRM) service, it is more effective to implement file screening to prevent the storage of executables in the first place.

To implement a Read capability while restricting executables, use the following command:

```
icacls.exe <path to folder> /grant <security principal>:(CI)RX <security principal>:(CI)(OI)R
```

# Implement a Browse To capability

There might be scenarios that require a user to connect to a resource deep within a folder hier-archy that the user should otherwise not be able to browse. Imagine a folder structure such as E:\Data\Finance\Team A\Communications. A user in the Communications department requires access to the files in the Communications folder. We need the user to be able to browse to the Communications folder, but we do not want the user to be able to browse par-ent folders.

To understand what the solution entails, you must know that if a user enters a path to a folder—for example, \\*servername*\departments$\finance\team a\communications—they require two capabilities for Windows Explorer to successfully display the folder. First, they require the ability to view the contents of the Communications folder.

This can be implemented as a Read capability, as described previously. The least-privilege ACEs required to support the Browse To capability are two permission entries: List Folder and Read Attributes. These can be allowed in the Permission Entry dialog box or by using icacls, as follows:

```
icacls <folder path> /grant <security principal>:(CI)(RD,RA)
```

Note this permission is not enough to enable users to open subfolders or files—it allows them only to view the contents of this folder. To allow users to actually open files, implement a Read capability on the target folder, Communications.

The second capability users require is to traverse parent folders in the path to the folder they are opening. In our example, that means users require the ability to traverse the folder shared as Departments$, the Finance folder, and the Team A folder. This capability can be implemented two ways: using a system privilege or an NTFS permission.

There is a system privilege, also known as a user right, called Bypass Traverse Checking, which is granted to Everyone by default. With this default user right in place, a user requires *only* the aforementioned permissions on the target folder, Communications. The ability to traverse parent folders is provided by the user right.

The second way to implement the capability to traverse folders is to grant the Allow::Traverse Folder ACE on each parent folder, using the Permission Entry dialog box or, again, icacls:

```
icacls.exe <folder path> /grant <security principal>:(CI)(X)
```

If you change the default configuration of the Bypass Traverse Checking system privilege so that users do *not* have the right to traverse folders, the NTFS Traverse Folder ACE must be granted on all parent folders, starting with the shared folder.

On subfolders that you do want users to browse to and open, apply the List Folder and Read Attributes permissions or the full Read or Read & Execute permission sets. To get them to those folders, the Traverse Folder, List Folder, and Read Attributes ACEs are part of the Read & Execute permission template. However, if you want to *prevent* a user from opening a parent folder—such as \\\\*servername*\\departments$\\finance—or its Team A subfolder, you need to grant the user *only* the Traverse Folder ACE on those parent folders. Using icacls, the Browse To capability is implemented as shown here:

```
icacls.exe <path to shared folder> /grant <security principal>:(CI)(X)
icacls.exe <path to target folder> /grant <security principal>:(CI)(RD,RA)
```

Again, this enables users to open the target folder when it is a subfolder in a folder hierarchy. To enable users to open *files* within that target, implement a Read capability:

```
icacls.exe <path to target folder> /grant <security principal>:(OI)[R or RX]
```

# Implement an Edit capability

The edit capability is commonly implemented for scenarios in which a team of users should be able to open each other's documents and make modifications to those documents. The problem is that most enterprises implement the edit capability using the Modify permission template. The Modify template includes the Delete permission entry. When a group is given Modify permission to a folder, any user in that group can, accidentally or intentionally, delete the folder and all of its contents or any subset of the folder's contents. This creates at best a denial of service: For a period of time, users cannot access the files they require while data is restored. At worst, data is lost—particularly data that has not yet been backed up or captured by Shadow Copies.

Even more dangerous is the Full Control permission template, which adds the Delete Sub-folders and Files, Change Permissions, and Take Ownership permission entries. Each of these entries opens up new opportunities for any member of the group to damage or destroy data in the folder tree, up to and including the entire folder tree. The Delete Subfolders and Files ACE is a unique container permission that enables a user to delete a folder and all of its contents, even if the user has explicit Deny::Delete permissions on those contents. It is an especially dangerous permission to apply to a group.

> **Best Practices**    Unless required by business needs, do not allow a group the Modify or Full Control permission templates on a folder, as both of those templates enable any user in the group to cause denial of service or data loss within the folder.

In many business scenarios, it is *not* appropriate for users to be able to *delete* each other's documents—it is only necessary for them to be able to *change* each other's documents. Thus, the edit capability should be implemented using one or more of the following:

**The Write permission template for the group**    The Write permission template, applied to a folder and assigned to a group, gives any member of the group the ability to make changes to, but not delete, other users' documents. It also enables any member of the group to create new files or folders.

**The Delete permission for a more restricted group**    Consider granting Allow::Delete to a subset of users on the team. Implement a folder cleanup or folder management capability that includes the Allow::Delete ACE or the Allow::Modify permissions template.

**The Modify permission template scoped to files, not folders**    Alternatively, grant a group the Allow::Modify permission on a folder, but change the inheritance flag so that it applies only to files, not to folders. The effect of doing this will be that users can still delete each other's documents, but folders will be protected.

**The appropriate permissions for Creator Owner**    When a user creates a file or folder using the Create File or Create Folder ACE (both of which are included in the Write permission template), that user becomes the Owner of the new object, and the user's account is given explicit ACEs equivalent to the inheritable ACEs assigned to the Creator Owner special identity on the parent folder. So, if you give the Creator Owner identity the Modify permissions template (which includes an Allow::Delete ACE, on the parent folder) and apply that template to Files, whoever creates a new file in the folder will be given Modify and, therefore, Delete permission on the new file. This is, in fact, the best practice for most business scenarios. Thereby, the person who created a file will have the ability to delete her own file, but users in the group cannot delete each other's files.

If you grant the Creator Owner identity Full Control (which is a standard practice and is, in fact, the Windows default), you take two risks. First, users can change permissions on the objects they create without such action triggering a Failure audit. We'll explore this issue in Solution 2-11, "Preventing Users from Changing Permissions on Their Own Files," on page 141. Second, if a user creates a folder, and thus inherits Full Control of that folder, the user can effectively take ownership of, change permissions of, or completely delete any files or folders that are later added to the folder he created.

When implementing an Edit capability, the best practice is to grant the Creator Owner the Modify permissions template, inheritable to files only; however, this is a squishy best practice that applies primarily to team shared folders, and even then should be fully evaluated to determine whether it works with your business requirements. The bottom line is that you need to carefully consider permissions granted to Creator Owner. Do so in light of the guidance in Solution 2-11 on page 141.

The method you use to implement an Edit capability will vary based on the business requirements for the data in a folder. A reasonbly secure Edit capability—implemented in such a way that users can change but not delete each others' documents and only the creator of a document can delete the document—can be implemented using icacls.exe:

```
icacls.exe <folder path> /grant <security principal>:(CI)(OI)(RX)
icacls.exe <folder path> /grant <security principal>:(CI)(WD,AD)
icacls.exe <folder path> /grant <security principal>:(OI)(IO)W
icacls.exe <folder path> /grant "CREATOR OWNER":(CI)(OI)M
```

# Implement a Contribute capability

An Edit capability enables users to modify each others' documents. A Contribute capability enables users to create or save documents in the shared folder, and to read but not change each others' documents.

Implement this capability by granting a group the ability to create files and folders within a folder and to read the contents of the folder. Here's how you do it using icacls.exe:

```
icacls.exe <folder path> /grant <security principal>:(CI)(WD,AD) <security
principal>:(CI)(OI)[R | RX]
```

Additionally, you must determine the capabilities you want users to obtain when they create a new file or folder. Refer to the earlier discussion of the Creator Owner permissions. For example, you can use the following command:

```
icacls.exe <folder path> /grant "Creator Owner":(CI)(OI)(IO)M
```

## Implement a Drop capability

A drop folder allows users to add files to the folder but not to access those files once they have been added. This is implemented by giving users the Create Files permission entry on a folder, but not the List Folder Contents permission:

```
icacls.exe <folder path> /grant <security principal>:(CI)(WD)
```

Because users don't have Read permission to the drop folder, the folder will not appear if you have ABE configured for the shared folder. ABE must be disabled for the share in which such a drop folder exists.

A variation of this capability allows users to drop files into the folder and then to have the ability to access their own files, but not to see files from other users:

```
icacls.exe <folder path> /grant <security principal>:(CI)(WD) <security principal>:(NP)[R | RX]
icacls.exe <folder path> /grant "Creator Owner":(OI)(IO)[R | RX | W | M]
```

This set of permissions gives a group the ability to add files to the folder and see the contents of the folder. The tricky part is that you enable ABE so that users will see only the files that they added. The user who added a file will have read, write, or modify permission, according to the permission switch you used on the second icacls.exe command.

## Implementing a Support capability

The support capability enables a user to perform administrative tasks on files and folders, including renaming, moving, or deleting. The capability is often implemented using the Full Control permission template. As discussed earlier, this template contains several dangerous permission entries, so it should be granted with extreme caution. If you do want to use a Full Control permission template, the following icacls.exe command enables you to do so:

```
icacls.exe <folder path> /grant <security principal>:(CI)(OI)F
```

Often, support personnel do not require the ability to take ownership or change permissions on a file or folder, and they rarely require the Delete Subfolders and Files permission. So you should consider implementing the support capability using the Modify permission template:

```
icacls.exe <folder path> /grant <security principal>:(CI)(OI)M
```

If you want to add any of the remaining three granular permissions that distinguish the Modify and Full Control permission templates, add the WO (write owner), WDAC (write discretionary access control), or DC (delete child) permissions. For example, to allow the support organization to modify and to take ownership, use the following command:

```
icacls.exe <folder path> /grant <security principal>:(CI)(OI)M(WO)
```

The Support capability might be called "support," "administer," or even "own." All three of those descriptions convey an ability to perform actions on resources in a shared folder.

## Create scripts to apply permissions consistently

To facilitate consistent application of ACLs to support the capabilities you implement in your organization, create scripts to ensure the correct permissions are applied. For example, the following script creates a Contribute capability for a folder by giving a group the correct permissions:

```
Folder_Capability_Contribute.bat
@echo off
Set GROUP=%1
Set FOLDER=%2
icacls.exe %FOLDER% /grant %GROUP%:(CI)(WD,AD) %GROUP%:(CI)(OI)R
icacls.exe %FOLDER% /grant "Creator Owner":(CI)(OI)(IO)M

@echo on
```

The script can be called with two parameters, the first specifying the group that should be given the Contribute capability and the second specifying the folder—for example:

```
Folder_Capability_Contribute.bat ACL_MyFolder_Contribute
    "\\server01.contoso.com\departments$\finance\team a"
```

Similar scripts, each using the icacls.exe commands described in this solution, can be prepared to implement capabilities you require.

## Manage folder access capabilities using role-based access control

Role-based access control (RBAC) is a common way to describe role-based management (RBM) as it applies to the management of resource access. Nowhere does RBM provide a bigger bang for the buck in terms of IT productivity than RBAC. Many organizations can benefit from the agility that is enabled by RBM: When a user is hired, the definition of that user's roles by HR and the user's manager results in instant and consistent resource access the day the user reports to work. When a user is promoted or moved within the organization, the redefinition of the user's roles (moving them between groups) results in a seamless transition from the resource access required by the previous roles and that required by the new roles.

Additionally, RBAC enables an IT organization to answer two critical questions: "What can the *user* access?" and "Who can access the *resource*?" Traditionally, when the first question is asked, it requires an administrator to scan multitudes of ACLs to locate ACEs assigned to groups to which the user belongs or directly to the user account. When the second question is asked, an administrator must make sense of ACEs such as Traverse Folder, Append Data, and Delete Subfolders and Files. RBAC revolutionizes your ability to analyze and audit resource security.

Solution 1-5, "Implement Role-Based Access Control," discussed RBAC implementation in detail, in the context of role-based management as a whole. The following list summarizes the best practices for RBAC:

- Role groups are implemented as global security groups. They define collections of users and computers based on common business characteristics.

- Resource access capabilities are implemented by adding permissions to ACLs.

- Those capabilities are managed by creating domain local security groups that represent a specific capability for a specific collection of resources—for example, ACL_Budget_Read and ACL_Budget_Contribute.

- Role groups and, occasionally, individual users or computers are given capabilities not by being added directly to the ACL, but by being nested within the appropriate capability management group.

## Solution summary

Grant a folder permissions based on the capabilities required by users for that folder. Unfortunately, capabilities required by today's information workers cannot be implemented with least-privilege access without managing granular permission entries (ACEs) and inheritance properties of those ACEs. Although these permissions can be applied using the user interface, you'll often be better served using icacls.exe to configure security, particularly because you can then automate icacls.exe using scripts to ensure consistent application of permissions. Be sure to manage resource access capabilities by creating a capability management group to represent a specific type of access to a collection of resources. That will enable you to leverage role-based management to implement role-based access control.

# 2-7: Understand Shared Folder Permissions (SMB Permissions)

## Solution overview

| | |
|---|---|
| **Type of solution** | Guidance |
| **Features and tools** | Shared folders, *net share* |
| **Solution summary** | In most scenarios, share permissions should be Everyone::Allow::Full Control, and NTFS permissions should be used to secure the folder according to business requirements. Unfortunately, the default SMB |

permissions applied to a new shared folder are usually Everyone::Allow::Read, which is too restrictive to be useful in most scenarios. The *net share* command can create a share with specific permissions, such as Everyone::Allow::Full Control.

**Benefits**          Increased manageability of shared folder security

# Introduction

The permissions associated with a shared folder have long been called *share permissions*. Because Windows Server 2008 natively supports sharing folders with NFS, these permissions are now referred to more specifically as *SMB permissions*. SMB permissions are challenging to use for the implementation of security because they affect resource access in unusual ways.

First, if the effective SMB permission for a user is more restrictive than the user's effective NTFS permission, the SMB permission will win out. So, even if a user has Allow::Full Control NTFS permissions, if the folder is shared as Everyone::Allow::Read, the user will only be able to read items when accessing the folder through the SMB share. And Everyone::Allow::Read is the default permission applied when you create a share with user-interface tools in Windows Server 2003 and later operating systems. Therefore, even Administrators creating the share will be unable to access the share with anything more than Read permissions.

Second, SMB permissions affect resource access *only* if the resource is accessed through that shared folder's UNC. If resources are accessed locally by logging on to the server interactively, or if resources are accessed by a user logging on with Remote Desktop and finding the resource on the file system, SMB permissions do not apply. The same physical folder can be shared several times, each with unique share permissions. So users accessing a file within that folder could have completely different effective permissions depending on which shared folder UNC they accessed.

Third, SMB permissions are weak. They are stored in the registry, not in the security descriptor of the shared folder itself. If the folder is moved or renamed, the share permissions are effectively lost because they now refer to a folder that no longer exists.

There are a number of other reasons why share permissions are not used by many organizations. Instead, these organizations set forth a policy under which every share is created with Everyone::Allow::Full Control SMB permission. Doing so does not expose any data within the shared folder because the same folder is secured using NTFS permissions to configure least-privilege access.

There are, in my experience, only a handful of salient scenarios under which SMB permissions should be anything other than Everyone::Allow::Full Control. Here is a list of those scenarios:

**Prevent users (even object owners) from changing permissions.**    Setting the SMB permission to Allow::Change prevents users from changing the permissions of resources in the shared folder, *even if they are the owner of the object*. Of course, the restriction applies only to remote access through the shared folder's UNC, not to local or remote-desktop access to the folder. Starting with Windows Server 2008, this business requirement can be met using the Owner Rights identity, which is described in Solution 2-11 on page 141.

**Create a hub-and-spoke distribution of resources.**    Some organizations want to distribute a copy of resources to multiple locations. DFS Replication (DFS-R) or the Robocopy command can be used to do just that. If your organization wants to ensure that changes are made to original documents in only one location, you have a challenge. DFS-R replicates NTFS permissions, and Robocopy can and should be configured to replicate permissions using the */copy:s* or */copyall* switches. Therefore, to allow changes in one place but not others, you must give users Write or Modify NTFS permissions and then further restrict such changes by applying an Allow::Read share permission to the shared folders that act as copies. This scenario is addressed in Solution 2-15 on page 151.

**Apply different SMB settings to different users for the same folder structure.**    SMB settings include ABE and caching settings. Suppose you have a departmental folder and you want to prevent all but a few users from taking files offline. You can achieve this by sharing the folder twice. The first share would have caching disabled. On the second share, enable caching and configure the share permissions so that only selected users can access the folder through the share's UNC name. Similarly, you might have a folder structure that should appear to some users with ABE enabled, but other users, such as the support staff, should see all files. Two separate shares, with two separate configurations and permissions would achieve this goal.

**Temporary lockdown.**    Typically, a shared folder is configured with Everyone::Allow::Full Control SMB permission, and access capabilities are implemented using more restrictive NTFS permissions. A scenario might arise that requires locking down a resource. Perhaps a security trigger requires freezing a folder—that is, preventing access or perhaps allowing only Read access. Changing the share permission from Allow::Full Control to Allow::Read or even Deny::Full Control can instantly prevent further changes to data in the shared folder. Changing the root-level folder's NTFS permission, however, would result in an ACL propagation that could be problematic for the following reasons:

❑ ACL propagation to all objects requires that all child objects inherit permissions, which might not be the case.

❑ An explicit permission on a child object might enable the very type of access that you want to prevent.

❑ ACL propagation touches files, which might affect the ability to effectively audit or perform forensic investigation on the files.

❑ ACL propagation takes time and, when a large number of files are affected, might allow access to files at the previous level for an undesirable length of time.

Locking down a folder using SMB permissions takes effect immediately, does not touch files or folders within the share, and can be easily reverted. Just remember the weaknesses of SMB permissions, such as the fact that they will not limit access to files by users logged on interactively or using Remote Desktop to access the file server.

## Scripting SMB permissions on local and remote systems

The easiest way to implement SMB permissions is to use the *net share* command to create the share:

```
net share sharename=path  /GRANT:user or group,[READ | CHANGE | FULL]
```

Because of its ability to create a share and apply SMB permissions simultaneously and effi-ciently, I recommend using the *net share* command, rather than the GUI, to create a share. But what if you need to create a share on a remote system? PSExec comes to our rescue. Originally developed by Mark Russinovich and friends at Sysinternals, which was subsequently acquired by Microsoft, PSExec is an extraordinarily important component of the administrator's tool-set, as it lets you execute commands on a remote machine. If you have not been fortunate enough to have been exposed to the tool previously, you're in for a happy day. You can download this tool from *http://www.microsoft.com/technet/sysinternals*. The basic syntax of PSExec is

```
psexec \\computername command
```

In this simple form, the PSExec command takes two arguments. The first is the computer name, preceded by two backslashes: \\*computername*–for example, \\*server01*. The second is the command you want to execute. You can use PSExec, to execute the *net share* command on a remote system with this command:

```
psexec \\computername net share sharename=path
    /GRANT:user or group,[READ | CHANGE | FULL]
```

The *net share* command allows you to assign permissions only when creating a share. You can-not modify permissions on an existing share using *net share*–you must delete and re-create the share. Custom scripts, such as those written in VBScript, can attach to the security descriptor for the SMB shared folder and modify its ACL at any time. Solution 2-9, "Provision the Cre-ation of a Shared Folder," (on page 126) presents just such a script.

## Solution summary

Shared folders should be secured for least-privilege access using NTFS permissions. There-fore, SMB permissions can be set to Everyone::Allow::Full Control. This best practice is in place in most organizations. There are only a handful of scenarios, some of which were detailed in this solution, that require setting share permissions to anything more restrictive. Because the Windows default share permission is Everyone::Allow::Read, when creating a share using GUI tools, it is recommended to use the *net share* command with the */grant:everyone, full* switch to create a share and set its permissions simultaneously.

# 2-8: Script the Creation of an SMB Share

## Solution overview

| | |
|---|---|
| **Type of solution** | Script |
| **Features and tools** | VBScript, PSExec, *net share* |
| **Solution summary** | Customize and use the Share_Create.vbs script to script the creation of an SMB share, including all of its properties. |
| **Benefits** | Increased manageability of shared folder security |

## Introduction

Because the Shared Folder user interfaces apply default share permissions and caching settings that are not desirable in most situations, I recommend creating a script that can be used to deploy shared folders based on your specifications.

## Using Share_Create.vbs

The Share_Create.vbs script, in the Scripts folder of the companion media, creates a share and assigns the Everyone::Allow::Full Control permission. The usage of the script is as follows:

```
cscript Share_Create.vbs /server:ServerName
    /path: "Path to folder on server's file system"
    /sharename:"Share name" [/cache:CacheSettings]
    [/username:AltCredsUsername /password:AltCredsPassword
```

In this script, *CacheSettings* specifies the caching settings and can be one of the following: *Manual*, *Documents*, *Programs*, or *None*; *AltCredsUsername* and *AltCredsPassword* are the user name and password, respectively, for credentials to be used for creating the share. If alternate credentials are not specified, the script runs under the security context of the currently logged-on user.

## Customizing Share_Create.vbs

Unfortunately, caching settings are not exposed in a way that can be accessed using VBScript. Therefore, we have to execute the *net share* command to configure caching settings. The Share_Create.vbs script relies on psexec.exe to run *net share* on remote machines.

You must specify, in the script's *Configuration* block, the full path to psexec.exe. The path is not required if psexec.exe is in the same folder as the script.

Optionally, you might want to change the share permissions assigned by the script to a new shared folder. By default, the script grants the Everyone::Allow::Full Control permission. You can modify this default or configure additional permissions to be applied to the new share.

# Understanding Share_Create.vbs

The core functional components of the script are described here:

```
Set oWMIService = ConnectWMI(sServer, "root\cimv2", sUsername, sPassword)
```

This line calls the *ConnectWMI* function to connect to the *root\cimv2* Windows Management Instrumentation (WMI) namespace on the server specified by the */server:* argument you specify on the command line when you run the Share_Create.vbs script file. Before creating a new shared folder, any previous share by the same name is removed:

```
Set oOutParams = oWMIService.ExecMethod("Win32_Share.Name='" & sShareName & "'", "Delete")
```

Then a security descriptor is generated that contains the SMB ACL for the shared folder. These lines of code can be modified to specify a different default ACL:

```
Set oSecDescClass = oWMIService.Get("Win32_SecurityDescriptor")
Set oSecDesc = oSecDescClass.SpawnInstance_()
Set oTrustee = oWMIService.Get("Win32_Trustee").SpawnInstance_
Set oACE = oWMIService.Get("Win32_Ace").SpawnInstance_
' CONFIGURATION (Optional)
' Use these three lines of code for "EVERYONE"
oTrustee.Domain = Null
oTrustee.Name = "EVERYONE"
oTrustee.Properties_.Item("SID") = Array(1, 1, 0, 0, 0, 0, 0, 1, 0, 0, 0, 0)
' For a user/group other than Everyone, use the following line
' instead of the previous three lines
' Set oTrustee = Trustee_Get("<domain>", "<name", "user | group")

' CONFIGURATION (Optional)
oACE.Properties_.Item("AccessMask") = 2032127
' 2032127 = "Full"
' 1245631 = "Change"
' 1179817 = "Read"

oACE.Properties_.Item("AceFlags") = 3
oACE.Properties_.Item("AceType") = 0
oACE.Properties_.Item("Trustee") = oTrustee
oSecDesc.Properties_.Item("DACL") = Array(oACE)
```

After the security descriptor has been prepared, the shared folder can be created:

```
Set oWin32Share = oWMIService.Get("Win32_Share")
Set oInParam = oWin32Share.Methods_("Create").InParameters.SpawnInstance_()
oInParam.Properties_.Item("Access") = oSecDesc
oInParam.Properties_.Item("Description") = sRemark
oInParam.Properties_.Item("Name") = sShareName
oInParam.Properties_.Item("Path") = sPath
oInParam.Properties_.Item("Type") = 0
Set oOutParams = oWin32Share.ExecMethod_("Create", oInParam)
```

Finally, the *net share* command is launched to configure caching settings for the shared folder:

```
sCommandLine = "net share """ & sShareName & """ /CACHE:" & sCache
PSExec_Run sCommandLine, sServer
```

## Solution summary

The Share_Create.vbs script provisions the creation of a shared folder including its ACL, description, share name, and more.

# 2-9: Provision the Creation of a Shared Folder

## Solution overview

| | |
|---|---|
| **Type of solution** | Tool |
| **Features and tools** | HTA, VBScript, PSExec, *net share* |
| **Solution summary** | Customize and use Folder_Provision.hta to fully provision the creation of a shared folder including role-based access control (RBAC). |
| **Benefits** | Automated, role-based provisioning of shared folders and security |
| **Preview** | Figure 2-9 shows a preview of the solution. |

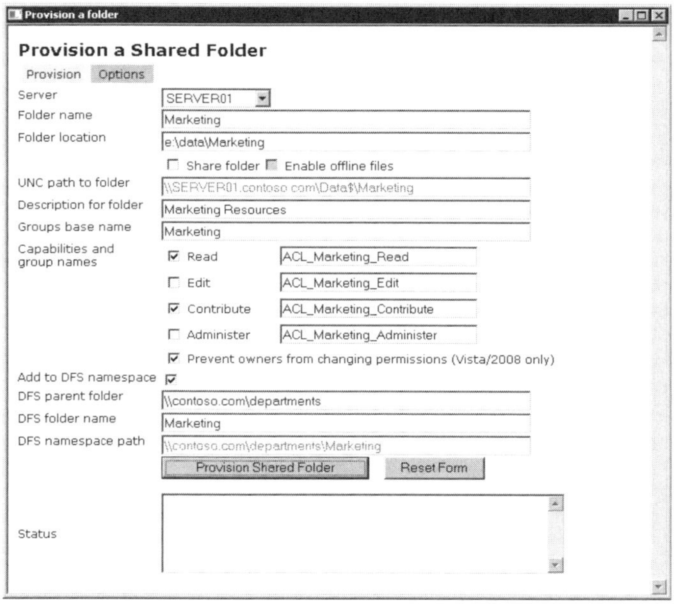

**Figure 2-9**   The Provision a Shared Folder tool

# Introduction

Provisioning a shared folder is not a one-step process. To provision a shared folder, you must do the following:

1.  Create the folder if it does not exist.

2.  Create resource access capability management groups with which to secure the folder, if you are following principles of RBAC and if the groups do not already exist.

3.  Implement resource access by modifying the ACL of the folder to include appropriate ACEs assigned to the capability management groups.

4.  Create an SMB share.

5.  Assign SMB share permissions.

6.  Modify properties of the SMB share, such as the description and caching settings.

Throughout this resource kit, we are applying the concept of provisioning to automate multi-step processes and to ensure consistent application of business rules. A process with as many moving parts as the provisioning of a shared folder is an ideal candidate for a custom administrative tool.

Figure 2-9 shows the interface for Folder_Provision.hta, located in the Scripts folder of the companion media. Folder_Provision.hta is an HTML Application (HTA) that provisions folders, automating all the steps just listed. It will require a moderate amount of customization to reflect your enterprise configuration and business logic. In this solution, we'll examine Folder_Provision.hta to understand its use, its customization, and the code that it leverages to achieve its task.

# Using Folder_Provision.hta

Folder_Provision.hta is located in the Scripts folder of the companion media. It requires the script Share_Create.vbs, discussed in the previous solution. It also requires psexec.exe, which can be downloaded from *http://www.microsoft.com/technet/sysinternals*, and icacls.exe, which is a native tool on Windows Server 2003 SP2, Windows Vista, and Windows Server 2008 systems. Place the script and HTA in the same folder. You'll also need to configure the HTA to know the path to psexec.exe unless you put it in the same folder as the HTA itself. We'll look at how to configure the HTA later in this solution.

To use the tool to provision a folder, you must have permission to do the following:

■   Create a folder in the specified location (unless the folder already exists).

   The folder you specify in the tool will be created beneath a root data folder. The root data folder must already exist. If the root folder doesn't exist, create it before running this tool.

- Create a share on the selected server (unless the share exists or you are not sharing the folder).

- Modify ACLs on the folder.

- Create groups in the organizational unit (OU) specified on the Options tab (unless the groups already exist).

When the tool opens, as shown in Figure 2-9, it displays a number of input controls that enable you to provision a shared folder.

To provision a folder, follow these steps:

1. Select a server from the Server drop-down list.

    This list can be customized to display your file servers.

2. Enter a name for the folder in the Folder Name text box.

3. The Folder Location field is populated automatically.

    The default location will be a first-level folder beneath a root data folder. The root data folder can be configured on the Options tab, accessed by clicking the Options button. You must have created and shared the root data folder prior to specifying it here.

    The folder must be created beneath the root data folder on the Options tab. However, it does not have to be a first-level folder beneath the root—it can be a folder several levels down.

    You can customize the HTA code to change the logic with which the folder location is populated, or to prevent the user from manually overriding the prepopulated Folder Location. See the next sections for details regarding customization of the tool.

4. Select the Share Folder check box to create a new SMB share for the new folder.

5. If you are creating a share, you can specify whether to enable offline files for the share by selecting the Enable Offline Files check box (cleared by default).

6. If you are creating a share, the UNC Path To Folder text box is populated automatically.

    ❑ By default, the UNC is a hidden share in the form \\*server name*\*folder name$*. You can configure whether or not the HTA creates hidden shares (the default) on the Options tab.

    ❑ You can customize the HTA code to change the logic with which the UNC path is created. See the next sections for details regarding customization of the tool.

7. Enter a description for the share in the Description For Folder text box.

8. Enter a name in the Groups Base Name text box.

    The HTA provisions the folder using RBAC. It creates capability management groups for selected capabilities, such as Read, Edit, Contribute, or Administer. Each group's name is in the form ACL_*Folder Name_Capability*. As soon as you change the value in the Groups Base Name box, the group names for each capability are automatically generated.

On the Options tab, you can change the prefix (ACL_ by default) used for the naming standard for resource access capability management groups. You can also specify the OU within which the groups are created.

You can customize the HTA code to change the logic with which group names are generated. See the next sections for details regarding customization of the tool.

9.  In the Capabilities And Group Names section, select the capabilities you want to implement for the folder.

    Only capabilities that are selected (checked) will be provisioned.

    When a capability is provisioned, the script modifies the ACL of the folder to add appropriate ACEs for the specified groups.

    You can override the prepopulated group name. This is particularly useful when you are creating a new folder in a collection of resources that have already been provisioned, so there are already appropriate groups in Active Directory. If a capability is being provisioned to a group that does not exist in Active Directory, the group will be created in the OU specified on the Options tab.

    You can customize the HTA to add or remove supported capabilities.

    In addition to the ACEs assigned to the selected groups, the HTA code assigns several default ACEs: Administrators::Allow::Full Control, System::Allow Full Control. If the Contribute capability is selected, Creator Owner is assigned the Modify permission. All of these additional permissions can be modified or removed in the HTA code.

10. If you want the folder to prevent the owner of a file or folder from changing the permission on that object, select Prevent Owners From Changing Permissions.

    This option is supported only if the system on which the folder is provisioned is running Windows Vista or Windows Server 2008. If you are creating the folder on a system running a previous version of Windows, do not select this option.

    The permission that makes this possible is discussed in Solution 2-11 on page 141.

11. To add the new folder to a DFS namespace, select the Add To DFS Namespace check box. You can then do the following:

    ❑ Enter the path of the DFS parent folder, which can be either an existing namespace or an existing DFS folder. The DFS Parent Folder text box is prepopulated with the DFS Namespace option on the Options tab.

    ❑ Enter the name of the new DFS folder that will target the folder you are provisioning. The DFS Folder Name text box is prepopulated with the name of the folder.

12. Click the Provision Shared Folder button.

13. Several command windows will open as the HTA calls the Share_Create.vbs scripts, along with psexec.exe and icacls.exe.

   The first time you run the HTA, you might be prompted to agree to the license agreement for psexec.exe.

14. The Status window will alert you to any errors, and a message box will appear indicating that the folder has been provisioned successfully.

To override the HTA defaults, click the Options button. The Options tab allows you to change the default behavior of the HTA until the HTA is closed. The defaults are themselves driven by the code in the HTA, so if you want to permanently change the defaults, you can customize the HTA code itself.

# Basic customization of Folder_Provision.hta

The folder provisioning tool will certainly require customization for your enterprise. There is a configuration block near the top of the script that contains values such as the domain name and paths to supporting scripts and tools.

## Customizing the behavior of option defaults

There is also a block labeled *Option Defaults*, which controls the default behaviors of the tool, such as the default root data share location, whether unique shares are created for each new folder, whether shares are hidden, the prefix used for the group naming convention, and so on. Each of these values is explained in comments in the code.

Each value in the Option Defaults section is displayed on the Options tab of the HTA and can be overridden when using the tool. The HTML for the Options tab of the tool is near the bottom of the HTA code.

There might be situations in which you don't want a user to be able to override one of the default values. For example, the HTA does not allow a user to change the prefix used in the group naming standard (ACL_, by default). The justification is that an administrator has configured the value of the prefix in the code of the HTA to enforce a naming convention. Someone using the tool should not be able to go outside of the naming convention.

To lock down a default value, you can delete the table row that displays the value in the Options tab by deleting the entire table row tag, from the *<tr>* opening tag up to and including the *</tr>* closing tag. Alternatively, you can allow the value to be displayed but not modified on the Options tab by adding an attribute to the *<input>* tag:

```
disabled="true"
```

You can see an example of this on the line of HTML that displays the group name prefix. This latter method is recommended over deleting the table row because, by disabling the control, a user of the tool can continue to see what is configured, which can be useful. That user just can't change it.

### Customizing the list of servers

The drop-down list of servers should display appropriate file servers in your enterprise. The list is hard-coded near the bottom of the HTA:

```
<select name="cboServer" />
<option value="">Select a server</option>
<option value="SERVER01.contoso.com">SERVER01</option>
<option value="SERVER02.contoso.com">SERVER02</option>
</select>
```

The *<select>* tag creates a drop-down list. Each *<option>* tag creates an item in the drop-down list. To modify, add, or remove servers, simply change, create, or delete *<option>* tags. It is important that the *value* attribute be set to the server's name. I recommend that you always use fully qualified domain names (FQDNs) when referring to any computer by name. The text between the opening *<option>* and closing *</option>* tags is the text that appears in the drop-down list. This is simply the user-friendly name of the server displayed in the form. You can use simpler (flat NetBIOS or host) names if you so desire.

## Understanding the code behind Folder_Provision.hta and advanced customization

To perform more advanced customization of the folder provisioning tool, you need to understand how the tool works. This section will be useful for you if you are experienced in scripting with HTML and VBScript. There are three major components of the HTA's functionality that we'll examine: the way the application is displayed, the form controls' behavior, and the code that actually provisions the folder.

### Application display

The application has two tabs: Provision and Options. Each tab is represented by a button generated by HTML code:

```
<table border="0" cellpadding="3" cellspacing="5">
   <tr><td id="btnProvision" onclick="ShowProvision()" style="background-color: #CCCCCC;
       width:60px; text-align:center;">Provision</td>
       <td id="btnOptions" onclick="ShowOptions()" style="background-color: #CCCCCC;
       width:60px; text-align:center;">Options</td>
   </tr>
</table>
```

Each tab is contained within a division (*<div>* tag), for example:

```
<div id="divOption" name="divOption">
<table border="0" cellpadding="0" cellspacing="0">
   <!-- OPTIONS PAGE of the HTA is below. If you don't want a user to be able to override the
   default value of one of these options, either delete the table row <tr>...</tr> entirely or
   add disabled="true" within the <input> tag -->
   <tr><td class="frmlabel">Root data folder</td><td><input type="text" name="txtRootPath"
   size="60" /></td></tr>
   ...
</table>
</div>
```

The *<div>* tag contains a table that lays out input controls for the tab's form.

When you click a button, such as the Options button, an *OnClick* event is fired. The *OnClick* event is wired up in the *<td>* tag for the button, shown earlier, and calls a subroutine such as the following one:

```
Sub ShowOptions()
   divProvision.style.display = "none"
   btnProvision.style.backgroundcolor = "#CCCCCC"
   divOption.style.display = "inline"
   btnOptions.style.backgroundcolor = "#EEEEEE"
End Sub
```

This simple VBscript turns on the tab represented by the button (*divOption.style.display = "inline"*) and turns off the other tab. It also changes the color of the buttons so that the lighter colored button represents the current tab.

When the application launches, the *Window_OnLoad* subroutine is automatically called. That subroutine resizes the application window to appropriate dimensions and then calls the subroutine that makes the Provision tab visible. Then it sets the values of the controls on the hidden Options tab.

No customization should be necessary to the code that controls the display of the application unless you add more controls and require a larger horizontal or vertical dimension for the HTA window.

## Form controls

The two forms of the HTA are the Options tab and the Provision tab. As I just described, each form is contained in a *<div>* tag that is displayed when the corresponding button is clicked. Each *<div>* contains a table that lays out input controls: text boxes, drop-down lists, and check boxes. Each input control has a name that can be used to refer to the control and its values.

If you decide to create additional input parameters, simply add table rows to the appropriate form and insert new input controls.

The default values on the Options form are hard-coded in the *Option Defaults* section of the script. You should configure the defaults in the code to reflect the correct values for your enterprise.

To make those values easier to override by a user of the HTA, each value is exposed in an input control on the Options tab. The default values are inserted into the controls by the *SetDefault-Options()* subroutine, which is called by the *Window_OnLoad* event when the HTA is opened and is also called when the Reset Options To Defaults button is clicked.

You can change the way options are displayed on the Options tab. For example, as described earlier, you can add a *disabled="true"* attribute to an *<input>* tag to disable the control and thereby prevent a user from overriding one of the defaults. You can also change a control type. If you have several OUs in which a resource access capability group can be created, you can change the *txtGroupOU* control to a drop-down list (*<select>* tag). Just be sure to modify other locations in the code that refer to *txtGroupOU*.

If you *add* new parameters to control the behavior of the tool, I recommend that you follow the model that is in place. Define a variable with the default value in the *Option Defaults* section of the script, add an input control to the Options *<div>*, and add a line of code to inject the default value into the control in the *SetDefaultOptions()* subroutine. You obviously need to modify other code in the HTA to actually *use* your new parameter to achieve your goals.

The values on the Provision form are displayed using input controls in a table in the Provision *<div>*. Controls are set to their default value (blank) by the *ResetControls()* subroutine, except for the folder name and server name controls. All controls, including the folder name and server name, are initialized by the *ResetForm()* subroutine, which is called when the Reset Form button is clicked. If you add any controls to the form, be sure to set them to their default value in the *ResetControls()* subroutine.

Some controls, when changed, trigger the autopopulation of values in other controls. This is achieved by using an *OnChange* event or, in the case of check boxes, an *OnClick* event. For example, if you change the value of the Groups Base Name box, all the names of the capability groups are autopopulated. The Groups Base Name box on the form is named *txtGroupBase-Name* in the HTML code. The following script wires up the *OnChange* event for that text box:

```
Sub txtGroupBaseName_OnChange()
  ' when the base name is changed, reconfigure the values in the capability group name boxes
  ' Here is where you can modify the code to reflect your capability gorup naming conventions
  If txtGroupBaseName.value > "" Then
    txtReadGroup.Value = txtGroupPrefix.Value & txtGroupBaseName.Value & "_Read"
    txtEditGroup.Value = txtGroupPrefix.Value & txtGroupBaseName.Value & "_Edit"
    txtContributeGroup.Value = txtGroupPrefix.Value & txtGroupBaseName.Value & "_Contribute"
    txtAdministerGroup.Value = txtGroupPrefix.Value & txtGroupBaseName.Value & "_Administer"
  Else
    txtReadGroup.Value = ""
    txtEditGroup.Value = ""
    txtContributeGroup.Value = ""
    txtAdministerGroup.Value = ""
  End If
End Sub
```

If the new value of the text box is not blank, the code constructs the four capability group names by taking the prefix from the *txtGroupPrefix* text box on the Options tab, appending the value entered into the Group Base Name box, and then appending the capability. On the other hand, if the value in the Group Base Name text box is blank, all the capability group text boxes are set to blank as well.

If you want to change any of the logic that determines how values are autopopulated, look for the appropriate *OnChange* or *OnClick* event in the HTA's code.

## Folder provisioning

The code that manages the provisioning process is the *ProvisionIt()* subroutine, called when the Provision Shared Folder button is clicked.

*ProvisionIt()* first calls the *CreateFolder()* function, which simply determines the path of the new folder and calls the *FolderPath_Create* subroutine, which then creates the specified folder. The *CreateFolder()* function takes values from input controls on the form, such as the folder name and path. *CreateFolder()* returns its results as a string, and *ProvisionIt* is able to examine the results to determine whether an error was encountered.

*ProvisionIt()* then applies default permissions to the folder. Administrators and System are each allowed Full Control. The permissions are assigned to the string variable named *sPermission*. *sPermission* is in the same syntax as switches for the icacls.exe command. In fact, *sPermission* is passed—along with the UNC to the folder—to the *ACLit()* subroutine, which simply calls icacls with *sPermission* as its switch.

If you want to change the default permissions applied to every folder created by the HTA, change the assignment of *sPermission*.

After default permissions have been applied, *ProvisionIt()* then looks at each capability that has been selected (checked). It first calls the *CreateGroup()* subroutine to create the group in Active Directory. There is business logic in *CreateGroup* that provisions the *Description* property of the group as the UNC to the resource controlled by the group. *CreateGroup* also is coded to create the group as a domain local security group.

*ProvisionIt* again assigns permissions by configuring *sPermission* as the switch for icacls and, again, calls *ACLit()* to execute icacls.exe.

As each selected capability is implemented, a variable named *sRolesConfigured* is appended with the friendly name of the capability. This variable is then used to create a summary event in the event logs.

If you want to modify the way capabilities are implemented, change the permissions assigned to *sPermission*. If you want to add capabilities to the existing four, you need to do the following:

- Add a row to the HTML table for the new capability. Use the existing capabilities as a template.

- Add code to the *txtGroupBaseName_OnChange* event to prepopulate the group name for the new capability.

- Add code to *ProvisionIt()* to evaluate whether the new capability is selected and, if so, to send the appropriate *sPermission* string to *ACLit()*.

The last permission applied by *ProvisionIt()* assigns the Modify permission to the Owner Rights identity. The effect of this permission, which is available only when you are provisioning a folder that is on a Windows Vista or Windows Server 2008 system, is to prevent the user who owns the file from being able to change permissions on the file. This permission is discussed in detail in Solution 2-11 on page 141.

*ProvisionIt()* then looks to see whether the check box is selected to indicate that an SMB share should be created. If so, the *ShareFolder()* function is called. *ShareFolder()* examines values on the form and creates a command line to call the Share_Create.vbs script.

Finally, *ProvisionIt()* determines whether the folder should be added to a DFS namespace, and then calls the *AddToDFS()* function. This function creates a DFS namespace folder targeting the UNC of the provisioned folder.

As *ProvisionIt* performs each major step, it updates the status box on the form, named *txtStatus* in the code. If the process is successful, a message box is generated informing the user of the successful provisioning of the shared folder.

## Solution summary

Folder_Provision.hta is an example of a powerful provisioning tool that automates a multistep procedure and encourages or enforces business logic and process. The tool also demonstrates some useful approaches to configuring default values, displaying separate tabs within an HTA, autopopulating input controls, and leveraging external scripts and tools. With basic customization, you can configure the HTA to provision folders, including the creation of RBAC. With slightly more advanced customization, you can leverage the approach to create a perfect solution for your enterprise.

# 2-10: Avoid the ACL Inheritance Propagation Danger of File and Folder Movement

## Solution overview

| | |
|---|---|
| **Type of solution** | Guidance |
| **Features and tools** | Robocopy.exe |
| **Solution summary** | Never use Windows Explorer to move files or folders between two locations in the same namespace with different permissions. Instead, use Robocopy or an alternative. |
| **Benefits** | Correct application of permissions |

> **Important**   This solution addresses what many (including all of my customers) consider to be a bug or design flaw in the security of files on Windows systems. Microsoft has documented the problem as the result of a known feature of the NTFS file system, but it has changed it nonetheless in Windows Server 2008. Whether you call it a "feature" or a "bug," you *must* educate your administrators to avoid the security implications. Do *not* skip over this solution.

## Introduction

Imagine that you have configured a shared folder for a department. Beneath that shared folder are folders for departmental teams. Each team folder is secure so that only members of that team can access the folder's contents. The departmental manager, who has access to all the team folders, accidentally puts a sensitive file into the wrong team's folder. She notifies you immediately, and you connect to the share and drag and drop the file into the correct folder. Unfortunately, you discover that members of the wrong team are still able to access the file in its new location, and members of the correct team are unable to access the file. You have created a security problem.

The bottom line of this solution is that you cannot use Windows Explorer to move a file between two folders with different permissions in the same namespace (for example, within the same share or on the same disk volume of a system you are logged on to interactively or through remote desktop). Moving a file using drag and drop, cut and paste, or any number of other methods can lead to the incorrect application of security permissions. Windows Server 2008 has corrected the problem, and, not surprisingly, Microsoft is not highlighting the potential security concern that was fixed eight years after it was introduced. But I'm glad, nonetheless, that it is fixed.

I'll go into some of the details of why this happens and how to avoid it. I will not cover *every* detail or exception to the rule, but you will understand the problem and a variety of solutions. You'll also learn best practices for moving files between folders on any Windows operating system.

# See the bug-like feature in action

A hands-on experience is worth a thousand words sometimes, and in this case the adage is absolutely true. The easiest way for you to understand the problem is to experience it yourself. Follow these steps to replicate the scenario on an NTFS volume on a Windows Server 2003 or Windows XP system:

1.  Create a parent folder—for example, C:\Data.

2.  Create a subfolder—for example, C:\Data\TeamA.

3.  Apply permissions to that folder so that TeamA has Modify permission.

4.  Create another subfolder—for example, C:\Data\TeamB.

5.  Apply permissions to this second folder so that TeamB has Modify permission.

6.  Add a file to the TeamA folder—for example, C:\Data\TeamA\TeamAInfo.txt.

7.  Add a permission to the file giving a user or group Full Control of that specific file.

8.  Drag the file into C:\Data\TeamB.

What do you expect the permission on the file to be after you've moved it? Common sense suggests that the explicit permission you added in step 7 would remain attached to the file, but that the file would now inherit its permissions from the new parent folder, TeamB. So TeamB would have inherited Modify permission, and TeamA would no longer have access.

Not so! Open the Security tab of the file's property dialog box and click Advanced. In the Advanced Security Settings dialog box, shown in Figure 2-10, you'll notice that TeamA still has access and TeamB does not. Even more interesting, the Permission Entries list cannot display where the permission is being inherited from.

Now let's make it even more interesting. Open the Security tab of the Properties dialog box of the TeamB folder. Clear the check box that allows TeamB Modify permission, click Apply, re-select the Allow Modify permission, and click Apply again. All you have done is removed and then reapplied the Modify permission for TeamB.

Open the Advanced Security Settings dialog box for the file. Notice, now, that TeamB does have inherited Modify permission, and TeamA no longer has permission.

The practical implication of this experiment is that, if you move files between two differently-permissioned folders in the same namespace (in this case, the C:\ volume) using Windows Explorer, the file will have an unexpected permission set until something happens to fix it! In short, whether it's a bug or a feature, it's both unexpected and inconsistent.

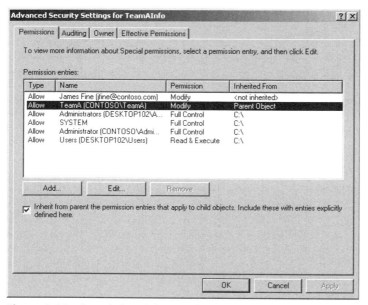

**Figure 2-10**   Permissions inherited from a file's *previous* parent

The same thing happens in a variety of scenarios, including moving files between two sub-folders of a remote share, or using tools other than Windows Explorer. Scary, huh?

# What in the world is going on?

This odd and potentially disturbing phenomenon is a result of the way ACLs are applied to NTFS resources. An object, such as our file, has a flag that enables the object to inherit permissions from its parent container that are themselves inheritable. The ACL on the file has specific, individual ACEs for each permission that applies to the file, including the inherited permissions.

But what actually *applies* those inherited permissions? Well, there's a process that I'll call the *ACL propagator* that, when triggered, goes from a folder to its subfolders and files and applies the inheritable ACEs into the ACLs of the child objects.

When you created the file in the TeamA folder, the instantiation (or creation) of the new object triggered the ACL propagator to apply inheritable permissions from the parent to the file. So the file's ACL contained ACEs allowing TeamA Modify permission. You then applied an explicit ACE to the file.

When you move a file in a namespace, you are basically renaming it, not moving it physically. So when you moved the file into the new folder, nothing triggered the ACL propagator to apply inheritable permissions (from the new parent folder) to the file. So its ACL kept its previously applied ACEs.

Then you made a change to the second parent folder. Changing permissions on a container triggers the ACL propagator, so the ACLs of child objects were opened and modified correctly.

 **Important**    Until the ACL propagator is triggered, permissions will be incorrect on the moved object.

Windows Server 2008 corrects the problem by triggering an ACL propagation when a file or folder is added to a folder.

## Solving the problem

There are several ways to solve this problem. One is to ensure that, whenever a file is moved into a new folder with different permissions in the same namespace, the ACL propagator is triggered. Use the following steps to do this:

1.  Move the object.

2.  Open the Advanced Security Settings dialog box for the object.

3.  Clear the Include Inheritable Permissions check box (Windows Server 2008 or Windows Vista) or the Inherit From Parent check box (Windows Server 2003 or Windows XP), and click Apply.

    If you are using a Windows Vista or Windows Server 2008 system with User Account Control enabled, you need to click the Edit button before you are able to clear the check box.

4.  When you are prompted to Copy or Remove inherited permissions, choose Remove.

5.  Re-select the same check box, and click Apply. This triggers the ACL propagator to apply inheritable permissions from the parent folder to the object.

That's a lot of steps, isn't it?

Another option is to *copy* rather than *move* the object. When you copy an object, you create a new instance of the object, which immediately triggers the ACL propagator. You then simply delete the original item.

The only potential pitfall with this method is that you might have explicit permissions assigned to the original object that you will need to maintain when you move the object. Therefore, rather than use copy and paste, use a command that can copy the object including its security descriptor. You can use xcopy.exe with the /x switch to copy a file with its security descriptor intact. On Windows Server 2008, you can also use robocopy.exe with the /copyall switch. By copying the entire security descriptor, you also maintain auditing and ownership information. Then delete the original file.

Any utility that can copy or back up and restore an NTFS object while maintaining its security descriptor will similarly solve this unusual feature of NTFS permissions.

## Change the culture, change the configuration

It is important to inform appropriate users and support personnel about the dangers of moving files between two folders with different permissions in the same namespace. Education can go a long way toward avoiding the inherited permissions trap.

You can also enforce success by aiming for a configuration in which each folder with unique permissions is, in fact, its own share. A connection to a share creates a unique namespace. So if you move a file between two folders in two different shares, you are in fact copying the file—so the inherited permissions problem will not rear its ugly head. Unfortunately, in these situations you might run into another challenge: By copying the file, you are not keeping the security descriptor (ownership, auditing, and explicit ACEs) unless you again use a security-descriptor-friendly tool such as *xcopy /x* or *robocopy /copyall*.

But aiming for a unique share for each folder with unique permissions is a decent idea. You might ask, "But won't that make my resource namespace very flat and wide?" To which I will reply, "Yes, except that users won't be going directly to shares—they'll view your resource namespace with DFS Namespaces, which create a virtual hierarchy within which you can organize your shares in any structure that aligns with your business."

You begin to see why even a question as seemingly simple as, "How should I organize the folders on my servers?" can only be answered by a consultant with the truism, "It depends." There are a lot of moving parts in Windows that must be aligned to your business requirements.

## Solution summary

NTFS permissions that are inherited from a parent folder will stick to a file (or folder) when you move it to another folder. The permissions of the new parent folder won't apply to the object until something triggers the ACL propagator. Therefore, it's critical for security that you do *not* just move files between folders with different permissions. You must either move the object and then remove and re-enable inheritance to the object; or you must use a security-descriptor-friendly tool—such as *xcopy /x* or *robocopy /copyall*—to copy the object to its new location and then delete the original. Although Windows Server 2008 has addressed the problem by triggering propagation immediately when a file is added to a folder, it is nevertheless important to follow best practices to ensure that security descriptors are moved correctly.

# 2-11: Preventing Users from Changing Permissions on Their Own Files

## Solution overview

| | |
|---|---|
| **Type of solution** | Guidance |
| **Features and tools** | The Owner Rights identity |
| **Solution summary** | New to Windows Server 2008, the Owner Rights identity enables administrators to prevent object owners from changing the permissions of objects. |
| **Benefits** | Decreased help desk calls, and reduced exposure to denial of service on file servers |

## Introduction

For as long as I can remember, Windows administrators have fought a battle to prevent users from changing permissions on their own files or folders. When a user creates a file on a Windows system, the user becomes the owner of the object. An object's owner has a built-in right to modify the security descriptor of the object. The idea behind that design is that there is always someone (the owner) who can unlock a resource, even if Deny permissions are preventing all other access.

A problem arises when users accidentally or intentionally change the ACL on an object they've created and thereby open an object to users who should not (based on the organization's information security policy) have access to the file or thereby restrict an object from users who should have access and thus generate a support call from those users.

Earlier in this Solutions Collection, I emphasized the importance of least-privilege access. In reality, the only users who should set permissions on files or folders in most organizations are IT or data security personnel. Restricting the ability to set permissions enables the organization to follow the best practices of configuring ACLs only on the first levels of a folder hierarchy and allowing inheritance to manage security below that.

Unfortunately, until recent versions of Windows, the only way to restrict an object owner from changing the ACL on the object was to restrict the SMB (share) permission to Change. Without a share permission of Full Control, an owner cannot modify the ACL. The problems with this approach are, first, not every Windows administrator knew that it was possible to do this, and second, share permissions have significant limitations, some of which were discussed in Solution 2-4, "Delegate the Management of Shared Folders," on page 110.

Windows Server 2008 solves the problem. A new well-known SID—the built-in identity called Owner Rights—was added specifically to address this scenario. ACEs assigned to the Owner Rights identity override the system rights assigned to the Owner of an object.

Imagine that you have created a shared folder with the default permission that allows the Creator Owner identity Full Control. When a user creates an object, an ACE is added to the object granting that user Full Control permission. If in any way the user is denied access to the object, the user can, as the object's owner, change permissions to grant himself or herself access.

Now, we make one small change to the ACL of the shared folder. We create an ACE with a single permission: Owner Rights::Allow::Modify. This is shown in Figure 2-11.

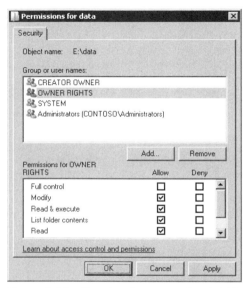

**Figure 2-11**  Denying the owner the right to change permissions by assigning the Owner Rights identity the Modify permission

If the owner attempts to change permissions, one of two things will happen, depending on the user's credentials and operating system. Either the controls that would enable the user to edit permissions are disabled, or if the controls are enabled, the user will receive an "Access Denied" error when attempting to change permissions. The permission assigned to the Owner Rights identity, which does not allow Change Permissions, is now overriding even the built-in system privilege that allows an owner to modify an object's ACL.

And as ownership of the object is transferred to another user, the new owner is similarly restricted by the Owner Rights ACE.

Now *that* is a great, new, small, important feature!

**Caution**  You, the administrator, can likewise lock yourself out of resources! If you are the owner of a file or folder, you will also be unable to change permissions. Use this feature wisely.

## What about object lockout?

You might be wondering now, if an object owner cannot change the ACL, isn't it possible to lock all users out of a resource? Apparently not. According to my testing, if you are a member of the Administrators group and are the owner of an object, you are not restricted by the Owner Rights ACEs. That caveat makes sense.

## Solution summary

In earlier versions of Windows, the only way to prevent users from changing permissions on their own files was to restrict the Share Permission to Change. Now a better solution, based on NTFS permissions, is available. Any permission assigned to the Owner Rights identity over-rides the permissions and system rights assigned to the owner of an object. So by configuring a folder with the ACE Deny::Owner Rights::Change permissions, you can effectively prevent any user who creates a file or subfolder from being able to alter that object's ACL.

# 2-12: Prevent Users from Seeing What They Cannot Access

## Solution overview

| | |
|---|---|
| **Type of solution** | Guidance |
| **Features and tools** | Access-based Enumeration (ABE) |
| **Solution summary** | The Windows Server 2008 file server role includes ABE, which enables you to hide from users the folders and files that they cannot access in a shared folder. |
| **Benefits** | Decreased help desk calls, and a security-trimmed view of shared folders |

## Introduction

On a traditional Windows folder, the List Folder Contents and Read Attributes permissions enable a user to see what the folder contains. The user sees *all* files and subfolders, whether or not the user can actually open those objects. The ability to open the object itself is managed by the Read or Read & Execute permissions.

When I began providing consulting and training to Windows IT professionals back in the early days of Windows NT Server, most administrators were approaching Windows networking after their experiences with Novell NetWare. That platform, as well as some other network operating systems, exposes shared folders differently than Windows. When you looked at a mounted volume on a Novell server, you would see only the files and subfolders to which you had permission. Those that you couldn't open were hidden from your view.

So for as long as I've been working with Windows, one of the most frequent questions I've been asked has been, "How do I hide files from users?"

This solution addresses that question.

# One perspective: Don't worry about it

One answer to the question, "How do I hide files from users?" is not to worry about it. Here's my take on the problem: If I were to tell one of your users that somewhere on your network there was a folder with the performance reviews of your company's employees, that would probably not surprise the user. Users know that on your network there is information—in fact, sensitive information and even information to which they cannot gain access. They know it's there.

So seeing the file really isn't that big of a deal, perhaps. It's not news to your users that it exists. What really matters is whether they can get to it or not. So the user shouldn't be able to open it, and, if you've applied your permissions correctly, they can't.

# A second perspective: Manage your folders

When a customer frequently runs into the problem of users being able to see a file they can't access, it suggests to me that the folder structure is not ideal. If users can see a lot of things they can't get to, those things should probably be somewhere else—in another folder—which itself cannot be accessed by users.

Folders should, ideally, contain objects that share common access requirements. That's the whole point, really: A folder is a container of like objects, controlled by one ACL that is inherited by all of those objects, with ACEs that define users' access to those objects based on least privilege. If you are having to manage multiple ACLs within a single folder, you probably should be rethinking your folder structure.

# A third perspective and a solution: Access-based Enumeration

Windows Server 2003 SP1 introduced Access-based Enumeration (ABE). ABE can be downloaded from the Microsoft Downloads site (*www.microsoft.com/downloads*) for Windows Server 2003, and it is available as a feature of the File Server role in Windows Server 2008.

ABE can be enabled for an entire server, affecting all of its shares, or for individually specified shares. When ABE applies to a share, users cannot see items to which they do not have Read permission. It's that simple! About time!

Figure 2-12 shows the same share, viewed by James Fine. On the left, he is viewing the share without ABE enabled. After an administrator enables ABE on the share, he cannot see the file or folder to which he does not have Read permission, as shown on the right.

**Figure 2-12**   A share viewed without (left) and with (right) ABE enabled

Note that ABE applies to an entire share, and it applies only when the share is accessed over an SMB connection. If James were to log on to the server with Remote Desktop and look at the folder directly on the local file system, he *would* see all files and folders.

## Solution summary

If you want to hide items from users, you have three options. The first is not to worry about it and, instead, focus on ensuring that the items are properly assigned permissions to prevent users from opening or viewing the items. The second option is to move the items to another folder to which the user does not have access. The third—a simple and elegant solution—is to enable ABE on shared folders. ABE will hide files and folders to which the user doesn't have Read access.

# 2-13: Determine Who Has a File Open

## Solution overview

| | |
|---|---|
| **Type of solution** | Script |
| **Features and tools** | VBScript |
| **Solution summary** | The FileServer_OpenFile.vbs script enables you to determine who has a file open on a file server. |

## Introduction

When you administer a file server with shared resources for users, it is not uncommon for multiple users to need a file at the same time. Some applications don't support multiple users opening a file concurrently. So occasionally one user will need a file and be unable to access it, and typically that user contacts the help desk.

If the user needs the file badly enough, the help desk might need to determine who is currently accessing the file so that person can be contacted and asked to close the file. FileServer_OpenFile.vbs, located in the Scripts folder of the companion media, enables you to do just that.

## Using FileServer_OpenFile.vbs

The script requires two parameters, *ServerName* and *FileName*. *ServerName* is the name of the server that contains the file–a fully qualified domain name is preferred but not required. *File-Name* is any part of the file name or file path–the script performs the equivalent of a wildcard search to locate matching files. Following is the syntax of the script:

```
cscript //nologo FileServer_OpenFile.vbs /server:ServerName /file:FileName
```

## Understanding FileServer_OpenFile.vbs

The script itself is straightforward and simple:

```
FileServer_OpenFile.vbs
sComputerName = WScript.Arguments.Named("server")
sFileName = WScript.Arguments.Named("file")

if sComputerName = "" or sFileName = "" then
   WScript.Echo "Usage: cscript FileServer_OpenFile.vbs " &_
            "    /server:SERVERNAME /file:FILENAME"
   WScript.Quit (501)
end if

Set oServer = GetObject("WinNT://" & sComputerName & "/LanmanServer")

for each oResource in oServer.resources
   on error resume next
   if (Not oResource.User="") AND (Not Right(oResource.User,1) = "$") Then
       if Instr(1, oResource.Path, sFileName, 1) >0 then
             WScript.echo "Path: " & oResource.path
             WScript.echo "User: " & oResource.user
             wscript.echo "Lock: " & oResource.lockcount
             wscript.echo
       end if
   end if
next
```

First, the script parses the arguments passed to the script. If one of the arguments is missing, the script prompts for better input.

Then the script connects to the file services (the LanmanServer service) on the server specified by the *server* argument. LanmanServer exposes a collection of resources–open files. We loop through that collection looking for any resource that contains a match for the file name provided to the script. If a match is found, the information about the matching resource is outputted.

## Solution summary

That was easy, wasn't it? A simple script looking for a match in the resources collection of the LanmanServer service enables us to answer the question, "Who has this file open?"

# 2-14: Send Messages to Users

## Solution overview

| | |
|---|---|
| **Type of solution** | Script |
| **Features and tools** | VBScript, PSExec |
| **Solution summary** | Leveraging PSExec and the Message_Notification.vbs script, you can once again send messages to users, which is particularly useful to notify users that a server will be taken offline. |

## Introduction

Back in the good old days, the Messenger and Alerter services allowed you to send a message to a user or computer. Then some bad guys got ahold of those services and started sending my mother messages, over her Internet connection, encouraging her to purchase their wares. Microsoft subsequently locked down those two services so that they now do not start automatically. OK, my mother probably wasn't the only person troubled by the security vulnerabilities exposed by the Messenger and Alerter services, but you get the idea.

If you're going to take a server offline or want (for some other reason) to send a network message to users, you can no longer expect the NET SEND command to succeed, because dependent services are not running. We need an alternative. In this solution, we'll assemble tools that allow us to notify users that they should close files that they have open from a server before we take the server offline. The tools will also help you send network messages in any other situation.

## Using Message_Notification.vbs

On the companion media, in the Scripts folder, you'll find a script named Message_Notification.vbs. To use the script, enter the following command:

```
cscript //nologo Message_Notification.vbs /message:"Message Text"
    [/title:"Title Bar Text"] [/time:[0 | n]
```

The message is a required parameter and must not be blank. The *title* parameter sets the text of the title bar, which, if the parameter is omitted, will be *Notification*. The *time* parameter can be zero, which causes the dialog box to appear until the user clicks the OK button, or it can be a number representing the number of seconds to display the message. If omitted, a default of 60 seconds is used. Because of the nature of this script, you can also easily use wscript.exe to execute the script, rather than cscript.exe.

This script can be used to create a message, but it's not quite enough to display a message on a remote machine. We'll solve that problem in a moment.

## Understanding Message_Notification.vbs

Here is the body of Message_Notification.vbs:

```
Message_Notification.vbs
Const PopupOK = 0
Const PopupWarning = 48

sMessage = WScript.Arguments.Named("message")
sTitle = WScript.Arguments.Named("title")
iWait = WScript.Arguments.Named("time")

if sMessage = "" then WScript.Quit(0)
if sTitle = "" then sTitle = "NOTIFICATION"
if iWait = "" then iWait = 60

Set WSHShell = CreateObject("WScript.Shell")
Call WSHShell.Popup (sMessage, iWait, sTitle, PopupWarning + PopupOK)
```

The script is a simple wrapper around an existing method of the *Shell* object: a method called *Popup*. The *Popup* method creates a dialog box that can have a title bar, message, buttons (such as OK, or Yes and No, or Retry and Cancel), and an icon (stop sign, question mark, exclamation point, or information mark). The dialog box can be set to time out so that after a specific time it disappears. Or you can configure the message to wait for user input. The Popup dialog box can also hold more than 1023 characters (the limit of messages produced by the *MsgBox* statement). This makes *Popup* an ideal candidate for communicating a message to a user in many situations.

In this particular script, we define the button that will be available (the OK button) and the icon (an exclamation point) at the beginning of the script. The script's arguments are then located and processed: If the message is empty, the script exits; if either of the other two arguments are missing, the values are set to defaults. Then a reference to the *Shell* object is created, and the *Popup* method is called.

If you want to adapt this script for popup messages with other buttons or icons, see the documentation of the *Popup* method at *http://msdn2.microsoft.com/en-us/library/x83z1d9f.aspx*.

## Using PSExec to execute a script on a remote machine

To send a message to a remote computer, we'll use PSExec to execute our Message_Notification.vbs script on the remote system. This requires you to be an administrator of the remote system and to be able to connect to the remote system (ports 445 and 139 must be open).

> **Note**    I am sure I'm not the only one who tests scripts on virtual machines. To save you the pain I encountered, let me warn you: This script does not seem to work when sending a notification to a Windows Vista installation within VMware Workstation 6.0. There appears to be a problem rendering the Popup message, so the script appears in the task bar or only the title bar appears. The script runs perfectly against Windows XP within VMware Workstation 6.0, and against Windows Vista on a physical box. So please don't bang your head against a wall (or e-mail me) if you have challenges in a virtual environment with testing this script.

Place the Message_Notification.vbs script in a shared folder on a server so that it can be accessed from the remote computer. Then use the following command:

```
psexec.exe \\computername -i -u DOMAIN\username -p Password -d wscript.exe
    "\\server\share\path\message_notification.vbs" /message:"Message"
    [/title:"Title"] [-time:0|n]
```

That's a lot of switches! Let's examine each:

**\\computername**    This specifies the computer on which to execute the script. The popup message will appear on this computer.

**-i**    The script runs under credentials that are for an administrator on the machine, but you want the message to appear to the currently logged-on user. The *−i* switch enables the process to *interact* with the user's session.

**-u DOMAIN\username and –p Password**    These two switches provide the credentials with which to execute the process. The credentials must be for a member of the local Administrators group on the remote computer. This member also must have read permission to the script in the network shared folder. You must provide credentials explicitly because you are passing the credentials to the remote system, which must then reuse those credentials to access the network.

**-d**    The *-d* switch instructs PSExec not to wait for the process to complete. This prevents PSExec from waiting for the amount of time specified and also prevents interference if the script does not run on the target computer.

**wscript.exe**    PSExec launches the process wscript.exe on the remote machine. Because wscript.exe is in the command path of Windows systems, no path is required. We're using *wscript* because if we use *cscript*, a black command-prompt window opens, which is not the aesthetic effect we want.

**"\\server\share\path\message_notification.vbs"**    This is the UNC to the script that will be executed by wscript.exe.

The remainder of the switches are arguments for the script, which were described earlier in this solution.

As a result of combining PSExec with a simple VBScript wrapper around the *Shell* object's *Popup* method, we have a useful replacement for the NET SEND command! And because

PSExec does its work securely and requires local administrative credentials on the remote machine to execute, it's a reasonably robust and secure solution!

## Listing the open sessions on a server

Now that we have a tool with which to send a network message, we simply have to identify *which* users to notify. In the previous Solutions Collection, we examined a script that looked at the open files on a server using the LanmanServer's resources collection. LanmanServer also has a collection for open sessions, which can be enumerated by the following code:

```
sComputerName = "SERVER02.contoso.com"
Set oServer = GetObject("WinNT://" & sComputerName & "/LanmanServer")
for each oSession in oServer.sessions
   wscript.echo "User: " & oSession.user
   wscript.echo "Computer: " & oSession.computer
next
```

Using this approach, we are able to identify the computer from which each user has connected to the server. That is the computer to which we send our notification.

## Using and customizing FileServer_NotifyConnectedUsers.vbs

By combining the code just shown that finds which computers are connected to a server with our PSExec command that launches the Message_Notification.vbs script, we are able to create the solution we require. The result is FileServer_NotifyConnectedUsers.vbs in the Scripts folder on the companion media.

Before you use the script, be sure to modify the configuration block with the path to Message_Notification.vbs and the path to PSExec.exe. (No path is required if PSExec.exe is in the same folder as the FileServer_NotifyConnectedUsers.vbs script.) You can also modify the title bar text and timeout that is used for the notification message.

The syntax used to run the script is as follows:

```
cscript FileServer_NotifyConnectedUsers.vbs /user:DOMAIN\username
   /password:password /server:SERVERNAME /message:"Message to send to users"
```

The username and password provided must be for an administrator on all systems to which messages will be sent. If it is not, those systems will not receive notifications, but the script will continue. The server name you provide points to the server that will be analyzed for open sessions. The message is what you want to communicate to users connected to the server.

The script determines which computers have open sessions with the server, and then it sends the specified message to each computer. As it does so, the script reports each computer name. Some computers might not respond as quickly as others—give the script time to execute.

The result is a reasonable effort to notify users. There is no guarantee that the user is paying any attention. Nor is there a guarantee that PSExec will be able to connect to each computer and successfully run the script. Firewall and other issues can prevent connections. The same concerns were characteristic of the old NET SEND notifications.

## Solution summary

It is common for network administrators to need to send a message to users. E-mail is an option, assuming users are checking their Inboxes. But there's nothing like a popup message, right in the middle of the desktop, to catch a user's attention. This solution leveraged a simple VBScript wrapper around the *Shell* object's *Popup* method and an incredibly useful tool, PSExec.exe, to execute that script on a remote machine.

In the event that you must take a server offline, you can notify all connected users of the impending change by running FileServer_NotifyConnectedUsers.vbs. This script identifies all open sessions on the server and then automates the execution of PSExec to run the notification script on the computer of each connected user.

# 2-15: Distribute Files Across Servers

## Solution overview

| | |
|---|---|
| **Type of solution** | Command and procedure |
| **Features and tools** | schtasks.exe, robocopy.exe, DFS-Replication, SMB (Share) permissions |
| **Solution summary** | Create a master/mirrors topology to distribute files from a single (master) source to multiple (mirror) destinations using Robocopy or DFS Replication. |

## Introduction

In a distributed organization, it is often necessary to distribute files to servers that are local to users. For example, you might need to copy a folder that contains drivers or applications to servers in branch offices; or you might need to distribute commonly accessed corporate documents to multiple servers. In such scenarios, organizations often desire a *single-source* model, where changes made to a folder in one location are distributed but changes cannot be made to the distributed copies. We'll refer to the single source as the *master* and to the distributed copies as *mirrors*. We'll solve the problem two ways: using Robocopy and using DFS Replication.

## Using Robocopy to distribute files

Robocopy.exe is available in the native, out-of-box toolset for Windows Vista and Windows Server 2008. It is a resource kit utility for previous versions of Windows. Many organizations have leveraged Robocopy to distribute or replicate files. Here is the most straightforward syntax for mirroring a folder to another location:

```
robocopy.exe Source Destination /copyall /mir
```

The *source* and *destination* parameters are the paths to the source and destination folders. You'll typically execute Robocopy on the source server, so the *source* parameter will be a local path and the destination will be a UNC, but both paths can be either local or UNC paths, as appropriate. The */copyall* switch specifies that all file attributes—including security, auditing, and ownership—should be copied. The */mir* switch directs Robocopy to mirror the source folder: Any file that is newer in the source will overwrite an older file in the destination; files that are missing in the destination are added; and any file that exists in the destination but not in the source will be deleted.

To create a master/mirror file distribution topology, simply create a scheduled task to execute the Robocopy command at a desired repetition interval. The schtasks.exe command can be used as follows:

```
schtasks.exe /create /RU DOMAIN\Username /RP password /TN TaskName /TR
"robocopy.exe source destination /copyall /mir" /sc MINUTE /mo Interval
```

The domain *username* and *password* are used to execute the Robocopy task. They must have NTFS Full Control permission on the source and destination folder and files. The *taskname* is a friendly name for the scheduled task. The *interval* is the number of minutes between repetitions. From a command prompt, type **schtasks.exe /create /?** for more detail about the parameters available for the schtasks command.

To ensure that the source (the master) is the only location where files can be added for distribution, you must use share permissions to control access. You should not use NTFS permissions because Robocopy replicates NTFS permissions to the mirrors. Instead, on the mirrors, configure share permissions so that *only* the account used by the scheduled task has Full Control. All other users requiring access to the mirrors should have Read share permission. The schtasks.exe account and other users requiring access to the master should have Full Control share permission on the master. Because a user's effective access is the most restrictive combination of NTFS permissions and share permissions, users who *can* create, change, or delete files based on their NTFS permissions will be able to do so only on the master share.

## Using DFS Replication to distribute files

DFS Replication (DFS-R), introduced in Windows Server 2003 R2, provides highly efficient and manageable replication, leveraging differential compression and bandwidth controls to ensure that replication of data has as small an impact on the network as possible.

One of the common misconceptions about a hub-and-spoke replication topology for DFS-R is that it provides a master/mirror functionality. That is not the case. With a hub-and-spoke topology, changes made at a spoke are replicated to the hub and then replicated to other spokes. To create a master/mirror topology, you start by creating the DFS-R topology, and then you change share permissions. The steps are as follows:

1. Open the DFS Management console.

2. Select and expand the Replication node.

3. Right-click Replication and choose New Replication Group.

4. The New Replication Group Wizard appears.

5. On the Replication Group Type page, select Multipurpose Replication Group. Click Next.

6. On the Name And Domain page, enter a name for the replication group, such as **Master-Mirror File Distribution**. Optionally, enter a description. Click Next.

7. On the Replication Group Members page, click the Add button and enter the name of the master server. Click OK. Repeat the process for each mirror server. Click Next after all servers are listed in the Members box.

8. On the Topology Selection page, select Hub And Spoke if you have at least three members. If you have two members, select Full Mesh. Then click Next. If you are using Full Mesh topology, skip to step 11.

9. On the Hub Members page, select the master server from the Spoke Members list and click the Add button to move the master server to the Hub members list. Click Next.

10. Accept the defaults on the Hub And Spoke Connections page, and click Next.

11. On the Replication Group Schedule And Bandwidth page, you can accept the default bandwidth (Full), or you can configure the bandwidth utilization for the replication. Remember that DFS-R is a highly efficient replication mechanism, so even at Full bandwidth usage it is unlikely that all available bandwidth will be used when replication occurs. Click Next.

12. On the Primary Member page, select the master server and click Next.

13. On the Folders To Replicate page, click the Add button and enter the path to the folder you want to replicate. All subfolders will be included in the replication. Optionally, give the folder a custom name, and then click OK. Repeat this step for each folder you want to replicate. Then click Next.

14. On the Local Path Of Shared Data On Other Members page, select the first mirror server, click Edit, and select Enabled. Enter the path to the folder on that server, and click OK. Repeat for each mirror server. Then click Next.

15. Review the settings you have configured.

16. Click Create.

17.  Confirm that the tasks completed successfully.

18.  Click Close to close the New Replication Group Wizard.

On the master, ensure that share permissions allow Full Control for all users who might require access to the folder. On the mirrors, users who might require access to the mirrors should be allowed only Read permission on the share. Unlike Robocopy, which uses an account to copy files between shared folders, DFS-R is a service, so no other changes to share permissions are required.

 **Important**   The process just described is the supported method to create one-way replication, from the master to the mirror. Numerous Web sites recommend deleting replication connections. This is *not* recommended, as it can have unintended side effects on DFS-R. Microsoft does not support deleting replication connections.

## Solution summary

Using a scheduled task that executes Robocopy, or using DFS-R, you can replicate files from a master to mirrors of a shared folder. To ensure that changes cannot be made directly to the mirrors, use share permissions on the mirrored copies that enable only Read access. NTFS permissions should not be modified on the mirrors, as the master's NTFS permissions will be replicated out to the mirrors and will thus override any modifications you might have made. Deleting DFS-R links is also not recommended.

# 2-16: Use Quotas to Manage Storage

## Solution overview

| | |
|---|---|
| **Type of solution** | Guidance |
| **Features and tools** | Quotas |
| **Solution summary** | Understand changes to the quota management capabilities of Windows Server 2008. |

## Introduction

The quota management capability of Windows servers was overhauled in Windows Server 2003 R2. Like that predecessor, Windows Server 2008 enables a powerful, flexible, and effective set of features for monitoring or enforcing storage utilization. This solution provides an overview of Windows quota management and highlights key concepts and tricks. Refer to the Help and Support Center for detailed documentation regarding quota management.

# What's new in quota management

The following discussion highlights changes to quotas compared to Windows Server 2003 and Windows 2000. No changes in functionality have been introduced since Windows Server 2003 R2.

Perhaps the most significant change is that quotas can now be enforced at the folder level as well as the volume level, and when a folder quota is configured, all users are subject to the quota. In other words, if you specify that the Marketing folder's quota is 100 MB, that is the maximum storage allocated to that folder, regardless of who has created files in the folder. As soon as 100 MB of data is in the folder, the next user who attempts to create a new file in the folder will be denied access.

The quota is also now based on the physical disk usage rather than the logical disk usage. So if a file is compressed using NTFS compression, the resulting (compressed) size counts against the quota.

Quota behavior is very flexible. Quotas can be defined as hard quotas, which prevent all users from adding data once the quota is reached, or soft quotas, which continue to allow data to be added to a folder that has reached its quota but can be used to monitor storage utilization. Each quota can have multiple notification thresholds, which define what happens at specific percentages of the quota. And at each threshold, one or more of the following actions can be triggered:

**E-mail Message**   An e-mail message can be sent to one or more administrators and/or to the user whose modifications to the folder caused the threshold to be breached. The message to the user is definable and can include a number of variables.

**Event Log**   A warning can be added to the event log. As with the e-mail message, you can define any text for the warning, and several variables can be included to ensure a detailed and understandable log entry.

**Command**   You can configure a threshold to execute any command. This makes the quota actions infinitely extensible.

**Report**   Storage utilization reports can be generated and sent by e-mail to administrators and/or to the user who exceeded the threshold. Reports are also saved in the %systemdrive%\StorageReports\Incident folder on the server.

## Quota templates

Although Windows' quota management functionality offers innumerable options for configuration, the chances are very good that you'll determine a small number of configurations that are desirable for quota management in your enterprise. You can decide, for example, that a departmental folder will have a certain quota, and, when 85 percent of the quota is reached, users will begin to receive e-mail messages instructing them to remove outdated files and administrators will be notified that the folder is nearing capacity. When 100 percent of the quota is reached, you can disallow further additions of files. You can define other configurations for a handful of various storage scenarios in your organization.

To implement your quota design decisions, you should create quota templates. A handful of default quota templates are available initially. You can create new templates in the File Server Resource Manager snap-in. Expand Quota Management, select and then right-click Quota Templates, and choose Create Quota Template. The new template can start as a copy of an existing template, or you can create all properties from scratch. Name the template, and specify the maximum size of the quota. Configure the quota as hard or soft, and then add notification thresholds. For each threshold, configure the e-mail messages, log entry, command, or reports to be triggered.

After you've defined a quota template, you'll *apply* that quota template to folders. You are likely to want to use similar quota templates across multiple servers. Use the dirquota.exe command with the */export* and */import* switch to transfer quotas between systems.

## Apply a quota to a folder

After you've created the appropriate quota templates, you can create quotas for specific paths. Select and right-click the Quotas node in the Quota Management branch of the File Server Resource Management snap-in. Choose Create Quota. Enter the path to which you want to apply the quota: It can be to a folder or an entire volume. Then select your template from the drop-down list in the middle of the Create Quota dialog box, as shown in Figure 2-13.

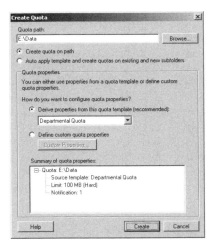

**Figure 2-13**    The Create Quota dialog box

Note that you are allowed to define a custom quota in the Create Quota dialog box, but by using quota templates you are able to manage quotas more effectively than using a one-off approach. In addition to simplifying the application of quota properties, quota templates also give you long-term flexibility. If you modify the properties of a quota template, all folders to which that template was applied are immediately updated to reflect the changes you have made.

The Create Quota dialog box has an Auto Apply Template option. This option is particularly useful when you have a top-level folder (typically with no quota) that will contain subfolders and, as each subfolder is created, you want to automatically apply a specific quota to the new subfolder. Consider a scenario in which a departmental folder will have subfolders for functions or teams within the department. You want each subfolder to have a specific quota. This option supports that goal. Another common scenario for this option is user data folders: A root folder exists above folders for each user. As user data folders are created, you want to apply a specific quota to them. This Auto Apply Template option will be discussed in detail in Solutions Collection 3, "Managing User Data and Settings."

## Solution summary

Windows Server 2003 R2 completely revamped the quota management capability of the Windows Server product line. You can now configure storage allocation using quotas that support threshold-based actions such as e-mail notification, event log entries, report generation, and command execution. Quotas are applied to a folder, rather than to a user, and quota templates provide a single point of management for defining and revising quota properties.

# 2-17: Reduce Help Desk Calls to Recover Deleted or Overwritten Files

## Solution overview

| | |
|---|---|
| **Type of solution** | Guidance |
| **Features and tools** | Shadow Copies of Shared Folders |
| **Solution summary** | Enable Shadow Copies, and provide users a method to recover previous versions of files in shared folders. |

## Introduction

When a user accidentally deletes or overwrites a file, the support intervention that is required can be significant—locating a backup, mounting the backup, and retrieving the file. Windows Server 2003 introduced the Shadow Copies of Shared Folders feature, which enables point-in-time snapshots of disk volumes, and the Previous Versions client, which allows users to restore files from those snapshots without administrative intervention.

The underlying Shadow Copies technology is important to understand in detail, so I recommend that you read the following Microsoft documentation:

■ Feature documentation: *http://technet2.microsoft.com/windowsserver/en/library/ 77a571cc-a360-468a-ad99-6c80049530db1033.mspx?mfr=true*

- Technical reference: *http://technet2.microsoft.com/windowsserver/en/library/2b0d2457-b7d8-42c3-b6c9-59c145b7765f1033.mspx?mfr=true*

- White paper: *http://www.microsoft.com/windowsserver2003/techinfo/overview/scr.mspx*

This solution provides guidance in specific areas to help you align the feature with your business requirements.

## Enabling shadow copies

Shadow copies must be enabled on Windows servers—they are not enabled by default. The feature is enabled per volume, not per folder or share. On the Shadow Copies tab on a volume's Properties dialog box, shown in Figure 2-14, click the Settings button.

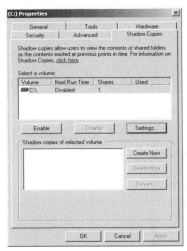

**Figure 2-14**    The Shadow Copies tab of the volume Properties dialog box

**Best Practices**    Do not click the Enable button.

The Enable button is a quick fix. It configures Shadow Copies with all default settings, and the default settings will not be appropriate for every scenario. Instead, click the Settings button. The Settings dialog box appears, as shown in Figure 2-15. After you configure the settings and click OK in the Settings dialog box, you simultaneously enable shadow copies and enforce your specific settings.

A shadow copy requires a storage area, which does not have to be on the same volume for which you are enabling shadow copies. In fact, it is a best practice to locate the shadow copy storage area on another volume that, itself, is not being shadow copied.

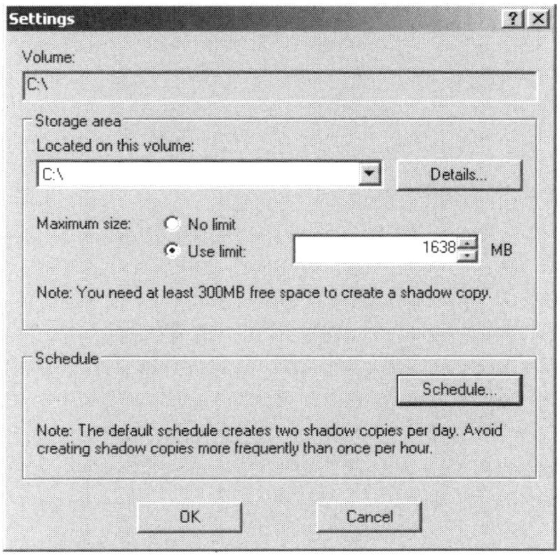

**Figure 2-15**  The Shadow Copies Settings dialog box

Click the Schedule button in the Settings dialog box to modify the schedule of shadow copies, also called *snapshots*. Using the Schedule tab, shown in Figure 2-16, you can configure multiple schedules. For example, you might create a snapshot at the end of each day, plus a snapshot at lunch time during weekdays.

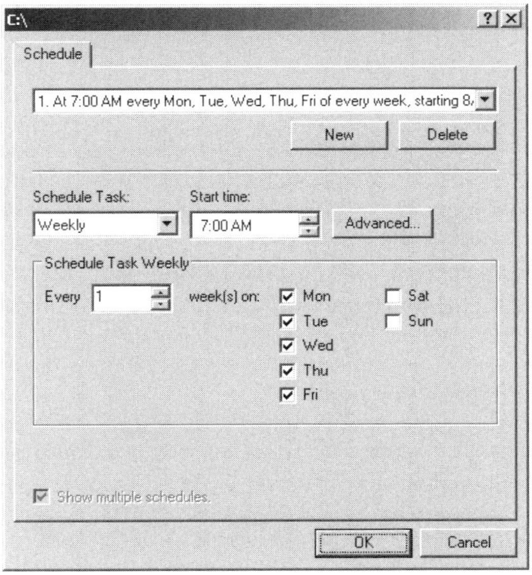

**Figure 2-16**  Shadow Copies Schedule dialog box

# Understanding and configuring shadow copies

The art and science of configuring shadow copies is detailed in the Microsoft references listed earlier. It boils down to balancing the desired functionality—specifically, a user's ability to restore a file—with performance and storage. We'll discuss how a user restores a previous version later in this solution, but to summarize, a user is able to restore a version as of the last snapshot time. *Not every change or version is available to restore*—only versions captured at each scheduled snapshot are available.

You might think to yourself, "I should configure frequent snapshots, then." But not so fast! You must also consider performance and storage. First, the good news: When a snapshot is created, Windows does *not* create a copy of the entire volume at that moment in time. Each shadow copy does *not* take an amount of storage equivalent to the size of the volume. Instead, a snapshot in effect freezes a volume's current state and creates a cache (in the snapshot storage area) for the snapshot. From that point forward, when a change needs to be written to the disk, the Volume Shadow Copy Service (VSS) intercepts the change and, before writing the change to the disk, takes what is currently on the disk and moves the information into the cache of the most recent snapshot. Then the new information is written to disk. So if snapshots are scheduled at 7:00 a.m. and 12:00 p.m., all changes written to the disk between 7:00 a.m. and 12:00 p.m. are intercepted, the current data (that existed at 7:00 a.m.) is moved into the storage area for the 7:00 a.m. snapshot, and then the change is made. The changes are at the block level, so they can be very efficient, depending on the application that is making the change to the disk. So the size of a snapshot reflects the amount of disk activity between the snapshot and the next snapshot.

Now, the bad news. You can maintain a maximum of 64 snapshots. So if you take one snapshot a day, you could possibly maintain 64 days worth of snapshots. On the sixty-fifth day, the first (oldest) snapshot would be deleted to make room for the next. A snapshot every three hours would mean eight per day, so you could possibly maintain eight days worth of snapshots. I say "possibly" because the amount of activity could be such that the storage area fills up before the sixty-fourth snapshot is taken. When the storage area fills, the oldest snapshot is removed. Now, perhaps, you can see the need for art and science to determine your snapshot schedule.

There are some additional guidelines I'd like to highlight:

■  Select a volume that is not being shadow copied for the shadow copy storage area whenever possible, and particularly on heavily used file servers.

■  Mount points and symbolic links (folders that expose data that is in another location) are not included in shadow copies. You must enable shadow copies on the volumes that host the data that is being mounted or linked to if you want to use the shadow copy feature on that data.

- Do not schedule copies more than once per hour, as it will have an impact on performance.

- If a volume will use the shadow copy service, format the source volume with an allocation unit size of 16 KB or larger. The shadow copy service stores changes in 16-KB blocks. Smaller allocation unit sizes will lead to inefficient storage. This is particularly important if you regularly defragment the volume. Sadly, this 16-KB cluster size recommendation means you cannot use NTFS compression on the volume. NTFS compression cannot be used with an allocation unit size larger than 4 KB. Put simply, format your volumes with 16-KB clusters and forget NTFS compression. Sorry for the bad news.

> **Important**    Shadow Copies of Shared Folders (Previous Versions or snapshots) should not be considered as an alternative to a comprehensive backup and recovery strategy.

Because shadow copies are not maintained indefinitely, you should use shadow copies only for these purposes:

- Recovering a file that was accidentally deleted

- Recovering a file that has been overwritten

- Comparing a version of a file to a recent version captured by a snapshot

Make sure you have designed, implemented, and (most importantly) validated your server backup and recovery procedures.

## Accessing previous versions

To access previous versions of files for the purposes just listed, you must use the Previous Versions client, also known as the *Shadow Copies client*. The client is built in to Windows XP SP2 and later. It is available from the Microsoft Web site for download to Windows 2000 and Windows XP clients. It is also found in the %systemroot%\System32\Clients\Twclient folder on a Windows Server 2003 or Windows Server 2008 server.

Clients work differently on various versions of Windows. Windows Vista and Windows Server 2008 allow you to go to the properties of any file and click the Previous Versions tab, as shown in Figure 2-17.

If a previous version exists, it will be listed. You can then click Open to open the file in its default application, or you can right-click the file to select an application with which to open the file. This allows you to *view* the file, and, of course, you could use the application to save a copy of the file to a specific location. From the Previous Versions tab, you can also click Copy to copy the file to a specific location. Finally, you can click Restore to restore the version to the original location, thereby restoring a deleted file or overwriting the current version.

**Figure 2-17**    The Previous Versions tab of a file's Properties dialog box

Windows 2000, Windows XP, and Windows Server 2003 support accessing previous versions *only* through a shared folder. If you have opened a folder using a UNC—that is, \\*server*\*share*\ [*path*]—you can go to the properties and see Previous Versions. You can then perform the actions described previously. You cannot get to Previous Versions from the properties of a local file on Windows 2000, Windows XP, or Windows Server 2003.

Here are some notes about Previous Versions:

■ If a file has not changed since the first snapshot, you will not see any previous version listed. Recall that shadow copies works when changes are made *after* a snapshot. So only files that have been changed at least once since the first snapshot will have previous versions listed.

■ If you rename a file, it will no longer display its previous versions.

■ When you restore a file, you are *not* restoring the permissions of the file. If you are restoring a deleted file, it will inherit its ACL from the parent folder. If you are restoring a file over the current version, it will use the ACL of the current version.

## Solution summary

Caveats and all, Shadow Copies of Shared Folders is a fantastic feature to address the solution we're discussing: reducing help desk calls that result from a deleted or overwritten file. Spend time reading Microsoft's documentation so that you can configure shadow copies effectively on your servers, deploy the Previous Versions client to any computers running Windows XP SP1 or earlier, and communicate to users the process with which to restore previous versions.

# 2-18: Create an Effective, Delegated DFS Namespace

## Solution overview

| | |
|---|---|
| **Type of solution** | Guidance |
| **Features and tools** | DFS Namespaces |
| **Solution summary** | Address business and technical intricacies of DFS namespace design. |

## Introduction

If you are familiar with the DFS Namespaces feature, you can skip this overview. If you are not, let me introduce you to DFS Namespaces, a component I like to call "The Role Service Previously Known as Distributed File System (DFS) and Known Before That as Distributed File System (Dfs)."

As you'll discover in this solution, the benefits provided by the DFS Namespaces feature make it as close to a no-brainer solution as anything Microsoft has provided. DFS Namespaces—and DFS before it, and Dfs before it—have, since Windows NT 4.0, provided the capability to abstract the physical location of files and folders from any pointer to those resources.

The fundamental challenge is that if you have a pointer—such as a shortcut, mapped drive, or other UNC to a share, folder, or file—it takes the form \\*server*\\*share*\\[*path*]\\[*file*]. If you restructure the physical storage of the file in any way, such as change the share name or move the folder tree to another share or server, you have to reconfigure the shortcut, mapped drive, or other UNC pointer. If there are numerous pointers, the management headaches increase exponentially. In a business of any size whatsoever, if data is moved between servers, it takes a mammoth effort to reconfigure everything that refers to the files and folders and shares.

DFS Namespaces solves this problem by creating a separate namespace—a folder hierarchy that can present enterprise resources in a *logical*, rather than physical, structure. For example, you might choose to represent the path to the Marketing department share as \\contoso.com\departments\marketing. Each folder in the DFS Namespace is a virtual entity. It points to, or *refers to*, the physical location of the folder. So the \\contoso.com\departments\marketing folder in the DFS namespace refers to the current location of the folder, \\server01\data$\marketing. All other references to the marketing folder—mapped drives, shortcuts, links between files, and so on—will use the DFS namespace. When a Windows client requests \\contoso.com\departments\marketing, the DFS client (built in to every recent version of Windows) contacts a DFS Namespace server. The DFS namespace server refers the client to the current location of the folder, and the client then connects to that server. All of this happens transparently to the user.

If the marketing folder is moved to server02, the only change that must be made is to the reference of the DFS namespace folder, pointing it now to \\server02\data$\marketing. Clients will continue to request \\contoso.com\departments\marketing, but now they will be referred to the new location.

Because the physical location of resources is abstracted, administration of those resources is significantly easier. In addition, it's easier for users to locate data they require as the data is presented in a logical format. Users can more easily determine that a Marketing folder is within a Departments folder than they can figure out that it must be on Server02.

Additionally, DFS namespace folders can refer to more than one target. In other words, the Marketing folder in DFS can point to copies of the folder that exist *both* on Server01 and Server02. The folders can be replicated using a closely related feature, DFS Replication. A folder that refers to more than one target provides a form of load sharing, as clients will get alternating referrals to the two servers. Or, if the servers are in different Active Directory sites, clients will be referred to the server that is *closest*, from a site link cost perspective, to the client. And as if that is not enough, if one of the servers fails, clients will be referred to the other server—producing a level of fault tolerance I refer to as "poor man's clustering."

# Creating DFS namespaces

Microsoft has documented DFS Namespaces in great detail, and I recommend that you check out the following resources:

- Feature documentation: *http://technet2.microsoft.com/windowsserver/en/library/ 77a571cc-a360-468a-ad99-6c80049530db1033.mspx?mfr=true*

- Technical reference: *http://technet2.microsoft.com/windowsserver/en/library/77a571cc- a360-468a-ad99-6c80049530db1033.mspx?mfr=true*

You should certainly read the documentation prior to implementing DFS Namespaces, but as with the other solutions in this resource kit, I would like to provide guidance in several specific areas that I have seen trip up many an experienced administrator.

Creating a DFS Namespace is detailed in the feature documentation. To summarize, open the DFS Management console, right-click the Namespaces node, and choose New Namespace. A wizard will step you through each task required to create the namespace. For the sake of example in the following sections, let's assume you create a namespace called "Human Resources."

# Delegating DFS namespaces

The Enterprise and Datacenter editions of Windows Server 2003 R2 and Windows Server 2008 can host multiple DFS namespaces. If your DFS server is a Standard or Web edition, you are limited to one DFS namespace. If you have more than one namespace, you'll likely want to delegate management of the namespaces.

This is where I see organizations make the first mistake—which is, in my experience, *not* to delegate the management of DFS namespaces. The typical argument I hear in such situations is, "Corporate wants to maintain control of the namespace to ensure a logical hierarchy of folders." That is, in my opinion, shortsighted to say the least, *unless* you are working with the Standard or Web editions and therefore can have only one namespace.

The DFS Namespaces feature is just that: namespaces—or if you prefer, a hierarchy or a folder tree. Does Corporate maintain control over what folders are on a file server? Do you have to call up a vice president before adding a subfolder to a share? Probably not. The organization of data should generally be pushed out to those who "own" the data and who can best evaluate how it should be presented.

Now, I'm not suggesting that Corporate doesn't have a good point: There is a lot of value in a centrally driven namespace that stays more consistent over time. We'll solve that problem in the next section, "Linking DFS namespaces." So Corporate will get its way *also*. But I highly recommend that those who know the data and the servers on which data is stored—and, most importantly, know how and why the data is accessed—will best be able to organize the data in a logical namespace.

Let's assume that you have a significant number of resources related to Human Resources, such as corporate policies, information about benefits, and so on. One or more individuals has been tasked with determining how that data is used and accessed, and that person creates a logical hierarchy of folders such as the following one:

```
HR
        Benefits
                        Vacation
                        Medical
                        Retirement
                        Corporate Discounts
        Policies
                        Diversity Statement
                        Information Technology Usage
                        Sexual Harassment Policy
        Compensation
                        Payroll Calendar
                        Direct Deposit Forms
```

I recommend that you delegate to that individual or team the ability to manage the namespace, so if new resources need to be added to the namespace, they can do it. To delegate a namespace, right-click the namespace in the DFS Management console and choose Delegate Management Permissions. Enter the name of the user or, preferably, of the group that should be given permission to manage the namespace. It's that simple! In previous versions of DFS, a delegation of namespace management required that the user or group be a member of the local Administrators group on the namespace server. That is no longer the case. The team can now manage the namespace.

From a change control perspective, you should manage a DFS namespace carefully. The whole point of a DFS namespace is to provide a stable, logical view of enterprise resources. Any change to the DFS namespace itself requires changing the references (mapped drives, shortcuts, and so on) to the namespace. So good planning should result in a structure that doesn't need to be changed regularly, or at all. However, *new* resources are likely to be added to the enterprise, and they can certainly be added to the namespace as long as existing structure (folders) remain stable.

## Linking DFS namespaces

Now let's address the concern we raised about Corporate, which wanted control of the namespace. Typically, that requirement arises from the desire to maintain a very stable namespace that creates a taxonomy—a way of organizing enterprise resources. This section employs a trick that will address this, and other, business requirements.

Earlier I presented a scenario in which the Human Resources department maintains a DFS namespace. Let's assume other departments also have unique, delegated DFS namespaces, including IT.

It is quite useful to present your enterprise application distribution points within a DFS namespace. For example, the path from which Microsoft Office is installed might be a UNC through a DFS namespace called "Software," such as \\contoso.com\software\microsoft\office\2007\. That DFS namespace folder might refer to several copies of the software throughout the enterprise, such as \\denverserver\software$\office2007. Using DFS folders for software distribution UNCs makes software management (including installation, repair, and removal) much more efficient. We'll discuss this further in Solutions Collection 9, "Improving the Deployment and Managementt of Applications and Configuration."

You might delegate the management of the Software namespace to a limited number of administrators who manage software installation. But because the software folders are often thought of as IT resources, you want to be able to locate software through the IT namespace.

That's where the trick comes in. Create a DFS namespace folder in the IT namespace—for example, \\contoso.com\it\software. The target of that folder is *another* DFS namespace—specifically, \\contoso.com\software. If a client navigates to the IT namespace, the client sees "Software" within it. When the client navigates to that folder, the client is actually (transparently) navigating an entirely different DFS namespace!

Figure 2-18 shows an example, as seen by a client, of the resulting namespace.

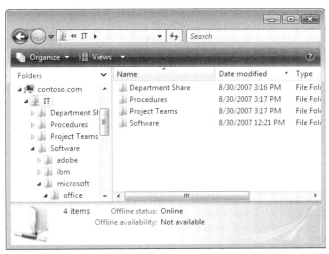

**Figure 2-18**   The IT namespace with a folder, Software, that exposes another DFS namespace

With that trick in mind, you can imagine a solution to Corporate's request. Corporate can create a namespace that it maintains, at a high level, such as this one:

```
\\Contoso.com\Corporate
            Departments
                    HR
                    IT
                    Finance
                    Marketing
                    ...
```

The folders in the corporate namespace target the departmental namespaces that have been delegated to the personnel who are best equipped to manage them.

This concept also can solve a common dilemma within an organization: Should the namespace be departmental or geographical? Why not both? You can certainly create a DFS namespace with multiple paths to the same resource. The goal is to make your resources easy to manage and, for users, easy to find. The only caveat I'd mention here is that if you do provide multiple paths to the same resource, you should train users to know that even though they see a file in two paths, it is still one file, and they should not delete the file because they believe it is a copy.

# Presenting DFS namespaces to users

Because DFS namespaces create a logical view of enterprise resources, it is reasonable to provide a way for users to navigate the namespace as a more intelligent form of browsing. There are several ways to incorporate DFS namespaces into the client user interface:

**Shortcuts**    Shortcuts, with location properties that reference a DFS namespace folder, can be placed in any location within the user's experience: the desktop, the Documents folder, the Start menu, and so on. Shortcuts provide access to users running any recent version of Windows.

**Mapped drives**    Similarly, network drives mapped to a DFS namespace folder can be accessed by users running any recent version of Windows. The advantage of a mapped drive over a shortcut is that the mapped drive exposes an expandable node within the Explorer folder tree. Additionally, it is easy to reference the S:\ drive as the location where users can find software, for example. But mapped drives are limited to the number of available letters and are in many ways a legacy form of connection to network resources.

**Network places and network locations**    Network places and network locations provide the best of both worlds for Windows XP and Windows Vista users, respectively. You can create a network place in the Windows XP My Network Places folder. Windows Vista replaced network places with network locations, which you can create by opening the Computer folder, not the Network and Sharing Center. After you create a network place or network location, you can move it to any other location, just as you can a shortcut. And, like a shortcut, the network place or network location can have any name. Like a mapped drive, a network place or network location expands within the Explorer folder tree, giving easy visibility to the hierarchy of the DFS namespace to which the network place points.  I recommend that you move the network places and network locations that users need most regularly on their desktops, and leave links to less commonly accessed targets in the My Network Places and Computer folders where they were created. The companion Web site, *www.intelliem.com/resourcekit*, provides scripts to generate network places and network locations automatically.

**Symbolic links**    Symbolic links, new to Windows Vista, provide an additional option. You can create a symbolic link to a DFS namespace. The link can be created in any folder—for example, Desktop, Documents—or in the user's profile; and it can have any name. When viewed in the Explorer folder tree, the symbolic link expands to show the DFS hierarchy. To create a symbolic link, use the mklink.exe command. You must be an administrator to create a directory link, which is necessary to refer to a DFS namespace. For example, to create a symbolic link for a user, James Fine, called Corporate that points to the Corporate DFS namespace, the syntax would be as follows:

```
mklink.exe /d "c:\users\jfine\Corporate" \\contoso.com\corporate
```

An example of the Corporate DFS namespace, exposed within the user profile of James Fine, is displayed in Figure 2-19.

**Figure 2-19** A DFS namespace exposed, through a symbolic link, within a User's profile

Both network locations and symbolic links appear as an expandable node in the Explorer shell. Symbolic links add the capability to refer to the DFS namespace within the local path. So you could refer to a folder in the Corporate DFS namespace as C:\Users\jfine\Corporate\ *subfolder*. Symbolic links are new to Windows Vista, so the use and benefits they provide are *terra nova*. I think they are worth testing! I'll be interested to hear about your experiences using symbolic links to present DFS namespaces—use the companion Web site, *www.intel-liem.com/resourcekit* to discuss this and other solutions.

## Solution summary

DFS Namespaces is a phenomenally useful feature of Windows servers that you can use to facilitate administration, user access to resources, and performance across servers and sites. If you haven't looked at DFS Namespaces yet, *look now*. It is a no-brainer, in my opinion. Refer to the Microsoft documentation listed earlier in this section to learn about the technology. If you are using the Enterprise edition of Windows Server, you can have multiple domain namespaces, and you can therefore create delegated namespaces that are managed by administrators who understand the data, its use, and its location. To create centralized or hierarchical namespaces, you can create a high-level DFS namespace with folders that target other DFS namespaces.

After you've created the perfect enterprise DFS Namespaces implementation, you can present the namespaces, or portions thereof, to users. Features such as shortcuts, mapped drives, network places (Windows XP), network locations (Windows Vista), and symbolic links (Windows Vista) will empower users to browse for resources efficiently, through the logical namespace you have designed.

# Managing User Data and Settings

In Solution Collection 2, "Managing Files, Folders, and Shares," we looked at best practices for creating, securing, and managing folders with shared business data. However, all business data is not necessarily shared—there is typically a vast quantity of business data that is created by and often accessible only by an individual user. User data—such as files and folders that would be stored in the Documents (or My Documents) folder, on the desktop, or in a home directory—is usually critical to the function that a user plays in the organization. In most business scenarios, users require and should be able to access their data whether they are logged on to their primary desktop or laptop, logged on to a shared computer such as a conference room system, logged on to a remote desktop (Terminal Services) session, or working while disconnected from the corporate network at home or on the road. Additionally, that data should be protected in such a way as to prevent it from being corrupted or lost in the event of hardware failure or if it's accidentally or intentionally deleted; and the data should be readily deployed so that if a user receives a new or replacement system, the user's data is immediately available.

A user's business files and folders are not the only data that is important to the user's effective and productive IT experience. Settings such as customizations, templates, favorites, and preferences should also be made available on any computer to which the user has a business need to log on, be protected against loss or corruption, and be readily deployed to new and replacement systems.

The management of user data and settings, which I will abbreviate as *UDS*, is a complicated undertaking that requires more than just a feature or two: It requires technologies, people, and processes. I encourage you to view any infrastructure that requires technologies, people, and processes as a framework—a collection of components that must themselves be designed, implemented, and supported, but that also must interoperate in defined, manageable, and supportable ways.

> **Note**    I refer to a *framework* as the collection of people, processes, and technologies assembled to attain a business objective—in this case, the management of user data and settings, abbreviated as UDS.

In this solution, I'll guide you through the business and technical challenges that you're likely to face as you implement a framework to support UDS.

## Scenarios, Pain, and Solution

The following common scenarios are symptomatic of a nonexistent or incomplete UDS framework in an organization:

- Users at Contoso, Ltd., regularly prepare management reports and presentations at their desktops, and then deliver the results in conference rooms. However, when they log on to conference room computers, they do not have access to the data on their desktops. So they are constantly having to copy the files they need from their desktop onto USB flash drives to transport those files to the conference room.

- Users at Blue Yonder Airlines regularly travel for work and require data from the corporate network on their local hard drive so that they can work while disconnected from the network. An employee in the Human Resources (HR) department copied some files to a folder on the root of his laptop's hard disk. Some weeks later, an HR intern logged on to the laptop to install an application and had immediate access to sensitive data in that folder—because folders on the root of a member computer's disk are, by default, readable by all users who can log on to the system, who, by default, are all domain users.

- Administrators at Adventure Works want to manage storage capacity by applying quotas to limit how much data users can store on the network. Unfortunately, the feature that automatically applies quotas ends up applying quotas to each user data folder, such as Desktop, Documents, Favorites, Pictures, Videos, and Music. They want to configure a quota that will manage those data folders within a single, combined limit.

- At Adventure Works, when a user moves to another site, administrators move the user's data to servers that are local to the new site. They must then change all references to the user's data locations, including the roaming profile path, targets of folder redirection and mapped drives, shortcuts, and links between documents.

- Northwind Traders is in the process of deploying Microsoft Windows Vista. The Information Technology (IT) team has found it difficult to support user data and settings when users have both Windows XP and Windows Vista clients, and it is looking for a way to unify management of user profiles and redirected folders in the heterogeneous desktop environment.

- Recently, an unfortunate series of disk crashes at Trey Research resulted in the loss of the Favorites folder for several key members of the Research team, who now must begin locating the Internet resources they had bookmarked for their research. The IT team at Trey has been tasked with finding a way to protect the productivity of the Research team by making users' Favorites folder redirected, both on Windows Vista and Windows XP.

- Wide World Importers attempted to implement Offline Files for its users several years ago, but users complained of excessively long synchronization times at logon and logoff, poor performance while remotely connected to the network using the company's virtual private network (VPN), and innumerable popup messages, so the effort was canceled.

- Producers and editors at Southridge Video edit and encode videos that, for performance reasons, must be stored on the local disk subsystem rather than on a network server. Management is concerned about the potential for data loss in the event of a disk failure and has asked the IT organization to back up videos to a server every one to two weeks. Because of the size of the files, the regular and frequent Windows Offline Files synchronization and roaming profile synchronization are not appropriate tools—an alternative must be located or developed.

- Traditionally, the process of upgrading computers at Fabrikam, Inc., has been problematic for users, who commonly complain that replacement hardware does not contain all of their data and settings, leading to lost productivity and, occasionally, loss of business-critical files.

In this Solution Collection, we'll examine technologies and features that can be assembled to address these pain points. We'll leverage, among others, folder redirection, user profiles, Offline Files, quotas, Group Policy, scripts, Robocopy, encryption, DFS Namespaces, and DFS Replication—in an effort to create an effective framework for managing user data and settings.

It is likely that you have examined, if not already implemented, one or more of the technologies and features just listed. If your experience was like that of every client I've served, you've had mixed results. The reason is simple: There are a *lot* of moving parts. Each of the individual technologies is simple enough to understand, design, implement, and support. But putting the pieces together in just the right way to support your business requirements is anything but simple. Let me warn you now: Don't try to implement just one piece of the framework set forth in this Solution Collection! Be sure you've considered each aspect of the UDS framework, because missing just one piece will lead to pain and make it appear as if the entire effort was misguided.

# 3-1: Define Requirements for a User Data and Settings Framework

## Solution overview

| | |
|---|---|
| **Type of solution** | Guidance |
| **Features and tools** | N/A |
| **Solution summary** | Identify the business requirements for the availability, mobility, resiliency, and security of user data and settings. |
| **Benefits** | Establishing clarity of requirements and consensus around them is a critical step to complete before embarking on the design of a complex framework. |

## Introduction

The first step to designing a user data and settings (UDS) framework is to identify the business requirements for the framework. In this solution, I'll set forth a common set of requirements for UDS management. We'll then develop solutions that meet those requirements later in this Solution Collection.

This solution is, therefore, a business exercise, not a technical one. I, and consultants like me, spend a lot of time guiding organizations through the requirements definition phase. The requirements definition phase is absolutely fundamental to the success of the effort. Do not underestimate its importance.

## Understand the business requirements definition exercise

The goal of the exercise outlined in this solution—defining the business requirements of a UDS framework—is to define the desired results. You can call these the "outcomes," the "requirements," the "end state," the "vision," or the "ideal world." Whatever term you use, the deliverable from this exercise should serve as the measuring stick to use for all designs and solutions to determine whether they do, indeed, meet the need. I find it helpful to brainstorm the desired end state with a team of constituents, including technical experts, management, financial decision makers, and even representatives of your customer base (end users).

Brainstorming with a diverse set of constituents achieves two things. First, you get a more big-picture or real-world view of requirements. Second, by including constituents in the requirements definition phase, you are much more likely to ensure that they understand and have bought in to the strategy and tactics used to meet those requirements, and thereby to the resulting UDS framework itself.

> **Guidance**   Brainstorm business requirements with a diverse set of constituents who will have an effect on or be affected by the UDS framework.

I caution you to focus on the goal of the exercise and, if possible, *not* get caught up in any particular methodology for requirements definition. I've watched clients waste so much time trying to follow Six Sigma or some other process improvement methodology so closely that they lose track of what they're really trying to *do*. Get it done. Define the end state. It's unlikely that every one of your constituents will be equipped to follow a single methodology (such as Six Sigma); and it is more likely that each constituent will be able to contribute more fully by helping to define the vision in his or her own unique way.

> **Guidance**   Don't get caught up in how you define requirements (that is, using a particular methodology such as Six Sigma). Instead, focus on eliciting the business requirements.

I also encourage you not to get caught up in the phrasing, wording, or "voice" of requirements. Sometimes it is easy to state a requirement simply: "Users should be able to log on to any computer and have access to their business data." At other times, however, it is easier to define a scenario that you want to be able to support. As long as all constituents understand what you're trying to achieve, you're in good shape.

> **Guidance**   Business requirements can be defined as requirements, as scenarios that you want to address, or in any other fashion that, in the end, creates a clear vision of what you are trying to achieve.

I'll propose a set of requirements for you as a starting point. You should examine the business requirements I propose in the context of your enterprise and IT environment. I expect you will agree with most or all of the requirements; however, where your requirements differ, you'll need to make modifications to the solutions to ensure they align with your specific needs.

> **Guidance**   Use the requirements in this solution as a baseline for discussion, but be sure to examine the unique requirements driven by your business and your IT environment.

One of the most important outcomes of a requirements definition exercise is to define not only the rules but the exceptions as well. We all know that there is rarely a single silver bullet—a single solution or approach—that solves all problems in all scenarios. If you can define exceptions and manage those exceptions, you'll create a framework that is capable of managing all users in all scenarios and that is more likely to support unexpected change over time—the definition of an *agile* environment.

 **Guidance**    Define the requirements not only for the majority—that is, for the rules—but also for the minority—that is, for the exceptions to the rules. By designing a management infrastructure that supports *all* scenarios, you'll be best served by the resulting framework.

Another important outcome of the requirements definition phase is consensus around the requirements. If you work on a team, ensure that the entire team understands the requirements. Also make sure that other constituents mentioned earlier have bought into the requirements that define the desired end state.

 **Guidance**    Build consensus around the requirements.

In the process of building consensus around requirements, do whatever you can to avoid having the discussion degenerate into a conversation about technologies, features, and designs. The number one downfall in the design of any framework occurs when design begins before requirements are understood. It is very easy to get so caught up in a discussion about the design and implementation of a feature, such as roaming profiles, and to get so embroiled in debate over a technology's strengths or weaknesses that the entire point gets lost: A framework is *not* a single technology, or even a collection of technologies—it includes people and process as well, all assembled to achieve a desired end state. Without the strategy, the vision, the definition of the end state, the requirements—whatever you choose to call it—you cannot begin to effectively design the solution. So focus on *what* you want to achieve, not *how* to achieve it.

 **Guidance**    During the requirements definition phase, focus on outcomes and scenarios that define the desired end state. Avoid getting caught up in *design*—in *how* you achieve the desired end state.

Finally, I encourage you to define an ideal world without constraints. Start with that vision. Then, after everyone has agreed to the vision and the requirements, begin to design components of the framework that attain the vision. During the component design phase, introduce constraints such as budget, time, network connectivity, bandwidth, and so on.

The reason I suggest this constraint-free approach to business requirements is that I've found, in almost every situation, the requirements *can* be met. There is rarely a constraint that creates an insurmountable obstacle. My experience has shown me that because of the very fact that there are a *lot* of moving parts in a UDS framework, you have a *lot* of options for how to put the pieces together. Therefore, it's highly likely you'll find a way to your goal. So do not introduce constraints too early in the process, because it tends to distract from the most critical task: defining the desired outcome.

> **Guidance**    Try not to introduce constraints in this phase of the framework design. Define your desired outcomes as exactly that—*desired* outcomes. Then, as you design components of the framework to achieve those outcomes, your constraints can be introduced and you can choose approaches that achieve the outcomes within the constraints.

Certainly, one of the most driving constraints you'll eventually have to introduce is financial constraints—that is, budget. I cannot emphasize enough how destructive to the overall framework it is to define requirements within budgetary constraints. Requirements are business-outcome driven—they should be enumerated in an ideal-world exercise. Hold discussions of budget (and technical design) at bay. It's a tough thing to do, but it is very important.

# Define the high-level business requirements

I have found that the definition of business requirements for a UDS framework is best approached in two phases. In this, the first phase, you should define requirements at a very high, broad level. In the upcoming sections, I've enumerated common requirements that you can use as a baseline for discussing requirements with your constituents.

> **Important**    The high-level business requirements for a UDS framework fall generally into these categories: availability and mobility (for roaming and laptop users), resiliency (to loss of the local disk), and security (against data exposure).

## Availability and mobility

**Availability and mobility: Users will be able to access data and settings from any computer.**    This requirement addresses a scenario mentioned in "Scenarios, Pain, and Solution" on page 172. Users should be able to log on to any computer, including a computer in a conference room, and have access to the same data and settings that are available on their primary client (desktop or laptop). This requirement is common to every UDS project with which I've been involved. It's the gold standard of business requirements.

However, this requirement is just a rule, and there will certainly be exceptions. For example, there are likely to be computers that should be out of scope, such as a public-facing kiosk or Internet-access computers in a building's lobby, or computers that are not connected regularly (or with sufficient bandwidth) to the corporate network. So we'll have to design a UDS framework that manages these and other exceptions.

Additionally, it is important to note that although this framework can ensure that a user's data and settings are available, it does *not* ensure that the applications required to open a user's files or implement a user's settings will be available. Software distribution is, I believe, best addressed as a separate framework, and this resource kit discusses software distribution in Solution Collection 9, "Improving the Deployment and Management of Applications and Configuration."

**Availability: When a user receives a new computer, his or her data and settings will be fully available with minimal delay at first logon.**   This requirement is really just a variation of the previous one. I've seen organizations in which users wait hours or days to obtain their data on a new computer and, even then, receive only a subset of what was on their previous system. With a well-designed UDS framework, getting a brand new system to function fully for a user should be as easy as a user logging on to another computer in the environment.

**Availability: A new employee will have a standard user data and settings experience from day one.**   When user accounts are created, their data stores should be initialized so that when a user arrives, he or she is able to get right to work. The initial user experience should reflect corporate standards for customizations, preferences, and policies.

## Resiliency

**Resiliency: In the event of hardware failure or loss, a replacement that contains all of the user's data and settings will be available within *x* hours.**   As another variation of the universal availability goal of UDS, this requirement will have implications on the framework, which might include a specification for how many extra systems are kept in stock in anticipation of such replacement scenarios. The number of hours that you use for the replacement scenario will vary based on whether the user is in-house or on the road. For example, it might be reasonable to expect a response of a few hours if the user is in the office, but 24 to 48 hours is more realistic if the user is on the road and therefore requires a computer to be shipped.

**Resiliency: Data loss will be limited in the event of client disk failure.**   If a user's hard disk fails, some data might be lost. For example, if the user recently added a Favorite to her profile and has not logged off, her roaming profile on a network share will not have a copy of the new Favorite, and therefore, that setting is lost.

However, the extent of data loss can certainly be managed through the UDS framework you implement. Many organizations allow users to store business-critical documents *only* on the user's disk. That is, to me, an unacceptable business risk because if a user's system fails or is lost or stolen, corporate knowledge is lost—knowledge that can *easily* be captured within a UDS framework. Our design efforts and solutions focus on deciding what "limited" means to your enterprise.

## Security

**Security: Business data created by users will be secure.**    Security is "Job #1" for most IT organizations, and the security of user data is high on the list of concerns for enterprises that don't want to become the next headline story when a user's system is stolen and sensitive information is leaked.

A user's profile comprises a set of folders and files that contain the user's data (documents and other files) and settings (customizations and configuration). The profile is discussed in detail in several solutions later in this Solution Collection. The profile's default access control list (ACL) ensures that only the user and members of the computer's local Administrators group have access to the profile. Other users will be denied access by the profile's ACL.

ACLs are not of use, however, if a disk is made physically vulnerable—for example, if a laptop is stolen. As soon as the computer's local Administrators group is compromised, any member of that group can effectively access all data on the disk. This can be done simply by installing a second instance of Windows on the computer. As an administrator of the second instance, one can access all data on the entire disk, even that which is part of the first instance. The only protection for data on a disk against local, physical access is encryption, which is also examined in later solutions.

With that background information covered, allow me to describe several scenarios I've encountered that can cause unnecessary exposure of business data. These scenarios can serve as business requirements for a UDS framework—the framework must address and resolve any of the following problems that exist in your enterprise:

**Data folders created outside the user profile**    Users are not always good stewards of their own data security. If a user creates a data file anywhere outside of the user's profile, it's a good bet that the data is exposed. A common example occurs when users create folders on the root of their C:\ drive. Some applications even encourage such a poor practice. If a folder is created on the root of the C:\ drive, *all* users who log on locally to the system have access to that folder. And, by default, all domain users have the right to log on locally to any member server or workstation. So, by default, any user in your organization can log on to any desktop or laptop and, when logged on, will have at least Read permission to any folder on the root of the C:\ drive. The UDS framework should encourage or enforce data management practices that are appropriately secure.

**Users who are local administrators**    Members of the local Administrators group have effective unfettered access to all unencrypted data on a system. It is important to remove users from the local Administrators group, but that entails implementing frameworks that support the business requirements that currently drive users into the local Administrators group: requirements such as the ability to install printer drivers, to change system time and IP configuration, and to install applications. You must also test applications to ensure that they do not require local administrative credentials to function properly, and you must address any applications that do require such credentials. These efforts are significant, and many of them are discussed in other Solution Collections in this resource kit. Until those solutions are in place and all users are removed from the local Administrators group, you have a data security exposure that can be ameliorated only through encryption.

**Access to the physical disk (for example, through theft)**    As mentioned earlier, if a disk can be physically accessed, data on the disk is exposed. Encryption is the technology we'll use to secure data against physical access.

# Determine key design decision that is derived from high-level business requirements

After you have reached agreement regarding the high-level business requirements, one implication of those requirements must be recognized: User data and settings must be stored on the network. This is, in a way, a design decision, but it is a requirement in that, without user data on servers, high-level business requirements cannot be met. I encourage you to set forth this requirement and discuss it with your constituents at this point in the process. Don't devolve the discussion into more specific design discussions, such as *which* data gets stored *where*, or *how* it gets accessed on the road. Keep the discussion on a high level, with a goal of building consensus around the simple fact that without this design decision, the high-level requirements listed previously cannot be met.

## User data and settings must be stored on the network

Only by storing user data and settings on the network can you achieve goals related to mobility, resiliency, security, and support. As we'll see in later solutions, this does not mean *all* data and settings are stored on the network: Some data and settings fall outside the scope of the high-level requirements and therefore do not need to be managed in the same way. Think about the items in your TEMP folder—they clearly are not subject to the same requirements. But data that needs to be managed to meet the high-level requirements will at some point or another need to be stored on the network. Nor are we saying that all user data will be *accessed* in real time from the server. What I've just pointed out are typical objections to this fundamental design decision. But these objections are about design *specifics* and, as such, should be set aside for now. Keep the discussion at a high level. Is it common sense that important data needs to be on a server (backed up, at the least) to be resilient against loss of a user's local disk? Yes. Move on.

If your organization is among the ones that do not yet host most or all user data somewhere on their network, you might have a sales job to do at this point. Network storage has cultural, political, and financial implications that we will address, next, as requirements that are derived from this architectural decision. If you have managed to build consensus around the high-level business requirements discussed earlier, recognition of this design implication will be a no-brainer. That's one reason why, in my opinion, you should work hard to focus on business requirements before discussing any design implications—sometimes design implications are, like this one, potentially significant and complicated.

I recommend that you bring your constituents to agreement that some form of network storage will be required to meet business requirements. I encourage you *not* to get more detailed than that. Don't talk about roaming profiles, redirected folders, Offline Files, or the backup of client data yet. Those are specific technologies, and it makes more sense to discuss them in light of more detailed requirements and design challenges later in the process. The bottom line is that each of those technologies will play a role in supporting a wide variety of user data scenarios, but we have not yet defined those scenarios. So focus solely on the big picture for the moment: Network storage will be a design element. Keep it simple because, shortly, we'll have a slew of new requirements derived from this decision and only then can we begin to design an effective UDS framework.

If you currently do not host user data on servers, you should also avoid getting too caught up in financial implications such as additional storage capacity. The best pieces of advice I can give you are, first, don't let the discussion go there. Keep it at a high level and constraint free. There will be *more* than enough time to discuss budgets and return on investment (ROI) later. Everyone knows the framework will not be designed or implemented without considering cost. But, again, we are not yet *designing* in detail—we're developing requirements. Yes, we've decided that network storage is required to meet the high-level business requirements, but we've not laid down any designs as to what that means, yet. That is for later.

The second piece of advice I can give you is to do your best to get your financial constituents—the decision makers—in on the previous discussion of high-level business requirements. If they've agreed that those high-level requirements (availability, mobility, resiliency, and security) are critical to the success of the enterprise—and I think that's an easy argument to make—you can easily position network storage as a critical role in each and every requirement. Without network storage, requirements cannot be met. The art and science of designing for requirements while balancing cost and other constraints are addressed in solutions that follow.

## Define requirements derived from key design decisions

Earlier, I encouraged you to bring your constituents to a consensus that in order to provide resiliency, availability, security, and agility for user data and settings, the data and settings must be stored on the network. That key design decision has implications that should be addressed by enumerating requirements that derive from the decision. In other words, if we've agreed that data needs to be stored on the network to meet primary requirements, what requirements need to be added in light of that design requirement? Again, do not yet discuss specific technologies or more detailed design. Focus on requirements.

### Security: The UDS framework will comply with the enterprise information security and information technology policies regarding network storage of files.

This security requirement reflects the reality that, in many organizations, certain types of files should not be stored on the network. For example, your information technology policy might state that storing music files such as .MP3s is not permitted. Your enterprise might also dictate that—for security, storage management, or compliance reasons—e-mail archives are not allowed to be stored on network servers. Or you might have certain classes of data that, per your organization's information security policy, should not be stored on certain servers.

What this requirement means to your UDS framework depends on what your specific policies dictate. We'll propose design elements of a UDS framework that support most common data-storage scenarios, including those that prohibit certain file types from being stored on servers.

### Mobility: Users who work while disconnected (for example, laptop users) will be able to access their files using the same namespace, whether they are connected or disconnected.

If all user data were stored on each user's machine, a user would always have access to that data, whether the user was at the office or on the road. But to meet high-level requirements, data will be stored, to some extent, on the network. When data is stored on the network, you can increase consistency (and thereby security) and reduce support costs by *rationalizing* the user experience.

When users go on the road, do they currently copy files from their home directory to the local disk and then copy them back on return? This is an example of a disjointed namespace experience: The user accesses the file one way while connected to the network (through his or her home folder mapped drive) and another way (by browsing the local disk folder structure) when disconnected. It is reasonable to suggest that users should be able to work the same way whether connected or disconnected. It's also reasonable to assume that if users are able to work the same way while connected or disconnected, their productivity will increase, the chance for error will decrease, and costs related to support will decrease.

Microsoft Outlook is an example of a rationalized user experience. With Cached Exchange Mode, it is transparent to users whether they are connected or disconnected. They can compose, read, and manage e-mail using the same namespace. A user's experience with Windows Explorer should be equally rationalized across connected and disconnected experiences. Windows Offline Files is a design recommendation we'll use to address this requirement.

## Availability: Performance shall be sufficient to meet business requirements.

This intentionally vaguely worded requirement needs to be defined in the context of your organization's needs. The genesis of this requirement is the recognition that if some user data is not always accessed from the user's local disk, and is instead accessed over the network, performance should be sufficient so as not to encourage the user to work around the UDS framework by storing all data locally.

There are several requirements I encourage you to define with as much specificity as possible:

**Framework uptime requirement.**   *Framework uptime* relates to the availability of user data and settings, not necessarily to the uptime of one server, as servers can be clustered or replicated. Uptime can be defined in minutes, hours, days, or as a percentage of time. An uptime requirement of the UDS framework could be specified as 99.6%, for example, which equates to 35 hours of downtime per year, including both planned and unplanned downtime. I believe this figure is achievable with a UDS framework hosted on single-server storage systems—it provides sufficient downtime for rebooting the server after updates have been applied and for occasional hardware troubleshooting. The bulk of downtime should be planned such that most of the 35 hours of downtime happen in off-peak time windows. But, of course, there is a possibility of unplanned downtime as well.

**Redundancy requirement.**   You might want to define a redundancy requirement such as, "User data stores will support the failure of a single disk or array." Such a requirement is complementary to an uptime requirement. For example, if the UDS framework withstands the failure of a single disk or array, such a failure will not create downtime for the UDS framework.

**Performance of accessing network storage from clients will be adequate to meet business requirements.**   This addresses the scenario discussed earlier: Some or most data is likely to be accessed directly from a network storage location, and working with such data should not be so painfully slow as to jeopardize business requirements or to cause users to look for workarounds. Workarounds generally entail users copying data to their local system and working with it locally—a step that goes against most high-level requirements of the UDS framework.

**The impact of the UDS framework on the network will be optimized.**   This is a service-side perspective on the same requirement. We want to optimize the UDS framework with network capacity in mind. Notice we're not saying "minimized," which would then put network infrastructure concerns at the *top* of the list, to the exclusion of other requirements. Instead, we are saying "optimized" in balance with other requirements.

**The UDS framework will support the management of exceptions.**   To describe this requirement, we need to reveal one design element: redirected folders. We'll detail redirected folders later in this Solution Collection, but they address user data in a manner similar to home directories: User data is stored on a server. For most user work scenarios, this approach is quite effective. But you can imagine there will be scenarios in which a user cannot, for one reason or another, work effectively with a file that is stored on a network server. The specifics of such scenarios depend on your organization and the applications you use. As one example, older versions of Microsoft Outlook did not support accessing .pst data files on network folders—they had to be accessed locally. As another example, a user editing large video files will likely require local access to those files; otherwise, performance will be dreadful. In situations that require local access to data, although most data is accessed from servers, the UDS framework should ensure that the locally accessed data is managed to meet UDS requirements, such as resiliency against local disk failure and availability on other computers. Rather than forcing users to find workarounds to meet their needs, the framework needs to support all work scenarios.

**Storage locations will be abstracted from configuration pointers.**   This requirement suggests that user profiles should not point to \\*server*\\*share*\\%username%, because if the profiles need to be migrated to another server—in a server consolidation effort, for example—all user profile paths would need to be updated. To make the management of storage easier, abstraction is useful. You might be reading ahead in your mind and, yes, the answer to this design requirement is to use DFS namespaces.

**Responsible use of network storage will be encouraged, enforced, or monitored as appropriate.**   To optimize total cost of ownership, network storage should not become a dumping ground for all data, good and bad, current and outdated. The UDS framework should provide options for managing user data storage utilization.

## Solution summary

This solution focused on the steps that lead to a requirements definition for a user data and settings (UDS) framework. Because a UDS framework is complex and involves numerous moving parts, which are detailed in subsequent solutions, it is critical that all constituents come to a consensus regarding the requirements *before* moving into design discussions. However, because one fundamental aspect of a UDS framework—the network storage of user data—has cultural, political, and financial as well as technical implications, I encourage you to drive your requirements discussion as I've outlined here: Focus first on high-level business requirements and the scenarios that a UDS framework should support. Get consensus on those high-level requirements. Then the need for network storage as a fundamental design decision becomes obvious. In the light of a framework that involves network storage, you can then further enumerate requirements for performance, redundancy, security, and mobility.

# 3-2: Design UDS Components That Align Requirements and Scenarios with Features and Technologies (Part I)

## Solution overview

| | |
|---|---|
| **Type of solution** | Guidance |
| **Features and tools** | Roaming profiles, redirected folders, Group Policy, Offline Files |
| **Solution summary** | Describe a typical best practice for the implementation of a user data and settings framework. |
| **Benefits** | The design described in this solution serves as a an overview and reference for a detailed discussion of each component of the UDS framework. Your specific design will be based on the analysis presented in Solution 3-11 on page 293. |

## Introduction

After requirements have been agreed upon, you can begin to move closer to the technology needed to support those requirements. The goal of this solution is to guide you through a design discussion that identifies the major components of the user data and settings (UDS) framework and how they can be aligned to address the requirements you've set forth and a variety of work scenarios. This solution is still high level, looking at the pieces and how they are put together. What we'll end up with is a preview of a typical, best-practice UDS framework implementation that allows you to see how the pieces are most effectively assembled for most organizations.

I want you to see the forest before we look at both the beautiful and ugly details of each tree. That will happen as we detail each component and specify how components are designed, implemented, managed, and supported in subsequent solutions. Then, in Solution 3-11, we revisit how all the pieces are assembled with an eye on why all the pieces are assembled that way. Solution 3-11 thus serves to wrap up our discussion of framework components and, hopefully, you'll come out of that solution with two things. First, you'll see why the structure I recommend in this solution will work well for most organizations. Second, you'll understand the requirements, the components, and their interactions so well that you'll be able to modify my proposed structure to meet the exact needs of your enterprise.

You are welcome, of course, to jump ahead to Solution 3-11—particularly if you are super expert at all at working with the technologies used by a UDS framework. But I encourage you to continue following this Solution Collection in order. So let's begin by looking at the components of a UDS framework from a high level.

# Understand UDS options

I like to refer to the first step as defining "options." These are the tools at your disposal as you design a management infrastructure for user data and settings. As you read this section, focus on the concepts and definitions, as each option is explored in much more detail in subsequent solutions.

## Data and settings

The UDS framework needs to support both data and settings:

**Data**   Refers to files that the user creates or uses: documents, spreadsheets, presentations, and so on.

**Settings**   Refers to files that applications create transparently to the user to support the user's customizations. Examples include Internet Explorer favorites, cookies, custom dictionaries, and so on.

We'll get more granular with this definition, looking at specific types, or *classes*, of data—such as documents, e-mail archives, music collections, and pictures.

> **Important**   In the context of a UDS framework, I refer to "classes" of data (or documents, or files) as items that share common requirements and common characteristics that enable you to manage them with common tools and processes.

## Windows user data and settings stores

Windows provides a number of stores for user data and settings, including the following ones:

- Documents (Windows Vista) or My Documents (Windows XP): User documents
- Desktop: Documents, shortcuts
- Favorites: Internet Explorer favorites
- AppData (Windows Vista) or Application Data (Windows XP): application settings and configuration files
- Ntuser.dat: The user's registry hive, containing settings

> **Important**   *User data stores* are interfaces that expose one or more classes of data. Most user data stores are Windows user-interface elements. You'll probably create one or several additional user data stores. The user data store is where the user interacts with the data.

## Network and local stores

User data and settings stores will be physically stored in one or both of the following locations:

**UDS servers**    To meet high-level business requirements, most user data and settings will be stored on the network on servers we'll call *User Data and Settings Servers* (UDS servers). Notice I said "stored on," not necessarily "accessed from." The subtle difference will be clarified in this solution. Performance requirements drive the placement of UDS servers—typically, they will be placed in distributed sites to provide local area network (LAN) access to data for users in that site, or in datacenters on highly connected networks.

**Local data stores**    To meet requirements related to performance and disconnected work scenarios, much user data will also be stored locally on the user's disk subsystem.

Again, we'll get into more detail about the specifics of these stores later in this and other solutions.

> **Important**    The physical data stores of a UDS framework are where the user data stores actually "live." The Documents folder, for example, is a user data store that can live on the local disk or on a server. A user data store can exist in more than one physical store. A server-based (redirected) Documents folder can also be stored in the local offline files cache.

## Primary data stores

The UDS design dictates the location from which various classes of data and settings will be accessed in a variety of work scenarios. I'll refer to the store from which users access files as the *primary data store* for the data class. For example, a user who is editing large video files will likely, for performance reasons, access those video files locally—the primary data store for the files will be a local store. However, if those video files are subject to the business requirements discussed in Solution 3-1 on page 174, including resiliency against the failure of the user's disk drive, they need to exist on the network as well. The network store will simply support availability, mobility, and resiliency requirements—it will not be a primary data store from which video files are accessed.

## Synchronization of data stores

That scenario leads to the question of how files get from one store to the other. There are several approaches to synchronizing the local and network stores:

**Windows' Offline Files**    Offline Files can synchronize resources in a primary store on the network to a local store (the *cache*) on the user's system. The user accesses files from the network while connected and from the cache when disconnected. (See Solution 3-6 on page 245.)

**Roaming profiles**     Roaming profiles synchronize user settings from the primary store on the user's system to a network store. The user accesses files from the local profile store. (See Solution 3-7 on page 257.)

**Robocopy or other file copy mechanisms**     Robocopy and similar tools can synchronize a local or network store, and it can do so on a schedule. Either store can be used for file access, depending on the requirements for the work scenario and the type of data. (See Solution 3-10 on page 279.)

**Copying**     There will even be some scenarios in which it makes sense to perform a copy operation on an as-needed basis.

**Excluding (not synchronizing)**     Finally, there are scenarios in which synchronization just isn't necessary. For example, I've not yet met a client that cared to do any sort of synchronization of users' Temp folders. (See Solution 3-9 on page 274.)

## Presentation (or *namespace*)

Users or their applications will need to access files from the appropriate local or network data store. Ideally, this should be as transparent to users as possible. They should be presented with a user-interface element in the Windows shell namespace that abstracts (hides) the complexities of the underlying UDS infrastructure. This is the link between the user data store that is visible to the user and the physical (local or network) data store where the data lives.

Luckily, there are several technologies to help us achieve effective presentation of user data and settings:

**Redirected folders**     Redirection enables a Windows shell folder to point to any one of a variety of physical data stores. The Desktop and Documents folders (My Documents prior to Windows Vista) are both redirected folders. They are exposed in the shell in a constant fashion, but they are abstract constructs—they don't really exist. Instead, they are pointers to a specific folder in the local disk subsystem or on a network server.

**Roaming profiles**     Roaming profiles mask the complexity of the feature's synchronization functionality by presenting profile components in a locally cached copy of the user's roaming profile that is in the exact same location in the Windows namespace as a local profile (for example, C:\Users\\*username* in Windows Vista and C:\Documents and Settings\\*username* in Windows XP).

**Offline Files**     The Offline Files feature synchronizes network resources to a local cache, as described earlier, but it becomes more useful and valuable as it presents those files in the exact same namespace whether the user is connected or disconnected. In other words, if a user has made a network file such as \\\\*server*\\*share*\\*filename.ext* available offline, the file can be accessed using the exact same path if the user is disconnected. The user doesn't need to, and in fact cannot, directly access files in the client-side cache.

**Symbolic links or junctions**   Symbolic links (new to Windows Vista) and junction points (Windows XP and Windows Server 2003) create folders in the Windows Explorer namespace that redirect to another location.

**Shortcuts**   Shortcuts enable a user to navigate to a target.

### Network and DFS Namespaces

Namespace considerations are also important for the back end so that administration, support, and management of the UDS framework are as effective and efficient as possible. In Solution 3-3 on page 193, we'll examine the configuration of physical stores of UDS on the UDS servers—the folder hierarchy, such as E:\Users\%username%\Documents—and in Solution 3-4 the SMB shares required to support the framework—for example, \\server23\users$ as a shared folder targeting E:\Users on SERVER23.

In Solution 3-1, we proposed that one requirement of the framework is, "Storage locations will be abstracted from configuration pointers." DFS Namespaces enable you to achieve this requirement. Rather than redirecting users' Documents folders to \\server23\users$\ %username%\documents, you can leverage a DFS Namespace to create a path such as \\contoso.com\users\%username%\documents, which itself targets the share on SERVER23. This allows you to migrate all user data to another server with only one management change—a new target for the DFS folder.

The bottom line of this "Network and DFS Namespaces" section is that the presentation (or *namespace*) mentioned earlier—the link between the user data store that is visible to the user and a network data store where the data lives—should be made through a DFS namespace.

For most of the solutions in this collection, I use DFS namespace Universal Naming Conventions (UNCs) to refer to user data and setting stores on the network. The DFS namespace you actually create will be based on design considerations discussed in Solution 3-4 on page 211.

## Align user data and settings options with requirements and scenarios

Now let's get a preview of how these options align with our requirements. To reiterate, this is still a very high-level discussion to help your constituents see and understand the forest before you define each tree. Said another way, we're going to look at the puzzle, already put together, and then we'll dissect each piece.

The following sketch describes what is a typical, best-practice configuration of UDS stores and synchronization technologies. It is *not* the only choice, nor is it even the best choice for every enterprise. Approach these recommendations as a *likely* solution; then, as we detail each component, you'll come to understand all the design considerations and you can make modifications appropriate for your enterprise. Solution 3-11 presents the details that lead to this UDS design:

- *The two most important stores of user settings–Application Data (the AppData\Roaming folder in Windows Vista) and the user's registry hive–will roam.* A roaming profile is the only mechanism with which to manage the user's registry hive that meets the high-level requirements for availability of user settings. Until all users are running Windows Vista, you are likely to find that a roaming Application Data folder is the only way to meet requirements for settings in that namespace.

- *The Desktop and Documents folders will be redirected* to primary network stores. The Documents folder and, to a lesser extent, the Desktop folder tend to be quite large and therefore provide a suboptimal experience if allowed to roam.

- *All redirected folders will be made available offline* for laptop users, to ensure availability while they are disconnected from the servers.

- *Pictures, Music, and Videos folders will be redirected or stored locally*, depending on your information technology policies.

- *Folders will be created to support scenarios that require a local primary store* for user data, such as the video files example described earlier. Files in these two folders will be accessed by users directly on the local disk.

    ❑ The Local Files folder: One folder will support data that should be managed to support all high-level requirements. This local folder will be a primary data store for user data, and it will be backed up regularly to a network store to support requirements for availability, mobility, and resiliency.

> **Important**    The Local Files folder is not a standard Windows folder. It is a folder you will create and manage, based on the guidance in Solution 3-9. *It supports scenarios in which data must be accessed from the local hard disk for compatibility or performance reasons.* Examples include users who work with large video files or Outlook .pst files that are not supported for access over the network in Outlook 2003 or earlier. Such data cannot be adequately synchronized to a network store with roaming profiles, yet it needs to be managed for mobility, availability, and resiliency. To cut to the chase, this means that users will access data locally and use a backup mechanism—such as the script presented in Solution 3-10 on page 279—to back up data to the network store. I'll refer to the network store as the user's Backups folder.

    ❑ The Local Only folder: Another folder will support data that should not be stored on the network because of information security or information technology policies or storage capacity issues. This folder will not be backed up to a network share.

> **Important**    The Local Only folder is not a standard Windows folder. It is a folder you will create and manage based on the guidance in Solution 3-8 on page 267. *It supports scenarios in which data should not be stored on network servers* for compliance with information security or information technology usage policies. Examples include personal music collections.

- *Favorites can be configured as a redirected folder or to roam.* Several considerations will be discussed to help you determine the best design for your organization.

- *Other user profile folders, particularly those that are new to Windows Vista, tend to be quite small*, so both redirected folders and roaming profiles are feasible management technologies.

## Validate the outcome for desktop, roaming, relocated, and traveling users

For users who work on desktop computers and for those who log on to computers other than their own, settings will be made available on a new computer by the user's roaming profile. Settings (AppData, Ntuser.dat and, potentially, Favorites) will be synchronized when the user logs on to and logs off of the network store. Because these folders tend to be of reasonable size, the impact on the network and on user logon time should be acceptable, even when a user logs on to a new system that then downloads a complete copy of the profile. If a user logs on to a system that he has used before, only updated files need to be synchronized, further reducing the impact on the network and on logon time. Large data folders, such as Documents and Desktop, will be immediately available through redirection—no files will be transferred at logon or logoff. Therefore, users will be able to log on to any system and have access to their data and settings, as stipulated by the high-level requirements.

For users working on laptops, the local cache of the user's roaming profile will provide access to the user's settings from any location, including offline. User data in the Documents and Desktop and other redirected folders will be cached using Offline Files. So laptops won't have much of a problem with mobility within the UDS framework. The benefit of the UDS framework for laptops is greater in the areas of resiliency and redundancy—to protect against the loss of data if a laptop is lost, stolen, or corrupted.

If a user logs on to a system (desktop or laptop) that has inadequate connectivity to the server hosting that user's data, performance could become a concern as files are transferred over the poor connection. There are several scenarios and solutions:

**Office relocation**    If a user is relocated to another site that has limited connectivity to the user's original UDS server, it would be prudent to transfer the user's data to a UDS server in the new site to ensure optimal performance.

**Traveling user (laptop)**     If a user travels to another site with limited connectivity to the user's UDS server, it is likely in most organizations that the user will have a laptop computer. Laptops will have a locally cached copy of the user's profile, so synchronization of the profile in the new site should be a trivial matter. To access data, traveling users will leverage Offline Files, so this scenario is revisited as we discuss Offline Files in Solution 3-6.

**Traveling user (no laptop)**     If a user travels to another site with limited connectivity to the user's UDS server and does *not* have a laptop, the user's profile will be loaded when the user logs on. In most situations, this approach is acceptable, as the profile size will be minimized by redirecting the Documents and Desktop folders—the profile will contain only Ntuser.dat, Application Data, and perhaps Favorites. If the loading of that profile across the slow connection is not acceptable, you should implement a workflow whereby the user profile store is moved or the roaming profile path is removed from the user account when the user goes on the road, and then reinstate the profile store or roaming profile path when the user returns.

The other issue in this scenario is access to data in the redirected Documents and Desktop folders while on the distant side of a slow connection to the UDS server. The only files that will be transferred over the connection to the client in the new site are those that the user opens. So, depending on the work that the user performs in the new site while traveling, there might not be a problem. If there is a performance problem, users will have to transfer the files they need manually, on a USB drive or other portable media—at which point, you should look at the possibility of providing the user a laptop, even if only temporarily, to support effective work from poorly connected sites.

## Solution summary

This solution provided an overview of how the key components of a UDS framework interact to deliver many of the high-level requirements. Large data folders will be redirected to optimize user and network performance. Settings stores such as AppData, which tend to be much smaller, will roam to provide absolute access and compatibility. Access to user data and settings is then enabled for desktop, laptop, roaming, relocated, and traveling users. Other solutions in this collection provide more detail on each of the components and design recommendations presented in this solution. Solution 3-11 then revisits the design discussion at a more detailed level, helping you to assemble all these pieces to meet your specific requirements.

# 3-3: Create, Secure, Manage, and Provision Server-Side User Data Stores

## Solution overview

| | |
|---|---|
| **Type of solution** | Guidance, scripts |
| **Features and tools** | NTFS folders, permissions, quotas, dirquota.exe, file screens, icacls.exe, xcacls.vbs |
| **Solution summary** | Create an efficient, secure, and managed namespace (folder hierarchy) for stores of user data and settings. |
| **Benefits** | Automate and provision storage management tasks to increase consistency and security. |

## Introduction

User data and settings (UDS) stores will be hosted, physically, on network servers as well as on the user's local disk. As you'll see in upcoming solutions, each class of data will be accessed from one primary store and most will be synchronized to the other. Deciding whether to address the user data stores or the server data stores first is a bit like deciding whether the chicken or the egg came first. So I'll start with what is probably the more straightforward configuration: the server data stores. In this solution, we'll look at the options you have for organizing UDS folders, for configuring shares, for establishing access control, for setting quotas, and for provisioning user data stores. I'm sure that, after the two design discussions in the previous solutions, you'll be happy to begin getting into the technology.

First, let's review some of the terminology we introduced in Solution 3-2 on page 185. This is terminology related to the design and implementation of a UDS framework, not necessarily Microsoft terminology. A *user data store* is an entry point to a collection of data as presented to the user through an interface element, such as the Documents folder or the Desktop. It can also be an actual folder, such as the Templates folder in which Microsoft Office templates are stored. The physical data store is where the data really lives, which in many cases can be either local or on a server. When a physical data store exists on both the local system and a server, and its content is synchronized between the two, I refer to the store from which the user accesses data as the *primary store*.

The term *namespace* appears throughout. The Application Data roots a namespace within which applications store their settings. The user profile is a namespace. The physical folder structure on the UDS server is a namespace. And the location of physical data stores can be abstracted into a logical view by DFS Namespaces.

For most organizations, the desired end state for the user data namespace is similar or identical to that shown in Figure 3-1. Underneath a root folder for users (which we'll call the user data store root folder or Users folder), there is a folder for each user (which we'll call the %username% folder) and, within that, there are folders for each user data store.

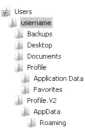

**Figure 3-1** User data and settings namespace

The user data stores beneath the %username% folder are those outlined in Solution 3-2: Desktop and Documents (redirected folders), Backups (backups of the user's Local Files), and Profile. The Profile folder, hosting the Windows XP profile, shows Application Data and Favorites as part of the roaming profile. The Profile.V2 folder hosts the Windows Vista user profile. Windows Vista adds the ".V2" extension to its profiles to ensure separation between the pre–Windows Vista profiles and the new Windows Vista user profile. This is discussed in Solution 3-7. Additionally, note that the Windows Vista profile folder named "Profile.V2" does not include Favorites. That is because Windows Vista supports redirecting Favorites, and you can redirect Favorites for a user to the user's Windows XP roaming profile Favorites store to maintain a unified experience for users working on both platforms. Note, however, that you *can* redirect Favorites with Windows XP using a trick I'll share with you in Solution 3-5 on page 224.

In this solution, your goal is to design a configuration for the physical namespace of data stores on the server (the folder structure). In the next solution, we discuss the Server Message Block (SMB) namespace of those stores (the shares), for a rationalized, logical view of the UDS namespace (through DFS Namespaces).You will then be equipped to answer the following three questions:

- How will folders for data stores be structured on the server itself? In other words, what will the folder namespace (hierarchy) be?
- What folders will be shared?
- How will that physical structure of data stores be presented to users and administrators?

There might very well be a difference between the physical namespace of the data stores on the server's disk volumes, the shares that are created, and the logical namespace as it is presented to users and administrators.

To answer these questions, you'll also need to be able to answer the following ones:

- What NTFS permissions need to be set?
- What SMB settings must be configured?

- What quotas will be applied?

- What folders will be created for users by administrators, and what folders will Windows create automatically?

# Create the user data store root folder

First, you must determine how to structure the server-based data stores for user data and settings. We'll start at the top of the UDS server's physical namespace: the user data store root folder (the Users folder shown in Figure 3-1). You must create at least one user data store root folder. If you decide to create it on the C:\ drive of the server (the drive on which the operating system is installed), use a name other than Users because you should reserve the Users folder on that drive for the local user profiles on that system. Hopefully, your server has a separate data volume on which you can create a Users folder, in which case you can call it *Users*. We'll start by examining how to secure that folder, and then we'll look at factors that determine how many user data store root folders you need on a UDS server.

## Apply least privilege permissions for the user data store root folder

You should secure the user data store root folder ("Users" in Figure 3-1) with least-privilege NTFS permissions, which are different than the permissions applied by Windows when you create a new folder. In the next section, I'll provide a script to automate the application of the permissions, which should be configured as follows:

**System::Allow:Full Control (Apply To: This folder, subfolder, and files).**    This enables services running under the System account to access the data store. Windows assigns this permission by default.

**Administrators::Allow:Full Control (Apply To: This folder, subfolder, and files).**    It is typical for organizations to grant Administrators the Full Control permission. Administrators have the right to take ownership of any resource, and thereby to gain access to any resource on the server. Therefore, it can be argued, there is no point in discussing "least privilege" in the context of users who already belong to the Administrators group. One must first manage that group's membership. Whether or not granting the Full Control permission to Administrators is appropriate for your organization should be determined by your information security policy. Modify the script as necessary to reduce the scope or level of access granted to Administrators.

**ACL_User Data and Settings_Admin::Allow::Create Folders and Allow:Read&Execute (Apply To: This folder only).**    This role-based access control entry (ACE) enables the group named "ACL_User Data and Settings_Admin" to create subfolders in the user data store root folder and to access the root with Read permission. The group name, of course, is up to you. To comply with the recommendations in Solution Collection 1, "Role-Based Management," I suggest using a name such as the following: ACL_User Data and Settings_ Admin (*Group Type_Scope_Capability*). This is not the group that determines that the user data store root folder does or does not belong on this server—that is up to the server's Administrators, as permissioned in the previous ACE. But after the user data store root folder exists, it is this group's job to create subfolders for users within the root. Of course, it's possible that the same roles (for example, Network Engineers) might be members of both Administrators and ACL_User Data and Settings_Admin.

**ACL_User Data and Settings_Admin::Allow::Full Control (Apply To: Subfolders and files only).**
This role-based ACE enables the same ACL_User Data and Settings_Admin group to have full control of all user data stores. With this permission, which applies to all objects below the user data store root folder, but not to the root itself, the group will have full control of the folders that it created using the Create Folders ACE discussed previously.

**ACL_User Data and Settings_Audit::Allow::Read (Apply To: This folder, subfolder, and files).**
Typically, organizations have a group that is allowed to audit (read) but not modify user data for security purposes. This permission enables that capability.

At this point, the permissions I've listed are sufficient if you, as a member of the ACL_User Data and Settings_Admin group, provision the creation of each user's %username% folder. In other words, if you create the subfolder within the Users folder for each user and give each user permission to his or her own individual folder, no "users" group requires NTFS permissions on the root folder! Now *that* is least privilege, I'd say! By default, Windows grants the Everyone group the Bypass Traverse Checking user right. This allows users to access a Universal Naming Convention (UNC) through one or more parent folders to which they do not have permission, as long as they have permission to the target of the UNC. So if James Fine's data stores are rooted at E:\Users\jfine, if he has permission to the jfine folder, if the Users folder is permissioned as I just described, and if it is shared, it will work perfectly.

> **Important**   It might sound like a lot of work to create a subfolder for each user. However, as you'll see, issues related to quotas and roaming profiles will put you in a position where you'll probably want to precreate each user's subfolder, anyway. And the ability to completely lock down the user data store root folder (the Users folder) is a great win for security. Additionally, precreating the %username% folder facilitates provisioning quotas, as I'll discuss later. This Solution Collection provides several scripts to automate the provisioning of user data folders.

If you do *not* precreate each %username% folder, Windows creates the folders for users automatically when the user logs on and first receives the configuration for a roaming profile or redirected folder. To do that, you need to add the ACEs in the following list to the Users folder:

**<Users Group>::Allow::Read & Execute (Apply To: This folder only).**   This permission is necessary for Windows to create the stores automatically. The group that you grant this permission to should contain only users with data stores on the server. You can use Authenticated Users if this is the only UDS server in your enterprise. Otherwise, select a more specific group. The Read & Execute permission enables users in the group to see their folder from the root.

**<Users Group>::Allow::Create Folders / Append Data (Apply To: This folder and subfolders; Apply permissions within this container only).**    This permission enables Windows to create data stores for users automatically. The group that you grant this permission to should contain only the users with data stores on the server. You can use Authenticated Users if this is the only UDS server in your enterprise. Otherwise, select a more specific group. The Create Folders/Append Data permission, assigned to a folder, allows the creation of subfolders. With the inheritance settings of "Apply To: This folder and subfolders" and "Apply permissions within this container only," we have enabled Windows to create a first-level folder ("%username%") and second-level folders (Documents, Desktop, Profile) on the user's behalf.

**Creator Owner::Allow::Full Control (Apply To: Subfolders and files only).**    This Windows ACE creates a permission template that is applied to the user who creates a file or subfolder. As each folder is created, the user inherits the Creator Owner permission (Full Control) for that folder.

## Provision the permissions of a user data store root folder with UDS_DataRoot_ACL.bat

Those permissions sound complicated, don't they? And they are a bit complicated to configure in the user interface, particularly with all the inheritance tweaks. Sounds like a good place for a script! In the companion media's Scripts folder, I've provided a script called UDS_DataRoot_ACL.bat that applies the permissions I just described to a user data store root folder. Call the script with a parameter that specifies the path to the user data store root folder—for example:

```
UDS_DataRoot_ACL.bat E:\Users
```

Run the script as an administrator of the server. The script is shown next:

```
UDS_DataRoot_ACL.bat
@echo off

:: CONFIGURATION
:: Define the groups that will be given permissions
Set GRP_ADMIN="ACL_User Data and Settings_Admin"
Set GRP_USERS="Authenticated Users"
Set GRP_AUDIT="ACL_User Data and Settings_Audit"

:: Check to see whether usage is requested or required
if "%1"=="?" goto usage
if "%1"=="/?" goto usage
if "%1"=="" goto usage

Set DIRA="%1"
cls
```

```
:: Create the folder
if not exist %DIRA% md %DIRA%

:: Reset folder to defaults in order to get rid of the explicit
:: ACE assigned to the user running this script as the creator
:: of the folder
icacls %DIRA% /reset 1>NUL

:: Attempt to remove inheritance with icacls
:: Requires version of icacls.exe included with
:: Windows Vista SP1 or Windows Server 2008
:: Create a flag to indicate whether or not it worked
set manualinherit=0
icacls %DIRA% /inheritance:r 1>NUL 2>NUL
if errorlevel==1 set manualinherit=1

:: Now assign permissions to the folder

:: CONFIGURATION
:: Customize these lines to reflect your security policy
:: System::Full Control (Apply To: This folder, subfolder, and files
icacls %DIRA% /grant SYSTEM:(OI)(CI)(F) 1>NUL

:: Administrators::Full Control
icacls %DIRA% /grant Administrators:(OI)(CI)(F) 1>NUL

:: Grant Full Control to the group that will administer
:: the user data folders. Also grant Read and Create Folders
:: permissions so that the group can create the first-level
:: subfolders (%%username%%) under the user data root folder
icacls %DIRA% /grant %GRP_ADMIN%:(OI)(CI)(IO)(F) 1>NUL
icacls %DIRA% /grant %GRP_ADMIN%:(NP)(RX,AD) 1>NUL

:: Grant Read permission to a group that represents security auditing
icacls %DIRA% /grant %GRP_AUDIT%:(OI)(CI)(RX) 1>NUL

:: If you are provisioning subfolders for each user so that
:: below the user data root there will be a folder for each
:: user BEFORE the user has a roaming profile or folder redirection
:: policy applied, then users do not need permissions at the user
:: data root itself--they need permissions only to their individual folder.
:: If, however, you want Windows to create the folders for each
:: user, then call the script with the AddUsers

if not "%2"=="AddUsers" goto complete
icacls %DIRA% /grant %GRP_USERS%:(NP)(RX) 1>NUL
icacls %DIRA% /grant %GRP_USERS%:(CI)(NP)(AD) 1>NUL
icacls %DIRA% /grant "CREATOR OWNER":(OI)(CI)(OI)(F) 1>NUL

:complete
if %manualinherit%==1 goto:fixinherit
echo Permissioning of %1 complete.
echo.
echo Resulting permissions for visual confirmation:
```

```
icacls %DIRA%
echo.
goto:eof

:fixinherit
:: Script was unable to remove inheritance with icacls
:: Prompt user to do it manually
echo Unable to remove inheritance using icacls.exe.
echo.
echo Remove inheritance manually.
echo ---------------------------
echo Open the security properties for %DIRA%
echo and click the Advanced button. On the Permissions tab,
echo deselect the check box that allows inheritance from the parent.
echo When prompted to Copy or Remove inherited permissions,
echo choose REMOVE.
echo.
echo Then return to this command prompt and
pause
echo Permissioning of %1 complete.
echo.
echo Resulting permissions for visual confirmation:
icacls %DIRA%
echo.
goto:eof

:: ============================================================================
:: USAGE EXPLANATION
:: ============================================================================
:usage
:: see UDS_DataRoot_ACL.bat for remainder of script
```

The script displays usage if it is called without a folder name or with a help switch, either *?* or */?*. The usage block is at the end of the script and is not displayed in the preceding code block. You can see it in the actual script on the companion media.

The script assigns three variables to represent the group names that are assigned administrative, user, and audit permissions later in the script. Modify those three Set lines to reflect your group names. The script then assigns the path you provide on the command line to a variable, DIRA.

Next, the script creates the folder if it does not already exist and runs *icacls* with the */reset* switch to reset the access control list (ACL) on the folder to the folder's default. This is done to remove any explicit permissions that are assigned to the folder, such as the permission granted to the user who created the folder. Then the script attempts to run *icacls* with the */inheritance* switch to remove inheritance. Because that switch is available only on Windows Server 2008 and Windows Vista SP1, the script checks to see if the command failed and, if so, notifies you that you must manually remove inheritance. To do so, open the Advanced Security Settings dialog box for your user data store root folder and clear the check box that allows inheritance from parent folders. When asked if you want to copy or remove inherited permissions, click Remove.

Then the script runs *icacls* to apply all permissions. The script applies the permissions in exactly the order discussed earlier in this section so that you can visually map our discussion to the permission parameters used by *icacls.*

If you will provision the individual %username% folders underneath the user data store root, users do not require permission to the user data store root. If you are not creating the %username% folders beneath the user data store root, and instead are letting Windows create the folders automatically, call the script with the *AddUsers* switch, and the script will grant necessary permissions to the users group represented by the variable *GRP_USERS* and to Creator Owner.

## Align physical namespace with management requirements such as quotas

It might seem strange that we have created only the user data store root folder (Users) and we're already talking about quotas. But now is the time to do it, because if you read the product documentation, you'll be led to believe that all you have to do is autoapply a quota template to the root folder and life will be beautiful. Not so fast!

First, because we already addressed quotas in Solution Collection 2, let's just review some fundamental concepts about quotas in Windows Server 2003 R2 and Windows Server 2008. Quotas are now folder based. Previously, quotas were volume based, they were applied to a user, and the *Owner* attribute of files was used to determine whether a user had exceeded a configured quota. Now, quotas are folder based. They set a maximum size for the folder regardless of who creates the data.

The new model actually makes sense for more business scenarios than the previous model. And in the context of a UDS scenario, it makes perfect sense to say, "A user can have *x*GB of data available for everyday use and *y*GB of data for archives, but we're not going to put a limit on the user profile—that way, the user profile synchronization won't run into problems." That is, in fact, what you're likely to want to say, if not now, then at some point in the future. If you know you will *never* have quotas, you can skip this discussion of quotas. But who can ever say "never"? The *possibility* of quotas in your future has a significant impact on how you structure your data stores now.

Enormous improvements were made to the management of quotas with Windows Server 2003 R2. First, quotas can have several thresholds, so as certain capacities are reached, warning e-mail messages can be sent, event log entries can be made, reports can be generated, or commands can be run. All of these properties can be stored in quota templates. So you can define a template that says, "Users can have this amount of storage, and here's what's going to happen as they near or reach that capacity." You can apply templates to multiple folders, and (this is my favorite part) if you change the template later, it changes the quotas on all the folders to which you ever applied that template! So if you get additional storage capacity and decide that every user can have 5 GB of additional storage, you can make one change to the template and you're done! Wow!

## Manage quotas collectively for the Desktop and Documents folders

Take a look at your data stores and determine where you will want, at some point in the future, to apply quotas. The first stores that come to mind are Documents and Desktop. Most organizations will, now or in the future, want to control how much data users store on network servers. Here's the first place where Microsoft's quota model doesn't work for us. Desktop and Documents are two separate folders. Do you set a quota on one but not the other? Do you set separate quotas on each? If so, how do you decide how much storage you should allocate for a user's desktop versus the user's Documents folder? You can see that it gets a bit sticky. You'll probably want to have the user's Desktop and Documents folders be subfolders of a single, parent folder. You can thereby apply a quota to the parent folder that manages the combined capacity of both the Desktop and Documents folders. The user can then decide, for himself or herself, how much to put in each user data store. Figure 3-2 shows an example.

**Figure 3-2**   Desktop and Documents folders arranged as subfolders of %username% so that you can apply quotas to %username%

## Create quota templates that give you wiggle room

Contoso, Ltd., has determined that users should be given 1 GB of storage for data in their Documents and Desktop folders. I'll forego the discussion of whether that's too much or too little—you'll need to analyze the current and desired usage levels within your own organization. Users will get e-mail messages as they approach the quota, and event log entries will be made to alert administrators when a user nears capacity. With a hard quota, a user would be unable to store any more data after the 100 percent quota threshold was reached. However, Contoso's IT department decided to give users (and therefore the help desk) some wiggle room, by giving the user a one-time, automatic extension of an additional 100 MB, along with a sternly worded e-mail message. If the user progresses to 1100 MB, the IT department will take a "no more Mr. Nice Guy" approach and additional storage will be prevented.

You can easily achieve this model by creating a custom quota template. Each new template you create can be a copy of an existing template. Windows Server 2008 includes two templates: "200 MB Limit with 50 MB Extension" and "250 MB Extended Limit." Just copy these two templates and modify their properties for the limits that are appropriate for your organization. Contoso's two templates are called "1 GB User Data Storage Limit with 100 MB Extension" and "1.1 GB Extended User Data Storage Limit."

The real magic of this model occurs in the first template—the one with the "Extension." In that template, when the 100 percent threshold is reached, a command is launched. The command is the dirquota.exe command, which is the command-line management tool for quotas. Specifically, the command shown in Figure 3-3 is executed:

```
%windir%\system32\dirquota.exe quota modify /path:[Quota Path]
    /sourcetemplate:"1.1 GB Extended User Data Storage Limit"
```

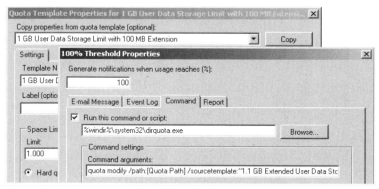

**Figure 3-3**    Quota template that executes Dirquota to apply a new template

The *dirquota quota modify* command changes the quota applied to a folder. The folder is represented by *[Quota Path]*. This is a variable that is replaced in real time by the server to the path that has reached capacity. The */sourcetemplate* parameter indicates the name of the template that should now be applied.

This is a slick approach, and the idea of chaining templates like this will come back to help us later.

## Autoapply quota templates

Here's the part that everyone likes to talk about (and that might not be all it's cracked up to be): autoapplication of templates. The idea is that you can configure a quota at the user data store root folder (Users) that will automatically apply quotas as each new subfolder is created. The configuration is shown in Figure 3-4. Specify the path of the root folder (E:\Users), specify the template to apply ("1 GB User Data Storage Limit with 100 MB Extension"), and be sure to select the Auto Apply Template And Create Quotas On Existing And New Subfolders option.

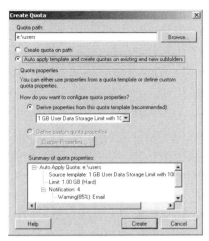

**Figure 3-4**  Autoapply a quota template

As I mentioned earlier, and as you probably know, if you configure a user for roaming profiles or redirected folders—for example, \\*namespace*\\*path*\\%username%\[documents | desktop | profile | etc.]—Windows creates the subfolders it needs to create. So if the *only* folder you have is E:\Users shared as Users$, and James Fine's Documents and Desktop folders are redirected to \\server01\users$\jfine\documents and \desktop when he logs on, Windows will create the jfine folder and the Documents and Desktop subfolders. The 1-GB quota template will automatically be applied to the jfine folder. The Desktop and Documents folders will be subject to that limit in their combined storage.

## Do not configure quotas for roaming profile stores

Along with the Documents and Desktop folders, a user's Application Data folder is a critical data store. This folder structure is likely to remain within the user profile for reasons we'll get to in later Solution Collections. The roaming user profile also contains the user's registry, Ntuser.dat. And it is likely to contain Favorites.

All of those folders, together, do not add up to a lot of storage space. I'm a power user on Windows Vista and my AppData\Roaming folder, Favorites, and Ntuser.dat files add up to less than 40 MB. That's not enough storage to warrant managing. Additionally, putting quota limits of any kind on a folder that hosts the registry hive of a roaming profile can lead to the possibility that, if the folder has reached its quota, the Ntuser.dat file might not be saved correctly. I suggest that there's too much at risk to put hard quotas on roaming profile folders.

Now you might choose to put *soft* quotas on profile folders. Soft quotas enable you to configure thresholds with e-mail messages, event log entries, reports, and commands—just like hard quotas. They just don't actually stop the user from storing data beyond the 100 percent threshold. So soft quotas might help you to monitor usage and watch for any unusual situations. But I think that as long as your roaming profiles do not contain user *data* stores—and instead contain only user *settings*—you're better served applying your energy to managing larger and more problematic stores than the roaming profile.

## Understand the problem with placement of profiles and other data stores

I've suggested you keep Desktop and Documents underneath a folder that has a single quota applied so that the user's combined storage in those two folders are managed with one limit. I also suggested that the parent folder should be the %username% folder (which will make configuration of folder redirection straightforward). But what if we want to put the user profile in the same physical folder namespace? What if we want our folders to look like Figure 3-5?

**Figure 3-5**   Documents, Desktop, and Profile underneath the %username% folder

This is a commonly envisioned structure. But there's a problem. If the quota applies to the %username% folder, now the Profile folder is part of that quota. That means we could end up in a situation where profile data cannot be stored, and that could be a problem! Add to the problem that there will be a Backups folder and, for any user who uses both Windows Vista and Windows XP systems, *two* user profile folders, as shown in Figure 3-6. Now the problem is easier to summarize: How do we manage the combined quota for Desktop and Documents if there are other folders at the same level of the physical namespace?

**Figure 3-6**   User data and settings namespace

> **Important**   The autoapply template functionality that automatically applies a template from the Users folder to the %username% folders does not align with a natural user data and settings folder namespace, in which a single folder for a user contains all of the user's data stores.

## Solution #1: Separate physical namespaces for different classes of data stores

This is where the concept of "classes of data stores" is first put to use. In Solution 3-2, I referred to classes of data (documents or settings) as items that share common requirements and therefore common management tools and processes. E-mail archives are a class of data. Users' music collections are another class of data. In this solution, I extend that concept to classes of data *stores*—entire stores of data that share common requirements and therefore are managed similarly. As an example, two user data stores—Desktop and Documents—will contain similar classes of data, specifically documents that are accessed directly by the user. Those two user data stores will be in separate physical data stores (separate folders) on a server, but they will likely be managed identically—with redirection, for example. For that reason, I refer to those stores as belonging to a *class* of (redirected) stores.

We now have a very salient example of this concept: One class of data store includes Desktop and Documents and is subject to a single quota template. Another class of data store (profiles) is subject to different, quota-free management.

If you want to use the autoapply quota template functionality, you need to separate top-level folders for these namespaces, as shown in Figure 3-7. The top-level folders named Users and Backups are configured to automatically apply appropriate quota templates to each %username% folder. The top-level Profiles folder either has no quota configuration or will autoapply a quota template with a soft quota that does not prevent storage past the 100 percent threshold.

**Figure 3-7**  Using separate namespaces for classes of data stores that are subject to diverse quotas

How many subfolders you have depends on how many data stores are part of each class of data store. User data, for example, is in two data stores: Desktop and Documents. These need to be subfolders of a single parent to support quota application with the autoapply functionality. On the other hand, if the Backup folder is the only data store for a user in the Backups namespace, you can get away without the subfolder, right? This is shown on the right side of Figure 3-7.

If there's any chance that users with a roaming profile might log on to Windows Vista and Windows XP machines in the course of their existence in your enterprise, it is wise to plan for the two separate profiles required for the two operating systems. The namespace can be provided as two separate folders under the %username% folder as shown on the left side of Figure 3-7, in which case the profile path property of users is set to \\*namespace*\*path*\%username%\profile. Alternatively, you can create users' two profiles as two folders with a user's name: %username% and %username%.v2. This is shown on the right side of the figure. The user object's profile path property is set to \\*namespace*\*path*\%username%. In either case, Windows Vista adds the ".V2" extension automatically. You do not need to, and should not, specify it yourself in the profile path of the user.

**The advantages**    The primary advantage of using separate physical namespaces for the different classes of data stores is that you can leverage automated management features. In the context of the current discussion, that means you can leverage the autoapply quota template feature. But there are likely to be other management tasks that are easier to accomplish if all data that shares the same management is in one place. Kind of makes sense, huh? Group similarly managed items together and you can manage them more easily. File screens, which allow you to specify what *types* of files users can store in a specific folder and are managed with templates in much the same way you manage quotas, are also easier to apply if you have grouped data together that is managed similarly. Later, we'll talk about a minor potential conflict between roaming profiles and offline files. Having profile stores, which should not allow caching, in a separate physical namespace from redirected folders facilitates managing that conflict.

> **Important**    Either physical namespace shown in Figure 3-7 allows you to use the feature to automatically apply quota templates for each %username% subfolder. Using separate physical namespaces for different classes of data stores facilitates managing those stores.

**The disadvantages**    The disadvantages of separate physical namespaces for different classes of data stores fall into two categories. The first category is cosmetic. Administrators don't like to see a single user's data in several places, as it is in Figure 3-7. I have two thoughts about that concern. The first is that you can abstract the physical storage namespace into a logical view of user data stores, such as that shown in Figure 3-8 (a figure that should be starting to look very familiar to you now!). Using DFS namespaces, you can present an organized, rational, logical—whatever you want to call it—view of your physical namespace. We'll talk more about that in just a bit. The only time you have to see the physical namespace is if you are connected to the server with Remote Desktop and look at the disk volume with Windows Explorer, or if you navigate to a parent folder, such as the hidden drive share (for example, E$) and drill down from there.

**Figure 3-8**    User data and settings namespace

My second thought about the "look" of diverse namespaces is that it's much more important that you can *manage* the data effectively. I know we are all used to thinking about "User Y's data" versus "User X's data." But when you look at data management tasks—such as security, quotas, offline use, synchronization, and so on—you find that there are more commonalities *across* users' data stores than *within* a single user's data stores. In other words, you're more likely to manage the music collections of User X and User Y the same way (for example, keep them off your servers) than you are to manage different classes of data for one user the same way (for example, you will probably not manage User X's music collection and her e-mail archives the same way).

So, to make a long explanation short, if you're concerned about how the physical namespace looks, I respectfully suggest you try to get over it.

There's a second challenge of working with separate classes of data stores. That is how, exactly, do you define and manage which data stores go in which class? What we've presented so far seems easy: Desktop and Documents as one data store, Profiles as another, Backups as a third. But there won't be just three. What about those e-mail archives? Are those managed the exact same way as Desktop and Documents? Or are they part of Backups? Or are they managed yet another way? You could easily end up with lots of different classes of data stores and therefore lots of root folders for those data stores.

**Working around the disadvantages**    DFS namespaces help you to present the physical namespace, based on data store classes, in a user-based logical namespace. There isn't really a workaround to help you add a new class of data stores in a slick, easy way. It will just have to be done.

## Solution #2: Manage individual data stores rather than data store classes

It gets complicated, doesn't it? So let's look at an alternative. The alternative is to keep the data stores for a user under a single parent folder, %username%, and then to manage the individual data stores. The result will look like Figure 3-9.

**Figure 3-9**    Data stores managed under %username%

Note that we've now recognized that Desktop and Documents are really components of a single data store of user data by placing them as subfolders of a Data folder. The Data folder will, of course, have the quota for the combined storage of the two subfolders. The advantages and disadvantages of the solution are the opposite of Solution #1.

By the time we're finished with this solution, we'll recognize that other data stores exist that you might want to store on the server and include in users' data quotas. As you include more user data stores, the single user namespace will end up looking more like Figure 3-10.

**Figure 3-10**    Additional data stores managed under %username%

**The advantages**    It now is easy to locate and work with a user's data stores within the physical namespace on the server. You also won't have problems with proliferation of classes of data stores. You'll be able to add new data stores within the single user-based namespace.

**The disadvantages**    However, you lose some of the automated management features that apply rules like umbrellas. There are few rules other than security permissions that you will apply to the %username% folder. You now have to manage James's Documents folder as a specific subfolder of James's folder, and Lorrin's Documents folder as a specific subfolder of Lorrin's folder.

**Working around the disadvantages**    To work around the disadvantage of having to manage items individually, you need to work to automate and provision the life cycle of those items.

### My recommendation

Throughout this book, you've heard and will hear me talk about automation and provisioning. I think it is the keystone to administrative productivity. So guess what? I recommend Solution #2. By building tools that automate the management of items, you have the ability to change those tools over time as your business requirements change. Microsoft's built-in management tools might allow you to automatically apply quota templates in a certain way that fits today. But if you build your framework around a technology you don't control, and that technology changes or your business requirements move away from the model supported by that technology, you are left high and dry.

## Provision the creation of data stores

There will be many reasons why you'll want to provision the creation of user data and settings stores. Let's use quota management as a first example and start building a solution that provisions a user's folders, including permissions, ownership, and quotas.

## Use the UDS_UserFolders_Provision.vbs script

In the Scripts folder of the companion media, you'll find several scripts that provision user data folders. The most sophisticated, and therefore the script you will probably want to use, is UDS_UserFolders_Extended_Provision_DFS.vbs. We will build up to that script from a more modest starting point: UDS_UserFolders_Provision.vbs.. You call this script with a single argument: the path to the %username% folder—for example:

```
cscript UDS_UserFolders_Provision.vbs e:\users\username
```

The script assumes that the last folder in the folder path is a username and that a user with the equivalent pre–Windows 2000 logon name already exists. It generates all subfolders to create the namespace shown in Figure 3-9. Along the way, it also does the following:

- Applies a quota to the Data folder, which contains Desktop and Documents. The quota template must already be defined.

- Ensures inheritance is enabled for the %username% folder and the Profiles folders. This is to overcome a bug-like behavior of roaming profile folder creation that we'll discuss later in the Solution Collection.

- Gives the user ownership of the %username% folder tree. Because the script will run under credentials other than the user's, the owner will be the account that executes the script. So at the very end of the script, ownership is given to the user.

There are some important notes about the script:

- Icacls.exe is used to assign ownership to the user. You must execute the script from a system running Windows Server 2008 or Windows Vista SP1 because the version of icacls.exe on other platforms does not perform the */setowner* command correctly.

- You can run the script remotely against either a Windows Server 2008 or Windows Server 2003 server, but the credentials with which you launch the script must have permissions to create the specified folder and Full Control permission of that folder and its subfolders. Additionally, the credentials must have the user right to Restore Files And Directories in order to successfully assign ownership to the user.

- You can also run the script directly on a Windows Server 2008 system as a member of the Administrators group if you are logged on locally or using Remote Desktop.

The script should be easy to follow if you have some scripting knowledge. There is a small block of code for each subfolder that, with an IF/THEN structure, creates each subfolder and, if the creation was successful, performs any management of that subfolder. Management tasks, such as setting a quota on the Data subfolder, are executed using command-line tools such as dirquota.exe.

> **Note**   See Solution 3-5 on page 224 for a script that generates all namespaces for a user: the NTFS folders (including quotas), the SMB shares, and the DFS namespace. It takes UDS_ UserFolders_Provision.vbs to the next level.

## Configure file screens

If your information security or information technology usage policies prohibit certain file types from being stored on network file servers, you might choose to implement file screens, which are supported in Windows Server 2003 R2 and Windows Server 2008. File screens are associated with a folder, and they determine what file extensions are prohibited and what actions to take if a user attempts to save a file of those types. The Windows documentation steps you through the process of creating file screens. The concepts are similar to quotas. You can configure templates, which specify the actions to take based on file types. Actions can include e-mail messages, reports, event log entries, or commands (just like quota thresholds). Templates can then be applied to folders. And there's a command-line tool, filescrn.exe, to manage the process as well as the GUI snap-ins and consoles.

## Solution summary

We've touched on a few points that I'd like to call out specifically regarding the physical namespace of user data stores on UDS servers:

- Before creating your physical namespace, consider the need to manage data stores. Do you want to separate different classes of data stores into unique namespaces as shown in Figure 3-7, or do you want to keep user data stores in a user-centric namespace as seen in Figure 3-9 and Figure 3-10? You might need more than one user data store root folder.

- You need to create and secure the user data store root folder (Users) with least-privilege permissions.

- By provisioning the %username% folder, at least, you can avoid giving any users permission to the Users folder—their right to Bypass Traverse Checking will enable them to reach their %username% folders.

- The UDS_UsersFolder_Provision script creates the %username% folder and all subfolders.

- Each user must have permission to his or her %username% folder. Specifically, the user should have Full Control and should be the Owner.

- Roaming profiles have an odd behavior. If a user's profile path points to \\*namespace*\ *path*\%username%\profile and the %username% folder does not yet exist, Windows creates the path correctly, but it turns off inheritance on the folders *and* it ignores the Group Policy setting Add The Administrators Security Group To Roaming User Profiles. The effect of this is that administrators are locked out entirely. You need to make sure at a bare minimum that the parent folder of the profile (%username%, in this case) is created, that inheritance is on, that the user is the owner, and that the user has Full Control permissions. Yet another reason to use the kind of provisioning scripts and tricks I've presented here.

■ The physical namespace does not need to be the namespace you present to the world. There is an SMB namespace and a DFS namespace yet to be built in the next solution.

With all those variables in the mix, the resulting recommended physical namespace for user data stores is something like *volume*:\Users\%username%[\*data store class*]\*data store*—for example, E:\Users\jfine\Profile or E:\Users\jfine\Data\Documents. The *data store class* component of the namespace was determined to be particularly necessary for Desktop and Documents, which generally need to be managed with a single cumulative quota.

# 3-4: Create the SMB and DFS Namespaces for User Data Stores

## Solution overview

| | |
|---|---|
| **Type of solution** | Guidance and scripts |
| **Features and tools** | DFS namespaces, shared folders |
| **Solution summary** | Design an SMB namespace and DFS namespace that will serve your organization's user data and settings requirements, and automate the creation of the namespaces for each user. |
| **Benefits** | Identify and thereby avoid common design mistakes that can increase the cost of supporting an agile environment. |

## Introduction

In the previous solution, we built the namespace for user data stores on the server—the physical namespace of NTFS folders. We learned that it could become necessary to separate user data stores into separate namespaces to support management that takes place at the NTFS folder level, such as quota management. We also learned the alternative was to automate and provision a user's data stores so that we could manage each one appropriately while still maintaining a user-centric physical namespace. The resulting physical namespace for user data stores was something like *volume*:\Users\%username%[\*data store class*]\*data store*—for example, E:\Users\jfine\Profile or E:\Users\jfine\Data\Documents.

We now move "up" a layer to the SMB namespace to determine what folders need to be shared and with what SMB settings; and we move even "higher" to the DFS namespace, which allows us to present our physical and SMB namespaces in whatever logical fashion meets our business requirements.

# Create the SMB namespace for user data and settings stores

Most organizations create a single SMB share for the user data store root, and often it has a simple share name such as "Users." With Windows 2000 and later clients able to map drives and connect below a share, there is no need to share each user's folder as there was in Windows NT 4.0. I do recommend hiding the Users share by adding a dollar sign ($) to the share name—for example, Users$.

However, one share is not enough. As we discussed in Solution Collection 2, SMB shares control connection settings, the most important of which is caching settings. You'll probably want to allow data and settings in redirected folders (such as Desktop and Documents) to be cached for offline use. But I expect you will not want the network backup of user's Local Files (the Backups folder) to be cached, as that goes against the whole purpose of local files. Also, it's very important that the files in the server copy of the user's roaming profile are never taken offline, because the synchronization mechanisms of offline files and of roaming profiles can cause problems with each other.

## Understand the undesirable interaction between roaming profiles and offline files

Solution 3-6 discusses Offline Files in detail. The Offline Files feature enables you to cache a copy of files from a network (SMB or DFS) namespace. It is a powerful and useful feature for user data stores such as Desktop and Documents, and it works very well *if* you design and implement it correctly. By default, a user can *pin* (make available offline) any file from any share on a Windows server.

Unfortunately, there are certain data stores that users should *not* be allowed to take offline. The server copy of a user's roaming profile is one of those stores. Because roaming profiles synchronize with a different mechanism than offline files, there can be conflicts if a system caches roaming profile items as offline files. I'll refer to this as the "cached copy of the roaming profile problem."

For more information, see the following three Knowledge Base articles on Microsoft's Support site (*http://support.microsoft.com*): 842007, 287566, and 325838. As the final article in the list explains, Microsoft thinks this problem is significant enough that Windows clients generate an event log warning (Event ID 1525) at each logon if Offline Caching is enabled on the roaming profile share.

## Design an SMB namespace that avoids the cached copy of the roaming profile problem

Because you can disable caching only at the share level and you have more than one configuration that you must implement, you'll need more than one SMB shared folder. In fact, you should create three SMB shared folders for each of these classes of data stores: profiles, redirected folders, and backups. You might decide to store profiles in a completely separate *physical* namespace, as in Figure 3-7, but that is not a requirement. Luckily, you can share a single NTFS folder multiple times, so the user data store root folder (Users) can be shared three times with appropriate configurations for each share. In other words, we'll share the exact same physical folder (E:\Users, for example) as Users$ (with caching enabled), Profiles$ (with caching disabled), and Backups$ (with caching disabled).

## Provision the creation of SMB shares for a user data store root

The script named UDS_DataRoot_Share.bat in the Scripts folder of the companion media creates the SMB shares we just discussed. Call the script with a parameter that specifies the path to the user data store root folder—for example:

```
UDS_DataRoot_Share.bat E:\Users
```

The script is presented in its entirety next. Simply customize the *Set* statements that reflect the names you want to apply for each share.

### UDS_DataRoot_Share.bat

```
@echo off

:: Check to see whether usage is requested or required
if "%1"=="?" goto usage
if "%1"=="/?" goto usage
if "%1"=="" goto usage

Set UserRoot="%1"
Set UserDataShare=users$
Set UserProfileShare=profiles$
Set UserBackupShare=backups$

cls
echo Creating User Data Root Shares

net share %UserDataShare%="%UserRoot%" /GRANT:Everyone,Full /CACHE:Manual
    /REMARK:"Root data share for all user data stores. Allows offline files."
net share %UserProfileShare%="%UserRoot%" /GRANT:Everyone,Full /CACHE:None
    /REMARK:"Root share for all user profiles. Does not allow offline files."
net share %UserBackupShare%="%UserRoot%" /GRANT:Everyone,Full /CACHE:None
    /REMARK:"Root share for all user backups. Does not allow offline files."

echo User Data Store Root Shares Created

goto:eof


:: =======================================================================
:: USAGE EXPLANATION
:: =======================================================================
:usage
:: see script for usage block
```

The *net share* commands used in the batch file create the share, apply the Everyone::Allow:: Full Control share permission, and configure caching settings for the share. Note the Backups$ and Profiles$ shares have identical caching settings. You could certainly get by with only one SMB share because of that. I simply prefer to have an SMB share for each class of data store even though the latter two (Backups and Profiles) share identical settings.

## Understand how a separate SMB namespace for profiles can prevent the cached copy of the roaming profile problem

We have created a best practice structure for the physical and SMB namespaces of our network data stores. But best practice does not mean "perfect from every perspective." We have designed our structure with one known weakness.

All data stores are under a common root, and that root is shared three times. Each share has caching settings configured. So a user whose Documents and Desktop folders are redirected to \\\\*servername*\\users$\\%username%\\[documents *or* desktop] will be allowed by the users$ share to take files offline. The user profile path directs to \\\\*servername*\\profiles$\\%username%\\profile.

As we discussed earlier, it's important not to allow items in the server copy of a user's profile to be taken offline. In this design, we've prevented that from happening because the profiles$ share has caching disabled.

A user could, theoretically, use Windows Explorer to navigate to \\\\*servername*\\users$\\%username%\\profiles and thereby get into his profile through the users$ share. Because that share allows files to be cached, the user could take a file from the profile offline. The very good news is that even though the file physically exists in the server copy of the roaming profile, to the client the file in the *users$* namespace is not in the same namespace as the roaming profile (profiles$). So the problem of potential synchronization conflicts is minimized. I imagine, however, that there are ways a particularly knowledgeable and malicious user could mess up his own profile if he tried hard enough. That's why our design is not "perfect from every perspective."

The alternative is to put users' profiles under a completely different *physical* root and share that root only once with caching disabled. But then there is a disjointed namespace for user data stores: Profiles are in one place, and everything else is in another. And most administrators I've met want to see all of a user's data in one place. So that approach isn't perfect from every perspective, either.

I recommend the approach we've built because it is simple, discoverable, effective, and resilient against all but the most intentional troublemaking. Finally, some IT pros have suggested to me that a user who goes that far out of line deserves to stay on hold with the help desk when such actions cause the computer to have hiccoughs. Luckily, NTFS permissions ensure that even a disruptive user can wreak havoc only on her own data and settings stores, not those of other users.

# Design the logical view of user data and settings stores with DFS Namespaces

DFS Namespaces, discussed in Solution Collection 2, allow you to create a logical or virtual view of enterprise resources. If you're not familiar with the distributed file system (DFS), you should read up about it. It plays critical roles in managing user data and settings. The first such role is to provide a logical view of user data and settings stores—one that is user-centric, not server-centric.

There are several design options for this logical view that I'll present to you. Each has advantages and disadvantages.

## Create a fully enumerated DFS namespace for user data and settings stores (DFS Design Option 1)

In this DFS namespace design, you create a DFS namespace folder for each user data store. There is a DFS folder for the user and subfolders for each of the user's stores. An example is shown in Figure 3-11.

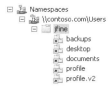

**Figure 3-11**    A fully enumerated DFS namespace creates a rational, logical view of all user data and settings stores

The path to a user's data store is quite rational: \\*domain*\\*dfs namespace*\\*username*\\*store*. For example, the path to James Fine's redirected Documents folder is \\contoso.com\users\jfine\documents. The path to which all users' desktops are redirected is, simply, \\contoso.com\users\%username%\desktop. The lowest-level folders in the namespace represent the data and settings stores, and they link to the physical store using a UNC through the UDS server's namespace. For example, the link targeted by James's documents folder is \\server01\users$\jfine\documents.

**Advantages**    The great advantage of this design is that you can easily move an individual physical data store for a user. Simply change the target of the DFS folder. No changes need to be made to Group Policy settings, user account attributes, group memberships, or anything else. That's agility!

Another key advantage is that the subfolders can target the correct SMB namespaces. The Profile and Backups folders in Figure 3-11 target the Profiles$ and Backups$ shares on SERVER01, which disable caching. The Documents and Desktops folders, however, target the Users$ share on SERVER01, which enables caching. Those two disparate SMB namespaces are rationalized into a single namespace that is focused on the user, represented by the user folder in the DFS namespace.

**Disadvantages**    There are a couple of disadvantages to this approach, however.

First, you must create the DFS namespace folders *prior* to configuring either the user's profile or the Group Policy redirected folder settings so that the namespace used by those paths exist before Windows clients attempt to access them. Second, Windows cannot automatically create all folders as it can with the other DFS namespace design options I'll discuss—you must create a few of the physical folders on the UDS server to host certain user data stores. In the previous solution, I created a script that provisioned the physical folders, and in this solution I'll extend that script to create a provisioning script that accomplishes all the steps so easily that you'll have no problem generating a powerful, agile, fully enumerated DFS namespace. Having a provisioned process that automates the many steps required to create a fully enumerated DFS namespace will address these two disadvantages.

However, there is one more technical challenge. On Windows Server 2003, DFS namespaces support only up to 5000 folders with targets. Because each user might have multiple subfolders that target data stores, you'll find yourself limited to 1000 to 2000 users. But I have some answers for that limit later in this solution, as well.

## Create a DFS namespace that redirects to each SMB namespace for the user data store root share (DFS Design Option 2)

The next alternative is to create a DFS namespace that targets each SMB share for the user data store roots on the UDS servers. Figure 3-12 shows the result.

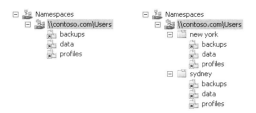

**Figure 3-12**    DFS namespaces that target root shared folders in the SMB namespace

On the left side of Figure 3-12, a DFS folder is created to point to each share (Users$, Profiles$, and Backups$). The DFS namespace thus ensures that users are accessing their resources through the shares that configure appropriate caching settings. A user's redirected documents folder is targeted to \\contoso.com\users\data\%username%\data\documents; and the roaming profile points to \\contoso.com\users\profiles\%username%\profile. The names looks a bit redundant, but remember you are traversing through two namespaces: The first "data" or "profiles" folder is the DFS namespace folder targeting the user data store root on SERVER01. The second "data" or "profile" folder is the actual subfolder underneath the top-level %username% folder—it's within the SMB or physical namespace. Refer to earlier figures that portray the *physical* namespace (folder hierarchy) on the server if you need to review. If you have only one UDS server, you can get by with the structure shown on the left of Figure 3-13.

If you have more than one UDS server, you need to group or organize the links, as suggested in the screen shot on the right side of Figure 3-12, which extends the namespace with parent DFS folders representing geographic sites. The resulting structure is one that is typical for many existing implementations, but I do *not* recommend it, for reasons detailed later in this solution.

> **Important** Figure 3-12 shows a *common*, but problematic, namespace on the right. Do *not* use sites or other real-world constructs in your DFS namespaces, for reasons I will discuss momentarily.

**Advantages** Because there are far fewer DFS folders, you will not have a problem supporting thousands of users. The %username% component of the resulting namespace is not within the DFS namespace; it's within the SMB (and physical) namespace.

**Disadvantages** Because the user folder and user store folder are no longer within the DFS namespace, you lose the management advantages of the DFS namespace. If you have to move a user's data stores, physically, to another server, you now have to adjust the elements that configure the user's experience: The folder targets of folder redirection Group Policy settings, the user's profile path, and any shortcuts or other pointers through the original DFS namespace.

### Compare DFS design options

Design Option 1 (the fully enumerated DFS namespace) provides the best support for a UDS framework, as long as you have a tool to automate the creation of the namespace and a plan for how to deal with more than 1000 to 2000 users until you are operating with Windows Server 2008 DFS namespaces, as discussed in the next section. Option 2, because it has fewer folders with targets, can support an unlimited number of users. Before you choose your design, consider the remaining pointers about DFS in this section.

## Build a DFS namespace to support thousands of users

Windows Server 2003 DFS namespaces are limited to 5000 links. What happens when you have more than 5000 links? Well, you could upgrade to Windows Server 2008 namespaces, which require Windows Server 2008 domain functional level and Windows Server 2008 DFS namespace servers. Windows Server 2008 does not have a technical limit to the number of links it supports in a DFS namespace. You simply have to monitor performance.

Or you could create new namespaces! In Windows Server 2003, each domain namespace can contain 5000 links, so you could have the following three DFS namespaces:

- \\contoso.com\usersa
- \\contoso.com\usersb
- \\contoso.com\usersc

Now each top-level namespace can contain up to 5000 links. Beneath each namespace you could implement Design Option 1, which contains the full path to the user's data store within the DFS namespace.

You would have security groups that contain the users who belong in each namespace, and you could use those security groups to configure folder redirection for those users through the appropriate namespace. Users are added to one group as they join the organization. As one group fills up, you begin to fill the next one. Alternatively, your namespaces might be based on employee numbers, making the groups and namespaces less arbitrary and facilitating the finding of users' data stores through DFS. Here's an example:

- \\contoso.com\users1xxx contains employees with IDs starting with 1.
- \\contoso.com\users2xxx contains employees with IDs starting with 2.
- \\contoso.com\users3xxx contains employees with IDs starting with 3.

> **Important**    Notice what I'm *not* using as groupings in my DFS namespace examples: sites, business units, or any other business construct. See the next sections for an explanation of why those elements should *not* be in your DFS namespace.

## Understand the impact of data movement and namespace changes

There are a number of pointers in your UDS framework that refer to specific data stores:

- The roaming profile path in the user account (the user object's *ProfilePath* attribute)
- Paths to targets of redirected folders, as configured in Folder Redirection policy settings

By using a fully enumerated DFS namespace (Option 1), each of the references to data stores can be abstracted from the physical stores. In the case of a redirected folder targeting a DFS namespace, the path might be something like \\contoso.com\users\jfine\documents. The redirected folder configuration is not dependent upon whether the physical data store is on SERVER01 in New York or SERVER02 in Sydney. In fact, if you moved the documents folder for jfine from New York to Sydney, you would only have to update the link targets of the DFS Namespace folder. You would not have to change any configuration in the user object, in GPOs, or anywhere else. That's one fantastic reason to use DFS.

However, that would be possible only with Design Option 1. Design Option 2 sets out a DFS namespace that goes only as deep as a folder that links to a specific server. The remainder of the path to the store is part of the SMB and physical namespaces. So with Design Option 2, if you moved James's data from SERVER01 in New York to SERVER02 in Sydney, you would be changing not the targets of DFS namespace folders, but the actual namespace within which James's data lives. You would have to change the pointers that configure James's environment. Roaming profiles would have to be changed from \\contoso.com\users\new york\jfine\profile to \\contoso.com\users\sydney\jfine\profile. Likewise, redirected folders would have to be configured to the new DFS namespace path.

But unfortunately, there are a lot of other more complex and painful configuration references and pointers you need to update from the previous namespace to the new namespace if you implement Design Option 2:

**Source paths of offline files**   The files in the cache are associated with the namespace from which the files were taken offline. If the namespace of the source files change, you must adjust those files so that they are associated with the new namespace; otherwise, Windows assumes they are different files altogether, from different sources, and the user will have to synchronize all the files from the new namespace. This issue is discussed later in this solution.

**Paths in custom tools**   Any custom tools that point to paths in the previous namespace will have to be updated. An example is the backup script built in Solution 3-10.

**Paths used in applications, by shortcuts, by mapped drives, and so on**   When a user's data is moved, it's highly likely that a number of references to that data will need to be updated, including the targets of shortcuts and mapped drives.

**Paths for links within and between documents**   For example, if a user has linked a Microsoft Office Excel worksheet to a PowerPoint presentation, the full path to the worksheet is stored within the presentation. If the namespace of that worksheet changes, you must update the presentation.

These references, particularly those discussed in the last bullet, are the most painful part of changing the namespace of a user's data—whether to another folder, another server, another share, or another DFS namespace.

The lesson to take away from this issue is that if you have a component in your DFS namespace path that might change over time, it will increase management effort. The most obvious example is a site-based DFS namespace such as that in Design Option 2. If a site name is part of a DFS namespace path—for example, \\contoso.com\users\new york\%username%\...—and changes to users' data or settings result in that site changing—for example, to \\contsoso.com\users\sydney\%username%—you have work to do to update user profile paths, change GPOs that configure redirection, tweak the client's offline cache, and locate and change all other embedded references to the previous namespace.

> **Important**    When using Design Option 1, changing the physical location of a user's data stores requires only that you change the targets of folders in the DFS namespace. Design Option 2 requires you to update all client-side references to the DFS namespace, which has an impact on applications and offline files as well.

## Consider the impact of %username% changes

We just addressed the important point that if the DFS namespace path to a user's data and settings changes, you have to change user attributes (specifically, the profile path), GPOs used to configure redirected folders, and many other client-side references as well. Any files that have been taken offline have to be rebuilt (Windows XP) or renamed with a script (Windows Vista). All of that is really fun to undertake...if you're paid by the hour.

But we've been making one very big assumption in our examples: that "%username%" translates to an actual user name, such as "jfine." If that's true, what if jfine's user name changes? It happens all the time: Think "marriage."

A change to a user logon name (pre–Windows 2000 logon name or *sAMAccountName*) has a significant impact on your infrastructure. It changes the namespace of *everything*. Redirection with Group Policy uses the %username% variable, so if the user logs on with a new name, the system will not find the old folder name—it will build new ones. So before your user logs on for the first time with the new logon name, you must do the following:

**Change DFS namespace folders.**    With Design Options 1 and 2, which include the user name in the DFS namespace, you need to change the names of DFS folders to reflect the new user name.

**Change the name of the physical NTFS folder that roots the user's data and settings stores.**
With DFS Namespace Design Option 2, which targets the user data store root, the change to the user name must be made to the actual NTFS folder on the user's UDS server.

**Change all other references to the previous namespace.**    As mentioned earlier, this means you must update all shortcuts, mapped drives, offline files, and, most problematically, links within and between documents that reference the previous namespace.

**Change attributes such as the *ProfilePath*.**    The roaming profile path is hard-coded in the user account. It will remain as the *old* path, which would work except that you had to rename the DFS or NTFS folder to the new user name because of redirection.

You do not need to rename the *local* user profile folder. Windows maintains a mapping between the security identifier (SID) of the user account and the folder that contains the local copy of the roaming profile. So even though the user logs on with the new name, Windows recognizes the SID and loads the correct profile.

However, not all applications are coded properly. Some applications and scripts look for the user's profile using the %username% variable rather than the %userprofile% variable. Those applications will look in the wrong place. So although you aren't forced by Windows to rename the local user profile, you might need to take action based on your applications.

Note that if you do rename the local user profile folder, you must also update the pointer to the profile in the registry. SID-to-Profile mappings are maintained in HKEY_LOCAL_ MACHINE\Software\Microsoft\Windows NT\CurrentVersion\ProfileList. Find the key that points to the profile with its old name and update it.

All of this discussion is to emphasize, again, how simple changes such as a new logon name can cause management headaches. For that reason, as discussed in Solution Collection 7, "Extending User Attributes and Management Tools," I highly encourage you to create a single-sign-on (SSO) type of logon name for your users, based on something neutral and unique—such as a payroll or Human Resources identification number. It appears less personal than a name-based logon, but it helps reduce management headaches from name changes, not to mention from scenarios in which two users have identical names.

**Important** Consider implementing pre–Windows 2000 logon names that are not based on the users' legal names, but rather on an abstract and unchanging construct such as Employee ID numbers.

I'd like to mention some pointers that we'll discuss again in Solution Collection 7. First, it is the pre–Windows 2000 logon name that is at issue. Remember that Windows supports authentication with the User Principal Name (UPN), which can be *anything* as long as it's unique. It could even be the user's e-mail address. So the UPN can become your user-friendly, name-based logon name.

Also, I've run into a number of clients that consider name changes only in the context of marriage. Their idea is, "If Jane gets married, she won't mind continuing to use the logon name based on her maiden name." That might be true, or it might not be. But consider also: divorce. Is it likely that Jane, if hired while already married, will want to continue to use her logon name based on her married name after a nasty split? Probably not.

## Build an abstract DFS namespace for user data and settings (no site-based namespace, preferably no human names)

In a complex organization with more than one UDS server, geographic site, or business unit, you might be tempted to create a DFS namespace for your UDS framework that reflects those entities. For example, Figure 3-12, on the right, proposes a site-based DFS hierarchy.

**Important** Including a site, business unit, or other business construct as part of your DFS namespace is highly discouraged!

We've discussed the challenges that arise when any part of the namespace to a file or folder changes; and the challenges grow logarithmically as you look at changing the namespace for entire data stores or classes of data stores.

Create a DFS namespace with abstract elements. Don't use sites, business units, or other elements that will change. And consider basing user logon names on employee numbers rather than names to avoid changes at the %username% level.

# Automate and provision the creation of user data stores and DFS namespaces

In Solution 3-2, I developed the UDS_UserFolders_Provision.vbs script, which created the physical namespace on the UDS server. In this solution, I've added a recommendation to create a fully enumerated DFS namespace. With that, we have a new script: UDS_UserFolders_Provision_DFS.vbs in the Scripts folder of the companion media. To use this script, you need to supply these arguments:

- The path to the user's top-level folder (%username%) on the UDS server.

- **/dfs:Y** (or Yes). This instructs the script to run in DFS namespace creation mode, which generates appropriate DFS folders and links for the user in a fully enumerated DFS namespace (Design Option 1). In DFS namespace creation mode, the next three parameters are required:

- **/server:*servername***. The name of the server on which the user's data is hosted.

- **/*userfirstname:User's First Name*** and **/*userlastname:User's Last Name***. These two arguments are used to create a comment in the DFS folder for the user. So if you can't tell who owns a folder based on the user name, you can examine the folder's comment.

Here is an example of a command that will fully provision all the network-side configuration for James Fine:

```
Cscript UDS_UserFolders_Provision_DFS.vbs e:\users\jfine
    /dfs:yes /server:server01 /userfirstname:James /userlastname:Fine
```

You can examine the folder structure that results under the user's folder (for example, E:\ Users\jfine) and in the DFS namespace. But before you run the script in production, be sure to follow the instructions in the next section to customize its behavior.

## Customize UDS_UserFolders_Provision_DFS.vbs

You will definitely need to customize this script. The *Configuration* subroutine defines all variables, including the entire physical, SMB, and DFS namespaces. Those variables are used to create a namespace as described in this and the previous solution.

You will see a lot of similarities with the previous script—this one simply adds DFS namespace generation, and, because the script is more lengthy and complex, I organized the code to make the flow easier to follow. I also put the configuration block into its own subroutine, because many script editors (including Sapien's PrimalScript 2007, which I use to edit scripts) automatically allows you to collapse subroutines and functions, making it easier to view and navigate lengthy scripts.

**Important**   Of all the scripts and tools in this book, UDS_UserFolders_Provision_DFS.vbs is probably one of the most useful. Spend time understanding, customizing, and putting the script to use. You can also use it in the method described in the previous solution: Trigger its launch using a quota template. You do not need to use UDS_UserFolders_Provision.vbs once you have UDS_UserFolders_Provision_DFS.vbs. There is one more variation of this script, UDS_UserFolders_Extended_Provision_DFS.vbs, which creates an even more fully enumerated namespace. See Solution 3-5 on page 224 for details about UDS_UserFolders_Extended_Provision_DFS.vbs.

## Solution summary

We have looked at the configuration of the namespaces related to the data stores. In the previous solution, we started with the physical namespace—the folder hierarchy on UDS servers, which is pretty straightforward, really. We also detailed the best practice ACLs for UDS root data store folders. Then we moved "up" to the SMB namespace that exposes the physical namespace to the network. We identified the need to have separate SMB shared folders to support disparate requirements for settings such as caching settings. You can, however, define multiple SMB shares for a single physical folder.

We then abstracted the server-based namespace created by shares and folders by implementing DFS namespaces, and we examined two design options. The first, a fully enumerated DFS namespace requires the most investment up front in scripts or other tools to provision the creation of namespace folders for each user data store, but we provided just such a tool with UDS_UserFolders_Provision_DFS.vbs. Now, you can simply run the script and create a fully enumerated DFS namespace (Design Option 1), which is ideal. After the user's client-side references, such as roaming profile and redirected folder targets, utilize that namespace, the namespace never has to change! All you have to do is change the *targets* of folders in that namespace if you move user data.

Windows Server 2003 DFS namespace servers can support only 5000 links per DFS namespace, so Design Option 1 (which has several folders per user) supports the fewest users per namespace. However, you can simply add more namespaces. We looked at ideas for how to create a DFS namespace to support thousands of users, and they entail using more than one DFS namespace.

Then we emphasized just how much you can help yourself by not including business constructs such as sites, business units, or even the friendly logon names of users in the namespace for your UDS framework. Instead, use abstract constructs that do not have to change over time. Otherwise, a change in the user's role or location that leads to a change in the namespace for that user's data stores could require complex and painful changes to all of the client-side references to the old namespace.

We wrapped up by examining UDS_UserFolders_Provision_DFS.vbs, which fully provisions a user's data stores, including the user's top-level folder, subfolders for each data store, quotas, permissions, ownership, and DFS namespace. With this important tool in your bag of tricks, creating and managing the network namespaces for your user data stores will be a breeze.

# 3-5: Design and Implement Folder Redirection

## Solution overview

| | |
|---|---|
| **Type of solution** | Guidance |
| **Features and tools** | Folder redirection, Group Policy, registry |
| **Solution summary** | Leverage folder redirection to relocate user data stores to servers, and learn to redirect Windows XP folders such as Favorites, Music, and Videos. |
| **Benefits** | Unify the storage of both Windows XP and Windows Vista clients. |

## Introduction

In the good old days, we had the concept of a user's home directory: a mapped drive in which users would store their data. Home directories, or "home folders" if you're hip, are exposed to the user by a drive letter, such as the "H:" drive (for "Home"), the "U:" drive (for "User"), or the "P:" drive (for "Personal"). It would be amusing to survey organizations to find out how many English-speaking organizations use one of those three letters. My guess: over 90 percent.

Folder redirection was the evolutionary next step. A standard, well-understood technology that has been part of the Windows platform since Windows 2000, folder redirection exposes data stores (physical storage locations) through standard user-interface (UI) elements, such as the (My) Documents folder, the Desktop, Favorites, and others. That is, users access their data with familiar UI elements that abstract the physical location of the data stores. The fact that these standard UI components, called *shell folders*, are redirectors makes redirection quite transparent to users.

With this redirected folders metaphor, the primary location for the storage of user data is on a network server. While users are connected to the network, the network store is also the primary location for accessing files. But files can also be made available when the user is disconnected from the network using another Windows feature, Offline Files, discussed in the next solution.

Redirected folders with offline files is generally an approach to managing user data that is preferable to roaming profiles because it allows users to have instant access to data when logging on to a new system. Redirected folders do not synchronize or download large quantities of user data. With careful design and management of offline files, the organization and users have more control over which files are synchronized and at what times compared to roaming profiles, which synchronize all files at each logon and logoff.

You will likely choose to redirect the (My) Documents and Desktop folders and enable laptop users to take files offline. This was the guidance set forth in Solution 3-2 as a recommended design. This solution and Solutions 3-6 through 3-9 provide the details you'll need to make an educated design decision.

You can also redirect Favorites, Videos, Music, and other shell folders to a network location. The method for doing so and the functionality is a bit different than with Documents and Desktop, but it works. Doing so can unify the data stores for both Windows XP and Windows Vista clients.

# Understand the role of folder redirection

Folder redirection is a client-side technology through which shell folders can target a local or network data store.

## What are the key benefits of folder redirection?

Folder redirection offers important benefits, including the following:

**Reduced profile size**    By targeting a network data store, the data in that folder can be separated from the user profile, reducing the size of the user profile. This is particularly true of a user's (My) Documents folder, which as the primary storage folder for user documents, can easily reach many megabytes or even gigabytes in size. The Desktop folder can, for some users, become a dumping ground for large files as well, in which case redirection of the Desktop offers similar value.

**Improved logon and logoff performance**    With Documents and Desktop redirected, the user profile size is reduced significantly, which also significantly reduces the time required to synchronize the profile at logon and logoff. In this way, folder redirection improves the user's experience of system performance—the user gets his or her desktop faster at logon.

**Significantly reduced possibility of profile corruption**    Windows 2000 overhauled the roaming profile behavior of previous versions of Windows. Before Windows 2000, profiles were downloaded in their entirety at user logon and were uploaded in their entirety at logoff. Windows 2000 introduced a synchronization algorithm, whereby it transfers only changed files. The algorithm has been further honed for better performance with subsequent versions of Windows. It is quite robust and reliable. However, the synchronization process is still challenged when a profile is enormous. The larger the profile, the more likely you are to experience profile corruption, which results in "garbage" files (partially synchronized files with random names) in the profile and, possibly, registry (Ntuser.dat) corruption.

My experience has been that as soon as large data stores (Documents and Desktop) are redirected and thereby removed from the user profile synchronization process, corruption is highly unlikely. By the way, Microsoft's Knowledge Base (*http://support.microsoft.com*) has a slew of articles to help you troubleshoot in the event of a corrupted profile. But you'll be best served by removing those large data stores from the scope of roaming profiles.

**Immediate access to data**    Users can log on to any computer and immediately access the data in their redirected folders, even if they have not logged off of another computer. With roaming profiles, changes are synchronized to the server only at logoff. With redirected folders, on the other hand, all computers in the domain will redirect the user to the user's central network store, allowing real-time access.

## What's new in Windows Vista folder redirection?

Windows Vista further enhances the folder redirection story by redirecting 13 folders of the user profile. Importantly, Favorites, Cookies, Pictures, Music, and Videos can now be redirected through Group Policy folder redirection. With Windows XP, redirecting these shell folders takes a bit of magic, which I'll share later in this solution. Redirecting these folders can provide a more managed experience for users accessing both Windows XP and Windows Vista systems.

## What is the downside of folder redirection?

Folder redirection results in using a network store as the primary storage and access location for data. Therefore, anything related to the connection to the server will introduce potential challenges.

If connectivity to the server is unavailable or inadequate, functionality and performance will suffer. For this reason, we will design our UDS framework to ensure that UDS servers are as local as possible to users. If the user is not connected to the network—for example, when on the road—the user will not have access to the server. The Offline Files feature addresses this scenario, but it introduces its own challenges related to synchronization. I address Offline Files in Solution 3-6.

Assuming you've accounted for compatibility, connectivity, and server availability in your requirements, as we did in Solution 3-1, folder redirection is certainly a critical component of your UDS framework.

# Configure folder redirection policies

We will now examine the steps required to configure folder redirection. We'll assume you will redirect Documents and Desktop, for the sake of example; but later discussions of offline files and roaming profiles will equip you to decide what's right for your enterprise.

We'll also assume you have at least one Windows Vista or Windows Server 2008 system in your enterprise. Windows Vista and Windows Server 2008 include the Folder Redirection Editor extension for the Group Policy Management Editor (GPME, formerly called the Group Policy Object Editor or "GPE") snap-in. The Folder Redirection Editor extension exposes important new redirection policy settings required by these versions of Windows. The extension, shown in Figure 3-13, also enables you to configure redirection for clients running Windows XP and Windows 2000.

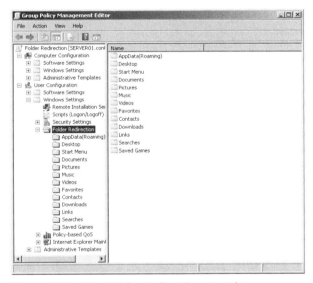

**Figure 3-13**   The Folder Redirection snap-in

> **Important**   Edit folder redirection policies using a Windows Vista or Windows Server 2008 system to expose the policy settings required by Windows Vista clients. The policies will, as detailed next, correctly manage previous versions of Windows as well.

Finally, we'll assume you understand the mechanics of Group Policy—specifically, how to apply a GPO to a site, domain, or organizational unit (OU); how to filter a GPO based on security group membership; how to evaluate resultant set of policy (RSoP); and how to use the Group Policy Management Console (GPMC) and GPME. If you need to bone up on Group Policy, start at *http://www.microsoft.com/technet/grouppolicy*. Or read *Windows Group Policy Resource Kit: Windows Server 2008 and Windows Vista* by Derek Melber (Microsoft Press, 2008) or *Group Policy: Management, Troubleshooting and Security: For Windows Vista, Windows 2003, Windows XP and Windows 2000* by Jeremy Moskowitz (Sybex, 2007). Solution Collection 10, "Implementing Change, Configuration, and Policies," contains advanced solutions related to Group Policy.

# Configure folder redirection targets

Windows Vista and later support redirecting 13 folders, shown in Figure 3-13. You can see the settings for yourself by opening a Group Policy object and navigating to User Configuration\ Windows Settings\Folder Redirection. For each folder, there are three possible settings: basic, advanced, and not configured. You choose one of these settings in the Setting drop-down list on the Target tab of the folder redirection policy, as shown in Figure 3-14. We'll look at each setting, but keep in mind that what matters is not the setting in any one Group Policy object (GPO), but the resultant setting that is applied to the client.

Unfortunately, the user interface exposing folder redirection target settings is poorly self-described and a bit quirky in its behavior.

### Basic – Redirect everyone's folder to the same location

This setting does not redirect everyone's folder to the *exact* same location; it redirects each user's folder to a user-specific folder within a single namespace. Figure 3-14 shows a common implementation of this setting.

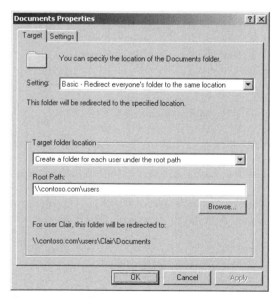

**Figure 3-14**    The Target page of a folder redirection policy

In Figure 3-14, the "same location" is a subfolder of the path configured in the Root Path text box—that is, \\contoso.com\users. But as you can see from the sample at the bottom of the dialog box, each user will receive a unique folder named with the user's pre–Windows 2000 logon name (the *sAMAccountName* property) and a subfolder called Documents. The resulting namespace for each user's redirected documents folder is, in this example, \\contoso.com\ users\%username%\documents.

The reason to choose the Basic setting is not because all users will go to the exact same location (they will not), but rather because all users within the scope of the policy will have a common *method* for configuring the target of the folder. The method used is based on your choice of the following options for the Target folder location:

**Create a folder for each user under the root path.**    This Target Folder Location option, shown in Figure 3-14, allows you to configure a Root Path, underneath which each user's folder will be created if it does not already exist and targeted. The root path should be a DFS namespace path to support the UDS requirement to abstract physical storage from UDS configuration pointers. The example path, \\contoso.com\users\, is a DFS namespace. The exact path you configure will be determined by DFS namespace design considerations in Solution 3-4.Underneath the root path, Windows automatically creates a folder for the user if it does not already exist, along with a subfolder with a name equivalent to the folder you are redirecting—for example, Documents.

Note that this namespace supports the exact DFS namespace that we created in Solution 3-4. In this target folder location option, there is no option to change the name of the subfolder (for example, Documents) or to prevent it from being created.

**Redirect to the following location.**    This Target Folder Location option provides a Root Path text box, into which you enter the target folder path. The text box control is a bit misleading, as it appears every user's folder will point to the *exact* same location. However, you are permitted to use certain environment variables (specifically, %username%, %userprofile%, %homeshare%, and %homepath%) as part of the path. So the root path, \\contoso.com\users\%username%, will in fact create a unique folder for each user. If you wanted to create a subfolder, you could specify additional information in the root path. For example, \\contoso.com\users\%username%\documents is valid and would produce a result identical to the Create A Folder For Each User Under The Root Path option.

> **Important**    If you are following the DFS namespace guidance from Solution 3-4, this target folder location option is the correct one. Specify \\*namespace*\%username%\ documents as the root path. By configuring this target folder location option, you enable both Windows Vista and Windows XP clients to redirect to a folder in the DFS namespace named Documents. There is more information about Windows Vista and Windows XP cohabitation later in this solution and in Solution 3-7.

Please be comforted if you start to think you're going crazy: The Redirect To The Following Location setting behaves strangely. If you enter a path with a variable, such as

\\contoso.com\users\%username%[\subfolder], it is perfectly valid and functional. But when you close and reopen the policy setting properties, the user interface will have changed your setting to Create A Folder For Each User Under The Root Path, and rein- terpreted your configuration—displaying it as, for example, \\contoso.com\users in the root path and \\contoso.com\users\clair[\subfolder] in the sample. You cannot make certain changes (for example, changes to a subfolder name) without changing the target folder option back to Redirect To The Following Location. My advice: Just know that the policy setting user interface is bizarre, but the results of the redirection are exactly what you originally configured and want them to be.

You can also use the Redirect To The Following Location option to redirect the folders of multiple users to a single location, to create a single user experience for those users.

**Redirect to the user's home directory.**  The Target Folder Location option is available only when redirecting the Documents folder. It enables you to redirect Documents to the location specified by the *homeDirectory* property of the user object in Active Directory. It's particularly useful while migrating from "old school" home directories to "new school" redirected Documents folders. Users will continue to have the mapped drive specified by the Home Directory in the user object, and the Documents folder will also redirect—both to the same location.

If you plan on removing the mapped drive in the near future, I recommend that, instead of choosing this option, you select the previous option (Redirect To The Following Loca- tion) and configure the path using the same template that you use for your user's home directories, such as \\*server*\\*share* \%username%. That way, when you remove the *homeDrive* and *homeDirectory* properties from the user account, the user's (My) Docu- ments folder continues to redirect to the correct location.

**Redirect to the local userprofile location.**  This Target Folder Location option redirects the folder to its Windows default location as a subfolder of the user profile.

## Follow the Documents folder

The Target Setting option—available only for the Pictures, Music, and Videos folders—specifies that the folder should be a subfolder of Documents. This is particularly useful for compatibil- ity with Windows XP, which cannot redirect My Music and My Videos. I'll talk more about this option later.

## Advanced—Specify locations for various user groups

The Advanced setting offers the same target folder location options just discussed. The differ- ence is that, unlike the Basic setting, this setting allows you to configure different target folder locations for various groups of users. The classic and typical usage scenario for this setting is to redirect groups of users to different servers. Instead of having to manage separate GPOs scoped to each user role, you can define redirection policies for all roles in one GPO. Figure 3-15 shows an example in which users in New York (who belong to the LOC_NYC location role group) and Sydney (in the LOC_SYD location role group) are redirected to appropriate servers.

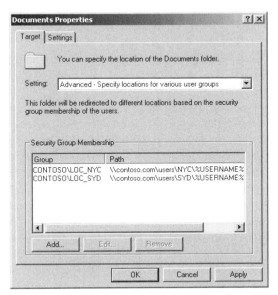

**Figure 3-15**    Folder redirection Advanced setting

You configure the groups and paths by clicking Add. Each group can have one of the four target folder options discussed earlier. In Figure 3-15, DFS namespace paths are once again used. The \\contoso.com\users\nyc and ...\syd folders are DFS folders that target servers in New York and Sydney, respectively.

I used a site-based example to make it easier to understand, but as we discussed in Solution 3-4, using site-based namespaces for UDS is highly discouraged. If you can, use a DFS namespace based on abstract or unchanging collections—you will be better served.

## Not Configured

The Not Configured setting redirects folders differently depending on the current state of the folder. If the folder was never redirected, the Not Configured state results in the default redirection to the folder's default location in the user profile—for example, %userprofile%\ *foldername*—except for My Pictures and My Music in Windows XP, which are subfolders of My Documents.

If, however, the folder was previously redirected and the resultant setting is changed to Not Configured, the folder is redirected to one of two places based on the setting of the *previous* resultant policy. On the Settings tab of a folder redirection policy, shown in Figure 3-16, the Policy Removal section has two options:

**Leave the folder in the new location when policy is removed.**   If this was the resultant setting and the policy is now Not Configured, the folder remains redirected to the location that was specified in the previously resultant policy.

**Redirect the folder back to the local userprofile location when policy is removed.**   If this was the resultant setting and the policy is now Not Configured, the folder is redirected to the folder's default location in the user profile.

The same pair of options determine the target of a redirected folder not only if the resultant policy setting becomes Not Configured, but also if there is no longer *any* policy specified for that folder.

## Configure folder redirection settings

Figure 3-16 also illustrates the most common initial configuration of these settings, which, unfortunately, are not the Windows defaults.

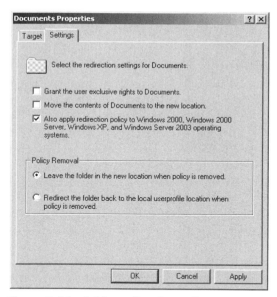

**Figure 3-16**   Folder redirection policy Settings page

### Grant the user exclusive rights to [*folder*]

If selected, this option performs two functions. First, if the folder *does not* exist, the folder will be created with explicit permissions only—inheritance of parent folder permissions is disabled. The explicit permissions allow Full Control only to the user and the server's System identity. Administrators, even, will not be allowed access to users' folders. These permissions are applied at the target folder, not at parent folders if they exist. This means, for example, that if you are using the target folder option Create A Folder For Each User Under The Root Path with \\contoso.com\users as the root path and \\contoso.com\users\clair\documents as the sample, only the Documents folder disables inheritance. The parent folder (for example, Clair) inherits permissions from the parent *and* adds explicit permission enabling the user to have Full Control.

Second, if the folder *does* exist, folder redirection verifies that the user is the owner of the target folder. If the user is not the owner, redirection fails for that folder.

If you clear the Grant The User Exclusive Rights check box, the ownership check does not occur. More importantly, folders created by folder redirection are created with inheritance enabled. The user is given explicit Full Control as well. By enabling inheritance, the security policy defined by the user data store root is able to apply throughout the user data structure. This approach is much more aligned with the needs of most organizations.

> **Important**    Typically, you will clear the Grant User Exclusive Rights To [*folder*] check box. It is selected by default. Solution 3-2 detailed the permissions for user data stores on the server.

This setting has no effect if the folders already exist. So if you use a prestaging process, such as our UDS_UserFolder_Provision_DFS.vbs script, you can specify the ACLs for each folder as you provision the folders and this policy will not change those permissions.

## Move the contents of [*folder*] to the new location

This setting is enabled by default. The result of this setting is that when this policy configures a new folder redirection target, the contents of the folder are moved to the target location. This results in a migration of data from the previous target of the folder to the new target. Imagine a user who is redirected to the New York server today and, after relocating to Sydney, is affected by a GPO that redirects folders to the Sydney server. The user's data is transferred from the New York server to the Sydney server. Similarly, if a user's folder is currently in his user profile and the folder is then redirected to a server, the contents of the folder are migrated to the server.

Do you really want this setting enabled? It depends. It is an effective way to migrate the folder automatically and transparently to the user. The question is, how likely is it to cause pain to the user or to break, causing pain to the administrator?

My recommendation is that with simple, granular folders, you enable this setting. For example, if you are redirecting Searches, Links, Contacts, Saved Games, or Favorites—each of which can be redirected in Windows Vista—this setting is likely to serve you quite well.

For larger or more complicated folders, such as Documents, you will likely want to ensure that migration is quick, painless, and complete. In these cases, I recommend that you clear this check box and implement a procedure whereby, immediately prior to being affected by your folder redirection policy, a user's Documents folder is moved to its new location. After the data has been migrated, the folder redirection policy is applied. This approach allows you to ensure that migration was successful and follows any rules or logic you establish for migration. Additionally, it ensures the user is not overly delayed the first time he logs on.

> **Important**    For large or complicated data structures such as Documents, Desktop, AppData, Pictures, Music, and Videos, clear the Move The Contents Of [*Folder*] To The New Location check box and move the folder contents using another mechanism.

Note that this redirection setting for a folder changes. If you've provisioned a fully enumerated DFS namespace, as described in Solution 3-4, and users' Documents folders are redirected using Group Policy to \\*namespace*\%username%\documents, when a user moves from New York to Sydney, there is no change to the client's redirection setting. The Documents folder still redirects to the same path—you simply change the folder target of the Documents folder in the DFS namespace. So this policy will not be of any use—you will need to move the data some other way, such as with a Robocopy script like that shown in Solution 3-10.

## Policy removal settings

The last choice you need to make when configuring folder redirection policies is what to do with the folder redirection setting on the client when the effective setting provided by Group Policy changes or is removed. There are four scenarios that could result in a policy removal:

- The GPO is deleted, or the User Settings of the GPO are disabled.
- The user is no longer within the scope of the GPO because the GPO link is disabled or because a GPO filter, such as a security group filter, no longer applies the GPOs policy settings to the user.
- The user's effective setting for the redirection of the folder is changed because another GPO takes precedence.
- The GPO's folder redirection setting is changed to Not Configured.

If you choose the Redirect The Folder Back To The Local Userprofile Location When Policy Is Removed option, the user interface folder (for example, Documents) is redirected to the default folder within the user profile *and* the data is copied (not moved) to the user profile location. The latter, significant behavior of this setting is not obvious in the user interface. So, to emphasize, all data in the redirected folder will be copied to the user profile location when the policy is removed. This behavior is effectively opposite of the Move The Contents Of [*folder*] To The New Location setting, which moves data to the new location when the policy is *first* applied.

The most common real-world scenario in which folder redirection policies are removed is when a user is transferred to another location. For example, a user in New York might be moved to Sydney, and, therefore, the Active Directory object representing the user is moved from a New York OU to a Sydney OU. Users in the Sydney OU are subject to a different GPO, which redirects folders to the Sydney server. You know by now, after Solution 3-4, that having site-based namespaces for user data and settings leads to other challenges.

In such scenarios, and in most others, you should choose the Leave The Folder In The New Location When The Policy Is Removed option. What this really means is "Keep the data in the folder specified by this GPO, and maintain redirection to this folder." If a GPO redirecting folders to a New York server no longer applies to the user relocating to Sydney, the user's data in those folders will not be copied to the local user profile.

However, if the Move The Contents Of [*folder*] To The New Location check box described earlier is selected in the *Sydney* GPO, that setting will effect the migration of the user's folders from the New York server to the Sydney server.

So, what the Policy Removal choices really mean is either "Copy the user's data to the local profile" or "Keep the data where it is" when this GPO no longer applies. If *another* GPO starts to apply, the folders will be redirected to the targets specified in the new GPO, and that GPO's Move The Contents Of [*folder*] To The New Location setting will determine whether data gets moved by folder redirection.

An interesting solution is provided if you select *both* options, Move The Contents Of [*folder*] To The New Location *and* Redirect The Folder Back To The Local Userprofile Location When The Policy Is Removed. Imagine a scenario with two locations: New York and Sydney. One GPO redirects New York users to the New York server. The GPO is linked to the New York OU, or filtered using a security group containing New York users (for example, LOC_NYC). Similarly, another GPO redirects Sydney users to Sydney servers. A third OU exists—let's call it "Users In Transit"—and users in that OU have no resultant policy setting for folder redirection.

A user in New York has her folder redirected to the New York server. She is going to be relocated to Sydney. She has a laptop computer. Before her last day in New York, her user object is moved to the Users In Transit OU. When she logs on, the New York redirection GPO no longer applies. The Policy Removal setting of the New York GPO causes her data to be copied to her local userprofile location. She then begins her relocation, and during that time her object is moved to the Sydney OU. When she arrives in Sydney and logs on, she is within the scope of the Sydney folder redirection GPO and the Sydney GPO's Move The Contents Of [*folder*] To The New Location setting causes the contents of her folder to be moved from her local profile to the Sydney server. In other words, these two settings, and the temporary placement of the user in an OU with no folder redirection policy, result in the user effectively creating her own migration. New York server data is moved to her laptop, which she takes to Sydney, and the data is moved to the Sydney server. That sounds great, and it is great. Just account for the issue that the data movement could take ages, particularly with large folders such as Documents.

Note that a similar transfer of data could be accomplished by configuring the Users In Transit OU with a GPO that specifies folder redirection targets with the Redirect The Folder Back To The Local Userprofile Location When The Policy Is Removed option.

# Support redirection for users on both Windows XP and Windows Vista

If there will be both Windows XP and Windows Vista users within the scope of a folder redirection GPO, it is important to configure the policy to apply both to all platforms, and to make sure that the Pictures, Music, and Videos are accounted for. Likewise, if you are planning to migrate from Windows XP to Windows Vista while supporting redirection, you need to design accordingly.

## Also apply redirection policy to Windows 2000, Windows 2000 Server, Windows XP, and Windows Server 2003 operating systems

This long-labeled option, which I will call the "Also Apply To Windows XP" policy for short, is visible in Figure 3-16. It is the most important configuration for supporting redirection on all platforms. When you select this check box, the redirection policy is written in a format that is compatible with the listed operating systems. When you clear this check box, the policy is written in a format compatible only with Windows Vista and Windows Server 2008. If any user within the scope of the GPO is likely to log on to a system running one of the listed operating systems, and you want the user to have access to his or her redirected folders, you should select this check box. If all users within the scope of the GPO need access to redirected folders only from Windows Vista or Windows Server 2008 systems, you can clear the check box.

The Also Apply To Windows XP setting is available only in folder redirection policies for Documents, Pictures, Desktop, AppData, and the Start menu, as these are the only folders that the previous versions of Windows are able to redirect using Group Policy.

> **Important**    I recommend that, unless a folder redirection policy will apply *only* to users of Windows Vista, you should always select the Also Apply To Windows XP check box.

## Side effects of the "Also apply to Windows XP" policy

It's important to note that if this setting is enabled, it affects the behavior of the folder target option Create A Folder For Each User Under The Root Path. With the Also Apply To Windows XP check box selected, the subfolder that is created beneath the root path will match the Windows XP name My Documents—for example, \\contoso.com\users\clair\my documents.

The functionality of the redirected folder will be completely intact, but the folder name itself will be a legacy name. This is problematic if you have followed my guidance and created a user data store provisioning process, such as the UDS_UserFolder_Provision_DFS.vbs script, which creates a consistent namespace for each user with Windows Vista–compatible names such as "Documents."

An even stranger effect of using both the Also Apply To Windows XP and Create A Folder For Each User policy settings is that, although the folder on the server will be a path such as E:\Users\\*username*\My Documents that includes the My Documents subfolder, Windows Explorer will show the path as E:\Users\\*username*\Documents. Windows Explorer shows the folder's alias name. This can be misleading, as I can tell you from personal experience. I was having trouble connecting a user to her redirected documents folder. I logged on using Remote Desktop to the server to double-check that I knew the path and it displayed in Windows Explorer as E:\Users\\*username*\Documents, but the UNC \\\\*server*\users$\\*username*\documents just wouldn't work. After 15 minutes of tearing my hair out, I found that \\\\*server*\users$\\*username*\my documents was what was necessary. And sure enough, viewing the folder from the command prompt required use of the CD command to change to the ...\My Documents subfolder.

You are better off, even in a mixed Windows XP and Windows Vista environment, just specifying the path of the folder target location to be \\\\*namespace*\%username%\documents so that all new folders are created in a fully compatible namespace. I encourage you to move forward using "new school" folder names, such as Documents instead of My Documents. To achieve this, use the folder target option Redirect To The Following Location, and specify \\\\*namespace*\%username%\documents. With this setting, the GPO will look for, use, and create if necessary a folder named Documents (instead of My Documents) for both Windows Vista and Windows XP clients. This will help you begin the transition into the Windows Vista profile namespace. Again, this is primarily a cosmetic rather than functional issue, but I am completely over the down-level love affair with the possessive pronoun "My." Remember your Windows XP users will still see the My Documents folder on their desktop—this is just to help us on the back end.

> **Important**   The best setting for a folder redirection target folder location is Redirect To The Following Location with your specific namespace entered as the Root Path—for example, \\\\*namespace*\%username%\[documents | desktop | etc.]. This will ensure a consistent front-end and back-end experience for users on both Windows XP and Windows Vista platforms.

## Pictures, Music, and Videos redirection policies

The Pictures, Music, and Videos folders deserve special attention. The My Pictures folder is, by default, a subfolder of My Documents in Windows XP, as are My Music and My Videos. As you know, Pictures, Music, and Videos are now subfolders of the user profile in Windows Vista.

If you redirect the Documents folder and a user affected by the policy logs on to both Windows XP and Windows Vista, you need to ensure—for compatibility with Windows XP—that the Music and Videos folders remain subfolders of Documents. Otherwise, the user will see disparate locations when logged on to each of the operating systems. Luckily, if you are redirecting Documents and you select the Also Apply To Windows XP check box, the Folder Redirection Editor automatically configures Pictures, Music, and Videos to Follow The Documents Folder as long as the policies are currently Not Configured. If a policy for one of those three folders is configured to Basic or Advanced redirection, the Documents policy setting to Also Apply To Windows XP will not change the configuration and, therefore, the folder (Pictures, Music, or Videos) will not follow Documents, and there will be two separate folders used for Windows Vista and pre–Windows Vista clients.

**Important**  One way to ensure that Pictures, Music, and Videos folders remain redirected and compatible for both Windows Vista and pre–Windows Vista clients is to ensure their redirection policies are set to Follow The Documents Folder.

## Redirect without Group Policy: Favorites, Music, Pictures, and Videos

There is one other option at your disposal: redirecting Favorites, Pictures, Videos, and Music for Windows XP clients without Group Policy. By pointing the appropriate Windows XP registry values to a network store for these folders, you *can* redirect them. You will then be able to use standard Group Policy settings to redirect those folders to the same network store for Windows Vista clients.

Folder redirection policy in Windows XP supported redirecting My Pictures to another location, though the user interface in the Folder Redirection Editor extension made it quite . . . interesting. Favorites, My Music, and My Videos cannot be redirected using Group Policy in Windows XP. Instead, you can use the registry to redirect shell folders. The concepts and approaches I lay out in this discussion can apply to other shell folders—such as SendTo, Net-Hood, PrintHood, and so on—but I have not run into a need to redirect anything other than the media folders and Favorites.

The redirection targets are defined in the registry, within HKEY_CURRENT_USER\Software\Microsoft\Windows\CurrentVersion\Explorer. There are two relevant subkeys: Shell Folders and User Shell Folders. User Shell Folders is the primary definition of the folder target. You can see in Figure 3-17 that each shell folder has a value of type REG_EXPAND_SZ. The value name is the name of the folder. The value is the folder target, which can use the environment variable %USERPROFILE% or %USERNAME%, such as %USERPROFILE%\My Documents\My Music—the default location for the My Music folder. As Figure 3-17 shows, you can redirect each folder, as we have redirected Favorites, My Music, My Pictures, and My Video to \\contoso.com\users\%USERNAME%\*folder*. Even though this is a Windows XP client,

I chose a folder name and location to match the structure of Windows Vista so that my migration to Windows Vista would be a bit easier.

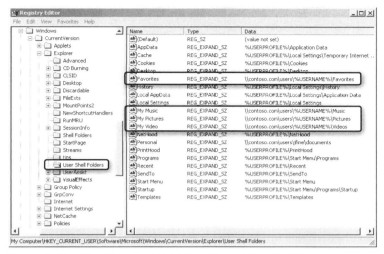

**Figure 3-17**   The User Shell Folders registry key

You can use any one of a variety of options to automate modifying the user shell folder registry values on clients, including registry merge files (.reg), VBScript scripts, or batch files with the REG command. I encourage you to migrate data to the new folder prior to changing the value, although I have not yet encountered problems from doing so afterwards. A user must log off and log on before Windows Explorer will fully utilize the redirected shell folders. Additionally, if users already have catalogs such as the Windows Media Player library database, they will have to be refreshed.

The easiest ways to test your success are, first, to drop an item in the Favorites folder on the server and then look in your Internet Explorer Favorites menu to see if the item appears. Then open Windows Media Player, choose Library, and choose Add To Library. Click Advanced Options, and you'll see the Monitored Folders. You should see your three redirected media folders, as in Figure 3-18. It is a good sign that Windows Media Player, which looks for the Music, Pictures, and Videos shell folders, reports it is monitoring your redirected folders.

There is another key in the registry, Shell Folders (seen just a few subkeys above User Shell Folders in Figure 3-17), which also resolves shell folders to targets. You'll find the same values—My Music, My Pictures, and so on—as you do in the User Shell Folders key. The only difference is Shell Folders takes hard-coded paths (for example, C:\Documents and Settings\ *userprofilename*\My Documents\My Music) rather than expandable strings. This is a legacy key, and it should generate new values for shell folders after the User Shell Folders values have been changed and a user has logged off and logged back on. But if something seems to be misbehaving, check to make sure Shell Folders values are, in fact, updated to reflect the new full path to the folder.

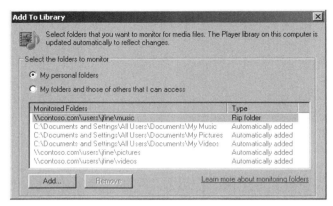

**Figure 3-18**    Windows Media Player showing redirected folders

## Quirks and bugs

These two keys have a couple of quirks. The most likely to affect you are the quirks related to My Videos. The folder in the user interface in the Windows XP My Documents folder is My Videos. The registry values in both the User Shell Folders and Shell Folders keys are named My Video (singular). If you create a value called My Videos, it won't work. The second quirk is that these values (My Music and My Video particularly) might not appear until after you've opened Windows Media Player. But luckily if you create them before opening Windows Media Player, Windows Media Player accepts them as authoritative. So you can create the value if it does not exist. The third quirk is that, even after opening Windows Media Player, you might not see a User Shell Folders value for My Video. But if you add the value as a REG_EXPAND_ SZ type, it will work perfectly in my experience, including performing an update to the Shell Folders value at the next logoff and logon.

Redirecting shell folders has numerous effects within the user interface. If you have the My Pictures link on your Windows XP Start menu and you redirect My Pictures to a folder named Pictures (a Windows Vista–like name without the "My"), the link on the Start menu will now also be displayed as Pictures. Don't be surprised.

This is not documented anywhere: For whatever reason, the name that appears in the user interface in Windows is not hard-coded (that is, Pictures or My Pictures). Nor is it the last element of the namespace path to the redirected folder—that is, if the folder target is \\contoso.com\users\%username%\pictures, it is not necessarily "Pictures." In fact, what is used to generate the visible name for the folder in the user interface is the *folder* itself—that is, *the DFS folder name* in a fully enumerated DFS namespace or *the physical folder on the server* if the folder target is deeper than the DFS namespace. So if you redirect a user's Pictures folder to \\contoso.com\users\%username%\pictures, but the DFS namespace folder is named "pictures" (lowercase), the user interface will show "pictures," lowercase, which looks really strange to most users. If you rename the DFS namespace folder to "Pictures" (initial-capped), the user interface will reflect the change at the next logon.

I emphasize this particularly because the scripts that accompany this book use the DFSUTIL command to create the DFS namespace. The DFSUTIL command is, as of Release Candidate 1 of Windows Server 2008, broken: It creates only lowercase names for DFS folders even if uppercase is specified in the command. So our scripts will create lowercase DFS namespace folders, which will lead to lowercase user-interface elements. Visit the Web site for this book (*www.intelliem.com/resourcekit*) and you will likely find a workaround for this problem after Windows Server 2008 is launched.

## Advantages of redirection with the registry

The first advantage of redirecting with the registry is, well, redirection! Assuming you want the user's data store to be on the network, you can get it there! My Music, My Pictures, and My Videos would have gotten there anyway, if you had allowed them to Follow The Documents Folder, which is the default behavior. But now you can get Favorites or any other shell folder up there as well.

Second, you can unify the physical and logical (DFS) namespaces used to host user data for both Windows Vista and Windows XP clients! Windows XP will use the registry to redirect My Music to a Music folder, My Pictures to a Pictures folder, and My Videos to a Videos folder. Group Policy folder redirection settings will redirect the Windows Vista folders to the same locations.

## Disadvantages of redirection with the registry

There aren't many disadvantages, really, assuming you do, in fact, want a particular shell folder to be redirected. You do have to work a little harder to achieve the redirection, using a script or .reg file or something similar to poke the Windows XP registry in the right places. You also don't get the slick functions of true folder redirection policies: You cannot specify Grant The User Exclusive Access and have it take effect automatically; you cannot specify Move The Contents; nor can you specify what to do if the policy is no longer in scope, because there is no policy. But, you'll remember, I recommended that you don't do those things anyway, not even when you can!

## Recommendation

Redirect, assuming you want these folders on the server in the first place. I expect that Favorites will be a no-brainer. Your IT security, usage policies, business requirements, and storage capacity will probably determine whether Pictures, Music, and Videos get redirected.

I suggest placing the *physical* stores for these folders in the Users\%username%\data folder, along with Desktop and Documents. These are, after all, just additional data stores. In most situations, they will be managed identically to Desktop and Documents and subject to the same quotas.

You'll also need to expand your DFS namespace if you are using the fully enumerated namespace design. We'll touch on that issue in a moment.

> **Important**   Another option for redirecting Favorites, Pictures, Music, and Videos folders for both Windows Vista and pre–Windows Vista clients is to redirect Windows Vista clients with Group Policy folder redirection and Windows XP clients with registry-based redirection.

### Get rid of the My Music and My Pictures subfolders

If you redirect My Music or My Pictures, Windows XP clients do not move or delete the My Music and My Pictures subfolders within the My Documents folder. You should manage those folders accordingly: Move data from them to the new, redirected location perhaps; then delete the folders to avoid confusion.

### Give users a way to browse to the folders

But when you delete the My Music and My Pictures subfolders (which you should), users might get confused if they are accustomed to seeing those folders in My Documents, and particularly if they're used to browsing through My Documents to reach the folders. I suggest that if you redirect My Music and My Pictures, you do two things. First, create *shortcuts* in the My Documents folder that target the new locations. That way there is a visible tool with which users can navigate just as they did before when the two folders were subfolders. Second, add My Music and My Pictures to the Start menu, which you can do by customizing the properties of the Start menu.

## Achieve a unified redirected folder environment for Windows XP and Windows Vista

To wrap up this solution, I'll present you with two *great* tools that should let you go all the way to unifying the redirected folders for Windows XP and Windows Vista.

### Provision the creation of all user data stores

The first is the logical next step of our provisioning script from Solution 3-4. This script is called UDS_UserFolders_Extended_Provision_DFS.vbs. It is called with the same syntax as the script from the previous solution, namely:

```
cscript UDS_UserFolders_Extended_Provision_DFS.vbs e:\users\jfine
    /dfs:yes /server:server01 /userfirstname:James /userlastname:Fine
```

The following arguments are provided on the command line:

- The path to the user's top-level folder (%username%) on the UDS server.

- **/dfs:Y** (or Yes). This instructs the script to run in DFS namespace creation mode, which generates appropriate DFS folders and links for the user in a fully enumerated DFS namespace (Design Option 1).

- **/server:***servername*. The name of the server on which the user's data is hosted.

- **/userfirstname:***User's First Name* and **/userlastname:***User's Last Name*: These two arguments are used to create a comment in the DFS folder for the user so that if you can't tell who owns a folder based on their user name, you can examine the folder's comment.

The only difference between this script and UDS_UserFolders_Provision_DFS.vbs from the previous solution is that this script has additional namespace definitions in the Configuration Sub and creates more folders in both the physical and DFS namespaces. The resulting namespaces are shown in Figure 3-19:

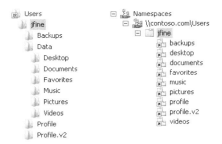

**Figure 3-19**   The extended physical and DFS namespaces to include redirected Favorites, Music, Pictures, and Documents

You will need to customize UDS_UserFolders_Extended_Provision_DFS.vbs. Refer first to the discussion of UDS_UserFolders_Provision_DFS.vbs in the previous solution, and then look at the comments in the script itself.

## Configure folder redirection for Windows XP Favorites, Pictures, Music, and Videos using Group Policy

Who said, "You can't use Group Policy to redirect Favorites, Music, and Videos?" Not I! I (hopefully) said, "You can't use Group Policy folder redirection policies." True, Group Policy folder redirection does not support all the folders in Windows XP that we want it to. But the registry does! And what can go in the registry can be put there with Group Policy. We just need to use the registry client-side extension (CSE), not the folder redirection CSE.

This involves creating a custom administrative template to enable the configuration of appropriate policy settings. The core of the template is shown next. You need the full version, called Registry Based Folder Redirection for pre-Vista Clients.adm, in the Scripts folder of the companion media. Add it to a Group Policy object, turn off filtering of unmanaged policies (otherwise, the settings will not appear), and you're good to go! If you're not familiar with how to work with administrative templates, see Solution Collection 10, where I detail the processes.

```
Registry-Based Folder Redirection for Pre-Vista Clients.adm
CLASS USER

CATEGORY !!Redirect

              KEYNAME "Policies\Software\Microsoft\Windows\
                      CurrentVersion\Explorer\User Shell Folders"

              POLICY  !!Favorites
              EXPLAIN !!FavoritesExplain
                      PART !!FavoritesPath EDITTEXT REQUIRED EXPANDABLETEXT
                      DEFAULT !!FavoritesDefault
                      VALUENAME "Favorites"
                      END PART
              END POLICY

              POLICY  !!Music
              EXPLAIN !!MusicExplain
                      PART !!MusicPath EDITTEXT REQUIRED  EXPANDABLETEXT
                      DEFAULT !!MusicDefault
                      VALUENAME "My Music"
                      END PART
              END POLICY

              POLICY  !!Pictures
              EXPLAIN !!PicturesExplain
                      PART !!PicturesPath EDITTEXT REQUIRED  EXPANDABLETEXT
                      DEFAULT !!PicturesDefault
                      VALUENAME "My Pictures"
                      END PART
              END POLICY

              POLICY  !!Videos
              EXPLAIN !!VideosExplain
                      PART !!VideosPath EDITTEXT REQUIRED  EXPANDABLETEXT
                      DEFAULT !!VideosDefault
                      VALUENAME "My Video"
                         ; That is not a typo: the value is My Video (singular)
                      END PART
              END POLICY

  END CATEGORY
  ; Definitions of all string variables (!!)follow.
  ; See the .adm file on the companion media
```

With the script and the administrative template, you can whip out data stores and redirect users to them in no time flat—Windows XP or Windows Vista. They said it couldn't be done! (Actually, "they" never said that . . . but they never made it easy.)

# Solution summary

This solution detailed the functionality, configuration, and business scenarios requiring various folder redirection policies. We looked at the nuances and quirks of the Folder Redirection Editor extension and the default settings that, more often than not, will be inappropriate for your implementation. We also examined redirection of Pictures, Music, and Videos using both Group Policy and registry-based redirection.

With the tools and guidance provided in this chapter, you could, if you so chose, create a comprehensive redirected folder implementation that supports all key user data and settings stores except for Ntuser.dat. Unfortunately, you don't quite yet have all the information you need to make the determination of which folders to redirect, so wait to configure redirection until you've considered the guidance in upcoming solutions.

Notice we did not discuss redirecting Application Data in this solution. You *can* redirect it, but you'll find that it's likely to be too early in the life cycle of your applications to be able to do so with 100 percent confidence. Solutions later in this collection discuss design considerations for roaming profiles, offline files, and local files. These solutions, together, will enable you to determine which folders should be redirected, which should roam, and which should remain local.

# 3-6: Configure Offline Files

## Solution overview

| | |
|---|---|
| **Type of solution** | Guidance |
| **Features and tools** | Offline Files, synchronization, csccmd.exe |
| **Solution summary** | Identify the nuances, tricks, and traps of Offline Files and synchronization so that you can align the technology correctly with your business requirements. |
| **Benefits** | Availability of user data and settings stored in redirected folders for laptop users. |

## Introduction

A requirement of the UDS framework is that it supports users who work while disconnected from the network. This means, in particular, laptop users. Any user data store that is accessed primarily from the network must be made available offline. Redirected folders are, of course, just such data stores. While connected to the network, users access files from redirected folders directly from the server. Those files must be accessible while the user is disconnected.

The Windows Offline Files feature is designed to support users who work while disconnected from the network. It provides access to and visibility of files and folders stored on network locations by caching files (including their permissions) in an offline cache (C:\Windows\ CSC, by default), which itself can be encrypted.

Network files are copied to the offline cache using a process called *synchronization*. During synchronization, changes are replicated between the locally cached files and the network files. Windows enables Offline Files by default; however, the feature can be configured by each user on a local machine or by a network administrator for a shared folder.

Although the Offline Files feature has potential uses and benefits in several scenarios, the UDS framework will apply it specifically to enable users with mobile computers to cache their redirected data stores. For this scenario, configuration and management are generally straight-forward. For example, if we are dealing with an individual user's data and settings being cached for offline access, we do not have to worry too much about the possibility of file change conflicts: There is only one user working on the file, and that user is either online or offline.

Behind the guidance I provide in this solution is a lot of technology and configuration. For comprehensive details on the Offline Files feature and its configuration, I highly recommend that you read Jeremy Moskowitz's discussions of Offline Files in his book, *Group Policy: Management, Troubleshooting and Security For Windows Vista, Windows 2003, Windows XP and Windows 2000* (Wiley, 2007).

## Understand the cache

The offline cache (C:\Windows\CSC, by default) is used to store files from network shares. The files are synchronized, including the access levels (permissions). But you cannot and should not open files directly from the CSC folder. Instead, you access the files using the same redirected folder, UNC, or mapped drive that you would use while connected. One of the most amazing capabilities of Offline Files is that while a user is offline it presents the files in the same namespace as when the user is connected.

If you want to see a flat list of the files you've taken offline, including the path from which the file originated and the current status of the file, you can choose to view offline files from the Offline Files tab of the Folder Options Control Panel application in Windows XP or the Offline Files Control Panel application in Windows Vista. This view of your offline files is useful for administration and support, but you should continue to access the files themselves from the files' own namespaces.

## Understand caching

Offline Files supports two types of caching: active and passive. Active caching occurs when a user pins a file by right-clicking it and choosing Always Available Offline from the context menu (or Make Available Offline for Windows XP). Actively cached files will remain available offline until a user deselects the Always Available Offline or Make Available Offline command for the file. Administrators can also configure a file to be Always Available Offline using Group Policy.

Passive caching synchronizes files to the cache when they have been accessed from a network share. Passive caching is meant to ensure that files deemed important by the mere fact that a user has recently accessed them will be available to the user when the user is disconnected from the network.

With Windows XP, the amount of files that can be passively cached is limited to a configurable percentage of the size of the volume hosting the CSC folder. By default, 10 percent of drive space is made available to passive caching. If that amount of storage is exceeded, the "oldest" files (those accessed least recently) are purged from the passive cache to make room for newly accessed files. Active caching is not subject to the cache size setting. A user can actively cache as many files as the local disk has room for.

Windows Vista changes the storage management for offline files. Now, there is a configurable amount of storage (a percentage of free disk space when the operating system is installed), and that storage is shared by both actively and passively cached files. Passively cached files can consume a configurable percentage of the offline files cache. If the store fills and the system passively caches a new file, the system will purge an older file that was passively cached. If the store is filled and a user attempts to actively cache a new file, the system will inform the user that the cache is filled.

## Understand synchronization

Windows XP synchronization is managed using Synchronization Manager. You can configure, per share and per network connection, when synchronization should occur: at logon, at logoff, on a schedule, or during idle time. You can also manually launch synchronization and select the shares you want to synchronize.

Windows Vista improves synchronization in almost every way. It is significantly more efficient and more robust. Most synchronization happens flawlessly and transparently in the background. In fact, there's no way in the user interface to instruct Windows Vista to synchronize at logoff—all files should *already* be synchronized. The Windows Vista Sync Center queues up any conflicts and allows you to manually launch synchronization. And Windows Vista synchronization provides a full set of application programming interfaces (APIs) that you can leverage to script just about anything (including logoff synchronization).

## Understand offline mode

When a server is not available, a file can be accessed from the cache. It's pretty easy to understand how, when you are on an airplane, the computer can detect that it is no longer on the network, transition into what is called "offline mode," and access files from the cache. But it gets more complicated in scenarios in which the user is connected to a server and the server goes offline or connectivity to the server fails. The computer then makes what is called a state transition to offline mode. More complicated still are scenarios in which the user is connected to the server over a slow link—if the client decides it should be online but performance while accessing the server copy of the file is heinously bad, how can the user convince the system to use the offline copy?

Among the many improvements Windows Vista made to offline files is the management of state transition, offline mode, and slow-link detection. Although there are settings and tricks you can play with Windows XP, you will have far fewer problems with Windows Vista than you would have had with Windows XP, and just about every setting can be managed through Group Policy.

# Leverage offline files for the UDS framework

Again, I *highly* encourage you to refer to Jeremy Moskowitz's books for comprehensive details about the concepts I just sketched out, and about all the configuration and management aspects of offline files. For purposes of our discussion of using offline files to support a UDS infrastructure, I'd like to focus on key points that organizations need to consider, and common mistakes that you can avoid.

## Allow redirected folders to be automatically made available offline

When you redirect a folder using Group Policy folder redirection for a Windows XP or Windows Vista client, that folder is made available offline, by default. In general, this is a desired effect for laptop users. The UDS requirements specify that users should have access to data and settings while disconnected. This default behavior ensures that the requirement is met.

There is a Group Policy setting Do Not Automatically Make Redirected Folders Available Offline. It is located in the User Configuration\Administrative Templates\System\Folder Redirection container in the Group Policy Management Editor. If you enable this setting, it prevents the system from automatically making redirected folders, such as Documents and Desktop, available offline.

## Recognize that folders redirected using the registry are not automatically cached

The preceding discussion applies to folders that are redirected using folder redirection policy settings. But, in Solution 3-5, we also found that we could redirect folders using registry settings in the User Shell Folders key. Those folders are not automatically cached, and you might very well want them to be! This is especially important for Windows XP clients because you might use registry-driven redirection to redirect Favorites, Music, Videos, and Pictures.

## Administratively assign ("push") specific files or folders to be available offline

Luckily, you can use the Administratively Assigned Offline Files policy setting to force these registry-redirected folders, or any other network resource, offline. The policy setting is found in User Configuration\Administrative Templates\Network\Offline Files. When you enable the policy, you can add UNC paths to resources you want to push offline to users within the scope of the GPO. Figure 3-20 shows the policy setting.

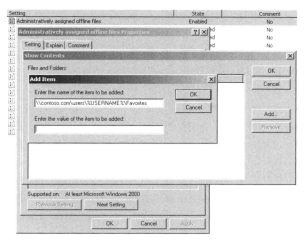

**Figure 3-20**   Administratively assigned offline files configured to push a folder offline

What the documentation doesn't make clear, and what is particularly great, is that you can use variables such as %USERNAME% in this policy setting! So if you've used registry-based redirection for Windows XP Favorites folders, you can ensure that Favorites are available offline with the type of setting shown in Figure 3-20.

### Plan for a long initial synchronization when large folders are made available offline

Think about the typical size of users' Desktop and, particularly, Documents folders. When a user's folders are first redirected, they are made available offline, which causes a synchronization to occur. That takes quite some time to complete, in many cases. Be sure to account for this fact when scheduling your rollout of redirected folders.

### Recognize that when folders are made available offline, they are synchronized to every machine to which the user logs on

When redirected folders are made available offline automatically by Group Policy, either with folder redirection policies or with the Administratively Assigned Offline Files policy, those policies apply to a user. And at that point, any computer the user logs on to attempts to cache the folders. This leads to the spread of data files as users roam in your organization. Sure, the offline files cache can be encrypted, but that encryption can be attacked (particularly with Windows XP, which encrypts the cache with the System account). It also means lots of wasted disk space.

## Determine that you don't want redirected folders to be automatically made available offline for every machine

This proposal should be self-evident by now. Imagine your poor conference room computer. Each time a user logs on to give a presentation, a full synchronization is launched. The hard drive fills up (literally, with Windows XP). Time is wasted. Data is potentially exposed. It's just not desirable.

## Identify where you *do* want redirected folders to be available offline

I recommend, and I'm sure you'll agree, that you configure your UDS framework to enable offline files for redirected folders where it really matters: for laptop users working on their own laptop.

## Manage offline files to that specification

After you've defined the scope of computers on which you do and do not want redirected folders to be made available offline, you can manage your environment to create the desired result. You have two major settings at your disposal:

**The Do Not Automatically Make Redirected Folders Available Offline policy setting.**    This setting, to reiterate, applies to users, not computers. That's unfortunate because it will require quite a bit of creativity to enable a user to have redirected folders available offline on her laptop but *not* on all the desktops she logs on to.

**The Allow Use Of Offline Files or Disallow Use Of Offline Files feature policy setting.**    This setting—located in Computer Configuration\Administrative Templates\Network\Offline Files—will, if disabled, completely turn off the Offline Files feature for clients within the scope of the policy setting. It's great that it is a computer policy, but it's unfortunate that it is an "all or nothing" switch.

You also have several tools at your disposal with which to define scopes of systems:

**Security groups.**    Groups can be used to filter Group Policy objects.

**Windows Management Instrumentation (WMI) filters.**    WMI filters are queries that are executed. If they return a logical "true," the Group Policy object is applied. WMI filters are expensive from a processing perspective because they take quite a few processor cycles to execute. They're also difficult to write and, depending on what you are querying, can be difficult to make precise enough to rely on.

Both of these tools are discussed in Solution Collection 10. With these settings and tools, I recommend one of the approaches in the following sections to manage the behavior of offline files and redirected folders in your environment.

## Disable offline files on all systems other than user laptops

One option is simply to turn off Offline Files on all systems other than laptops. There are a number of decent arguments for this approach. The Offline Files feature, although it has the *possibility* to benefit other scenarios, is *practically* best suited for laptop work scenarios.

If your OU structure is such that all laptops are in a manageable number of dedicated OUs, you could disable offline files for *all* computers with a GPO scoped very high in your Active Directory—perhaps even in the entire domain. Then create a GPO that *enables* offline files (by *enabling* the Allow Use Of Offline Files or Disallow Use Of Offline Files feature) and scope that GPO to your laptop OUs. The enabling GPO will have higher processing precedence because it is scoped to the OUs that host the laptop objects, so laptops will be an exception to the rule and will allow offline files.

If your OU structure is more complicated and it is difficult to isolate laptops, create a GPO that disables the setting Allow Use Of Offline Files or Disallow Use Of Offline Files. This effectively turns off offline files entirely. Scope the GPO to apply to all machines except user laptops by filtering the GPO with security groups or a WMI filter.

**Scope with security group filtering**    Use a security group that represents laptops, and apply a Deny::Apply Group Policy permission to the group that represents user laptops. The policy will be applied by all systems that are *not* members of the group. I prefer to manage my environment by specifying what is *allowed* versus what is *disallowed*. It tends to be a more secure, more manageable approach. Thus, I like this approach. Although it sounds like I'm disallowing something, what I'm disallowing is a policy that disables offline files—a double negative. That means by adding a computer to the group, I'm actually *enabling* that computer to use offline files.

Of course, the alternative is to use a security group that represents all desktop and other computers for which you want to disable offline files. Filter the GPO to apply only to that security group.

**Scope with a WMI filter**    You can also use a WMI query that identifies all systems that should not have offline files enabled. For example, you could try to create a query that identifies desktop systems by their *SystemEnclosure* property. Jeremy Moskowitz's book has an example. But it is tricky to expect such a complex query to work every time. You can learn more about WQL (SQL for WMI) at *http://msdn2.microsoft.com/en-us/library/aa394606.aspx*.

Here's a tip that leverages WMI queries that just might work for you: Query against the computer name. If you're lucky enough to have a naming convention like some of my clients, where every laptop name begins with the letter "L" followed by the asset tag of the laptop, you can create a WMI query that works pretty well:

```
Select * From Win32_ComputerSystem Where Name LIKE 'L%'
```

The percent sign is a wildcard, much like an asterisk is at the command prompt. This query will return *true* for any computer with a name that starts with "L." You've now identified your laptops!

With this accomplished, you create *two* GPOs. The first disables offline files by disabling the Allow or Disallow policy setting. It applies to *all* computers through the default GPO ACL that includes Authenticated Users::Allow::Apply Group Policy. A second GPO, with *higher precedence*, enables offline files by enabling the Allow or Disallow policy setting. This GPO uses the WMI filter I just listed.

The disadvantages of the WMI approach are, first, you might not be so lucky to find an easy way (such as a computer name) to identify systems with the scopes you are trying to manage. Furthermore, there might be a time when you want a desktop to have offline files—or more likely, when you want one or more laptops *not* to use offline files. The security group approach is more manageable in the long run. One group defines who *can* use offline files, and that group is *denied* the permission to apply the GPO that disables offline files. Computers in that group therefore exhibit the default Windows configuration for offline files, which is enabled.

## Disable the automatic caching of redirected folders for systems other than laptops

This approach leverages the user-side policy setting Do Not Automatically Make Redirected Folders Available Offline. You create a GPO that enables this setting, thereby disabling the caching of redirected folders, and you apply it to all systems other than laptops. Because this is a user setting and is applied at logon using the user's credentials, you cannot use a security group containing computer objects to filter the GPO. You have to use either a WMI query or loopback policy processing.

**Scope with a WMI filter**   WMI queries are the easy way to cause a user GPO to be filtered based on computer properties, *if* you can create a WMI filter that works for you. Remember our WMI query from the previous section that identified laptops? Well, now we have a GPO that is turning *off* the automatic caching of redirected folders. We need it to apply to all systems *other than* laptops:

```
Select * From Win32_ComputerSystem Where NOT  Name LIKE 'L%'
```

**Use loopback group policy processing**   We'll discuss loopback group policy processing in detail in Solution Collection 10. If you configure loopback policy processing for your desktops and laptops, you can use security groups that represent the systems that should, or should not, allow automatic caching of redirected folders. This is similar to the security group filtering approach suggested earlier, except that option turned off offline files completely using a computer-side policy setting. Now we're being more targeted, specifying only that we do or do not want redirected folders automatically cached, which is a user-side policy setting. So, with Group Policy loopback mode enabled for your clients (in merge mode so that users' Group

Policies continue to apply correctly), you can take either one of the following courses of action:

■ Create one GPO that enables the policy Do Not Automatically Make Redirected Folders Available Offline, thereby turning off automatic caching of redirected folders. Filter the GPO to apply only to a security group representing systems that should not cache redirected folders.

■ Create two GPOs. The first enables the policy Do Not Automatically Make Redirected Folders Available Offline and is scoped to apply to *all* clients, perhaps even to the entire domain. The second GPO *disables* the same setting, thereby *enabling* the caching of redirected folders. The second GPO is filtered with a group that represents systems that should cache redirected folders and has higher precedence than the first GPO.

As we'll see in Solution Collection 10, loopback policy processing in merge mode is a great way to manage your systems. It can be used here to prevent the unnecessary caching of users' redirected folders on conference room computers and other systems.

### Throw in the towel: Manually cache redirected folders

The third option is to just say "no" to trying to make it work. Configure a domain-wide policy that enables the Do Not Automatically Make Redirected Folders Available Offline setting. Then instruct your laptop users to right-click their Documents, Desktop, and other folders and choose Make Available Offline. Although this is a manual effort, it has big benefits:

■ Folders and files are cached only on the systems and by the users who need them.

■ Users get a quick and easy introduction to the concepts of offline files, synchronization, caching, and working offline.

■ When the initial (potentially long) synchronization occurs, it is under the full control of the user.

■ Users can choose to take subfolders, rather than their entire redirected folders, offline.

If you'd like, you can use csccmd.exe, which is part of the Windows Server 2003 Resource Kit (for Windows XP) to script the pinning of the Desktop and Documents folders. For Windows Vista, you can use VBScript to do the same. Visit the solutions Web site for this book for examples.

Now that we've talked about how to *prevent* offline files from running rampant, let's talk about issues that will arise once files are being cached.

### Prevent Windows XP from synchronizing all files at logoff

Imagine you have taken your entire Documents folder offline. That can be quite large and can contain hundreds if not thousands of files. By default, Windows XP systems synchronize all files (and the keyword is *all*) at logoff. Now the synchronization process will copy only files that have changed, but this process scans all files on both the server and the local cache to determine what has changed. Even if only one file has changed, the scanning can take *ages*. This is a big pain point of offline files for Windows XP.

The trick is to turn off the setting Synchronize All Offline Files Before Logging Off. This setting is on the Offline Files tab of the Folder Options dialog box, as seen on the left side of Figure 3-21. This is different than the setting Automatically Synchronize The Selected Items When I Log Off My Computer that appears in Synchronization Manager's Synchronization Settings dialog box, on the right side of Figure 3-21. If the option to synchronize *all* files is enabled, the scanning is painful. If that option is disabled and synchronization happens at all at logoff (as specified by Synchronization Manager), only files that the user actually touched on the server are synchronized to the cache.

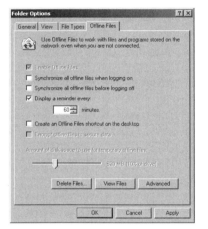 

**Figure 3-21** Options for managing synchronization at logon and logoff

**Important** I recommend configuring synchronization with the Automatically Synchronize The Selected Items When I Log Off My Computer setting in the Synchronization Settings dialog box for Windows XP clients. Just be sure that you clear the Synchronize All Offline Files Before Logging Off check box in the Folder Options dialog box for the relevant folder.

The Synchronize All Offline Files Before Logging Off setting can be managed through Group Policy. Disable the policy setting Synchronize All Offline Files Before Logging Off. It can be found in both the User Configuration and Computer Configuration folders, in the path Administrative Templates\Network\Offline Files.

## Eliminate unnecessary error messages from blocked file types

Before Windows Vista, synchronization of certain file types was discouraged. Specifically, most database formats, including .pst and .mdb files, were blocked from synchronization by default. That was based on the assumption that users might take such files offline from shared folders. While on the road, the user could make certain changes, and other changes could be made to the server copy. Resolving conflicts in such scenarios would be excessively difficult, so the file types were blocked altogether.

But we are using offline files for the UDS framework. A user will only be taking his own files on the road, so changes will not be made separately to the copies of those files on the server. There is no practical opportunity for conflicts to arise. So, with Windows XP, you can specify which file types are blocked by enabling the policy setting Files Not Cached. This setting is in Computer Configuration\Administrative Templates\Network\Offline Files. If you enable the policy and leave the list of blocked file types blank, all file types are allowed to be cached.

You can also specify certain file types that you do want to block by entering a semicolon-delimited list. If you specify a list, you need to re-enter any of the default file types that you want to block: Your list overrides the defaults. The default file types that are blocked are these: *.slm; *.mdb; *.ldb; *.mdw; *.mde; *.pst; *.db?.

I've had good experiences just enabling the policy and leaving the list blank, thereby unblocking all file types and getting rid of those pesky blocked file type errors. Of course, as with all solutions and recommendations in this resource kit, you'll want to test it thoroughly in your environment.

## Provide Windows XP users a way to force themselves offline

Both Windows XP and Windows Vista work to detect the speed of a connection when a server is online. The settings that can be used to manage slow-link detection are detailed in Jeremy Moskowitz's book. The Windows Vista settings are quite sophisticated and should really serve you well. Windows XP's . . . not so much. I've run into numerous clients who implemented Offline Files and then had problems when connecting to the network through a virtual private network (VPN). The VPN connection was fast enough to convince Windows XP that it was online, triggering synchronizations and online use of files. But the connection was slow enough that those activities were painfully slow.

To force a share offline when Windows thinks it should be online, you can use the csccmd.exe command. This command was recently updated by Microsoft. See Knowledge Base article 884739 at *http://support.microsoft.com/kb/884739*. Check to make sure your clients have the latest version of the command. Then create batch files for users that disconnect them from the namespaces that are being taken offline. Here is an example:

```
csccmd /DISCONNECT:"\\contoso.com\users\%username%\documents"
csccmd /DISCONNECT:"\\contoso.com\users\%username%\desktop"
```

### Manage offline files notifications

Windows XP also throws an inordinate number of interruptions and messages at you. Balloon messages inform you that you are offline (or online, or in need of synchronization). Dialog boxes inform you of the progress of synchronization. The list goes on. Use the settings in the Offline Files folders of Group Policy (both the User Configuration and the Computer Configuration) to manage which messages appear.

### Remember cached files when sources are moved

In Solution 3-4, we discussed that when users are moved to another server or site and the namespace of their redirected folders changes, Offline Files might need to be tweaked. Offline Files keeps track of the full UNC of files it has cached. If that UNC changes, the Offline Files feature considers the new location to be a new source, and it considers the old location simply to be unavailable. You need to tell Offline Files that the files it believes come from location A are now at location B.

Csccmd.exe, discussed earlier, has a /MOVE command that allows you to do just that. But csccmd.exe works only with Windows XP. For Windows Vista clients, you need a script. The script can be found at *http://blogs.technet.com/filecab/archive/2007/03/29/updating-your-offline-files-cache-in-windows-vista-to-point-to-a-new-server.aspx*.

## Put offline files to use

I'd like to reiterate that I am a huge fan of offline files. If well implemented, they perform a great service, particularly for laptop users. That's a big IF, however. As you see from the list presented, there are a lot off issues to consider and a lot of defaults that don't really align with taking large folders (such as Documents or Desktop) offline. You can, and should, manage all the configuration of offline files so that it yields the results you're after. It does a darned good job on Windows XP, once all is said and done, and a really great job on Windows Vista clients.

### Design thoroughly

Spend time reading Jeremy Moskowitz's book with an eye on the key issues I've raised in the preceding sections. But examine all the details he discusses and the options you have for configuring and managing offline files, synchronization, offline mode, and slow-link detection.

### Communicate and train effectively

Be certain that you have developed a plan for end-user training and communications. Get laptop users excited about the productivity benefits of offline work and the ease of synchronization. Be sure that you are training users to understand how to take files offline, when to synchronize, and how to work offline. Most importantly, make sure users know what types of data should or should not be cached.

### Remember that the Offline Files feature is not for all files

Some file types simply will not perform satisfactorily within the scope of offline files. There are some applications that might not appreciate state transition from online to offline use while a file is open. Some files might be so large that they take forever to synchronize, although Windows Vista improves that story tremendously with a block-level synchronization engine. And some applications might not do well working offline.

Although redirected folders made available offline will be the solution for most classes of user data, the 80/20 rule ensures that there will be exceptions. The folders in the user's roaming profile (discussed in Solution 3-7), and the Local Files folder (discussed in Solution 3-9) provide the necessary alternative data stores for files that cannot be managed effectively with offline files.

## Solution summary

The Windows Offline Files feature is a tremendous boon to laptop users. It caches files from network shares and enables their use while the user is offline from the same namespace (user data stores, mapped drives, and UNCs) that would be used while online. Synchronization is, if well implemented, effective and efficient. And Windows Vista really kicks it up a notch with improvements to every aspect of the technology. While the roaming profile and Local Files folders discussed later in this Solution Collection will serve to manage files that do not fit well with offline files, you will find that offline files are a valuable and welcome component of your UDS framework.

# 3-7: Design and Implement Roaming Profiles

## Solution overview

| | |
|---|---|
| **Type of solution** | Guidance and scripts |
| **Features and tools** | Roaming user profiles |
| **Solution summary** | Manage user settings stored in the registry and, likely, in Application Data (AppData\Roaming in Windows Vista) by configuring roaming profiles. |
| **Benefits** | Provide availability, mobility, and resiliency for user settings and customizations. |

## Introduction

Roaming profiles will be implemented to support the requirements of the UDS framework that relate to user settings. Roaming profiles ensure that a user's primary settings stores—the AppData folder (technically, in Windows Vista, the AppData\Roaming folder—previously known to its fans as "Application Data") and registry file (Ntuser.dat)—are accessible when a user logs on to any computer in the domain. If a user logs on to a new system, the profile is synchronized to the new system before the desktop appears. At logon and logoff, profile synchronization ensures that the network store and the locally cached copy of the profile are updated. After the user logs on, the user accesses files in the settings stores using the locally cached copy of the profile. At logoff, any changes are transferred to the server-based roaming profile folder.

The recommended configuration of the UDS framework is to configure roaming profiles to support AppData and Ntuser.dat. You learned in Solution 3-5 that you can redirect Favorites using Group Policy folder redirection for Windows Vista and with registry values (that can even be driven through Group Policy) for Windows XP. If you're not redirecting Favorites, you will probably want it to roam. You can also opt to allow Cookies to roam. All other folders will be excluded from roaming. By doing so, the size of the user profile will be minimized and performance should be sufficient.

But these recommendations are just guidelines that I expect will apply to most readers. After considering other solutions in this collection, you might even decide that your environment is an exception to the rule, and that data folders such as Documents or Desktop or even Start Menu should roam.

## Analyze the structure of the Windows Vista user profile

A user profile is a namespace of folders to isolate and organize user data and settings. Each user's profile is stored, by default, under a single root folder on the local disk of the client. Prior to Windows Vista, the root folder was named Documents And Settings. Beginning with Windows Vista, the root is named Users.

To provide backward compatibility, Windows Vista maintains an NTFS junction named Documents And Settings that targets the Users folder. Junctions are redirectors to another namespace. So if a legacy application is hard-coded to look for C:\Documents and Settings\*username*\*folderpath*\*filename*, it will navigate transparently to C:\Users\*username*\*folderpath*\*filename*.

Beneath the Users folder is a collection of intuitively named folders. The Windows Vista user profile rationalizes some of the folders that were nested several layers down in the user profile of previous versions of Windows. The result is that navigating to common locations is more intuitive and faster. Figure 3-22 shows the structure of a user profile.

**Figure 3-22**   User profile structure

Table 3-1 shows the names of common user data folders and their location in Windows Vista and in Windows XP.

**Table 3-1   Common Data Folders in Windows Vista and Windows XP**

| Windows Vista | | Windows XP | |
|---|---|---|---|
| Folder name | Location (Users\*username*\...) | Folder name | Location (Documents and Settings\*username*\...) |
| Desktop | Desktop | Desktop | Desktop |
| Documents | Documents | My Documents | My Documents |
| Favorites | Favorites | Not applicable | Favorites |
| Pictures | Pictures | My Pictures | My Documents\My Pictures |
| Music | Music | My Music | My Documents\My Music |
| Videos | Videos | My Videos | My Documents\My Videos |
| Downloads | Downloads | Not applicable | Not applicable |
| Contacts | Contacts | Not applicable | Not applicable |
| Searches | Searches | Not applicable | Not applicable |
| Links | Links | Not applicable | Not applicable |
| Saved Games | Saved Games | Not applicable | Not applicable |

A number of other profile folders were moved from their pre–Windows Vista location to subfolders of AppData in Windows Vista. The Windows Vista AppData folder is divided into three subfolders: Roaming, Local, and LocalLow. Roaming contains computer-independent settings that are specific to the user and should follow the user as part of the roaming user profile. Local and LocalLow contain computer-dependent settings that do not need to roam, such as the %TEMP% folder and the user's temporary Internet files. Both folders are automatically excluded from roaming profiles. LocalLow is one of the few locations that can be written to by applications running at the low integrity level (the most secure integrity level), such as Internet Explorer 7 in Protected Mode.

Table 3-2 maps Windows XP folders to their equivalent in Windows Vista and later.

**Table 3-2   Windows Vista Equivalents to Windows XP Folders**

| Windows XP folder | Windows Vista folder |
| --- | --- |
| Application Data | AppData\Roaming |
| Local Settings | AppData\Local |
| Local Settings\Application Data | AppData\Local |
| Local Settings\History | AppData\Local\Microsoft\Windows\History |
| Local Settings\Temp | AppData\Local\Temp |
| Local Settings\Temporary Internet Files | AppData\Local\Microsoft\Windows\Temporary Internet Files |
| Cookies | AppData\Roaming\Microsoft \Windows\Cookies |
| Nethood | AppData\Roaming\Microsoft\Windows\Network Shortcuts |
| PrintHood | AppData\Roaming\Microsoft\Windows\Printer Shortcuts |
| Recent | AppData\Roaming\Microsoft\Windows\Recent |
| SendTo | AppData\Roaming\Microsoft\Windows\Send To |
| Start Menu | AppData\Roaming\Microsoft\Windows\Start Menu |
| Templates | AppData\Roaming\Microsoft\Windows\Templates |

In the root of the profile is Ntuser.dat, the registry file that is loaded into HKEY_CURRENT_USER when the user logs on. Of course there are innumerable settings in the registry that reflect the user's configuration and customizations. It's an important file to maintain if your goal is to provide the availability, mobility, and resiliency of user settings.

You will also find compatibility junctions that represent legacy folder names. These include a Default User junction that links to Default for the default user profile, a symbolic link for All Users that exposes C:\ProgramData, and many junctions in the root of the user profile (Application Data and My Documents among them) that target the new equivalent namespaces. List access is denied to the application compatibility junctions that exist in Windows Vista, such as "My Documents." If this were not so, junction-unaware applications might misbehave. The folder that these junctions point to, Documents in this case, is not restricted in that way.

## Review the components that create the user profile

When a user logs on to a Windows system, Windows either synchronizes a roaming profile or builds a local profile for the user. Let's look very briefly at the profile generation process. You should be familiar with it from earlier versions of Windows, but I'll use this review to update you on changes that were introduced by Windows Vista.

## Default user profile

If a user logs on to a computer, Windows checks to see if the user has a local profile. If not, Windows creates a profile for the user based on the contents of the default user profile, which is stored either in the NETLOGON share of the domain controller or on the local disk subsystem as C:\Users\Default (or, in versions of Windows prior to Windows Vista, C:\Documents and Settings\Default User).

## Shell folders

Windows also ensures that shell folders—including those listed in the tables earlier in this solution—are created. If the user's copy of the default profile is missing its Links folder, for example, Windows will create it.

## Roaming profile synchronization

Windows then examines the *ProfilePath* property of the user account to determine whether a profile should be found on a network server. If the server-based profile exists, it is synchronized with the local user profile, using the profile merge algorithm to ensure that any files updated since the last logon to the computer are updated locally. If the local profile did not exist previously, the effect of synchronizing the server with the user's new copy of the default profile is that the roaming profile is downloaded through a full synchronization. But items that are unique to the default user profile are preserved and become a part of the user's profile.

## Public profile

The public profile contains data stores that are designed to be available to all users on a computer. The public profile data stores include Public Documents, Public Downloads, Public Music, Public Pictures, and Public Videos. Items in the Public Desktop folder appear on the desktop of all users who log on to the computer—it is the equivalent of the All Users\Desktop folder from pre–Windows Vista systems.

The All Users\Start Menu folder in Windows XP and Windows Server 2003 is also merged with the user's own Start Menu folder. This public Start Menu folder is relocated to C:\ProgramData\Microsoft\Windows\Start Menu.

The C:\ProgramData folder itself is equivalent to the All Users\Application Data folder in earlier versions of Windows. Application settings that apply to all users on a computer are stored in C:\ProgramData.

## Profile generation, summarized

In the end, every user profile begins as a copy of another profile: the default profile in the NETLOGON share of the domain controller or on the local disk, or a copy of a server-based profile indicated by the *ProfilePath* property of the user object. The user experience merges items in the public profile's Public Desktop and Start Menu folders into the user's own desktop and Start menu. Files in the user's profile are accessed locally unless those folders have been redirected. Changes to the profile are synchronized with the user's roaming profile, if it is configured, when the user logs off.

## Configure the folders that will not roam

You have the ability, with Group Policy, to specify that certain folders will not roam in addition to the folders that Windows excludes by default: Local Settings (in Windows XP), and App-Data\Local and AppData\LocalLow (in Windows Vista). The Group Policy setting you require is Exclude Directories In Roaming Profiles, and it is located in User Configuration\Administrative Templates\System\User Profiles. Because this setting is user based, you could have different folders roaming based on a user's role. Specify folder names relative to the user profile, such as AppData\Roaming\Microsoft \Windows\Cookies. Figure 3-23 shows an example that excludes the Cookies folder on both Windows XP and Windows Vista.

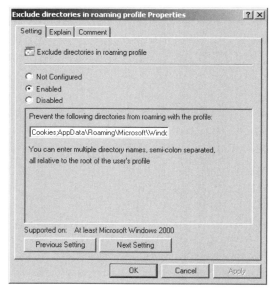

**Figure 3-23**    Policy excluding the Cookies folder from roaming

The specific folders you choose to exclude will depend on your UDS design, but I encourage you to exclude all Windows XP profile folders other than Application Data and Favorites. (Remember that Desktop and My Documents are redirected.) So I generally exclude folders such as Nethood, Printhood, Recent, Send To, Start Menu, and Templates (which holds only Windows templates, not templates such as those in Microsoft Office). In Windows Vista, new profile folders are introduced, and you should decide based on your business needs whether each should be roaming, redirected, or excluded (kept as local-only).

# Configure roaming profiles

To provide a user with a roaming profile, you must simply put the path to the folder in the user's *profilePath* attribute, which is exposed on the Profile tab of the user account, as seen in Figure 3-24.

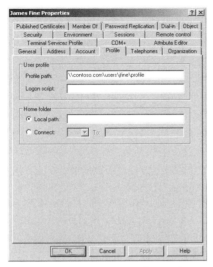

**Figure 3-24**   A user's profile path

Use a DFS namespace path to meet the requirement for abstracting a physical storage location from UDS configuration pointers. Note the use of the %username% variable in Figure 3-24. This is replaced automatically with the user's pre–Windows 2000 logon name (*sAMAccount-Name* property).

To upload a user's profile to the location, the user must first log on to his computer (*after* you have configured the profile path). Then, when the user logs off, the local profile is synchronized to the server.

> **Important**   After configuring the profile path for a user, be certain that the user logs on to, and then logs off of, the computer that reflects the profile he wants to roam. When populated, the roaming profile overwrites locally cached profiles for the same user as the user logs on to other computers.

# Recognize the "V2" of Windows Vista roaming profiles

The namespace of the Windows Vista user profile is incompatible with Windows XP profiles. Therefore, when a user on a Windows Vista client has a profile path configured, Windows Vista appends a ".V2" extension to the profile path. For example, if James Fine in Figure 3-24 logs on to a Windows Vista client, the profile it actually looks for is \\contoso.com\users\ jfine\profile.v2. There is no way to change this behavior, and you should not add the .V2 in the user account's profile path.

## Unify the experience of Windows XP and Windows Vista users

Although Windows XP and Windows Vista profiles are incompatible, that is not to say you cannot create a fairly unified experience for users who log on to both platforms. Folder redirection is the key. Whatever folders you have redirected will be available to users on both platforms, no problem. So redirect as many folders as you can: Documents and Desktop, for sure; Application Data *if* it works for you (see the following discussion); and Favorites, Pictures, Music, and Videos (using folder redirection policies for Windows Vista and registry redirection for Windows XP, as detailed in Solution 3-5). You can even go so far as to redirect other shell folders such as Cookies, Send To, and others (using policy for Windows Vista and registry for Windows XP).

The only thing that really cannot be shared is Ntuser.dat. It's just as well. My experience with trying to share registry files across operating systems is that even when it can be done, it doesn't produce the results to make it worth the effort.

If you are not using registry-based redirection for Favorites and other shell folders for Windows XP clients, you can allow them to be part of the Windows XP roaming profile. Then you can use folder redirection policies for those folders—policies that apply only to Windows Vista clients—and target the folders to their location in the Windows XP roaming profile. In other words, Windows XP gets the folders by roaming and Windows Vista redirects the folders into the roaming profile stores.

## Work through the FOLKLORE of roaming profiles

Implementing roaming profiles is simple from a technical perspective. It's the politics that can be problematic. If your organization has not yet implemented roaming profiles, it is probably because of at least one of a collection of dynamics I refer to as FOLKLORE:

- F—Fantasy or lack of fact
- O—Ownership
- L—Leadership
- K—Knowledge
- L—Legend or history
- O—Obsolete ways or thinking
- R—Religious influence
- E—Excuses/Expectations

Each of these dynamics can result in a perfectly good design or component being thrown out. In my experience, it is generally "L: Legend or history" that is most likely to derail roaming profiles. Roaming profiles got a bad reputation—partially deserved—in the days of Windows NT. They are now a reliable component of a UDS framework if implemented correctly in alignment with UDS requirements and design. There were significant problems with both the design and the performance of roaming profiles.

First, there was no merge algorithm or synchronization. Instead, the entire profile was copied to the client at logon and copied back to the server at logoff. This could lead to painful logon and logoff delays.

Second, because of the lack of synchronization, if a user logged on to more than one computer at a time, the last computer from which the user logged off would win for all files, which could be disastrous. The merge algorithm has, since Windows 2000, ensured that each individual file is synchronized correctly. The only file for which there is still a problem arising from multiple logons is the registry file. Because all user settings are stored in a single file, Ntuser.dat, the last computer from which the user logs off will upload its copy of Ntuser.dat, overwriting copies of the file from other computers. The likelihood of this causing significant or even apparent pain is quite low.

Third, no folders were excluded from roaming, so even junk folders such as Temp and Temporary Internet Files roamed, further bloating the server folder size and further increasing logon and logoff time. And if user documents were stored in the user profile, rather than in the user's network home directory, the profile could be enormous.

Fourth, large profiles were, and to some extent always will be, more prone to corruption, leading to help desk intervention and costs.

So IT professionals felt justifiably burned by roaming profiles in the 1990s. But hey . . . we're almost in the teens here in the twenty-first century. It's a new world. It just ain't the same.

The "K" in FOLKLORE, Knowledge, is another dynamic that can take discussions of roaming profiles off course. You now know that folders can be excluded from roaming profiles and that folders can be redirected out of the roaming profile entirely. Therefore, you know that roaming profiles can be managed to the point where even the most sophisticated power user has a profile that is small enough to synchronize very quickly, even to systems that the user is logging on to for the first time. A smaller profile also means reduced requirements for profile storage and a significantly reduced likelihood of profile corruption and the need for troubleshooting. Applying knowledge to create an effective design for roaming profiles will head you toward success.

# Identify the benefit of roaming profiles

Roaming profiles are the *only* practical option for meeting requirements for the availability and resiliency of user settings stored in the registry. Any customization that affects HKEY_CURRENT_USER is stored in the user's Ntuser.dat file in the root of the user profile. That registry file, if nothing else, must be accessible from the network.

But there are other folders in the profile, as well, that need to be made available in the same way. Favorites is the prime example. If a user performs Internet research as part of his job and for any reason loses his Favorites, you're likely to have an angry customer. Favorites cannot be redirected with Group Policy folder redirection in Windows XP, so allowing it to roam is one practical solution for meeting UDS requirements for this data store in Windows XP. You might also choose to allow Cookies to roam, although I view Cookies as an expendable folder and exclude it from roaming in most scenarios. But, in case you were skipping solutions, don't miss the coverage in Solution 3-5 of how to redirect shell folders such as Favorites, Cookies, and others in Windows XP using the User Shell Folders registry key.

A number of new user profile folders were introduced with Windows Vista. You can evaluate these folders in light of the discussion in this solution and in Solution 3-6 to determine whether those folders should roam, redirect, or remain local.

# Manage the Application Data (AppData\Roaming) folder

The big deal for roaming profiles, after Ntuser.dat, is Application Data (or AppData\Roaming in Windows Vista and later). The Application Data folder contains numerous important settings and customizations—including custom dictionaries, templates, and other Microsoft Office settings—encryption keys and more. If the data in Application Data is lost, it can be detrimental to productivity.

Although Windows clients support redirecting Application Data, the reality in my experience is that some applications still do not do well with a redirected Application Data folder. Furthermore, to make application data available while a user is disconnected from the network (for example, for laptops), Application Data must be cached with offline files. Again, some applications don't do well in the transition, particularly in the event that a client with cached Application Data experiences network connectivity problems that causes the client to switch between online and offline modes.

To summarize, the issues with Application Data are related, first, to applications themselves (and particularly to whether they work with a redirected Application Data folder), and then, to challenges related to going offline. Issues related to caching Application Data and working offline are more significant with Windows XP than with Windows Vista, which greatly improved every aspect of offline files. Before you attempt to make Application Data a redirected folder, which requires taking it offline for disconnected (laptop) users, applications need to be fully tested to determine whether they support network redirection and offline mode.

One other note: Windows Vista introduces a new Group Policy setting, Network Directories To Sync At Logon/Logoff Time Only. You can use this setting, discussed in Solution 3-9, to address applications that do not perform well when AppData is redirected to a network folder.

## Solution summary

To meet requirements for the UDS framework, roaming profiles will be implemented to manage availability and synchronization to a network store of the user's registry file, Ntuser.dat. Additionally, until applications have been fully tested for their support of redirection and offline mode, the Application Data (or AppData\Roaming in Windows Vista) folder will be included with the roaming profile. For Windows XP clients, Favorites will either be redirected by modifying the Favorites value in the User Shell Folders registry key (see Solution 3-5 on page 224), or it will roam.

Because large user data stores (Documents and Desktop) are being redirected, the size of the roaming profile will be minimal—it contains only settings and, perhaps, Favorites. Traditional complaints about roaming profiles, related to the time required to synchronize and the possibility of corruption, are all but eliminated by removing gigabytes of user data from the roaming profile feature. Group Policy can also be used to restrict other folders—such as Printhood, Nethood, and Cookies—from roaming.

With roaming profiles configured this way, user settings are stored and accessed primarily on the user's system. At logon and logoff, profile synchronization ensures any changes are transferred to the server-based roaming profile folder. If a user logs on to a new system, the profile is synchronized to the new system before the desktop appears.

# 3-8: Manage User Data That Should Not Be Stored on Servers

## Solution overview

| | |
|---|---|
| **Type of solution** | Guidance and scripts |
| **Features and tools** | Folder redirection, shortcuts, roaming profile folder exclusion |
| **Solution summary** | Create data stores for user data that should not be stored in network stores, and redirect any shell folders that fall into that category. |
| **Benefits** | Comply with information security and technology usage policies. |

## Introduction

When I work with clients to implement user data and settings frameworks, one of the first objections that is raised is, "But we don't want users storing <insert file type here> on the network!" The implication of the objection is that all user data must be managed the same way. And the reason some administrators believe that is because pretty much all user data is stored within the user profile, which we seem to be saying will either be redirected or will roam, resulting in a copy on network servers.

That is exactly why one requirement of a user data and settings framework should be: "The UDS framework will comply with the enterprise information security and information technology policies regarding network storage of files." There are, in fact, two driving reasons *not* to store certain data on servers: information security policies and information technology usage policies. Information security policies should be set forth in such a way to clearly define how specific information classes are managed. There might be particularly sensitive data that, for whatever reason, should not be on a network server or should not be accessible from any machine in the environment. However, my experience has been that files that fall under information security policies are typically the most valuable information assets of an organization, so they *should* be protected, backed up, and closely managed. Those tasks are accomplished more effectively when the data *is* on a server. It's really more a question of restricting access to that data—a security or permissioning question. It might very well be that such data should not be in a roaming profile or redirected folder, but rather should be in a separate data store.

It's more likely that it is information technology policies and usage concerns that will drive what can and cannot be stored on network servers. I'll use the example of employees' music collections. Most of the organizations I've worked with have concerns about allowing users' music to be stored on servers—concerns that relate both to storage requirements and potential copyright violations. Often, companies consider most or all media files—pictures, music, and videos—as personal data rather than business data. And information technology policies often require users to refrain from storing personal data on servers.

I'll refer to such data that should remain stored *only* on a client system, neither roaming nor redirecting, as *local-only* user data.

 **Important**    Local-only user data is a concept that is unique to our presentation of a UDS framework. It is not an official Microsoft term. It means data that will neither roam nor be redirected.

In this solution, we'll look at options for managing local-only user data that should "never" be stored on servers. I use quotation marks when I say "never" because there are few hard-and-fast rules in IT, and I believe you should support the migration of *all* user data when a user gets a new computer—including files such as personal music collections. I say this solely because users are our customers in IT, and deleting or losing a user's music certainly creates an unhappy customer. So what we will really be managing in this solution is user data that should not, on a day-to-day basis, be stored on servers.

# Identify the types of data you want to manage as local only

The first step is to identify the specific classes of data that should be managed to prevent their storage on network servers. I'll use the examples of music, pictures, videos, and miscellaneous personal (that is, non-business-related) files, and I'll refer to the whole of such data as local-only data.

The types of data you consider local only should be driven directly by information security and information technology policies. If you do not have such policies, or if you are including certain classes of data as personal files that are not addressed by the policies, you are likely to run into political and cultural resistance. I recommend creating the policies if they don't exist or extending existing policies if necessary, so there is a corporate mandate behind your decision to manage these classes of data separately.

# Design a local-only data folder structure

The folders you create to host local-only data will depend first, I suggest, on the parallels between your classes of local-only data and the profile folders on Windows Vista, along with your roadmap to Windows Vista.

## Media folders as local only

If you are considering pictures, music, and videos as local only, keep in mind Windows Vista has folders explicitly created to host such files. So you will easily be able to use the existing folders and exclude them from roaming. Windows XP, unfortunately, stores those folders as subfolders of My Documents. In this solution, we assume that Windows Vista is somewhere in your future. So we'll create, later in this solution, a Windows XP profile folder structure that mimics that of Windows Vista and therefore eases the migration to Windows Vista. We will then treat those folders as local only.

## Nonmedia personal files

You might have classes of data other than pictures, music, and videos that you want to treat as local only. In our example, we use one: miscellaneous personal files. You might have more than one.

You need to design a folder structure to host those nonmedia classes of local-only data. The goals of the design should be to communicate the purpose of the folder and the type of data it is to contain. Ideally, you should also communicate to users that the data is not the responsibility of the organization to maintain.

If you have only one nonmedia class, as in our example, I recommend creating one folder named Personal Files. Other names I have seen proposed or in use include Local Data, Local Data Not Backed Up, and My Local Data. I could also imagine Local Only Data.

So we'll create a folder called Personal Files. It will be a first-level folder within the user profile, it will not be redirected, and it will be excluded from the roaming profile by using the Group Policy setting discussed in Solution 3-6. We create it within the user profile so that it is secured using the profile ACL, which ensures that only the user and the computer's Administrators group have access to the folder. The Personal Files folder should *not* be created on the root of the disk drive, for reasons addressed in the requirements in Solution 3-1.

I have always recommended implementing the Personal Files folder as a first-level profile folder—for example, C:\Users\\*username*\Personal Files in Windows Vista or C:\Documents and Settings\\*username*\Personal Files in Windows XP. Technically, you run a risk of conflicting with an application that expects to have its own folder named Personal Files in that location. The risk is small, and obviously you would identify the issue as you evaluate the new application.

You could reduce the risks from such a technicality by creating a folder within the user profile with your company name and then placing Personal Files within it—for example, C:\Users\\*username*\\*company*\Personal Files. There is some elegance to that approach because there might be other user-specific folders you want to create, and you can centralize them under a common parent folder. Solution 3-9 discusses the Local Files folder, which, if you implement it, might be more elegant as a peer folder under a common parent—for example, C:\Users\\*username*\\*company*\Local Files.

If you have more than one nonmedia class of personal files, you have a choice: You can create a top-level profile folder for each class of files, or you can create a folder within a root folder, such as Local Only, and thereby centralize all personal files. Figure 3-25 shows these two options.

**Figure 3-25**    Two options for personal file structures

Which option should you choose? I suggest that it is more a matter of personal taste than anything else, and you could of course have a hybrid of first-level folders and subfolders of a common parent.

**Note**    If you have developer resources, you might ask them to look at MSDN's documentation of Known Folders in Windows Vista. Windows Vista enables you to create official profile folders, called *known folders*, which can have properties including flags that prevent roaming. Known folders that you create can also support redirection. You can easily take this idea to the next level with a set of known folders specific to your organization.

# Implement local-only file folders

After you've identified what file types you will manage as local only and you've designed a folder structure to support such data, you are ready to implement the changes. There are several steps you need to undertake:

**Create the folders:**    You need to generate the actual folders on the file system.

**Migrate data to the new folders:**    User data can then be moved to the folders.

**Ensure that applications can locate the new folders:**    Any application that looks for its data in a location that has moved will need to be updated.

**Redirect Windows XP shell folders that you are treating as local only:**    Media folders such as My Music, My Pictures, and My Videos in Windows XP can be redirected to the new location you've created for those files.

**Provide a way for users to find relocated folders:**    Make sure there's a visible, easily discovered path to the folders you've created.

**Exclude local-only folders from roaming profiles:**    Use the Group Policy setting Exclude Directories In Roaming Profile, which is located in User Configuration\Administrative Templates\System\User Profiles.

The first two steps are simple enough. The last four we will examine next.

# Ensure that applications will find relocated media folders

Let's assume you have a class of data that you are treating as local only. You have created a folder for it within the user profile and you have migrated the files out of the Documents folder to the newly created folder. Certain applications might remember the previous location of the files, so some redirection might be necessary. How you point the application to the new location depends entirely on the application. Often, there are registry values that might need to be updated or a configuration file such as an .ini or .xml file to modify.

Generally, applications find folders either with a hard-coded path or by resolving the location of a shell folder. Shell folders are discussed in the next section, and you can apply the concepts there to any application that uses shell folders. Hard-coded paths can be located with great success by searching the registry for instances of the old path, and then searching the hard disk (including system and hidden files and folders) for files with the old path in their contents.

As you design your UDS framework, you'll want to test applications that might be affected by relocating their data stores. You'll want to ensure that they can be redirected to a custom location and that they continue to function as expected. This shouldn't be *too* daunting of a task, however, because the whole point of "local-only" folders is that they are exceptions to redirection and roaming. So you probably won't have too many business applications that need to interact with such a narrow scope of data types.

## Redirect Windows XP media folders that you are treating as local only

If you are treating Windows Vista folders as local only, you should be in fine shape. All you need to do is ensure that they are not subject to folder redirection policies, and then exclude them from roaming profiles, as discussed later.

But with Windows XP, you will have to redirect the media folders that you want to treat as local only so that they are no longer subfolders of My Documents, and then exclude the new locations from the roaming profile.

To redirect shell folders such as Pictures, Music, and Videos for Windows XP clients, see Solution 3-5 on page 224. I even provided a custom Group Policy template (.adm file) with which to redirect the media folders. Just redirect them to a location within the user profile, such as %USERPROFILE%\\*foldername*, rather than to a network store, as shown in Figure 3-26.

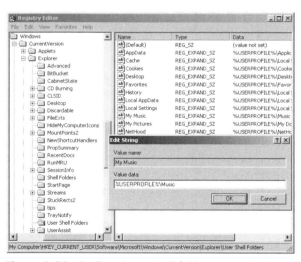

**Figure 3-26**   Redirecting a shell folder to another local location

## Provide a way for users to find relocated folders

The two previous sections stepped you through how to ensure that applications will find your local-only folders: redirecting shell folders by changing their registry values or locating the settings that each specific application uses to point to its data stores. But if you move folders—for example, the music, pictures, and videos folders—users will no longer know where to browse for them. You need to provide discoverable paths in the user interface to the relocated folders. I'll discuss two approaches that should give you enough ammunition to design an approach that works in your situation.

First, we'll use the My Music folder as an example, but similar concepts and techniques can be used for any other folder you are relocating. Windows XP users are accustomed to seeing My Music and friends inside the My Documents folder. If you have now created a new folder for music—for example, %USERPROFILE%\Music—to manage it as local only, you must provide some way for users to click their way to their music collection.

I recommend deleting the original My Music folder. The music files should have already been migrated to the new location. Then create a shortcut called My Music pointing to the new location. That way, users see the same thing they have always seen: something that looks like a folder and reveals their music collection.

The second example applies in Windows Vista, which has an overlooked and highly productive element of the user interface called the Favorite Links pane, the upper-left pane in Figure 3-27. To provide a visible, discoverable path for users to locate where we want them to store personal files, I've created a link in the links pane that targets our local-only personal files folder—for example, %userprofile%\Personal Files. To create a link in the Favorite Links pane, simply add a shortcut to the Links folder in the Windows Vista user profile.

**Figure 3-27**    The Favorite Links pane in Windows Vista

**Note**    User-interface hooks are a great place to communicate messages to users. Although the local-only folder might be named Personal Files, we could name the shortcut that creates the Favorite Link, Personal Files—Back Up Regularly, and thereby remind users it is their responsibility to back up the contents of the folder.

## Communicate to users and train them regarding local-only data

As with all aspects of a user data and settings framework, you should provide resources to communicate to users, and train users, about how to work with the UDS data stores. Local-only data is there for a reason—to support specific classes of data that are not to be roaming or redirected because of information security or information technology use policies. Make sure users know which types of data those are and what stores you've created for them to save such data. Additionally, because local-only data is stored only on the user's system, users should be reminded that it is their responsibility to back up any data they don't want to lose in the event of hardware failure or loss.

## Solution summary

In many organizations, there are types of data that should not be stored on network servers and therefore needs to be saved only on a user's local disk. This local-only data often includes users' music collections (the Music or My Music folder), sometimes extending to pictures and videos and certain types of personal files. To encourage compliance with information security and information technology user policies, you need to manage this data, meaning you need to move it so that it does not roam or redirect. You also need to make it easy for users and applications to locate the new folders.

# 3-9: Manage User Data That Should Be Accessed Locally

## Solution overview

| | |
|---|---|
| **Type of solution** | Guidance and scripts |
| **Features and tools** | Roaming user profiles, Offline Files, Group Policy, shortcuts |
| **Solution summary** | For data that needs to be accessed locally but still must be managed to meet the availability, mobility, and resiliency of the UDS framework, create one or more local folders within the user profile, but that are excluded from roaming. |
| **Benefits** | Support applications or workflows that require local data access. |

## Introduction

In the business requirements for a user data and settings (UDS) framework set forth in Solution 3-1, most requirements focused on the security, resiliency, and mobility of user data, which led to a design in which user data stores such as Documents and Desktop are redirected to servers as their primary storage location. For most user data on networks with reasonable connectivity between users and the UDS servers, this should serve to meet the requirements.

But there will always be exceptions to the rule. We used examples, earlier, of users who edit video files. That type of job task will be painful, if not impossible, with a network connection between the application and its data, so such data should be stored and accessed locally. Another example I see in some organizations is the desire to access Outlook or other e-mail archives locally for improved performance.

That is why one requirement for the framework was, "The UDS framework will support the management of exceptions." If we assume that data in these scenarios is important for the user and valuable to the organization, we must provide a managed way for users to opt out of the redirected folder model for such data so that they can access it locally; but we must also ensure the data is backed up to meet requirements for that data's resiliency and mobility.

In this solution, we look at options for managing data that should be accessed locally but must be regularly backed up to the network. This differs from the local-only data discussed in Solution 3-8, which remains *only* on the client disk. In the next solution, we'll learn exactly how to back the data up to the network stores.

## Determine the name for a local files folder

Regardless of which design you select after evaluating the options presented next, you need to determine what to name the folder or folders you will use to manage data in this category. The folder name or names should communicate one or more of the following:

- Data will be accessed from the local disk and not over the network.

- Data will be backed up with some regularity.

- The folder or folders should not become the new, local store for *all* user data—*only* for that which must be accessed locally.

- The folder or folders should not be treated as a "local-copy" alternative for offline files when a user is working while disconnected.

- The folder or folders should be used for data only while that data is being actively accessed. Once the user is finished working with the data, it should be moved into a store that is managed with redirected folders.

- The type or types of data users might maintain in the folder or folders.

I've not yet seen a name for this type of folder that was a clear winner. The kinds of names that seem to work include such names as the following:

- Local Files (or Data)

- Local Files (or Data) Backed Up

- Local Work or Work Local

- Local Business Files (as opposed to Personal Files)

In this solution, we'll pick one name—Local Files—and stick with it.

# Option 1: Use a roaming profile folder

The first option is the most straightforward: Use a folder that is managed using roaming profiles. As discussed in Solution 3-7, roaming profiles synchronize files between the network store and the local cached copy of the user profile at logon and logoff. While a user is logged on, access is from the local cache.

You could, for example, create a new Local Files folder in the user profile. As long as the folder is not specifically excluded from roaming using Group Policy, it will roam.

The disadvantage of roaming is that the synchronization happens at each logon and logoff and cannot really be stopped. That becomes a particular problem when the files in the Local Files folder are large: When users shut down their system, the transfer of that file to the server takes a long time. Users who are impatient might perform a cold shutdown or might learn that they can disconnect from the network and shut down more quickly. In either scenario, the integrity and viability of the user profile on the server is threatened.

If, however, the number and size of files that you expect to be stored in a Local Files folder are reasonable, a roaming profile folder is certainly the most straightforward solution.

# Option 2: Leverage offline files (Windows Vista only)

This approach has become possible only with Windows Vista, and it is a great approach to address scenarios in which accessing a file from a network share is problematic. Windows Vista introduced a new Group Policy setting: Network Directories To Sync At Logon/Logoff Time Only.

The policy works for redirected folders that have been made available offline. As discussed in Solution 3-6, when user folders are redirected, Windows makes them available offline automatically, by default. So if the Documents folder is redirected, Windows Vista takes it offline by default. You can then use this Group Policy setting to specify subfolders of Documents (or any other network folder such as AppData, Desktop, and so on) that should be *accessed* offline, even when the server is available. Changes made to files in the specified folders are synchronized only at logon and logoff. The effect is a roaming profile like a subfolder within an otherwise redirected folder. Nifty, huh?

The policy is located in User Configuration\Administrative Templates\System\User Profiles—a nonintuitive location for an offline files setting. Enable the policy and then specify folders using network folder names and paths to subfolders, as shown in Figure 3-28, which configures the Documents\Local Files folder to be accessed locally and synchronized only at logon and logoff.

The full path in the text box in Figure 3-28 is \\contoso.com\users\%username%\documents\local files.

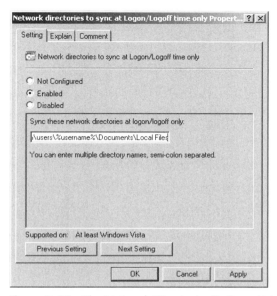

**Figure 3-28**    The Network Directories To Sync At Logon/Logoff Time Only option

Using this policy also enables you to redirect AppData in scenarios where applications do not perform well when the server is not available. This challenge was discussed in Solution 3-7. You could simply specify that the AppData subfolder for the problematic application is synchronized only at logon and logoff. This does *not* solve problems with applications that use hard-coded paths such as C:\Documents and Settings\*username*\Application Data to find the AppData folder.

OK, so what's the downside? First, it works only for Windows Vista. Second, it will synchronize at every logon and logoff (assuming the user is connected), which could again lead to challenges when the files in this class of data are large.

Third, the paths that must be entered into this policy are full UNCs, which might make your folder redirection GPO implementation tougher than it should be. Let me explain. If you use basic folder redirection, where all users' folders are redirected to a common root path—for example, \\contoso.com\users\%username%\documents—you are in luck. You can put the exact same path in the Network Directories To Sync At Logon/Logoff Time Only policy setting.

If, however, you want to use Advanced redirection, where various security groups have different target locations—such as \\contoso.com\users\sydney\%username%\documents and \\contoso.com\users\new york\%username%\documents—it gets more difficult. Either you need to put *every* possible path (in this example, the two paths including "sydney" and "new york") in the Network Directories To Sync At Logon/Logoff Time Only policy setting, *or* you need to forego advanced folder redirection and, instead, have separate GPOs—one for each security group, filtered to apply only to that security group, with basic folder redirection and the same UNC path in both the redirected folder target location setting and the Network Directories To Sync At Logon/Logoff Time Only setting. Yet one more good reason to keep the DFS namespace for your UDS framework fully enumerated and not based on things like sites.

# Option 3: Create a local folder that is backed up to a network store

The third choice for working with local files is to create a primary store on the local disk, from which files are accessed, and then to back up those files to the network. This option is the most complex to configure, but it gives you the most flexibility and control. It also allows you to support both Windows XP and Windows Vista (and any other version of Windows).

Because there can be so many flavors of this option depending on specific requirements, I'll step you through a scenario that touches all the key issues. You can then analyze your needs and build a design that addresses the issues while meeting your needs. In this scenario, we'll assume we have several types of data that need to be accessed locally: large video files and Microsoft Outlook .pst files. These are important assets to both the user and the business, so we don't want these to be local-only data that could be lost entirely in the event of hardware failure or loss. We do want to ensure there's a copy of the files on the network.

## Create the local folder

The first step is to create the local folder to act as the root for data in this class. You can choose to have more than one folder, of course. To reflect the Windows Vista namespace, we'll create a folder %userprofile%\Local Files. The folder is created outside of all redirected folders—we can't allow it to be redirected. It is also created within the user profile so that it is permissioned to allow only the user access to the folder.

## Exclude the folder from roaming

We then exclude the folder from users' roaming profiles using the Exclude Directories In Roaming Profile" policy discussed in Solution 3-7.

## Determine a backup or synchronization strategy and tools

Because data in this category is managed by the UDS framework, you must ensure that it is, with adequate regularity, backed up to or synchronized with a network store so that the data is available on other machines and is resilient in the case of hardware failure or loss on a user's system. Solution 3-10 addresses backup and synchronization options.

## Create visible navigation and access points in the user interface

Because the Local Files folder will not be in a redirected or roaming folder, you need to ensure it is easy for users to locate. You can do this by placing shortcuts or, in Windows Vista, symbolic links in appropriate user shell folders. For example, you might create a shortcut (or symbolic link) in the Documents folder called Local Files, and configure the shortcut to target the correct path on the local disk.

With Windows Vista, you can also use the Favorite Links pane, shown earlier in Figure 3-29. To create a link in the Favorite Links pane, simply add a shortcut the Links folder in the Windows Vista user profile.

## Solution summary

This solution provided guidance toward creating a store of data that will be accessed locally, to support scenarios in which data cannot be effectively supported by the core UDS management components: redirected folders, offline files, and synchronization. The first option is to create a new folder in the user profile and to allow the standard mechanism of profile merge to synchronize changes made locally with the server-based roaming profile. The second option, available only with Windows Vista, is to configure subfolders of a redirected folder to synchronize only at logon and logoff and to be accessed locally while logged on. The third option is the most flexible: It can be implemented both on Windows XP and Windows Vista, and it does not rely on any of the standard mechanisms to synchronize the local data store with the server-based store, so you have the ability to fully configure and manage synchronization based on the needs of that particular class of data. Solution 3-10 presents several tools for synchronizing local and server stores.

# 3-10: Back Up Local Data Stores for Availability, Mobility, and Resiliency

## Solution overview

| | |
|---|---|
| **Type of solution** | Guidance and scripts |
| **Features and tools** | Robocopy, VBScript, scheduled tasks, Group Policy logon and startup scripts |
| **Solution summary** | Create a mechanism through which data that must be accessed locally can be backed up to the network stores with full management control over the timing of synchronization. |
| **Benefits** | Enable management of UDS data that is not managed well through redirected folders, offline files, and roaming profiles. |

## Introduction

You will likely encounter a small number of classes of user data that cannot be supported effectively by redirected folders or offline files. Such data must therefore be accessed from a primary store on the local system. If these files are to be managed by the UDS framework—and are therefore subject to the framework requirements, including availability, mobility, security, and resiliency—there must be a mechanism to back them up to the server-based data store. But this cannot be a monolithic backup file, such as a .BKF or .WIM file—it needs to be a file-based copy on the server to provide for easy access to individual files when needed.

In this solution, we examine the components of a data backup solution. The exact solution you build will be specific to your enterprise's requirements, and it's likely you will have several variations of data backup solutions to support diverse classes of data—for example, you might back up certain classes of data every three days and other classes of data every two weeks.

Windows supports many business scenarios with roaming profiles, offline files, and roaming profiles. If your scenario can be supported by a native technology or feature, do use it. But there will likely be exception scenarios, and this solution will help you to address them.

## Define the goals of a synchronization solution

This solution is designed to meet requirements for maintaining the availability, mobility, and resiliency of data (that is, to make sure data is backed up on a server) when that data needs to be accessed locally and when the automatic synchronization options available through roaming profiles (synchronization at logon and logoff) and offline files (configurable in Windows XP, background in Windows Vista) are not yielding desirable results. The types of scenarios that fall into these categories are listed here:

- Files that do not perform acceptably when accessed over the network.
- Documents for applications that do not transfer to offline mode acceptably when a server goes offline.

In each of these scenarios, if the files are small, they can be part of a roaming user profile or, in Windows Vista, a subfolder of a user data store such as Documents that is configured to synchronize at logon and logoff. So the challenge is really to deal with large files that create unacceptably long delays when synchronizing. Therefore, the major goal of the solution is to enable an administrator or user to flexibly manage when backup or synchronization happens. Ideally, our solution should enable several timing options:

- Back up on a schedule
- Back up at startup, logon, workstation lock, or another event trigger
- Back up when idle
- Perform manual backup

Additionally, I propose these requirements:

- A single toolset is used for all backup operations.
- Backup can be done for a configurable set of folders within the user profile or for any subfolder of those folders.
- Results are logged, so we can monitor the success or (more importantly) failure of a backup.

- The namespace and files should be identical on the server and on the local client so that individual files can be accessed for support and recovery.

- Backup operations should leverage synchronization technologies to eliminate backing up files that have not changed.

If your backup model is complex, you will want to explore utilities that enable synchronization of files and folders. My personal favorite is BeyondCompare (available at *www.scootersoft-ware.com*). Microsoft SyncToy 1.4, available for free download from the Microsoft Downloads Web site, runs on Windows XP and Windows Vista and is a reasonably feature-rich tool that can be customized and automated.

Our backup model, however, is simple: Mirror the local data store to the server. The server acts as a backup to meet our needs for resiliency and availability. We are not expecting to have to resolve conflicts that occur from mutually exclusive changes in the local and server stores—just, simply, backing up. Because of that, we can leverage simple tools and scripts to achieve our needs. And with a modicum of customization, you can extend these tools and scripts to address the specifics of your situation.

## Utilize Robocopy as a backup engine

The Windows Server 2003 Resource Kit Tools (*http://www.microsoft.com/downloads/info.aspx?na=22&p=1&SrcDisplayLang=en&SrcCategoryId=&SrcFami-lyId=&u=%2fdownloads%2fdetails.aspx%3fFamilyID%3d9d467a69-57ff-4ae7-96ee-b18c4790cffd%26DisplayLang%3den*) include robocopy.exe, which can be copied to Windows XP machines. Windows Vista and Windows Server 2008 include Robocopy in the native command set.

Robocopy is to XCopy what XCopy was to Copy—the logical next step. Robocopy is a robust, feature-rich synchronization tool that is used in some environments as a replacement for File Replication Service (FRS) replication of DFS folders, and as a replacement for offline file synchronization or similar offerings from third parties. Robocopy is desirable over more standard copy tools because it does, in fact, synchronize. You can instruct it to skip files that have not changed, resulting in a significantly faster backup experience in folders where some data changes and other data does not.

As with all commands, the best way to start learning about Robocopy is to type, at a command prompt, **robocopy.exe /?**. To synchronize two folders, the following syntax is used:

```
robocopy.exe <source> <destination> /MIR [options...]
```

Without switches, the command works to synchronize the destination with the source directory. The result is that the destination is identical to the source—any files that differ are resolved by the source file, any files that exist in the source but not in the destination are copied to the destination, and any files in the destination but not in the source are deleted. In the event of problems connecting to either the source or destination, Robocopy attempts the operation every 30 seconds for one million attempts. With options, you can modify all of these behaviors and more. I find three options particularly useful:

**/COPYALL or /COPY:DATSO**   The */COPYALL* option instructs Robocopy to copy the file along with all attributes, including the DACL (permissions), SACL (auditing), and ownership information. If a standard user tries to use the */COPYALL* switch, Robocopy fails because the user does not have the right to copy auditing settings. For standard users, the maximum copy option is */COPY:DATSO*, which copies all attributes except auditing: data, attributes, time stamp, security (ACLs), and ownership.

**/R:x**   The */R* switch specifies the number of retries. I doubt you really want Robocopy running one million times if it cannot access a location.

**/W:t**   Use */W* to configure the delay, in seconds, between retries.

When Robocopy runs, it produces a verbose log of its actions—perfect for meeting our requirement to log and monitor synchronization.

## Leverage Folder_Synch.vbs as a wrapper for Robocopy

I've seen a lot of scripts that attempt to synchronize two folders, but my feeling is that if there's a Microsoft tool—particularly one that is now *supported*—I'm going to use it! So I've built a script around Robocopy that helps us to meet the requirements of our synchronization solution. The script is named Folder_Synch.vbs and is in the Scripts folder of the companion media. A simple usage of the script is as follows:

```
cscript //nologo Folder_Synch.vbs /source:"Source Folder"
    /target:"Target Folder"
```

When called from the command line, the script mirrors the source to the target. The target ends up being identical to the source. The most important lines of the script are shown here:

```
' CONFIGURATION BLOCK
sRobocopyOptions = "/COPY:DATSO /R:1 /W:30"
iRobocopyTimeout = 10
' END CONFIGURATION BLOCK
sSource = <code to determine what the source folder is>
sTarget = <code to determine what the target folder is>
sCommand = "robocopy.exe """ & sSource & """ """ & sTarget & """ /MIR " & sRobocopyOptions
aResults = Execute_Capture(sCommand, iRobocopyTimeout * 60, True)
```

In the configuration block, you specify the options for the *Robocopy* command. As mentioned in the previous section, I prefer to use */COPY:DATSO*, */R*, and */W*, which instruct Robocopy to copy all file attributes except auditing, because standard users will not have sufficient privilege to do so, and to retry the copy operation a specified number of times after a specified waiting period in the event of errors. You also specify how long in minutes to allow Robocopy to run before terminating it. You should make sure this timeout is sufficient for the largest folders that will be synchronized.

The source and target folders are determined, and then a command line is built for Robocopy. The command is run by a custom function I wrote, "Execute_Capture," which executes the command, allows it to run for a period of time before terminating it, and then returns the output of the command.

If you compare the handful of lines of the preceding code to the size of the Folder_Synch.vbs script, you'll see a huge difference. The remainder of the code is designed to profile support for a variety of scenarios—each of which provides the source and target folders differently—and to handle logging and error notification. We go into details about these portions of the code later in this solution.

So with a few lines of code, we've created the foundation for a useful mechanism with which to synchronize folders out of band from roaming profiles and redirected folders. In following sections, we'll look at the use and customization of the tool for several synchronization scenarios.

## Deploy Folder_Synch.vbs and Robocopoy

Before using Folder_Synch.vbs to back up local data stores to network servers, you must deploy Folder_Synch.vbs and robocopy.exe. Because the script will be executed in a variety of scenarios, it is recommended to put the script in a known path on each client—for example, in the Windows, System32, in a subfolder of Program Files or AppData. I recommend a subfolder of either Program Files or AppData (Application Data on Windows XP), as there are likely to be other custom tools you'll want to create and manage for all clients. The advantage of Program Files is that it is a well-known path that can be discovered using an environment variable (%PROGRAMFILES%). The advantage of AppData is that it, too, can be discovered using an environment variable (%APPDATA%), *and* it can be redirected or part of a roaming profile. Think about the benefits there: If you need to deploy a new version of a script, all you need to do is drop it into users' AppData folders in their roaming profiles on the server or servers. You don't have to touch every client! As long as the tool or script is not so large that it causes unacceptable delays while synchronizing, and as long as the tool or script doesn't have to be installed (for example, an MSI or setup.exe scenario), pushing scripts to users via AppData is an effective and efficient option.

In addition to making the script available, you must also make Robocopy available to Windows XP (and Windows Server 2003) systems. Robocopy.exe is in the Windows Server 2003 Resource Kit Tools. Copy it into the system path (System32) on Windows XP and Windows Server 2003 systems. Do *not* copy the version of robocopy.exe you'll find on Windows Vista and Windows Server 2008 machines—it is not compatible with previous versions of Windows.

## Determine how and when to run Folder_Synch.vbs for each local store

When the script and robocopy.exe are available to clients, you can begin to determine how and when you want to use Folder_Synch.vbs to back up folders from the local system to the network share. How often you want to synchronize and which folders you want to back up will be completely dependent on your business requirements. There's no best practice other than to say that the "how often" should be less frequently than daily. If you are going to back up a folder daily, you should probably consider allowing the folder to roam or, if you're using Windows Vista, to configure an offline folder that synchronizes only at logon and logoff.

The script can be launched manually, or it can be launched automatically. We'll look at various options in the following sections.

## Launch Folder_Synch.vbs manually

The first choice we'll examine is launching the script manually. You can place the script in any folder and even rename it something more discoverable, such as Back Up This Folder.vbs. Note I changed terminology from "synchronize" to "back up." The reason is that, from a *technical* perspective, when the script runs it is using Robocopy's synchronization algorithm, so it is synchronizing. However, I prefer to present this tool to users as a "backup" tool to separate it from the Synchronization Manager (Windows XP) or Sync Center (Windows Vista). Particularly if users are going to double-click the tool, as we're discussing in this section, I think it is helpful to communicate about the tool in a way that emphasizes that data on the local machine is being backed up to the server.

When double-clicked, the script synchronizes the folder in which the script is found. The script always synchronizes the entire folder tree because the */MIR* switch is used in the Robocopy command within the script. The key lines of code that enable this behavior are as follows:

```
bInteractive = (WScript.FullName <> WScript.Path & "\cscript.exe")

' EVALUATE SOURCE & DESTINATION
If Not bInteractive Then
    ...
Else
    ' Not interactive - called from WScript
    If WScript.Arguments.Count = 0 Then
        ' The script has been double-clicked
        ' or otherwise called with no arguments.
        ' This supports a scenario in which user runs the script "Back Up This".
        ' We assume, then, that we are to back up the script's parent folder.
        sSource = FSO.GetParentFolderName(Wscript.ScriptFullName)
```

First, the script examines the command with which the script was launched. If the command does not start with cscript.exe, the script sets a global variable, *bInteractive*, to *True*, which flags the script as having been launched interactively (for example, by double-clicking). The *sSource* variable is then set to the parent folder of the script itself. Robocopy uses *sSource* to indicate the source folder that is being synchronized to a target folder.

So where is the target itself? If the script is called with *cscript*, as discussed in later sections, the */source* and */target* switches are specified, so the source and target can be anything, really. But if the script is launched interactively, by double-clicking, for example, it behaves differently. The script is built with the assumption that it will be used interactively only within a UDS framework—that is, only subfolders of the user profile root will be allowed to be synchronized. The assumption is also made that there is a single folder for the user on a network server within which all synchronized folders will be created. That network folder is called the *user's synchronization root*, and it is represented by a variable in the script, *sUserSyncRoot*. Said another way, each user has a root folder for backing up his or her local files. The user's synchronization root on the server is equivalent to the user's local profile root folder, and the namespace beneath *sUserSyncRoot* will be identical to that under the user's local profile root.

It will be easier to understand with an example. Let's assume we've created a folder called "Backups" within each user's redirected folders root—for example, \\contoso.com\users\ %username%\backups. An example is shown in Figure 3-29. If, for example, you have a folder with the path %userprofile%\Local Files and you synchronize that folder, it will synchronize to a folder named Local Files underneath the user's synchronization root (*sUserSyncRoot*), "\\*path to synchronization root for the user*\local files." In our example, that would be "\\contoso.com\users\%username%\backups\local files" as seen in Figure 3-29.

**Figure 3-29**   A user's synchronization root

Not every folder will be synchronized using the script, but folders that are synchronized this way will appear beneath the user synchronization root in the same hierarchy they appear in beneath the user profile.

The target folder is represented in the script by the variable *sTarget*. To determine the target folder when the script is run interactively, these lines of code are used:

```
Set WSHShell = CreateObject("WScript.Shell")
sUserProfile = WSHShell.ExpandEnvironmentStrings("%userprofile%")
sUser = WSHShell.ExpandEnvironmentStrings("%username%")
sUserSyncRoot = "\\contoso.com\users\" & sUser & "\backups"
sUserLocalRoot = sUserProfile
sTarget = sUserSyncRoot & Mid(sSource, Len(sUserLocalRoot)+1)
If Not FolderPath_Create(sTarget) Then …
```

The first two lines identify the path of the user's local profile (for example, C:\Users\*user-name*). The third line identifies the username, which is then used to determine the path to the user's synchronization root, stored as *sUserSyncRoot*. The *sUserLocalRoot* variable is set to the user's profile path.

The magic happens on the last two lines, which ensure the same namespace appears in the user's synchronization root folder as in the user profile. The source folder path represented by *sSource* is effectively stripped of the part of the path that is the user profile path, leaving only the relative path to the source beneath the user profile, and that is appended to the user's synchronization root path. The last line shown in the preceding code snippet calls the *FolderPath_Create* function. This function checks to see whether the target path exists and, if it does not, it creates the folder structure. This is important the first time that the script is run so that the target folder actually exists before being used by Robocopy.

## Enable users to right-click a folder and back it up using a shell command

The Folder_Synch.vbs script also supports being used as a shell command. You can allow users to right-click a folder and choose a command, such as Back Up, to launch the script and synchronize the selected folder to the synchronization root. Of course, you don't want users to be able to back up *every* folder—just stores of local files within the user profile—so that the script has logic to determine which folders are allowed to be backed up.

Although this method is slick in its integration into the user interface, the disadvantage is that the Back Up shell command will be *visible* on any folder. When executed, the command notifies the user if the selected folder is not allowed to be backed up, but there is no way to limit the command's visibility without significantly greater development efforts.

To add a shell command, you must modify the Folder key of *HKEY_Classes_Root*, which requires administrative credentials. In the Registry Editor, locate HKEY_Classes_Root\Folder\shell and create a new key with the name Back Up (or whatever name you want to use for the command). Create a new string value that calls wscript.exe followed by the full path to the script (in quotes, because the path to the script might contain spaces) followed by "%1" (in quotes, because the source path might have spaces).

Alternatively, create a registry merge file in Notepad with the following text:

```
Windows Registry Editor Version 5.00
[HKEY_CLASSES_ROOT\Folder\shell\Back Up\command]
@="wscript.exe \"%APPDATA%\\Contoso\\Utilities\\folder_synch.vbs\" \"%1\""
```

Modify the command (Back Up) in the registry path to reflect the command name you want to use, and modify the path in the last line ("%APPDATA%\Contoso\Utilities\folder_synch.vbs") to point to the path to which you've deployed the script. Save the file with a .reg extension and then merge it by double-clicking or by running **regedit.exe /s** *filename*.

If you're not familiar with registry merge files, you might be surprised by the plethora of back-slashes in the preceding example. Quotation marks are technically supposed to be used only at the beginning and end of the string value. When the string value needs to contain quota-tion marks, that is achieved by escaping (flagging) the internal quotation marks with the escape character, which happens to be a backslash. So \"%1\" translates to "%1" when it is merged into the registry. Because the backslash is the escape character, if you actually want to include a backslash in the string you have to escape the backslash, leading to two backslashes. So %APPDATA%\\contoso\\utilities becomes %APPDATA%\contoso\utilities as it is merged into the registry.

The shell command appears on every object of class *Folder*. When the command is selected, it launches the script, passing to it as the %1 parameter the path to the folder that was selected.

After you've added the shell command that launches the script, you must also configure the script to specify which folders are allowed to be backed up in that way. The following lines of code are used to validate whether the folder that was selected and passed to the script is a valid folder:

```
sUserLocalRoot = sUserProfile
aSyncFolders = Array("Local Files","Videos")
bSyncSubFolders = True
sSource = WScript.Arguments(0)
   bAllowed = False
   For Each sSyncFolder In aSyncFolders
         ' For each subfolder specified in aSyncFolders
         ' underneath the root specified by sUserLocalRoot
         ' check to see if there's a match with the sSource
         sAllowedFolder = sUserLocalRoot & "\" & sSyncFolder
         If StrComp(Left(sSource, Len(sAllowedFolder)), sAllowedFolder, _
         vbTextCompare) = 0 Then
               If ((bSyncSubFolders) Or _
                     (Len(sSource) = Len(sAllowedFolder))) Then
                     bAllowed = True
                     Exit For
               End If
         End If
   Next
   If Not bAllowed Then <tell the user that they cannot back up this folder>
```

The script is hard-coded in the logic of the *For/Next* loop to allow backup only for subfolders of the user profile, represented by the variable *sUserLocalRoot*. The specific subfolders that are allowed are stored in the array *aSyncFolders*. These folders are excluded from the roaming pro-file and are not to be redirected—they are managed within the UDS framework by this syn-chronization effort. All you have to do to customize the behavior of the script in this (shell command) scenario is to modify the contents of *aSyncFolders* to represent which folders you want users to be able to back up.

The *bSyncSubFolders* variable, if *true*, means that a user can choose the shell backup command for the entire folder tree, starting at the folder specified in *aSyncFolders*, or for any individual subfolder. For example, a user might want to back up only %userprofile%\Local Files\ Projects\Team A, without backing up the entire Projects folder or the entire Local Files folder. If you set *bSyncSubFolders* to *false*, a user can launch backup only from the folders specified in *aSyncFolders*, not from one of the subfolders. In either case, once the backup begins, the same namespace will be created in the user synchronization root and all subfolders of the source folder are synchronized.

## Compare manual options for Folder_Synch.vbs

We've seen two options for allowing users to manually trigger the synchronization of data in their local files stores to the server. The first entails putting the script in a folder, and when the script is launched, that folder is backed up. The second involves adding a shell command to the context menu of every folder, and when the script is launched, it backs up the folder but only if the folder is allowed to be backed up.

If your synchronization model is simple, I recommend the first option. If, for example, you have all local files in a single root—for example, %userprofile%\Local Files—put the script in that folder and name it something discoverable like Back Up This Folder. There's no need to add a shell command to every folder if only one folder is going to be allowed to be backed up. If, however, you plan to use this approach on multiple folders in diverse areas of the user profile, you might be better served by the shell command approach.

There are two other options to discuss. First, you can modify the script so that it can be launched once and it automatically backs up all folders that need to be backed up, even if those folders are in different parts of the user profile. For example, the script might back up %userprofile%\Local Files *and* %userprofile%\Videos. In this scenario, users launch the script once to fully back up all files that are not being saved on the UDS server up by roaming profiles or redirected folders. I recommend putting a shortcut to the script someplace very discoverable, such as on the desktop or in the Start menu.

The other option is *not* to provide a manual option and to run the script on a schedule, thereby ensuring that user data is being backed up. Of course, you could run the script on a schedule *and* provide the user the ability to trigger synchronization manually, as well. In the next sections, we look at ways to launch the script automatically.

## Run Folder_Synch.vbs automatically

There are several issues related to Folder_Synch.vbs that must be addressed while designing a way for it to run automatically. The most important issue is that when Folder_Synch.vbs executes, it can take quite some time for the local files to synchronize with the server. Robocopy copies only changed files, but if a changed file is large, the file copy time could be significant. Also, if the folder being synchronized has an extremely large number of files, it can take time to scan the files to determine what has changed. Hopefully, you're not in the latter boat, because you shouldn't be having to manage *that* many files outside of the scope of roaming profiles or redirected folders. But you need to be aware that either quantity or size of local files can cause synchronization to take time.

During synchronization, it is important that files are unlocked so that they can be copied successfully. Ideally, users should not work with files that are being synchronized. When the script runs interactively, it notifies users to that effect. But if you plan to run the script automatically, particularly if the user is logged on, you need to consider whether locked files will prevent successful synchronization and, if so, how to ensure the user doesn't have files locked until after the process is complete.

Similarly, you want to be sure that the synchronization runs to completion. If synchronization is running at logoff or shutdown, for example, the user might disconnect the machine from the network or perform a hard power down.

Finally, you need to ensure that synchronization actually does occur; otherwise, local files that should be managed by the UDS framework are not backed up to the server. How often synchronization needs to happen and for which folders are, again, questions that will best be answered in the light of your business requirements.

With these issues on the table, you are ready to decide how to run the script. You will use the following syntax:

```
cscript //nologo "Path\Folder_Synch.vbs" /source:"Source Folder"
    /target:"Target Folder" /interval:Days
```

Note the addition of the */interval* argument. This argument specifies the number of days that must have elapsed since the previous successful backup. Only if that number of days has passed is synchronization launched. An interval of zero, or a missing interval argument, causes synchronization to occur without regard to the last successful synch.

## Run Folder_Synch.vbs as a scheduled task

You can configure a scheduled task to execute the script. The many settings and practical examples of task scheduling are beyond the scope of this discussion and are detailed in other solutions in this resource kit. So I'll keep the discussion at a high level for our current purposes.

You can configure scheduled tasks on Windows XP, Windows Server 2003, Windows Vista, and Windows Server 2008. The latter two platforms support many more configurations and options, so you will need to consider which operating systems are in use to determine how to configure scheduled tasks appropriately. Tasks are launched based on a trigger, which can be a schedule, startup, logon, or idle time. Windows Vista and Windows Server 2008 add many more triggers, including connection to a session, workstation lock and unlock, or on the detection of an event log event.

The following tips will help you align the task scheduler with your needs:

- Tasks can be scheduled from the command line using the schtasks.exe command.

- A task can launch a script that performs an action, deletes the task, and creates another task. Using this trick, you can create a script that backs up local files and then schedules itself to run again starting at an appropriate date in the future. This provides possibilities for more flexible scheduling than a calendar-based (daily, weekly, or monthly) schedule.

- Windows Vista tasks have an option that allows the machine to execute tasks that were missed because the machine was offline.

Microsoft TechNet has an excellent discussion of task scheduling and how it has changed in Windows Vista and Windows Server 2008 at *http://technet.microsoft.com/en-us/windows-vista/aa906020.aspx.*

Also keep in mind that just because a task executes doesn't mean something has to happen! You could, for example, configure a task to launch synchronization at each logon. You can customize the script to recognize when the last successful synchronization occurred and to launch synchronization only if the backup interval you determined has been exceeded. Options for enabling the script to self-manage its execution are presented in the next section.

## Run Folder_Synch.vbs as a logon, logoff, startup, or shutdown script

The script's execution can also be managed by assigning the script as a startup, shutdown, logon, or logoff script within a Group Policy object. In this event, you need to ensure that synchronization doesn't actually occur at each logon, logoff, startup, or shutdown. The script needs to be able to identify when the last synchronization occurred and trigger a new backup only if the determined backup interval has been exceeded.

```
sSuccessFlagFile = "_Contoso Synchronization Success.txt"
sFailureFlagFile = "_Contoso Synchronization Failure.txt"
' Self-management.
' Determine the backup interval (in days) passed to the script
If WScript.Arguments.Named("interval") = "" Then
   iBackupInterval = 0
Else
   iBackupInterval = CInt(WScript.Arguments.Named("interval"))
End If
' Check flag file for most recent successful synch.
sSuccessFlag = sSource & "\" & sSuccessFlagFile
sFailureFlag = sSource & "\" & sFailureFlagFile
If ((iBackupInterval > 0) And (FSO.FileExists(sSuccessFlag))) Then
  Set oFile = FSO.GetFile(sSuccessFlag)
  ' Determine the date on the Success flag.
   ' I found LastModified was more reliable than Created.
  dLastSuccess = oFile.DateLastModified
  iInterval = Int(Now()- dLastSuccess)
  If iInterval < iBackupInterval Then
       ' This should be a scheduled backup,
```

```
        ' and the interval has not yet passed, so quit
        sMessage =  "The last successful backup occurred on" & VbCrLf & _
                      Cstr(dLastSuccess) & "." & VbCrLf & _
                      "The next backup should be made on or after" & VbCrLf & _
                      CStr(dLastSuccess + iBackupInterval) & "."
        Call Notify (sMessage, "SYNCHRONIZATION NOT NEEDED", 30, 64)
        If UCase(WScript.Arguments.Named("schedule"))<>"IGNORE" Then
              WScript.Quit(0)
        End If
    End If
End If
```

The preceding code looks at the */interval* argument provided to the script and saves it in the variable *iBackupInterval*. It then looks at the timestamp on the success flag file (the name of which can be customized in the configuration block) to determine whether synchronization is not needed. A backup interval of zero, a missing */interval* argument, or a missing flag file causes synchronization to proceed.

The flag files are created when synchronization completes. By default, they are hidden files. You can, in the configuration block, configure the files to be superhidden (*system* and *hidden* attributes) or unhidden.

## Log and monitor synchronization

The script is quite long relative to its simple task to launch Robocopy to back up a local folder to a server. The length is because of the business logic that supports running the script interactively or using *cscript* with a variety of different parameters and because of the logging activity that the script supports.

Folder_Synch.vbs creates a log in the root of the folder that is synchronized. The name of the log is set in the configuration block and assigned to a variable, *sSyncLogFileName*. I recommend using a name such as "_Contoso Synchronization Log.txt" so that it appears at the top of the list of files in a folder and has an extension that can easily be opened in Notepad. Because the file would be in the way for users and is really only meant for support personnel who need to monitor or troubleshoot synchronization, the file is configured as a hidden file. In the configuration block are two parameters that determine whether the file is just hidden (by default) or superhidden (*system* and *hidden* attributes) or neither.

Each synchronization operation is logged at the beginning of the log, so older operations are further down in the file. To prevent the log from becoming too large, you can configure a size limit (2 MB by default). When the log reaches the size specified by *iSyncLogMaxSize*, it purges the oldest information to reduce the file size. The amount of information that is deleted is set in the call to the *TextFile_Purge* function: 25%. This isn't the world's slickest first-in, first-out (FIFO) logging, but it works to keep the log size manageable.

The script also creates a flag file based on the success or failure of the synchronization operation. The names of the success and failure flag files are also specified in the configuration block. Again, I recommend a name starting with an underscore and with a .txt extension. Like the log, these files are hidden by default and can be set to superhidden in the configuration block.

The logs and flag files are copied to the server *after* the synchronization operation. So the synchronization copies the most recent log. After synchronization, the log and flag files are updated locally and then copied to the server using xcopy.exe. That way, if connectivity or other problems are preventing effective file operations on the server, as much information as possible can be captured on the local machine.

The fact that log and flag files are on the server allows you to monitor synchronization. Let's assume you are synchronizing only users' Local Files folder (%userprofile%\Local Files) as created in Solution 3-9. Each user, on the server, has a backup folder in the path "\\contoso.com\users\%username%\backup". It is fairly trivial to create a script that looks in each user's Backup folder, in the Local Files subfolder, determines whether a file with the name of the synchronization success flag exists, and then examines that file's time stamp. The existence of a success (or failure) flag and the file's timestamp can be used to determine whether something is wrong with the synchronization framework for a particular user.

You could also configure the script to log its success or failure in a centralized database as simple as an Excel file on an accessible network share or as sophisticated as a central SQL database. Alternatively, with Windows Vista, you could create event log entries that are subscribed to for central logging.

I highly recommend visiting the solutions Web site for this resource kit. I expect the community of IT professionals reading this resource kit solution will extend it to provide monitoring and reporting capabilities.

## Solution summary

This solution was a big one, and it has the opportunity to provide a lot of value in several scenarios. Windows' roaming profiles, redirected folders, offline files, and synchronization are tremendous technologies, and they should be used whenever they address your requirements. However, there will be scenarios in which a particular class of data cannot be accessed by the user directly from a server (redirected folders), does not transition well to offline use (offline files), or causes pain when synchronized (roaming profiles or offline files synchronization) generally because of file size.

This solution built a script that wraps around Robocopy to enable you to back up a local data store with a folder on the network. Folder_Synch.vbs can be launched manually by double-clicking it in a folder that you want to back up or through a shell command allowing you to right-click a folder and back it up. It also can be launched as a scheduled task or logon/logoff/startup/shutdown script, during which the script can determine whether synchronization is necessary or not based on a configurable backup interval. The script has moderate levels of error checking and logging to enable monitoring of users' backup operations.

> **Important**    This solution gets users' local files onto the server to meet the requirements for resiliency (backup) of business data within the UDS framework. We have not yet provided for *roaming* capabilities to meet the mobility requirements of the framework. In other words, when a user logs on to a new system and wants his or her local files, how do those files get *down* from the server to the client? The Folder_Synch.vbs can be turned around to provide a mechanism with which data can be synchronized from the user's backup on the network to the user's local profile. The solutions Web site for this resource kit (www.intelliem.com/resourcekit) provides that script.

# 3-11: Design UDS Components That Align Requirements and Scenarios with Features and Technologies (Part II)

## Solution overview

| | |
|---|---|
| **Type of solution** | Guidance |
| **Features and tools** | Redirected folders, offline files, roaming user profiles, Group Policy |
| **Solution summary** | Analyze the data stores and types of data within your organization to identify the ideal design for managing user data and settings. |
| **Benefits** | Go beyond best practice to identify what is really necessary in your environment. |

## Introduction

We've now completed a fairly exhaustive (and, perhaps, exhausting) tour of the components of a user data and settings (UDS) framework. Believe it or not, we've only scratched the surface. But hopefully you've learned enough about the components to be able to create an intelligent, effective design for the UDS framework in your enterprise.  Solution 3-2 set forth my proposal for a framework—what I think will work in many organizations. Now you've seen all the pieces of the puzzle and it's time to put them together to create the perfect picture given your requirements.

## Recognize the crux of the challenge

Microsoft gives us a lot of technologies and features to support UDS: profiles, roaming profiles, redirected folders, offline files, synchronization, Robocopy, quotas, file screens, DFS, shared folders, and NTFS folders. Some of those pieces just don't play well together. We have more than two classes of data: some data that performs well redirected and offline, some that is OK to redirect but doesn't make a graceful state transition to offline, some of which does not synchronize acceptably, some of which we need to access locally, and some of which we don't want on servers at all. That's a big matrix of variables, and we have only a few data stores, most notably Desktop and Documents, with which to support those variables.

# Identify the desired classes of data stores

I propose that we can identify five types of data stores, based on the business requirements and behaviors of data:

- Data that does not need to be managed to meet the availability, mobility, security, and resiliency requirements of the UDS framework. The following types of data fall into this category:

    - Data or settings currently in the user profile that we simply don't care about. This data will continue to be stored in the user profile but *excluded* from roaming.

    - Data that the user needs to access but that we do not want on servers to comply with information security or information technology policies. (Personal Files or Local Only). This data, too, will be in managed locations within the user profile that are excluded from roaming.

- Data that does need to be managed to meet the availability, mobility, security, and resiliency requirements of the UDS framework. The following types of data fall into this category:

    - Data that can live in redirected folders and be available when a user is disconnected using offline files. If data can be managed with those two features, it should be. (Redirected Folders)

    - Data that cannot live in redirected folders but for which regular synchronization is acceptable. This data will live in the user profile and will roam. (Roaming Profile)

    - Data that cannot live in redirected folders and for which regular synchronization mechanisms (roaming and offline files synchronization) are not acceptable. This data will live in the user profile and will not roam, but it will be backed up regularly to the network. (Local Files)

Notice there are at least two stores—Local Files (that are backed up) and Local Only or Personal Files (that are not)—for which Windows provides no direct management path. We needed to create management capabilities for those stores from scratch. We created subfolders of the user profile, excluded them from roaming, and developed a script to back up Local Files to the user's Backups folder on a regular basis. If we were treating a typical shell folder—such as My Music—as Local Only or Personal Files, we learned that we could redirect that folder to a local location so that it would not be targeted to a network store.

# Analyze and classify your user data stores and data

To help you design your UDS framework, I created a necessarily complex decision diagram shown in Figure 3-30. It steps you through a series of questions to determine how to manage a particular data store or file.

You use this diagram by executing it in two phases.

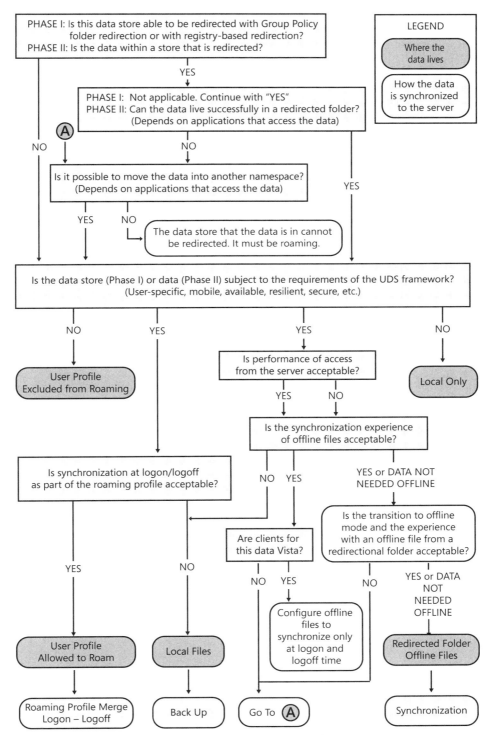

**Figure 3-30**   User Data and Settings framework decision diagram

## Phase I: Analyze how to manage your user data stores

In the first phase, you run through the decision diagram for each Windows user data store. Your goal is to determine where that data store, as a whole, should live. The stores you should analyze include Documents, Desktop, Application Data, Favorites, Pictures, Videos, Music, and the registry file (Ntuser.dat). You should also analyze any other user data store that is to be managed by your UDS framework. Some organizations might choose to manage Cookies, for example. You might also choose to manage the new Windows Vista profile folders such as Saved Searches, Downloads, Links, and so on.

It will be difficult to think about the store without thinking about the specific data that lives in it. But in Phase II, you'll look at the data in each data store to determine whether that data can continue to live in that data store, needs to be relocated to another store, or necessitates relocating its parent store. So as you go through Phase I, approach the questions with an 80/20 rule perspective. For example, when you get to the question, "Is performance of access from the server acceptable?", don't answer it by thinking of the largest, slowest, most heinous piece of data in the store—think about the general population of files. This phase identifies the rules—the way you will manage the store as a whole. Phase II will help you identify and manage the exceptions.

I'll provide you with my answers here, as a way of providing perspective and guidance for getting through this phase:

- All key user data stores can be redirected, except for Ntuser.dat. Ntuser.dat, as a store, will land squarely in the User Profile Allowed To Roam bucket.

- We learned that you can redirect all key user data stores—including Favorites, Pictures, Music, and Videos. Where there are not folder redirection policies, there is registry redirection. In general (80 percent of the time), data in these folders can live in redirected folders, performance will be acceptable, synchronization will be adequate, and the transition to offline mode will be acceptable. So I expect that all user shell folders will end up in the Redirected Folder bucket. The exceptions will be folders that you peel off because you don't want them on the network at all. If you don't want users' music collections on your servers, those stores will end up in the Local Only bucket. The other exception will be for Windows XP shell folders that you can't redirect with Group Policy folder redirection. If you for some reason don't want to redirect them with the registry, they will end up in the User Profile Allowed To Roam bucket.

- Application Data (AppData\Roaming in Windows Vista) will be tricky. You might not know enough about how data in that store behaves in your environment, so you might not be comfortable that even 80 percent of it can live in a redirected folder. You might end up, as I proposed, dumping Application Data into the User Profile Allowed To Roam bucket for the time being, until you have had time to adequately test it as a redirected folder.

## Phase II: Classify data

Phase II is about the exceptions to the rules. This is where your answers will likely be very unique to your organization. In this phase, you repeat the decision diagram for each type of data you support. You first need to come up with a healthy list of data types based on your business. I'll suggest just a few:

**Large work files.**   These files are very large. Throughout this Solution Collection, we've referred to the example of users who work with large video files. Those might not perform or synchronize acceptably from the server side of a redirected folder.

**E-mail archives.**   E-mail archives, too, are very large. They could be considered as part of the large work files collection just mentioned. But I'll break it down even further to help you get a feeling for how to identify data types in your enterprise:

**Outlook 2003 .pst files.**   You can take .pst files from Outlook 2003 (and earlier) through the decision diagram. Early on, you are asked, "Can the data live in a redirected folder?" The answer is "No" in the case of Outlook 2003, as it does not support accessing .pst files from the network. (Although I know some people do it, it's not supported.) Then you are asked, "Can it be moved into another namespace?" Sure. You can move Outlook 2003 .pst files anywhere you want them to be and, because of support issues, they probably should be in a local store. But those files are large, and synchronizing one back to the network at each logoff's profile synchronization will likely not be acceptable. I expect you'll decide that Outlook 2003 .pst files belong in the Local Files bucket.

**Outlook 2007 .pst files.**   Microsoft now supports accessing Outlook 2007 .pst files from the network. So "Yes," the data can live in a redirected folder, and "Yes," we want to manage them, and (let's assume), "Yes," performance is acceptable. What about synchronization? Windows XP clients will detect that the file has changed just by touching it with Outlook (even if no items were added, modified, or deleted). Windows XP's synchronization will then want to copy the *entire* .pst file down to the local cache, which will bog the system down. So regular synchronization might not be acceptable, landing Outlook 2007 .pst files in the Local Files bucket as well.

# Solution summary

By walking the decision diagram in Figure 3-30, you will be able to analyze, first, each user data store and, second, each type of data you support. You will see why I recommended the framework we laid out in Solution 3-2. More importantly, you'll be able to modify my suggestions to create the best possible storage and management framework for the user data and settings in your enterprise. The decision diagram allows you to reconcile the requirements for mobility, availability, resiliency, and security with the realities of diverse and sometimes problematic classes of real-world data and technologies.

Solution Collection 4

# Implementing Document Management and Collaboration with SharePoint

For the first decade or more of Microsoft Windows technologies, collaboration around documents has been supported through shared folders. Because they will still be necessary in some scenarios, I provided detailed coverage of shared folders in Solution Collection 2, "Managing Files, Folders, and Shares." The addition of Windows SharePoint Services version 3.0 (WSS) as a feature of Windows Server 2003 and a downloadable component for Windows Server 2008 enables advanced collaboration and document management capabilities that shared folders can only dream of.

WSS provides valuable functionality to enterprises, including support for document libraries (the subject of this Solution), lists (both preset and custom), wikis, blogs, discussion forums, calendars, tasks, issue tracking, surveys, and more. All of this is accessible through Web applications provided by WSS, with a back-end data source in an instance of Microsoft SQL Server, and authentication from Active Directory or any other .NET 2.0 authentication providers. Microsoft also released Microsoft Office SharePoint Server 2007, which you can obtain through separate (and not free) licensing. Office SharePoint Server builds upon the foundation of WSS to provide Web content management, enterprise search, business intelligence, portals, and support for business process and forms. Although Office SharePoint server is a truly phenomenal product, don't be so distracted by it that you overlook the incredible value to be found in WSS.

> **Note**    When speaking of tasks or features applicable to both Windows SharePoint Services 3.0 and Office SharePoint Server 2007, I'll use the term "SharePoint" rather than WSS.

In this Solution Collection, we configure a secure, fully functional document library; demonstrate key document management and collaboration functionality; and learn about the interaction between SharePoint and applications, including applications within Microsoft Office 2007 and 2003. Because you are probably less familiar with SharePoint than you are with some other technologies, I'll start from square one, to ensure that you, your IT organization, and your end users are able to go from A to Z. Along the way, I'll point out and solve some of the common challenges faced by organizations implementing WSS document libraries. So if you are familiar with SharePoint technologies already, I encourage you to glance through each solution with an eye out for headings and tips that will help you take your existing implementation to the next level of manageability, usability, and efficiency.

## Scenarios, Pain, and Solution

The scenarios that drive implementation of SharePoint Products and Technologies, such as WSS document libraries, revolve around collaboration and document management:

- In preparation for a merger, the legal department of Adventure Works needs to analyze existing agreements of all kinds, including contracts with vendors and customers. Unfortunately, locating contracts dispersed across a large number of shared folders is challenging. Once contracts are located, they must be opened and read individually to determine critical information such as the contract termination date and the parties to the contract. The legal department asks the IT organization to support a method for making key pieces of information about a contract more visible and accessible so that reports and analyses can be generated more easily in the future.

- Employees, managers, and accounting personnel at Northwind Traders have supported a manual process for routing expense reports for approval and reimbursement. The process is manual, lengthy, and prone to problems when someone involved is busy or on vacation. To improve productivity, the company decides to implement an automated workflow for this common and important process.

■ The business development department at A. Datum Corporation wants to ensure the consistency of proposals to prospective customers by managing a single set of templates for marketing, proposals, agreements, and follow-up.

■ As product plans are developed at Trey Research, the complexity of documentation requires that only one user make changes at a time; otherwise, the reconciliation of multiple changes is nearly impossible. The IT organization needs to find a way to ensure only one user is editing such documents at any time.

■ The communications department at Proseware, Inc., wants to ensure that outgoing marketing collateral is accurate and representative of the company's branding and messaging. They have assigned a small committee to be responsible for approving any changes to collateral, and have asked IT to make sure that users in the organization can see and use only approved versions.

■ Tailspin Toys has discovered some unethical behavior on the part of one of its employees, who management believes has introduced questionable data into important Microsoft Office Excel documents. They've asked IT to provide a complete audit trail of changes to the document, but IT can provide only versions that were backed up and preserved on a weekly backup rotation.

■ Product Managers at Contoso, Ltd., are preparing for the launch of the next big thing. As deadlines approach and as documents, worksheets, and presentations related to the project near completion, they want to be immediately informed of any changes made to the documents.

■ Users and IT professionals everywhere want a way to search for information more easily, across and within document stores and documents.

These are some of the scenarios that SharePoint document libraries can address. I think you'll find that libraries are easy to create, configure, and manage—so easy that you will be amazed at the rich functionality they provide.

# 4-1: Create and Configure a Document Library

## Solution overview

| | |
|---|---|
| **Type of solution** | Procedures |
| **Features and tools** | SharePoint sites, document libraries, permissions, and groups |
| **Solution summary** | Create a SharePoint site and a document library, and configure a library's settings, permissions, and template. |
| **Benefits** | Implement a secure, well-configured, URL-friendly site and document library. |

# Introduction

Before we dive into a more advanced configuration of a document library, we have to get one up and running. In this solution, we cover the procedures for creating a site and a document library. We then look at some of the library settings you'll want to configure before releasing a library into the wild, the most important of which is, not surprisingly, the library's permissions.

The procedures we'll cover are fairly rudimentary. If you are an experienced SharePoint administrator, you'll be well served to quickly skim the solution and look at the tips that are called out. If you are new to SharePoint, I recommend you practice these procedures in a test environment to gain hands-on experience with them.

> **Note**   You can download WSS from the Microsoft Web site at *http://technet.microsoft.com/windowsserver/sharepoint*. On that site, you'll find documentation detailing the installation of WSS.

# Create a site

To create a site for the document library, you must sign in to the site with credentials that have the Create Subsites permission. This permission is assigned to the site's Owners group and is part of the Full Control permission level. To accomplish this, follow these steps:

1. In Internet Explorer, connect to the default site for SharePoint Services by typing **http://your_server_name** in the Address text box. Then choose the Create command. This can be done several ways:

   ❑ Click the Site Actions button on the right side of the Team Site page, and then choose the Create command.

   ❑ Click the View All Site Content link in the Quick Launch bar on the left side of the Team Site page, and then click the Create button in the toolbar.

2. Below Web Pages, click the Sites And Workspaces link.

3. Enter a title for the site.

4. Optionally, enter a description.

5. Enter the URL for the site.

> **Note**   Avoid using spaces wherever possible in URLs.

6. Select the Team Site template or a custom template that you have created for your enterprise.

7. Choose whether to Use Same Permissions As Parent Site or Use Unique Permissions. The WSS security model is discussed later in this solution.

8. Make Navigation and Navigation Inheritance choices based on your site user-interface design.

9. Click Create.

# Create a document library

To create a document library, you must sign in to the site with credentials that have the Manage List permission. This permission is assigned to the site's Owners group and is part of the Design permission level. Follow these steps:

1. Choose the Create command. This can be done several ways:

   ❑ Click the Site Actions button, and then choose the Create command.

   ❑ Click the View All Site Content link in the Quick Launch bar, and then click the Create button in the toolbar.

2. Below Libraries, click Document Library (or Picture Library if you are creating a library for photos and graphics).

3. The New page for the document library appears. In the Name text box, enter a name for the library.

   Most settings on the page are easily changed after the library has been created, as we'll see later in this Solution Collection. The Name field, however, is a bit tricky and must be configured correctly the first time on the New page for the document library. The Name field is used to create the library's title and the library's URL. The title is easy to change after the library is created. Modifying the URL, however, is not straightforward. The URL that is created is http://*sharepoint.server.fqdn*/*site*/*name*, where *name* is what you enter in the Name field on the New page for the document library.

> **Note**   I recommend that you create a name that is URL friendly—specifically, follow these guidelines:
>
> ❑ Keep the name short.
>
> ❑ Create the name in the desired case (uppercase or lowercase).
>
> ❑ Avoid spaces, because spaces are sometimes necessary to represent as the escaped space, %20. For example, when you navigate to the document library that is created in the default team site, you'll see this URL: *http://sharepoint.server.fqdn/ Shared%20Documents*.
>
> After the library is created, you can change the library's title to a more user-friendly name, including capitalization and spacing, in the library's settings. I describe the steps for this process later in the solution.

4. Optionally, enter a description in the Description text box. This description will appear below the document library heading on the library's page.

5. In the Navigation section, specify whether you want the library to appear as a link on the site's Quick Launch.

6. If you want to e-mail–enable the library, click Yes in the Incoming E-mail section and enter a unique mailbox name for the library. This option will not be visible if you have not enabled incoming e-mail using SharePoint Central Administration. I'll discuss e-mail–enabling libraries in Solution 4-5 on page 329.

7. You can enable version history by selecting Yes in the Document Version History section. I'll discuss version history in Solution 4-11 on page 345.

8. Select a document template from the Document Template drop-down list.

   If a document library will generally or exclusively contain one type of document—such as generic Microsoft Office Word, Excel, or PowerPoint documents—and if that type is in the Document Template drop-down list, select it. But in most situations, such as the following ones, you should choose None as the template:

   ❏ The template for the type of document you want to create when clicking the New button in the document library is not listed.

   ❏ The library will contain documents created with a custom document template (for example, Contracts, Expense Reports).

   ❏ The library will be used to create multiple document types.

   ❏ A document library will be populated only by *uploading* documents, not by clicking the New button.

   I'll examine custom templates in this solution and multiple templates in Solution 4-4 on page 327.

9. Click Create.

## Configure document library settings

After you create the document library, you should configure its settings. The library will open immediately after creation, or you can navigate to the library using the Quick Launch: Either click the document library's link, if you enabled it, or click the View All Site Content link and then click the link to the library. After you open the library, click the Settings button in the library toolbar and choose Document Library Settings, as shown in Figure 4-1.

**Figure 4-1**    The Document Library Settings command

To manage the settings of a library or list, you must have the Manage Lists permission, which is assigned to the Owners group and is part of the Design permission level. Without this permission, the Settings button will not appear.

The Customize page for the document library appears, as shown in Figure 4-2. I've eliminated the details beneath each section heading in the figure to make it more readable. You will not see the Content Types section unless you've enabled content types as discussed in Solution 4-3 on page 321.

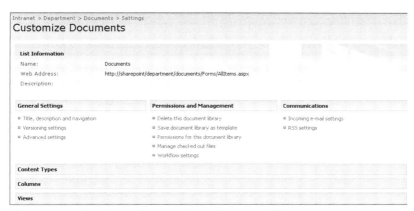

**Figure 4-2**    The Customize page for a document library

You should configure many settings of the document library prior to announcing the library's availability. The following guide will point you to the solutions in this collection that address each setting:

■ Title, description, and navigation: later in this solution

■ Versioning settings:

❑ Content approval: Solution 4-12 on page 347

❑ Version history: Solution 4-11 on page 345

❑ Require checkout: Solution 4-10 on page 341

- Advanced settings:
  - ❑ Content types: Solution 4-3 on page 321
  - ❑ Document template: later in this solution
  - ❑ Folders: Solution 4-14 on page 353
  - ❑ Search: Solution 4-15 on page 355
- Delete this document library: Self-explanatory.
- Permissions for this document library: later in this solution
- Manage checked-out files: Solution 4-10 on page 341
- Workflow settings: Solution 4-13 on page 349
- Incoming e-mail settings: Solution 4-5 on page 329
- Really Simple Syndication (RSS) settings: Solution 4-9 on page 339
- Content types: Solution 4-3 on page 321
- Columns: Solution 4-2 on page 312
- Views: Solution 4-14 on page 353

## Configure the document library title

The document library title appears in the heading of the library page, as shown in Figure 4-3. As mentioned earlier, it is initially derived from the name you entered in the Name field when you created the library. The name is used for both the library's title and URL, and I recommended that you create the library with a URL-friendly name and then change the library title after you create the library.

**Figure 4-3**   Document library title

To change the library title, follow these steps:

1. Click the Settings button in the library toolbar, and choose Document Library Settings.
2. The Customize page appears. In the General Settings section, click the Title, Description And Navigation link.
3. In the Name box, enter the library title.
4. Click Save.

> **Note**   If you are showing the library on Quick Launch and if the only change you are making in the Name field is to change the case—for example, from "documents" to "Documents"—the change will not appear in Quick Launch. To remedy this problem, you must remove and re-add the library to Quick Launch. The easiest way to do this is by following these steps:
>
> 1. On the Customize page for the library, click the Title, Description And Navigation link.
> 2. Choose No in the Navigation section.
> 3. Click Save.
> 4. Once again, click the Title, Description And Navigation link.
> 5. Choose Yes in the Navigation section.
> 6. Click Save.

The document library should now appear in the correct case in the Quick Launch.

## Enable or disable folders within the document library

Another setting that you should configure immediately is the ability for users to create folders within the library. We discuss folders in more detail in Solution 4-14. By default, folders are enabled. If you choose to disable folders, you can follow the procedure shown next:

1. Click the Settings button in the library toolbar, and choose Document Library Settings.
2. The Customize page appears. In the General Settings section, click the Advanced Settings link.
3. In the Folders section, choose the No option for the Display "New Folder" Command On The New Menu.
4. Click OK.

> **Note**   If you disable folders and there is no document template or content type associated with the document library, the New button disappears from the library toolbar. Users with appropriate permissions can, however, upload documents using the Upload button.

## Change the default template for the library

If, when you created the document library, you configured the correct template for all documents in the library, you might want to skip this section. But because most document libraries will not use a generic Word, Excel, or PowerPoint template, you'll likely want to configure a custom template for the library. The steps in this section show you how to create a template for documents users create by clicking the New button in the document library. If you want more than one template to be available, you'll have to wait until Solutions 4-3 and 4-4 for our discussion of content types and multiple templates.

There are two major steps to creating a specific, customized template for a document library. First, you have to get the template into the library's Forms folder. Then you have to configure the library to use the template.

The first step can be the trickiest. You must navigate to the library's Forms folder so that you can copy your template into it. I recommend entering the Universal Naming Convention (UNC) of the library's Forms folder:

> **Note** Choose Start and then Run. Then enter the UNC of the library in the following form: \\*sharepointserver*\*site*\*library*\forms—for example, \\sharepoint.contoso.com\department\documents\forms. Then, when this folder opens, copy the template into it.

Alternatively, you can do the following:

1. Open the document library in Internet Explorer, and be sure you are signed in as a user with Full Control permission to the library.

2. Click the Actions button, and choose Open With Windows Explorer.

   This is the step that is most likely to be problematic. If the library won't open with Windows Explorer, use a Windows Vista or Windows XP client—as of this writing, I have been unable to successfully open the library in Windows Explorer while working directly on a Windows Server 2008 system. If you are prompted to sign in, you must enter credentials that have permission to the site. Also be certain that the SharePoint server is in your Trusted Sites or Local Intranet security zone and that Internet Explorer 7 is not running in Protected Mode. The browser status bar will inform you of the site's security treatment. You can double-click the indicators shown in Figure 4-4 as a shortcut to the Security page of the Internet Options dialog box, where you can change the settings.

3. Navigate to the Forms folder within the library. It is a hidden folder, so you might need to enable the Show Hidden Files And Folders option in your system's Folder Options. (To do so, click Organize and then choose Folder And Search Options. Click the View tab, select Show Hidden Files And Folders, and then click OK.)

Local intranet | Protected Mode: Off

**Figure 4-4** Internet Explorer security settings for a SharePoint site

After you have opened the Forms folder, copy your template into it. Then configure the library settings as shown in the following steps so that it uses the template.

1. On the Customize page for the document library, click the Advanced Settings link in the General Settings section.

2. In the Template URL text box, enter the template URL in the form *library*/Forms/*templatename.ext* (where *library* is the name of your library and *templatename.ext* is the name of the template).

   Note there is no protocol ("http://") or root ("/") prefix. Just type the URL relative to the site itself.

3. Click OK.

The custom template in the Forms folder is now used when a user chooses the New Document command in the document library. The logical next step is to centralize templates across multiple libraries so that you do not have to maintain multiple copies of the same template in each document library; or to provide more than one template option to users of a library. Both of these goals are addressed in Solution 4-3 as we discuss content types.

## Configure security for a document library

SharePoint's model of securable objects is straightforward and is illustrated in Figure 4-5. A site can contain libraries, lists, and other sites. Libraries and lists can contain documents and items, respectively, and folders. Folders can also contain library documents or list items, and other folders.

**Figure 4-5**    SharePoint securable object model

Each object in the model inherits its permissions from its parent object, by default. But you can specify permissions for any object, at which point changes to permissions of its parent will no longer be inherited. A user must have the Manage Permissions permission, part of the Full Control permission level, to change permissions on an object.

There are minor differences in the application of security concepts to SharePoint as compared to a shared folder, discussed in Solution Collection 2. In SharePoint, inheritance is all or nothing—there is no mix of inherited and explicit permissions for an object. SharePoint also does not allow a user who owns an object by creating it to change the object's permissions.

But the basic approach to security management in SharePoint should be the same as in shared folders: Assign permissions to groups, grant permissions on containers—not on individual documents or items—wherever possible, and use role-based access control as described in Solution Collection 1, "Role-Based Management."

## Manage permissions for a document library, folder, or document

To manage permissions on a document library, click the Permissions For This Document Library link on the Customize page for the document library. By default, a new document library inherits its permissions from its site. To assign unique permissions to the library, you must break inheritance. Click the Actions button directly above the list of users and groups with permissions to the site, and choose Edit Permissions. You will be prompted to confirm that you want to break inheritance. The permissions that had been inherited will be applied as the default permissions for the library. Click OK to confirm this action.

The New button allows you to add a user or group and specify its permissions. To modify the permissions for a user or group already listed, or to remove the permissions assigned to a user or group, use the Actions button.

**Note**  Although the user interface suggests you are adding, removing, or editing users, you can add, remove, or edit permissions for groups as well. In fact, managing permissions with groups is a best practice. It's unfortunate that the interface is both unclear and misleading.

To manage permissions for a folder or document, in the library, click the drop-down arrow that appears when you hover over a folder or document name. From the menu that appears, choose Manage Permissions.

**Note**  This menu is called the *edit menu*. If you are unfamiliar with SharePoint's edit menu, see "Use SharePoint's edit menu" on page 317.

The same rules apply: You must first click the Actions button and choose Edit Permissions, and confirm that you want to break inheritance Then you can add, remove, and modify permissions.

## Assign permissions to SharePoint or Active Directory groups

A common question is whether to assign permissions directly to an Active Directory group or to create a SharePoint group and then assign permissions to this group. The answer relates to how you will use the group beyond simply granting access to your Active Directory users.

If you assign permissions to an Active Directory group, members of that group gain access at that level. You can manage access by managing the membership of the Active Directory group. You can also give the Active Directory group access to other resources, such as shared folders, printers, and applications. However, if you configure alerts for the same group, the alerts go to the e-mail account of the *group*, not to each user in the group. Of course, your mail system could forward the mail to all members, but SharePoint will send just one e-mail notification—to the group.

If you assign permissions to a SharePoint group, members of the group gain access at that level. When alerts are sent, each member is notified directly. Additionally, you can leverage SharePoint features that allow users to request membership in the group. This membership management capability can reduce support costs related to resource access requests. But the SharePoint group is not visible using Active Directory management tools, nor can you assign permissions to it outside of SharePoint.

One of the biggest disadvantages of Active Directory groups is that they can contain only users with Active Directory accounts. If you extend your SharePoint site to include users logging on with other authentication providers, such as forms-based authentication, those users will have to be given permission using a SharePoint group.

So there is no easy answer. If you simply cannot decide what to do, I suggest creating a SharePoint group to manage permissions and then nesting an Active Directory group into it. That way, you can continue to manage access using Active Directory tools, but your SharePoint group has the flexibility to support extension to other authentication providers, and you can, if you so choose, enable the group membership management functionality for the group to allow individual users to request access.

To learn more about planning and implementing SharePoint security, visit the Windows SharePoint Services Tech Center at *http://technet.microsoft.com/windowsserver/sharepoint*.

## Solution summary

In this solution, we covered the fundamental procedures for creating a site and a secure document library. Along the way, I offered some tips and pointed out some common traps to avoid. A document library configured to the extent presented in this solution is more or less equivalent to a shared folder. The following solutions start to apply SharePoint's document management functionality.

# 4-2: Manage Document Metadata Using Library and Site Columns

## Solution overview

| | |
|---|---|
| **Type of solution** | Procedures |
| **Features and tools** | SharePoint library and site columns, Microsoft Office applications |
| **Solution summary** | Create custom columns to support document metadata at this library or site level. |
| **Benefits** | Describing documents with metadata is a core construct of content management that enables views, search, reporting, and other document management functionality. |

## Introduction

SharePoint columns are what other databases call fields, attributes, or properties. They are data points for a record, where the record is a document in a library or an item in a list. Columns can be managed from a library's settings page—the Customize page—in the Columns section shown in Figure 4-6.

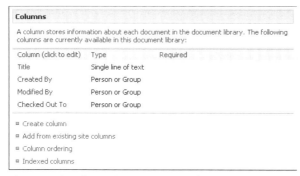

**Figure 4-6**   The Columns section of a document library's settings

Columns in a document library can be used to describe, organize, locate, and manage documents. Content management resources often refer to such data points as *metadata*. By default, a document library supports more than a dozen columns, such as Title, Name, Created, Created By, Modified, Modified By, File Size, Version, and Checked Out To.

You can modify the columns in a library to support other properties that you want to keep track of for each document. For each column, you are given a wide range of options for the type of data the column should support, the user-interface controls provided for entering data into the column, default values, and whether the column is a required field for new documents. A document will not be visible in the library to users if any required column is not configured.

In this section, you'll learn how to create and manage columns in a library. You'll also learn how end users interact with custom columns in both the SharePoint Web interface and in Microsoft Office clients. Finally, you'll learn how to manage columns, both at the library level and at the site level, where columns can be made available to multiple lists or libraries.

## Create a column

To create a column, follow these steps:

1.  Click the Settings button in the library toolbar, and choose Document Library Settings.
2.  The Customize page appears. In the Columns section, click the Create Column link.
3.  In the Column Name text box, enter the column name.
4.  Choose from the options that appear underneath the heading The Type Of Information In This Column Is. The choice you make affects not only the type of data that the column will contain but also the type of control that is displayed in the user interface.
5.  Your choice for the type of information you want to store in the column produces an appropriate selection of Additional Settings. Configure the settings and click OK.

For more information about configuring columns and the variety of column types that are available, see *Microsoft Office SharePoint Server 2007 Administrator's Companion* (Microsoft Press, 2007). Figure 4-7 shows the configuration of a drop-down list that will contain project names. To make the figure more readable, I edited the figure to show only the options that were used. The Description field is worth completing. The description appears in the edit item form shown in Figure 4-13 beneath the text box for the Project column.

> **Note**   For any property that is not self-explanatory, configure the column's description.

> **Note**   The default value for a new Choice column will be the first item in the list. Often, you will want to ensure that there is no default so that the user must make an appropriate selection. I recommend you make the Default Value field blank, as shown in Figure 4-7.

You might be thinking ahead and considering scenarios in which you have multiple document libraries. Imagine if you have more than one library that requires the Project column, for example. It would be painful, if not downright dreadful, to configure the same columns in each library. Site columns and content types, discussed later in this solution and in Solution 4-3, allow us to centrally define content options for multiple lists, libraries, or sites.

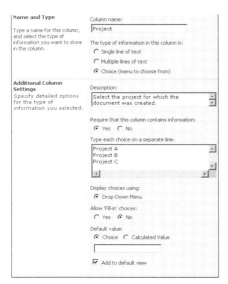

**Figure 4-7**    Creating a column for Project

# Work with custom columns from Microsoft Office clients

When a document library has a custom column, the user can enter the properties for a document using several methods, depending on which version of Microsoft Office is being used. Microsoft Office 2003 and Microsoft Office 2007 both integrate directly with SharePoint Products and Technologies.

## Create a new document from the document library with Office clients

If you create a new document using the New button in the document library toolbar, and you use Microsoft Office 2003 or 2007 clients, the client ensures that you complete the custom properties as required. Office 2003 clients prompt you with the Web File Properties dialog box shown in Figure 4-8 when you save the document.

You can also use the Document Information page of the Shared Workspace task pane in Office 2003 clients to configure document properties. The task pane is shown in Figure 4-9. To open this task pane, choose Tools and then Shared Workspace.

Document properties are displayed by Office 2007 clients in the document information panel, shown in Figure 4-10.

> **Note**    If the panel does not appear, click the Microsoft Office Button, click Prepare, and then choose Properties.

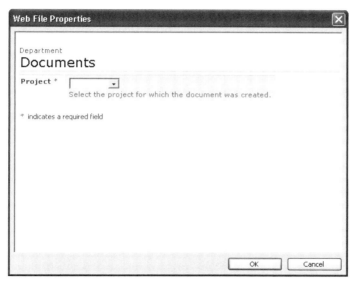

**Figure 4-8**    The Web File Properties dialog box appears when an Office 2003 client saves to a document library

**Figure 4-9**    The Shared Workspace task pane, Document Information page

**Figure 4-10**    Document information panel in an Office 2007 client

## Save a document to a library with custom columns from Microsoft Office clients

If you create a document without using the New button in the document library, Office clients will not know of the custom properties until you attempt to save the document to the document library. Office 2003 clients prompt you with a Web File Properties dialog box shown earlier in Figure 4-8. Required properties must be filled in, or you will not be able to save the document to the library.

With Office 2007, if you try to save a document with missing properties, you receive the error message shown in Figure 4-11, which is clear and helpful—it opens the document information panel for you. The document information panel, in Figure 4-12, provides controls with which to configure the missing properties, at which point the Retry Save button becomes enabled.

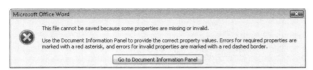

**Figure 4-11**    Word 2007 error message when saving a document with missing required properties

**Figure 4-12**    Office 2007 document information panel with required properties

# Work with document properties from the SharePoint Web interface

If you create a document with a version of Microsoft Office prior to Office 2003 or with any other application that is not compatible with Windows SharePoint Services, you save the document to the library by uploading it.

## Upload a document with custom columns

If a user uploads a document to the library, the site prompts the user to complete document properties, as shown in Figure 4-13. If the user does not specify the required properties indicated by a red asterisk, the document remains in the library checked out to the user who uploaded it. The document will not be visible to normal users until the properties are set and the document is checked in. This is one of several reasons discussed in this Solution Collection that justify the best practice of requiring checkout on document libraries.

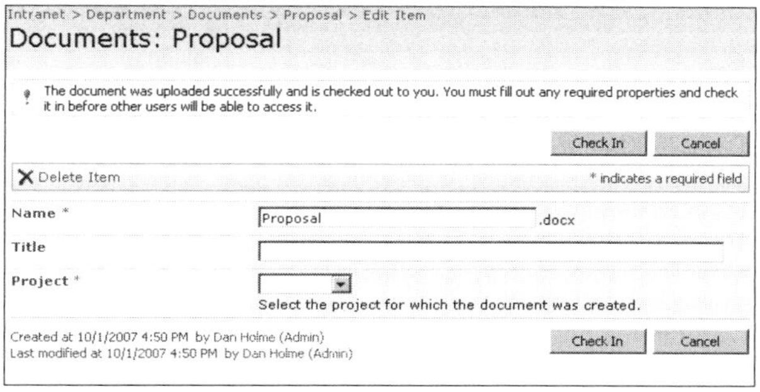

**Figure 4-13**   Required columns for an uploaded document

## View document properties

Document properties can be viewed using the View Properties command in the document's edit menu. The view item page, also called the *view properties page*, lists each column, as shown in Figure 4-14.

**Figure 4-14**   A document's view properties page

## Use SharePoint's edit menu

Because this is the first mention of a document's *edit menu*, let me ensure that we're on the same page. You perform most actions in a document library using either toolbar buttons or the edit menu. What can be confusing is that there is no menu labeled Edit. The edit menu appears when you hover over a document and click the drop-down arrow that appears. The contents of the menu vary based on the content type you selected and your permissions within the library. A typical edit menu is shown in Figure 4-15. It is similar to the context menu or right-click menu in Office applications in that the commands it contains affect the selected document.

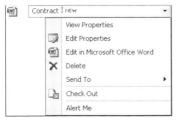

**Figure 4-15**   A document's edit menu

 **Note**   A tip is also warranted here: You do not have to click the tiny drop-down arrow at the rightmost edge of the link. You can click anywhere between the text and the arrow—in the blank space. The drop-down arrows are small. The white space is much easier to target with a mouse click. Perhaps I'm too used to playing by the rules and clicking only things that I see, but I worked with SharePoint for *months* before realizing that I could access the edit menu by clicking anywhere to the right of the name of the document.

### Edit document properties

To change document properties, click the Edit Properties command in the document's edit menu or the Edit Item button on the document's properties page, as seen earlier in Figure 4-14. As you can see in Figure 4-16, there are controls for each property and required properties are called out with an asterisk.

**Figure 4-16**   A document's edit item form

## Modify or delete library columns

Now that you've seen how to create columns and how they affect the user's experience, you're ready to dive deeper into the topic of columns. To manage columns, you'll return to the columns section of the document library's Customize page. You can click any column to open its Change Column page. There are certain properties of a column that you cannot modify after the column has been created—the specific properties depend on the type of column. Any properties you can change will be available on the Change Column page. You can also delete the column by clicking the Delete button on the Change Column page.

# Reorder columns

The view and edit item pages display columns in the column order specified by the document library settings. Click the Column Ordering link in the Columns section of the Customize page for the document library and use the drop-down lists to modify the column order.

> **Important**    The Column Ordering link affects the pages that allow you to view edit document properties, such as the edit item form shown in Figure 4-16. Column Ordering does *not* have an impact on the order in which columns appear in document library views. The order of columns in a library view is part of the view definition, as we'll see in Solution 4-14.

# Manage site columns

We have discussed how you can create, manage, and use custom columns in a document library. We used a simple example of a Project column that provided a choice—a drop-down list control. It's reasonable to expect that such a column would be useful in multiple document libraries, perhaps even in multiple sites. Site columns are much like library or list columns, except that they are scoped to an entire site and its subsites.

# Create site columns

To create a site column, you must first determine the site that will contain the column. Site columns are available to a site and its subsites. To create a site column, follow these steps:

1.  From the site that you want to contain the column, click Site Actions and choose Site Settings.

2.  In the Galleries section, click Site Columns.

3.  Click Create.

4.  Configure the settings for the column.

5.  Click OK.

> **Note**    It is recommended that you create site columns in the top-level site of the site collection.

Settings for a site column are identical to those of a list or library column as described earlier in this solution. Additionally, you must specify a group for the column. Groups are simply an organizational tool that makes it easier to locate the column when you are managing it or adding it to a list or library.

# Use a site column in a list or library

To add a site column to a list or library, open the Customize page for the list or library and, in the Columns section, click the Add From Existing Site Columns link. Use the Select Site Columns From drop-down list and the Available Site Columns list box to select a site column. Then click the Add button. An example is shown in Figure 4-17. Click OK when you have selected all the columns you want to add to the site.

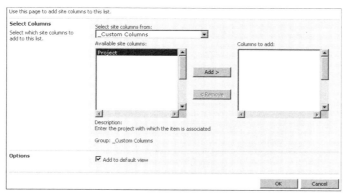

**Figure 4-17**    The Add Columns From Site Columns page

The newly added site column inherits its properties from the definition of the site column. You can view and modify the properties by clicking the column name in the Columns section of the list or library's Customize page. It is highly recommended that you do not change any of the properties, for reasons discussed in the next section. If a site column is not well suited for use in a list or library, create or select another site column, or create a list or library column.

# Modify and delete site columns

After you create a site column, you can click the link for the column in the Site Column Gallery and the Change Site Column page appears, on which you can modify or delete the column. When you change the properties of a site column, SharePoint, by default, updates every instance of the column in lists and libraries. For example, if we add a project to the list of choices in our Project column, the new project appears as a choice in all libraries and lists in the site. You can prevent this updating by selecting No in the Update Lists section of the Change Site Column page; however, it is recommended that you leverage, not disable, this powerful capability.

**Note**    The ability to make changes to a column in one place and to have those changes reflected in all libraries and lists that use the column is a big advantage of site columns.

When you use a site column in a list or library, the column in the list or library inherits all of its properties from the site column. You can override the properties for that specific list or library. For example, you can have a generic description in the site column and change the description in the list or library to be more specific. But your changes to the list or library column settings will be replaced if you take advantage of the automatic updating of list and library columns when the site column is modified. Therefore, I discourage you from overriding properties of site columns in a list or library.

## Solution summary

Library columns provide the fields, or metadata, with which documents can be described and exposed within the library. Metadata enables us to create views that sort, filter, and group our data in useful ways (Solution 4-14), and those views can be used to generate alerts (Solution 4-9). Metadata is also used to support search, reporting, and just about every other core functionality of document management. When you create columns, and particularly when you configure them as required, you need to understand how users will interact with and fill in those columns, based on the applications they are using to access SharePoint. And when metadata must be defined for more than just one list or library, it should be defined at the site level, as a site column.

# 4-3: Implement Managed Content Types

## Solution overview

| | |
|---|---|
| **Type of solution** | Procedures |
| **Features and tools** | SharePoint site and library content types |
| **Solution summary** | Create and configure site and library content types. |
| **Benefits** | Centralized definition of columns (metadata), settings, and workflows to fully describe a type of content for use in one or more libraries or lists in one or more sites. |

## Introduction

Content types are one of the most powerful features of SharePoint. A content type is a definition for an item or document. It contains all the properties (columns), settings, and workflows that the content type should have wherever it is used. You define it once, as a site content type, and then you can use it in any list or library within that site. Changes to the definition of the content type update any instance of that content type.

For example, Contoso.com wants to keep track of contracts and agreements it has made with customers, partners, and vendors. Such contracts and agreements can be made in any business unit or department, so the documents can be found in any number of libraries. Therefore, Contoso will create a content type that drives the definition of what a contract is, what template it uses, and what metadata (columns) are needed to manage contracts.

# Create a content type

To create a content type, you must first determine what site should contain the content type. After you create it, you can use a content type within that site and its subsites. To create a content type, follow these steps:

> **Note** It is recommended that you create content types in the top-level site of the site collection to centralize the management of content types for the collection.

1. From the site that will contain the column, click Site Actions and choose Site Settings.

2. In the Galleries section, click Site Content Types.

3. Click Create.

4. The New Site Content Type page appears, as shown in Figure 4-18.

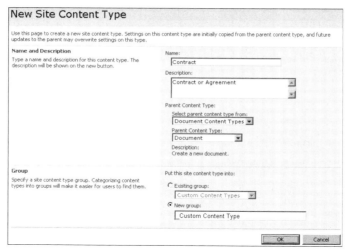

**Figure 4-18** The New Site Content Type page

5. Configure the Name and Description for the content type.

6. Select the parent content type using the two drop-down lists: Select Parent Content Type From and Parent Content Type.

   In the context of this Solution Collection regarding document libraries, we use the Document Content Types to derive new content types. Document and Picture are self-explanatory and will be the most commonly selected options. The Dublin Core Columns is an alternative. Dublin Core Columns is a standard collection of metadata that you can use to describe just about any kind of content. The only disadvantage of Dublin Core Columns is that there are 15 columns, which might be more than your content type really requires.

7.  Select an existing group, or create a new group for the content type.

    Groups are simply an organizational tool that makes it easier to locate the content type when you are managing it or adding it to a list or library. The default group for new site content types in SharePoint is Custom Content Types. However, when you work with column groups, they are presented in alphabetical order. Therefore, I recommend creating a group that will appear at the top or bottom of lists of content types, such as _Custom Content Types.

8.  Click OK.

The Site Content Type page appears, as shown in Figure 4-19.

**Figure 4-19**   Site Content Type page

The page looks similar to a library or list settings page, does it not? That is no coincidence. A list or library is nothing more than a container for content. Each list or library has, by default, one content type that defines the items or documents for that list or library. Plus, the list or library has container-level settings, such as permissions, RSS settings, and views.

From the Site Content Type Settings page, you can manage the content type, including the following items:

**Name, Description, and Group settings**   These settings allow you to change the properties given to the content type when it was created.

**Advanced settings**   These settings define the Document Template associated with the content type. This will be discussed more in Solution 4-4.

**Workflow settings**   These settings allow you to configure workflows associated with the content type. Workflows will be covered in Solution 4-13.

**Delete This Site Content Type**   This setting is self-explanatory.

You can also manage site columns so that you can add the metadata or properties associated with the content type. Figure 4-19 shows some examples of properties (columns) defined for the Contract content type. Each column associated with a content type is a site column.

## Add one or more content types to a list or library

After you define your content types, you are ready to use them in your libraries and lists. You can do so by following these steps:

1. From the list or library's Customize page, click the Advanced Settings link.

2. In the Content Types section, for Allow Management Of Content Types, choose Yes.

3. Click the OK button.

The settings page now displays the Content Types section, as you can see in Figure 4-20.

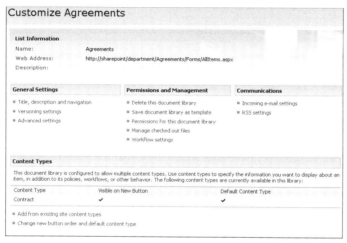

**Figure 4-20**    Settings page with the Content Types section

Use the commands in the Content Types section to add a content type. To remove a content type that already exists in the list or library, click the content type's name and then click the Delete This Content Type link. If your library will have more than one content type, you can change the order with which they appear on the library's New button menu, and you can specify the default content type that will be used if the user clicks the New button itself.

## Understand child site and list content types

Content types are hierarchical. When you create a custom content type, such as the Contract content type we created earlier (shown in Figure 4-19), it is derived from a parent content type (usually Document or Picture). Properties of the parent are inherited by the new child content type. When you create a content type based on a parent content type, you are able to extend the definition of the parent with additional columns, with settings such as a template, and with workflows. We added several columns to our Contract content type that were not part of its parent content type, Document.

To take the example a step further, let's assume you've created the Contract content type, and you create another content type derived from Contract for purchase agreements over a specific value. You name the new content type "High Value Contracts" and add appropriate columns, such as the value of the contract and notes as to how the contract was negotiated.

Changes to content types cascade through child content types. Using our Contracts example, let's imagine you decide to add a column to the contract content type to specify who signed the contract or agreement. When you add the Signed By column to the Contract content type, you can update child content types, such as the High Value Contracts content type.

The propagation of updates through child content types is exciting and valuable in most scenarios, as it provides a great way to manage content definitions. However, if you have modified a setting or column in a child content type, your customizations will be overwritten when you change a parent content type and specify that SharePoint should make updates to child content types.

> **Important** The nuance is that updates from a parent to a child content type will overwrite *changes* you made to the child; but if you *added* columns to the child, those columns unique to the child content type will not be changed or removed.

When you add a content type to a list or library, you are in fact creating a new content type that is derived from the site content type. Said another way, each list or library content type is a child of its site content type. The list or library content type is available only within the scope of that list or library, of course—site content types are scoped to the site and its subsites.

So the same rules regarding content type hierarchy and updates apply:

- You can change columns, settings, or workflows.
- You can add columns or workflows.
- When changes to the parent (site) content type update child list and library content types, changes (but not additions) you previously made to the library or list content type will be overwritten.

> **Important** The SharePoint user interface does not make it completely intuitive that the content type you add to a library is, in fact, a child content type—not just a reference to a site content type.

## Protect a content type by making it read-only

You can configure any content type—at the site or list/library level—to be read-only. This setting is on the Advanced Settings page for the content type. If a content type is read-only, changes cannot be made—you cannot add, remove, or modify columns, settings, or workflows. Users with the permission to edit the content type can remove the read-only setting to make changes, so the setting is more of a safety stop, ensuring that changes from a parent content type cannot update the child content type. The read-only setting is particularly important when you are basing workflows or other code on the definition of a content type because it ensures that changes to the content type that could throw off other processes are avoided.

If you set a child content type to read-only, changes to parent content types that enable updating children will produce an error: The parent content type will be successfully updated, but any read-only child objects will not be. The exception to this rule is the read-only setting itself. If the read-only setting on a parent object is changed, it will propagate to child objects.

> **Note**   By turning the read-only setting on a parent object on and then off, you can effectively enable changes to all child objects and then make a change to the parent that will successfully propagate to all children. The only challenge, then, is going to the individual child content types that should be read-only and re-enabling the setting.

If this sounds complicated: It can be. I recommend that you enable read-only for entire branches of content types—starting with the parent content type that you create. Try to manage the environment to avoid situations where child content types are read-only, but parent content types are not.

## Do not change default SharePoint content types

Do not change settings, columns, or workflows on any of the default SharePoint content types. If you believe you need to make changes to a default SharePoint content type, first evaluate whether you can achieve your goals by creating a child content type derived from the default content type. If that's not possible, refer to the SharePoint software development kit and all other in-depth technical content on SharePoint to fully understand the ramifications of your proposed change.

## Solution summary

By creating content types for a site collection, you can create a definition of the content that you will support in libraries and lists. The centralized and hierarchical nature of content types provides the basis for efficient content and document management.

# 4-4: Configure Multiple Templates for a Document Library

## Solution overview

| | |
|---|---|
| **Type of solution** | Procedures |
| **Features and tools** | SharePoint content types and document libraries |
| **Solution summary** | Enable a document library to expose multiple templates on the library's New button menu. |
| **Benefits** | Users can generate new documents with templates appropriate for the library. |

## Introduction

Many document libraries will not be specialized to one type of document. If a library should support the creation, storage, and management of multiple document types, it is reasonable to want the New button to support creating each supported document. In this solution, we use content types to achieve that goal.

Content types aren't useful only because of the columns they associate. Each content type also defines the template that should be used to create a document of that type. Perhaps you can already see where we are going—at a high level, you will do the following:

- Create a document library for templates.
- Create a content type for each class of document. Configure the content type with the template for that document class.
- Configure a library to support the content types.

## Create a central library for templates

First, create a library to host the templates themselves. I recommend creating a document library at the top-level site of a site collection. Because this library will be used behind the scenes, you should not make it visible on Quick Launch—doing so might lead to confusion among users as to where they should go to start a new document. Ensure that permissions are set to allow read permission to all users who will require any of the templates. Upload your templates into the library. Earlier solutions detail the steps for creating a library and uploading documents to it.

You can also skip this step. As you'll see in the next section, you can choose to upload a template as you create a content type. SharePoint saves templates uploaded this way into a hidden folder, _cts, in the site. The _cts folder therefore acts something like a template library. However, I prefer to have my templates easily accessible for editing and visibility to support personnel and administrators.

# Configure a content type for a template

In Solution 4-3, we discussed the process for creating content types and created a content type for contracts. In the advanced settings of a content type, you can specify the URL for its template:

1. Click Site Actions, and choose Site Settings.

2. In the Galleries section of the Site Settings page, click the Site Content Types link.

3. Create a new content type (refer to Solution 4-3 for details), or click the name of an existing content type to edit it.

4. On the Site Content Type Settings page, click the Advanced Settings link.

5. In the Document Template section, shown in Figure 4-21, enter the URL to the template.

> **Note**    You can upload a template in this step; however, you have no control over where the template is stored. It will be stored in a hidden folder named _cts. I prefer to maintain a central library of templates for easy access and editing, particularly in WSS implementations, so that I can use the templates for content types defined in other site collections and servers. The previous section provides guidance for creating a central library of templates.

6. Click OK.

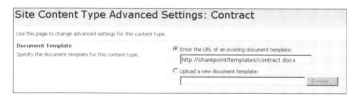

**Site Content Type Advanced Settings: Contract**

Use this page to change advanced settings for this content type.

| Document Template | |
| --- | --- |
| Specify the document template for this content type. | ⦿ Enter the URL of an existing document template: |
| | http://sharepoint/templates/contract.docx |
| | ○ Upload a new document template: |
| | [                    ] Browse... |

**Figure 4-21**    The Document Template setting for a content type

# Configure a library to support the content types

In the document library where you want the content type to be available, open the library's settings, click the Advanced Settings link, and select the Yes option for the Allow Management Of Content Types in the Content Types section. Then, on the Customize page for the document library, add site content types to the library. The details for these steps were presented in Solution 4-3. When you have finished, the New button displays any content types you have added to the library, as you can see in Figure 4-22.

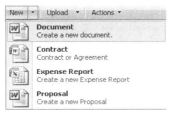

Figure 4-22    The New button with multiple content types

The order of the content types on the New button menu is determined by the order in which content types are listed in the document library settings. To change the order, click the Change New Button Order And Default Content Type link. The first-listed content type is the library's default content type, and it will be used if the user clicks the New button itself rather than choosing from the button's drop-down menu.

## Solution summary

To enable a document library to expose multiple templates, you must create a content type associated with each template. Storing the templates in a central library makes it easy for template editors to access and modify those templates.

# 4-5: Add, Save, and Upload Documents to a Document Library

## Solution overview

| | |
|---|---|
| **Type of solution** | Procedures |
| **Features and tools** | SharePoint document libraries, Microsoft Office applications, Windows Explorer, e-mail |
| **Solution summary** | Explore the options for populating a document library, through the Web interface, from Office applications, and even by e-mailing the library. |
| **Benefits** | Users can add documents to SharePoint libraries using familiar applications and interfaces, thereby increasing the libraries' usability and adoption. |

## Introduction

A document library's New and Upload buttons enable you to add documents to the library. In addition, you can use simple Windows Explorer copy-and-paste operations, Office applications, and e-mail attachments to get documents easily into a document library.

# Create a new document with the New command

The New button will appear if you have permission to Add Items to the document library and one of the following is true:

- The document library has a template specified (in the library's advanced settings).

- The document library has one or more content types with templates.

- The document library allows new folders to be created (in the library's advanced settings).

As we saw in Solutions 4-3 and 4-4, you can configure a document library with multiple content types and any content type that has a template will be displayed as a "New *content type*" in the New button menu, shown in Figure 4-22. When a document is instantiated from a document library, the application associated with the template is launched on the client. If the application is not available to the client, an error is displayed. If the application is installed and is compatible with WSS 2.0+ (Office 2003 or Office 2007, for example), the application remembers that the document should be saved to the document library. So when you choose the Save command, the Save dialog box is focused on the library as the default location to save the document.

# Upload documents with the Upload commands

The Upload menu is straightforward enough. It supports two commands: Upload Document and Upload Multiple Documents.

## Upload one document

If you choose Upload Document or click the Upload button itself, you are given a Web interface from which you can browse to locate the document you want to upload. When a document library contains multiple content types, users are asked to select the content type after a document has been uploaded. Similarly, the user is prompted to complete properties (columns) associated with the library or content type.

## Upload multiple documents

If you have appropriate WSS 2.0+ client software installed, which includes Office 2003 and Office 2007, the Upload Multiple Documents command is available. This command allows you to select one or more documents from a single folder on your system, and to upload them all.

> **Note** You cannot use the Upload Multiple Documents command to select multiple items from separate folders—it only supports selecting multiple documents from a single folder. Be sure that you communicate this nuance to your users.

If Upload Multiple Documents is used, the user is *not* prompted to select the content type or to specify document properties.

> **Important**    After the documents have been placed in the document library, properties of the documents might need to be completed. In addition, if the library manages multiple content types, you will need to associate documents with the correct content type. SharePoint enforces the configuration of required properties for uploaded documents. See Solution 4-7 on page 336, for important guidance regarding managing multiple document uploads.

## Upload specific content types

A trick that is less well publicized is the ability to provide users a way to select the type of content they want to upload. This is achieved by providing a content type with no template configured. If a template is not specified for a content type in a library, the New button command changes to Upload A New *Content Type*, as seen in Figure 4-23. Although the process begins with the New button, rather than the Upload button (certainly a user-interface peculiarity worth highlighting to your users), the remainder of the process is like a document upload, except that users will not have to select the content type for the uploaded document after it has been uploaded.

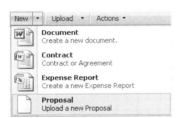

**Figure 4-23**    A content type with no template appears as Upload A New *Content Type*

> **Note**    The ability to provide users an Upload A New *Content Type* option is particularly useful when the content type is produced by an application that is not WSS 2.0+ compatible. Users can create and manage the document locally, and then use this command to upload it to the library as the appropriate content type.

# Add documents to document libraries with Windows Explorer

Document libraries can be opened using Windows Explorer. After they have been opened with Windows Explorer, you can use standard Windows copy and cut-and-paste methods to copy (or move) documents into a document library.

To open a document library with Windows Explorer, click the Actions button and choose Open With Windows Explorer. A new Windows Explorer window opens, focused on the document library. The Windows Explorer address bar displays the library's address. In Windows

Vista, the address appears as http://*server/site/library*. In Windows XP, the address appears as \\*server\site\library*. The address reveals a less-well-publicized secret, which is described in the following Note.

> **Note**   You can open a SharePoint library in Windows Explorer directly by entering the address as a UNC (\\*server\site\library*) in the Windows Explorer address bar, in the Run command (choose Start and then Run), or in the Search box in the Windows Vista Start panel.

Unfortunately, opening a library with Windows Explorer can be problematic if your environment is not configured correctly. Over 80 percent of the problems I've seen boil down to problems related to Internet Explorer security zones. Be sure that your SharePoint site belongs to the Trusted Sites security zone or the Local Intranet security zone. Turning off, at least temporarily, Internet Explorer's Protected Mode for the zone can also be helpful to identify problems when troubleshooting access to a document library from Windows Explorer.

> **Important**   After the documents have been placed in the document library using Windows Explorer, properties of the documents might need to be completed. In addition, if the library manages multiple content types, you will need to associate documents with the correct content type. See Solution 4-7 on page 336, for important guidance regarding managing multiple document transfers.

## Save to a document library from a SharePoint-compatible application

Applications that are compatible with WSS 2.0 or later can save directly to the document library. Such applications include Office 2003 and Office 2007. Simply choose the Save command and enter the URL to the document library, in the form http://*server/site/library*, and press Enter to navigate to the library.

> **Note**   Be sure to see Solution 4-6 on page 334 to learn how to create shortcuts for your users to navigate to the library so that they are not required to enter the library's URL.

## E-mail–enable a document library

Another way to populate document libraries is to send documents via e-mail. The library is given an e-mail address in the form *LibraryAlias@server.domain.com*. Users can send e-mail messages with attachments to the address. SMTP routing is configured to direct the message to the SMTP Server running on the SharePoint server. The incoming e-mail drop folder is monitored for any messages containing the library's address. When a message is detected, it is moved into the library. You can configure the library to take only the attachment or to keep the message, and you can even tell the library to save the document in a folder based on the e-mail's sender or subject line. Sound's great, doesn't it?

The basic steps that are required are as follows:

- Configure incoming and outgoing e-mail settings using SharePoint Central Administration's Operations page.

- Configure outgoing e-mail settings for the application using SharePoint Central Administration's Applications page.

- Install Windows SMTP Server on the SharePoint server. In Windows Server 2003, this is done using Add Or Remove Programs and then Add/Remove Windows Components. In Windows Server 2008, SMTP Server is a Feature that can be added through Server Manager.

- Create an MX record in your domain's DNS zone for *sharepointserver.domain.com* that points to the same FQDN.

- E-mail–enable the library using the Incoming E-mail Settings link on the library's Customize page.

A number of planning and configuration issues warrant close study prior to enabling incoming e-mail for a library. Most importantly, security is a concern: You need to determine who can send documents to the library and how to ensure that messages received by a document library are not spam and are virus free. Detailed information regarding planning and configuration of e-mail–enabled libraries can be found at *http://technet2.microsoft.com/Windows-Server/WSS/en/library/ac36dcfa-d3ac-4269-934d-4e52a1df5e141033.mspx* (Planning) and *http://technet2.microsoft.com/windowsserver/WSS/en/library/445dd72e-a63b-46d0-b92d-bcf0aa9d8d061033.mspx?mfr=true* (Configuration).

 **Note** If you e-mail–enable a document library, add the library's address to its Description field so that the address is visible to users who visit the page.

## Solution summary

One of the most common causes of failure for any collaboration or document management technology is when users find it difficult to use and therefore don't use it. With its tight integration into familiar interfaces, such as Web browsers, Office applications, Windows Explorer, and even e-mail, you are able to provide one or more very easy ways for users to get their documents into SharePoint document libraries.

# 4-6: Create Shortcuts to Document Libraries for End Users

## Solution overview

| | |
|---|---|
| **Type of solution** | Procedures |
| **Features and tools** | Network places and network locations |
| **Solution summary** | Create network places for Windows XP and network locations for Windows Vista clients, and put those links into the correct locations for Microsoft Office Open and Save dialog boxes. |
| **Benefits** | Easier navigation to document libraries for end users. |

## Introduction

When you use the Open or Save command of a client to access a document library, you need a way to navigate to the document library that is effective, efficient, and user friendly. Asking users to enter a URL such as http://*server/site/library* or even a UNC such as \\*server*\\*site*\\*library* is not a recipe for usability and adoption. Instead, anticipate users' need for easy navigation and provide visible shortcuts in the right locations that provide one-click or two-click links to libraries they access.

 **Note**  Create Network Places (Windows XP) and Network Locations (Windows Vista) as user-friendly shortcuts to document libraries.

## Create Network Places (Windows XP)

Windows XP supports network places, which are a combination of a shortcut and a mapped drive. They are like shortcuts in that they can have a user-friendly name and can be placed anywhere: on the desktop, in the My Network Places folder, or in any other folder. They are like mapped drives in that they expose the target namespace in the Windows Explorer folder tree: They are nodes of the tree that expand and collapse.

To create a network place, follow these steps:

1. Open the My Network Places folder.

2. Click the Add A Network Place command in the Network Tasks panel.

   If you don't see the tasks pane on the left side of the window, first be sure that your folder tree is off (by clicking the Folders button), choose Tools and Folder Options and, on the General page, select Show Common Tasks In Folders and then click OK.

3. The Add Network Place Wizard appears. Click Next.

4. Click Choose Another Network Location and then click Next.

5. Enter the URL or UNC to the document library—for example, http://*server*/*site*/*library* or \\*server*\*site*\*library*. Click Next.

6. Enter a friendly name for the network place. Click Next.

7. Click Finish.

After you create the network place, you can move the network place to the desktop, the My Documents folder, or any other folder. If you expect to have multiple network places representing various document libraries, I recommend keeping them in the Network Places folder as a container. When you open or save documents, Network Places is easily accessed in the places bar on the left side of the Open or Save dialog box. If you are in Office 2007 and choose the Publish To Document Management Server command, you will see a dialog box that is focused on the Network Shortcuts or My Network Places folder, from which you'll be able to navigate to your document library.

## Create Network Locations (Vista)

Windows Vista offers functionality equivalent to network places in its network locations. You create network locations within the Computer window in Windows Explorer, not within the Network window. (If that's not surprising to you, you've been working with Microsoft technologies for awhile!). To create a network location, follow these steps:

1. Open Computer from the Start menu.

2. Right-click in an empty part of the window, and choose Add A Network Location.

3. The Add Network Location Wizard appears. Click Next.

4. Click Choose A Custom Network Location and then click Next. (Come on, doesn't *everyone* in your enterprise use MSN Communities?)

5. Enter the URL or UNC to the document library—for example, http://*server*/*site*/*library* or \\*server*\*site*\*library*. Click Next.

6. Enter a friendly name for the network location. Click Next.

7. Click Finish.

The network location will be visible in two places: in the Computer namespace and in the Network Shortcuts folder. The latter folder is the Windows Vista replacement for My Network Places. It is also the equivalent of the former NetHood folder. Network Shortcuts is located in %*userprofile*%\AppData\Roaming\Microsoft\Windows. You can also copy or move the network location to other folders, such as the desktop.

When you access the Open or Save dialog box on a Windows Vista computer, Computer is easily accessed in the Favorite Links bar on the left. Network locations then become visible. If you are in Office 2007 and click the Microsoft Office Button, click Publish, and then click the Document Management Server command, you'll see a dialog box that is focused on the Network Shortcuts folder, from which you'll be able to navigate to your document library.

## Solution summary

Network places (Windows XP) and network locations (Windows Vista) can be placed in strategic locations to enable easy navigation to document libraries from Open, Save, and Publish dialog boxes.

# 4-7: Quarantine and Manage Uploads to a Document Library with Multiple Content Types

## Solution overview

| | |
|---|---|
| **Type of solution** | Guidance and procedures |
| **Features and tools** | SharePoint site columns, content types, document libraries, and views |
| **Solution summary** | Create a content type to receive documents that are uploaded or copied to a library without an association to the correct content type. |
| **Benefits** | Prevent documents from becoming visible to users until they have been assigned to the correct content type and have had required properties configured. |

## Introduction

If you use Windows Explorer to copy one or more documents into a document library, or if you use the Upload Multiple Documents menu command, the documents are uploaded to the library. But you will not be prompted to identify the content type or configure metadata for the documents. Instead, the uploaded documents will be associated with the default content type and, if that content type has required properties, the documents will remain checked out to you and invisible to other users until those properties are configured.

The default content type is the first content type listed in the Content Types section of the Customize document library page. To modify the order of content types on the New button and to set the default content type, click the Change New Button Order And Default Content Type link.

The worst case scenario is that the default content type does not have required properties and is not the correct content type for an uploaded document. The document will be associated with the default content type and will become immediately visible to all users. But in any event, if a library supports multiple content types, it's likely that uploaded documents might need to be assigned to a content type other than the default and that properties should be configured prior to releasing the document into the library. I refer to this as "quarantining" an uploaded document—not because it has a virus, but because it is not yet managed content, assigned to the correct content type and with properties configured.

To quarantine documents uploaded using Windows Explorer or the Upload Multiple Documents command, you should perform the following tasks:

1. Create a site column that is configured as required. It actually doesn't matter what type of column you create because it will be used only to trap content that is uploaded using Windows Explorer or the Upload Multiple Documents command.

2. Create a site content type—I recommend a name such as Upload Control—based on the Document content type as its parent. Click the Add From Existing Site Columns link, and add the site column you created in step 1 to this content type. Click the Advanced Settings link, and configure the content type as Read Only.

3. In a document library that supports multiple content types, open the Customize page and add the new content type (Upload Control) and configure it as the default content type.

4. On the Customize page for the library, scroll down until you see the Views section. Click the Create View link, and then create a datasheet view that shows the document name and content type columns. (No other columns are necessary.). I call this view Upload Control. Configure the view to have the following filter: Content Type Equals Upload Control.

The result of this effort is that when users upload documents using Windows Explorer or the Upload Multiple Documents command, the documents are assigned to the default content type, Upload Control. That content type has a required column, so the documents remain checked out to the user. This is the "quarantine."

The user then opens the Upload Control view and, because it is a datasheet, is easily able to assign the items to the correct content type. The user still has to configure any required properties for the newly assigned content types and check in the documents. You might consider adding those columns to the datasheet view to reduce the number of steps required to move a document out of quarantine.

Finally, you can create workflows that are triggered when a new document is added to the document library, or associate a workflow with the Upload Control content type. The workflow can remind users to finish the upload by assigning the correct content type, editing metadata for the content type, and checking in the documents.

## Solution summary

When multiple documents are transferred to a document library through the Upload Multiple Documents command or through Windows Explorer, the documents are assigned to a default content type, which might not be the correct content type and might allow those documents to become visible prior to the configuration of important document metadata. The procedures outlined in this solution create a type of quarantine to ensure that documents transferred to the library using these methods are trapped until fully configured by the user.

# 4-8: Work with Documents in a Document Library

## Solution overview

| | |
|---|---|
| **Type of solution** | Procedures |
| **Features and tools** | SharePoint document libraries and Microsoft Office applications |
| **Solution summary** | Understand the nuances regarding opening a document for viewing or editing. |
| **Benefits** | Provide clear training to users of document libraries. |

## Introduction

Document libraries aren't particularly useful if you cannot view the documents they contain. This section covers the tasks and tips related to viewing and editing documents in a library. These are rudimentary procedures that should be communicated to all end users.

## View a document in a document library

To view documents in a document library, simply click the link for the document. It opens in the appropriate application on your system. If an application is not available for the document type, an error is displayed.

## Edit a document in a document library

To open a document for editing, the "foolproof" method suggests you should click the edit menu for the document and choose the Edit In *Application* command. The edit menu, remember, is the name for the menu that appears when you hover over a document and click the drop-down arrow that appears. You can also click in the white space between the document name and the arrow.

Unfortunately, this two-click process for opening a document for editing is not intuitive. Users typically just click the link for the document itself, which will often open the document in read-only mode.

 **Note** Be certain to train your users to click the edit menu and choose Edit In *Application*, and to understand the difference between opening a document for viewing and for editing.

## Open a document with Office 2007 clients installed

The behavior you experience when you click the link for a document varies depending on the application associated with that document type. If you have Office 2007 installed on your system, for example, clicking the link for an Office document produces a prompt: You will be asked whether you want to open or edit the document. The prompt is shown in Figure 4-24. It solves the user training issue for Office 2007 document types. However, users will still have to know to click the edit menu's Edit In *Application* command for documents managed with other applications.

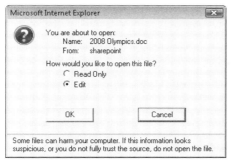

**Figure 4-24**   Office 2007 clients will prompt you when you click the link for a document

## Solution summary

Although the standard method for opening a document for viewing is to click its link and you should use the document's edit menu to choose Edit In *Application*, there are in fact differences in behavior when opening a document based on the document type and the application that is used to open it. Understanding these differences, and communicating both the options and the best practices to users, can reduce frustration and increase the usability of a document library.

# 4-9: Monitor Changes to Libraries or Documents with Alerts and RSS

## Solution overview

| | |
|---|---|
| **Type of solution** | Guidance |
| **Features and tools** | E-mail notifications and RSS |
| **Solution summary** | Configure alerts for changes to a library or document, or monitor a library by subscribing to its RSS feed. |
| **Benefits** | Stay informed of important changes to SharePoint libraries and documents. |

## Introduction

SharePoint provides two great ways for you to monitor what is going on in a library or with a specific document: e-mail alerts and RSS feeds.

# Subscribe to e-mail alerts for a library or document

E-mail alerts can be sent to notify you of changes to a library or document. To configure alerts for a library, click the Actions button and choose Alert Me. To configure alerts for a single document, open the document's edit menu and choose Alert Me, or click the Alert Me button on the document's view properties page. The New Alert page centralizes all options for the alert. For a document library, options include the following:

**Alert Title.**   This becomes the subject line of the e-mail notification, which can then be used by rules-processing logic in your e-mail client.

**Send Alerts To.**   Most users will be able to configure an alert to be sent only to themselves. However, users with the Create Alerts permission can configure alerts to be sent to any user or group. This is an important functional update from previous versions of SharePoint. Note that the interface suggests that you can enter user names, but you can also enter group names. Alerts sent to a SharePoint group will be sent to each member of the group. Alerts sent to an Active Directory group will go to the *group object*'s e-mail address.

**Change Type.**   You can specify what types of changes should trigger a notification.

**Send Alerts For These Changes.**   In previous versions of SharePoint, you would receive alerts for changes made by anyone—even yourself. In WSS 3.0, that option is called Anything Changes. But you can also configure alerts for other than your own changes (with the Someone Else Changes A Document option) or when someone changes documents you either created or most recently modified. If you have more than one view configured for the library, you can also configure alerts to be sent when a change affects a document that would appear in a specific view.

> **Note**   Use alerts associated with specific views to create filters or rules for sophisticated alert configuration. For example, if you are interested in being notified when someone changes a document that has been marked as Final in a custom Status column, create a view that filters for documents whose status is Final. Then create an alert that sends notifications for changes to documents based on that view.

In lists, you will also see options in the Send Alerts For These Changes section that are specific for that type of list. In a Calendar list, for example, you can choose to be notified when a time or location of a meeting changes.

**When To Send Alerts.**   Finally, you can configure the frequency and schedule with which notifications are sent.

When you create an alert for a document, you will see a subset of these options, without the options that apply to a collection such as a library.

> **Note**    If you use an Office 2003 application, you can configure alerts for a document using the Shared Workspace task pane on the Document Information page. Office 2007 lost this functionality, somehow.

## Monitor library activity using RSS

You can also watch library activity using an RSS reader. All document libraries and lists are RSS-enabled by default in SharePoint. Click the Actions button in the document library, and choose View RSS Feed. You can then use your favorite RSS reader, including the RSS reader functionality built into Internet Explorer 7 or Microsoft Office Outlook 2007 to subscribe to and monitor the feed.

> **Note**    If you want to configure or disable RSS feeds for a list or library, click the RSS Settings link on the Customize page for the list or library.

## Solution summary

After users start making changes to lists and libraries, as outlined in Solutions 4-5 and 4-8, you can leverage the e-mail notification and RSS capabilities of SharePoint to monitor and audit activities of other users, reducing the need to manually examine changes.

# 4-10: Control Document Editing with Check Out

## Solution overview

| | |
|---|---|
| **Type of solution** | Procedures |
| **Features and tools** | SharePoint document libraries, optional and required checkout, and Microsoft Office applications |
| **Solution summary** | Configure and manage document check out and check in. |
| **Benefits** | Provide managed control over document editing to eliminate conflicting changes from multiple users. |

## Introduction

When you check out a document, the document can be edited only by you. This prevents problems that can arise when multiple users try to make changes to a document at the same time. Check out places a lock on the file. While the document is checked out and locked, the changes you make are visible only to you. When you check in the document, changes you made become visible to other users and other users can in turn edit the document.

## Require document checkout

Checkout is an important function for a document-management system. In most scenarios, it is critical. Previous versions of SharePoint didn't allow you to require document checkout, which significantly reduced the usefulness of the feature. WSS 3.0 does allow you to require checkout. On the library's Customize page, click Versioning Settings. At the bottom of the page that appears, you'll find the Require Check Out option. Select Yes and then click OK.

## Check out a document

There are numerous ways to check out a document. The most common are discussed next.

### Using the document library

You can check out a document from a document library by clicking the document's edit menu and choosing Check Out. There are also Check Out command buttons on pages such as the page you see when you click the document's edit menu and choose View Properties.

If you have Office 2003 installed and checkout is required, clicking a document opens the document in read-only mode. You can make changes, but when you attempt to save the file you receive a file permission error. To work around the error, you must save the file locally, check out the file from the document library, and then upload your changed file.

If Office 2003 is installed, checkout is required, and you use the Edit In *Application* command on the document's edit menu, you are prompted to check out the document before making changes.

Office 2007 clients are more user friendly than their predecessors. If checkout is required and you click the document link, you are provided the option to open the document for read-only viewing or to check out and edit the document. The prompt is shown in Figure 4-25. Note that Office 2007 clients also give you the ability to save the document to your local drafts folder for offline editing, which will be discussed in Solution 4-16 on page 359. Even if you choose the Read Only option, a bar appears in the Office application allowing you to check out the document.

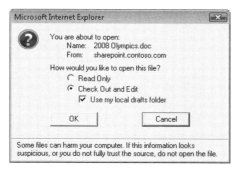

**Figure 4-25** Office 2007 prompt when a document is opened with checkout required

If Office 2007 is installed, checkout is required, and you choose the Edit In *Application* command, Office 2007 checks out the document for you automatically.

### Using Office applications

Microsoft Office 2003 and 2007 offer additional options for checking out documents that are built in to the application interface itself. Office 2003 users can check in and check out documents using the Shared Workspace task pane's Document Information page. Office 2007 users can do the same using the Server menu under the Microsoft Office Button.

## Understand the user experience while a document is checked out

While a document is checked out, a green checked-out arrow appears on the document in the document library. If you try to edit a checked-out document, you are informed that the document is locked for editing and by whom. You are given the choice to open the document as read-only, create a local copy for editing, or receive an e-mail notification when the user checks the document in. The second of those options, Create A Local Copy And Merge Your Changes Later, is not recommended for most scenarios because it might be difficult to reconcile the changes made by two different users to the same document.

One of the most important things to know, and to communicate to users, is that when you check out a document, changes you make are not committed to the document and made visible until you check the document in. While you are making changes and saving those changes, the document is updated and the changes are visible to you, but nobody else will see those changes until you check in the document.

> **Important**    Communicate to users that while a document is checked out, changes will not be visible to any other user until the document is checked in.

Office 2007 clients make this behavior more discoverable. When you close a checked-out document, Office clients prompt you with a message that reads: "Other users cannot see your changes until you check in. Do you want to check in now?"

## Manage document check in

It is important to understand what can be done with a document that one has checked out and to train users how to best use those alternatives.

### Save changes to a checked-out document

As you modify a document you've checked out, you obviously need to save your changes. Just remember that those changes are visible only to you until you check in the document.

## Check in the document

You can check in a document directly from a WSS-compatible application: Office 2003 clients can check in the document using the Document Information page of the Shared Workspace task pane; and Office 2007 clients can check in using the Server menu under the Microsoft Office Button.

Checkin can be also performed on the document library for any application, not just Office or WSS-compatible applications. Click the document's edit menu and choose Check In. The Check In command button is also available on the document's view properties page.

When a document is checked in, the following actions occur:

■ If the document was checked out to the Local Drafts folder, it is uploaded to the server. The Local Drafts folder is discussed in Solution 4-16.

■ Changes made to the document are made visible to users with permission to read the document.

■ If versioning is enabled, the user is prompted for a version and for version comments. Versioning is discussed in Solution 4-11.

■ If content approval is enabled and the version is set to a major version, the approval status is changed to Pending.

**Important**    A user can check in a document that she checked out. In addition, any user with the Override Check Out permission can check in a document on behalf of other users. This effectively commits all changes made to the document to that point and makes the changes visible to users. However, the user who originally checked out the document might have made changes that were not yet saved to the server. Those changes can no longer be saved. Changes will have to be manually identified, reconciled, and made to the server.

## Check in the document but keep it checked out

When you check in a document, you are given the following option: Keep Document Checked Out After Checking In This Version. That might seem counterintuitive and confusing. It boils down to those uncommitted changes. By checking in a document, you make those changes visible to other users. But by keeping the document checked out, you maintain the editorial lock on the file.

## Check in without saving changes

You can also choose to check in the document without saving changes. This effectively reverts the document to the state it was in when you originally checked it out.

### Discard check out

A user with the Override Check Out permission, or the user who checked a document out, can choose Discard Check Out from the document's edit menu in the document library. This command removes the lock from the file and discards all changes that have been made since the document was checked out.

## Solution summary

You can reduce the possibility that multiple users will make conflicting changes to a document by requiring checkout—a best practice for most document libraries. Checkout and checkin can be requested using the SharePoint Web interface or from compatible applications, such as Microsoft Office. The sheer variety of ways to check out and check in documents, along with the behavior and visibility of changes to a checked-out document, require thorough understanding and communication to your end users.

# 4-11: Implement and Maintain Document Version History

## Solution overview

| | |
|---|---|
| **Type of solution** | Procedures |
| **Features and tools** | SharePoint document libraries, version history, and Microsoft Office applications |
| **Solution summary** | Configure and manage SharePoint's capability to maintain major and minor versions of documents as they are revised. |
| **Benefits** | Audit trail of document changes, version comparison, the ability to hide drafts, and easy restoration of corrupted documents. |

## Introduction

Version history is a valuable feature of any document-management system. It serves several business purposes:

**Audit trail.**   By maintaining previous versions of a document, you can identify changes that were made over its life cycle.

**Recovery.**   If a user makes changes that corrupt a document, you can recover the document's previous version.

**Visibility.**   There are scenarios in which you want to control who sees particular versions of a document. For example, you might want the users in your organization to see only final versions of a document, not the drafts that bounce back and forth between the document's editors.

# Configure version history

To enable version history, click the Versioning Settings link on the document library's Customize page. In the Document Version History section, shown in Figure 4-26, you can configure the library to maintain only final or major versions (in the form 1.0, 2.0, 3.0...) or to maintain draft or minor versions of a document as well (in the form 1.1, 1.2, ...). You can also specify how many previous major and minor versions to maintain, based on your business requirements. These settings support the requirements for audit trail and recovery.

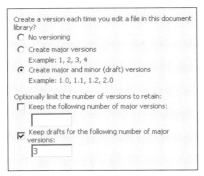

**Figure 4-26**    The Document Version History options

To support requirements for visibility, choose from the options in the Draft Item Security section. Figure 4-26 shows a typical configuration, whereby drafts are visible only to users who have edit items permission for the drafts. Other users will see only the most recent major version of the document.

# Manage the creation of major and minor versions

After you enable versioning, users can save documents as major or minor versions. The interaction between major and minor versions, application behaviors, check out and check in, and content approval (discussed in Solution 4-12) are somewhat complex.

When you are editing a document and save your changes, each save creates a minor version. Even though the document has not been checked in, users who can view drafts are able to open any but the most recent minor version. To see the most recent minor version, the document must be checked in.

When you choose the Publish A Major Version command from the document's edit menu in the library, you create a major version.

Office 2007 applications prompt you when you check in a document for whether the document should be checked in as a minor version or as a major version. Office 2003 will check in a minor version, and then you can use the document library to publish a major version.

# Manage document versions

When versions are maintained in a library, you can manage the versions using the Version History command. This command is found in the document's edit menu, in the view properties page, in the Document Information page of the Shared Workspace task pane in Office 2003, and in the Server menu of Office 2007.

With the Version History command, you can open (view) and restore a version of the document. You can also delete a version. In the document library's Versions page, you can delete all versions of a document or delete minor versions. Unfortunately, these commands are mislabeled. What you are really doing is deleting all versions *previous to the current major version*, or deleting all minor versions *previous to the current major version*. You are cleaning out the backlog, so to speak. The current major version and any drafts since that major version remain. To delete those versions, you must delete the document itself from the document library.

# Compare document versions

To compare document versions, you need to open the versions and use the appropriate application to perform a comparison. For example, you can use Word to compare two Word documents. Word 2007 takes it a step further: You can compare versions directly from the library's history. Open the current version of a document, click the Office button and, from the Server menu, choose Version History. In the Versions dialog box, choose the previous version against which you want to compare, and click the Compare button.

# Solution summary

Version history is a valuable feature of any document management system, and SharePoint's version history capabilities are easy to configure for administrators, and easy to access and understand for end users.

# 4-12: Implement Content Approval

## Solution overview

| | |
|---|---|
| **Type of solution** | Procedures |
| **Features and tools** | SharePoint document libraries, content approval, and Microsoft Office applications |
| **Solution summary** | Configure content approval functionality. |
| **Benefits** | Manage the visibility of draft and final versions of documents. |

## Introduction

Content approval is a workflow through which changes made to a document are not made public until approved. In this short section, we cover both the procedures and the behavior of content approval.

# Configure content approval

To configure content approval, open the Customize page for the document library and click the Versioning Settings link. In the Content Approval section, click Yes.

When Versioning is enabled, you can limit who is able to see unapproved drafts of the content. The Draft Item Security section allows you to grant read permissions for drafts to any user who can read items, only users who can edit items, or only users with the Approve Items permission. In each case, the author of the item can see the draft as well. The second and third options are best aligned with most content approval scenarios. Users who are not permitted to see unapproved drafts see only the most recent approved version of the document.

You then manage content approval using the Approve/Reject Item command, which is available on the document's edit menu and the view properties page. When you choose the Approve/Reject Item command, you are able to specify approved, rejected, or pending, and you can enter comments.

# Understand the interaction of content approval, versioning, and checkout

Content approval is technically distinct from versioning and document checkout, which are in turn distinct from each other. But in most document management scenarios, you'll use all three if you want to implement content approval. The interaction of the three warrants a brief overview.

When required checkout, versioning, and content approval are all enabled, the concept of a *draft* remains the minor version. However, draft item security becomes tricky. If there is only one author for documents, it probably makes sense to limit draft item visibility to the author and to users with the Approve Items permission, which is included in the Design permission template. If there is more than one author, drafts should be visible to anyone who might need to edit the minor version as well.

The process for finalizing a document when all three functionalities are in place is as follows:

1. The author must check in the document.
2. The document must be published as a major version.
3. A user with the Approve Items permission must approve the document.

# Solution summary

Content approval is a straightforward feature that is easy to configure and to use. However, its interaction with checkout and version history can be somewhat more nuanced and should be well tested, understood, and communicated to end users.

# 4-13: Implement a Three-State Workflow

## Solution overview

| | |
|---|---|
| **Type of solution** | Procedures |
| **Features and tools** | The three-state workflow |
| **Solution summary** | Create a three-state workflow, with an example for supporting the submission, approval, and reimbursement of expense reports. |
| **Benefits** | Automate business processes using SharePoint. |

## Introduction

I would certainly describe content approval as a workflow. Certain steps must happen before an item becomes visible to readers of the document library. However, SharePoint Products and Technologies reserve the word "workflow" for a process that is driven by more sophisticated logic. There is only one workflow supported out of the box by WSS: the three-state workflow. We'll examine it in this solution. Microsoft Office SharePoint Server 2007 adds a more robust content approval workflow. Sophisticated workflows can be developed using SharePoint Designer. Just about anything can be done by developing a .NET workflow using tools such as Microsoft Visual Studio.

> **Important**    Workflows can be created for a document library, or they can be associated with a managed content type.

A three-state workflow involves a document that moves through three milestones. When the first milestone (or "state") is reached, certain users can be notified that action is required. When that action is completed, the second milestone is reached, and a notification can be sent to users—typically another group of users. And when their action is complete, the document reaches its third state.

A common example is an expense report. An expense report is submitted by an employee (state #1). The manager must then be notified that the report must be reviewed and accepted. When the expense report is approved (state #2), accounting is notified to cut a reimbursement check. When the expense report has been reimbursed (state #3), the workflow is complete.

## Configure the choice field for the state

A three-state workflow requires a field that indicates the state of the document. This is called the *choice column*. The choice column must have at least three choices. For example, our expense report workflow has these three states: submitted, approved, and reimbursed. In the settings of the document library or content type for which you are creating the workflow, add a column that is a Choice column, and enter the three states as choices.

## Configure the three-state workflow

After the choice field has been created, you can create the workflow itself by following these steps:

1.  Click the Workflow Settings link on the Customize page for the document library or content type.

2.  If you are associating a workflow with a content type, click Add A Workflow.

3.  The Add A Workflow page appears.

4.  In Windows SharePoint Services 3.0, your only choice for the workflow template, by default, is Three-State.

5.  Enter a name for the workflow, such as Expense Report Approval.

6.  When the first and second milestones, or states, are reached, tasks are generated for the users, who must take action to move the document to its next state. Choose the task list that will be used for this workflow, or select New Task List to create a new list.

7.  A workflow history list will be maintained in the library or list. Choose a history list. If this is the first workflow you are creating, SharePoint will create a new workflow history.

8.  Configure the options for how the workflow will be initiated.

    The default setting is that a user with Edit Items Permission can trigger the workflow using the Workflows command on the document's edit menu. You can elevate the required permission to the Manage Lists permission. Alternatively or additionally, you can specify that the workflow should be triggered when a new item is created. If a document library contains only one type of document, and you want the workflow to apply to every document as it is added, this is a great way to automate the launching of the workflow. Similarly, if you are assigning a workflow to a content type and you want the workflow to begin whenever a new item is added of that content type, to any library or list that uses the content type, you can select the Start This Workflow When A New Item Is Created check box.

9.  Click Next.

10. In the Workflow States section, select your choice field and the three choices that mark the three states or milestones for the document.

    When a workflow is initiated, either by launching the workflow manually or as an automatic response to the creation of a new document, its choice field is set to the first state.

11. Configure the action to take when the workflow is initiated. A task is generated, and you can configure the details of the task. Optionally, you can also send an e-mail message. An

example is shown in Figure 4-27. In our case, we notify the employee's manager by task and by e-mail that approval of the expense report is required.

> **Note** If users are being alerted to changes in the task list using SharePoint alerts, or if they have integrated the SharePoint task list into Outlook 2007, it might be unnecessary to configure e-mail alerts as part of the workflow.

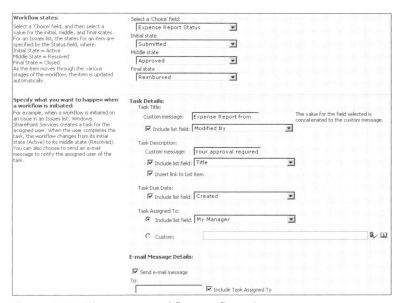

**Figure 4-27**   Three-state workflow configuration

Note we are using a column named My Manager (a Person or Group column) in the document library or content type. When an employee submits an expense report, the employee indicates his manager in this required column. The information in that column is used to assign the task and to send the e-mail message.

Users are notified by the SharePoint task or by e-mail that action is required.

When the action has been performed and the choice field has been changed to the second state, the workflow triggers a second action. In our example, a manager changes the choice field to Approved and then we want to notify one of our accountants to cut the check.

12. Configure the second action for the workflow. Again, you can configure the task that will be assigned and, optionally, an e-mail notification.

13. Click OK.

> **Note**   Be careful to test the interaction between your three-state workflow and any other SharePoint processes, such as required checkout, version history, or content approval.

# ιunch and manage workflows

When workflows are in place, users with appropriate permissions can start a workflow by choosing the Workflows command from the document's edit menu or the view properties page. Or, in Office 2007, they can choose it from the Server menu in the Office button.

The Workflows command also displays the status of workflows that are currently running for a document. Figure 4-28 shows that a recently submitted expense report is being run through the Expense Report Approval workflow.

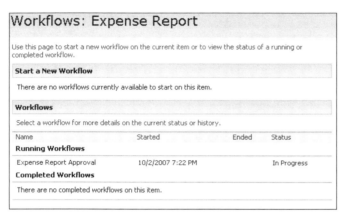

**Figure 4-28**   The Workflows report for a document

Clicking the link for a workflow, such as the Expense Report Approval link shown in Figure 4-28, produces a detailed report of the workflow's progress. On this Workflow Status page, you can see the events that have occurred in the workflow. In the case of a three-state workflow, they are the initiation of the workflow and two state changes. You can also see tasks that have been created that are associated with the workflow. And, importantly, you can terminate the workflow if something has gone wrong.

## Solution summary

This solution introduced the three-state workflow, the only workflow available out of the box in WSS 3.0. As you learned, workflows enable you to support a business process with SharePoint, by specifying conditions and actions to take based on those conditions. Microsoft Office SharePoint Server offers several more out-of-the-box workflows. But I highly recommend you examine Microsoft Office SharePoint Designer, with which you can create custom workflows without a single line of code. If you are a developer, you can go all the way using Visual Studio to build sophisticated workflows.

# 4-14: Organize and Manage Documents with Folders and Views

## Solution overview

| | |
|---|---|
| **Type of solution** | Guidance |
| **Features and tools** | SharePoint document library folders and views. |
| **Solution summary** | Understand the purpose of folders and of views, and the value of each to the organization and presentation of document library contents. |
| **Benefits** | Enable effective access to and visibility of documents. |

## Introduction

Documents can be managed in a document library using folders or metadata (columns). Folders are a familiar metaphor. Views can leverage metadata (columns) to manage the display, sort, filter, grouping, and summary of the contents of a document library.

 **Note**   It is recommended that you use metadata (columns) to organize and manage documents whenever possible.

## Use folders to scope document management

There are several reasons to use folders as organizational and management containers within document libraries:

**Unique security permissions.**   Folders can have unique permissions applied, which will then be inherited by documents within the folder. Folders with specific permissions might be easier to manage than specifying permissions on individual documents.

**More than 2000 items.**   It is recommended that lists and libraries be kept to less than 2000 items per folder. So, if you have 5000 documents in a library, you should divide them among several folders so that no folder has more than 2000 documents. This is a performance issue, not a technical one, and there are workarounds and guidance you can find on the Internet for lists or folders that need to have more than 2000 items.

**Outlook Synchronization.**   You can take the contents of a document library offline with Outlook 2007. When you do, the library or folder you connect to, and all subfolders, will be synchronized. If you want to control the scope of documents that users synchronize with Outlook, organize the documents into folders.

In these situations, be sure to enable folders in the library's advanced settings. Then you can create folders with the New button.

> **Note**    If content approval is required for a library, even new folders must be approved.

## Use views to scope the presentation and management of documents

Views are an extraordinarily flexible and powerful way to manage documents because they are independent of the containers (folders) you have created within your document library. The settings for a view specify the following:

- Whether the view is available to you, only, or to the public
- Which columns are visible and in what order
- How documents are sorted
- What criteria is used to determine whether a document appears or not
- Whether or not documents appear in expandable and collapsible groups
- Which columns (if any) are totaled using *Sum*, *Count*, or other functions
- How items are displayed

All of these settings result in a view that can be presented as a standard view, a datasheet view, or other view types, such as a Gantt chart or calendar. I could easily write an entire book on SharePoint views, but I just don't have the space or time here. Begin your exploration of views at *http://office.microsoft.com/en-us/sharepointserver/HA100215771033.aspx*.

> **Note**    As presented in Solution 4-5, views can be used as the basis for e-mail notifications. You can configure alerts for changes to documents that would appear in a specific view, so you can leverage the filtering capability of views to define which documents generate alerts.

## Solution summary

Folders, a familiar metaphor, are useful for scoping permissions and synchronization with Outlook 2007. Views are a more powerful way to manage document libraries, as they define through a variety of settings which documents and properties are visible.

# 4-15: Configure WSS Indexing of PDF Files

## Solution overview

| | |
|---|---|
| **Type of solution** | Procedures |
| **Features and tools** | SharePoint search, indexing, iFilters, and icons |
| **Solution summary** | Configure the indexing of PDF files and the association of an icon for PDFs. |
| **Benefits** | Enable search of the popular PDF file format within WSS sites. |

## Introduction

Windows SharePoint Services indexes documents and enables a user to search within a list or library, or within a site and its subsites. The maximum scope of a search in WSS is the site collection. You cannot search across site collections in WSS 3.0—Microsoft Office SharePoint Server 2007 provides that functionality.

## Disable search within a library

When you perform a search, the results include only hits that you have permission to read: Results are security trimmed. Therefore, there is usually not a need to disable search within a library. However, some scenarios might warrant disabling search. To do so, click the Advanced Settings link in the Customize page for the library. In the Search section that appears, choose No and then click OK.

## Enable indexing of PDFs

Indexing is automatic and hands-free. However, SharePoint cannot index every type of document. PDF files, for example, are not indexed by default, and I expect you'll want to enable indexing of this popular file format.

For example, Figure 4-29 shows a document library with a Word document and a PDF. Note the PDF does not display an icon. This does not relate directly to indexing—there is a *second* problem: WSS doesn't know what icon to display for PDFs. We'll solve that.

**Figure 4-29**   SharePoint library with a PDF and a Word document

Both of these documents contain the word "iFilter." When I perform a search, however, only the Word document is returned, as shown in Figure 4-30.

**Figure 4-30**    Search does not return PDF matches because PDFs are not yet indexed

Microsoft Office file formats can already be indexed by SharePoint. For formats that SharePoint does not recognize, you must install an iFilter on your SharePoint servers. iFilters are plug-ins that enable indexing of file types. Although iFilter is a Microsoft specification, it is generally through vendors or third parties that you'll get iFilters—not through Microsoft itself.

After you add the iFilter, you must configure SharePoint to index the file type (.pdf). But then, you still have two problems. The biggest is that SharePoint indexes only the files that are added or existing files whose properties change. So SharePoint will not index existing PDFs when you add the PDF iFilter. You must rebuild your index. The second challenge, purely a cosmetic one, is that you enable SharePoint to display an appropriate icon for PDFs.

## Install the PDF iFilter

To install the PDF iFilter, follow these steps:

1.   Obtain the following two downloads from Adobe:

❑   The Adobe PDF iFilter version 6.0, available at *http://www.adobe.com/support/ downloads/detail.jsp?ftpID=2611*. As of the writing of this solution, the only 64-bit iFilter for PDFs is a for-fee download from Foxit Software (*www.foxitsoft.com*).

❑   An icon for PDFs, also available from Adobe. Check the Adobe licensing page at *http://www.adobe.com/misc/linking.html#producticons* and then download the gif at *http://www.adobe.com/images/pdficon_small.gif*.

2.   Install the iFilter on the SharePoint server by double-clicking it and stepping through the setup wizard.

3.   Add a registry entry for the .pdf extension in the registry:

a.   Open the Registry Editor, and navigate to HKEY_LOCAL_MACHINE\SOFT-WARE\Microsoft\Shared Tools\Web Server Extensions\12.0\Search\Applications\<GUID>\Gather\Search\Extensions\ExtensionList.

b.   Identify the highest number value in the key. On a default installation of WSS, the highest entry is 37. Note they are not sorted in numeric order because registry value names are strings.

c.   Create a registry value for the next number—for example, 38—by choosing Edit, New, and String Value, and then naming the value the next highest number (for example, 38).

d.   Double-click the value you just created and, in the Value Data box, type **pdf**. Note there is no dot preceding the extension.

4.   There are two registry keys with specific values that must exist. Verify that these exist and, if they do not, create them as follows:

❏   HKEY_LOCAL_MACHINE\SOFTWARE\Microsoft\Shared Tools\Web Server Extensions\12.0\Search\Setup\ContentIndexCommon\Filters\Extension\.pdf

   ●   Value Name: Default

      ○   Type: REG_MULTI_SZ

      ○   Data: {4C904448-74A9-11D0-AF6E-00C04FD8DC02}

❏   HKEY_LOCAL_MACHINE\SOFTWARE\Microsoft\Shared Tools\Web Server Extensions\12.0\Search\Setup\Filters\.pdf

   ●   Value Name: Default

      ○   Type: REG_SZ

      ○   Data: (value not set)

   ●   Value Name: Extension

      ○   Type: REG_SZ

      ○   Data: pdf

   ●   Value Name: FileTypeBucket

      ○   Type: REG_DWORD

      ○   Data: 0x00000001 (1)

   ●   Value Name: MimeTypes

      ○   Type: REG_SZ

      ○   Data: application/pdf

5. Restart the Windows SharePoint Services Search service using the following steps:

   a. Open a command prompt.

   b. Type **net stop spsearch**.

   c. Type **net start spsearch**.

### Rebuild the index

After you install the iFilter, newly added or modified PDFs will be indexed. However, existing PDFs will not be indexed and will therefore not appear in search result lists. The solution is easy: Rebuild the WSS search index. Depending on the number of items on the server, this could take quite some time, and search results quality might suffer during the re-indexing, which therefore should be performed in an appropriate time window. To trigger a rebuilding of the WSS search index, follow these steps:

1. Open a command prompt.

2. Navigate to Program Files\Common Files\Microsoft Shared\web server extensions\12\BIN.

3. Type the following command: **stsadm.exe -o spsearch -action fullcrawlstop**

4. Type the following command: **stsadm.exe -o spsearch -action fullcrawlstart**

# Assign an icon to unrecognized file types

After you rebuild the index, existing PDFs will, after being indexed, appear in search results. But they will still not have correct icons. So, while your site is being indexed, keep going with these steps to configure the icon:

1. Open the folder Program Files\Common Files\Microsoft Shared\Web Server Extensions\12\Template\Images.

2. Copy the .gif file you downloaded from Adobe in an earlier section into the folder.

3. Open the folder Program Files\Common Files\Microsoft Shared\Web Server Extensions\12\Template\Xml.

4. Right-click the file docicon.xml and choose Open With and select Notepad.

5. In the *<ByExtension>* element, you'll see a number of *<Mapping Key>* elements. You will add one for PDF. It does not have to be in alphabetical order. The element you need to add is  **<Mapping Key="pdf" Value="pdficon_small.gif" OpenControl=""/>**

6. Save that file and close Notepad.

Now, the moment of truth. A search now provides the results shown in Figure 4-31.

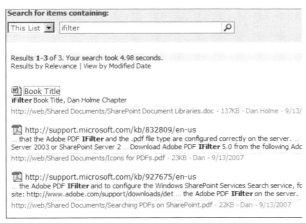

**Figure 4-31**    Search results returning PDFs

## Solution summary

SharePoint does not index PDFs by default, but you can install the iFilter to expose PDF contents, and configure SharePoint to rebuild its index to include the contents of existing PDFs. These procedures enable users to search files in the popular PDF format within libraries and sites.

# 4-16: Work with SharePoint Files Offline

## Solution overview

| | |
|---|---|
| **Type of solution** | Guidance |
| **Features and tools** | SharePoint document libraries, Microsoft Office 2007 applications |
| **Solution summary** | Identify the options for working with documents in SharePoint document libraries while offline. |
| **Benefits** | Gain access to documents while disconnected from the server. |

## Introduction

SharePoint provides fantastic functionality for collaboration and document management within an organization. But, of course, users are not always connected to the network and to the SharePoint server. In this solution, we examine the options for taking a document offline for reading and editing.

# Download a copy of a file

The first way to work with a file offline is to simply download a copy. This works identically to downloading any file from a Web site. You can right-click the link for a document and choose Save Target As. Or, using the document's edit menu, choose Send To and then Download A Copy. If you plan to make changes to the document, it is recommended that you check out the document to prevent other users from making changes that could be difficult to reconcile with the changes you will be making concurrently.

The copy you now have downloaded locally is completely disconnected from the copy on the server. You can make changes to it. If you want to save your changes to the server, you need to use the application's Save command and enter the URL to the document library. Or you can use the library's Upload command to upload your document. You can decide whether to overwrite the copy in the document library and, if versioning is enabled, to save the document as a new version.

# Provide offline access to files using the local cache

WSS 3.0 and Office 2007 team up to provide the first built-in option for taking files offline from SharePoint. If checkout is required and if Office 2007 clients are installed, when you choose to edit an Office document you are given the option to save the file to your local cache. This option appears when you click a document's link in the library or when you choose the Edit In *Application* command from the document's edit menu. Figure 4-32 shows an example.

**Figure 4-32**   The Use My Local Drafts Folder option

Technically, this is the SharePoint drafts folder in your (My) Documents folder. While you are editing the document, you will use the copy in your local cache, which is available when you are disconnected from the network. When you check in the document, it is automatically uploaded to the SharePoint server.

This fantastic functionality is sadly limited to Office 2007 clients editing Office documents when checkout is enabled. It does not address scenarios where users want to take non-Office documents offline for editing or take files offline for viewing.

# Use Outlook 2007 to take libraries and lists offline

Outlook 2007 is, surprisingly, the engine that has been equipped to take document libraries offline. I would have expected such functionality to be part of Windows Vista, but it made it into Outlook 2007. That's good enough for me, but it might not be for the millions of users running previous versions of Outlook.

The good news is that this feature is fantastic. It's built into a tool that every Office user lives on: Outlook. And it's very easy to use. Just open a document library, click the Actions button, and choose Connect To Outlook. A new node is created in Outlook: SharePoint Lists. Below that will be the libraries or lists to which you've connected. Figure 4-33 shows an example.

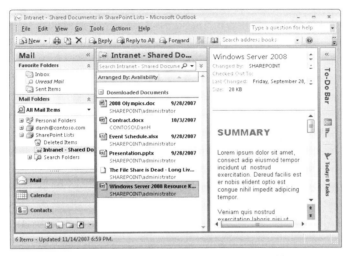

**Figure 4-33**   Outlook client showing a SharePoint library

Behind the scenes, an offline storage database has been created. Outlook synchronizes the library once per hour. If you're leaving the office in a rush, just click Outlook's Send/Receive button to be sure you've received any updates from the library. You are able to open Office documents for editing offline. The application prompts you to save a copy in the local cache (the SharePoint Drafts folder). The document is flagged in Outlook with a red up arrow to remind you that the document needs to be uploaded when you are once again online. When you are connected to the SharePoint server, open the modified document from Outlook, and the application will prompt you to update the server.

Unfortunately, you cannot check out a file using Outlook. This must be done from the document library's Web interface. So if you believe you'll be editing a file while offline and that other users might want to make changes during the same timeframe, be sure to check out the file before you leave the office.

> **Important**   When you check out a file for editing offline with Outlook's synchronized document library, be sure to select Use Local Cache.

There are a number of nuances to using Outlook with document libraries. I highly recommend you skim through the end-user training on this topic at *http://office.microsoft.com/training/Training.aspx?AssetID=RC102338501033&CTT=6&Origin=RC102338501033*.

## Other options for offline use of SharePoint document libraries

Microsoft Office Groove provides native support for offline use of documents from document libraries. See *http://office.microsoft.com* for more information about Groove.

In addition, third-party vendors offer tools to enhance the offline experience of SharePoint users. Colligo Networks, at *http://www.colligo.com/*, is one such vendor.

## Solution summary

SharePoint and Microsoft Office applications are integrated to provide several options for working with the documents in a document library while disconnected from the SharePoint server. The business value of these options is similar to that of the Windows Offline Files feature, discussed in Solution Collection 3, "Managing User Data and Settings," which allows you to take files offline from SMB shared folders. With the ability to take documents offline from SharePoint document libraries, even users who travel away from the network can continue to leverage the collaborative capabilities of Windows SharePoint Services.

# Active Directory Delegation and Administrative Lock Down

Because Active Directory is critical to the security and integrity of a Microsoft Windows network, it is very important to secure the directory service itself. Unfortunately, many organizations have not had the time, resources, or knowledge with which to plan and implement their administrative models with least-privilege permissions in Active Directory. In this Solution Collection, I explain the ins and outs of Active Directory security, the tools available to manage permissions on Active Directory objects, and the steps you can take to implement a role-based delegation that supports your current administrative model and is agile enough to adapt to organizational changes over time. I also show you how to delegate the ability to administer computers to your support organizations, and why it's important to empty as many of Active Directory's built-in groups as possible.

## Scenarios, Pain, and Solution

If you have not already implemented a role-based delegation of administrative tasks in Active Directory, you might or might not experience the resulting pain on a day-to-day basis. Consider the scenarios outlined in the following four bullet points:

■ Contoso, Ltd., migrated to Active Directory from a multidomain environment built during the days of Windows NT 4.0. During the migration, the administrators of the

Windows NT domains expressed great concern that the new directory service would remove their ability to maintain independent control over their environments. Contoso migrated each domain into a separate organizational unit (OU) to represent the distributed administration model and gave each of the administrators full control over the OU that corresponded to their previous Windows NT 4 domain. To mollify administrators' concerns over loss of control, Contoso added all administrators to the Domain Admins group.

In an enterprise where all or too many administrators belong to the Domain Admins group, you might not experience pain because all the administrators can do everything. Of course, the reality is that they can do more than they should be able to do. Such an environment is highly overdelegated. Any of the administrators could, accidentally or intentionally, perform domain-level actions that jeopardize the integrity of the entire directory service.

■ The team responsible for managing regulatory compliance at Contoso notified the Information Technology (IT) organization that the extensive membership of the Domain Admins group posed an unacceptable security and compliance exposure. Contoso's IT team must now evaluate the administrative model of the organization to define job tasks and roles so that a least-privilege implementation of the administrative model can be put in place.

In my experience, the most difficult aspect of delegating Active Directory is neither the access control lists (ACLs) nor the tools used to manage security, but rather the business exercise that is necessary to evaluate requirements and design an effective administrative model.

■ At Adventure Works, Active Directory was designed in 2001 by an administrator who delegated numerous security permissions to Active Directory objects. That administrator has since left the organization, and today the IT team finds it very difficult to understand exactly which administrators have been delegated which permissions to which OUs.

The distributed nature of ACLs on Active Directory OUs, and the tools available with which to evaluate those ACLs, make it very difficult to understand, report, or audit the existing delegation in an Active Directory domain. In this Solution Collection, I'll share with you my favorite tools and processes for reporting and evaluating ACLs in Active Directory. A role-based approach to delegation, similar to the role-based access control for shared folders presented in Solution Collection 1 and 2, will greatly facilitate these tasks, as well as the general manageability of Active Directory security.

■ Blue Yonder Airlines growth is skyrocketing. The company is hiring new members of its help desk team every few weeks. The effort required to train these team members in the use of Active Directory administrative tools and specific procedures required at Blue

Yonder Airlines is placing a great strain on the limited resources of IT management. Management wants to create administrative tools that will enable new help desk team members to get up to speed independently, and to perform administrative tasks in full compliance with organizational procedures.

When you have locked down Active Directory ACLs to delegate control in a way that fully supports the demonstrated model, the next logical step is to customize administrative tools to provide easy access to exactly the tasks that you have delegated to a particular set of administrators. Solution 7-3 on page 499 will do just that.

# 5-1: Explore the Components and Tools of Active Directory Delegation

## Solution overview

| | |
|---|---|
| **Type of solution** | Guidance and procedures |
| **Features and tools** | The Active Directory Users and Computers snap-in, Active Directory ACL editor interfaces, the Delegation Of Control Wizard |
| **Solution summary** | Explore the basic tools, concepts, and guidelines involved with the delegation of control within Active Directory. |
| **Benefits** | Understand the capabilities of out-of-the-box methods for managing ACLs in Active Directory. |

## Introduction

The delegation of administrative tasks within Active Directory is achieved by managing the access control lists (ACLs) of Active Directory objects. For each task, such as resetting a password, there is a permission—in this case, Reset Password—that can be allowed or denied, inherited or explicit, just like the Read or Write permissions on a file or folder. However, the number of Active Directory permissions can be mind-boggling, so Microsoft provides the Delegation Of Control Wizard to hide the underlying complexity. In this solution, I'll introduce you to the Active Directory ACL editor interfaces and the Delegation Of Control Wizard.

## Use Active Directory object ACLs and ACL editor interfaces

Each object in Active Directory includes a security descriptor, which itself contains an ACL. Just as an ACL on a file or folder specifies who can read, modify, or delete that resource, an ACL on an Active Directory object specifies who can perform actions on that object. Also, as with a file or folder, you access the ACL of an Active Directory using the ACL editor interfaces that begin with the Security tab of the object's Properties dialog box, shown in Figure 5-1.

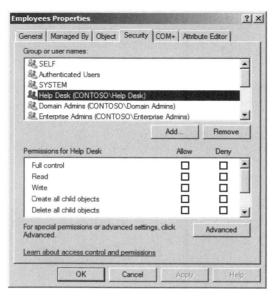

**Figure 5-1** The Security tab of the Properties dialog box for the Employees OU

Unlike a file or folder, the Security tab does not appear by default when you open an object's Properties dialog box. You must turn on the Advanced Settings in the Active Directory Users and Computers snap-in. To enable the visibility of the Security tab, follow these steps:

1. Open the Active Directory Users and Computers snap-in.

2. Click the View menu, and choose Advanced Settings.

The change affects the currently open console, and it will persist as you close and reopen that console. However, if you access the Active Directory Users and Computers snap-in in another console, you need to enable Advanced Settings there, separately. Unfortunately, Server Manager does not remember your customizations.

The ACL editor for Active Directory objects supports several interfaces, each of which provides a different level of information about an access control list. The first interface appears on the Security tab, shown in Figure 5-1. It displays common permissions templates. However, the complexity of Active Directory permissions renders the information provided by the Security tab virtually useless—the tab provides nowhere near enough detail for most activities. Clicking the Advanced button reveals a more detailed enumeration of permissions in the access control list in the Advanced Security Settings dialog box, on the Permissions tab, shown in Figure 5-2.

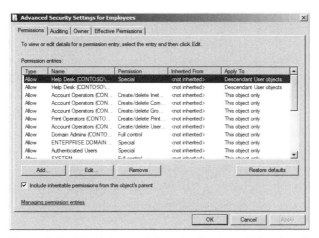

**Figure 5-2** The Advanced Security Settings dialog box for the Employees OU

**Best Practices** Always go to the Advanced Security Settings dialog box to manage ACLs in Active Directory.

Selecting one entry in the Permissions list of the Advanced Security Settings dialog box and clicking the Edit button provides the complete detail for that particular entry. In Windows Server 2008, you might need to click Edit twice—once to change the mode of the Advanced Security Settings dialog box to edit mode, and a second time to open the permission entry in the Permission Entry dialog box.

## Manage access control entries on Active Directory objects

If you navigate to the Permission Entry dialog box for an object, you will discover that the sheer number of permissions available can be overwhelming. Each attribute of each object is assigned permissions individually. You could allow a group to modify only the *carLicense* attribute of a single user object if you wanted to, which I hope you do not. Figure 5-3 shows the Permission Entry dialog box of an organizational unit for which the Help Desk group is assigned permission to modify the *carLicense* attribute for user objects.

There are as many permissions as there are attributes—actually a few more. There are so many permissions, in fact, that Microsoft split the display of permissions between the Properties tab shown in Figure 5-3 and the Object tab shown in Figure 5-4. Permissions on the Object tab relate to what you can do with the object as a whole. Figure 5-4 shows the Object tab of an organizational unit. The tab displays permissions that include the types of objects you can create within the organizational unit.

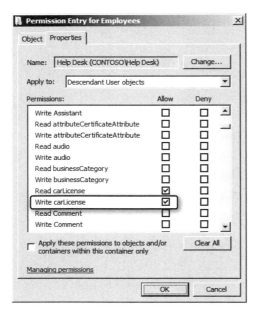

**Figure 5-3**   The Permission Entry dialog box with the Write permission selected for *carLicense*

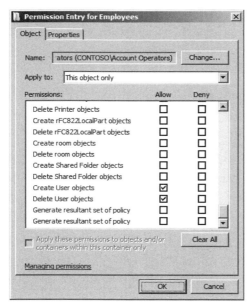

**Figure 5-4**   The Object tab of the Permission Entry dialog box

# Adhere to the golden rules of delegation

As you delegate permissions within Active Directory, you should keep in mind the rules explained in the following sections.

## Configure permissions on OUs, not on individual objects

As with individual files on a server, you should not set the permissions on an individual user, group, or computer in Active Directory. Instead, you should set permissions on OUs. Much like permissions on a folder, ACLs on an OU are inherited by objects within the OU. So although you could take each user in an OU and grant your help desk the Allow permission to Reset Password, you are better off applying the permission to the OU containing the users. Even though it's not possible to reset the password on an organizational unit itself, you can set the permission on the OU and specify that it apply to users within the OU. An ACL propagator thread ensures that inheritable permissions on an OU are applied to appropriate objects within that OU. Figure 5-2, which we saw earlier, shows exactly the scenario we're addressing: the help desk is granted the Allow::Reset Password permission on the Employees OU—shown as Special in the Permission Entries list—and the permission is configured to Apply To Descendant User Objects.

By the way, I advise against performing delegations at the domain level, at least for the types of standard administrative delegations we're discussing in this Solution Collection. Although there are some delegations that might be appropriate to delegate at the domain level, most delegations are object specific, so they should be limited to a scope representing that object class in your OU structure.

## Assign permissions to groups, not users

Continuing to follow best practices for permissions on files and folders, you should manage permissions in Active Directory using groups. Assign the Allow::Reset Password permission to the help desk group, for example. Even if a particular administrative task is performed by only one individual in your organization today, that individual might change tomorrow, or more individuals might need to perform the task. By establishing a group that has been granted a permission such as Allow::Reset Password, you need only manage the membership of that group to control who can or cannot perform that task. In Solution 5-7 on page 403, we take this rule to the next step by implementing role-based management of Active Directory administration. The outcome of that discussion is the recommendation that you create a capability management group, as described in Solution Collection 1, "Role-Based Management," to represent the management of a particular administrative capability, such as resetting user passwords. You can, for example, create a group called AD_Users_Reset Passwords. Delegate permissions to that group, and then assign the capability to role groups or individual users by nesting them into the capability management group.

### Manage delegation with Allow permissions and inheritance

As with folders on a file server, the best practice for managing security in Active Directory is to configure Allow permissions on a high-level organizational unit and let inheritance propagate the permissions to child objects and OUs. If you find yourself needing to block inheritance or to assign Deny permissions, re-examine your OU structure to determine whether it is truly reflecting your administrative model.

### Document your delegation

Active Directory permissions are complex and critical to the security of your enterprise. It is not at all easy to dig through the ACLs on your OUs to reverse engineer the delegation you've applied. Document what you do, how you do it, and why you're doing it. You'll be glad later! In Solution 5-8 on page 408, I discuss using scripts to implement delegation—scripts are useful because they serve as documentation of how you applied delegation.

## Apply permissions with a friend: The Delegation Of Control Wizard

The complexity of access control entries (ACEs) and ACLs on Active Directory objects means that it can be difficult to correctly configure ACLs to achieve a particular desired result. In fact, it is not generally recommended to implement delegation using the ACL editor interfaces. Because so much granularity is exposed, you can easily make a simple mistake that can be disastrous to a weekend you had planned not to spend troubleshooting, if not disastrous to your entire directory. That's where the Delegation Of Control Wizard comes in. The wizard masks the complexities of ACL modification and is one of the good wizards behind the gates of the Emerald City.

You launch the wizard by right-clicking a major container (including, but not limited to, sites, domains, or OUs) and choosing the Delegate Control command. Notice that the context menus for other Active Directory objects do not provide the Delegate Control command. "But," you ask, "don't all Active Directory objects have ACLs and therefore support delegation?" Yes, but you can imagine (and as I discussed earlier) it is not a best practice to modify ACLs on individual leaf objects in Active Directory. Such an approach is unruly and difficult to document, analyze, and troubleshoot. It is a better practice to use containers as points of delegation and allow ACL inheritance to modify the ACLs of the objects within those containers.

By launching the Delegate Control command from a container, you have specified the *scope* of the delegation. The wizard therefore asks you two remaining questions:

1.  To whom do you want to delegate an administrative task? You specify this recipient by adding security principals—specifically, the administrative group that represents the role or, as discussed in Solution 5-7, a group that represents the capability. Figure 5-5 shows that the Help Desk is going to be delegated an administrative task.

2. What task do you want to delegate? Notice in Figure 5-6 that the wizard even uses the word *task* here. When the wizard is asking about the task, you can select from a list of what it determines are common tasks, or you can create a custom task. Your definition of common tasks will likely be very different from the defaults, and yes, you can customize this wizard to show your common tasks. More on this in a moment.

You've now specified the group, task, and scope—the OU or other container from which you launched the wizard—for the delegation. The wizard has all it needs to perform its job. The wizard then applies the appropriate ACEs to the selected OU or container.

So, to summarize, here are the steps for delegating with the Delegation Of Control Wizard:

1. Open the Active Directory Users and Computers snap-in.

2. Right-click the node (domain, OU, or container) for which you want to delegate administrative tasks or control.

3. Choose Delegate Control.

   The Delegation Of Control Wizard appears.

4. Click Next.

   You are asked to select the group to which you are granting privileges.

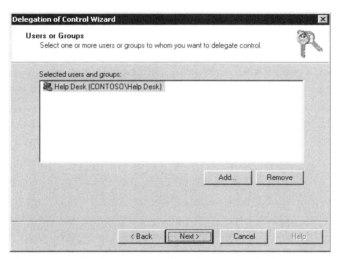

**Figure 5-5**   The Delegation Of Control Wizard's Users Or Groups page

5. Click Add and select the appropriate group. Click OK.

6. Click Next.

   You are then asked to specify the task you want to assign to the selected group.

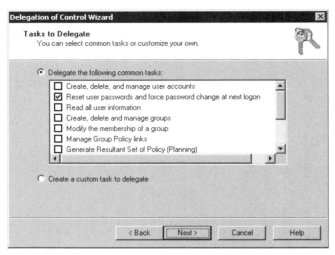

**Figure 5-6**    The Delegation Of Control Wizard's Tasks To Delegate page

7.  Select the check box for the appropriate task or tasks. Click Next.

8.  Review the summary.

9.  Click Finish.

## Manage the presentation of your delegation

What you can do within the Active Directory Users and Computers snap-in is, of course, a result of the permissions you have been assigned. Unfortunately, there is no consistent presentation within the user interface to help a user understand what she can or cannot do as an administrator. Some administrative tasks—such as the creation of users, groups, or computers—appear on the New menu of the Actions menu or the context menu. These commands appear only if you have permission to perform those tasks. Other administrative tasks appear on the menus, and some even let you complete all the information required to perform the task and then present an Access Denied error.

For these reasons, I'm not a big fan of the Active Directory Users and Computers snap-in from an administrative delegation perspective. I recommend that you create administrative task-pads that contain, as tasks, exactly the commands that you have given a set of administrators. That way, they can become accustomed to seeing the tasks in the task pane of the taskpad—it becomes a visual indicator of what they can do in Active Directory. It is certainly a bit more work up front—creating taskpads and distributing them—but it pays off in the long run, I think. Unfortunately, there's no way to remove the context menu—it will always be there when an administrator right-clicks, presenting some commands that the administrator cannot actually perform. Just train your users to look to the tasks in the taskpad. In Solution 7-3, I explain the steps for creating taskpads for your administrative teams.

## Solution summary

Active Directory security is managed with ACLs, exposed in the GUI by the ACL editor interfaces, very much like files and folders on a file system. The number of permissions available to configure is mind-boggling—each attribute of each object can be assigned permissions individually. To manage and abstract the complexity of the underlying security implementation, Microsoft provides the Delegation Of Control Wizard. The wizard guides you through the steps required to give a group permission to perform a task within a specified scope of Active Directory. Whether you use ACLs or the Delegation Of Control Wizard, you should give permissions to groups rather than users, assign permissions at the organizational unit level, allow inheritance to apply the permissions to objects within the container, and document your delegation.

# 5-2: Customize the Delegation Of Control Wizard

## Solution overview

| | |
|---|---|
| **Type of solution** | Customized template for the Delegation Of Control Wizard |
| **Features and tools** | The Delegation Of Control Wizard and Delegwiz.inf |
| **Solution summary** | Customize the tasks that are available in the Delegation Of Control Wizard using delegation templates including a ready-to-use template that provides delegation for 70 common tasks. |
| **Benefits** | Align the Delegation Of Control Wizard with your administrative model so that it supports delegating exactly the tasks that are performed in your enterprise. |

## Introduction

The Delegation Of Control Wizard allows you to delegate a small handful of tasks, but the options it provides are far from adequate for most organizations. For example, it would be reasonable for most organizations to want to allow the help desk to unlock user accounts. The Delegation Of Control Wizard does not provide that option by default. It is also normal, particularly in larger organizations, to strictly control the deletion of objects—particularly users, groups, and computers—because the deletion of a security principal results in the loss of the security identifier (SID). The wizard's common tasks provide for the creation, management, and deletion of user objects. What if you want to divide those tasks? In this solution, you learn how to customize the options presented by the wizard so that you can delegate exactly the tasks that are required to support your administrative model.

# Locate and understand Delegwiz.inf

The options presented by the Delegation Of Control Wizard as Common Tasks are driven by a simple text file called Delegwiz.inf. The file is located in %windir%\system32 on Windows Server 2008 system, and %windir%\inf on Windows Server 2003. If you are using Windows XP or Windows Vista to administer your domain, look in both locations—the location depends on which version of the administrative tools you installed. You can open this file in Notepad. The first part of the file is shown here:

```
[Version]
signature="$CHICAGO$"
[DelegationTemplates]
Templates = template1, template2, template3, template4, template5, template6,
template7, template8, template9,template10, template11, template12, template13
;--------------------------------------------------------
[template1]
AppliesToClasses=domainDNS,organizationalUnit,container
;Description = "Create, delete, and manage user accounts"
Description = "@dsuiwiz.dll,-301"

ObjectTypes = SCOPE, user
[template1.SCOPE]
user=CC,DC
[template1.user]
@=GA
;--------------------------------------------------------


;--------------------------------------------------------
[template2]
AppliesToClasses=domainDNS,organizationalUnit,container
;Description = "Reset user passwords and force password change at next logon"
Description = "@dsuiwiz.dll,-302"

ObjectTypes = user
[template2.user]
CONTROLRIGHT= "Reset Password"
pwdLastSet=RP,WP
;--------------------------------------------------------
```

The file is a kind of script or configuration file for the wizard. Each administrative task that you can delegate is contained in a *task template* (or, simply, *template*) within the file. The template begins with the template name in brackets—*[template2]*, for example. The template tells the wizard where to make the task available for delegation, how to describe the task in the wizard's interface, and what permissions to apply if the user selects the task. For example, the task shown earlier as *template2* allows you to delegate the task of resetting user passwords and forcing the user to change passwords at the next logon. You can delegate this task by right-clicking and launching the wizard from a domain, an organizational unit, or a container, as specified by the first line: *AppliesToClasses*. The *Description* line specifies the friendly name of the task that appears in the wizard's list of Common Tasks. The *Description* line can be a literal string of text, in quotes. In this case, however, Microsoft is making it easier for itself to localize the wizard by having a dynamic-link library (DLL) that provides the localized string for a specific task, which they refer to as "@dsuiwiz.dll,-301." If you create your own tasks, you'll do so with the text in quotes. As you might guess from reading the template, a line that starts with a semicolon is a comment, not actual code.

The real magic happens in the last few lines of the template that specify the ACEs to apply to the domain, OU, or container. In this case, the wizard applies ACEs that will be inherited by user objects, as indicated on the *ObjectTypes* line. The *ObjectTypes* line indicates that there will be a permission entry in a subsection of the template named *[templatename.ObjectType]*— [template2.user], for example. The specific permissions that will be applied are listed in the corresponding permission entry section: the *Reset Password* control access right, and the permission to read and write an attribute called *pwdLastSet*. Here are some key facts about these items:

**Reset Password**    The *Reset Password* right is self-explanatory. *Reset Password* is implemented as a *control access right*. As you know, permissions are implemented as ACEs on the access control list. Although a control access right is implemented elsewhere in the security descriptor (SD) of the object, the net effect is the same as a permission—you are granting the ability to manipulate the object in some way.

**pwdLastSet**    A somewhat obscure attribute of user objects, *pwdLastSet*, maintains a timestamp of the last time a user changed his password. When the password is older than allowed by the domain's maximum password age policy, the user is prompted to change his password. If the value of *pwdLastSet* is zero, the user is prompted to change the password at logon. If you are working in the Active Directory Users and Computers snap-in and you select the check box labeled User Must Change Password At Next Logon, what you are doing is putting the value zero into *pwdLastSet*. So, to delegate the ability to force the user to change his password at next logon, you must allow that property to be changed.

Just having the task template—*template2*, for example—is not enough. The Delegation Of Control Wizard has to be told that the template exists. This occurs at the top of the Delegwiz.inf file: the *Templates* value in the *[DelegationTemplates]* section lists all the templates within the INF file that should be presented by the wizard. If you add or remove a template from the body of the file, you should add or remove the template name from this section.

Table 5-1 summarizes the components of a delegation of control template.

Table 5-1   Components of Delegwiz.inf

| Component | Description |
|---|---|
| [templatex] | A unique template name, in square brackets, marks the beginning of a task template. The number represented by x ensures the name of the template is unique in the Delegwiz.inf file. The name of the template can actually be anything. But Microsoft uses the word "template" followed by a number, so you might as well follow its lead. |
| AppliesToClasses=objectClass | This line determines the scope of delegation, where objectClass is a comma-delimited list of one or more object types. The most common objectClass for customizing the wizard is organizationalUnit. That means that your custom task will appear when you launch the Delegation Of Control Wizard from an OU. |
| Description="description" | Not surprisingly, Description specifies the friendly name for the task. This is the label that appears in the Delegation Of Control Wizard's Common Tasks list. |
| ObjectTypes=objectType | This line indicates the object classes to which permissions will be scoped, where objectType is a comma-delimited list of object types. For example, an objectType of user indicates that a permission entry will be made that will apply to user objects. The specific permissions that will be made are found in the [templatex.objectType] section described next. When the objectType is the keyword SCOPE, that represents the object—typically an OU—from which the wizard was invoked. |
| [templatex.objectType]<br><br>*Permission entries for objectType* | This indicates the beginning of a permission entry template, where x is again your task template number, and objectType is the type of object that must inherit ACL changes for the task to be effective. If multiple types of objects must be modified, you will have multiple objectType entries in the ObjectTypes= list and multiple [templatex.objectType] sections—one for each object type. |

Let's look at one example to reinforce your understanding of the task templates. The listing presented next shows *template1* from the standard Delegwiz.inf file of Windows Server 2008. The first line of the template indicates that the template will apply when the wizard is invoked from a domain, OU, or container object. Its user-friendly description follows. In Windows Server 2008, Microsoft has commented out the English language string description and is instead leveraging its new DLL to present the description in the local language. The *Object-Types* line indicates that if the task is selected, permissions have to be modified on the scope—the domain, OU, or container that was selected—and on user objects. Then there are two permission entry templates: one for the scope that allows the creation and deletion of user objects, and another permissions entry for user objects that assigns full control (GA) to all properties of user objects.

```
[template1]
AppliesToClasses=domainDNS,organizationalUnit,container
;Description = "Create, delete, and manage user accounts"
Description = "@dsuiwiz.dll,-301"

ObjectTypes = SCOPE, user
[template1.SCOPE]
user=CC,DC
[template1.user]
@=GA
```

## Customize Delegwiz.inf

Now that you have seen the syntax of the file, you are ready to customize Delegwiz.inf. The file can be found in the windows\inf or windows\system32 folder, depending on the version of the administrative tools installed on the client. In Windows Vista and Windows Server 2008, the file is protected—you will not be able to change it by default. You must take ownership of the file—a task that requires administrative credentials—and then give yourself permissions to modify the file.

You can implement one of the most common tasks that Microsoft missed when designing the wizard (unlocking locked user accounts) using the template shown next. Remember the template name must be unique in your Delegwiz.inf file. I've used *template14* as the name, because the default Delegwiz.inf has 13 existing templates. However, if you find that your Delegwiz.inf already has a *template14*, choose another name and use it in both the template header *[template14]* and in the permission entry header *[template14.user]*. You must also add the template name—*template14*, for example—to the *TEMPLATES* line near the top of the file.

```
[template14]
AppliesToClasses=organizationalUnit
Description = "NEW TASK: Unlock locked user accounts"
ObjectTypes = user
[template14.user]
lockoutTime=RP,WP
```

This template allows you to delegate the ability to unlock user accounts for users within an *organizationalUnit*. It assigns the Read Property (RP) and Write Property (WP) permissions to the *lockoutTime* attribute of user objects.

*lockoutTime*    The *lockoutTime* value keeps track of when an account was locked out. If it is zero, the account is unlocked. To delegate the ability to unlock an account, you must give the permission to change the *lockoutTime* value to zero.

Remember to close and reopen the Active Directory Users and Computers snap-in to see the effect of your change. As you can see in Figure 5-7, the wizard now displays our custom common task.

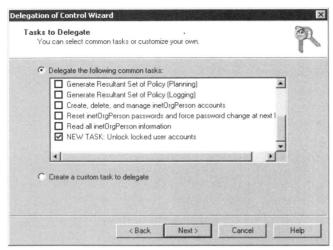

**Figure 5-7**   The Delegation Of Control Wizard with a new custom task

You modify Delegwiz.inf on the computer from which you administer Active Directory. It does *not* have to be modified in the forest or on any one domain controller—its effects are seen totally on the client of the administrator. If you want multiple administrators to use a customized Delegwiz.inf, distribute it appropriately. A service pack or operating system upgrade can possibly overwrite your file, so be sure to back it up somewhere too.

## Use Microsoft's super-duper Delegwiz.inf

Manually changing Delegwiz.inf might seem a bit daunting to you, particularly if you do not yet know the exact properties and permissions you need to configure within a permission entry template. Luckily, in 2003 Microsoft published a white paper, "Best Practices for Delegating Active Directory Administration." In Appendix O of that white paper (yes, it had that many appendices), there is a sample Delegwiz.inf file that provides 70 task templates. You can obtain the white paper from the Microsoft Download Center site (*http://www.microsoft.com/downloads/Search.aspx?displaylang=en*)—search for *Best Practices for Delegating Active Directory*. Or, better yet, you can find it on the companion media. Find Appendix O, and copy and paste the contents of the Delegwiz.inf file it illustrates to Notepad. Save the file as "delegwiz.inf" in the correct (system32 or inf) folder. Remember that Windows Vista and Windows Server 2008 protect this file, so you have to take ownership of it and give yourself permission to modify it before replacing it with the contents of the white paper's Delegwiz.inf. Also remember to save the file using quotation marks around the name, "delegwiz.inf," so that Notepad does not add a *.txt* extension.

Although the 13 tasks provided by the default Delegwiz.inf file are not sufficient to support the delegation models in most organizations, the 70 tasks provided by this new and improved Delegwiz.inf files might be a bit of overkill. Ideally, when you run the Delegation Of Control Wizard, you should be given the options that are used within your organization—no more and no less. Therefore, I recommend you use the Delegwiz.inf file in the appendix of the white paper as a reference, and from that you can build a Delegwiz.inf file that is best for your enterprise with the subset of tasks that you need to be able to delegate.

**Best Practices**   Use the Delegwiz.inf file found in the delegation white paper to build a Delegwiz.inf file that contains exactly the tasks you need to delegate to support your administrative model. In most scenarios, you'll be able to simply remove tasks from the sample file to meet your needs—it's likely you will not need to add any new tasks. If you do need to add tasks, use the white paper to identify the permissions required to delegate effectively. You can also visit the Web site for this resource kit (*http://www.intelliem.com/resourcekit*) and post a question if you need help identifying the necessary permissions.

To find out more detail about the structure of Delegwiz.inf, check out Knowledge Base article 308404 (*http://support.microsoft.com/kb/308404/en-us*). Information about specific Lightweight Directory Access Protocol (LDAP) property and object names, and permissions specifiers can be found in TechNet (*http://technet.microsoft.com/en-us/default.aspx*) and MSDN (*http://www.msdn.com*).

## Solution summary

The Delegation Of Control Wizard is a useful tool because it masks the complexities of the permission entries required to delegate administrative tasks in Active Directory. However, the 13 tasks that it provides by default will not meet the needs of most organizations as they attempt to implement an effective administrative model. Luckily, you can customize the wizard by modifying Delegwiz.inf. This solution explains the syntax of that file so that you can customize it with tasks you need to delegate. I also recommend that you leverage the sample Delegwiz.inf file provided in Appendix O of the white paper, "Best Practices For Delegating Active Directory Administration."

# 5-3: Customize the Permissions Listed in the ACL Editor Interfaces

## Solution overview

| | |
|---|---|
| **Type of solution** | Customized template for the ACL editor interfaces |
| **Features and tools** | The ACL editor interfaces and Dssec.dat |
| **Solution summary** | Customize the permissions that are visible when examining permissions using the ACL editor user interfaces. |
| **Benefits** | Ensure that permissions you have delegated are, in fact, visible in the user interface. Windows hides many permissions from the ACL editor interfaces, which could make it difficult to know what permissions are actually applied to an Active Directory object. |

## Introduction

In Solution 5-1 on page 365, I examine the ACL editor interfaces, which expose the ACLs of Active Directory objects and point out the vast number of permissions available for Active Directory objects. For better or worse, when you look at the Permission Entry dialog box, you are not actually seeing all the available permissions. There are dozens of additional permissions for objects that are hidden by default, in an effort to simplify the user interface where possible. Unfortunately, this means that it is possible you are not seeing all the permissions applied to an object. Furthermore, you might need to delegate a permission that you cannot even find in the ACL editor. In this solution, I reveal the secrets behind the permissions list in the ACL editor and show you how to ensure you see all the permissions that you have delegated.

## Recognize that some permissions are hidden

In Solution 6-6 on page 450, I suggest using the *manager* property of a computer object to track the user to whom the computer is assigned. If you choose to implement that solution, you need to delegate permission to change the *manager* property to the group that will enter that information. Unfortunately, when you look in the ACL editor for the *manager* property for computer objects, you do not see that permission, as shown in Figure 5-8. *managedBy* is visible, *manager* is not.

The *manager* property is an example of a permission that exists for computer objects but is hidden from the user interface. To properly delegate the permission and to provide visibility and reporting for the permission after you delegate it, you must unhide the permission.

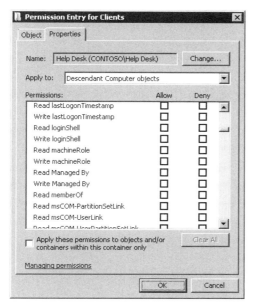

**Figure 5-8**    Permissions for Descendant Computer Objects do not list the permissions for *manager*.

## Modify Dssec.dat

The Dssec.dat file is responsible for determining which permissions are and are not visible in the user interface. The file is located in the system32 folder, and you can open it in Notepad. The file is divided into sections, each section beginning with a section name in square brackets. The section name represents an object class, and the entries below the section name are properties of the object class that will or will not be exposed in the ACL editor. A portion of the *[computer]* section of the file is shown next:

```
[computer]
accountExpires=7
accountNameHistory=7
aCSPolicyName=7
adminCount=7
adminDescription=7
adminDisplayName=7
allowedAttributes=7
allowedAttributesEffective=7
allowedChildClasses=7
allowedChildClassesEffective=7
altSecurityIdentities=7
assistant=7
badPasswordTime=7
badPwdCount=7
bridgeheadServerListBL=7
c=7
canonicalName=7
catalogs=7
```

```
co=7
codePage=7
comment=7
company=7
controlAccessRights=7
countryCode=7
createTimeStamp=7
dBCSPwd=7
defaultClassStore=7
defaultLocalPolicyObject=7
desktopProfile=7
destinationIndicator=7
directReports=7
displayName=7
displayNamePrintable=7
distinguishedName=7
division=7
. . .
mail=7
managedObjects=7
manager=7
masteredBy=7
maxStorage=7
mhsORAddress=7
middleName=7
mobile=7
modifyTimeStamp=7
. . .
```

Notice the *Description* property is not listed. If a property is not listed, that property will appear in the ACL editor. If a property is listed and the value of that property is 7, the property will be hidden. Sure enough, the *manager* property is listed and its value is 7. That's why permissions for the *manager* property are not visible in the ACL editor. To make the permissions visible, simply set the value to 0 (zero) or delete the line entirely. I prefer to set the value to zero because it allows me to look at the Dssec.dat file and quickly recognize changes I have made to the defaults provided by Microsoft. Always be sure you are changing the property in the correct section—the *manager* property in the *[computer]* section, for example—because the property might appear in several object class sections.

Changes made to Dssec.dat are visible only after you have closed and reopened the Active Directory Users and Computers snap-in. Dssec.dat is responsible not only for the permissions visible in the Properties tab of the Permission Entry dialog box, but also in the Custom Tasks page of the Delegation Of Control Wizard. Figure 5-9 shows the Manager property permissions now visible in the Permission Entry for Descendant Computer Objects permissions list.

The Dssec.dat file must be changed on the machine from which you are managing Active Directory permissions, not the domain controllers themselves, unless you are actually running the Active Directory Users and Computers snap-in on the domain controller while logged on locally or using Remote Desktop. Because Dssec.dat can possibly be replaced by service packs or other operating system updates, you should always keep a backup of your custom file.

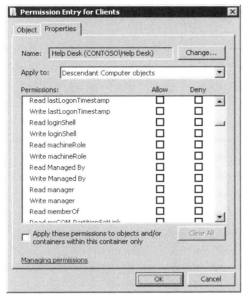

**Figure 5-9**   Permissions for Descendant Computer objects now show permissions for the *manager* property.

## Ensure the visibility of permissions that you are delegating

You must make sure that permissions you are delegating are visible in ACL editor interfaces. Otherwise, someone examining the permissions on Active Directory objects will not be getting the full story. In Windows 2000, the *lockoutTime* property was hidden, so if you delegated the ability to unlock accounts, that permission wasn't visible in the ACL editors. That problem and other problems like it were solved in Windows Server 2003. There are few if any properties that appear in the native user interface that are not also visible in the ACL editors.

But as soon as you begin to customize Active Directory, you need to be sure to give visibility to the properties you are working with. For example, if you decide to use the computer object's *manager* property, which is not visible in the user interface, you should make the property visible in the ACL editors. If you add new attributes to Active Directory, you should also be sure they are appearing correctly.

## Solution summary

Windows does not display every property in the permissions lists of the ACL editors. Permissions that are hidden can be displayed by changing the Dssec.dat file. You should make sure that any permission you delegate is, in fact, visible in the ACL editors.

# 5-4: Evaluate, Report, and Revoke Active Directory Permissions

## Solution overview

| | |
|---|---|
| **Type of solution** | Tools and guidance |
| **Features and tools** | Dsacls, ACLDiag, ADFind, DSRevoke, Effective Permissions |
| **Solution summary** | Apply a variety of tools to evaluate, document, and remove administrative delegations. |
| **Benefits** | Gain understanding of the current state of your Active Directory delegation. |

## Introduction

Although Windows makes it relatively easy to delegate permissions within Active Directory using the Delegation Of Control Wizard, it is not as easy to un-delegate permissions. Nor is it easy to report existing permissions or evaluate the effective permissions of a specific user or group. In this solution, we discuss some of the options you have for performing these tasks.

## Use Dsacls to report Active Directory permissions

Dsacls (dsacls.exe) is the first tool you can turn to for managing Active Directory permissions from the command line. Dsacls is part of the Support Tools for Windows Server 2003, which can be downloaded from *http://go.microsoft.com/fwlink/?LinkId=100114*. Dsacls is now a native command in Windows Server 2008. I leverage Dsacls for many of the solutions in this Solution Collection. As with other commands, you can learn the syntax of Dsacls by entering the command **Dsacls /?**.

Let's apply Dsacls first to the task of reporting the permissions that have been applied to an OU. The first parameter passed to the Dsacls command is always the distinguished name of an object, in this case an OU. The following command, for example, will report the permissions applied to the People OU:

```
dsacls "ou=people,dc=contoso,dc=com"
```

The output of Dsacls is fairly verbose. But it does the trick of reporting permissions. A portion of the output of Dsacls is shown here:

```
Inherited to user
Allow CONTOSO\Help Desk
                                      SPECIAL ACCESS for pwdLastSet
                                      WRITE PROPERTY
                                      READ PROPERTY
Allow CONTOSO\Help Desk
                                         Reset Password
```

You can identify the permissions we assigned to the help desk in an earlier solution: The help desk can reset passwords and can unlock user accounts, which entails changing the *pwdLast-Set* attribute, and these permissions apply to user objects in the People OU.

# Use ACLDiag to report Active Directory permissions

Although Dsacls does a good job of dumping the permissions that are applied to an object in Active Directory, its verbose output is not always easy to interpret. For example, if you did not know that the *pwdLastSet* attribute was related to unlocking user accounts, you would not be able to understand the report produced by Dsacls shown earlier.

Enter another tool from the Windows Server 2003 support tools: acldiag.exe. ACLDiag can also be used to report Active Directory permissions by providing the distinguished name of an Active Directory object as the first parameter. But the more interesting feature of ACLDiag is its ability to compare the permissions applied to an Active Directory object against the permission templates used by the Delegation Of Control Wizard. ACLDiag uses the same Delegwiz.inf file discussed in the previous solution to translate an object's permissions into plain English. Just add the */chkdeleg* switch to the ACLDiag command line:

```
acldiag.exe "ou=people,dc=contoso,dc=com" /chkdeleg
```

Part of the output of this command is shown here:

```
Delegation Template Diagnosis:

    Create, delete, and manage user accounts

        Status: NOT PRESENT

    Reset user passwords and force password change at next logon allowed
    to CONTOSO\Help Desk

        Status: OK
        Applies on this object: YES
        Inherited from parent: NO
```

Notice that ACLDiag uses the descriptions of tasks that would be visible in the Delegation Of Control Wizard. If you follow the guidance provided earlier in this Solution Collection and customize Delegwiz.inf to reflect the exact administrative tasks you need to delegate in your enterprise, that file then becomes the source for both the application of delegation, through the wizard, and for reporting delegation using ACLDiag.

ACLDiag was designed to run on Windows Server 2003 and Windows XP. My experience is that it works on Windows Vista and Windows Server 2008, but it is not supported on those platforms. Use it on those platforms at your own risk.

# Use ADFind to report Active Directory permissions

I believe the best tool available for reporting Active Directory delegation is ADFind, one of the many incredible utilities created by Joe Richards of joeware.net (*http://www.joeware.net*). Joe is an Active Directory MVP who contributes an amazing amount of expertise to the Windows community, including freeware tools such as ADFind.

ADFind is so powerful that it has several levels of help documentation. You can type **ADFind -?** for basic help or **ADFind -??** for advanced help. I recommend redirecting the outputs to a text file—ADFIND -?? >adfind.txt, for example—so that you can print out the documentation and study it carefully. Don't be overwhelmed by the sheer number of parameters that ADFind supports. I'll give you some suggestions for how to use it for specific solutions, and you can find a lot of discussion about the command by searching the Internet for ADFind or by searching the archives of the ActiveDir.org mailing list (*http://www.activedir.org*), which Joe Richards moderates and on which I and other Active Directory MVPs participate.

To use ADFind to report the permissions on an Active Directory object, use the following syntax:

```
adfind -b ObjectDN -s base ntsecuritydescriptor -sddl++ -resolvesids
```

The following switches are illustrated in this command:

**-b ObjectDN**    The base domain name (DN) to search—for example, "OU=people,DC=contoso,DC=com"

**-s [base | onelevel | subtree]**    The scope of the search, which can be any of the following:

- *base*: Search only the object specified by *ObjectDN*.

- *onelevel*: Search the object and its immediate child objects.

- *subtree*: Search the object and all child containers.

***attribute list***    A list of attributes that you want to return. *ntsecuritydescriptor* is the security descriptor that contains the ACL of the object.

***-sddl++***    Specifies that ADFind should perform the best possible translation of the security descriptor.

***-resolvesids***    Instructs ADFind to translate SIDs into security principal names.

ADFind also has switches to control the output of the report. You can use the *-csv* switch, for example, to produce the report in comma-delimited format. If you change the scope parameter (*-s*), you can return the ACLs of Active Directory objects in a branch of your OU structure, or even in your entire domain. Be careful, though, because you will get the permissions of every object, not just of organizational units. To return the permissions of OUs only, you need to add a filter parameter to the command line:

```
adfind -b ObjectDN -s base -f (objectClass=organizationalUnit)
    ntsecuritydescriptor -sddl++ -resolvesids
```

The *-f* switch directs ADFind to perform an LDAP query—in this case, for objects whose class is *organizationalUnit*. If you are reporting permissions for more than just one OU, you might not require the report to include inherited permissions that are repeated on child objects.

Although the *-f* switch specifies the filter with which to perform the search in Active Directory, there are also switches to control the output of ADFind. For example, you can add an output filter to the ADFind command to filter out inherited ACEs:

```
-sddlnotfilter ;inherited
```

You can also add a filter to return only ACEs assigned to a specific security principal:

```
-sddlfilter [allow|deny|<blank>];;;;;"DOMAIN\user or group"
```

Finally, the *-recmute* switch instructs ADFind to suppress returning the distinguished names of objects that match the search filter, but whose attributes are empty based on output filters such as *-ssdlfilter*.

Putting all these switches together, you can use a command similar to the following to report all the permissions explicitly assigned to OUs for a particular user or group:

```
Adfind -b "dc=contoso,dc=com" -s subtree -f (objectClass=organizationalUnit)
    ntsecuritydescriptor -sddl++ -resolvesids
    -sddlfilter ;;;;;"CONTOSO\Help Desk" -sddlnotfilter ;inherited -recmute
```

Just change the distinguished name of the domain and the name of the user or group you want to report. Remember that ADFind is reporting permissions assigned directly to the specified user or group. It is not evaluating permissions for a user or group based on indirect or nested memberships in other groups. For more information on the usage of ADFind, consult its help documentation.

## Use DSRevoke to report Active Directory permissions

DSRevoke is yet another tool that can report permissions in Active Directory. It can be downloaded from the Microsoft Download Center site (*http://www.microsoft.com/downloads*). Much like the last variation of the ADFind just presented, DSRevoke can be used to identify the permissions you've assigned to a specific security principal. The following command reports permissions assigned to the help desk in the Contoso domain:

```
dsrevoke /report /root:"dc=contoso,dc=com" "CONTOSO\Help Desk"
```

The command provides the following report (minus a few blank lines I removed to make it more readable):

```
ACE #1
Object: OU=People,DC=contoso,DC=com
Security Principal: CONTOSO\Help Desk
Permissions:
  EXTENDED ACCESS
ACE Type: ALLOW
```

```
ACE does not apply to this object
ACE inherited by all child objects of class User

ACE #2
Object: OU=People,DC=contoso,DC=com
Security Principal: CONTOSO\Help Desk
Permissions:
  READ PROPERTY
  WRITE PROPERTY
ACE Type: ALLOW
ACE does not apply to this object
ACE inherited by all child objects of class User

# of ACEs for CONTOSO\Help Desk = 2
```

Although DSRevoke does identify that permissions are assigned to the Help Desk group, it does not specify which extended access (*ResetPassword*) or which property (*pwdLastSet*) are involved. Therefore, I suggest sticking with ADFind or Dsacls for reporting permissions.

## Evaluate permissions assigned to a specific user or group

All the commands I've examined in this solution report permissions assigned directly to a user or group. None of them account for permissions that apply to a user or group indirectly, through nested group memberships. In Solution 5-7, we apply the concepts of role-based management to solve this problem. Until then, a partial solution can be found on the Effective Permissions tab of the Advanced Security Settings dialog box, shown in Figure 5-10.

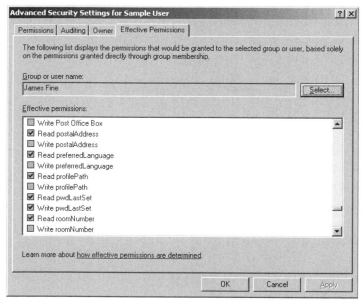

**Figure 5-10**   The Effective Permissions tab of the Advanced Security Settings dialog box

This dialog box does a good job of evaluating the permissions that apply to the specified user or group. There are a few rare scenarios in which the permissions reported will not be accurate, because the tool does not evaluate membership in certain special groups such as Network and Interactive. You can click the link How Effective Permissions Are Determined to learn more about those scenarios.

The bigger trick to using the Effective Permissions tab is understanding which permissions are reported in the Effective Permissions list. The list shows only permissions that apply to the object itself, not permissions that are inherited by child objects. So, for example, if we were to open the Advanced Security Settings dialog box for our People OU and use the Effective Permissions tab to evaluate the capabilities of our help desk, we would not see the permissions to reset user passwords and unlock accounts. That's because those permissions apply to user objects and we are viewing the Effective Permissions of an organizational unit. To determine what the Help Desk group can do with user objects, we need to examine the Effective Permissions on a user object, as shown in Figure 5-10.

Therefore, although the Effective Permissions tab can be useful, its view is very granular indeed. I highly recommend that you implement role-based management of Active Directory delegation, as presented in Solution 5-7.

## Revoke Active Directory permissions with DSRevoke

As I showed you earlier, DSRevoke can report the permissions assigned to a specific user or group, but its output leaves a lot to be desired. DSRevoke shines, however, when it comes to un-delegating permissions assigned to a specific security principal. The following command removes all permissions delegated to the help desk within the People OU:

```
dsrevoke /remove /root:"ou=People,dc=contoso,dc=com" "CONTOSO\Help Desk"
```

The command casts a wide net. It removes all ACEs assigned to the Help Desk on the People OU, on all child OUs, and on all objects within.

## Revoke Active Directory permissions with Dsacls

You can also use Dsacls to remove permissions assigned to a security principal. Just use the /R switch as in the following example, which removes permissions assigned to the help desk on the People OU:

```
dsacls "ou=People,dc=contoso,dc=com" /R "CONTOSO\Help Desk"
```

 **Important**  Switches used by the Dsacls command in Windows Server 2003 are case sensitive. /R removes the permissions assigned to a security principal; /r produces an error. The switches in Windows Server 2008 are now case insensitive.

Dsacls with the /R switch removes permissions assigned to the group for the specified object only. Assuming you are managing permissions with OUs, this might be all you require. However, if you need to remove permissions assigned to the group throughout a branch of your OU structure, use DSRevoke.

## Reset permissions to Schema defaults

Several tools make it possible to reset the permissions on an Active Directory object to their defaults. When a new object is created in Active Directory, its initial permissions are determined by the schema. When you reset permissions of an object to the schema defaults, you effectively remove any explicit permissions that are not in line with those defaults.

The Advanced Security Settings dialog box provides the Restore Defaults button on the Permissions tab, shown in Figure 5-11. Note that when you click the Restore Defaults button, you are not prompted to confirm your action, so be sure that you have considered the effect you will have.

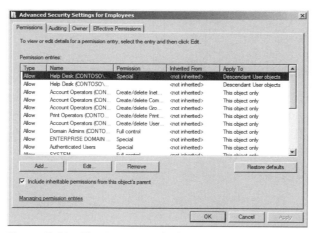

**Figure 5-11**   The Restore Defaults button on the Permissions tab

The schema default permissions for an organizational unit allow inheritance of permissions from the parents of the OU. Therefore, if you reset the permissions of a child OU, the effective permissions on that OU might still not be identical to the schema defaults, because nondefault permissions on the parent will be inherited by the child.

You can also reset permissions to schema defaults using Dsacls with the /S switch. If you also add the /T switch, Dsacls resets permissions to schema defaults on the entire subtree. Therefore, you can use the following command to completely un-delegate the People OU of the Contoso domain:

```
dsacls "ou=people,dc=contoso,dc=com" /S /T
```

Be very careful before resetting permissions to schema defaults. Make sure that you have documented existing permissions, particularly permissions that have been applied by Active Directory applications in your enterprise. Microsoft Exchange, for example, applies a number of permissions in Active Directory to support its functionality. Those permissions are applied directly to existing objects, not to the schema defaults. So if you reset permissions to the schema defaults, you effectively wipe out the permissions required by Exchange.

## Solution summary

Several tools make it possible for you to evaluate, report, and revoke permissions that you have delegated on Active Directory objects. Dsacls, DSRevoke, ACLDiag, and ADFind are among the best. I prefer to use ADFind to report and document existing permissions in Active Directory. ACLDiag is also useful for its ability to translate ACEs using the task templates defined in Delegwiz.inf. Dsacls is my tool of choice for most situations requiring the revocation of permissions. Role-based management of Active Directory delegation, which I discuss in Solution 5-7, provides the ultimate support for the application, management, reporting, and auditing of delegation.

# 5-5: Assign and Revoke Permissions with Dsacls

## Solution overview

| | |
|---|---|
| **Type of solution** | Guidance and command-line scripts |
| **Features and tools** | Dsacls |
| **Solution summary** | Leverage Dsacls to manage the delegation of administrative tasks in Active Directory. |
| **Benefits** | Understanding the use of Dsacls allows you to build scripts to apply delegation, as discussed in Solution 5-7. |

## Introduction

In the previous solution, I introduced Dsacls, a command-line tool that enables the reporting and revocation of permissions on Active Directory objects. Dsacls is even more useful for applying Active Directory permissions. In this solution, I walk you through learning the most important switches and uses of the Dsacls command. I also present the permissions syntax used to perform many common Active Directory delegations. This solution creates a foundation from which, in Solution 5-7, I will build a framework to automate the application of Active Directory permissions.

# Identify the basic syntax of Dsacls

In the previous solution, I used Dsacls to report permissions on an Active Directory object. The following command does the trick:

```
dsacls ObjectDN
```

*ObjectDN* is the distinguished name of an Active Directory object. I also showed you how to use Dsacls to reset permissions on an Active Directory object to the schema defaults, using the */S* switch for schema defaults and the */T* switch to reset the entire tree of objects below an organizational unit, container, or domain specified by *ObjectDN*. Because best practice suggests that you delegate at the OU level, we'll use the placeholder *OUDN* to refer to the distinguished name of an organizational unit, rather than the more general *ObjectDN*.

> **Important**  Remember that the switches for Dsacls are case sensitive in Windows Server 2003—they must be uppercase. Switches are no longer case sensitive in Windows Server 2008.

As we start to apply Dsacls to grant and deny permissions to Active Directory objects, we will be using the */G* switch to grant permissions and the */D* switch to deny permissions, using the syntax shown here:

```
dsacls OUDN /G "DOMAIN\groupname":permissions
```

These two switches are followed by the name of the security principal to which permissions are assigned. The name of the security principal can be in the form "DOMAIN\\*group or user name*" or "*username@upnSuffix*"—the user principal name (UPN) of the account.

Best practice dictates that the security principal is a group, so we'll approach our explanation of Dsacls using groups. However, other security principals can also be referred to by a */G* or */D* switch.

The group name is followed by a colon and then by the permissions. The next sections explain how permissions are indicated.

# Delegate permissions to manage computer objects

Let's use an example as a way to learn about important switches for the Dsacls command. The IT organization at Contoso, Ltd., has decided to give the desktop support organization full control over computer objects for user desktops and laptops. Such objects are contained in the Clients OU. Two Dsacls commands are required to perform this delegation. First, the desktop support team must be able to create and delete computer accounts in the Clients OU. The following command is used:

```
dsacls "ou=Clients,dc=contoso,dc=com" /I:T
    /G "CONTOSO\Desktop Support":CCDC;computer
```

The permissions assigned to the desktop support team are specified as *CCDC;computer*. *CC* and *DC* enable the creation and deletion, respectively, of child objects. If only *CCDC* were specified, the group could create objects of any class. But only computer objects should be created within the Clients OU; so, following a semicolon, the object class is specified. Therefore, the desktop support organization can create only computer objects within the Clients OU.

Notice there is an additional switch in the command just listed: */I:T*. The */I* switch specifies the scope of inheritance for the permission. Without an */I* switch, the permission would apply to the specified object only. One of three inheritance flags can be used with the */I* switch:

*T*    Permissions apply to this object and all child objects.

*S*    Permissions apply to child objects only, not to this object.

*P*    Propagate inheritable permissions one level only.

By using the */I:T* switch, the desktop support team is able to create computer objects in any sub OUs of the Clients OU.

Getting the desktop support team permission to create child computer objects in the Clients OU is not sufficient to meet the requirements of Contoso. The team must also be able to join computers to those accounts, reset computer accounts, disable and enable computer accounts, and modify all properties of accounts. This is attained with the following command:

```
dsacls "ou=Clients,dc=contoso,dc=com" /I:S
    /G "CONTOSO\Desktop Support":GA;;computer
```

This command grants the desktop support team full control of computer objects in the Clients OU. It uses *GA*, which represents the Full Control permission. (I like to remember it as "grant all" or "global access.") The *CC* and *DC* permissions discussed earlier are object permissions. You'll remember that they are followed by one semicolon and the object class to which they apply. *GA* is a property permission. Property permissions adhere to this syntax: *Perm;Property;ObjectClass*, where *Perm* is a valid permission presented in security descriptor definition language (SDDL). *Property* is the name of the property to which the permission applies, and *ObjectClass* is the type of object to which the permission applies. Because Full Control (*GA*) implies all properties, the *Property* part is left empty. The object class in this example is *computer*.

 **Note**    A nice overview of SDDL and a reference to SDDL syntax can be found at *http://www.washington.edu/computing/support/windows/UWdomains/SDDL.html*.

You'll notice here that I used the */I:S* switch. This instructs Dsacls to assign the permission at the OU but to apply the permission to child objects only. This is the correct switch for delegating permissions to a property of a child object.

# Grant permissions to manage other common object classes

You can easily modify the two Dsacls commands described in the previous section to delegate to a group effective Full Control permissions for other object classes by changing the *Object-Class* parts of the commands, as shown here:

| | |
|---|---|
| **Computers** | `dsacls "OUDN" /I:T /G "DOMAIN\group":CCDC;computer`<br>`dsacls "OUDN" /I:S /G "DOMAIN\group":GA;;computer` |
| **Users** | `dsacls "OUDN" /I:T /G "DOMAIN\group":CCDC;user`<br>`dsacls "OUDN" /I:S /G "DOMAIN\group":GA;;user` |
| **Groups** | `dsacls "OUDN" /I:T /G "DOMAIN\group":CCDC;group`<br>`dsacls "OUDN" /I:S /G "DOMAIN\group":GA;;group` |
| **Printers** | `dsacls "OUDN" /I:T /G "DOMAIN\group":CCDC;printQueue`<br>`dsacls "OUDN" /I:S /G "DOMAIN\group":GA;;printQueue` |
| **Organizational units** | `dsacls "OUDN" /I:T /G "DOMAIN\group":CCDC;organizationalUnit`<br>`dsacls "OUDN" /I:S /G "DOMAIN\group":GA;;organizationalUnit` |

# Use Dsacls to delegate other common tasks

You can use Dsacls to delegate common administrative tasks with one or two lines of code.

## Unlock user accounts

As I discussed in Solution 5-2 on page 373, the *lockoutTime* attribute of the user object keeps track of the time at which a user account was locked out. When you unlock a user account using the Active Directory Users and Computers snap-in, you are setting the *lockoutTime* attribute to zero. To delegate a group the ability to unlock user accounts, use the following command, where *rp* and *wp* represent reading and writing the property, respectively:

```
dsacls "OUDN" /I:S /G "DOMAIN\group":rpwp;"lockoutTime";user
```

Technically, the quotes are necessary only when there are spaces, but I have a habit of using quotes all the time so that I never get caught without them.

## Force users to change passwords at the next logon

In the Active Directory Users and Computers snap-in, when you select the check box to force a user to change passwords at the next logon, you are changing the *pwdLastSet* attribute of the user account. I also discussed this attribute in Solution 5-2. So, to delegate the ability to force users to change passwords at the next logon, use the following command:

```
dsacls "OUDN" /I:S /G "DOMAIN\group":rpwp;"pwdLastSet";user
```

## Reset user passwords

Resetting a user's password is not directly analogous to changing a single property of the user account. This capability is managed by a control access right. Therefore, the SDDL code *CA* is used in the command to delegate a control access right, and the right is specified where a property would normally appear. The following command is used to delegate the right to reset user passwords:

```
dsacls "OUDN" /I:S /G "DOMAIN\group":CA;"Reset Password";user
```

## Disable user accounts

To delegate the ability to disable and enable user objects, use the following command:

```
dsacls "OUDN" /I:S /G "DOMAIN\group":rpwp;userAccountControl;user
```

*userAccountControl* is a binary attribute that controls several properties of the account, so you are in fact over-delegating somewhat by allowing a group to modify *userAccountControl*. However, there's no other option, at least using Active Directory permissions.

## Change the logon names for a user account

When a user logon name changes, one or both of the *userPrincipalName* and *sAMAccountName* (pre–Windows 2000 logon name) attributes are changed. You can delegate the ability to change the logon names for a user account with this command:

```
dsacls "OUDN" /I:S /G "DOMAIN\group":rpwp;userPrincipalName;user
    "DOMAIN\group":rpwp;sAMAccountName;user
```

## Change user properties

You can delegate a group the ability to manage multiple properties of an object class. For example, the following command delegates the ability to change five of the user phone numbers:

```
dsacls "OUDN" /I:S
    /G "DOMAIN\group":rpwp;telephoneNumber;user
    /G "DOMAIN\group":rpwp;mobile;user
    /G "DOMAIN\group":rpwp;pager;user
    /G "DOMAIN\group":rpwp;otherPager;user
    /G "DOMAIN\group":rpwp;facsimileTelephoneNumber;user
```

Similarly, you can assign *rpwp* to other sets of related properties, such as the following:

**Address attributes**     *postOfficeBox*, *streetAddress*, *l* (that's lowercase "L" for "locale," or city), *st* (state or province), *postalCode*, *c* (for *countryName*, the two-character country code defined in ISO 3166), *co* (for friendly country name)

**User profile information**    *profilePath*, *homeDrive*, *homeDirectory*, *scriptPath*

**User names**    *userPrincipalName*, *givenName* (first name), *initials* (middle name), *sn* (surname or last name), *cn* (common name), *mail* (e-mail address), *displayName*

The bottom line here is that you should examine which attributes are being managed in your Active Directory and delegate those attributes to appropriate groups.

> **Note**    If you are unsure of the purpose of a specific attribute, you can consult an excellent reference for Active Directory attributes at *http://msdn2.microsoft.com/en-us/library/ms675090.aspx*.

## Delegate with property sets

Active Directory enables you to easily delegate collections of attributes using *property sets*. Property sets are defined in the schema and can be modified. You have probably seen the property set called *Personal Information*, which contains 46 attributes in Windows Server 2008 including a user's address attributes. There are also property sets such as *General Information*, *Public Information*, *Web Information*, and *Logon Information*. There are two benefits that are derived from the existence of property sets. First, you can delegate permissions to a collection of attributes with one ACE. For example, if you give a group the Write Logon Information permission, you effectively give them permission to change the 12 attributes that are associated with that property set. Second, property sets can reduce the size of the Active Directory database. Each ACE on each object requires storage in the database. By using property sets, the number of ACEs are reduced, so the size of the database is reduced.

Property sets are defined in the schema. Each has a *rightsGUID* attribute. An attribute is associated with a property set with the attribute's own *attributeSecurityGUID* attribute. Attributes can belong to only one property set. You can change the association of attributes—for example, you might take an attribute and move it from *Public Information* to *Personal Information*. You can also create new property sets, although that is well beyond the scope of this book.

The most important thing for you to be able to do is visualize the attributes that are associated with each property set. If you install Active Directory Lightweight Directory Services (AD LDS), you will find (in the C:\Windows\ADAM folder) a tool called ADSchemaAnalyzer. It provides an excellent way to see property sets and their attributes. To explore property sets, perform the following steps on a system that has AD LDS installed, or copy ADSchemaAnalyzer.exe to a remote client.

1.    Open ADSchemaAnalyzer from the C:\Windows\ADAM folder.

2.    Choose File, and then Load Target Schema.

3.    Enter the name of a domain controller in the Server[:Port] text box.

4.    Enter your username, password, and domain in the respective text boxes.

5. Choose AD DS/LDS in the Server Type section.

6. Click OK.

7. Expand Property Sets.

Inside the Property Sets folder, you'll find each property set listed. In each property set, you'll see an indicator of the object classes to which the property set applies and the attributes of object classes that are associated with the property set. You might be surprised at what you find—the names of the property sets are not crystal clear. For example, when I first started to examine property sets, I expected to see *sAMAccountName* and *userPrincipalName* associated with the *Logon Information* property set. They are actually associated with *General Information* and *Public Information*, respectively.

For more information about ADSchemaAnalyzer, see *http://technet2.microsoft.com/windowsserver/en/library/7fac5191-27d3-43dd-99c6-bb8ad044e7b91033.mspx?mfr=true*.

To delegate a property set with Dsacls, use the *rpwp* permission (Read Property and Write Property), and the property set in the property position of the command syntax, as in the following example:

```
dsacls "OUDN" /I:S /G "DOMAIN\group":rpwp;"Logon Information";user
```

The concept of property sets applies to computers, groups, and other object classes. Particularly in larger or more complex organizations, you should consider using property sets to enable more efficient delegation of administrative permissions.

## Manage group membership

Group membership is maintained in a group's *Member* attribute. You can use the following command to delegate the ability to add and remove members of groups within an OU:

```
dsacls "OUDN" /I:S /G "DOMAIN\group":rpwp;"member";group
```

## Join computers to the domain

The lengthy list of permissions required to allow a group to join computers to a domain can be applied with the following Dsacls command:

```
dsacls "OUDN" /I:S
    /G "DOMAIN\group":WS;"Validated write to DNS host name";computer
    "DOMAIN\group":WS;"Validated write to service principal name";computer
    "DOMAIN\group":CA;"Reset Password";computer
    "DOMAIN\group":WP;"Account Restrictions";computer
    "DOMAIN\group":WP;sAMAccountName;computer
```

**Important**  In Windows Server 2003's version of Dsacls, even the permissions are case sensitive.

### Prestage a computer account

If you want to allow a group to create computer accounts, use the following Dsacls command:

```
dsacls "OUDN" /I:S /G "DOMAIN\group":CC;computer
    "DOMAIN\group":WO;;computer
```

### Disable and enable computer accounts

To delegate the ability to disable and enable computer objects, use the following command:

```
dsacls "OUDN" /I:S /G "DOMAIN\group":rpwp;userAccountControl;computer
```

The *userAccountControl* is a binary attribute that controls several properties of the account. So you are in fact over-delegating somewhat by allowing a group to modify *userAccountControl*, but there's no other option, at least using Active Directory permissions.

### Rename computers

To rename computer objects successfully, multiple properties must be changed. Therefore, the Dsacls command is fairly complex:

```
dsacls "OUDN" /I:S
    /G "DOMAIN\group":WS;"Validated write to DNS host name";computer
    "DOMAIN\group":WS;"Validated write to service principal name";computer
    "DOMAIN\group":CA;"Reset Password";computer
    "DOMAIN\group":WP;"Account Restrictions";computer
    "DOMAIN\group":WP;SAMAccountName;computer
```

See Solution Collection 6, "Improving the Management and Administration of Computers," for information about renaming computers, and about the Computer_Rename tool provided on the companion media.

### Reset computer accounts

Solution Collection 6 also discusses resetting computer accounts. To delegate authority to do so, use the following command:

```
dsacls "OUDN" /I:S /G "DOMAIN\group":CA;"Reset Password";computer
```

### Manage group properties

The following command delegates a group permission to change the membership, name, and description of a group:

```
dsacls "OUDN" /I:S
    /G "DOMAIN\group":rpwp;member;group
    /G "DOMAIN\group":rpwp;cn;group
    /G "DOMAIN\group":rpwp;name;group
    /G "DOMAIN\group":rpwp;SAMAccountName;group
    /G "DOMAIN\group":rpwp;description;group
```

## Link GPOs to an OU

I commonly see larger organizations in which certain Group Policy objects (GPOs) are available for use anywhere in the enterprise. They might represent a collection of configurations, such as a GPO that defines a standard user interface. Owners of specific OUs in the organization are able to leverage OUs of standard GPOs by linking them to their OU. The OU owners cannot modify the settings within the GPO, but they can link the GPO and modify link options. You can delegate the ability to link GPOs to an OU with the following command:

```
dsacls "OUDN" /I:S /G "DOMAIN\group":rpwp;gpLink
```

To delegate the ability to modify link options, use this command:

```
dsacls "OUDN" /I:S /G "DOMAIN\group":rpwp;gPOptions
```

## Run resultant set of policy reports

I encourage many of my clients to delegate to the help desk the ability to run resultant set of policy (RSoP) reports. RSoP is discussed in Solution 5-10 on page 416. Because group policy has the ability to change the configuration of a user's experience, you need to understand the policies that are being driven from higher levels of the organization when performing certain desktop support activities. To delegate the ability to run RSoP logging reports, use the following command:

```
dsacls "OUDN" /I:S
    /G "DOMAIN\group":CA;"Generate Resultant Set of Policy (Logging)";
```

Notice the extra semicolon at the end of the command. That semicolon is required—the *objectClass* part of the permission is empty.

## Delegate the ability to move objects

Just as you were beginning to think Dsacls can do it all and that all tasks can be delegated, I have some bad news: Moving objects cannot be delegated with least privilege. In large, distributed organizations, it is common to see organizational units that reflect business units, geographic locations, or departments. In the course of day-to-day operations, users and computers are reassigned or relocated. It would be nice if the help desk could simply move a computer or user object from one OU to another in response to such changes.

Unfortunately, there is no Active Directory permission for "move object." Instead, if you want to move an object between OUs, you must have a variety of permissions on both OUs, including the ability to delete objects from the source OU and create objects in the target OU. In many of the organizations I work with, the need to move objects has been implemented by granting a group full control of both the source and target OUs. This is hardly a least-privilege solution.

Even if you were to apply only the bare minimum permissions, there is a problem. If a group has been given the delete objects permission on the source OU, members of the group will be able to move objects out of the OU, but they will also be able to delete all objects in the source OU accidentally or intentionally. This represents a vulnerability to denial of service.

How then should you effectively manage the permissions required to move an object? I have two recommendations:

**Escalate the capability to move objects**   The best answer for many organizations is this: Do not allow your front-line administrators to move objects. Instead, escalate requests for moving objects to administrators who, for other reasons, have levels of delegation that support moving objects. I know this is not a pretty answer; however, if we are not managing our directory service with least privilege, how can we expect the rest of our enterprise to accept a drive towards least privilege?

**Proxy requests to move objects**   The best answer for my clients, and for you as a reader of this resource kit, is to create a process through which requests to move objects are automatically executed with special credentials that have appropriate permissions. See Solution 8-7 on page 570 for a discussion of proxying.

### Delegate the ability to delegate

Your ability to delegate administrative control is dependent on your ability to change the ACL of the target Active Directory object. You must be allowed the Change Permission permission on the OU. The following command delegates to a group the ability to change permissions on the sub-OUs of the specified OU:

```
dsacls "OUDN" /I:S /G "DOMAIN\group":rcwd;;organizationalUnit
```

The *rc* and *wd* permissions are SDDL codes for reading permissions and modifying permissions. The */I:S* switch applies these permissions to child OUs of the specified OU. This is useful if you have created the specified OU and want to delegate another group the ability to delegate within your OU. If, instead, you use the */I:T* switch, you will delegate to the specified OU and all child OUs.

### Tightly control the delegation of OUs

In general, the creation of OUs in a domain should be a tightly controlled activity. Someone who creates an OU is the owner of that OU, and therefore has the capability to create any class of object and to set permissions of any kind. In Active Directory, you have the ability to hide objects if you are able to change object permissions. Unless your organization is prepared with the right auditing and monitoring tools, it can be very difficult to identify that such hidden objects exist in your Active Directory. If these hidden objects are security principles, such as users, they can act as a back door into your directory service and enterprise. Therefore, you should restrict and manage processes that result in the creation of an OU or in the modification of the OU ACLs.

## Solution summary

In this solution, you learned how to use the Dsacls command to delegate control in Active Directory. You learned the syntax of the command, and you saw a number of specific examples that will help you delegate specific administrative tasks. In a later solution, I propose using Dsacls to script, automate, and document the administrative model for your entire domain.

For more information about Dsacls, see "Dsacls Overview" at *http://technet2.microsoft.com/ WindowsServer/en/library/ffd71dba-386e-463e-9529-f0b77d708ca01033.mspx*.

# 5-6: Define Your Administrative Model

## Solution overview

| | |
|---|---|
| **Type of solution** | Guidance |
| **Features and tools** | Business analysis |
| **Solution summary** | Define an administrative model that thoroughly reflects the current state and supports changes in the future. |
| **Benefits** | You must completely understand and document the current and desired administrative models before you can implement role-based, least-privilege Active Directory delegation. |

## Introduction

With the right tools and knowledge, the technical processes used to delegate control in Active Directory are fairly straightforward. What I find to be more difficult for most organizations are the business aspects of the delegation project. Specifically, few organizations have defined their administrative model to a level of detail that supports granular, least-privilege delegation. In this solution, I provide guidance to help you and your organization define an administrative model that not only supports current operations, but is also agile enough to support changes in the future.

## Define the tasks that are performed

First, define the administrative tasks that are performed in your environment and that have an impact on Active Directory. The list of common tasks in the previous solution, as well as the task templates in the super-duper Delegwiz.inf file discussed in Solution 5-2, give you a great starting point. Think of each major object class: users, groups, computers, printers, and GPOs.

Don't bundle the tasks yet. That is, as you consider what tasks are performed for user objects, think about resetting a user's password and forcing that user to change her password at next logon as two distinct tasks.

Also remember that in the context of this discussion, you are concerned only with tasks that result in a change in Active Directory. You are not concerned with tasks that relate to rights or permissions to other resources or to users' computers. For example, do not worry about who is able to support particular software and hardware on client computers because that task is delegated by giving the appropriate support team membership in each computer's local Administrators group. Don't worry about who can change permissions on shared folders because that is implemented by granting the Change Permission ACE on the NTFS folder.

## Define the distinct scopes of each task

Next, look at each task defined in the previous step and determine whether the task is likely to be performed by different individuals for different scopes of objects in Active Directory. For example, the task of resetting a user password is usually delegated to front-line administrators for normal user accounts. However, resetting passwords for service accounts or for the accounts used by administrators is generally a more privileged activity. This implies two or three scopes for this task: normal user accounts, administrative accounts, and service accounts.

## Bundle tasks within a scope

For each scope you identify in the previous step, bundle tasks that you expect will always be performed together. This is a tricky step that affects the ability of your administrative model to support changes in your organization with least-privilege delegation. For example, your help desk might currently create user objects and support them by resetting passwords and unlocking accounts. It might seem perfectly reasonable, today, to bundle all these tasks together. But consider the possibility that, someday, your organization might implement a user account provisioning tool, whereby when a user is hired and her information is entered into the HR database, a user account is created automatically. The credentials used by that tool are not likely to require the ability to unlock accounts or reset passwords—only the ability to create user objects is required. Similarly, after such a tool is in place, it would be reasonable to remove from the help desk the ability to create user accounts. For such reasons, I suggest that you always separate the tasks related to the creation and deletion of objects from the tasks of maintaining, managing, and changing properties of objects.

## Identify the rules that currently perform task bundles

After you have identified tasks, scopes, and bundles of tasks within each scope, it is time to map the task bundles to the current administrative roles in your organization. Job descriptions of each role, as well as internal knowledge of how IT administration is managed, should make this step fairly straightforward.

## Solution summary

This solution outlines the process required to define an administrative model that reflects your current environment and is agile enough to support a change in your future. After you have a good handle on your administration of the model, you can translate that model into a role-based management implementation of Active Directory delegation.

# 5-7: Role-Based Management of Active Directory Delegation

## Solution overview

| | |
|---|---|
| **Type of solution** | Guidance and tools |
| **Features and tools** | Role-based management, Active Directory groups, delegation, Delegation_Report.hta |
| **Solution summary** | Apply concepts of role-based management to Active Directory delegation so that the assignment of administrative tasks can be accomplished by changing group memberships rather than ACLs on Active Directory objects. |
| **Benefits** | By representing delegations with capability management groups, it becomes significantly easier to assign and revoke administrative tasks. You can also use tools such as Delegation_Report.hta and Members_Report.hta to audit and report delegation. |

## Introduction

In Solution Collection 1, I presented the concepts and tools related to role-based management (RBM). RBM enables an organization to define and control capabilities of users based on the roles those users play in the organization. Role-based access control (RBAC), a flavor of RBM, is used to manage access to resources such as shared folders. The same tenets can be applied to improve the manageability of Active Directory delegation. In fact, I propose that the sheer complexity of delegation in Active Directory makes it the perfect candidate for RBM.

## Identify the pain points of an unmanaged delegation model

ACLs on Active Directory objects are complex. Let's take, for example, the permissions required to join a computer to the domain:

- Change password
- Reset password
- Write account restrictions
- Validated write to DNS host name
- Validated write to service principal name
- Create\delete all child objects

In Figure 5-12, you can see the Advanced Security Settings dialog box for an OU for which the help desk has been given permission to join computers to the domain. Can you interpret this dialog box? Can you tell exactly what permissions the help desk has? Would you be able to recognize whether one required permission were missing? Can you identify what additional permissions have been delegated to the help desk on this OU?

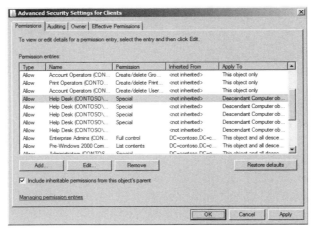

**Figure 5-12**   The Advanced Security Settings dialog box of an OU for which the Help Desk has been delegated permissions to join computers to the domain

What if another group—desktop support, for example—is also delegated permission to join computers to the domain in this OU? Figure 5-13 shows the resulting mess. Permissions get completely out of hand, making it difficult to interpret, audit, report, or modify the delegation model.

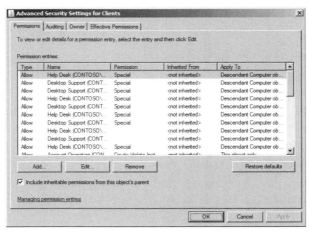

**Figure 5-13**   The Clients OU with the Help Desk and Desktop Support teams delegated permissions to join computers to the domain

And, finally, how would you answer the question, "What can [insert name of administrator] do?" Would you have to go looking at every ACL on every OU (or object) in your Active Directory to find out?

# Create capability management groups to manage delegation

One of the concepts of role-based management introduced in Solution 5-1 was that of the capability management group. A capability management group represents a specific type of access for a specific scope of control. If the basic question we are trying to answer as we attempt to manage security within our enterprise is, "Who can do what, where?", the capability management group represents the *what* and the *where*. The members of the group represent the *who*.

In our example, the *what* is the ability to join computers to the domain. The *where* is the Clients OU. The *who* is the help desk and the desktop support team. We implement a capability management group as a security group, typically with domain local scope. I recommend a rigorous naming convention that communicates the group's purpose—such as, to delegate permissions in Active Directory—the task that is being delegated, and the scope of delegation. Specifically, in our example, I suggest the following name: *AD_Clients_Join Domain*.

The name represents a naming convention with three parts:

**AD**  A prefix such as *AD*, for Active Directory delegation, that represents the purpose of the group.

**Clients**  The type of object for which we are delegating control. Technically, of course, we are delegating permissions for computer objects. But I prefer to be more specific, indicating the business purpose of the objects: user desktops and laptops. If you followed the recommendations in the previous solution, this part of the name is the scope.

**Join Domain**  The task we are delegating, which can be a single task or a task bundle as described in the previous solution.

An underscore character acts as a delimiter between the three parts of the group name. You can imagine that we might have additional groups to manage the delegation of other tasks related to computer objects. For example, an AD_Clients_Move group might be created to manage who can move client computers between OUs. Another group, AD_Clients_Create, would manage who could actually create computer objects in Active Directory.

# Assign permissions to capability management groups

After you've created the capability management groups, you assign permissions to those groups, not to role groups. For example, you would assign the permissions required to join computers to the domain in the Clients OU to the AD_Clients_Join Domain group. You'd assign the same permissions to your file servers OU to your AD_File Servers_Join Domain group. On your Employees OU, you would assign the permissions to reset user passwords, force users to change passwords at the next logon, and unlock user accounts to a group named AD_Users_Account Support. Again, these are just examples. The main point is that you are assigning permissions to the groups that represent each distinct capability and scope.

**Best Practices**   The capability management groups that you create and to which you delegate Active Directory permissions should have a one-to-one relationship with the scope-based task bundles defined in the previous solution.

## Delegate control by adding roles to capability management groups

You've created the foundation for role-based management of Active Directory delegation. Now, to delegate both the help desk and the desktop support teams the ability to join user desktops and laptops to the domain, you do not need to change any ACLs in Active Directory. Instead, nest those groups in the AD_Clients_Join Domain group. If next summer you hire interns to help with a rollout of new clients, you can add the interns group to the same AD_Clients_Join Domain group. And when the summer ends, you can pull the group out to un-delegate the capability.

## Create granular capability management groups

I recommend basing your capability management groups on what are, to your organization, logical bundles of related administrative tasks—*not* on which tasks are performed by roles within your organization today. The former are less likely to change; the latter are more likely to change. Let me clarify by way of an example.

Your help desk might be able to reset user passwords, unlock accounts, add users to groups, and join computers to domains. Don't create a capability management group that represents all those tasks, because later your environment might change. You might add a Web application that allows users to reset their passwords directly—that Web application will need the ability to reset passwords but will not need the ability to join computers to the domain. Similarly, the day you decide to use those interns to help out with deployment, they will need to join machines to the domain, but they will not need the ability to reset passwords on user accounts. By having granular capability management groups, perhaps one for each of the tasks performed today by the help desk, you have the flexibility, later, to grant individual tasks to meet your business requirements without having to change any ACLs in Active Directory.

On the other hand, don't go overboard, either. For example, I might create a group called AD_Users_Contact Info Change that represents the ability to change basic contact information for users: phone numbers and addresses. I would not create a group called AD_Users_Postal Code Change and AD_Users_City Change. Those two tasks are tightly related and are unlikely to be delegated separately in the future.

For more guidance, refer to the delegations discussed in Solution 5-5 on page 391 and in the previous solution.

# Report permissions in a role-based delegation

In Solution 5-4 on page 384, I discussed a number of tools that could be used to report permissions in Active Directory. None of them were perfect. Most listed individual permissions without interpreting what those permissions really mean. None could include nested group memberships to evaluate the effect of permissions of a user or group. With a role-based implementation of Active Directory delegation, you no longer need to enumerate the ACLs of Active Directory objects to determine who can do what. Instead, you simply evaluate group memberships with tools similar to those presented in Solution Collection 1.

## Use Delegation_Report.hta

Delegation_Report.hta can be found in the Scripts folder of the companion media. It is a variation of the My Memberships.hta tool presented in Solution Collection 1. The HTML Application (HTA) enumerates the nested group membership of a user or group, and reports groups with names that match the naming convention you have established for your Active Directory delegation groups. The tool is written to look for groups with the prefix *AD_*. You can change this prefix in the *ReportGroups* subroutine of the HTA. Figure 5-14 shows Delegation_Report.hta in action.

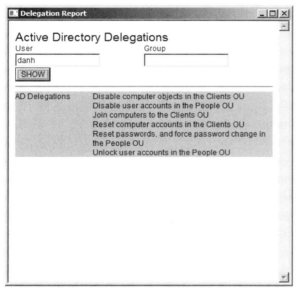

**Figure 5-14**   Delegation_Report.hta

Delegation_Report.hta answers the question, "What can [insert name of user or group] do in Active Directory?" To answer the other question, "Who can [insert name of task] for [insert scope of objects]?", you can use the Members_Report.hta tool presented in Solution Collection 8, "Reimagining the Administration of Groups and Membership." Enter the name of an Active Directory capability management group, such as AD_Clients_Join Domain, and the tool will enumerate all nested members of that group, as shown in Figure 5-15.

**Figure 5-15**   The Members report tool displaying the users and groups delegated permission to join computers to the domain

## Solution summary

The permissions that you assign to delegate control within Active Directory are critical to the security and integrity of your directory service. The implementation of an administrative model requires a lengthy and complex set of ACLs be applied to numerous OUs in your domain. Such complexity makes it difficult to evaluate, report, and audit your administrative model and delegation. I cannot overemphasize the value that role-based management plays in establishing an effective, secure, agile, and manageable Active Directory delegation. There is absolutely a great investment of time to define the administrative model, as discussed in the previous solution, and to implement it using role-based management principles. But the investment pays off.

# 5-8: Scripting the Delegation of Active Directory

## Solution overview

| | |
|---|---|
| **Type of solution** | Guidance |
| **Features and tools** | Scripting, Dsacls |
| **Solution summary** | Understand the importance of scripting the delegation of Active Directory, and identify a simple approach that uses Dsacls. |
| **Benefits** | Scripting the delegation of Active Directory provides numerous benefits to the enterprise, the most important of which are consistency, transferability between lab and production environments, and documentation of delegation. |

# Introduction

In the early days of Windows 2000, I sat in a room with the top Microsoft administrators of a major Fortune 500 company. Our goal was to apply permissions to implement the corporate administrative model across a distributed organizational unit structure. We divided the world of this organization between us, and each of us was to delegate a prescribed set of tasks within our part of the world using the Delegation Of Control Wizard. It seemed like a simple job, and the folks in the room were nothing short of genius-level minds. However, the result was that each of our divisions were slightly different, and none precisely matched the complex permissions we had been asked to configure. That day, it became clear to me that expecting administrators to correctly interpret and apply the permissions required to delegate Active Directory in a sophisticated, least-privilege way was expecting too much of human beings. Since then, I have been a major proponent of scripting Active Directory delegation. In this solution, I outline the benefits and the steps of this approach.

# Recognize the need for scripted delegation

Applying permissions to Active Directory objects by hand is a tedious, complex, error-prone activity. By scripting the application of permissions, you can obtain the following valuable and, in my opinion, critical benefits:

**Consistency**   Because a script lays out, step-by-step, the permissions that need to be applied, those permissions can be applied consistently across similar scopes of control. In the story I shared in the introduction to this solution, we could have applied a script within each region that would have ensured identical permissions were applied.

**Ease of modification and rollback**   With a script, it is easy to modify permissions at a later date. You can simply make a change to the script and rerun it. You can also create a script that has the ability to roll back changes if those changes have unintended effects.

**Transferability between lab, pilot, and production**   If you use a script to delegate permissions in your lab environment, you can then use the script to apply the same permissions to a subset of your production Active Directory to perform a pilot implementation, and then use the script to fully delegate the entire directory service. Because the script applies the same permissions each time, you can be assured that human error and other inconsistency will not be introduced.

**Accuracy**   You've seen in this Solution Collection that delegating certain administrative tasks can require a great number of permissions. If any one of those permissions is not applied correctly, your delegation will either fail to function or fail to be least privilege. While testing your delegation, you can refine the script that applies permissions until you obtain exactly the results you desire. You can then be confident that when the script runs, permissions are being accurately applied. You could even code a script to double-check resulting ACLs to make sure they match the desired permissions.

**Provisioning**    If you have invested the time and effort to create a script that delegates permissions for a specific type of OU, you can then leverage that code to create a script that provision new OUs of the same type. For example, assume you have divided your Clients OU that contains user desktops and laptops into geographic sites to delegate local desktop support teams specific capabilities for their site. If you have scripted the application of permissions to your site OUs, you can create a script that allows you to instantly, accurately, and consistently create new OUs for new sites as your organization grows.

**Documentation**    Very few organizations have thoroughly documented the granular implementation of their administrative models. I understand why that is the case—we are all that busy—but lack of documentation is a showstopper when it comes to auditing, reporting, or modifying the environment. A script is one of the best forms of documentation. Although a script might be light on descriptive text, it clearly indicates exactly how the environment was built. You can always return to the script as a reference for the administrative model.

## Script delegation with Dsacls

In Solution 5-5, I described the use of the Dsacls command for delegating administrative control. You can be served perfectly well with a long batch file containing Dsacls commands as a script for delegating your environment.

A more advanced approach could leverage a database that describes the administrative model. A script could interpret the model and apply appropriate permissions to Active Directory. I have performed just such delegations with several clients, and it has served us well. The database enables us to provide reports and to easily modify the administrative model, at which point we simply rerun the script.

The delegations I have scripted all leverage the Dsacls command to do the heavy lifting of modifying the security descriptor on Active Directory OUs. So, from my experience, if Fortune 500 companies can be delegated effectively by iterating through an administrative model and applying appropriate permissions with Dsacls, so can your organization.

There are other ways to apply permissions, however, by using code that directly accesses the *ntSecurityDescriptor* and modifies the ACL. Whether your solution directly modifies permissions or drafts off the capabilities of Dsacls, create a solution that is capable of fully implementing the ACLs required by your administrative model.

See the companion Web site, *http://www.intelliem.com/resourcekit*, for examples of scripts that can help you delegate your Active Directory.

## Solution summary

Applying the permissions required to delegate administrator tasks in Active Directory is a time-consuming, complex, and error-prone undertaking. I highly recommend creating a script—even if just a lengthy batch file containing Dsacls commands—to implement the ACLs required by your administrative model. The script gives you the ability to test and refine permissions in your lab, and to apply exactly the same permissions in production. You can also use such a script as a basis for tools that provision OUs. And, perhaps most importantly, a script acts as an authoritative document that describes to a very granular level how you implemented your administrative model in Active Directory.

# 5-9: Delegating Administration and Support of Computers

## Solution overview

| | |
|---|---|
| **Type of solution** | Guidance and procedures |
| **Features and tools** | Local Administrators group, Group Policy Restricted Group policies |
| **Solution summary** | Manage the delegation of administrative rights on client and server computers so that you can control who is able to administer and support individual systems. |
| **Benefits** | Increase the security of your environment by removing the Domain Admins group from the local Administrators group and replacing it with a group that enables managed control of local Administrators credentials. |

## Introduction

As organizations recognize the need to secure their servers and the desktops and laptops of end users, and as they come to understand the importance of least privilege, they are scrambling to regain control of the local Administrators groups on client computers. This solution presents a role-based approach to managing the delegation of administration and support for servers and client computers. It is a simple approach that combines two components. First, you define scopes of computers that are administered by the same team or teams. Those scopes are represented by capability management groups in Active Directory. Then you implement the delegation using Restricted Groups policies.

## Define scopes of computers

Most organizations allow a limited number of skilled, trusted administrators to support servers, whereas administration of user desktops and laptops is generally delegated to less senior roles. This approach implies that servers and clients are two separate scopes of management. It is certainly possible that the individuals who can manage servers are also able to manage clients, but probably not vice versa.

Larger organizations tend to have IT teams that are more specialized. For example, one team might be dedicated to support Web servers, and another to support e-mail servers. These tasks then become separate scopes of management. Similarly, geographically dispersed enterprises often have one or more support personnel in local sites who are capable of performing administrative tasks on client systems in their sites. These sites then also become scopes of management.

To effectively delegate administration of computers in your environment, you must first identify your scopes of administration. In each of these scopes, you will manage the membership of the local Administrators group identically.

# Create capability management groups to represent administrative scopes

Next, create security groups to represent each scope of management. Best practice suggests that the groups should be domain local groups, although global groups will serve equally well in most scenarios. Refer to Solution Collection 1 for details regarding the advantages and disadvantages of global and domain local groups.

Adhere to a rigorous naming convention for these groups. I recommend using a prefix such as *SYS_* to reflect the group's purpose: to manage rights on systems. After the prefix, I have found it best to indicate the scope to which the group applies. Finally, the group name should communicate the rights that the group's membership provides. For example, the group SYS_Exchange_Local Admins would be used to manage the delegation of local administrative privileges on servers running Microsoft Exchange Server, and the group SYS_NYC_Client Admins would manage the membership of the local Administrators groups of clients in New York.

If you have overlapping or hierarchical scopes of management, reflect that in your capability management groups. For example, a company-wide desktop support model could be implemented by nesting the SYS_Contoso_Client Admins group in each of the site-based capability management groups: SYS_NYC_Client Admins, SYS_LAX_Client Admins, SYS_SYD_Client Admins, and so on.

# Implement the delegation of local administration

After you have created the capability management groups representing each scope of local administration, you can use group policy to drive those groups into the local Administrators groups of client systems in those scopes. You need a group policy object for each scope. Edit an existing GPO that applies to each scope, or create new GPOs. Then, for each GPO, follow these steps:

1.  In the Group Policy Management Editor, navigate to Computer Configuration, Windows Settings, Security Settings, Restricted Groups.

2.  Right-click Restricted Groups and choose Add Group.

3.  Click the Browse button, and in the Select Groups dialog box, enter the name of the appropriate capability management group—for example, SYS_NYC_Client Admins—and click OK.

4.  Click OK to close the Add Group dialog box.

   A Properties dialog box appears.

5.  Click the Add button next to the This Group Is A Member Of section.

6.  Type **Administrators** and click OK.

   The group policy setting Properties should look something like Figure 5-16.

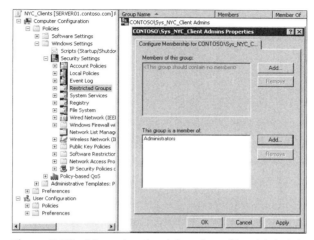

**Figure 5-16**   Managing the delegation of local Administrators credentials using the Member Of policy setting

7.  Click OK again to close the Properties dialog box.

Delegating the membership of the local Administrators group in this manner adds the specified capability management group to the local Administrators group. It does not remove any existing members of the Administers group. The group policy simply tells the client, "Make sure this group is a member of the local Administrators group." This allows for the possibility that individual systems could have other users or groups in their local Administrators group. This group policy setting is also cumulative. If multiple GPOs configure different security principals as members of the local Administrators group, all will be added to the group.

To take complete control of the local Administrators group, follow these steps:

1.  In the Group Policy Management Editor, navigate to Computer Configuration, Windows Settings, Security Settings, Restricted Groups.

2.  Right-click Restricted Groups and choose Add Group.

3.  Type **Administrators** and click OK.

   A Properties dialog box appears.

4.  Click the Add button next to the Members Of This Group section.

5. Click the Browse button, and enter the name of the capability management group—for example, SYS_NYC_Client Admins—and click OK.

6. Click OK again to close the Add Member dialog box.

The group policy setting Properties should look something like Figure 5-17.

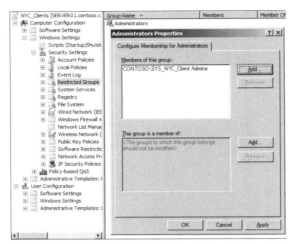

**Figure 5-17**   Managing the delegation of local Administrators credentials using the Members policy setting

7. Click OK again to close the Properties dialog box.

This version of the group policy setting configures the effective membership of the local Administrators group. Only the members listed in the group policy setting will be members of local Administrators. All other members will be removed. If multiple GPOs configure the membership of the Administrators group this way, only the GPO with the highest precedence will take effect. This setting also rules out the possibility of exceptions. Every computer within the scope of the GPO will have exactly the same membership for the Administrators group. Therefore, this setting is used in only the most tightly controlled and managed environments within an organization.

## Manage the scope of delegation

After you've configured the GPOs that specify the membership of the local Administrators groups for each scope of your enterprise, you need to deploy those GPOs to appropriate systems. If an organizational unit matches a scope of local administration, you can link the GPO for that scope to the organizational unit. Figure 5-18 shows the OUs for two sites: New York and Beijing. A GPO configuring client settings for each site is linked to the OU. Within the GPO is a Restricted Groups setting that specifies the membership of the local Administrators group for that site.

⊟ 🗐 NYC
   🗐 NYC_Clients
⊟ 🗐 PEK
   🗐 PEK_Clients

**Figure 5-18**   GPOs linked to OUs

Often, the scope of delegation will not align perfectly with your organizational unit structure. This is the natural result of the fact that OUs are designed first and foremost to manage the effective delegation of permissions within Active Directory. Luckily, there are other ways to scope GPOs, such as security group filtering.

Let's assume that in each site, your organization has training rooms. A role group named CMP_Training Room is created to represent the computers, and the training room computers from all sites are made members of the group. The PCs in the training rooms are managed by a central support team. A capability management group is created to reflect the centralized support function: SYS_Training Room_Client Admins. But you also want local site support teams to be able to administer the training room PCs when required.

You create a GPO, and configure a Restricted Groups policy that specifies that SYS_Training Room_Client Admins is a member of the local Administrators group. You could link this GPO to a Training Room OU in every client site, but it is generally easier to manage an environment when there are fewer points of management. Therefore, you link the GPO to the Clients OU— the parent OU to each of the sites. The link causes the settings to apply to all clients and all sites, so you use security filtering to limit the scope to the training room PCs. In the Security Filtering section of the Scope tab of the properties of the GPO, select Authenticated Users and click Remove. Then click Add, and select the role group representing the training room PCs, *CMP_Training Room*. An example is shown in Figure 5-19.

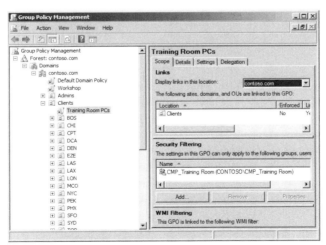

**Figure 5-19**   Scoping local administration with a GPO filtered by a computer role group

The result is beautiful indeed. The GPO linked to the Clients OU and filtered to apply only to the CMP_Training Room role group will add the SYS_Training Room_Client Admins group to the local Administrators group of all training room PCs. Additionally, the site-based policies will add the local site support teams to the local Administrators groups. So, for example, training room PCs in New York will have as administrators the SYS_Training Room_Client Admins group and the SYS_NYC_Client Admins group.

## Get the Domain Admins group out of the local Administrators groups

I'd like to close this solution with one final recommendation: Get the Domain Admins group out of your local Administrators groups. Domain Admins should be a role that is managed to delegate capabilities to support Active Directory Domain Services and domain controllers. The user accounts that are members of Domain Admins should be few and highly controlled. In larger organizations, it's not uncommon for an individual with Domain Admin credentials to have *three* user accounts: one nonprivileged user account that is used to log on to his or her computer; a second that provides credentials to perform day-to-day data administration tasks in Active Directory; and a third that is used only when performing significant operations on the directory service or domain controllers.

It might be perfectly reasonable, based on your administrative model, to have a group with the capability to log on to all clients and perhaps even all servers. If that's the case, create a custom capability management group—CMP_Global_Local Admins, for example—that is made a member of the local Administrators groups of all systems. Just don't use the Domain Admins group as that group.

## Solution summary

This solution outlines the process of delegating local administrative authority on domain member computers. Identify scopes of computers that are administered similarly, and create a capability management group that represents that scope. Use a Group Policy object that applies to the same scope to place the capability management group into the local Administrators group.

# 5-10: Empty as Many of the Built-in Groups as Possible

## Solution overview

| | |
|---|---|
| **Type of solution** | Guidance |
| **Features and tools** | Protected built-in groups, adminSDHolder |
| **Solution summary** | Remove the members of built-in, protected groups. |
| **Benefits** | Gain more granular, managed control over Active Directory delegation, and prevent the user accounts that belong to protected groups from being exempted from the normal inheritance of Active Directory permissions. |

# Introduction

To support rapid deployment of Active Directory, Windows provides several default administrative groups with preconfigured permissions and rights in the domain. Most of those groups—including Account Operators, Backup Operators, Print Operators, and Server Operators—can be found in the Built-in OU. Wherever possible, you should delegate those permissions and rights to custom groups and empty out the membership of the built-in groups. Doing so will make your delegation more manageable and help you avoid problems associated with membership in protected groups.

# Delegate control to custom groups

In this solution, you have learned how to delegate Active Directory by assigning permissions to capability management groups. After Active Directory is delegated to a line with your administrative model, there should be no need for administrators to belong to most of the built-in groups.

# Identify protected groups

Active Directory uses a protection mechanism to make sure ACLs are set correctly for members of specific highly sensitive groups, including the following ones:

- Administrators
- Account Operators
- Server Operators
- Print Operators
- Backup Operators
- Domain Admins
- Schema Admins
- Enterprise Admins
- Cert Publishers

If your user account is a member of one of these groups, called *protected groups*, your user account is exempt from the normal mechanisms of ACL inheritance in Active Directory. Instead, the ACL applied to your user account is configured by the ACL on the special container, *adminSDHolder*—for example, CN=adminSDHolder,CN=System,DC=*domain*,DC= . . . . The idea is that if your user account is moved into a container or OU where a malicious user has been delegated permissions that could be used to modify your user account, the entire domain is at risk. So Active Directory protects all members of protected groups by disabling inheritance on the objects and applying the ACL specified by adminSDHolder. You can see this in action by adding a user account to one of the protected groups. Within about one hour, you will see that the ACL on the object has been changed.

This is another good reason for emptying out the membership of these groups. You can delegate most of the rights and permissions assigned to these groups to custom groups. Other groups, such as Schema Admins, can be empty until the day a specific task such as modifying the schema must be performed. Perhaps only the Domain Admins and Administrators groups will need to have a small number of persistent members. Earlier, I suggested that top-level administrators in an organization should have a third user account that belongs to Domain Admins. The fact that Domain Admins member accounts will be protected is yet another justification for this guidance.

Interestingly, if an account has at one point been a member of a protected group, it will continue to be protected with inheritance disabled even after it has been removed from the group. This will affect you if you have used these groups in the past. Be sure to read Knowledge Base article 817433 (*http://support.microsoft.com/kb/817433/en-us*) for information about protected groups, adminSDHolder, and how to restore inheritance to objects that were once members of protected groups.

## Don't bother trying to un-delegate the built-in groups

I've had a number of clients ask me if it makes sense to remove the delegations assigned to built-in groups such as Account Operators. From a purist standpoint, it might make sense. But from a practical standpoint, that entails modifying the ACLs specified by the schema for many Active Directory objects. Instead of fighting that battle, just make sure that the groups are empty.

## Solution summary

Active Directory comes preloaded with a number of built-in groups that have been delegated permissions and rights within a domain. Because the permissions assigned to these groups are broad and wide reaching, I recommend that you focus on delegating permissions to custom groups that will support the administrative model, and then empty out the membership of these built-in groups. Because user accounts that are members of these groups are subject to ACL protection, you are also ensuring that all user accounts are managed based on the inherited permissions of the apparent OUs.

# Improving the Management and Administration of Computers

Computers in an Active Directory domain are security principals, which means, like users, they each have an account (an object in Active Directory) with an internal username and password and, of course, a security identifier (SID). Like a user, a computer uses its account to authenticate and access domain resources. Unfortunately, most enterprises do not invest the same kind of care and process in the creation and management of computer objects as they do for user objects. In this Solution Collection, I share the best practices related to creating, provisioning, maintaining, and deleting computer objects in Active Directory. I also share steps you can take to integrate commonly used computer management tools and scripts into custom Microsoft Management Console (MMC) consoles.

## Scenarios, Pain, and Solution

Managing computers—both the objects in Active Directory and the physical devices—is part of the day-to-day tasks of most IT professionals. Whether you're supporting client systems or servers, desktops or laptops, local area network (LAN) or remote systems, there are certain problems you and your organization are likely to encounter:

■ Support personnel at Adventure Works regularly join computers to the domain by logging on to the system, opening System Properties, and changing the machine's membership to the domain. Unfortunately, when they do that, the computers end up in the default Computers container. The systems do not receive the Group Policy settings that are specified for client computers because those settings are scoped to the Servers organizational unit (OU) and the Clients OU, not the Computers container. Corporate security officers are concerned that security templates are not being applied correctly because of this problem.

- IT personnel at Contoso are preparing to reorganize their Active Directory. They want to ensure that computers are moved to the correct OU in the new structure, but there is no way to identify the users to whom the computers are assigned or the sites in which the computers are being used. A systems management tool, Microsoft System Center Configuration Manager 2007, is being deployed next year. The company needs some way to gather basic information about a computer before Configuration Manager is rolled out.

- The Help Desk team at Litware has asked for help to make desktop support more productive. They want to find a way to do more from the standard Active Directory Users And Computers console.

- Over at Proseware, the team has read Solution Collection 3, "Managing User Data and Settings," and are ready to roll out redirected folders and offline files. They want to disable offline files on desktop computers, but their OU structure is site-based, not object-based, so they need a way to scope the Group Policy object (GPO) that will configure that setting. They decided to filter the GPO with a security group, so they want to create groups for desktop and laptop computers and to keep those groups dynamically updated as systems are added to and removed from the environment.

- The IT organization at Fabrikam has decided to start managing computer accounts because they are Microsoft Windows security principals just like user accounts. They want to lock down who is able to create accounts, manage who is able to join systems to the domain, and enforce standards for computer names and the contents of attributes such as *description*.

- Trey Research uses Configuration Manager 2007 to deploy software. It uses Active Directory security groups to manage the computers that should have applications. But when a user's computer is replaced, the new computer does not automatically receive the same applications as the previous computer—the user has to enter a request for the applications. Management has asked IT to improve this process so that when a user gets a new system, it serves the same role and gets the same applications as the computer it replaces.

- The IT team at The Phone Company has found it very difficult to support users without knowing what computer a user is using. The first question the help desk asks is typically, "Can you read me the name of your computer that is on the sticker on the back?" To improve manageability, the IT team wants to create a way to associate computers with the users to which the computers are assigned.

These are some of the pain points I'll address in this Solution Collection. Quite a lot of pain is caused by legacy practices used to join systems to the domain. I'll guide you to best practices, equip you to lock down the environment to restrict or prevent bad practices, and give you a tool that makes it easy to provision computer objects in Active Directory and join a new computer to the domain—in its correct OU.

I'll also begin in this Solution Collection to leverage Active Directory as a database capable of supporting the information requirements of an enterprise. I'll show you how to assign computers to users using one of several existing attributes and, better yet, how to extend Active Directory with a custom attribute designed specifically for that purpose. You'll discover how to create a self-reporting environment, where computers submit information to Active Directory, such as their site and the last user who logged on. And I'll show you a few amazing tricks for your administrative toolset that should trigger a burst of creativity and productivity for your day-to-day support tasks.

# 6-1: Implement Best Practices for Managing Computers in Active Directory

## Solution overview

| | |
|---|---|
| **Type of solution** | Guidance and scripts |
| **Features and tools** | OUs, Dsacls, naming conventions, the registry |
| **Solution summary** | Explore the detail of each step involved with creating a computer account and joining a computer to the domain. Implement best practices for Active Directory design, delegation, computer account creation, and joining computers to the domain. |
| **Benefits** | Increased consistency and manageability of computer objects. |

## Introduction

Computer objects are security principals and include properties similar to users and groups, such as a logon name (*sAMAccountName*) and a password that is established when the computer joins the domain and is changed automatically by the computer every 30 days. The security principal properties make up what many administrators call the computer account. After an account has been established, an administrator of the computer can change the membership of the computer to the domain, at which point the computer changes its SID and sets its password in the domain.

In this solution, we'll examine best practices for creating computer accounts and joining computers to the domain.

# Establish naming standards for computers

Your enterprise should establish a strict naming convention for computers, particularly for client systems—desktops and laptops. Establish standards for computer names that will support the ongoing management of computers. I recommend that you design your naming standards for client computers to meet the following requirements:

- The computer name is guaranteed to be unique.

- The computer name can be derived by knowing properties of the system.

- The computer name is not dependent on the current location of the system—so that you can move the system without renaming it.

- The computer name is not dependent on the user to whom the computer is assigned—so that you can reassign the computer without renaming it.

- The computer name can be generated automatically.

- The computer name reflects fixed properties of the system that are otherwise difficult to derive.

A common basis for computer names is the asset tag or serial number of the system. This approach to naming meets the first four requirements. Additionally, most modern computers expose the asset tag or serial number in the system BIOS, which can be read by the Windows Management Instrumentation (WMI), meeting the fifth requirement.

The sixth requirement leads to a specific recommendation: The name should indicate whether the device is a desktop, laptop, or other class of device. That's because it's very useful to know a system's class for inventory and configuration management. It's also very difficult to derive this information using WMI or any other method. I've seen a number of approaches, none of which are guaranteed to be accurate 100 percent of the time. WMI exposes properties such as *ChassisType*, the presence of PCMCIA cards or batteries, and many other characteristics of a system. However, today more than ever, as devices blur traditional categories, nothing is as good as a manual, intentional classification of a system.

Therefore, the naming convention that I prefer and that I recommend to you is to establish the class of the device with a single character prefix, such as *D* for desktop or *L* for laptop, and to follow that prefix with the asset tag or serial number of the system. In Solution 6-4 on page 442, I demonstrate how you can create dynamically maintained groups of desktops and laptops, which you can then use to scope Group Policy as suggested in Solution 3-6 on page 245 and in Solution Collection 10, "Implementing Change, Configuration, and Policies."

# Identify requirements for joining a computer to the domain

Three things are required for you to join a computer to an Active Directory domain:

- A computer object must be created in the directory service.

- You must have appropriate permissions to the computer object. The permissions allow you to join a computer with the same name as the object to the domain.

- You must be a member of the local Administrators group on the computer to change its domain or workgroup membership.

The next sections examine the permissions required and the steps to achieving each of these requirements.

# Design Active Directory to delegate the management of computer objects

Most organizations create at least two OUs for computer objects: one to host computer accounts for clients—desktops, laptops, and other user systems—and another for servers. These two OUs are in addition to the Domain Controllers OU created by default during the installation of Active Directory. In each of these OUs, computer objects are created. There is no technical difference between a computer object in a clients OU and a computer object in a servers or domain controllers OU: Computer objects are computer objects. But separate OUs are typically created to provide unique scopes for delegation and configuration. The desktop support team is delegated the ability to create computer objects in the clients OU, but not in the servers or domain controllers OU; and a group representing server administrators is delegated the ability to create computer objects in the servers OU. Additionally, GPOs that specify configuration for clients are linked to the clients OU, and server configuration GPOs are linked to the servers OU.

Your administrative model might necessitate further dividing your client and server OUs. Many organizations create sub-OUs beneath a server OU to collect and manage specific types of servers—for example, an OU for file and print servers and an OU for database servers. By doing so, the team of administrators for each type of server can be delegated permissions to manage computer objects in the appropriate OU. Similarly, geographically distributed organizations with local desktop support teams often divide a parent OU for clients into sub-OUs for each site. This approach enables each site's support team to create computer objects in the site for client computers and join computers to the domain using those computer objects. As discussed in Solution Collection 5, "Active Directory Delegation and Administrative Lock Down," you should design your OU structure based on your administrative model so that your OUs provide single points of management for the delegation of administration.

Figure 6-1 illustrates a typical OU design for an organization whose server administration teams are centered around specific types of servers and whose desktop support teams are focused on clients in specific geographical areas.

After your OU design fully reflects and supports your administrative model, you might want to further divide OUs to support the scoping of GPOs that drive configuration for computer objects. I commonly see Active Directory design in which client objects are separated into desktop and laptop OUs. GPOs specifying desktop or laptop configuration can then be linked to appropriate OUs.

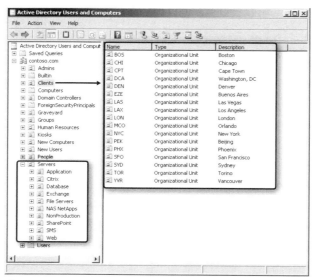

**Figure 4-1**    A common OU design illustrating site-based administration of clients and role-based administration of servers

If an organization has decentralized, site-based administration and wants to manage unique configurations for desktops and laptops, it faces a design dilemma: Should it divide its clients OU based on administration and then subdivide desktops and laptops, or should it divide its clients OU into desktop and laptop OUs and then subdivide based on administration? The options are illustrated in Figure 6-2. For the reasons I outline in Solution Collections 5 and 10, you should base your OU design first on administration, and then for configuration. So the design on the left side of Figure 6-2 would be more appropriate in this scenario.

**Figure 4-2**    OU design options

## Delegate permissions to create computers in the domain

After an appropriate OU structure is in place, you can delegate the ability to create computer objects to appropriate administrators or support personnel. The permission required to create a computer object is Create Computer Objects. This permission, assigned to a group or an OU, allows members of the group to create computer objects.

> **Note**   In Solution Collection 5, I discussed the Dsacls command, which you can use to delegate permissions in Active Directory from the command line. Throughout this Solution Collection, I will indicate the command line syntax that you can use to delegate permissions required to perform tasks I discuss. See Solution Collection 5 for more information about Dsacls. Dsacls is a native command for Windows Server 2008. On earlier versions of Windows XP and Windows Server 2003, you must install the Windows Server 2003 Support Tools. Dsacls is added to Windows Vista when you install the Remote Server Administration tools.

The following Dsacls command delegates permissions to create computer accounts:

```
dsacls "DN of OU" /I:T /G "DOMAIN\group":cc;computer
```

> **Important**   Switches used by the Windows Server 2003 version of Dsacls are case sensitive. In Windows Server 2008, Dsacls is no longer case sensitive.

There is a simple batch file on the companion media called ComputerOU_Delegate_Create.bat. It wraps the preceding command so that you can use the command to delegate the creation of computers:

```
computerou_delegate_create.bat "DN of OU" "Domain\group"
```

## Create a computer object in Active Directory

With the permissions described in the previous section, you can create a computer object using the following procedure:

1.  Open the Active Directory Users and Computers snap-in.

2.  Right-click the OU or container in which you want to add the computer.

3.  Choose New and then Computer.

4.  The New Object – Computer dialog box appears, as shown in Figure 6-3.

5.  Type the computer's name in the Computer Name box.

    Follow your enterprise naming convention.

6.  Click the Change button next to the User Or Group box.

7. In the Select User Or Group dialog box that appears, enter the name of the user or group that will be allowed to join the computer to the domain.

   The permissions that are applied to the user or group you select are more than are necessary to join a computer to the domain. The selected user or group is given the ability to modify the computer object in other ways. I recommend that you just use Domain Admins (the default) and apply the least-privilege permissions required for joining the machine to the domain, as described in the next section.

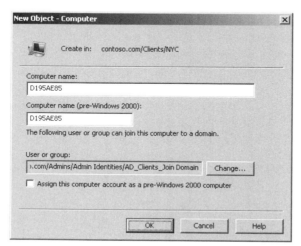

**Figure 4-3**　The New Object – Computer dialog box

8. Complete the process. If you are using the newer versions of the Active Directory Users and Computers snap-in, click the OK button. If you are using older versions, click Next, click Next again, and then click Finish.

A computer object contains properties you might want to configure right away. Right-click the computer and choose Properties to change the object's attributes. I'll discuss some of the more useful properties later in this Solution Collection.

> **Best Practices**　I highly recommend that you create computer accounts before joining machines to the domain. This is a process called *prestaging a computer*.

# Delegate permissions to join computers using existing computer objects

The individual who creates a computer account has the ability to join that computer to the domain. You might also want certain support personnel to be able to join computers to the domain, but only when computer objects have been prestaged. This allows you to maintain control over the provisioning of new computer objects, which are security principals, while delegating the ability to join individual computers to the domain. You can delegate permissions to join computers using existing computer objects in one of two ways:

- When you create a computer object, you can delegate to another user or group the ability to join a computer to the domain with the same computer name. This process was described in steps 6 and 7 in the previous section and can be seen in Figure 6-3. As I mentioned in that discussion, Windows actually over-delegates the object, assigning more permissions than are truly required to join the machine to the domain.

- You can assign the necessary permissions on the OU to enable a user or group to join computers to the domain using any prestaged computer objects in the OU.

The specific access control entries (ACEs) that enable joining a computer to the domain are: Reset Password, Write Account Restrictions, Validated Write To DNS Host Name, and Validated Write To Service Principal Name. The following Dsacls commands delegate to the specified group the ability to join computers to the domain where the computer objects have been prestaged in an OU:

```
dsacls "DN of OU" /I:S /G "DOMAIN\group":
    "Validated write to DNS host name";computer
dsacls "DN of OU" /I:S /G "DOMAIN\group":
    "Validated write to service principal name";computer
dsacls "DN of OU" /I:S /G "DOMAIN\group":CA;Reset Password;computer
dsacls "DN of OU" /I:S /G "DOMAIN\group":WP;Account Restrictions;computer
```

**Important**    The Windows Server 2003 version of Dsacls is case sensitive—even the permissions must be entered as shown.

You can also give a specific user or group the ability to join a single, specific computer to the domain. For example, we might want James Fine to be able to join the new computer we gave him to the domain. The delegation could be implemented using these commands:

```
dsacls "DN of computer" /G "CONTOSO\jfine":
    WS;"Validated write to DNS host name";
dsacls "DN of computer" /G "CONTOSO\jfine ":
    WS;"Validated write to service principal name";
dsacls "DN of computer" /G "CONTOSO\jfine ":CA;Reset Password;
dsacls "DN of computer" /G "CONTOSO\jfine ":WP;Account Restrictions;
```

Note that when you use Dsacls to apply permissions to a single object, you do not use the /I (inheritance) switch, nor do you specify the object class to which the permissions are inherited—you leave that placeholder empty after the final semicolon.

The ComputerOU_Delegate_Join.bat file in the Scripts folder of the companion media applies all four of these permissions. Call the command with the following syntax:

```
computerou_delegate_join.bat "DN of OU" "Domain\group"
```

# Join a computer to the domain

By prestaging the computer object, you fulfill the first two requirements for joining a computer to a domain: The computer object exists, and you have specified who has permissions to join a computer with the same name to the domain. Now, a local administrator of the computer can change the computer's domain membership and enter the specified domain credentials to successfully complete the process. Here are the steps for doing so:

1.  Log on to the computer with credentials that belong to the local Administrators group on the computer.

    Only local administrators can alter the domain or workgroup membership of a computer.

2.  Open the System properties using one of the following methods:

    ❑  Windows XP: Right-click My Computer and choose Properties (or press Windows+Pause).

    ❑  Windows Vista: Right-click Computer and choose Properties (or press Windows+Pause) and then, in the Computer Name, Domain, And Workgroup Settings section, click Change Settings. Click Continue when prompted.

3.  Click the Computer Name tab.

4.  Click Change.

    Avoid the evil Network ID Wizard, which forces you through multiple steps to accomplish what you can do quite easily with from the dialog box.

5.  Under Member Of, select Domain.

6.  Type the name of the domain you want to join.

 **Best Practices**   Use the full DNS name of the Active Directory domain. Not only is this more accurate and more likely to succeed, but if it does not succeed, it indicates there could be a problem with DNS name resolution that should be rectified before joining the machine to the domain.

7.  Click OK.

8.  Windows prompts for the credentials of your user account in the domain.

    The domain checks to see if a computer object already exists with the name of the computer.

    If the object exists and a computer with that name has already joined the domain, an error is returned, and you cannot join the computer to the domain.

If the object exists and it is available—a computer with the same name has not joined the domain—the domain confirms that the user account you entered has the permissions required to join the machine to that account. These permissions were discussed earlier in this Solution Collection.

If the computer does not yet have an account in the domain, Windows checks to see if you have permissions to create a new computer object in the default computers container. These permissions are discussed in the next solution. If you do have permissions to create a new computer object in the default computers container, the object is created with the name of the computer.

The computer then joins the domain by assuming the identity of its Active Directory object. It configures its SID to match the domain computer account's SID and sets an initial password with the domain. The computer then performs other tasks related to joining the domain. It adds the Domain Admins group to the local Administrators group and the Domain Users group to the local Users group.

 9. You are prompted to restart the computer. Click OK to close this message box.

 10. Click Close (in Windows Vista) or OK (in Windows XP) to close the System Properties dialog box.

 11. You are prompted, again, to restart the computer.

The very first time you start a computer that has just joined the domain (including newly deployed systems), you need to click the Options button in the Log On To Windows dialog box and select the appropriate domain from the Log On To drop-down list.

## Ensure correct logon after joining the domain

When you join a computer to the domain and restart the system, Windows expects you to log on as the same local account with which you last logged on. Typically, you'll want to log on with a domain account instead.

On Windows Vista clients, when you restart, the logon user interface presents you with the user name of the previously logged-on local user. You can click Switch User and log on as a domain user, but that is more awkward than it needs to be. The *LogonUI* registry key, found in the registry in the path HKEY_LOCAL_MACHINE\SOFTWARE\Microsoft\Windows\CurrentVersion\Authentication\LogonUI, contains the *LastLoggedOnUser* value that, not surprisingly based on its name, keeps track of the username of the user who last logged on to the system.

If you delete this value, when Windows Vista restarts, the logon user interface presents Other User, which when clicked allows you to enter a username and password. The reg.exe command allows you to manipulate the registry from the command prompt. (You'll need to open this command prompt with elevated privileges.) You can use the following command to delete the *LastLoggedOnUser* value:

```
reg delete HKLM\SOFTWARE\Microsoft\Windows\CurrentVersion\
    Authentication\LogonUI /v LastLoggedOnUser /f
```

You can also prepopulate the value with the name of the user to whom the computer will be assigned. Simply enter the username in the format *DOMAIN\username*. When the machine restarts, that username will be prepopulated in the logon user interface. Use the following command:

```
reg add HKLM\SOFTWARE\Microsoft\Windows\CurrentVersion\
    Authentication\LogonUI /v LastLoggedOnUser /t REG_SZ
    /d "DOMAIN\username" /f
```

Windows XP's behavior is even more problematic. When you join a Windows XP client to the domain and restart it, its logon interface prompts you for a username and password, but the Log On To drop-down list is, most unfortunately, set to log on to the local computer. So it is quite common that the first user to log on to a computer newly joined to the domain is denied logon, because the system attempts to authenticate the user with the local security accounts manager (SAM) database.

Windows XP manages the logon user interface in a different key than Windows Vista: HKEY_LOCAL_MACHINE\SOFTWARE\Microsoft\Windows NT\CurrentVersion\Winlogon. Change the *DefaultDomainName* value to match your domain name, and change the *DefaultUserName* value to the name of the user who will log on to the system, or delete the contents of the value, leaving it blank. You can use the following commands:

```
reg add "HKLM\SOFTWARE\Microsoft\Windows NT\CurrentVersion\Winlogon"
    /v DefaultDomainName /t REG_SZ /d "DOMAIN" /f
reg delete "HKLM\SOFTWARE\Microsoft\Windows NT\CurrentVersion\Winlogon"
    /v DefaultUserName /f
```

Instead of the second command, which leaves the user name box empty in the logon dialog box, you can prepopulate a user name with this command:

```
reg add "HKLM\SOFTWARE\Microsoft\Windows NT\CurrentVersion\Winlogon"
    /v DefaultUserName /t REG_SZ /d "username or blank" /f
```

In Solution 6-3 on page 435, we provision joining a system to the domain. The configuration of the Windows Vista and Windows XP logon user interfaces are part of the provisioned process.

## Solution summary

This solution details the best practices for implementing a managed, delegated framework for the creation of computer objects in your domain. First, you must design an OU structure that reflects and supports the administrative model for computers—both servers and clients—in your enterprise. Then you can delegate the permission to create computer objects within specific OUs to appropriate administrators and support personnel. As you create a computer object, you can grant a specific group or user the ability to join a computer with the same name to the domain. Or, by setting permissions on the OU, you can delegate the ability to join computers to any available objects in the OU. Finally, as a member of the local Administrators group, you can change the domain membership of a computer. During that process, you are prompted to enter the credentials of a domain account which is then used to authorize joining the computer to its account. I wrapped up the solution with a small but very helpful tip to ensure that the first logon to the domain is as user friendly as possible.

# 6-2: Control the Addition of Unmanaged Computers to the Domain

## Solution overview

| | |
|---|---|
| **Type of solution** | Guidance and scripts |
| **Features and tools** | Redircmp.exe, Computers_SetQuotas.vbs, Group Policy, Active Directory permissions |
| **Solution summary** | Manage, reduce, and eliminate the addition of computers to your domain using legacy practices that result in computers in inappropriate containers and OUs. |
| **Benefits** | Increased compliance of computer objects with security and configuration policies. |

## Introduction

Solution 6-1 on page 421 described how to create OUs and delegate permissions so that new computers can be created and joined to the domain. Unfortunately, you must also discourage or prevent administrators from using legacy practices to join computers to the domain, as such practices will result in computer accounts that are not managed according to the policies you implemented. In this solution, we examine such legacy practices and identify the steps required to manage their impact on your environment.

In Solution 6-1, I stated that three things are required for you to join a computer to an Active Directory domain:

- A computer object must be created in the directory service.

- You must have appropriate permissions to the computer object. The permissions allow you to join a computer with the same name as the object to the domain.

- You must be a member of the local Administrators group on the computer to change its domain or workgroup membership.

That list of requirements is presented in an order reflecting the best practice described in Solution 6-1: prestaging the computer object, delegating it, and joining the computer to the domain.

Unfortunately, Windows allows you the ability to join a computer to a domain without following best practices. I've seen it happen many times: An administrator joins a computer to a domain by opening the computer's Properties dialog box and changing the computer's domain membership before creating an account for the computer in Active Directory. On the fly, Windows creates a computer object in Active Directory, gives the administrator permission to join a computer to that object, and then proceeds to join the system to the domain.

There are three disturbing aspects of this feature of Windows. First, a computer account created automatically by Windows is placed in the default computer container. Second, by default, any domain user can also do this—no domain-level administrative permissions are required. The following sections detail these first two issues.

The third problem is that you must move the computer from the default computer container into the correct OU. As I explain in Solution 7-6 on page 523, delegating the ability to move objects is problematic. In a well-delegated and secure Active Directory, you strictly limit or even prevent administrators' ability to move computers. This means you want to ensure computer objects are in the correct OU in the first place. See Solution 7-6 for more detail.

## Configure the default computer container

When you join a computer to the domain and the computer object does not already exist in Active Directory, Windows automatically creates a computer account in the default computer container, which is called Computers. The problem with this goes back to the discussion of OU design in Solution 6-1. If you have implemented the best practices described there, you have delegated permissions to administer computer objects in specific OUs for clients and servers. Additionally, you might have linked GPOs to those OUs to manage the configuration of these computer objects. If a new computer object is created outside of those OUs, in the default computer container, the permissions and configuration it inherits from its parent container will be different from what it should have received.

The solutions in this Solution Collection help you to prevent computer objects from being created in the default computer container. However, I am not suggesting that you can guarantee a computer account will never be created in the default computer container. Therefore, I recommend that you create a framework to manage what happens to computer objects that are created outside the boundaries of your best practices.

First, you should create a custom OU to serve as the default container for new computers. When you install Active Directory, Windows creates a container object called Computers, CN=Computers,DC=*domain*. It is not possible to link GPOs to an object of a class *container* such as the Computers and Users containers. By creating an organizational unit, you enable yourself to manage the configuration computer objects within the OU. After you have created the OU, you can instruct Windows to use that OU as the default computer container. The redircmp.exe command is used redirect the default computer container with the following syntax:

```
redircmp "DN of OU for new computer objects"
```

Now, if a computer joins the domain without a prestaged computer account, Windows creates the computer object in the specified organizational unit.

You can now be creative with how you manage computer objects in the OU. For example, you might configure security auditing on the OU so that new objects created in the OU generate an event log entry. You could then configure a trigger on the event log to send an e-mail message informing appropriate personnel that a computer account has been created in the wrong location. You might even trigger a script that disables the computer object.

Alternatively, you might configure the OU as a kind of jail, using GPOs. Configure user rights so that only administrators, not domain users, have the right to log on locally. Create a logon banner, which appears when you press Ctrl+Alt+Delete, that informs the user logging on to the system that the system's functionality will be limited, and provide a phone number to call appropriate support personnel. You can repeat the message in a logon script. You can even use Group Policy to specify that after logon the command prompt is launched as the user shell rather than Windows Explorer. I can almost guarantee that behavior will cause the user to call the help desk.

By configuring the access control list (ACL) of the OU, you can strictly limit which users are able to create computer objects in the default computer container that you've created. However, if the approach laid out in this section is new to your organization, consider allowing creation of computer objects within your custom default computer container for the short term (a few weeks or months) so that you can monitor how computers end up there. You can identify the legacy practices and the users whose practices should be corrected. As long as you are managing the objects that do get created in this OU, you can guide your enterprise to better practices.

Over the long term, you should strive to eliminate the practices and tools that result in the creation of computers in the default computer container. Instead, prestage computer accounts in the correct OU prior to joining the computer to the domain. Solution 6-3 provides a tool that makes following the best practice even easier than joining computers to the domain the old, less preferred way.

## Restrict the quota that allows any user to join computers to the domain

You now know that Windows creates a computer account automatically in the default computer container when you join a computer to the domain without a prestaged computer object. The most disturbing aspect of this feature of Windows, in my opinion, is that you don't need to have any domain-level administrative permissions to do so. You can join a machine to the domain without a prestaged computer account if either of the following conditions exist:

■ You have been delegated the ability to create computer objects in the default computer container. By default, Account Operators, Domain Admins, and Enterprise Admins have permissions to create computer objects in any new OU or container, including the Windows default Computers container, and the custom organizational unit described in the previous section.

■ You are a user in the domain.

You read the latter condition correctly: Any user in the domain—any member of the Authenticated Users group—can add 10 computers to the domain without any delegation whatsoever.

This leads to one of two problems. First, users can add machines to the domain without delegation, approval, or any other control. A computer is a security principal and is a member of the Authenticated Users group, so the computer account is instantly able to access any resource to which the Authenticated Users group has access. The result is similar to letting a user create a new user account without any delegation, approval, or control—it's a significant security hole. Second, if you have not correctly delegated the ability for your desktop support team to join computers to the domain—as they should be able to do—a desktop support member will be able to join 10 computers to the domain, and then all of a sudden that member will no longer be able to join other machines to the domain.

You should therefore eliminate the ability for Authenticated Users to join computers to a domain and correctly delegate appropriate support personnel permissions to create computer objects in specific OUs.

The 10-computer quota is configured by the *ms-DS-MachineAccountQuota* attribute of the domain. To change *ms-DS-MachineAccountQuota*, follow this procedure, which applies to Windows Server 2008:

1. Open the ADSI Edit MMC console from the Administrative Tools folder.

2. Right-click ADSI Edit and choose Connect To.

3. In the Connection Point section, choose Select A Well Known Naming Context, and from the drop-down list choose Default Naming Context.

4. Click OK.

5. Expand Default Naming Context.

6. Right-click the domain folder—"DC=contoso,DC=com", for example—and choose Properties.

7. Select ms-DS-MachineAccountQuota, and click Edit.

8. Type **0**.

9. Click OK.

On Windows Server 2003, install the Support Tools from the product CD's Support folder, run Adsiedit.msc, and open the properties of the Domain node. From there, continue with step 7.

Alternatively, you can use the Computers_SetQuota.vbs script on the companion media to set the quota to zero. Just change the domain distinguished name in the *Configuration Block*.

> **Best Practices**    Enterprises should reduce the *ms-DS-MachineAccountQuota* attribute to zero. This attribute can be accessed using ADSIEdit to open the properties of the Domain NC node, or by using Computers_SetQuota.vbs.

Additionally, the Authenticated Users group has the user right to add workstations to the domain, but you do not have to modify this right if you have changed the default value of the *ms-DS-MachineAccountQuota* attribute.

After you have changed the *ms-DS-MachineAccountQuota* attribute to zero, you can be assured that the only users who can join computers to the domain are those who have been specifically delegated permission to join prestaged computer objects or to create new computer objects. These permissions are detailed in Solution 6-1.

## Solution summary

The best practice is to prestage a computer's account prior to joining it to the domain. Sadly, however, Windows allows administrators to join a computer to the domain without prestaging the computer object—in which case, the computer object is created automatically in the default computer container. The problem with that approach is that the default computer container is generally not delegated with the same ACL as a custom OU created specifically to host computer objects. Similarly, most enterprises link the Group Policy objects that configure computers to OUs that host computer objects for clients and servers. Usually, enterprises are less careful about the GPOs scoped to a generic computer container. You should proactively address this scenario by creating a custom organizational unit to act as the default computer container and managing the computer objects that are created in it.

# 6-3: Provision Computers

## Solution overview

| | |
|---|---|
| **Type of solution** | Custom HTML Application (HTA) |
| **Features and tools** | Computer_JoinDomain.hta |
| **Solution summary** | Implement a tool that provisions the process of creating computer objects and enforces business logic for attributes such as the computer name. The tool also acts as a replacement for the standard Windows interface for joining a computer to the domain and makes it possible to create a computer account in the correct OU and to join it, on the fly. |
| **Benefits** | Consistency, manageability, and security. |

# Introduction

In Solutions 6-1 and 6-2, I detailed the mechanisms through which you can join a computer to the domain by providing the credentials of any user in the domain. I also discussed the problems that result from allowing a computer to join the domain without a prestaged computer account: The computer object is created in the default computer container, rather than in the OU that is delegated and configured correctly for the type of computer you are joining. Unfortunately, many administrators do join computers to the domain without prestaging the computer object in the correct OU.

I believe there are two primary reasons why administrators continue to join computers to the domain without prestaged computer accounts. The first is, "Old habits die hard." The second is that Windows XP makes it so easy to open the System Properties dialog box, click the Computer Name tab, click Change, enter the domain name and domain user credentials, and join the domain. Windows Vista makes it even easier: Just open the System window and click Change Settings. To change behavior, I recommend you follow the carrot-and-stick approach. The stick is described in Solution 6-2 on page 431, which details the steps you can take to discourage or prevent administrators from joining computers to the domain without prestaged computer accounts—steps that, over time, will change those old habits. The carrot is presented in this solution: a tool that makes it even easier to follow the best practice than to follow the legacy practice.

To make it easy for administrators to follow the best practice, consider the requirements of joining a machine to the domain: You must be an administrator of the computer, a computer object must exist in Active Directory, and you must have permissions to join the computer to the domain using the object with the same name. You can meet these requirements with a simple GUI administrative tool that provisions the computer correctly.

The tool I present also addresses two other common scenarios. In the first, you are joining a computer to the domain, but the computer has a generic name that must be changed. Using standard procedures, you have to rename the computer, restart the computer, join the domain, and restart again. We will eliminate a reboot. In the second scenario, you want to prestage a computer object in the domain but do not want to join the computer to the domain.

# Use Computer_JoinDomain.hta

Computer_JoinDomain.hta is just such a tool. You can find it in the Scripts folder of the companion media. Double-click the HTML Application (HTA) and you are prompted to enter the minimum properties required to fully provision the computer object, as seen in Figure 6-4.

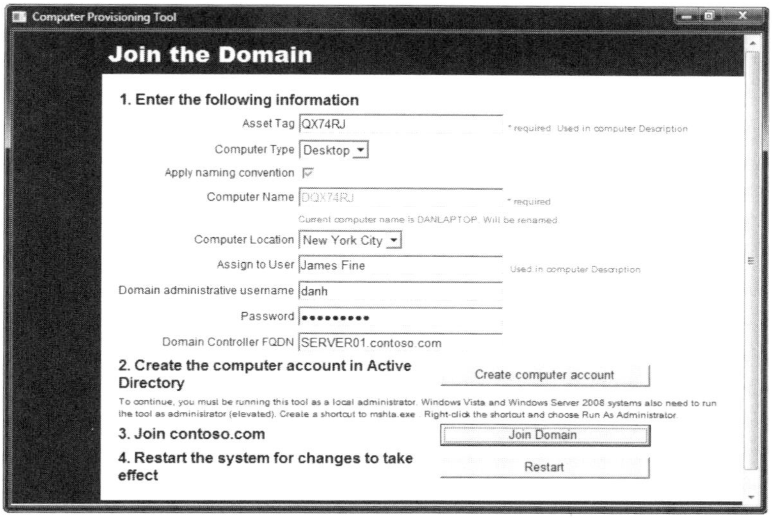

**Figure 4-4**    Computer_JoinDomain.hta

The code I've written reflects the recommendations of Solution 6-1. You are prompted to do the following:

- Configure the computer's asset tag.

- Select whether the computer is a desktop or laptop.

- Choose whether naming conventions should be followed to create the computer's name. I provide detail on this option later.

- Change the default computer name.

- Specify the OU within which the computer object will be created using a user-friendly Computer Location drop-down list.

- Enter the name of the user to whom the computer will be assigned.

- Enter your username and password, which must have permission to create computer objects in the specified OU. If you are joining the machine to the domain, you must also have permissions to join the domain.

When you have completed the form, click the Create Computer Account button. The tool is coded with business logic that derives the computer name (*Function Calculate_ComputerName*) and the OU within which the computer is created (*Function Calculate_TargetOU*). By default, the first letter of the computer type is used as a prefix for the computer name—*D* for a desktop and *L* for a laptop—and the rest of the computer name is the Asset Tag of the system. The computer object is created in a Desktops or Laptops OU within the OU selected on the form. For example, if the Sydney OU is selected, the computer account for a laptop will be created in the Clients\Sydney\Laptops OU. If you have an environment that does not require an intermediate level of OUs, such as geographic sites, you can modify the code as instructed in the code comments so that the computer object is created in a Desktops or Laptops OU immediately below the Clients OU.

The HTA notifies you that the computer object has been created successfully or that an error prevented the creation of the account. Then, if you are logged on to the computer as a member of the local Administrators group, you can click the Join Domain button. The computer joins the domain and then, if necessary, is renamed. You are then prompted to restart the computer.

Like most other scripts and tools provided in this resource kit, Computer_JoinDomain.hta requires some customization. The customization that you must perform is located in the *Configuration Block*. Read the documentation in the *Configuration Block* for guidance. Additionally, there are several subroutines and functions that drive the business logic of the tool. If you want to change the rules with which the tool determines computer names, descriptions, and OUs, you need to make additional modifications.

It will be easiest to understand the steps to customize the tool by stepping through its functionality. The tool works in two basic modes. The first is *computer provisioning* mode, which is the tool's default. The second mode is *local join domain* mode. You can change to local join domain mode by setting the variable *bLocalJoinMode* to *TRUE*.

> **Important**   Computer_JoinDomain.hta works in two modes: local join domain mode and computer provisioning mode. Change the value of *bLocalJoinMode* in the *Configuration Block* to set the mode. After you have configured the tool to work in your enterprise, I recommend saving two separate copies—one preset in local join domain mode and the other preset in computer provisioning mode.

## Provision computer accounts with Computer_JoinDomain.hta

When the variable *bLocalJoinMode* is *FALSE*, the tool operates in computer provisioning mode. In this mode, the interface of the tool is simpler than what you saw in Figure 6-4. In computer provisioning mode, only the computer account fields and commands are visible, as shown in Figure 6-5. The tool provisions a computer account following business logic that dictates the computer's name, description, and the OU in which the computer is created.

The computer object's name will be set to the value of the Computer Name text box. Notice in Figure 6-5, the Computer Name box is disabled. That's because the tool can be set to use business logic to determine the computer's name. The computer name logic uses a prefix of *D* or *L* based on the selection of Desktop or Laptop in the Computer Type drop-down list, followed by the contents of the Asset Tag field. The mapping of the options in the Computer Type list to prefixes used in the computer name is managed by the *maComputerTypes* variable, the third element of which is the prefix. See the *Configuration Block* of the tool for more detail. The function *Calculate_ComputerName* builds the computer name with this logic, and you can customize that routine if you want to change the rules with which computer names are created.

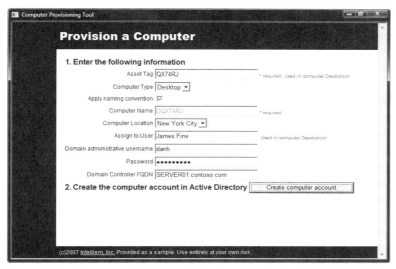

**Figure 4-5**   Computer_JoinDomain.hta in computer provisioning mode

To enforce business logic for the computer name, set the variable *bEnforceName* to *TRUE*, its default value. If you set the variable to *FALSE*, the user has the ability to enter any name into the Computer Name box. When you are not enforcing computer name conventions with *bEnforceName*, an administrator using the tool can manually enable naming conventions by selecting the Apply Naming Convention check box. This check box is the equivalent of *bEnforceName*, but it can be turned on and off at will. By setting *bEnforceName* to *TRUE*, you can ensure that computer names adhere to naming conventions—the check box is selected and disabled when you enforce naming conventions.

The computer's *description* attribute is constructed by the *Calculate_Description* function. By default, the description is *[AssetTag]: Assigned to [User Name]*, where *[AssetTag]* is the value in the Asset Tag box and *[User Name]* is the name in the Assign To User box. You can change the logic of this routine to apply other business logic to the creation of the computer's *description*.

> **Note**   The Assign To User box is used only to create the computer's *description* attribute. It does not affect the ACL or any other field of the computer object.

The OU in which to create the computer is determined by the *Calculate_TargetOU* function. By default, the OU is determined by the selection in the Computer Location drop-down list, which is associated with a site-based OU. The mapping of friendly site names to OUs is managed by the *maTargetOUs* variable in the *Configuration Block*. The computer is created in either the Desktops or Laptops sub-OUs of the site OU based on whether the computer is a desktop or laptop, as selected in the Computer Type box. The mapping of computer types to sub-OUs is managed by the *maComputerTypes* variable, the second element of which is the OU. See the *Configuration Block* of the tool for more detail.

You must enter your username and password in the Domain Administrative Username and Password boxes. These credentials must have permission to create computer accounts in the domain. You must also enter the fully qualified domain name (FQDN) of a domain controller so that Active Directory can be located by the application.

When you have configured all values in the form, click the Create Computer Account button. The *cmdCreateComputer_OnClick* function is called. That function validates that you did, in fact, enter an Asset Tag and Computer Name so that those two fields are required properties. The computer account is then created.

## Create an account and join the domain with Computer_JoinDomain.hta

While in local join domain mode, you can launch the Computer_JoinDomain.hta tool on a workgroup computer running Windows XP or later operating systems. (You configure this script to use the local join domain mode by setting the *bLocalJoinMode* variable to *TRUE*.) The functionality in this mode enables you to provision the computer account and join the domain. It also supports renaming the local computer. All of this is achieved with a single reboot. Local join domain mode is illustrated in Figure 6-4.

The provisioning of the computer account is identical to the process described in the previous section. The one customization that is worth mentioning is that you can instruct the HTA to query the local computer for its asset tag and to automatically populate the Asset Tag field. To do this, set *bAssetTag* to *TRUE*. Then locate the *Calculate_AssetTag* function. This function is used to determine the asset tag of the system, but it does that by calling one of three WMI functions later in the script. The three WMI functions each query a different property of the system's BIOS for asset tag and serial number information. Unfortunately, not all manufacturers put the information in the same place. Dell, for example, puts its Express Service Code for newer models in the property queried by the function *Computer_BIOSSerialNumber*. You might need to use *Computer_EnclosureSerialNumber* or *Computer_AssetTag* for other models or manufacturers. Just call the appropriate function from the *Calculate_AssetTag* function. You might have to experiment with each to determine what works best for your systems. To summarize, the goal of the *bAssetTag* variable and the *Calculate_AssetTag* function is simply to save you the time of looking for and entering the local system's asset tag.

In local join domain mode, after creating the computer account, click the Join Domain button. This calls the *cmdJoinDomain_OnClick* event, which makes sure you have entered domain credentials, joins the domain, and then, if necessary, renames the computer. Last but not least, the system is rebooted.

Typically, you want a system to reboot after joining the domain, and the tool does that by default while the variable *bNoChoiceReboot* is set to *TRUE*. However, if you set *bNoChoiceReboot* to *FALSE*, the HTA prompts you to restart after joining the domain, but you are not forced to do so.

To join the domain and, if necessary, rename the machine, you must be a local administrator of the system, and you must enter a domain credential in the Domain Administrative Username and Password boxes that has permissions to join the computer to its prestaged account.

Additionally, you must run the HTA as an administrator in Windows Vista and Windows Server 2008 when User Account Control is enabled. This is, unfortunately, not an easy task, as HTAs do not expose a Run As Administrator command on the context menu. One of the easier ways to achieve elevation for the HTA is to create a shortcut with the target by typing **mshta.exe <*path to HTA*>**. By specifying mshta.exe, you can now right-click the shortcut and choose Run As Administrator.

> **Important**    On Windows Vista and Windows Server 2008 systems, you must run the HTA as an administrator, using the instructions in the previous paragraph. Otherwise, you will receive errors if you attempt to join the domain while User Account Control is applied.

As I mentioned earlier, the tool allows you to rename a computer and join a domain with a single reboot. This is useful when you have imaged systems with a computer name that you need to change before joining the systems to the domain. The process that is required for this to work with a single reboot is that the computer account must be created for the computer's current name. The computer is joined to the domain with that account. Immediately thereafter, the computer is renamed and, using the credentials you supplied in the HTA, the domain account is able to be renamed simultaneously. The computer is then rebooted.

## Understand Computer_JoinDomain.hta

The workhorses of the HTA are three subroutines: *Computer_CreateObject*, *Computer_Rename*, and *Computer_JoinDomain*. These routines are heavily commented within the code of the HTA. Most of the other code manages the user interface or prepares parameters that are used by those three routines.

## Distribute Computer_JoinDomain.hta

This tool is trickier than most to deploy, simply because it is used before a computer joins the domain. After the computer joins the domain, you can more easily copy tools to systems using methods described in Solution Collection 9, "Improving the Deployment and Management of Applications and Configuration." I recommend building the tool into your image. For example, you could copy the tool to the computer as part of the image, and then launch the tool as a task within a task sequence created using the Microsoft Deployment Tool. Alternatively, place the tool in an intranet Web site so that administrators can download it on demand using Internet Explorer, which is installed prior to joining the domain.

## Solution summary

Computer_JoinDomain.hta is two tools in one. It allows you to provision computer objects, enforcing business logic regarding their names, descriptions, and OUs. It also allows you to provide a replacement for the legacy practices of opening the System Properties dialog box, clicking the Computer Name tab, and clicking Change. With Computer_JoinDomain.hta, you can ensure that best practices are followed: A computer account is created in the correct OU, and then the computer is joined to that prestaged account. The tool makes it all possible with a minimal number of clicks and navigations.

# 6-4: Manage Computer Roles and Capabilities

## Solution overview

| | |
|---|---|
| Type of solution | Guidance and scripts |
| Features and tools | Computer_DesktopsLaptops.vbs, Active Directory groups |
| Solution summary | Apply the concepts of role-based management to computers so that you can manage their configuration and the applications that are deployed to them. Use a script to dynamically maintain role groups, such as groups for desktops and laptops. |
| Benefits | Manageability |

## Introduction

Prior to Windows 2000, groups did not contain computer accounts. For that reason, many organizations have been slow to adopt and adapt to computer groups. You can use groups that contain computer objects for numerous management tasks, including software deployment, patch management, asset inventory, and the management of configuration. In this solution, I present some of the tools and tricks related to computer groups.

## Automate the management of desktop and laptop groups

I find that it is invaluable to be able to readily identify and manage desktops and laptops in an enterprise. Typically, different configurations are managed using GPOs deployed to each type of computer. In Solution Collection 3, for example, I suggested disabling on desktops the default behavior that makes redirected folders automatically available offline, which can be done using a GPO scoped to desktop computers. The easiest way to accomplish these goals is to maintain a security group for desktops and another for laptops. Ideally, soon after a desktop or laptop is added to the domain, it will automatically be made a member of the correct group.

There are three major steps to such a solution. First, you must determine how you can identify that a computer object is a desktop or a laptop. Second, you must decide how to monitor

Active Directory for the addition of new computer objects. Later, I will explain how to create a recurring scheduled task that queries Active Directory for new computer objects that represent desktops and laptops. Third, you need to update the membership of the Desktops and Laptops groups. You should not completely rebuild the group membership because it would trigger more replication than necessary. Simply add desktops and laptops that are not currently members of those groups.

## Determine how to identify desktops and laptops

In Solution 6-1, I recommended that you establish a computer naming convention that allows you to identify the computer type, using a *D* as the first letter for all desktops and an *L* for all laptops. You might choose to develop another method for identifying the type of computer, but this is one situation in which I've found a manual configuration is most reliable. In this solution, I'll assume you are following my recommended naming convention, but I'll also point out where you can replace my logic with your own method for identifying desktops and laptops.

## Decide how to monitor Active Directory for the addition of new computer objects

There are slick ways to monitor changes in Active Directory, and there are simple ways to monitor changes in Active Directory. To provide a solution that can be used in almost every enterprise, customized by almost every reader, and extended to other scenarios, I'm keeping it simple.

We'll create a scheduled task that runs at a regular interval. The task will execute a script, the script will look for desktop and laptop objects, and the script will ensure these objects are members of the correct groups. Of course, this is not the most elegant way of doing this—you could do much more if you were a .NET code jockey. But it works.

## Update the membership of the Desktops and Laptops groups

The script adds new desktops and laptops to the appropriate groups. The script is not written to remove computers from those groups, because when you delete the computer object for a desktop or laptop, it is automatically removed from all of its groups. The script adds only computers that are not already members of the correct group, so membership is built incrementally as new computers are detected. This approach helps to minimize the impact of this tool on Active Directory replication.

Of course, the assumption is that you have already created two groups: one for desktops and one for laptops.

## Customize and use Computer_DesktopsLaptops.vbs

Computer_DesktopsLaptops.vbs is located in the Scripts folder of the companion media. You must customize the script to reflect your naming standards, OU design, and groups. This configuration is in the *Configuration Block* of the script, shown here:

```
' CONFIGURATION BLOCK
sDesktopNameMatch = "D*"
sDesktopGroupDN = "CN=CMP_Desktops,OU=Systems, OU=Groups,DC=contoso,DC=com"
sLaptopNameMatch = "L*"
sLaptopGroupDN = "CN=CMP_Laptops,OU=Systems, OU=Groups,DC=contoso,DC=com"
sSearchDN = "ou=clients,dc=contoso,dc=com"
```

*DesktopNameMatch* and *LaptopNameMatch* are criteria used in the script's Lightweight Directory Access Protocol (LDAP) query strings to locate desktops and laptops, respectively, based on their names. The asterisk is, of course, a wildcard. Desktops are added to the group with the distinguished name assigned to *sDesktopGroupDN*, and laptops are added to *sLaptopGroupDN*. The script limits its search to the portion of your domain specified by *sSearchDN*—that scope, and its entire subtree, are searched.

The script can be run from any domain member computer by a user account with permission to change the group membership of the Desktops and Laptops groups. I suggest running it once manually to ensure that it is working properly before configuring it as a recurring scheduled task.

To configure a scheduled task to run the script, use the following schtasks.exe command on a Windows Vista or Windows Server 2008 system:

```
schtasks /create /S ServerName /SC MINUTE /MO 15
    /TN "Update Desktops and Laptops Groups"
    /TR "cscript.exe path\Computer_DesktopLaptops.vbs"
    /RU DOMAIN\username /RP Password
```

Add the switch */V1* to schedule the task on a Windows XP or Windows Server 2003 system. The sample command shows typical switches, which are described in the following list. Enter the command **schtasks /create /?** for detailed help regarding the syntax of schtasks.exe.

S       The server or workstation on which to schedule the task. You must be an administrator of that system to create the scheduled task. If your current credentials are not elevated sufficiently, add the */U username* and */P password* switches to specify your administrative credentials so that the scheduled task can be created successfully.

SC      The basis of the schedule, such as MINUTE, HOURLY, or DAILY. This is the repetition frequency unit, which is further modified by the */MO* switch.

MO      The modifier of the */SC* switch. In the case of a MINUTE schedule basis, values of 1 through 1439 (one minute less than 24 hours) are supported.

*TN*    The friendly task name.

*TR*    The task to run. In this case, we are executing a VBScript with cscript.exe.

*RU*    The name of the user account with which to execute the task. The user must have rights to log on to the computer specified by the */S* switch. Additionally, for this script, the user must have permission to change the membership of the Desktops and Laptops groups.

*RP*    The password for the user account with which to execute the task.

# Deploy software with computer groups

Software deployment is typically managed by assigning software to computers, not users. That approach might seem counterintuitive, so let me explain with a scenario. At Contoso, Microsoft Office Visio 2007 is a managed application, deployed through a software deployment infrastructure such as Microsoft System Center Configuration Manager 2007. James needs Visio. However, Visio is not assigned to James. It is assigned to his computer. That's because it is licensed per machine, and so it should not be installed on every computer to which James logs on.

Therefore, collections used to manage applications are best managed as security groups with computers as members. If you create a group named APP_Visio, for example, your software deployment tools can ensure that each member of the group gets Visio. Add James's computer to the group, and James's computer receives Visio. The mechanisms for doing this are detailed in Solution Collections 9.

Often, application deployment is related to the role a user plays in the enterprise. For example, you might need to deploy your accounting application to all users in the Finance department. In reality, you need to deploy the application to the computers in the Finance department. The group that represents computers playing a finance role is an example of a role group for computers. Create a group such as CMP_Finance—I recommend a prefix such as *CMP* to designate role groups containing only computers. The CMP_Finance group would then be a member of the group managing the accounting application—for example, APP_Office Accounting 2007. Through the nested membership, computers in the finance role would obtain the accounting application.

# Identify and manage other computer roles and capabilities

We've identified desktops, laptops, and applications as likely candidates for computer groups. What other groups might be created to manage computer roles and capabilities?

In many organizations, configuration is driven to users and computers based on their geographic location. Users at a site might be directed to an appropriate proxy server for Internet access, and computers at the site might be configured to use a site-specific DNS suffix search order. Therefore, I recommend that you consider implementing what I call location groups—security groups that represent, document, and manage users and computers based on their location. You might have an OU structure that represents locations to some extent, but typically users and computers are, and should be, in completely separate OUs. Groups allow you to collect both users and computers in a single collection. I suggest a naming convention such as LOC_*location name*—LOC_SYD for the Sydney location group, for example. Again, such groups would contain both users and computers in the location.

Location groups can be manually maintained so that when a user's office is relocated, their user account and computer account are manually moved to a new location group. Or you might leverage attributes of the user object—such as an address attribute or the *Office* attribute—to programmatically maintain group membership.

You should also manage the application of security updates. In a well-designed update infrastructure, certain machines are used to pilot a newly released update so that the organization can validate the update against its environment before proceeding with a broad deployment. There are often machines in an environment that should be exempt from the standard update deployment. For example, an engineering workstation might be regularly used to run lengthy computations that cannot be interrupted by the reboot caused by the installation of an update, so that machine might have a different update schedule or reboot behavior. All of these configurations can be driven through Group Policy. The real question is, how do you manage them? With groups.

Create a group, such as UPD_Pilot, that contains computers used for update testing—ideally, the group should contain a mix of servers and clients that enable a reliable evaluation of new updates—and a group such as UPD_ManualReboot and UPD_UpdateExceptions to contain computers that have various types of exceptions to the standard update deployment configuration. Leverage these groups to filter update-related GPOs, to create computer groups in Windows Server Update Services (WSUS), or to otherwise manage configuration using the update infrastructure in place in your enterprise.

## Solution summary

There are several scenarios that drive organizations to begin managing computers, as well as users. This solution discussed the need to configure settings for desktops that are different from settings for laptops, to deploy applications, to manage software updates, and to manage configuration for computers by geographic locations or departmental functions. Role-based management and groups—they aren't just for users anymore!

# 6-5: Reset and Reassign Computers

## Solution overview

| | |
|---|---|
| **Type of solution** | Guidance |
| **Features and tools** | Computer accounts, group memberships |
| **Solution summary** | Implement best practices throughout the life cycle of a computer account to ensure that security and role assignments are preserved. |
| **Benefits** | Reduced effort and increased success during computer repair, refresh, and replacement. |

## Introduction

Solution 6-4 proposed that computers can and should be members of groups, just like users, so that the capabilities of computers can be managed using a role-based management approach. Because computers will be members of increasing numbers of groups in your enterprise, it is dangerous to delete a computer account because you lose its group memberships. Unfortunately, that's just what happens when you move a computer from the domain to a workgroup, and then rejoin the domain. Removing the computer usually results in the computer account being deleted. When you rejoin the domain, even though the computer has the same name, the account has a new SID, and all the group memberships of the previous computer object must be re-created. In addition, it is possible (though not common) that the computer might have been assigned permissions to a resource directly. The new SID will not match the SID of the previous computer in such ACLs, and so access levels will not be correct. This solution provides the best practices for managing computer accounts throughout their lifespan.

 **Important** Far too many IT professionals have grown accustomed to removing a machine from a domain and placing it into a workgroup. Be sure to train your team to follow the procedures in this solution.

## Rejoin a domain without destroying a computer's group memberships

You have probably had the occasion to remove a machine from the domain, put it into a workgroup, and then rejoin the domain. There are scenarios that warrant such an action—scenarios that are beyond the scope of this book. The point is how to do it correctly, without destroying the SID and group memberships of the computer object in Active Directory. When you go to the System properties of a computer and change the membership of the computer to a workgroup, Windows attempts to delete the computer account in Active Directory. Just say no!

To rejoin a domain correctly, follow these steps:

1.  Open the Active Directory Users and Computers snap-in and locate the computer object.

2.  Right-click the computer object and choose Reset Account.

    Reset Account is to a computer what Reset Password is to a user. It prepares the computer account to receive a new password and effectively frees the account from its association with the actual computer.

3.  On the computer that needs to be rejoined, change the machine's membership to a workgroup.

4.  When prompted for credentials, enter incorrect credentials. I recommend entering a username that does not exist (so that you don't lock out a real user) or just entering blank credentials. You might be prompted to do so several times—just continue to enter incorrect credentials.

    The purpose of this step is to prevent the computer object from being deleted. You can also achieve the same result by disconnecting the computer from the network entirely before joining the workgroup. This step should not be necessary, because if the account has been reset, it should not be deleted. However, I am overly cautious at this step, so I recommend you be the same.

5.  Restart the machine as prompted.

6.  Make sure the machine is connected to the network, and join the domain using the domain's FQDN—for example, contoso.com, not just contoso.

    Using the FQDN is a best practice explained in Solution 6-1.

The computer will locate the computer account that is in Active Directory and has been reset. Then the computer will configure a new password and assume the SID of the computer object—the same SID as it had before. All group memberships are maintained.

 **Important**    When rejoining a domain, always reset the computer account in Active Directory, and do not allow the computer to delete its own computer object.

## Replace a computer correctly by resetting and renaming the computer object

Another event in the lifespan of a computer is the loss, theft, or corruption of a computer that results in the computer's replacement. When a computer is replaced entirely, and the new computer will play the same role, for the same user, you should allow the new computer to adopt the account previously held by the previous computer. That way, the computer's SID, group memberships, and other attributes remain intact.

You will certainly need to reset the computer account of the previous computer. Locate the object in Active Directory, right-click, and choose Reset Account. As explained in the previous solution, this process frees the account to be used by the new computer. If the new computer has the same name as the previous system, it will join the domain using that account.

However, if you followed my earlier recommendations regarding the computer name, the new computer will not have the same name: It will have a new name because the asset tag or serial number of the machine is new. The new computer would not join the account that has the old computer's name. Therefore, you must also rename the computer account. This is not a task that is exposed within the Active Directory Users and Computers snap-in. You must use a script to rename a computer account.

### Use Computer_Rename.hta

Computer_Rename.hta, found in the Scripts folder of the companion media, renames a computer object—there are several names that have to be changed. The script is written so that it can be used as a stand-alone tool that will prompt for the old and new computer names, or as a task or context menu item. See Solutions 1-3 and 6-7 for guidance for integrating Computer_Rename.hta into the Active Directory Users and Computers snap-in.

## Replace a computer by copying group memberships and attributes

Another replacement scenario occurs when you replace a user's existing computer with a new system—not because the previous system was lost or stolen, just because it's time to give the user a new computer. The challenge in this scenario is that it is likely that both computers will be online at the same time while you migrate applications and data. If this is the case, the computers need unique computer accounts.

In this scenario, you should ensure that all important attributes of the old computer account are copied to the new one. These attributes would certainly include group memberships, but they also might include attributes such as the custom *ComputerAssignedTo* attribute created in Solution 6-7 on page 454. The following command line can be used to copy group memberships from one account to another:

```
dsget computer ComputerADN –memberof | dsmod group –addmbr ComputerBDN
```

The *Dsget* command retrieves the memberships of the computer with the distinguished name indicated by *ComputerADN*. The output of *Dsget* is a list of distinguished names of the computer's group memberships. That output is piped to the *Dsmod* command, which for each group adds the computer specified by *ComputerBDN*—also a distinguished name.

## Solution summary

Because computer objects are becoming increasingly managed—with more populated attributes, with group memberships, and perhaps even with permissions assigned directly to the computer—it is unwise to delete a computer object. If you are required to move a computer into a workgroup and then to rejoin the domain, reset the computer account first, and enter blank credentials when prompted for domain credentials while moving the computer into a workgroup. If a computer is lost, stolen, or otherwise directly replaced, reset the computer account and rename it to match the name of the new computer, if necessary. And if a computer's role is being migrated to a new system, be sure to copy group memberships and any other important attributes to the new computer object.

# 6-6: Establish the Relationship Between Users and Their Computers with Built-in Properties

## Solution overview

| | |
|---|---|
| **Type of solution** | Guidance |
| **Features and tools** | Computer object *manager* and *managedBy* attributes |
| **Solution summary** | Use the *manager* and *managedBy* attributes to associate a computer with the user to whom it is assigned. |
| **Benefits** | Increased understanding of asset utilization. |

## Introduction

One of the most common complaints I hear regarding Active Directory is the lack of support within Active Directory to relate a user to the computer or computers that she has been assigned. Administrators are often required to know the relationship between computers and users—that is, which computers are assigned to a specific user, or which users are assigned a specific computer. This is one of the most fundamental requirements of asset management. It is also one of the first questions asked of any user who calls the help desk: "What is your computer name?" In this solution, I provide several options for keeping track of who has been assigned a specific computer. Because there is no single, obvious answer, you should examine each option and its advantages and disadvantages. You should also consider the tools I provide in the next two solutions for tracking to whom a computer is assigned and who is currently logged on to a system, which might or might not be the user who was originally assigned the computer. With the tools and guidance in this and the next two solutions, you should be able to identify the answers you need in these situations.

There are two properties of computer objects that can be used to support tracking the assignment of a computer to a user: *manager* and *managedBy*. Each has its advantages and disadvantages.

## Use the *managedBy* attribute to track asset assignment of a computer to a single user or group

You might have seen the *managedBy* attribute in the Managed By tab of a computer object's Properties dialog box, as illustrated in Figure 6-6.

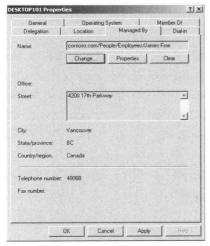

**Figure 4-6**   A computer's Managed By tab, exposing its *managedBy* attribute and the properties of the object the attribute refers to

Click the Change button to select a user, and the contact information of that user's object is automatically displayed on the Managed By tab. The information is linked dynamically—if you change the user's contact information, it will automatically change on the computer's Managed By tab. You can therefore use the *managedBy* attribute as a way to link the computer to the user to whom it is assigned.

You could also link the computer to a group. It might be that several users share the system. Or you might use the *managedBy* attribute to specify a support organization responsible for the computer. However, there is a trick. When you click the Change button, the dialog box that appears enables you to search for users only, by default. Click the Object Types button and then select the Groups check box to indicate that you want to include groups in your search. Additionally, group objects do not have contact information, so no contact information is displayed on the Managed By tab.

# Use the *manager* attribute to track asset assignment of computers to a user

The *manager* attribute is even more interesting. You've probably seen the *manager* attribute of a user object—it appears on the Organization tab. When you specify a user's manager and then open the properties of the manager, you see the user listed as a direct report. That's because *manager* is a special type of Active Directory property called a forward link, and *directReports* is a type of property called a back link. Windows calculates and updates the back link (*directReports*) automatically based on other objects' forward link (*manager*) attributes.

Few people know that computer objects also have a *manager* attribute. That's because Microsoft doesn't expose the *manager* attribute in the user interface. The tool Computer_Manager.hta, which you can find in the Scripts folder of the companion media, allows you to assign the *manager* attribute of a computer. Although you can open the HTA directly, I recommend that you create a taskpad task for computer objects that launches the HTA. The steps for creating a taskpad and a task that launches an HTA are in Solution 6-7. Computer_Manager.hta is shown in Figure 6-7, where I have assigned DESKTOP101 to James Fine.  Enter the pre–Windows 2000 logon name (*sAMAccountName* attribute) of the new manager.

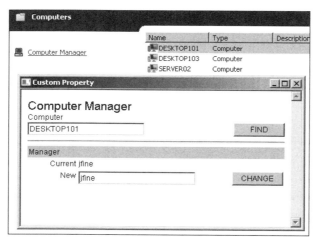

**Figure 4-7**    Computer_Manager.hta

If we now open the properties of the user James Fine and click the Organization tab, we see DESKTOP101 listed in the direct reports section, as shown in Figure 6-8. James has also been assigned LAPTOP324. This demonstrates the fact that although each computer can have only one manager, the manager can have many direct reports.

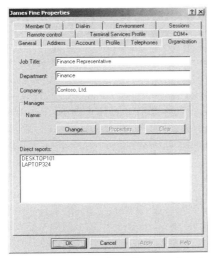

Figure 4-8    The Direct Reports list showing the computers assigned to James Fine

## Solution summary

The *manager* property supports a one-to-many relationship between users and computers. You can assign one or more computers to a single user, and identify those computers in the user's Direct Reports section. Unfortunately, the *manager* attribute does not appear in the user interface of computer objects, so you must extend your toolset with custom scripts to enter and retrieve the *manager* property of the computer. The property does not allow you to assign one computer to multiple users.

The *managedBy* attribute, on the other hand, appears in the Properties dialog box of computer objects and even shows contact information for the user. However, it does not create a back link to the user object, so there is no true relationship between objects—just a pointer from the computer to a user. The property is a one-to-one pointer: The computer cannot have multiple users as its *managedBy* property.

In the next solution, I explain how to extend the schema to support true, many-to-many assignments of computers to users.

# 6-7: Track Computer-to-User Assignments by Extending the Schema

## Solution overview

| | |
|---|---|
| **Type of solution** | Script and guidance |
| **Features and tools** | Custom schema attributes and object classes, Computer_AssignTo.hta |
| **Solution summary** | Extend the schema with a custom attribute to associate a computer with one or more users. |
| **Benefits** | Improved system inventory control. |

## Introduction

In the previous solution, I presented two built-in properties that can be used to track the assignment of a computer to a user. Neither solution is perfect, and neither supports assigning one computer to many users. In this solution, I provide guidance and tools to extend the schema with custom attributes and object classes. Doing so allows you to add to Active Directory exactly the data you need to support your business requirements.

## Understand the impact of extending the schema

In the 1990s, every time Microsoft shared information about modifying the registry, the information was preceded with a lengthy warning about just how dangerous it can be to modify your registry. In the early twenty-first century, similar warnings of impending doom accompany any discussion of changing the Active Directory schema. Although it is certainly true that extending the schema is a serious operation that must be undertaken with care, I find that the doomsday forecasts have the effect of petrifying IT professionals to the point that they don't take full advantage of Active Directory. There's no need to be scared—just careful.

The schema is the blueprint for the objects and attributes in Active Directory. It defines attributes, such as the *Description* attribute, by specifying how the attribute is constructed, stored, indexed, and replicated. For example, the schema determines that the *Description* attribute will be a string rather than an integer. The schema also defines object classes—such as users, groups, and computers—and creates relationships between attributes and object classes and between multiple object classes so that, in the end, users, groups, and computers all include the *Description* attribute. Then every instance of an object class that you create—each user, computer, or group, for example—can support the attributes, such as *Description*, that have been specified in the schema.

When you extend the schema, you define attributes or object classes, or create new relationships. The result is that instances of object classes support new capabilities. This is a very good thing—not something to be scared of.

There are only a few major concerns that need to be kept in focus. First, after you have added an object class or attribute to the schema, you cannot delete it. It will always be defined. You can make the new object class or attribute defunct, which prevents it from being used in the future, but you cannot delete it entirely. That means that if you are careless and create attributes or object classes that you don't really need, the definitions of those changes cannot be entirely removed from Active Directory. As long as you plan and test your changes in a lab prior to deploying them in production, you should be fine.

Second, you must be careful that your extensions to the schema do not conflict with the extensions you later introduce into the schema. When you add an Active Directory–aware application to your portfolio, it generally extends the schema. If it adds attributes or object classes that conflict with yours, you will have a problem—the application will fail to install. Therefore, there are strict guidelines to ensure that application developers don't bump into each other in the schema: Each attribute and object class has a unique identifier and name. As long as you follow the rules, you should be safe.

Third, because of the first two concerns, Microsoft has done a great job of both scaring the heck out of most administrators and locking the schema down like Fort Knox. The result is that the ability to write to the schema is highly restricted. Therefore, most organizations are reluctant—perhaps too reluctant—to extend the schema. Political inertia and fear might be the biggest obstacles to attaining the functionality you desire from Active Directory.

With all that said, my recommendation is to thoughtfully extend the schema to meet your business requirements. Read up on the schema so that you are comfortable with the issues related to doing so. Plan your changes. Test them in a lab. Then deploy confidently.

To learn more about the schema, see *http://technet2.microsoft.com/windowsserver/en/library/ 160ffb83-bbbd-4a56-aec0-7c495866c45f1033.mspx?mfr=true.*

# Plan the *ComputerAssignedTo* attribute and *ComputerInfo* object class

In this solution, I guide you through the steps to create a new attribute that supports linking users and computers to track the assignment of one or more computers to one or more users. The attribute is called *ComputerAssignedTo*, although you can certainly change the name if you'd prefer another name. The attribute is neither a string nor an integer—it is a type of attribute called *DistinguishedName*, which accepts valid distinguished names (DNs). So you enter the DN of a user to assign the computer to that user. The attribute is multivalued so that a computer can be assigned to more than one user.

Although we could add the *ComputerAssignedTo* attribute to the existing object class for computers, it is a best practice not to change the attributes of existing object classes. Rather, we need to create a new object class, which I call *ComputerInfo*, assign the attribute to that object class, and then associate the new object class (*ComputerInfo*) with the existing object class (*Computer*) so that the existing object class inherits the attributes of the new object class. If that doesn't seem quite clear yet, you'll understand it perfectly after you've stepped through the process in a lab environment.

# Obtain an OID

Each attribute and object class requires a unique identifier—a long numeric identifier. The identifier is called a schema globally unique identifier (schemaGUID) or object identifier (OID). It used to be that you would contact Microsoft to obtain a valid OID. Now you can generate your own using a script, OIDGen.vbs, provided on the Microsoft Web site. Find OID-Gen.vbs at *http://www.microsoft.com/technet/scriptcenter/scripts/ad/domains/addmvb03.mspx?mfr=true*. Copy and paste the script into Notepad, and save it as "OID-Gen.vbs." Be sure to include quotes so that Notepad doesn't add a .txt extension. I've also included OIDGen.vbs on the companion media.

The script generates a unique root OID, which is very, very long.

You won't want to have to write it down, so dump the output of the script to a text file using the following command, run from the command prompt:

```
cscript oidgen.vbs >oidinfo.txt
```

For example, I ran the script once and obtained the following OID:

1.2.840.113556.1.8000.2554.56948.10142.18417.18856.35303.3760594.9317226

You can then open the text file, oidinfo.txt, which contains your OID and some explanatory information.

Each time you run OIDGen.vbs, you will obtain a different result—and although theoretically you could use any or all resulting OIDs in your schema extensions, you should follow convention and use one root OID for all changes to the schema.

I say "root OID" because OIDs are hierarchical, very much like DNS. Theoretically, an organization must register its OID, but that is not necessary because you are creating an OID that is a child of Microsoft's own OID: 1.2.840.113556.1.8000.2554. The script creates a GUID (which is unique) and appends it to Microsoft's OID so that a unique OID can be provided to your organization. Your organization can then use a subset of this OID space for your schema modifications. The best practice is to create a subset of your root OID for attributes and another for object classes. For example, I might use 1.2.840.113556.1.8000.2554. … .9317226.1 for object classes, with the first object class being 1.2.840.113556.1.8000.2554. … .9317226.1.1. Then, I might use 1.2.840.113556.1.8000.2554. … .9317226. … .2 for attributes—in which case, the first attribute I create will have 1.2.840.113556.1.8000.2554. … .9317226. … 2.1 as its OID, and the second will be 1.2.840.113556.1.8000.2554. … .9317226.2.2.

# Register the Active Directory schema snap-in

After you've obtained your root OID, you are ready to dive into the schema, which is done by opening the Active Directory Schema snap-in. This snap-in is available if you've installed the administrative tools (available with Windows XP, Windows Server 2003, and Windows Server

2008) or remote server administration tools (available with Windows Vista or Windows Server 2008), but the .dll might not be registered. Open a command prompt and enter the following command:

```
regsvr32 schmmgmt.dll
```

Then create a custom MMC console by clicking Start, selecting Run, and typing **mmc.exe** into the Open text box and clicking OK. Then add the Active Directory Schema snap-in to the console.

## Make sure you have permission to change the schema

Only members of the Schema Admins group have permission to change the schema. If you're not sure whether you are a member of Schema Admins, open a command prompt and enter the command **whoami /groups**. If you are not a member of Schema Admins, add your user account to the Schema Admins group. You will, of course, have to log off and log on again for the change to be incorporated into your access token.

## Connect to the schema master

When you open the Active Directory schema, the changes you make are written to the directory by the schema master. One and only one domain controller acts as the schema master, ensuring that there is no potential for conflicting changes to be made to the schema on two different domain controllers. You need to connect to the Schema Operations Master. The Windows Server 2008 Schema Management snap-in makes it easy. Select and then right-click Active Directory Schema. Then choose Connect To Schema Operations Master.

In earlier versions of the snap-in, you must first identify the operations master. Right-click the root node of the snap-in, Active Directory Schema, and choose Operations Master. Make a note of the schema master, as you will connect to that domain controller. Close out of the Operations Master dialog box, right-click Active Directory Schema again, and choose Connect To Domain Controller. Select the schema master, and connect to it.

The schema might be write protected, even on the schema master. If you find that you cannot create a new attribute in the next section, see the Help file for the Active Directory Schema snap-in for directions for write-enabling the schema.

## Create the *ComputerAssignedTo* attribute

To create the *ComputerAssignedTo* attribute, perform the following steps:

1. Expand the Active Directory Schema snap-in and select the Attributes node.
2. Right-click Attributes and choose Create Attribute.

A warning appears to strike fear in your heart about the fact that schema changes cannot be removed. Be sure that you have read the preceding section so that you understand the impact of changing the schema.

3.  Click Continue.

    The Create New Attribute dialog box appears.

    The Common Name and LDAP Display Name attributes must be unique in your forest's schema. It is very important that the names do not conflict with an attribute that you add later. Therefore, the best practice is to create the name with a prefix based on your company or domain name, followed by a hyphen, followed by the name of the attribute. For example, if my company is Contoso, Ltd., my attribute can be named contoso-ComputerAssignedTo or contosocom-ComputerAssignedTo. Your goal is a unique prefix—if your company has a name that is not unique in the world, add your domain DNS suffix— for example, *contosocom*. The prefix should be all lowercase, with no dots, spaces, or other punctuation. The prefix should be separated from the name using a hyphen. The name, too, should contain no spaces or other punctuation. Keep it simple and unique.

4.  Enter the Common Name in the form *domain*-ComputerAssignedTo—for example, contoso-ComputerAssignedTo.

5.  Enter the same name in the LDAP Display Name box—for example, contoso-ComputerAssignedTo.

    The Windows Server 2008 Schema Management snap-in automatically populates the LDAP Display Name box but removes the hyphen. That is perfectly fine, as well. The goal is a unique name.

6.  In the Unique X.500 Object ID box, enter the OID for the attribute, based on the root OID you obtained earlier using OIDGen.vbs.

    Remember that the OID you obtained is a root ID. You should append identifiers to ensure your OIDs are unique. I recommend you add a .1 for object classes and a .2 for attributes. So this first new attribute should be your OID plus .2.1—for example: 1.2.840.113556.1.8000.2554.....9317226.2.1.

7.  For the Description, enter **Computer-Assigned-To**.

8.  From the Syntax list, choose Distinguished Name.

9.  Select the Multi-Valued check box.

    The result should look similar to Figure 6-9.

> **Important**   Because you cannot delete an attribute after it has been created, look carefully to confirm that you have configured all settings correctly.

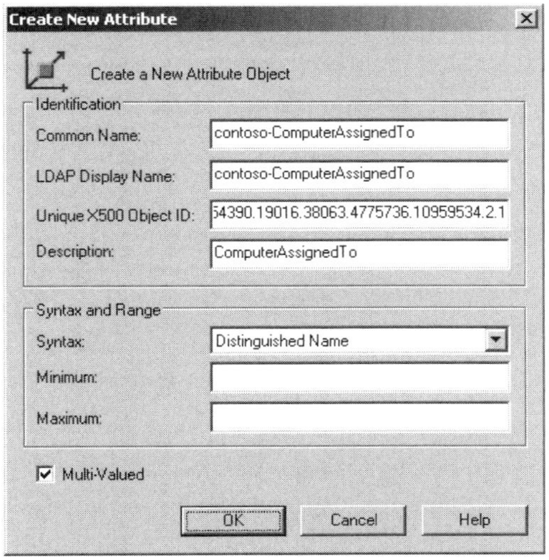

**Figure 4-9**   Creating the *ComputerAssignedTo* attribute

10.   Click OK.

   After creating the attribute, make sure that it can be used for searches.

11.   Refresh your view of the Attributes container. If you do not see the new attribute, right-click Active Directory Schema in the tree pane and choose Reload Schema.

12.   Double-click the attribute to open its properties.

13.   Select the Index This Attribute check box (in the Windows Server 2008 snap-in) or the Allow This Attribute To Be Shown In Advanced View check box (in the Windows Server 2003 snap-in).

   This enables you to perform searches based on the attribute.

14.   If necessary, select the Attribute Is Active check box.

15.   Select the Replicate This Attribute To The Global Catalog check box.

   The attribute will be replicated to the global catalog, making searches even more efficient.

16.   In Windows Server 2003, also select the Allow This Attribute To Be Shown In Advanced View check box.

17.   Click OK.

## Create the *ComputerInfo* object class

Next, create an object class to host this and other custom attributes for computers.

1.   In the Active Directory Schema snap-in, select the Classes node.

2. Right-click Classes and choose Create Class.

3. Click Continue if you are prompted with a message regarding the dangers of schema modification.

4. For the Common Name, enter *domain*-ComputerInfo—for example, contoso-ComputerInfo.

5. In the LDAP Display Name box, enter the same name used in the previous step.

   The Windows Server 2008 Active Directory Schema snap-in removes punctuation such as the hyphen. That is OK as well.

6. In the Unique X.500 Object ID box, enter the OID for the object class, based on the root OID you obtained earlier using OIDGen.vbs.

   Remember that the OID you obtained is a root ID. You should append identifiers to ensure your OIDs are unique. I recommend you add a .1 for object classes and a .2 for attributes. So this first new object class should be your OID plus .1.1—for example: 1.2.840.113556.1.8000.2554.56948.10142.18417.18856.35303.3760594.9317226.1.1.

7. For the Description, enter **Computer-Custom-Information**.

8. From the Class Type drop-down list, choose Auxiliary.

   The result should look similar to Figure 6-10.

> **Important**    Because you cannot delete an object after it has been created, look carefully to confirm that you have configured all settings correctly.

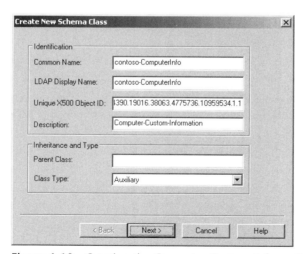

**Figure 4-10**    Creating the *Computer-Custom-Information* object class

9. Click Next.

10. Click the Add button next to the Optional Attributes section.

11. Select the attribute you created in the previous procedure, *domain*-ComputerAssignedTo.

12. Click OK.

13. Click Finish.

14. Refresh your view of the Classes container. If you do not see the new object class, right-click Active Directory Schema in the tree pane and choose Reload Schema.

15. Double-click the new object class to examine its properties.

16. Make sure that the Class Is Active check box is selected.

17. Click OK.

## Associate the *ComputerInfo* object class with the *Computer* object class

You now have a custom object class with a custom attribute, but we want that attribute to be part of the computer objects in our Active Directory. We could have added the *ComputerAssignedTo* attribute directly to the computer object class, but it is a better practice to allow the built-in object class to inherit our new attribute by relating the existing object class to the new object class:

1. In the Active Directory Schema snap-in, select the Classes node.

2. Double-click the Computer object class to open its properties.

3. Click the Relationship tab.

   Object classes in the schema are related. A child object class inherits properties from its parent object classes. An object class can also inherit properties from associated object classes.

4. Click the Add Class button in the Auxiliary Class section.

5. Select *domain*-ComputerInfo.

6. Click OK.

7. Click OK.

## Give the *ComputerAssignedTo* attribute a friendly display name

You will need to perform actions on the new attribute, such as delegate who can modify the attribute. When you go to the Permission Entry dialog box to allow a group the ability to change the attribute, you might want the attribute to appear with a friendly name rather than *domain*-ComputerAssignedTo. Follow these steps:

1. Open the ADSIEdit console.

   This console is available in Windows Server 2008 in the Administrative Tools folder. Windows 2003 includes ADSIEdit.msc in the Support Tools, which can be installed from the Support folder of the Windows Server 2003 CD.

2. Expand the Configuration node.

   If you do not see the Configuration node, right-click the root of the snap-in, ADSIEdit, and choose Connect To. In the Select A Well Known Naming Context drop-down list, select the Configuration container. Click OK.

3. Expand the Configuration container and the Display Specifiers node.

4. In the console tree, select CN=409, which contains the display specifiers for English.

   If you are using a non-English installation of Windows, you need to open the display specifier for your language. See *http://msdn2.microsoft.com/en-us/library/ms776294.aspx* for more information.

5. Double-click CN=Computer-Display to open its properties.

6. Double-click attributeDisplayNames.

7. In the Value To Add box, type ***attributeName, displayName***—where *attributeName* is the name of your custom attribute and *displayName* is a friendly name for the attribute. In our example, the value for *attributeDisplayName* is contoso-ComputerAssignedTo,Computer Assigned To.

8. Click Add.

9. Click OK.

10. Click OK to close the Properties dialog box for CN=computer-Display.

## Allow the changes to replicate

The new class and attribute need to replicate, which could take quite some time in your domain. If you are testing this procedure on a single domain controller in a test environment, you can reboot the domain controller. In a production environment, you should just wait until the attribute becomes visible in the ACL editor as described in step 12 in the procedure shown in the next section.

## Delegate permission to modify the attribute

You can delegate permission to modify the new attribute just as you would delegate any other activity in Active Directory. The most direct path to delegation is to open the ACL editor of an OU and assign permissions. Follow these steps:

1.  Close the Active Directory Users and Computers snap-in if it has been open while you were making the changes described previously. The snap-in will see the new property, assuming that the schema has replicated, when the snap-in is reopened.

2.  Open the Active Directory Users and Computers snap-in.

3.  Click the View menu and make sure that Advanced Features is selected.

4.  Right-click an OU containing computers and choose Properties.

5.  Click the Security tab.

6.  Click Advanced.

7.  If the Add button is not visible, click Edit.

8.  Click Add.

9.  Select the group that you want to give permission to modify the attribute. Click OK.

10. In the Permission Entry dialog box, click the Properties tab.

11. In the Apply To drop-down list, select Computer Objects (for Windows Server 2003) or Descendant Computer Objects (for Windows Server 2008).

12. In the Property list, select the Allow check boxes next to Read Computer Assigned To and Write Computer Assigned To.

13. Click OK three times to close the security interfaces.

## Integrate the Computer_AssignTo.hta tool with Active Directory Users and Computers

Congratulations! You've just finished extending the schema, and computer objects now support the *ComputerAssignedTo* attribute! Unfortunately—and you might have already discovered this yourself if you poked around—that attribute still doesn't appear anywhere. Just because an object has an attribute does not mean that the Active Directory Users and Computers snap-in exposes that attribute. You would have to do some serious coding to add a tab to the Properties dialog box of computer objects in the Active Directory Users and Computers snap-in.

The Active Directory Users and Computers snap-in included with Windows Server 2008 does add the Attribute Editor tab. This tab is visible when Advanced Features are selected in the View menu, and it shows a raw view of all attributes of an object. In Figure 6-11 you can see the *contoso-ComputerAssignedTo* attribute of a computer object.

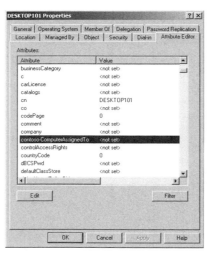

**Figure 4-11**   The Attribute Editor tab of a computer object showing the *contosoComputerAssignedTo* attribute

Instead of doing any heavy coding, you can use Computer_AssignTo.hta, an HTA written specifically to allow you to assign computers to users. If you open the HTA directly, a form appears (shown in Figure 6-12) on which you can enter a computer name and the logon names of the users to whom the computer is assigned.

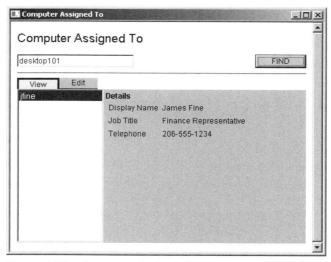

**Figure 4-12**   Computer_AssignTo.hta

To make this tool more useable, you must customize it. Then you can integrate it directly into Active Directory as a task or a context menu selection.

## Customize Comptuer_AssignTo.hta

Computer_AssignTo.hta provides a text box into which a computer name can be entered. The tool then retrieves the values in the *ComputerAssignedTo* attribute, translates those user names into a list of pre–Windows 2000 logon names (the *sAMAccountName* attribute). On the View tab, you can see the current assignments. When you select a user, some of the user's details are displayed. On the Edit tab, you can modify the list—one user per line, indicated by the user's pre–Windows 2000 Logon Name (*sAMAccountName* attribute)—and then click Update, and the tool updates the *ComputerAssignedTo* attribute.

The only modifications that must be made to the tool are in the *ConfigurationBlock*. Be certain to identify the name you assigned to your custom attribute. If you want to see other details of users in the Details section of the View tab, change the *lstResults_OnChange* routine.

## Create a task for computer assignment

Tasks and taskpads were introduced in Solution Collection 1, "Role-Based Management." The following steps create a taskpad for an OU of computers, with a task that launches Computer_AssignTo.hta for a selected computer. If you already have a taskpad, you can skip these steps:

1. Open a custom console with the Active Directory Users and Computers snap-in, or create a new console with the snap-in. To create a new console, follow these steps:

   a. Click Start and choose the Run command (Windows XP), or click in the Search box (Windows Vista/Windows Server 2008) type **mmc.exe**, and then press Enter.

   b. An empty MMC console appears. Choose File, choose Add/Remove Snap-In, and add the Active Directory Users and Computers snap-in.

   c. Save the console by choosing File and then choosing Save. You should save it in the network share where the HTA is located, or in some other shared folder that is easily accessed by administrators.

2. Expand the console tree of the console to an OU that contains computers.

3. Right-click the OU, and choose New Taskpad View.

4. The New Taskpad View Wizard appears. Click Next.

5. On the Taskpad Style page, accept all defaults and click Next.

6. On the Taskpad Reuse page, select Selected Tree Item and click Next.

7. On the Name And Description page, accept the defaults—although you can change the name and description if you want to—and click Next.

8. On the Completing page, be sure the check box is selected and click Finish.

You have actually finished creating the taskpad, and a second wizard launches to help you create the task on the taskpad.

You now create the task on the taskpad. If you are changing an existing taskpad, right-click the OU and choose Edit Taskpad View, click the Tasks tab, and click the New button.

1. The New Task Wizard appears. Click Next.
2. On the Command Type page, choose Shell Command and click Next.
3. In the Command box, type **mshta.exe**.
4. In the Parameters box, type "*Path to the HTA*\Computer_AssignTo.hta".

    If you are saving the tool in a shared folder, use the FQDN of the server—for example: **\\server01.contoso.com\admintools\computer_assignto.hta**. But to reduce security prompts when running the HTA, I recommend distributing the HTA to administrators by copying it into a custom folder—for example, C:\Program Files\*Company* Tools.

5. After the path to the HTA, type a space.
6. With the cursor positioned after the space, click the arrow, which is a browse button.
7. Select Name.
8. The Parameters box should look like this:

    ```
    "Path to the HTA\Computer_AssignTo.hta" $COL<0>
    ```

9. In the Start In box, type the path to the folder in which the HTA is stored.
10. Click Next.
11. On the Name And Description page, in the Task Name box, type **Computer Assignments**. Optionally, enter a description, such as "Show or change the users to whom this computer is assigned."
12. Click Next.
13. On the Task Icon page, select an icon.

    If you click Custom Icon, you can browse to find an icon that is part of an executable or from one of the icon libraries—such as C:\Windows\System32\Shell32.dll, or in Windows Vista and Windows Server 2003, C:\Windows\System32\Imageres.dll.

14. Click Next.
15. Click Finish.

The task will now be visible when you select a computer object in the OU.

 **Important**   Tasks will not appear until you select an object in the details pane.

### Add computer assignments to the context menu

Solution 1-3 on page 35 details the process of adding a custom command to the context menu, including the permissions required to do so. To add Computer_AssignTo.hta to the context menu, use AdminContextMenu.hta, found in the Scripts folder.

Open AdminContextMenu.hta and fill in the following:

**Language**    Select from the drop-down list. The HTA is coded to support a limited number of languages. You can extend the HTA to include more.

**Object Class**    Select Computer.

**Menu Command**    Enter the command you want to appear on the context menu—for example, **Computer Assignments . . .**

**Command Line**    The path to Computer_AssignTo.hta.

Then click Add To Administrator Context Menu. The change is made for you. If you received an Access Denied error, see Solution 1-3. You need to close and reopen any instance of the Active Directory Users and Computers snap-in before your change will be visible.

## Add other attributes to computer objects

What other attributes would you like to keep track of regarding the computers in your environment? You can use what you learned in this solution to add other attributes to computers—just create additional custom attributes and add them to the *ComputerInfo* object class. In the next solution, I use the computer's *description* and *comment* attributes to keep track of the computer's location and the users who have logged on to the computer. You could easily add custom attributes to support those bits of information and more. Solution Collection 7, "Extending User Attributes and Management Tools," continues the exploration of schema extension.

## Solution summary

This solution introduced the concepts and procedures required to extend the Active Directory schema to support your business requirements—in this case, the need to know which user or users have been assigned to a specific computer. By adding a custom attribute and object class, and associating the object class with the *computer* class, you can add attributes such as the *ComputerAssignedTo* property presented in this solution. After you've added a property, you can delegate it using the same steps as you would for default Active Directory attributes. Then you can access the attribute using custom tools such as Computer_AssignedTo.hta.

# 6-8: Establish Self-Reporting of Computer Information

## Solution overview

| | |
|---|---|
| **Type of solution** | Scripts, tools, and guidance |
| **Features and tools** | Computer_InfoToDescription.vbs, Computer_Comment.hta, startup scripts, logon scripts, and scheduled tasks |
| **Solution summary** | Leverage Active Directory to gather, distribute, and expose information about computers, such as their location and the last user who logged on. |
| **Benefits** | Improved visibility of asset location and easier support. |

## Introduction

Enterprises benefit from knowing as much as possible about a computer, including information that changes over time, such as the user who is logged on to a computer. In this solution, I propose a simple and elegant solution for gathering this kind of information. You can create a script that is executed at startup or logon and reports what you want to know by changing attributes of the computer object in Active Directory. For example, the computer can report the user who last logged on and the computer's Active Directory site by changing its *Description* attribute. That way, when you look at the computer in the Active Directory Users and Computers snap-in, you can immediately see where the computer is located and who is using it. Although Systems Management Server (SMS) and Configuration Manager 2007 are the best tools for inventorying and querying your computers, you might not have those tools. And even if you do, you might decide you want certain information instantly accessible within the Active Directory Users and Computers snap-in.

## Determine the information you wish you had

Give some thought to the types of information you wish you had at your fingertips—information that would make supporting computers easier. In this solution, I will use the following examples:

- The last (or current) user to log on to a system
- The site in which the system was last used

These two pieces of information make it easier to locate a computer that might be lost, and to support a computer—it's always good to know where the computer is and who is using it! You can certainly extend this list to gather other information from a computer. Keep in mind that some information, such as the computer's current IP address, can be found in other data stores—such as DNS, assuming you have enabled dynamic DNS for your clients.

# Decide where you want the information to appear

The information you identify for reporting will be pushed into attributes of the computer object in Active Directory. Computers have a number of attributes that are underutilized, including *description* and *comment*. The *description* attribute is advantageous because it is visible in the results pane of the Active Directory Users and Computers snap-in. Other attributes are less easy to access without a custom tool, but we will introduce just such a tool—Computer_Comment.hta—later in this solution.

For the sake of brevity in this solution, we'll focus on the *description* attribute, which is highly visible and accessible, and the *comment* attribute, which is not. With those two attributes at opposite ends of the usability spectrum, you'll learn the concepts and tricks you need. In Solution Collection 7, I discuss how to extend Active Directory using unused, underutilized, and custom attributes. Refer to that Solution Collection for more information.

# Report computer information with Computer_InfoToDescription.vbs

On the companion media, you'll find Computer_InfoToDescription.vbs. It's a powerful script not only because it helps you identify where a computer is located and who is using it, but also because it opens the door to system reporting and inventorying capabilities using Active Directory.

Copy the file to your system, and change the distinguished name of the domain in the *Configuration Block* to be appropriate for your domain. You can then run the script by double-clicking the script .vbs file or by entering this command:

```
cscript <path>\Computer_InfoToDescription.vbs
```

You'll find that the *description* and *comment* attributes of your computer object have been updated. If not, there's a delegation problem that I'll address later in this solution. So that you can see where we are going with this script, we'll execute the script as a startup or logon script so that the information is constantly up to date.

# Understand Computer_InfoToDescription.vbs

The script uses the *ADSystemInfo* object to determine the site in which the computer is located. It then calls two routines, *GetComputerName* and *GetLastUserLoggedOn*, to determine the computer name and the name of the last user to log on. These two functions are not shown in the preceding code block, but they are included in the script on the companion media. The *GetLastUserLoggedOn* routine queries the *DefaultUserName* value of the *Winlogon* key in the registry. This value is updated each time a user logs on interactively to the computer. So it represents the last user who logged on to the system. I use that method because I prefer to deploy this script as a startup script, and during startup, there is no user logged on to the system. In fairly static environments, the last user to log on is probably the same as the next user who will log on, so that information is good enough. Later in this solution, I describe how to report the currently logged-on user.

After all the information has been gathered, the script creates the value for the *description* attribute and stores it in the variable *sDescription*. You can customize that line of code if you want to format the information differently or include other information. Next, the script locates the computer's object in Active Directory using the *ADObject_Find_UCG* function, also not shown in the code block presented earlier. It updates the *description* attribute.

The next lines of the script are interesting and should serve as food for thought. I'd like to keep track of several recent logons for each computer. The script therefore uses the *comment* attribute as a kind of log field. The new information, stored in *sDescription*, is appended to the current value of the *comment* attribute. To prevent the *comment* attribute from getting too long, I pick an arbitrary length (255 characters), and if the current attribute is longer than that, I remove the first (oldest) entry in that field.

## Expose the report attributes in the Active Directory Users and Computers snap-in

After the computers in your environment begin to report information to their Active Directory attributes, you need to be able to locate the information in the Active Directory Users and Computers snap-in. The *description* attribute is simple enough—it's visible by default in the details pane of the snap-in; if it is not visible, you can add the column using the Add/Remove Columns command in the View menu.

The *comment* attribute is trickier. It is not visible in the user interface of the snap-in, so you need a tool to see and edit the attribute. Computer_Comment.hta is just the tool. This HTA is ready to use. Just open it up, and you'll be able to start viewing and editing the *comment* attribute of computer objects. You can then add the tool as a task in an MMC taskpad or as a right-click menu command.

## Delegate permissions for computer information reporting

Before you can deploy the Computer_InfoToDescription.vbs script, you need to delegate permissions so that the attributes you use—for example, *description* and *comment*—can be successfully changed. You must delegate the ability to read and write each property.

There's one problem. The *comment* attribute is not visible in the ACL editor interfaces of the Active Directory Users and Computers snap-in. You cannot see the *comment* attribute in the security dialog boxes to delegate permission to that attribute.

If you're not familiar with this problem, follow these steps to see it for yourself:

1. Open the Active Directory Users and Computers snap-in.
2. Make sure Advanced Features is selected in the View menu.
3. Open the properties of a computer object.
4. Click the Security tab, and then click the Advanced button.

5. Select any ACE in the Permissions List, and click Edit to open the Permission Entry dialog box.

   You might need to click Edit a second time if user account control (UAC) is enabled.

6. In the Permission Entry dialog box, click the Properties tab.

You will see lots of properties there, including *description*, but you will not see *comment*.

In Solution 5-3 on page 380, I discussed the DSSec.dat file, which determines which properties are and are not visible in the ACL editor. To enable the *comment* attribute to be visible, follow these steps:

1. Locate DSSec.dat in the Windows\System32 folder.

   You must change DSSec.dat on the computer that you use to manage and delegate Active Directory.

2. On Windows Vista and Windows Server 2008, DSSec.dat is protected. You must take ownership of the file and ensure you are allowed a minimum of Write permission to the file.

3. Open DSSec.dat with Notepad.

4. Search for the text **[computer]**. Be sure to include the brackets.

5. Within the *[computer]* section, find the line *comment=7*.

   If a property is listed and set to 7, it is hidden from the ACL editor interfaces for that class of object.

6. Change the 7 to a 0 (zero).

7. Save and close the file.

You need to close and reopen any instance of the Active Directory Users and Computers snap-in for the change to take effect. You can then follow the procedure at the beginning of this section to verify that *comment* is now visible in the Permission Entry dialog box. See Solution 5-3 for more details.

You will delegate Read and Write permissions for the attributes you are using for information reporting: *description* and *comment*. The security principal to whom you delegate permission depends on whether you choose to run the script at startup or at logon.

If the script runs at startup, it runs under the context of the System account. When the script attempts to make a change to Active Directory, it uses the credentials of the computer account itself. Therefore, the computer must have permission to change its own *description* and *comment* attributes. There is a special identity you use for just this purpose: Self. If you delegate the ability to change a property of an Active Directory object to Self, the computer or user can modify its own property but not the properties of any other object. It is the ultimate example of least privilege.

To delegate permission to Self to change the *description* and *comment* attributes, follow these steps:

1. Open the Active Directory Users and Computers snap-in.

2. Make sure Advanced Features is selected in the View menu.

3. Open the properties of the OU that contains the computers that will be reporting.

4. Click the Security tab, and then click the Advanced button.

5. Click the Add button.

   You might need to click the Edit button before the Add button will appear if user account control (UAC) is enabled.

6. Type **Self**, and click OK.

7. In the Permission Entry dialog box, click the Properties tab.

8. In the Apply To list, select Descendant Computer Objects or Computer Objects.

   The text displayed in the list depends on the version of the Active Directory Users and Computers snap-in.

9. Select the check boxes for Allow Read Comment, Write Comment, Read Description, and Write Description.

10. Click OK three times to close the security dialog boxes.

If you want to deploy the Computer_InfoToDescription.vbs script as a logon script, all users need the ability to modify the reporting attributes, *description* and *comment*. Follow the same procedures just shown, but instead of choosing Self as the security principal, choose a group that represents all users. I recommend Authenticated Users. This is a reasonable approach in many environments, but obviously there's a security exposure when you delegate properties to all users.

# Automate computer information reporting with startup and logon scripts or scheduled tasks

Now you have a script that allows a computer to update its own attributes in Active Directory with useful information, and you have delegated permissions for that to happen. The final step is to actually push the script to computers as a startup script or a logon script. Solution Collection 10 details the steps for deploying startup and logon scripts.

I recommend using a startup script, rather than a logon script, purely for delegation reasons. I am not as comfortable with delegating Authenticated Users the right to change the selected attributes of every computer object as I am with delegating Self the ability to change its own attributes.

There is another approach: scheduled tasks. Scheduled tasks can run under the System account, which would achieve the same effect as a startup script but would run more regularly. It's likely that a computer might not restart often enough to make the information gathered by the script relevant. A scheduled task can run regularly.

## Take it to the next level

I hope this solution has not only provided a great tool, but has also seeded your imagination with the possibilities for system management and particularly for information gathering and reporting without requiring SMS or Configuration Manager 2007.

There's so much more I'd like to share with you, but because of space limitations we'll have to continue this discussion online at the resource kit community site, *http://www.intelliem.com/resourcekit*. Let me summarize two possibilities:

■ In this solution, we used existing attributes of computer objects, *description* and *comment*, to store information gathered from the computer. In Solution 6-7, I detailed how to add new attributes to Active Directory, such as the *ComputerAssignedTo* attribute of a custom *ComputerInfo* object class. If you have added such attributes to your environment, I highly recommend you use the approach we've outlined in this solution to populate them. You can add custom attributes such as *LastLogonRecord*, *CurrentlyLoggedOnUser*, or *CurrentADSite* to the *ComputerInfo* object class. Those attributes are inherited by the *computer* object class, and you can change the Computer_InfoToDescription.vbs script to save its discovery into those attributes.

■ If you use a scheduled task or a logon script, you can use WMI to query for the logged-on user rather than using the *DefaultUser* value of the registry. The resource kit Web site, *http://www.intelliem.com/resourcekit*, has an example.

## Solution summary

This solution suggests a framework with which you can gather valuable information about computers, such as where they are located and the last user who logged on to the system. The framework includes a script, such as Computer_InfoToDescription.vbs, that causes a computer to discover information and report it to attributes of the computer's object in Active Directory. Those attributes must be appropriately delegated to the computer, represented by the special identity Self, or to a group representing the security principals that will run the script. Finally, the script has to be deployed using startup scripts, logon scripts, or scheduled tasks.

# 6-9: Integrate Computer Support Tools into Active Directory Users and Computers

## Solution overview

| | |
|---|---|
| **Type of solution** | Guidance and a custom HTA |
| **Features and tools** | MMC console taskpads, Remote_Command.hta, command-line tools |
| **Solution summary** | Incorporate the tools you need to support computers directly into the Active Directory Users and Computers snap-in. |
| **Benefits** | Increased security, more productive support. |

## Introduction

Throughout this resource kit, I've encouraged you to make more use of the MMC. In this solution, I help you further elevate the sophistication and functionality of your administrative toolset. Often, as IT professionals, we come across great tools, scripts, and utilities that we want to be able to fully leverage. Too often, though, such tools are underutilized. In my own experience, part of the reason is that I find a great utility, download it, try it a few times, and then forget that I even have it. In this solution, we're going to bring those great tools front and center, and integrate them directly into the Active Directory Users and Computers snap-in. This will make the tools easier to use and provide a significant benefit, as they'll be launched with the elevated credentials with which you run the console itself. We will use two examples: Remote Desktop and PSExec.

## Add a "Connect with Remote Desktop" command

IT professionals often need to connect to a system with Remote Desktop to perform support tasks. The MSTSC.exe command allows you to connect with a remote system from the command prompt. Here is its basic syntax:

```
mstsc /v:ServerName [/h:WindowHeight /w:WindowWidth | /full] [/console]
```

The /h and /w switches control the size of the window, or you can use /full to connect with a full-screen view. The two most important switches are /v, which indicates the system to which you will connect, and /console, which connects to the console session (Session 0) on the system. Knowing that command, we can enable the Active Directory Users and Computers snap-in to allow us to connect to a selected computer.

First you must create a taskpad for an OU that includes computer objects. The steps for creating a taskpad are listed in Solution 6-7. You can then create the task on the taskpad. Follow these steps:

1. In the Active Directory Users and Computers snap-in, right-click the OU with the taskpad and choose Edit Taskpad View.

2. Click the Tasks tab, and click the New button.

3. The New Task Wizard appears. Click Next.

4. On the Command Type page, choose Shell Command and click Next.

5. In the Command box, type **mstsc.exe**.

6. Type /**v:** in the Parameters box.

7. With the cursor positioned after the /v: switch, click the arrow, which is a browse button.

8. Select Name.

9. Click Next.

10. On the Name And Description page, in the Task Name box, type **Connect With Remote Desktop**. Optionally, enter a description.

11. Click Next.

12. On the Task Icon page, select an icon.

   If you click Custom Icon, you can browse to find an icon that is part of an executable or from one of the icon libraries—such as C:\Windows\System32\Shell32.dll, or in Windows Vista and Windows Server 2003, C:\Windows\System32\Imageres.dll.

13. Click Next.

14. Click Finish, and then click OK to close the Properties dialog box for the OU.

The task will now be visible when you select a computer object in the OU.

**Important**    Tasks will not appear until you select an object in the details pane.

**Important**    You can use these steps to create a task for any command-line tool that supports remote administration.

## Add an "Open Command Prompt" command

A powerful method for performing support tasks on a remote system is to open a command prompt on the remote system. PSExec allows you to do just that. Use this command:

```
psexec \\computername cmd.exe
```

PSExec must be in the system path (%PATH%—for example, C:\Windows\System32). You can download PSExec.exe from *http://technet.microsoft.com/sysinternals*. If you don't put PSExec in the system path, simply include the correct path to PSExec in the command just shown.

Knowing this trick, you can add a task, using the steps in the previous section. The command (step 5) is **psexec.exe**, including the path to PSExec if it is not in your system path. The parameters (steps 6 through 8) are **\\$COL<0> cmd.exe**, where *$COL<0>* represents the computer name. You can either type **$COL<0>** or use the browse button and select Name.

When you select a computer in the details pane of the MMC, the task will appear. Click the task and a command prompt will open. The command prompt is actually running on the selected computer—any commands you execute will be performed on that system.

## Execute any command remotely on any system

On a number of occasions, I've needed to run a command on a remote system. For example, I have wanted to know the IP configuration of the system. PSExec lets you run any command on a remote computer. In the previous section, we used it to launch a command prompt that would then allow you to execute commands on that system.

In this section, I'd like to introduce you to a great little tool, Remote_Command.hta. This simple HTA, shown in Figure 6-13, is a wrapper around PSExec. Enter a computer name in the Computer box and a command in the Command box, and click Execute. The tool runs the command against the specified computer using PSExec, and it returns the output to the HTA itself.

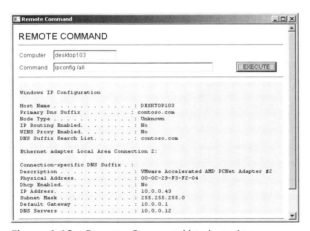

**Figure 4-13**   Remote_Command.hta in action

As with other HTAs in this resource kit, you need to make some changes to the *Configuration Block* before running the tool in your environment.

Use the steps shown earlier for adding commands to add this task to your taskpad. The command (step 5) is **mshta.exe**. The parameters (steps 6 through 8) are **"*path*\Remote_Command.hta" $COL<0>**. When you launch the tool from a taskpad task, the Computer box is automatically populated with the computer you selected in the Active Directory Users and Computers snap-in.

# Use Remote_Command.hta to create specific command tasks for remote administration

Remote_Command.hta is written so that you can create a copy of the tool that performs a single, specific command. For example, I can customize a copy of the tool to run *ipconfig /all* as the command. I can then save this copy as a separate HTA named, for example, Remote_IPCONFIG.hta. I can then create a task that calls this specific HTA. When the HTA is configured with a preset command and launched from a taskpad task, it executes the command on the selected computer with no further action required from the administrator.

 **Important**    If you've been skimming this resource kit, *stop now* and read this section. This tool, Remote_Command.hta, with preset commands, can open up a world of productive options for your day-to-day administration.

To configure Remote_Command.hta with a preset command, change the value of the constant *msCommand* in the *Configuration Block*. You can also change or delete the contents of the value of *msInstructions*—don't delete the entire variable, just set it to blank: **msInstructions = ""**.

If you enter a command in *msCommand*, the command will be run on the remote system using PSExec. Some commands do not require PSExec to run on a remote system. As a simple example, let's assume you want to be able to get a listing of shares on a specific system. That can be done using this command:

```
net view \\computername
```

This command is actually executed on your local computer but remotely touches the specified system. It does not require PSExec. For commands such as this that do not require PSExec, configure the constant *msCommand* with the full command, and use the text **%COMPUTERNAME%** to represent the position in the command where the computer name should be inserted. For example, you could configure *msCommand* as follows:

```
Const msCommand = "cmd.exe /c net view \\%COMPUTERNAME%"
```

Note that I preceded the *net* command with the *cmd.exe /c* command. This is required because the *net* command is not a shell executable—it runs only within the context of a command prompt. Therefore, the command prompt must be opened. Additionally, I used the %COMPUTERNAME% token to represent the location of the computer name. If I launch this version of Remote_Command from a task, it will do the rest: I will get a listing of shares on the specified computer.

**Important** Remember that not all commands are meant to be run remotely. This tool is not a silver bullet for every scenario, but it empowers you to easily perform a number of common support tasks. Treat it as a sample and as a seed for your own creativity.

## Solution summary

This solution introduced some important tricks that allow you to incorporate common administrative tasks into your MMC taskpad. We saw some useful examples that provide an easy way to launch a remote desktop session to a system, open a remote command prompt, retrieve IP configuration, and run almost any command. I hope that those examples caused you to think about the commands, tools, and scripts that you use for day-to-day administration, and how you might be able to integrate them with the Active Directory Users and Computers snap-in.

There are also a lot of attributes that computer objects inherit because they are actually a derivative of user objects. So a computer object has *employeeID* and *employeeType* attributes. Really!

Explore the properties of a computer object to discover these useable attributes. In Windows Server 2003, use ADSIEdit.msc—one of the Windows Server 2003 Support Tools—to look at the properties of a computer object. In Windows Server 2008, open the Active Directory Users and Computers snap-in and enable Advanced Features from the View menu. Then open the properties of a computer object and click the Attribute Editor tab.

Solution Collection 7

# Extending User Attributes and Management Tools

**In this chapter:**

It occurs to me that if there were not users in our enterprises, we would not have much to do. Luckily, they do keep us busy. They are hired, they are terminated, they change names, they move locations, they log on to one or more computers, and—oh, yes—they have problems that require us to know where they are and what computer they're on.

The default properties of a user object in Active Directory are straightforward enough. You're certainly familiar with standard properties such as the user's logon names (the *sAMAccount-Name* and *userPrincipalName* attributes), password, logon script, and home directory properties, among others. In this Solution Collection, I'll take you way beyond what Active Directory gives us by default, to leverage hidden attributes, to add new attributes, and to create customized consoles and HTAs that allow you to make much better use of Active Directory both as an enterprise database and as a data source for administration. Many of the concepts and solutions presented in this Solution Collection apply to other object classes—computers and groups, for example.

## Scenarios, Pain, and Solution

Active Directory is a database that almost every Microsoft Windows enterprise has in place. Unfortunately, few enterprises leverage Active Directory to its fullest potential, and some have antiquated account management practices in place that, in fact, make it more difficult than it should be to administer users. Let's examine a few scenarios that we'll address in upcoming solutions:

- At Trey Research, administrators want to find users based on their last name, even though the Active Directory Users and Computers snap-in displays users sorted by first name.

- Contoso, Ltd., recently hired a new employee named James Fine. Unfortunately, there is already a user named James Fine. Administrators are having problems deciding what user name, display name, and common name to give to this second James Fine.

- Ann Bebee, an accountant at Coho Winery with the username abebee, recently married Mike Danseglio. When her pre–Windows 2000 logon name is changed to adanseglio, a long list of changes must be made to her home folder, roaming profile path, redirected folders, and links between the Microsoft Office Excel files with which she works. Such changes are required any time a user's name changes, and the administrators at Coho Winery want to find a better way to work with user names.

- The security audit at City Power and Light identified several administrators who had set their passwords to not expire. The security director has required that the Information Technology (IT) department provide monthly reports that list user accounts that have nonexpiring passwords, are disabled, or are locked out.

- The Phone Company is about to expand its help desk organization, which it is bringing back in house after several years of outsourcing. Administrators have been asked by the project leadership to create easy-to-use administrative tools that are task-specific and that incorporate company procedures so that training costs can be reduced for the new support team.

- Woodgrove Bank's Human Resources (HR) department recently discovered that Active Directory has attributes for employee identification, and it has asked the IT department to leverage those attributes for HR functions.

- When a new user is created at Litware, Inc., there's no guarantee that all user properties will be populated, or that attributes such as the common name, display name, or user principal name will be created according to naming conventions. It's really up to the administrator creating the user to follow procedures, and few administrators follow the procedures perfectly, every time. The new security initiative has tasked the IT organization to increase consistency and compliance with corporate procedures and conventions.

- The IT team at Northwind Traders was intrigued by the possibility of associating computers with users, as presented in Solution 6-7 on page 454. But the team wants the relationship to be a two-way link, whereby when a computer is assigned to a user, the computer object shows the associated user and the user object displays the associated computer.

In this Solution Collection, we'll examine best practices for managing user objects and for increasing the value of Active Directory as an enterprise database. You'll learn how to leverage hidden attributes, such as *employeeID* and *employeeNumber*, and how to create custom tools that allow you to expose and modify those attributes. You'll also learn how to extend the Active Directory schema with a back link attribute, which opens up a world of possibilities for creating relationships among computers, users, and other objects.

# 7-1: Best Practices for User Names

## Solution overview

| | |
|---|---|
| **Type of solution** | Guidance and scripts |
| **Features and tools** | User object name attributes, attribute clean-up scripts |
| **Solution summary** | Follow best practices for user name attributes, and clean up the vestiges of legacy practices to standardize user names with manageable naming conventions. |
| **Benefits** | Decreased risk of broken functionality, reduced administrative overhead because of user name changes, improved user experience at logon, and better administrative experience. |

## Introduction

User objects in Active Directory are, above all else, accounts used to provide authentication and management of users in the enterprise. Because many IT professionals began managing user accounts early in their careers and have done so, potentially, across several network operating systems, a variety of practices have been applied to manage user accounts in Active Directory. Unfortunately, some of these practices are not constructive in terms of the health of the directory service or the productivity of administrators. In this Solution Collection, I address a few best practices in the hopes of ensuring the highest level of productivity and sanity for Microsoft Windows administrators.

## Establish best practice standards for user object name attributes

When you create a user account in Active Directory, the first property you are prompted to configure is the user's name: the first name, middle name, and last name, which create a field called Full Name in the New Object – User dialog box shown in Figure 7-1.

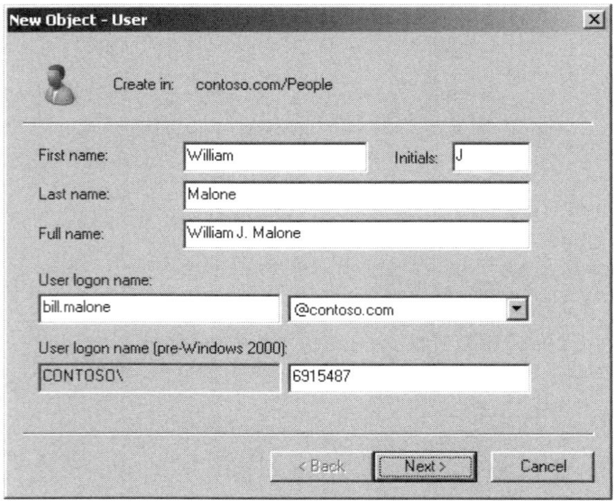

**Figure 7-1**   The New Object – User dialog box

As you know, Active Directory is a database, with a history based in a standard called X.500 and a structure that allows it to be accessed using Lightweight Directory Access Protocol (LDAP). Each of the properties you configure for an object are stored in an *attribute* associated with that instance of the *object class*. Object classes define the types of objects that can exist in the directory—users, groups, computers, organizational units (OUs), and Group Policy objects (GPOs), for example.

Objects of class *user* have a number of properties related to the user's name, and it's useful to know how the properties map to the user interface, shown earlier in Figure 7-1, and the user Properties dialog box, shown in Figure 7-2.

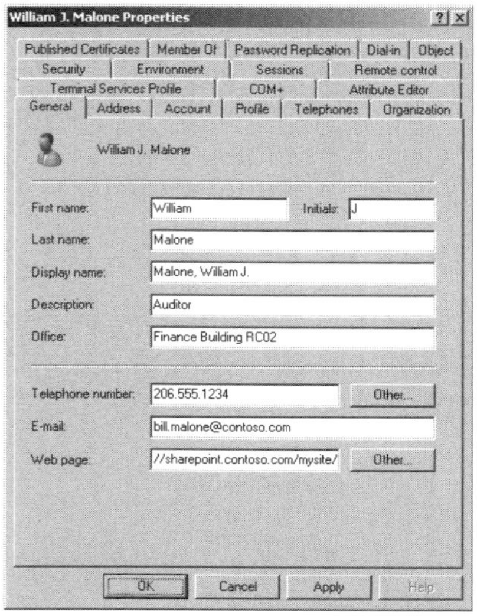

**Figure 7-2**   The user Properties dialog box

In Table 7-1, I summarize the most important name properties and where they appear in the user interface.

**Table 7-1   User Name Properties**

| LDAP Property Name | Label Used in New User | Label Used in User Properties | Description |
|---|---|---|---|
| *givenName* | First name | First name | The given name, or first name. |
| *initials* | Initials | Initials | The initials for parts of the user's full name. Used as the middle initial in the Windows Address Book. |
| *middleName* | | | The middle name attribute is mysteriously absent in the user interface, though it does exist. |
| *sn* | Last name | Last name | The family name, surname, or last name. |
| *displayName* | Full Name | Display name | The display name. Appears in the global address list (GAL) of Microsoft Exchange Server and in other address books. |
| *cn, name* | Full Name | n/a | The name that appears in the details pane of the Microsoft Management Console (MMC) in the Name column. |

Some of these properties must be unique—*cn*, for example—and some are not required to be unique. One of the most challenging aspects about the Active Directory Users and Computers snap-in's user interface is that it masks the properties that are really being configured by combining several attributes into one text box in the user interface, making it difficult to achieve the best practices. When you configure the Full Name text box in the New User dialog box, you are actually populating both *cn* (which must be unique and should be in the form *First-Name LastName*) and *displayName* (which is not required to be unique and should be in the form *LastName, FirstName* to make its listing in address books easier to find).

## Do not configure common name (*cn*) attributes as *LastName, FirstName*

It's unfortunately common for organizations to name the user objects based on a *Last Name, First Name* pattern. The reason for doing so is simple: If you have a lot of users in an OU, it's typically easier to locate a user by last name. For example, if I have been asked to reset the password for Bill Malone, do I look for him as Bill or William? It is easier if I look for him by his last name, Malone. So the reason for naming users *Last Name, First Name* is understandable—but doing so is a bad practice.

The reason is that although the user interface looks like you've named the user *Last Name, First Name*, that's not exactly what happened behind the scenes in the *cn* attribute. In Figure 7-3, you see, on top, two users in the Active Directory Users and Computers snap-in. Below them, you see the same two users using ADSIEdit. Notice the problematic distinguished name. It is not *CN=LastName,FirstName,OU=People,DC=contoso,DC=com*, but rather *CN=LastName\,FirstName,OU=People,DC=contoso,DC=com*.

| Malone, William J. | User | Auditor |
| William J. Malone | User | Auditor |

| CN=Malone, William J. | user | CN=Malone\, William J.,OU=People,DC=contoso,DC=com |
| CN=William J. Malone | user | CN=William J. Malone,OU=People,DC=contoso,DC=com |

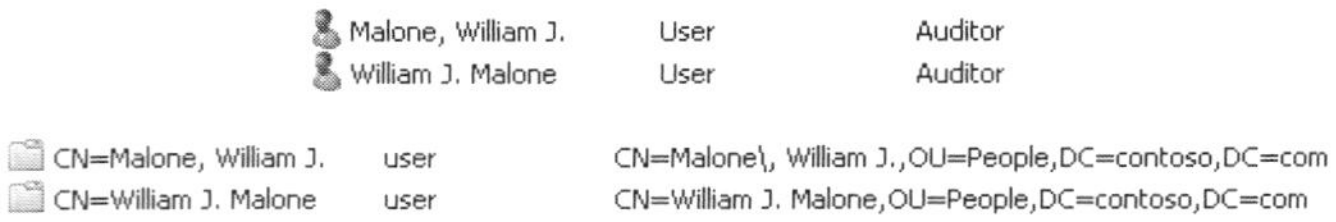

**Figure 7-3**   User names in the Active Directory Users and Computers snap-in and ADSIEdit

The reason is that the comma is a delimiter in the object's distinguished name, separating the components of the name. Therefore, if you embed a comma in the common name, which is the first component of the user object's distinguished name, Active Directory must flag that comma as an embedded character rather than as a delimiter, which it does using the backslash.

You can imagine the potential havoc this behavior can wreak on your scripts and tools. Even some third-party commercially available applications have had challenges with escaped characters in a distinguished name. This behavior even can mess up Active Directory itself—domain controllers can have trouble adding users with escaped characters in their names to groups in another domain (as explained in Knowledge Base Article 276266, which is available at *http://support.microsoft.com/kb/276266/en-us/*). Just don't do it!

## Add the Last Name column to your view to sort and find by last name

Instead of naming objects using a *Last Name, First Name* pattern, add the Last Name column to your view in the Active Directory Users and Computers snap-in. Follow these simple steps:

1. Choose View, Add/Remove Columns.

2. Below Available Columns, select Last Name.

3. Click Add.

4. Optionally, use the Move Up and Move Down buttons to determine the order of columns.

5. Click OK.

With the Last Name column visible, you can sort by last name and more easily find users. I can, for example, find the user with the last name Malone. Unfortunately, you cannot search for a user by beginning to type the name—for example, typing **Mal**. The Active Directory Users and Computers snap-in uses the Name column to provide that functionality.

## Add the Last Name column to views of saved queries

The next failing of the snap-in to align with the real world is the fact that when you add the Last Name column, it becomes visible in the details pane throughout the snap-in. So when you open an OU that contains groups or computers, you still see the Last Name column, which is, of course, a useless waste of on-screen real estate. Therefore, my recommendation is to add the Last Name column not to the details pane view of an OU or container, but rather to the details pane view of a saved query. Saved queries provide many advantages for day-to-day administration, and one of them is that the details pane settings of one saved query are independent from other saved queries. Saved queries are examined in Solution 7-2 on page 491. See that solution for more detail.

## Change Display Name to *LastName, FirstName*

When you create a user object and enter the Full Name as shown in Figure 7-1, you populate two attributes: *cn* and *displayName*. As you just learned, *cn* should not have a comma. But the Display Name field, seen in Figure 7-2, can have commas. The *displayName* attribute is used in address books, including the GAL of Exchange Server, so it is useful to display users as *Last-Name, FirstName*. That is perfectly reasonable for *displayName*. Unfortunately, you have to make the change after creating the user. Create the user with *FirstName LastName* as the Full Name, and then open the user's Properties dialog box and change the entry in the Display Name text box.

## Alternately use *LastName FirstName* as a common name without a comma

The real issue here is not the order of name fields in the common name—it is the use of the comma, which is a special character within a distinguished name. As an alternative, you can use a format such as *LastName FirstName*, with a space as a delimiter, or *Last Name − FirstName*.

The characters that must be escaped with a preceding backslash in a distinguished name are shown in the following list:

- Backward slash (\)
- Comma (,)
- Double quotation (")
- Equals sign (=)
- Left angle bracket (<)
- Plus sign (+)
- Pound sign (#)
- Right angle bracket (>)
- Semicolon (;)

The characters in the next list are allowed in distinguished names and do not need to be escaped:

- Ampersand (&)
- Asterisk (*)
- "At" sign (@)
- Carat (^)
- Closing parenthesis ")"
- Closing square bracket "]"
- Colon (:)
- Dollar sign ($)
- Grave accent (`)
- Hyphen (-)
- Opening parenthesis "("
- Opening square bracket "["
- Percent sign (%)
- Question mark (?)
- Tilde (~)
- Underscore (_)
- Vertical line (|)

Some of these characters are not allowed at all in a user's pre–Windows 2000 Logon Name (*sAMAccountName* attribute)–specifically, the following characters:

- Asterisk (*)
- Closing square bracket "]"
- Colon (:)
- Double quotation (")
- Equals sign (=)
- Left angle bracket (<)
- Opening square bracket "["
- Plus sign (+)
- Question mark (?)
- Right angle bracket (>)

- Semicolon (;)
- Vertical line ( | )

I suggest you stick with minimal punctuation in your common names—perhaps a hyphen between the last name and the first name, or just a space.

### Clean up sins of the past

Two scripts can be found in the Scripts folder of the companion media. The first, User_Fix_-DisplayNames.vbs, processes an OU of user objects and, for each, changes the format of the *displayName* attribute to *LastName, FirstName* format. The second, User_Fix_CommonNames.vbs, processes an OU of user objects and, for each, changes the format of the *cn* attribute to *FirstName LastName* format.

Launch the scripts from the command prompt using cscript.exe. Each script requires one argument: the distinguished name of an OU containing users. The scripts process all user objects within the OU—they do not recursively process child OUs. For example, to change the *displayName* attribute of all users in the People OU, use this command:

```
cscript User_Fix_DisplayNames.vbs "ou=People,dc=contoso,dc=com"
```

You can modify the scripts to change the logic they use to generate display names and common names. In fact, User_Fix_CommonNames.vbs is ready to convert from *FirstName LastName* to *LastName FirstName* with no comma. Read the comments in the script to learn how to make the change.

## Implement manageable user logon names

Users in an Active Directory domain can authenticate to the domain with one of two user names: the pre–Windows 2000 logon name, called the *sAMAccountName* attribute, or the user principal name (UPN), called the *userPrincipalName* attribute. The UPN is used primarily for authentication, unlike the *sAMAccountName*, which is represented by the %username% environment variable and used to determine innumerable user-specific settings, such as the profile folder name and redirected folder names. For this reason, I recommend that enterprises transition to using UPN for logon and relegate the *sAMAccountName* to user management and configuration needs.

### Assign unique and memorable user principal names

The UPN consists of two parts—the logon name and a suffix—separated by the at sign (@). Although UPNs have been available as logon names since Windows 2000, few organizations have made use of them as the standard logon name. But they can be used. When a user enters his UPN in the Log On To Windows dialog box, shown in Figure 7-4, he does not need to select a domain to log on to, nor does he need to enter the domain component of *DOMAIN\username*. That's because UPNs are unique in an Active Directory forest.

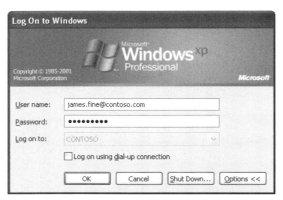

**Figure 7-4**    Log on using the user principal name

I recommend instituting a standard whereby UPNs are equivalent to users' e-mail addresses. This standard might not be achievable in every environment, depending on the complexities of e-mail addresses, but where it is possible, it achieves a unique logon name that users should have very little difficulty remembering.

To implement e-mail addresses as UPNs, you must first be sure that the suffix that will appear after the at (@) sign has been defined. By default, the only UPN suffixes that will be available are the DNS names of the domains in the Active Directory forest. If your e-mail suffix is equivalent to your Active Directory domain name, you have nothing else to do. However, if your Active Directory domain name is different from your e-mail suffix, you must add the suffix following these steps:

1.  Open the Active Directory Domains and Trusts snap-in.

2.  Right-click the Active Directory Domains and Trusts snap-in and choose Properties.

3.  In the Alternative UPN Suffixes text box, enter your e-mail address suffix and click the Add button. Repeat this step for any additional e-mail address suffixes.

4.  Click OK.

Adding the UPN suffix makes it available when you create new users in the Active Directory Users and Computers snap-in. If you want to convert existing UPNs so that they meet the same standard, use the User_Fix_UPNs.vbs scripts on the companion media. Run it using cscript.exe from the command prompt, supplying the distinguished name of an OU containing users. For example, this command will correct the UPNs of all users in the Employees OU:

```
cscript user_fix_upns.vbs "ou=Employees,ou=People,dc=contoso,dc=com"
```

In most environments, users know their e-mail address. Using it as a logon name improves user support while meeting Active Directory's requirement for UPNs that are unique within the forest.

## Assign pre–Windows 2000 logon names that are manageable

The pre–Windows 2000 logon name (*sAMAccountName* attribute) becomes the %username% environment variable, which is in turn used to manage many settings and configurations. When a user's pre–Windows 2000 logon name changes, the IT department must make numerous adjustments to accommodate the change, such as the following:

- Change the name of the user's roaming profile folder. If the user's profile setting (*profilePath* attribute) refers to a Server Message Block (SMB) namespace—for example, \\server14\profiles$\\*username*—the name of the user's folder must be changed. If the user's *profilePath* refers to a DFS namespace folder—for example, \\contoso.com\users\\*username*\profile or \\contoso.com\profiles\\*username*—the name of the DFS namespace folder must be changed.

- Change the user's *profilePath* attribute to refer to the location by its new name.

- Make changes to the namespace that supports the user's redirected folders.

- Change the name of the folder used by the local cache of the user's roaming profile. Because many scripts and tools look for hard-coded paths such as C:\Documents and Settings\%username% and C:\Users\%username%, IT is likely to need to change the name of the folder when the user's name changes.

- Redirect the *ProfileImagePath* registry value that points to the location of the user's local profile to the newly named folder. This value is located in HKEY_LOCAL_MACHINE\ Software\Microsoft\Windows NT\Current Version\ProfileList\\*userSID*, where *userSID* is the security identifier (SID) of the user account.

- Modify links between documents, worksheets, and other files created by the user. If a user linked two Excel worksheets in different folders within her Documents folder, the link in the destination worksheet will contain the full path to the source file, including the user's previous logon name in that path. In relation to the other changes listed here, this is by far the most excrutiating change to make—it is difficult if not impossible to complete thoroughly or efficiently without third-party applications.

These are just some of the difficulties that arise when a user's pre–Windows 2000 logon name changes. I discussed many of these issues in more detail in Solution 3-4 on page 211. The bottom line is that any changes to %username% will be time consuming and painful to implement.

Therefore, to improve manageability and productivity, I highly recommend that you implement pre–Windows 2000 logon names that will not change over time. In other words, the logon names should not be related to characteristics of the user that are not permanent. A logon name that indicates the user is a temporary employee by adding a prefix such as _TMP will be problematic if that user is hired full time. Logon names that reflect the business unit, geographic location, or status of a user are equally problematic. Even logon names related to users' actual names are a bad idea, because users get married, get divorced, and find various other reasons to change their names. Names and initials as logon names are not manageable in the mid to long term.

Determine or create an attribute of users in your environment that will not change during the life cycle of a person's involvement with your organization. The most obvious recommendation is to use an employee ID or payroll number, assuming that these will not change over time.

### Use User_Rename.vbs to rename user objects

In the companion media, you'll find the User_Rename.vbs script. It allows you to change many of the common name attributes of user objects. Be sure to change the *Configuration Block* so that it is appropriate for your environment. Read the comments in the script, or use this command to learn about the script usage:

```
cscript.exe user_rename.vbs /?
```

## Prepare to add the second "John Doe" to your Active Directory

One of the ultimate tests of your naming conventions is to consider how your environment would respond when a user is added who has the exact same name as an existing user. For example, if you already have a user named John Doe, what will happen when you add the second John Doe?

You will encounter these major restrictions when adding a user with the same name as an existing user:

- The *sAMAccountName* attribute must be unique for the entire domain. If you are using initials or some combination of first and last name, you will have to make adjustments if your existing user is *jdoe* because your new user cannot also be *jdoe*. Many organizations have naming standards that result in the new user having a name such as *jdoe2*. I've seen companies whose naming rules have so many exceptions that they can hardly be called rules. This problem is solved if the employee number or some other unique attribute of the users is used for the *sAMAccountName*.

- The *userPrincipalName* must be unique for the entire forest. E-mail addresses, which must be unique for the whole world, certainly meet that requirement. Consider using e-mail addresses as UPNs.

- The *cn* attribute must be unique within the OU. This can be a tricky one. If you have a single, flat OU for users, a second John Doe cannot have the same common name as the first John Doe. Unfortunately, there's no perfect answer for all organizations to this problem. Design a naming standard that applies a single rule for all CNs. Perhaps the CN should include an employee's number—for example, *John Doe (645928)*. If your OU structure for user accounts is flat, be prepared to address this challenge.

Consider these requirements, issues, and recommendations as you evaluate your naming standard's ability to cope effectively with a second John Doe.

## Solution summary

User name attributes, including both human names and logon names, are somewhat misunderstood and misused because of the quirks of the user interfaces that Windows provides. Whether it's a field such as Full Name that doesn't really exist but populates two other attributes with diverse requirements, or missing fields such as *middleName*, the Active Directory Users and Computers snap-in doesn't make it as easy as it could to work with names. In addition, both users and administrators continue to use legacy logon names rather than the user principal name, which can be more easily remembered and supported if set to the user's e-mail address. You should set the pre–Windows 2000 logon name to a value that is unique and will not change over the life cycle of the user in your enterprise.

# 7-2: Using Saved Queries to Administer Active Directory Objects

## Solution overview

| | |
|---|---|
| **Type of solution** | Tools and guidance |
| **Features and tools** | Saved queries, LDAP filters, custom MMC consoles |
| **Solution summary** | Rather than administer your environment using the OU structure of your Active Directory, use saved queries as a foundation for administrative tasks. |
| **Benefits** | Virtualized views improve productivity, decrease confusion, and increase manageability of Active Directory objects. |

## Introduction

In Solution Collection 5, "Active Directory Delegation and Administrative Lock Down," I discussed delegation of administrative tasks—for example, allowing the help desk to reset user passwords and unlock user accounts. During that discussion, I emphasized that the primary driver for the design of your OU structure should be efficient propagation of access control lists (ACLs) on Active Directory objects. In other words, your OU design should reflect your administrative model. It's quite possible that you will end up with user objects in more than one OU. When that happens, you need a way to administer a user's account that does not require you to hunt and peck through your Active Directory to locate the OU where that user exists. In addition, you might need to perform tasks on user objects that are dispersed across OUs.

The Saved Queries node in the Active Directory Users and Computers snap-in enables you to realize tremendous administrative productivity. Saved queries allow you to virtualize Active Directory so that you can see a unified view of objects across multiple OUs, or a filtered view of objects that meet specific criteria. Saved queries also enable you to control the columns that are visible in the details pane. For these reasons, saved queries form the basis for custom tools for all levels of administrators. In this solution, you'll learn what it takes to put saved queries to work—a set of skills that will help you administer not only users but also other objects more efficiently. The best way to learn about saved queries is to create them. I recommend you follow along if you are unfamiliar with saved queries. The next sections guide you through the creation of saved queries both as a learning exercise and as a way to produce a powerful custom console.

## Create a custom console that shows all domain users

I find it's helpful to have a one-stop shop for administering users in my domain, without having to dig through OU branches to find a specific user and without having to use the Find command in the Active Directory Users and Computers snap-in, which does not give me the same administrative commands and shortcuts as my console. To create a virtualized view of all users in your domain that abstracts the OU structure in which they are placed for delegation, use these steps:

1. Open a new Microsoft Management Console. In Windows Vista, click the Start button and, in the Search box, type **mmc.exe** and press Enter. In Windows XP, Windows Server 2003, and Windows Server 2008, click the Start button, click Run, type **mmc.exe**, and press Enter.

2. Click File, Add/Remove Snap-in.

3. Select the Active Directory Users and Computers snap-in, and click the Add button.

4. Click OK.

5. Expand Active Directory Users and Computers, and select Saved Queries.

6. Right-click Saved Queries, and choose New, Query.

7. Enter a name for the saved query—for example, **All Users**. You can optionally enter a description for the query in the Description text box.

8. Click the Browse button, select the domain, and then click OK.

9. Click the Define Query button.

10. On the Users tab, from the Name drop-down list, choose Has A Value.

    This results in a query that shows all users, because all users have values in their *Name* attribute, which is the user's common name (CN).

11. Click OK to close the Find Common Queries dialog box.

12. Click OK again to close the New Query dialog box.

13. Click the View menu, and choose Add/Remove Columns.

14. Because the query is showing only user objects, the Type column is not necessary. Select it and click Remove.

15. Custom tasks that you create, such as My Memberships.hta that I introduced in Solution Collection 1, "Role-Based Management," use a user's pre–Windows 2000 logon name as a parameter. Add that column by selecting Pre–Windows 2000 Logon Name and clicking the Add button.

16. Add the Last Name column so that you can sort users by last name.

   Consider using the Move Up button to move Last Name to the second position. I prefer to have it be the second, rather than the first, column because the user icons appear as part of the Name column, and I want icons to be the leftmost items in the details pane.

17. Add other columns that are useful for you to view, and then click OK.

18. Because it's often easiest to locate users by last name, click the Last Name column heading to sort by that column.

The result should appear similar to Figure 7-5.

| Console Root | Name | Last Name ▲ | Description | Pre-Windows 2000 |
|---|---|---|---|---|
| Active Directory Users and Comp | Administrator | | Built-in account for admini… | Administrator |
| Saved Queries | Guest | | Built-in account for guest … | Guest |
| All Users | krbtgt | | Key Distribution Center Se… | krbtgt |
| contoso.com | Jesper Aaberg | Aaberg | Sales | 615531029 |
| | Lene Aalling | Aalling | Manufacturing | 669500964 |
| | Syed Abbas | Abbas | Marketing Manager | 652303900 |
| | Kim Abercrombie | Abercrombie | Finance Representative | 697400047 |
| | Lina Ãbola | Ãbola | Sales | 613427265 |
| | Hazem Abolrous | Abolrous | Manufacturing Manager | 622472632 |
| | Sam Abolrous | Abolrous | Research | 627977733 |
| | Humberto Acevedo | Acevedo | Vice President, Research | 648511248 |
| | Gustavo Achong | Achong | Operations Representative | 614162177 |
| | Pilar Ackerman | Ackerman | Operations | 605015511 |
| | Terry Adams | Adams | Sales | 662192564 |
| | Stephan Adolphi | Adolphi | Sales | 629638575 |
| | Karina Agerby | Agerby | Marketing Manager | 661729151 |
| | David Ahs | Ahs | Manufacturing Represent… | 660923370 |
| | François Ajenstat | Ajenstat | Sales Manager | 660951308 |
| | Kim Akers | Akers | Finance Representative | 659042059 |
| | Cigdem Akin | Akin | IT | 692107456 |
| | Kweku Ako-Adjei | Ako-Adjei | Legal Manager | 667353164 |
| | José Ignacio Peiro Alba | Alba | Manufacturing Represent… | 672396736 |
| | Amy E. Alberts | Alberts | Finance | 686004455 |

**Figure 7-5**   A saved query showing all users in the *contoso.com* domain

# Control the scope of a saved query

In the first example, I created a saved query that shows all domain users. For my help desk, however, I do not want or need them to be viewing administrative user accounts. The administrative user accounts at Contoso are in the Admins OU, whereas standard user accounts are in the People OU and its sub-OUs. The help desk needs a view that flattens the list of users within the People OU. To achieve this, I simply have to manage the scope of my saved query.

I'm going to assume you have separated your administrative user accounts from your standard user accounts. If not, you should. Administrative accounts should be delegated much more tightly than standard user accounts—for example, the help desk should not be able to reset passwords on administrative accounts. After you've separated the two types of accounts, you can create a saved query showing only the standard accounts. To do so, follow the same procedure just listed, except in step 7, give the saved query another name, such as "Standard

Users," and in step 8, select the top-level OU for your standard user accounts, rather than the entire domain. When you have defined the query in step 11, the New Query dialog box should appear similar to Figure 7-6. The resulting query displays all users within the selected OU and its sub-OUs. To prevent the query from displaying objects in child OUs, deselect the Include Subcontainers check box shown in Figure 7-6.

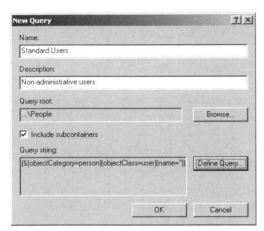

**Figure 7-6**   A query with limited scope

## Build saved queries that target specific objects

So far, we've looked at saved queries that show all users using a query that specified that the *Name* value (the *commonName*) has a value. Obviously, you might want to create queries that target more specific subsets of users. To do this, begin by creating a new query. In the New Query dialog box, provide a name and description for your query and then select the container you want to query. Next, click the Define Query button. The Find *query_type* dialog box shown in Figure 7-7 allows you to build a query one of several ways, as described in the following list, based on your selection in the Find drop-down list.

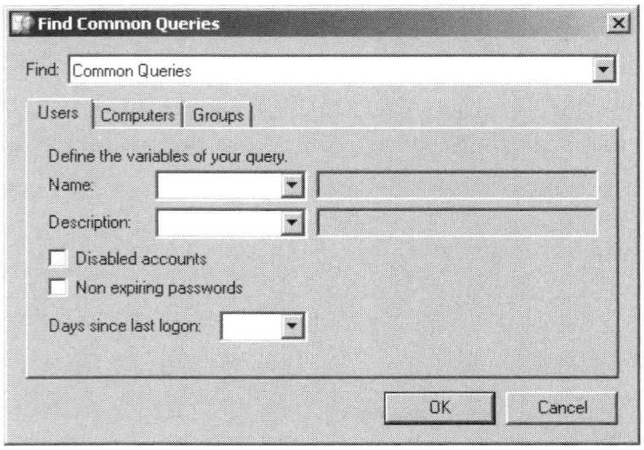

**Figure 7-7**   The Find Common Queries dialog box

■ The Common Queries option exposes several queries that are useful to most administrators, including the ability to locate disabled accounts, accounts with passwords set to never expire, and accounts that have not been used for logon for a specified number of days. Note that there are also tabs for common queries for computer and group objects.

■ If you choose an object-specific option from the Find drop-down list, you see options that help you further refine your search for objects of that class. Try choosing Users, Contacts, And Groups as an example. Two tabs appear, as illustrated in Figure 7-8. The Users, Contacts, And Groups tab has text boxes for Name and Description. I've never understood what the advantage is to using this tab rather than the Users tab of the Common Queries dialog box, shown in Figure 7-7. The Advanced tab is more useful. It allows you to select any one of a number of attributes and to perform searches on those attributes. Click the Field button, choose the object class, and then click the field you want to search on. You can use the Condition and Value controls on the form to build the query.

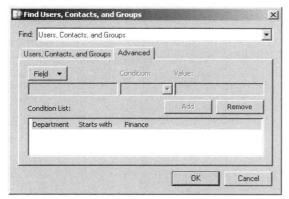

**Figure 7-8**   An Advanced query can use many of an object's attributes, such as a user object's *Department* attribute

■ If you choose Custom Search from the Find drop-down list, two tabs appear as shown in Figure 7-9. The Custom Search tab behaves similarly to the Advanced tab shown in Figure 7-8. I've rarely found a need for this tab, except for when I was trying to create a query that showed several object classes in one view. The Advanced tab of the Custom Search form, shown in Figure 7-9, is very useful. In this text box, you can enter any LDAP query. Figure 7-9 shows a query that displays locked user accounts. In the next section, I'll explain LDAP query syntax.

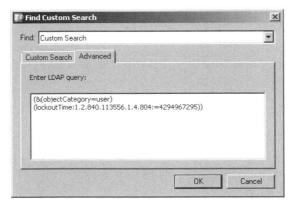

**Figure 7-9**   The Find Custom Search Advanced tab allows you to enter any LDAP query

## Understand LDAP query syntax

You can enter a custom query in the Advanced tab of the Find Custom Search dialog box, shown in Figure 7-9. Use LDAP query syntax to define the query. To specify a criteria, called a *comparison*, use the syntax (<attribute><operator><value>), such as (*objectCategory=user*) or (*department=Finance*). The *<attribute>* component is the LDAP attribute name as defined in the schema. The value is the value that you want to use as a basis for comparison. It can include the asterisk wildcard (*) to represent zero or more characters. Numeric values must be represented in decimal form—hexadecimal or binary values must be converted into decimal form for use in the query. The *<operator>* component is a *comparison operator* that can be one of those shown in Table 7-2.

**Table 7-2   LDAP Query Comparison Operators**

| Operator | Description |
| --- | --- |
| = | Equals |
| ~= | Approximately equals |
| <= | Less than or equal to |
| >= | Greater than or equal to |

You can have more than one comparison in a query—in which case, you must specify whether all or any one of the comparisons must be met for an object to be returned by the query. This is achieved using *logical operators* to represent logical AND, OR, and NOT. The logical operators are shown in Table 7-3.

**Table 7-3   LDAP Query Logical Operators**

| Operator | Description |
| --- | --- |
| & | Logical AND |
| \| | Logical OR |
| ! | Logical NOT |

One of the unusual aspects of LDAP query syntax is that logical operators are placed *before* the comparisons. So, if we want to find all users whose department included the string "finance," we use the following query:

```
(&(objectCategory=user)(department=*finance*))
```

Notice that the logical AND operator appears within a single comparison group, indicated by the parentheses, but before the individual comparisons. Wildcards are used for the department value. And *objectCategory* is used to look for users. You'll see many queries that use *objectClass*, but I prefer *objectCategory*. Both users and computers are *objectClass*=user. Only users are *objectCategory*=user.

If we want to query for users whose *department* value is either Marketing or Sales, we can use this query filter:

```
(&(objectCategory=user)(|(department=*marketing*)(department=*sales*)))
```

This query specifies that the *objectCategory* must be *user* and that either the *department* attribute contains the string "marketing" or the *department* attribute contains "sales."

To learn more about LDAP query syntax, see *http://msdn2.microsoft.com/en-us/library/ms675768.aspx*.

## Identify some useful LDAP queries

The following are examples of useful LDAP queries:

- Locked-out user accounts:

  ```
  (&(objectCategory=user)(lockoutTime:1.2.840.113556.1.4.804:=4294967295))
  ```

  The crazy looking 1.2.840.113556.1.4.804 is an example of an LDAP matching rule object identifier. Don't get too caught up in what that means—you'll only run into a few of them, including those shown in this section.

- Users who have never logged on:

  ```
  (&(objectCategory=person)(objectClass=user))(|(lastLogon=0)(!(lastLogon=*)))
  ```

- Users with expired passwords:

  ```
  (&(objectcategory=user)(userAccountControl:1.2.840.113556.1.4.804:=8388608))
  ```

- Users in a specific group:

  ```
  (&(objectCategory=user)(memberOf=cn=Finance,ou=Roles,ou=Groups,dc=contoso,dc=com))
  ```

- All users created after January 1, 2008:

  ```
  (objectCategory=user)(whenCreated>=20080101000000.0Z)
  ```

  Generalized time values such as the one shown here are in the format YYYYMMDDH-HMMSS.0Z, where *0Z* indicates Greenwich Mean Time. For more information about this format, see *http://msdn2.microsoft.com/en-us/library/ms676930.aspx*.

And although I know this Solution Collection is about user objects, saved queries are very useful for other types of objects as well. So let's cover some useful queries for computers and groups:

- Groups with no members:

    ```
    (&(objectCategory=group)(!member=*))
    ```

- Mail-enabled groups:

    ```
    (&(objectCategory=group)(mailNickName=*))
    ```

- Computers that have never logged on:

    ```
    (&(objectCategory=computer)(!lastlogon=*))
    ```

- Computers running Windows XP:

    ```
    (&(objectCategory=computer)(operatingSystemVersion=5.1*))
    ```

> **Note**  Did you know you can use DSQuery.exe with custom LDAP filters such as those just listed? It took me *years* to realize that DSQuery had this capability. OK . . . I'm a bit slow. To learn more, open a command prompt and type **dsquery.exe * /?**. The key is the asterisk. You'll use it with switches such as *-filter "LDAP filter"* to specify the query, *-attr attribute list* to configure the attributes you want returned, and *-limit [0|limit]* to control how many results are returned (0 is unlimited; the default is 100). Use this syntax to query Active Directory from the command line and to pipe its results to other DS commands—Dsget, Dsmod, Dsadd, Dsmove, and Dsrm.

# Transfer saved queries between consoles and administrators

There are three ways to use a saved query created in one console elsewhere. The first way is simply to share or distribute the console itself. Saved queries are attached to the definition of the Active Directory Users and Computers snap-in in the console, so they go with the console.

The second way is to paste the query directly into the Advanced tab of the Find Custom Search dialog box. To do so, create a new saved query, click Define Query, choose Custom Search from the Find drop-down list, and click the Advanced tab. Then paste the query into the text box. You can therefore copy queries you find online or send queries to other administrators via e-mail.

The most elegant way to save and distribute queries is to export them from the console in which they were created, and import them into other consoles. To export a saved query, right-click it and choose Export Query Definition. The query is exported as XML. To import a saved query into another console, right-click the Saved Queries node and choose Import Query Definition.

## Leverage saved queries for most types of administration

I strongly encourage you to create a number of saved queries that support the various administrative teams, tasks, and scopes of management in your enterprise. A particularly useful view of your enterprise can be to look at users who belong in a specific group:

```
(&(objectCategory=user)(memberOf=distinguishedName of group))
```

You could, of course, open the group object and see its members. But a saved query allows you to perform administrative tasks on those members. You cannot use a wildcard in this type of query—the group must be specified by its complete distinguished name.

## Solution summary

Saved queries are an immensely useful tool with which to boost administrative productivity. They enable you to create customized views of your enterprise objects that support particular tasks, such as identifying locked-out users or stale accounts that have never logged on to the domain, or user accounts that have had the Password Never Expires flag set. They also allow you to virtualize your perspective of Active Directory so that you can view objects in a format that abstracts the underlying complexity of your Active Directory OU structure. Finally, they let you add columns that are unique to the query so that you don't end up with a Last Name column in your computer and group OUs, as you would in the rest of the Active Directory Users and Computers snap-in.

# 7-3: Create MMC Consoles for Down-Level Administrators

## Solution overview

| | |
|---|---|
| Type of solution | Tools |
| Features and tools | MMC console taskpads, saved queries |
| Solution summary | Create administrative tools for down-level administrators that give high visibility to the tasks that you have delegated to them. |
| Benefits | Reduce confusion regarding what is and is not possible for administrators of various levels. Integrate documentation into administrative tools for improved training and compliance with procedures. |

## Introduction

The delegation of permissions on Active Directory objects, detailed in Solution Collection 5, determines what an administrator can and cannot do in Active Directory. I recommend, however, that you take the next logical step, which is to provide administrative tools that make it as easy as possible for administrators to perform the tasks they have been delegated. This is particularly important for front-line administrators, who are typically less familiar with Active

Directory and with the specific procedures of your organization. By creating productive MMC consoles, you can provide visibility to tasks, tools, and documentation that will empower your administrative teams.

## Create a console with saved queries

First, open a blank MMC and add the Active Directory Users and Computers snap-in. Although you can create taskpads using your OU structure, you will be better served by creating saved queries.

Saved queries were detailed in the previous solution. They are, in my opinion, the foundation for effective administration in the Active Directory Users and Computers snap-in. Use the procedures in Solution 7-2 to create saved queries that display views of objects based on the scopes of management for your administrators. For example, for your Help Desk you can create views of all nonadministrative users (as described in Solution 7-2), all client computers, and all groups. For a team that supports users in a particular site or department, you can create views that show the users and computers in that scope of management based on those objects' membership in a relevant group.

When you create a saved query for user objects, I recommend adding the pre–Windows 2000 logon name as a column because many of the tools and scripts in this resource kit can be added as taskpad tasks and pass the pre–Windows 2000 logon name as a parameter.

Figure 7-10 shows a saved query that displays all nonadministrative users in the domain.

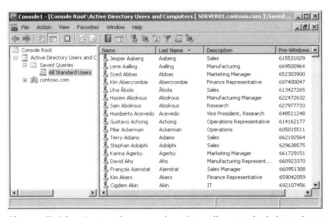

**Figure 7-10**     A saved query showing all nonadministrative users as the basis for a taskpad

## Create a taskpad with tasks for each delegated ability

Next, for each saved query, create a taskpad view with tasks for the capabilities that you have delegated to the team that will use the console. For example, if you have delegated the ability to reset user passwords, provide a task for the Reset Password menu command. Taskpads were introduced in Solution Collection 1 and are used in a variety of solutions in this resource kit. The following steps summarize how to create a taskpad view for a saved query displaying user objects:

1. Right-click the saved query that displays the objects for which you have delegated administrative tasks, and choose New Taskpad View.

2. The New Taskpad View Wizard appears. Click Next.

3. In the Taskpad Style page, click Next.

4. In the Taskpad Reuse page, select the Selected Tree Item option button and click Next.

5. In the Name And Description page, accept the default name and click Next.

6. Clear the Add New Tasks To This Taskpad After The Wizard Closes check box, and click Finish.

After you create the taskpad view, add tasks for each delegated ability. When adding tasks for commands such as the Reset Password command, you add menu command tasks. The following steps illustrate the process for adding menu command tasks:

1. Right-click the saved query for which you created the taskpad, and choose Edit Taskpad View.

2. Click the Tasks tab.

3. Click the New button.

4. The New Task Wizard appears. Click Next.

5. Select the Menu Command option button, and click Next.

   The Menu Command page appears, as shown in Figure 7-11.

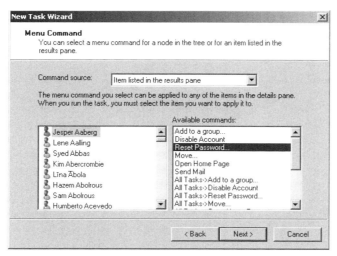

**Figure 7-11**  The Menu Command page of the New Task Wizard

6. Select a command from the Available Commands list.

   The list of menu commands in the Available Commands list is based on the type of object selected on the left side of the dialog box. This is one of the trickiest and most frustrating parts of building taskpads. For example, notice in Figure 7-11 that the Disable Account command is available but there is no Enable Account command. That's because the selected object is an enabled user. If you select a disabled user on the left side, the Enable Account command appears but the Disable Account command disappears. So you must select the correct type of object before the command you want becomes available.

7. Click Next.

8. Enter the name for the task in the Task Name box. This name will be the label of the hyperlink to the task.

9. Optionally, enter a description in the Description box. This description will appear below the task hyperlink in the taskpad.

10. Click Next.

11. Select an icon or click the Custom Icon option button, and then click Browse to choose an icon. There are more interesting and colorful icons in the file C:\Windows\System32\Shell32.dll. Windows Vista and Windows Server 2008 also have a plethora of icons in C:\Windows\System32\Imageres.dll.

12. After you have selected your icon, click the Next button.

13. Click Finish, and then click OK to close the Properties dialog box for the query you selected.

The resulting taskpad should appear similar to Figure 7-12. I added several more tasks.

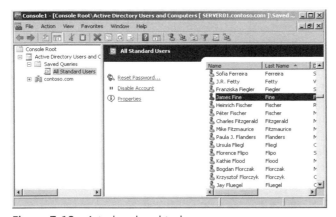

**Figure 7-12**   A taskpad and tasks

**Important**   Remember that tasks are context sensitive—the tasks you've added to the task-pad appear only when you select an object in the details pane.

## Add productive tools and scripts to the taskpads

Make sure to integrate into the taskpads links to useful tools and utilities from Microsoft, from this resource kit, and from third parties. Also add shell commands that can launch common applications such as the command prompt. The administrator who uses this console will log on to her system with a nonprivileged user account. She will then proceed to launch this console with the elevated credentials of her administrative account. Any processes launched from the console will inherit elevated credentials, allowing easy access to administrative tools without the need to reenter the secondary user name and password. These concepts are discussed in detail in Solution Collection 1.

## Add procedures and documentation to the console

I recommend that you integrate documentation of your environment and of procedures related to Windows administration directly into the MMC. This can be done one of two ways. First, you can add a shell command task to a taskpad that launches a document with the appropriate application. For example, a shell command can launch winword.exe with a parameter that opens procedural documentation. Second, if the documentation is available on your intranet, you can integrate the documentation using a Link to Web Address snap-in.

## Create an administrative home page within the console

Create a node in the console that can be used as a home page for the console. Because of the awkward way in which navigation between taskpads is implemented, you will find it much easier to have this home page as a kind of home base or hub from which you can navigate to individual taskpads. Each task will have a single navigation link back to this page.

You can use any taskpad as this home page, but if you happen to have an intranet site for your administrators, such as a SharePoint or IT portal, I suggest you add that into the MMC using a Link to Web Address snap-in and then create a taskpad using that snap-in. A folder snap-in can also serve as a home page if you use a taskpad with the *no-list* format.

At one client location where we leveraged such consoles, the administrative home page of the MMC was a taskpad for a Link to Web Address snap-in, which itself pointed to the home page of our IT administration SharePoint site. SharePoint then allowed us to easily manage Web content that was then integrated directly into the console. For example, we included a schedule of help desk shift assignments and important announcements on the SharePoint home page so that information was regularly visible to administrators as they navigated between taskpads.

# Add each taskpad to the MMC favorites

Navigate to each taskpad in the console that you want to make available to the administrators who will use the console. Add the node to your Favorites in the console using the Favorites menu. Be sure to add the administrative home page to your Favorites folder as well.

# Create navigation tasks

Edit the taskpad view of the administrative home page, and add navigation tasks to each of the nodes that you added to your Favorites folder. Then edit each taskpad, and add a single navigation link back to the administrative home page. After you have completed these steps, you should be able to use the navigation tasks on each taskpad to navigate between the administrative home page and each taskpad in the console.

Figure 7-13 shows an example of the resulting administrative home page. Each of the other taskpads in the console can be reached using navigation tasks on the left-hand side of the taskpad.

**Figure 7-13**   An intranet site exposed in a taskpad view of a Link to Web Address snap-in acts as the hub for the console, using navigation tasks.

# Save the console in User mode

To prevent users from modifying your task pad, you need to save the console in User mode. To change a console's mode, choose File, Options. By default, new consoles are saved in Author mode, which enables users to add and remove snap-ins, view all portions of the console tree, and save customizations. User mode, on the other hand, restricts the functionality of the console so that it cannot be changed. There are three types of user modes, described in Table 7-4. User Mode–Full Access is commonly selected for a console provided to skilled administrators with diverse job tasks requiring broad use of the console's snap-ins. User Mode–Limited Access is a locked-down mode and is therefore selected for a console provided to administrators with a more narrow set of job tasks.

Table 7-4   MMC Modes

| Mode | Use when |
| --- | --- |
| Author | You want to continue customizing the console. |
| User Mode—Full Access | You want users of the console to be able to navigate between and use all snap-ins. Users will not be able to add or remove snap-ins, or change the properties of snap-ins or the console. |
| User Mode—Limited Access, Multiple Windows | You want users to navigate to and use only the snap-ins that you have made visible in the console tree, and you want to preconfigure multiple windows that focus on specific snap-ins. Users will not be able to open new windows. |
| User Mode—Limited Access, Single Window | You want users to navigate to and use only the snap-ins that you have made visible in the console tree, within a single window. |

When a console is no longer saved in Author mode, you—the original author—can make changes to the console by right-clicking the saved console and choosing Author.

# Lock down the console view

This last step enables you to lock down the console completely. If you click the View menu and choose the Customize command, you can choose to hide some or all of the components of the MMC window. By hiding the console tree, for example, you discourage administrators from browsing the directory by restricting them to the taskpads and navigation links you have provided.

# Distribute the console

Save the highly customized console to a location that can be accessed by all administrators. That will make it easier for you to manage revisions to the console. Remember that consoles are basically a set of instructions that are interpreted by mmc.exe—instructions that specify which snap-ins to add and which computers to manage with those snap-ins. Consoles do not contain the snap-ins themselves. Therefore, a console will not function properly if the snap-ins it contains have not been installed. So be sure you have installed appropriate snap-ins from the Administrative Tools (adminpak.msi in Windows XP and Windows Server 2003) or the remote server administration tools (RSAT in Windows Vista or Windows Server 2008).

## Solution summary

After you have fully implemented a least-privilege delegation model in Active Directory, you can give visibility to the tasks that can be performed by administrators, and support those tasks with documentation, by creating highly customized MMCs. The consoles will consist of taskpads, and the taskpads will quite often be derived from saved queries rather than from organizational units or containers in the Active Directory hierarchy. Integrate procedural documentation directly into the console, along with an administrative home page that can serve as both the opening page of the console and the hub for navigation to each taskpad.

# 7-4: Extending the Attributes of User Objects

## Solution overview

| | |
|---|---|
| Type of solution | Guidance |
| Features and tools | Underused and unexposed attributes of user objects, schema extensions, linked attributes |
| Solution summary | Discover attributes that already exist in Active Directory but are not exposed by the standard Windows user interfaces, and apply a schema extension to user administration and management. |
| Benefits | Leverage the value of Active Directory as a distributed, efficiently replicated database to increase manageability and administrative productivity. |

## Introduction

User objects contain dozens of attributes and, unfortunately, not all of them are exposed in the user interface (UI). Even attributes that most organizations would describe as fundamental are absent in the UI: *employeeID*, *employeeNumber*, *assistant*, and *division*. And other attributes could be very useful for certain applications: *carLicense* and *employeeType*, for example. There are also attributes that could be extremely helpful but are not available by default in Active Directory. Can you imagine how much easier it would be to support a user if you could identify, immediately, the computer to which the user is logged on? In this solution, I discuss the options available to you to extend your use of user attributes. You'll learn how to identify existing, underused attributes and how to work with those attributes using custom administrative tools. And you'll learn about extending the schema to add attributes, such as an attribute that identifies the computer to which the user most recently logged on. In the next solution, I describe how to go about exposing these attributes in useful administrative tools.

# Leverage unused and unexposed attributes of user objects

User objects support a number of attributes that could be of use to your organization:

- *employeeNumber*
- *employeeID*
- *employeeType*
- *assistant*
- *secretary*
- *carLicense*

There's even a *photo* attribute, which could be used to store an actual picture of the user! Unfortunately, these attributes are not exposed in the user interface of the Active Directory Users and Computers snap-in. It's possible to create additional tabs in the user Properties dialog box, but that takes serious programming effort that is beyond the scope of this book. I recommend, instead, that you use simple scripts and HTML Applications (HTAs) to access the properties. I'll introduce such tools later in this solution.

## Discover unused attributes

To identify attributes that are unused and unexposed, open the attributes of a user object with the Active Directory Users and Computers snap-in. In Windows Server 2008, this can be done using the Attribute Editor tab of a user object's Properties dialog box. This tab appears when you have enabled Advanced Features in the View menu.

You can also use ADSIEdit.msc. This console is available by default in Windows Server 2008 and is installed with the Support Tools for Windows Server 2003. If you do not see the domain naming context, you need to connect to it. To connect to the domain naming context, follow these steps:

1. Open the ADSI Edit console (ADSIEdit.msc).
2. Right-click the root node, ADSI Edit, and choose Connect To.
3. In the Connection Point section, select the Select A Well Known Naming Context option and choose Default Naming Context.
4. Click OK.

Expand the domain naming context—for example, DC=contoso,DC=com—and browse to locate a user object in your environment. Right-click the user object and choose Properties.

After you have opened the attributes of a user object using ADSI Edit or the Attribute Editor tab, you can examine the list of available attributes to identify attributes that are of interest to your management goals.

## Evaluate unused attributes

Before you use an attribute for your own purposes, evaluate whether it is an appropriate attribute to leverage. The issue is that if you start using an attribute that exists in Active Directory and later install an Active Directory–aware application, that application might start using the same attribute for its purposes. With that in mind, I recommend the following approach:

**Understand the attribute itself**    Open the attribute using the Active Directory Schema Management snap-in. Look at the attributes of the attribute. What type of data does it hold: numeric, string, distinguished names? What is the maximum length of the value? Is the attribute single-valued or multivalued? Is the value replicated to the global catalog? Are these properties appropriate for your use of the attribute?

**Research the use of the LDAP attribute**    Most of the unused attributes you will discover are standard LDAP attributes. I recommend going online and researching their purpose. Use the following type of keyword search: **LDAP** *attributeName*—for example, *LDAP employeeType*. If you get too many results, try using "**LDAP attribute**" (including quotes) to create a phrase-based search for definitions of the specific attribute as an LDAP attribute. Identify how the attribute is meant to be used and how other organizations use it.

**Use attributes as they are meant to be used**    As long as the properties of an attribute support your requirements, you can put an unused attribute to work for any purpose. For example, you could use the *employeeNumber* property, which is a 512-character string, to keep track of an employee's diet preference. However, I don't recommend doing that, as it increases the chance that, one day, an application will expect to use that attribute to store employee identification. Instead, create your own attribute, as described later in this solution.

**Document what you do**    When you decide to start leveraging an attribute that is not exposed by the standard Active Directory tools, document what you do for posterity. Someday the enterprise might need to know what was done when you are not available.

**Evaluate all Active Directory–aware applications before deploying them**    This is a no-brainer, but warrants mention in this context. Whenever you install an application that is Active Directory aware, evaluate the attributes that the application uses to make sure there is no conflict with the existing use of those attributes in your organization.

If you have used this approach, you are likely to be very safe as you apply unused attributes to meet the needs of your organization. Remember the issue—potential conflicts with Active Directory–aware applications. If you've used the attribute as it was meant to be used, and if you've evaluated Active Directory–aware applications prior to deployment, you should not have a problem. This is especially true because most Active Directory–aware applications add their own attributes to the schema, rather than assuming that a customer's schema and use of attributes will support the application. So most commercial applications do everything that they can to avoid conflicts with your environment, as well.

# Extend the schema with custom attributes and object classes

The best way to avoid conflicts with other applications, including Microsoft's own technologies, is to extend the schema with a custom attribute that meets your requirements exactly. To extend the schema with a custom attribute, follow these procedures:

- Obtain a base object identifier (OID).
- Create an attribute.
- Create at least one custom object class.
- Associate the attribute with your custom object class.
- Associate your custom object class as an auxiliary class with the standard object class, such as *user*, *computer*, or *group*.

Your attribute ends up associated with the built-in object class indirectly, through the auxiliary relationship between the built-in object class and your custom object class. The steps for these procedures are detailed in Solution 6-7 on page 454.

That solution also discusses the concerns that arise about schema extension, the most salient of which is that after you have added an attribute or object class to the schema, you cannot delete it, only make it defunct (that is, make it unavailable for future use). The bottom line is that schema extension works—that's why there are commercial applications such as Microsoft Exchange that extend the schema. If you do your research, follow best practices, and test everything in a lab environment that simulates your production environment, you should be able to avoid problems. Most IT professionals are too cautious about schema modification, at the cost of foregoing the increased productivity and decreased cost of ownership that can come from customizing the vanilla Active Directory schema to support the unique characteristics of their enterprise. See Solution 6-7 for more information.

There are many ways you can take advantage of schema extensions to increase the value of Active Directory for administrative productivity. Although I don't have enough room to detail every step of these examples, I'd like to be sure you've considered them as a way to seed your creativity.

## Create an attribute that exposes the computers assigned to a user

In Solution 6-7, I described how to create an attribute associated with computer objects that tracks the users to whom a computer is assigned. I also provided the Computer_AssignTo.hta tool to manage assignments. What if you want to look at a user and see the computers assigned to that user? You can do that in two ways. First, you can create a tool that queries Active Directory to look for computers with a *computerAssignedTo* property that matches a specific user. Alternately, you can create an additional property associated with users that exposes the information automatically—we'll call it the *assignedComputers* attribute.

This attribute can be created as a *back link*. Back links are easy to understand because you are already familiar with the *memberOf* attribute, which is also a back link. The *memberOf* attribute of a user shows the groups to which the user belongs. When you add a user to a group, you are actually changing the group's *members* attribute—it is the *members* property that is a writeable property, and it is what is called a *forward link* attribute. When *members* changes, Active Directory automatically updates the *memberOf* property of the new member. Similarly, when you remove a user from a group, it is the group's *members* property that changes, and Active Directory updates the user's *memberOf* attribute.

We can construct the computer object's *computerAssignedTo* attribute as a forward link, and the user's *assignedComputers* as a back link. You could reverse the construction if you wanted to, as well. The key to creating linked values is the *linked* attribute. In Windows 2000 domains, it was laborious to create *linkID*s correctly. As long as your domain controllers are running Windows Server 2003 or Windows Server 2008, it is now automatic. The high-level steps to create a linked attribute are as follows:

- Create the forward link attribute (*computerAssignedTo* in this case), and make a note of its *attributeID* because you will use it in the next step. Configure the *linkID* of the forward link attribute to 1.2.840.113556.1.2.50. The system will automatically generate a new *linkID*.

  The challenge is that *linkID* is not accessible in the user interface when creating an attribute. You need to use a script or an LDIF file to create attributes with *linkID*s. I'll say more about this in a moment.

- Reload the schema cache. The schema cache is reloaded on demand, within approximately five minutes or when the domain controller (DC) is rebooted. The script Schema_Reload.vbs in the Scripts folder forces the schema cache to be reloaded immediately. If you are creating several back-linked attributes, create all forward links and then reload the schema cache; then create all back links.

- Create the back link attribute (*assignedComputers*, for example), and for its *linkID*, enter the *attributeID* or *ldapDisplayName* of the forward link attribute. Back link attributes are always multivalued. Again, the challenge is that the *linkID* is not available in the UI, so a script must be used.

- Create a custom class for each of your custom attributes. For example, create a *domain-ComputerInfo* class that contains the *computerAssignedTo* attribute, and a *domain-UserInfo* class that contains the *assignedComputers* attribute.

- Associate the custom classes with the built-in object classes using an auxiliary relationship. For example, associate *domain-ComputerInfo* with the *computer* object class, and *domain-UserInfo* with the *user* object class. Alternately, it is common practice to associate the back link attribute as an optional attribute for the object class top, because theoretically any object (not just users, for example) can be referred to by a forward link.

Now, when you assign a computer to a user with the Computer_AssignTo.hta tool, the computer's *computerAssignedTo* attribute is changed. Active Directory automatically updates the user object's *assignedComputers* attribute.

As I mentioned in the summary earlier, the major challenge is that *linkID* cannot be filled in manually when creating a schema attribute. Therefore, you must use a script. In the companion media's Scripts folder, you will find the script Schema_Create_AssignedComputers.vbs. This script demonstrates how to create a forward link attribute, reload the schema, and create the back link attribute. Read the script's comments for more information. Note that the script is configured to prevent it from being run accidentally in an enterprise so that inadvertent schema changes are avoided. The script's comments explain how to configure *bSafetySwitch* to *False* to allow the script to be run in a lab environment.

Another challenge with creating back link attributes is that, by default, they do not appear in the properties of an object viewed with ADSI Edit or the Windows Server 2008 Attribute Editor. You must click the Filter button and enable Backlinks.

## Create an attribute that exposes the computer to which a user is logged on

When a user calls for support, one of the first questions asked by the help desk is often, "What computer are you logged on to?" In Solution 6-8 on page 468, I described how to configure the environment so that when a computer starts up, it updates one of its own attributes—*description*, for example—to record information about the computer's location and the last user to log on to the system. Now I want more up-to-date information about where a user is currently logged on.

To achieve this goal, follow these procedures, each of which is very similar to those detailed in Solution 6-7:

- Decide the type of information you want to record. Do you want the computer's name, fully qualified domain name, distinguished name, or Active Directory services path? Do you want other information to be recorded, such as the time of logon or the current temperature? (Just checking to see if you were reading closely. But who knows—maybe you would want to record the current temperature.)

- Determine which attribute you will use to store the information. You can decide to use the user's *description* attribute, which is advantageous because you can view it in the details pane of the Active Directory Users and Computers snap-in. Or you can use another user attribute.

  If you are extending the schema, I recommend adding a custom attribute called *lastLogonComputer*, for example. Create the custom attribute and associate it with a custom class, such as the *domain-UserInfo* class proposed in the previous section. Then associate that object class with the user object class in an auxiliary relationship. See Solution 6-7 for details on these procedures.

- Delegate users the Write permission to the selected attribute.

- Create a logon script that updates the attribute. You can use the startup script in Solution 6-8 as a starting point.

- Deploy the logon script using a GPO scoped to the users for whom you want to record this information.

# Create an attribute that supports users' software requests

In this solution and in Solutions 6-6 and 6-7, I've addressed methods for associating computers with users. The schema extensions I proposed result in a many-to-many relationship in which one computer might be associated with multiple users, and one user might be associated with multiple computers. This structure is useful for computer tracking and inventory management. But it might not be ideal for software deployment.

As you'll see in Solution Collection 9, "Improving the Deployment and Management of Applications and Configuration," it is generally a best practice to deploy software to a computer rather than to a user. There are two major justifications for this best practice. First, most software is licensed by computer, not by user. Second, you generally do not want an application to follow a user and install itself on each computer that the user logs on to. So when a user requests an application, the application should be provisioned to the user's computer, not to the user herself.

If a user has more than one computer association, how do you determine which computer or computers should be targeted for installation of the requested application? If the custom *computerAssignedTo* attribute is sufficient, use it. If not, create another custom attribute to manage this information. You can create an attribute called *softwareInstalledOn*, for example. The attribute would be associated with the *user* object class through an auxiliary relationship with a custom object class—*domain-UserInfo*, for example.

It can be single-valued if your business requirements are such that a user's software installation requests should target only one system. But I recommend that you create it as a multivalued attribute even if you currently target only one system. You don't have to use more than one value in the attribute, but it might come in handy in the future. The attribute can be a *distinguishedName* type or a *string* type, depending on whether you want to maintain references as distinguished names or as host names or FQDNs.

After you've created the attribute to match users with computers for software installation, when a user request a particular application, you can easily add both the user and his targeted systems into the group that manages that application's deployment. Using groups to manage software deployment is covered in Solution Collection 9.

## Solution summary

There is a lot of value to be gained from increasing the usefulness of Active Directory as a management and administrative database. Active Directory already supports a number of useful attributes that Windows does not expose in the user interfaces. You can use those attributes to maintain information about employee identity and organizational relationships including *assistant* and *secretary*. When you need to manage information that is not already supported by Active Directory attributes, you can extend the schema with those properties. Solution Collection 6, "Improving the Management and Administration of Computers," detailed the steps for schema extension and self-reporting attributes. In this solution, we examined applications of those skills to user administration and management.

# 7-5: Creating Administrative Tools to Manage Unused and Custom Attributes

## Solution overview

| | |
|---|---|
| **Type of solution** | Scripts |
| **Features and tools** | VBScript, HTAs, taskpad tasks, display modifiers |
| **Solution summary** | Create custom administrative tools to manage user attributes that Microsoft does not expose or that you have added to the schema. |
| **Benefits** | Manageability of custom attributes |

## Introduction

In solutions throughout this resource kit, I've provided scripts and HTAs that manage custom properties. In this solution, I guide you through the creation of a script and an HTA that enables you to access one or more properties of a user object. This functionality allows you to expose the unused and custom attributes discussed in the previous solution. If you are somewhat comfortable with the fundamentals of scripting with VBScript, this chapter gives you the insight you need to create administrative tools for custom attributes. If you are less comfortable with scripting, I recommend that you jump to the section on how to use the scripts I provide in this solution. Specifically, jump to the section, "Use the Object_Attribute.vbs script to display or edit any single-valued attribute."

We will explore the creation of custom tools from the inside out. We'll start with the simplest possible scripts that display and allow the modification of custom attributes. We'll then layer on complexity as we introduce issues related to multivalued attributes and HTML applications (HTAs). Along the way, we'll look at how to integrate the tools with the Active Directory Users and Computers snap-in.

# Display and edit the value of an unexposed attribute

Let's start by learning how to grab hold of an attribute of a user object and display it. I recommend that you follow along. We'll use the *employeeNumber* attribute as the first example. This attribute is defined in the schema as a string, with a maximum length of 512 characters. Because we're starting with the display of the attribute, I suggest that you populate the *employeeNumber* for a user manually so that there is some information to display.

To populate the *employeeNumber* of a user in Windows Server 2008, follow these steps:

1. Open the Active Directory Users and Computers snap-in.

2. Click the View menu, and make sure that Advanced Features is selected.

3. Open the properties of a user.

4. Click the Attribute Editor tab.

5. Select the *employeeNumber* attribute, and click Edit.

6. Enter any value, up to 512 characters. It will be used only for testing and learning purposes in this lesson.

7. Click OK to close the Properties dialog box.

To populate *employeeNumber* of a user in Windows Server 2003, follow these steps:

1. Open the ADSI Edit console by clicking Start, clicking Run, and entering the command **ADSIEdit.msc**.

   ADSI Edit is part of the Windows Server 2003 Support Tools, which must be installed from the Windows Server 2003 CD-ROM Support Directory, or they can be downloaded from the Microsoft Downloads site (*http://www.microsoft.com/downloads*).

2. Expand the root node of the tool, expand the domain node, and navigate to and select an OU that contains users.

3. Select a user object in the details pane.

4. Right-click it, and choose Properties.

5. Select the *employeeNumber* attribute, and click Edit.

6. Enter a value, up to 512 characters. It will be used only for testing and learning purposes in this lesson.

7. Click OK to close the Properties dialog box.

I know this seemed laborious. By the time this solution is complete, you will have tools that allow you to edit the property more easily. That's the whole point of this solution. But we have to have something to start with.

## Latch on to an object

Now that the attribute is populated, we're ready to display the attribute. The first step to do this in VBScript is to grab the user object so that you can then extract the attribute. To latch on to the user object, you create what's called an *object reference*. The following line of code creates an object reference for the user object of James Fine:

```
Set oObject = GetObject("LDAP://cn=James Fine,ou=People,dc=contoso,dc=com")
```

An object reference is nothing more than a variable—*oObject*, for example—that represents an object (in this case, a user in Active Directory). The object is retrieved using the *GetObject* statement, which uses the Active Directory services path (ADSPath) to locate the object. The ADSPath is the distinguished name of the object preceded by *LDAP://*. So everything to the right of the equals sign in the line of code just shown results in a reference to James Fine's user object. That reference is assigned to the variable *oObject* using the *Set* statement. As you know, if you assign a value to a variable, you simply use the syntax *variable = value*. When you use a variable as an object reference, you start with *Set*.

For what it's worth, the variable name can be anything. It's conventional to prefix variable names to indicate the variable type—*o* for *object*, for example—but that's all it is—convention—it's not required. Variables are case insensitive, as are statements such as *GetObject* and *Set*. Even the ADSPath is case insensitive. And spacing doesn't matter in VBScript, except within a literal—for example, within a string. So VBScript is a very forgiving scripting language.

## Display an attribute of an object

Now you are representing the Active Directory object by a variable. You manipulate the Active Directory object indirectly by manipulating the variable. User objects in Active Directory support a *SetPassword("newpassword")* method. Methods are actions—things you do to an object. To change James Fine's password, you can apply that method to the object reference: *oObject.SetPassword("newpassword")*. Objects also have attributes, of course. So to find James Fine's *employeeNumber*, we can look at *oObject.employeeNumber*, as in the following line of code:

```
WScript.Echo oObject.employeeNumber
```

The *WScript.Echo* statement creates output—to the *StdOut* stream that is returned in the command prompt using cscript.exe to launch the script, or to a dialog box if the script was launched using wscript.exe.

There's another way to get the attribute from the object, and that is to use the object's *Get* method. The *Get* method takes the attribute name as its argument. The following line of code produces a result that is identical to the aforementioned *oObject.employeeNumber* code:

```
WScript.Echo oObject.Get("employeeNumber")
```

Try it! Save the following two lines of code as "User_ShowEmployeeNumber_v1.vbs." Be sure that Notepad doesn't add a .*txt* extension by enclosing the name in quotes when you save it. Change the ADSPath of the sample user, James Fine, to match the user for whom you changed the *employeeNumber* earlier:

```
Set oObject = GetObject("LDAP://cn=James Fine,ou=People,dc=contoso,dc=com")
WScript.Echo oObject.Get("employeeNumber")
```

Run the script from the command prompt by entering the command **cscript.exe User_ShowEmployeeNumber_v1.vbs**. Then try double-clicking the script.

## Make a script more flexible using variables

Now let's make the script just a touch more sophisticated by abstracting the hard-wired elements of the script into variables. Examine the following code:

```
sAttribute = "employeeNumber"
sObjectADsPath = "LDAP://cn=James Fine,ou=People,dc=contoso,dc=com"
Set oObject = GetObject(sObjectADsPath)
sValue = oObject.Get(sAttribute)
WScript.Echo sValue
```

The advantage of *abstracting*, or separating a component of the script, is that the components can be managed separately. The preceding code can display any single-valued attribute of any object in Active Directory by changing the first two lines. The functional lines—the third through fifth—do not need to be modified any further. Note that I also assigned the value of the attribute to a variable, *sValue*. Chances are good that if you're going to the trouble of grabbing an attribute, you're going to want to do more with it than just display it, so we might as well store it in a variable.

Many coders tighten their scripts by *declaring* variables before they are used. This practice, along with using the *Option Explicit* statement at the beginning of a script, help to prevent script errors that are a result of typographic mistakes made in variable names. For example, the following code produces an error:

```
sAttribute = "employeeNumber"
sObjectADsPath = "LDAP://cn=James Fine,ou=People,dc=contoso,dc=com"
Set oObject = GetObject(sObjectADsPath)
sValue = oObject.Get(sAtribute)
WScript.Echo sValue
```

There's nothing wrong with the code itself, but the variable *sAttribute* is mistyped in the *Get* method in the fourth line. Adding *Option Explicit* and declaring variables using the *Dim* statement produces a specific error that explains that a variable is used that was not declared. So the next step for our script is to add these two lines at the beginning:

```
Option Explicit
Dim sObjectADsPath, oObject, sAttribute, sValue
```

Variables can be declared on separate lines, with separate *Dim* statements, or they can be combined in a comma-delimited list as shown in the preceding code.

## Enable a script to use arguments

We need to make our script more flexible so that we can use it to display the *employeeNumber* attribute of any user we specify. This is achieved by enabling the script to accept arguments. Let's assume that the script will be sent the ADsPath of a user as the argument. You call the script with this syntax:

```
cscript "User_ShowEmployeeNumber_v1.vbs" "ADsPath of User"
```

A script's arguments are represented as a collection of zero or more items by the *WScript.Arguments()* collection. The index of arguments is zero-based, so the first argument passed to the script is actually *WScript.Arguments(0)*. We assign that to our *sObjectADsPath* variable, as shown here:

```
Option Explicit
Dim sObjectADsPath, oObject, sAttribute, sValue
sAttribute = "employeeNumber"
sObjectADsPath = wscript.Arguments(0)
Set oObject = GetObject(sObjectADsPath)
sValue = oObject.Get(sAttribute)
WScript.Echo sValue
```

## Handle errors

If the script is called without an argument, it will throw an error. We proactively avoid that problem with the following code:

```
If WScript.Arguments.Count = 0 Then
    WScript.Echo "Usage: cscript.exe " & WScript.ScriptFullName & _
        " <ADsPath of user>"
    WScript.Quit(0)
End If
```

This code looks at the *Count* property of the *Arguments* collection. If it is zero, meaning no arguments were passed, a message is displayed that reminds the user how to call the script. The message uses the ampersand (&) to concatenate several pieces into one message. *WScript.FullName* returns the path and filename of the current script. The underscore character (_) preceded by a space is used to continue a single line of code on a second line of the script. And *WScript.Quit(0)* causes the script to exit with an exit code of zero. Exit codes are discussed in Solution Collection 9. They aren't particularly important in our lesson. The conditional *If Then* block is closed with the *End If* statement.

We could also run into an error if the argument is an invalid path. We won't know that until we try to get the object using that path. We can trap that error using the following code around the *GetObject* statement:

```
On Error Resume Next
Set oObject = GetObject(sObjectADsPath)
If Err.Number <> 0 Then
    WScript.Echo "The ADsPath provided is invalid:" & vbCrLf & _
        sObjectADsPath & vbCrLf & "Error " & Err.Number & _
        vbCrLf & Err.Description
    WScript.Quit(0)
End If
On Error Goto 0
```

The *On Error Resume Next* statement tells the script processor that if any error is encountered, the script should continue on the next line rather than throw an error. So if *GetObject* fails, the script continues on the next line. On the next line, the *If Err.Number<>0 Then* statement determines whether an error occurred. There is an object, *Err*, that is used to represent errors. If the *Number* property of the *Err* object is zero, no error occurred. If any other value is displayed, there was an error. So if the value is not zero, the code creates a message. The message is a long one, with several line continuations (underscores). It also creates line breaks in the message using the intrinsic constant *vbCrLf* (also not case sensitive). The message displays the error number and any description provided by the error in the *Description* property of the *Err* object. Then the code quits. On the line after the *End If* statement, the *On Error Goto 0* command resets the script to its default error-processing mode, which is to throw an error if an error occurs.

You'll see in many scripts that if the script processing continues, rather than quits, an *Err.Clear* statement is used. This statement clears out the contents of the *Err* object. It's important to do that after handling an error so that the next time you examine *Err.Number* it does not continue to reflect the error that you've already handled.

In our code, there is yet another opportunity for an error. When you get an attribute of an object and that attribute has never been populated, the *object.PropertyName* or *object.Get("PropertyName")* method throws an error. Active Directory creates storage for an attribute for a user only when the attribute actually has a value. You can experience this by running your script, User_ShowEmployeeNumber_v1.vbs, with the path to a user that does not have an *employeeNumber* configured. So we have to intercept, or trap, that error and handle it, as well. The following code achieves that result:

```
On Error Resume Next
sValue = oObject.Get(sAttribute)
If Err.Number <> 0 Then
    WScript.Echo "There is no value for " & sAttribute
    WScript.Quit(0)
End If
On Error Goto 0
WScript.Echo sValue
```

The same structure is used. Prepare to trap an error with *On Error Resume Next*, execute code that might produce an error, examine the *Err.Number* attribute to determine whether an error occurred, handle the error accordingly, and then reset error processing to identify unanticipated errors using *On Error Goto 0*.

The final code is available as User_ShowEmployeeNumber_v2.vbs in the Scripts folder of the companion media.

## Edit an unexposed or custom attribute

To edit the value of *employeeNumber* or any other attribute, you need to provide a method for input. VBScript's *InputBox* function does just that. It produces a dialog box that can include a message, a title bar, and a default value for the input. Here is the basic syntax of *InputBox*:

```
InputBox(prompt, title, default)
```

For our purposes in this lesson, we can use *InputBox* both to show the current value and to accept input for a new value. Look at the following code:

```
On Error Resume Next
sValue = oObject.Get(sAttribute)
If Err.Number <> 0 Then
    sPrompt = "There is no current value for " & sAttribute
    sValue = ""
Else
    sPrompt = "The current value for " & sAttribute & " is" & vbCrLf & _
            sValue
End If
On Error Goto 0
sNewValue = InputBox(sPrompt, sAttribute, sValue)
```

First, we prepare for the possibility that the attribute does not yet have a value. If this is the case, an error is produced by the *Get*(attributeName) method and we prepare a message that indicates there's no current value. I also set the value of *sValue* to blank, which isn't really necessary but adds clarity to the script. If the *Get* method was successful, the prompt is prepared to communicate the current value.

The important line is the one that contains the *InputBox* function. The *InputBox* function creates the dialog box with a prompt that communicates the current value and a title bar showing the attribute name. The default value is set to *sValue* so that, if the user doesn't want to change the attribute, he can just click OK and the original value of *sValue* will be maintained.

## Save the new value

Finally, we need to save the new value entered by the user. To optimize replication, however, we should save the value only if it has changed. The following code can be used:

```
If sNewValue <> sValue Then
    On Error Resume Next
    oObject.Put sAttribute, sNewValue
    oObject.SetInfo
    If Err.Number <> 0 Then
        WScript.Echo "Error changing value of " & sAttribute
        WScript.Quit(0)
    End If
End If
```

If the new value is different from the attribute's current value, we attempt to save the new value. This is done by using the *Put* method of the object, which takes the attribute name and value as its arguments. Changes to objects are made to the local representation of the object, which is specified by the object reference variable *oObject*. To commit the changes to Active Directory, we must use the *SetInfo* method. These steps could fail for a variety of reasons—the most likely reason is that the user does not have Write permission on the attribute. If there was an error, we communicate that to the user. We could evaluate the error number to determine exactly what went wrong, but for now we'll just handle all errors with a generic message.

There is another issue. Ideally, if the attribute value is erased, the attribute should be cleared from the user object, not just set to blank. The following lines of code do just that:

```
oObject.PutEx 1, sAttribute, 0
oObject.SetInfo
```

The *1* and *0* are required. The *PutEx* method can be used to perform several types of changes to attributes, one of which is to clear the attribute. The *1* indicates the operation, which is often represented by a constant, *ADS_PROPERTY_CLEAR*. The name of the constant relates to a development concept that is beyond the scope of this book. Just think of it as a variable that has a specific (though not required) name to provide consistency across development languages. So earlier in the script, we would define the constant using this code:

```
Const ADS_PROPERTY_CLEAR = 1
```

We could then use the constant name in our *PutEx* method:

```
oObject.PutEx ADS_PROPERTY_CLEAR, sAttribute, 0
oObject.SetInfo
```

But wait! There's one more challenge caused by the *InputBox* function. It provides an OK button and a Cancel button. If the user clicks Cancel, the function returns a blank string, just as if the user deleted the text in the input box and clicked OK. So if the new value comes back blank, we don't know whether it is intentionally blank (indicating that the user wants to delete the value) or whether the user simply looked at the current value and clicked Cancel.

Therefore, we should use a prompt to confirm what the user wants to do. The following code prompts a user to confirm deletion, and if the user clicks Yes, the deletion proceeds:

```
If MsgBox("Do you want to delete the current value, " & _
    sValue, vbYesNo, "Confirm deletion") = vbYes then
    oObject.PutEx ADS_PROPERTY_CLEAR, sAttribute, 0
    oObject.SetInfo
End If
```

So the code that supports changing and deleting the value of an attribute is as follows:

```
Const ADS_PROPERTY_CLEAR = 1
If sNewValue <> sValue Then
    On Error Resume Next
    If sNewValue > "" Then
        oObject.Put sAttribute, sNewValue
        oObject.SetInfo
    Else
        If MsgBox("Do you want to delete the current value, " & _
            sValue, vbYesNo, "Confirm deletion") = vbYes then
            oObject.PutEx ADS_PROPERTY_CLEAR, sAttribute, 0
            oObject.SetInfo
        End If
    End If
    If Err.Number <> 0 Then
        WScript.Echo "Error changing value of " & sAttribute
        WScript.Quit(0)
    End If
End If
```

The resulting code is the User_ShowEmployeeNumber_v3.vbs in the Scripts folder. The code includes declarations for the new variables introduced in version 3: *sPrompt* and *sNewValue*. You can change the value of *sAttribute* to apply the script to any single-valued attribute.

## Use the Object_Attribute.vbs script to display or edit any single-valued attribute

The Object_Attribute.vbs script is found in the Scripts folder of the companion media. It allows you, with minimal customization, to display and edit any single-valued attribute. Just change the two lines in the *Configuration Block*. Then call the script with this command:

```
cscript Object_Attribute.vbs [DN | ADSPath | name]
```

 **Note**  Add Object_Attribute.vbs as a custom task or context menu item in your MMC task-pads. Solution Collection 1 details the steps required for adding a shell command task that calls a script with arguments.

The script accepts a user name (pre–Windows 2000 logon name or *sAMAccountName*), a distinguished name, or the ADSPath. It can accept the same arguments for groups. For computers, use the computer's name, distinguished name, or ADSPath.

To support these options, the script uses several routines from my library: ADObject_Find_Generic, ADObject_NameType, ADObject_Search_Array, ADObject_Search_RS, and ADObject_Validate. These routines are used to translate the argument passed to the script into a common denominator: the ADSPath of the object.

# Use Object_Attribute.hta to view or edit single-valued or multivalued attributes

One of the more powerful tools in this resource kit is Object_Attribute.hta. This generic HTA can be customized using values in the *Configuration Block* to allow you to view or edit any single-valued or multivalued attribute. It also provides lookup capabilities so that you can see details about an attribute, such as the details about a user who is a member of a group.

> **Important**    This tool is powerful enough that it is highly likely to be updated as readers provide feedback. Be sure to visit the resource kit Web site, *www.intelliem.com/resourcekit*, for the latest version before you proceed to customize it for your enterprise.

The tool allows you to define the attribute that will be modified, as well as user-interface characteristics such as the title bar, heading, prompt, and popup message text. You can also select the layout of the tool—which can be *SIMPLE* (a text box to edit a single-valued attribute) or *MULTIDETAILS*, which shows a list of values in a multivalued attribute (such as the *member* attribute of a group)—and, when an item is selected, details of that item are shown in the details pane. You can also control whether the tool allows you to edit the attribute. Of course, even if the tool allows editing, changes will not be committed successfully to Active Directory unless you have Write permission for the attribute.

The easiest way to learn about the configuration options for the tool is to experiment with the *Configuration Block*. I have included several samples in the Scripts folder that are summarized here:

**Object_Attribute_GroupMembers.hta**    Displays and allows editing of the *member* attribute of groups. This tool demonstrates the list and details view layout, specified by setting *sUserInterface* to *MULTIDETAILS*.

**Object_Attribute_UserMemberOf.hta**    Displays the *memberOf* attribute of users. Back linked attributes cannot be changed, so you must set *bAllowEdit* to *FALSE* when using Object_Attribute to manage back links.

**Object_Attribute_EmployeeNumber.hta**    Displays the *employeeNumber* attribute of users. Demonstrates managing an attribute that is not otherwise revealed in the Active Directory user interface.

**Object_Attribute_ComputerAssignedTo.hta and Object_Attribute_AssignedComputers.hta**

Demonstrate accessing the custom attributes created in Solution 7-4 and in Solution 6-7. These HTAs will not work in your environment because you will not have added attributes named *contoso-computerAssignedTo* or *contoso-AssignedComputers* in your schema. These two HTAs are for demonstration purposes only. Note that the HTA for the back link *assignedComputers* attribute does not allow editing of the attribute because back links cannot be modified directly—you must change the forward link. If you have added custom attributes for computer assignment to the schema, change the *Configuration Block* to reflect the attributes' names.

To create your own derivation of Object_Attribute.hta, change the *Configuration Block* to support the attribute you are managing.

The HTAs are written to work in three modes: stand-alone (double-click the HTA), execution as a shell task in a taskpad, or execution as a context menu command. Review Solution 1-3 on page 35 for details regarding the creation of taskpad shell tasks and context menu commands.

## Solution summary

In this solution, I stepped you through the VBScript code required to access and manipulate attributes of user objects. I also provided sample scripts and HTAs to help you manage attributes that might otherwise be unexposed in the user interface of the Active Directory Users and Computers snap-in. Although these concepts and skills were discussed in the context of user objects, they also apply to computers, groups, and other Active Directory objects. By creating custom administrative tools to work with attributes in Active Directory, and integrating those tools with the Active Directory Users and Computers snap-in using taskpad tasks or context menu changes, you can further extend the value your organization gets out of Active Directory as an enterprise directory service.

# 7-6: Moving Users and Other Objects

## Solution overview

| | |
|---|---|
| **Type of solution** | Guidance |
| **Features and tools** | Active Directory ACLs, proxying |
| **Solution summary** | Delegating the ability to move users or computers between OUs also delegates the ability to delete one or more such objects, accidentally or intentionally. You should design your delegation to restrict the ability to delete objects. |
| **Benefits** | Decreased risk of denial of service; decreased potential for deleted object recovery requirements. |

# Introduction

The ability to move users or other objects between OUs in Active Directory is commonly required by administrators to support the movement of employees and computers around an organization. Unfortunately, it is somewhat dangerous to allow administrators to move objects, because the permissions required to move objects out of an OU also enable the intentional or accidental deletion of all objects, leading to an accidental or intentional denial of service. In this short solution, I outline the problem of object movement in Active Directory. In Solution 8-7 on page 570, I discuss the use of proxied tasks, which can be a solution to the problem.

# Understand the permissions required to move an object in Active Directory

To move an object in Active Directory, you need to have delegated permissions on the object. For users, computers, and groups, you must have Write Property permission for the relative distinguished name (*name*) and common name (*cn*) attributes. Additionally, you need the permission to create child objects of the object class on the destination OU. For example, if you're moving a user from the New York OU to the Sydney OU, you must have Create User Objects permission on the Sydney OU.

In addition, and most problematically, you must have Delete permission for the object you are moving or Delete Child Objects permission on the source OU. Continuing our example, you must have permission to delete users in the New York OU to move a user from New York to Sydney. When you move an object between OUs, you are *not* deleting it and re-creating it—the object is the same and all of its attributes remain intact—but the permissions required to move an object are the Delete permission in the source OU and the Create Object permission in the destination OU.

# Recognize the denial-of-service exposure

I hope you can already see the problem. Many organizations allow their help desk to move users and computers between site-based, departmental, or other divisional OUs. That means that any member of the help desk can, accidentally or intentionally, delete one or more (or all!) users and computers. If that were to happen, whether for one or more objects, those users and computers would be unable to authenticate properly and could experience a denial of service. Additionally, the Active Directory administrators would need to dust off the Active Directory deleted object recovery procedures (do you know where yours are?) and begin the arduous process of recovering objects and repopulating lost attributes, or performing an authoritative restore of an object from a snapshot or other backup mechanism. It's not pretty.

# Carefully restrict the delegation to move (delete) objects

Your enterprise delegation plan should tightly restrict who is allowed to delete objects from your directory service. Solution Collection 5 details the ins and outs of delegation, but I deferred discussion of this particular issue to now so that we could examine it in light of the potential for deleted user objects. Although users are painful to lose, groups can be more painful, and computers aren't so fun either. Object deletion, and therefore object movement between OUs, should be delegated to a tightly scoped subset of your administrative team.

## Delegate highly sensitive tasks such as object deletion to tertiary administrative credentials

For administrators who are delegated permission to delete objects, assign the delegation to a third administrative account that is created in addition to their secondary logon administrative account. The secondary logon can be used for day-to-day administration. The tertiary account is reserved for high-impact administrative tasks. Even if you are in a small business, you can follow this last recommendation—create a tertiary account for yourself that has the most sensitive privileges assigned to it, to help shield you from mistakes that could result in object deletion and resumé generation.

## Proxy the task of moving objects

So if you have restricted the ability to delete, and thereby to move, objects in Active Directory, does that mean every time a user needs to be moved to another OU that the request must be escalated to the very top? Not necessarily.

In Solution 8-7, I introduce the concept of proxying. Proxying results in a task being performed on your behalf by a middle-man process that uses credentials different from, and more elevated than, your own. If you implement a form of proxying—such as the simple approach outlined in Solution 8-7—you can allow the help desk to enter requests for object movements. The proxy performs the move using credentials with appropriate delegation in Active Directory. The help desk member is not able to perform the task directly using the Active Directory Users and Computers snap-in, as her credentials do not carry sufficient permissions. But the proxy does the task on her behalf.

## Solution summary

Unfortunately, there is no way to directly delegate the ability to move objects in Active Directory. Instead, to move an object, you must have permissions that include the ability to delete objects in the source OU and create objects in the target OU. It seems bizarre because you are not actually deleting and re-creating the object—you are just moving it—but that's the way the ACL cookie crumbles. The ability to delete objects opens up a nasty exposure to denial of service. Therefore, you must strictly limit the users who have permission to delete objects, which would thereby limit those who can move objects. To enable object movement without exposure to denial of service, implement object movement as a proxied task, as outlined in Solution 8-7.

# 7-7: Provisioning the Creation of Users

## Solution overview

| | |
|---|---|
| Type of solution | Scripts and tools |
| Features and tools | User_Provision.vbs, User_Provision.hta, provisioning concepts |
| Solution summary | Provisioning the creation of users with custom tools allows you to inject business logic and rules into the process. |
| Benefits | Increased compliance with standards and conventions for objects and attributes; support for automated object creation and management. |

## Introduction

When you create or manage an object using native Windows tools such as the Active Directory Users and Computers snap-in, you are using an attribute editor that has almost no data validation and incorporates none of the rules specific to your business. Let's assume, as suggested elsewhere in this resource kit, that you've adopted standards for specific attributes. For example, you've determined that *displayName* will follow the *LastName, FirstName MiddleName* format and that *cn* will be *FirstName MiddleName LastName*. You might also have determined what information is put into a user's *description* attribute. And you might want to ensure that fields such as *employeeID*, *employeeType*, and *employeeNumber* are populated for every user. The Active Directory Users and Computers snap-in will not enforce that logic. It lets you enter pretty much whatever you want into the attributes it exposes.

The only way around this limitation is to create custom tools that are used instead of, or alongside, native tools such as the Active Directory Users and Computers snap-in. By creating custom tools, you can enforce data validation and business logic—you can *provision* changes rather than just enter them. In this solution, I provide an example of key concepts related to provisioning using a script and an HTA that enables the provisioning of new users.

## Examine a user-provisioning script

In the Scripts folder of the companion media, you'll find User_Provison.vbs. This script illustrates the components of a provisioning process. You can customize its configuration block so that it is appropriate for your environment, but you'll also want to customize its *BusinessLogic* and *Validate* subroutines. I recommend you treat this script as an illustration and extend it significantly to provision users based on your requirements, conventions, and business logic.

The script is called with a series of arguments listed both in the comments at the top of the script and in the *Usage* subroutine. The syntax the script expects is the following:

```
cscript user_provision.vbs /firstname:John [/initial:Q]
    [/middlename:Franklin] /lastname:Doe /samaccountname:"jdoe"
    /ou:"ou=Employees,ou=People,dc=contoso,dc=com"
    [/description:"Accountant in Sydney"]
```

Note that each argument is named with a forward slash, the argument name, and a colon. This format allows the script to make much more effective use of the arguments, and it adds clarity to the command line. Several arguments are required: *firstname*, *lastname*, *samaccountname*, and *ou*.

Let's look at each component of User_Provision.vbs to learn what it takes to create a provisioning script.

## Structure the script in subroutines and functions

The script declares variables and assigns some variables in the *Configuration Block*. Other than that, the script contains only two lines of code in the active flow of the script:

```
Call MainRoutine()
WScript.Quit
```

In other words, the only code that is run directly is code to call the *MainRoutine* subroutine and then to exit the script. All other code is contained in subroutines and functions that branch off of *MainRoutine*. This approach, called *encapsulating* routines, is helpful when you move the code into other applications—HTAs, for example.

## Declare important configuration variables in the global scope

At the top of the script, you'll see a number of variables declared with *Dim* statements before and outside of the subroutines. I find it useful to declare all the important configuration variables in this location. Doing so creates the variables in what is called *global scope*, which makes them available to all subroutines and functions. Think of it as reserving the name and memory for the variable so that, wherever that variable is referred to, the code is reaching up into the shared definition of the variable. My rule is that I declare all variables that are assigned in the *Configuration Block*, passed as arguments, or created by business logic in global scope.

## Identify arguments passed to the script

The *MainRoutine* code first calls the *Arguments* subroutine. The job of *Arguments* is to extract all the arguments passed to the routine. *Arguments* puts the values passed to the script into the globally declared variables. Notice that it does not try to interpret or do anything else with the arguments. It is just transferring them from the command line to the script's variables.

```
Sub Arguments()
    Dim oArgs
    ' Check for "HELP"
    If (WScript.Arguments.Count = 0) Or _
        (WScript.Arguments.Named.Exists("?")) Then Call Usage()
    Set oArgs = WScript.Arguments.Named
    sFirst = oArgs("firstname")
    sInit = oArgs("initial")
    sMiddle = oArgs("middlename")
    sLast = oArgs("lastname")
```

```
    sSAM = oArgs("samaccountname")
    sDescription = oArgs("description")
    sTargetOU = oArgs("ou")
End Sub
```

The *Arguments* subroutine also checks to see if the person executing the script needs help, indicated by calling the script with no arguments or a */?* switch. In that case, the code branches to the *Usage* subroutine, which simply dumps an explanation of the script's usage.

## Apply business logic to derive additional attributes

When *Arguments* completes, execution returns to *MainRoutine*, which then calls *BusinessLogic*. The job of *BusinessLogic* is to derive additional information that was not provided by the arguments. For example, you might specify that the user principal name is derived by using *First-Name.MiddleName.LastName@domain.com.*

In User_Provision.vbs, *BusinessLogic* calls a separate subroutine, *CalculateNames*, which does the job of calculating all the name attributes that are derived from the first, middle, and last names passed as arguments. Examine that code to identify how the names are used to derive the following:

- *cn*: *FirstName MiddleName LastName*
- *displayName*: *LastName, FirstName MiddleName*
- *userPrincipalName*: *FirstName.MiddleName.LastName@UPNSuffix*

Notice as each attribute is derived, it is assigned to the appropriate variable declared globally.

*BusinessLogic* also derives the user's profile path. It uses the *Replace()* function to replace the %username% token in the profile path template, *sProfileNamespace*, with the *samAccountName* passed to the script on the command line.

In a more sophisticated provisioning script, you could perform lots of additional business logic. You could even tap into other data sources to drive toward the outcome of the provisioning process.

## Validate the attributes prior to making changes

After *BusinessLogic* has derived the remaining attributes, the *MainRoutine* calls the *Validate* function. *Validate* uses conditions to determine whether all required attributes have been completed. It returns Boolean *True* if the required attributes have values and *False* if one or more do not. *MainRoutine* uses the Boolean value returned by the *Validate* function to decide whether to quit or continue processing.

In a more sophisticated provisioning script, you could not only test the existence of values in required fields but also perform tests to make sure the actual values fell within prescribed ranges or patterns.

### Execute the task

With all the attributes identified or derived, the script then creates the user object and assigns all attributes. It also assigns a random password to the account.

### Provision object creation and management

This example illustrates the components of provisioning. To ensure that the business process is followed, you must accept appropriate input, derive any additional attributes of the change you are provisioning, ensure that all the rules are being followed, and then, and only then, perform the task. These concepts apply to all provisioning tasks.

## Create graphical provisioning tools

In the Scripts folder, you'll find User_Provision.hta. The purpose of this HTML Application is to illustrate how you can port a scripted provisioning process into a graphical HTA. I recommend you perform a line-by-line comparison of the scripts. In fact, in the Scripts folder, look for User_Provision_Compare.pdf for just such a comparison.

You'll see that the core of the provisioning code is identical between the script and the HTA. The only differences are those related to input and output. Scripts take input from arguments and provide output through statements such as *WScript.Echo*. HTAs get input from controls, such as text boxes, in the HTML form, and provide output by dynamically changing a *span* or *div* tag in the HTML itself.

The major difference between the script and the HTA is not the workhorse code, but the HTML itself. There is a control—a text box or drop-down list—for each parameter. Some controls trigger changes, using *OnChange* subroutines in the script, so that as you enter name attributes, the derived attributes are updated visually on the form. To enforce business rules, the *Window_OnLoad* event disables controls that cannot be changed by a user.

## Solution summary

HTML and VBScript instruction is beyond the scope of this resource kit, but I think you'll find that by using User_Provision.hta as a kind of template, you can derive useful administrative tools to align Active Directory administration with your business requirements, processes, and standards. In this solution, I provided two examples of tools—one script, and one graphical HTA—that incorporate business rules and data validation to support a provisioned creation of user objects.

The logical next step is to consider that although such tools encourage administrators to follow a process, the tools themselves cannot *enforce* a process. Why? Because an administrator can just open the Active Directory Users and Computers snap-in and make an unprovisioned change directly. That's where proxying comes into play. See Solution 8-7 for information about proxying.

Solution Collection 8

# Reimagining the Administration of Groups and Membership

I'm sure you've heard the message loud and clear in the solutions presented in this resource kit: It's time to elevate the sophistication of your group management framework. We've relied on groups to implement role-based management using Active Directory, secured files and folders and applied quotas using groups, configured user data and settings redirection based on groups, created document libraries with group permissions, and managed the otherwise unwieldy delegation of permissions in Active Directory itself with groups. We discussed groups of computers, groups of users, and capability management groups that contain role groups. In the next two Solution Collections, we deploy software to groups and scope Group Policy (which actually has very little to do with groups) using global security groups. Every single Solution Collection in this resource kit has something to do with groups.

## Scenarios, Pain, and Solution

I've seen very few organizations that have fully actualized the potential administrative productivity that can be found by creating a rule-based, automated, data-driven management infrastructure. Groups provide that engine. Without advanced, nuanced approaches to group management, you might find yourself in these scenarios:

- At Contoso, Ltd., Mike Danseglio is the lead for a large new engineering program. The program maintains its resources in a shared folder on a file server, and there is a capability management group—ACL_Engineering Program_Contribute—that allows program members to add their resources to the folder and to view each other's resources. The role group called Engineering Program contains users in the program and is a member of the ACL_Engineering Program_Contribute group.

With this role-based access control model, when new hires are added to the program, they immediately gain appropriate access to the shared folder. When users who are not in the program need access to the share, they call the help desk, which creates a support ticket. A member of the IT organization then contacts Mike to get Mike's approval. If the request is approved, the IT employee adds the user to the ACL_Engineering Program_Contribute group and closes the support ticket. In the end, it's really up to Mike to approve or reject the user's request for access. Neither the help desk nor the IT organization is adding value to the process. There are many other similar scenarios throughout Contoso. To reduce help desk costs and increase responsiveness to its internal customers, the IT organization wants to empower users such as Mike to directly manage the membership of groups for which they have business ownership.

- A recent security audit resulted in a mandate to remove unnecessary groups from Active Directory, and to understand and justify the purpose of the remaining groups. The IT organization needs to evaluate each group to list all the users who belong to the group, whether directly or indirectly, and to list all the groups to which the group belongs, both directly and through nesting.

- Concurrently, the IT organization wants to establish standards whereby when a group is created, its description clearly indicates the purpose of the group, its name complies with naming standards, and for capability management groups, its *info* field lists all the resources managed by the group. They also want to keep a record of groups, the individual who created each group, and the person or team that is responsible for determining group membership.

- Contoso, Ltd., isn't the only company feeling pain. Last week, at Blue Yonder Airlines, an important group was deleted accidentally. This week, object recovery plans are being developed, and the support team is working to determine who had belonged to the deleted group. IT management has required that all new groups be protected from accidental deletion.

- Application developers at Litware, Inc., have asked to be given the ability to manage the membership of groups that determine who receives their applications.

- In an effort to increase responsiveness, the IT organization at Fabrikam, Inc., has identified groups for which users should be able to join and leave without IT intervention.

- After a recent security incident involving a compromised administrative account, the Board of Directors at Trey Research has required management to implement a much stricter password policy for members of the Domain Admins group.

In this Solution Collection, we will deliver tools to make the administration of groups easier, allow visibility and even management of group membership to nontechnical owners, create groups that allow users to join and leave at will, and configure group membership that is synchronized with the objects in an organizational unit (OU) or with other Active Directory attributes. Perhaps most importantly, in this Solution Collection I introduce you to the concept of proxying, which has the potential to revolutionize not only the way you manage groups but also the way you conduct other Active Directory and Microsoft Windows administration.

# 8-1: Best Practices for Creating Group Objects

## Solution overview

| | |
|---|---|
| **Type of solution** | Guidance |
| **Features and tools** | Group object attributes, protection from deletion, Dsmod, and Dsacls |
| **Solution summary** | Configure additional attributes and properties of user objects, and explore scenarios that warrant deviating from conventional group management guidelines. |
| **Benefits** | Increased manageability of groups, reduced risk of group deletion, increased total group membership for users. |

## Introduction

Groups are a fundamental object class in any Active Directory enterprise. Whether you use groups as extensively as envisioned by some of the solutions in this resource kit or use them on a more limited basis, it is important that you manage them efficiently and effectively. In this solution, I review some of the best practices related to group management and position them against real-world constraints to help you determine when best practices are or are not practical.

## Create groups that document their purpose

Creating a group in Active Directory is easy. It is not so easy to make sure that the group is used correctly over time or to audit a group to determine how it is used or whether it is used at all. You can facilitate the management of a group over its entire life cycle by helping administrators understand the group's purpose. So when you do create a group in Active Directory, I recommend that you follow the best practices in the following sections.

### Establish and adhere to a strict naming convention

Solution 1-5 on page 55 provides guidance related to group naming conventions. Establishing and following group naming standards enables measurable increases in productivity and automation. I highly recommend that your convention include a prefix that indicates the purpose of the group. For example, the prefix *APP* can be used to designate groups that are used to manage applications, and the prefix *ACL* can be used for groups that are assigned permissions on access control lists (ACLs). With such prefixes, it becomes easier to locate and interpret the purpose of groups named APP_Accounting versus ACL_Accounting_Read—the former is used to manage the deployment of the accounting software, and the latter to provide read access to the accounting folder. Be sure to read Solution 1-5 for details about naming conventions.

## Summarize the purpose of the group in its description

The *description* attribute of a group object is an ideal place to summarize the purpose of the group. Because the Description column is enabled by default in the details pane of the Active Directory Users and Computers snap-in, the group's purpose can be highly visible to administrators.

## Detail the purpose of the group in its notes

When you open the properties of a group object, the Notes text box is visible on the General tab, shown in Figure 8-1. This field maps to the attribute *comment* with the Lightweight Directory Access Protocol (LDAP) display name *info* in the schema. Interestingly, there is also an attribute with the LDAP display name *comment* but with the common name *User-Comment*. Yes, it's confusing! To access the property programmatically, you can use the following code:

```
sGroupDN = "cn=ACL_Budget_Edit,ou=resource access,ou=groups,dc=contoso,dc=com"
Set oGroup = GetObject("LDAP://" & sGroupDN)
oGroup.Put "info","\\contoso.com\finance\budget (EDIT)"
oGroup.SetInfo
WScript.Echo oGroup.Get("info")
```

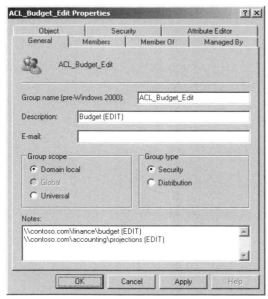

**Figure 8-1**  A group's Properties dialog box, showing the Notes field that maps to the *info* attribute

You can see from the code just shown that I enter the Universal Naming Convention (UNC) path to the resource that is managed by the group, and indicate the capability that is provided—for example, *(EDIT)*. I place the capability in parentheses so that I can identify and extract the capability programmatically. If the group manages access to resources in more than one location, separate the paths with a carriage return and line break, represented by the intrinsic constant *vbCrLf*, as shown here:

```
oGroup.Put "info","\\contoso.com\finance\budget (EDIT)" & vbCrLf & _
    "\\contoso.com\finance\projections (EDIT)"
```

I recommend that you use the *info* attribute similarly for groups that manage other types of resources. For example, groups that are used to scope Group Policy objects (GPOs) should list the GPOs in the *info* attribute.

## Protect groups from accidental deletion

The accidental deletion of a group object has a high impact on administrators and a potentially serious impact on security. Consider a group that has been used to manage access to resources. If the group is deleted, access to that resource is changed. Either users who should be able to access the resource are suddenly prevented from access, creating a denial-of-service scenario, or if you had used the group to deny access to a resource with a Deny permission, inappropriate access to the resource becomes possible.

Additionally, if you re-create the group, the new group object will have a new security identifier (SID), which will not match the SIDs on ACLs of resources. So you must instead perform object recovery to reanimate the deleted group before the tombstone interval is reached. When a group has been deleted for the tombstone interval—60 days by default—the group and its SID are permanently deleted from Active Directory. When you reanimate a tombstoned object, you must re-create most of its attributes including, importantly, the *member* attribute of group objects. That means you must rebuild the group membership after restoring the deleted object. Alternatively, you can perform an authoritative restore or, in Windows Server 2008, turn to your Active Directory snapshots to recover both the group and its membership.

You can learn more about recovering deleted groups and their memberships in Knowledge Base article 840001, which you can find at *http://support.microsoft.com/kb/840001/en-us*. In any event, it is safe to say that recovering a deleted group is a skill you should hope to use only in disaster recovery fire drills, not in a production environment.

Protect yourself from the potentially devastating results of group object deletion by protecting each group you create from deletion. Windows Server 2008 makes it easy to protect any object from accidental deletion. To protect an object, follow these steps:

1. In the Active Directory Users and Computers snap-in, click the View menu and make sure that Advanced Features is selected.

2. Open the Properties dialog box for a group.

3.  On the Object tab, select the Protect Object From Accidental Deletion check box.

4.  Click OK.

> **Note**    This is one of the few places in Windows where you actually have to click OK. Clicking Apply does not modify the ACL based on your selection.

The Protect Object From Accidental Deletion option applies an access control entry (ACE) to the ACL of the object that explicitly denies the Everyone group both the Delete permission and the Delete Subtree permission. If you really do want to delete the group, you can return to the Object tab of the Properties dialog box and clear the Protect Object From Accidental Deletion check box.

You can also protect objects from deletion by applying the ACEs directly. This can even be done from the command prompt using the Dsacls command. The following command applies the ACEs required to protect the ACL_Budget_Edit group from deletion:

```
dsacls "cn=ACL_Budget_Edit,ou=resource access,ou=groups,dc=contoso,dc=com"
    /D Everyone:SDDT
```

You can use this command both in Windows Server 2008 and Windows Server 2003 domains. It's a bit more difficult to remove the protection using Dsacls because the command does not allow you to remove an individual ACE. Instead, you must remove all permissions assigned to the Everyone group using this command:

```
dsacls "cn=ACL_Budget_Edit,ou=resource access,ou=groups,dc=contoso,dc=com"
    /R Everyone
```

However, before you enter this command, you must be certain that you have documented any other permissions explicitly assigned to the Everyone group. After revoking the permissions of the Everyone group using the preceding command, you need to re-create any of the permissions that had been assigned to the Everyone group that you want to maintain. Fortunately, it is unusual for the Everyone group to have any explicit permissions for an object, so most often the only permissions you'll be removing will be the Deny ACEs that protected the object.

## Consider the group type: security vs. distribution

You are certainly familiar with the fundamental difference between security groups and distribution groups. When you are authenticated by a Windows system, the security access token that is generated to impersonate you to the local security subsystem includes the SIDs of security groups to which you belong, but it does not include SIDs of distribution groups. Therefore, security groups can be used to manage access to resources such as files and folders on an NTFS file system, printers, and registry data. Both security and distribution groups can be e-mail enabled.

## Remember group membership limitations

In Solution 1-7 on page 77, I discussed one of the management challenges in larger organizations: implementing role-based management within the constraints of the maximum token size. To summarize, the security token generated for a user by current releases of Windows operating systems can store SIDs for several hundred groups, in the range of 200 to 400. If a user belongs to more groups than that, a wide variety of bizarre errors and problems will arise. In environments where users belong to more groups, the *MaxTokenSize* registry value must be increased from its current default of 12,000 bytes to the recommended maximum of 65,535 bytes, which can support several thousand group memberships for a user.

Unfortunately, although you can increase the size of the local security token, you cannot increase the size of the Kerberos Privileged Access Certificate (PAC), which maxes out at 1024 SIDs. The PAC is included with the Kerberos service ticket that is presented by a client to a service. The server uses the SIDs in the PAC to generate the local token, adding local group memberships and privileges to the memberships indicated by the PAC. Because the PAC limit is 1024 SIDs, that is the effective ceiling for the number of domain group memberships for a user. Luckily, although I've seen environments with several hundred group memberships, I've not yet run into one that has required more than 1000 groups for a user.

Another concern is introduced with non-Windows devices. Some network-attached storage (NAS) devices have somewhat lower limits to the number of group memberships they allow for a user. So even if these devices are using Active Directory as their authentication database, they might run into trouble if users belong to a higher number of groups than the devices support.

Be sure to read Solution 1-7 for more details regarding group membership limitations.

## Convert security groups to distribution groups

Many enterprises use only security groups because they provide the benefits of both security management and e-mail distribution. As you begin to leverage Active Directory for role-based management and introduce more groups into your environment, you should review existing groups to determine which, if any, you can convert to a distribution group. If a group is used only for e-mail, change it to a distribution group so that it is no longer loaded into users' PACs and tokens. The switch can be made in the Active Directory Users and Computers snap-in in the properties of the group, or using the Dsmod command with the following syntax:

```
dsmod group "DN of group" -secgrp { yes | no }
```

You can actually convert a group from a security group to a distribution group and back again. The *objectSID* attribute of the group remains intact. The change simply modifies whether the group's SID is used to generate the user's PAC and thereby the user's token. When you convert a security group to a distribution group, it affects users the next time they log on. If a user has already logged on, the SID of the group will already be in his PAC and tokens.

The fact that you can switch back and forth is good news. If you have a group that you believe is used only for e-mail, but you are unsure if it has also been given permissions to resources, you can convert the group to a distribution group and monitor the environment to determine whether any users are unable to access resources. Of course, this is a slightly risky tactic. If the group was used to deny users access to a resource, access to that resource will be opened up inappropriately. You are also risking a temporary denial of service for users that require access to the resource. But I know that in the real world there are times in which, to learn how your environment works, you sometimes have to make a change and see what happens. In this case, if you find that the group is actually used for security, you can change the group back to a security group, and when users log on again, their access will be restored.

## Reduce token and PAC size

By changing groups that are not used to manage ACEs or local group membership to distribution groups, you can reduce the number of groups that must be packed into the PAC. Additionally, if a group is used by an application, rather than by Windows, you can possibly configure the group as a distribution group. You must know how the application evaluates group membership.

Some applications determine whether a user is in a group by drilling down through the user's memberships. Later in this Solution Collection, some scripts provide examples. The code connects to the user object in Active Directory, looks at the *memberOf* attribute for the user, and for each group that the user belongs to, recursively analyzes the *memberOf* attribute for the group. The result is an exhaustive list of groups to which the user belongs, including nested groups. The scripts in Solution Collection 1, "Role-Based Management," performed *memberOf* enumeration in this way, as does the Dsget command with the *–memberof* and *–expand* switches discussed in Solution 1-1 on page 11.

An application that evaluates a user's memberships in this way identifies both security and distribution groups. So if the application uses a group to grant a permission or capability, you can create the group as a distribution group. The group can be used by the application, but it will not add an unnecessary SID to the user's PAC or token.

Other applications use methods to determine group membership that do rely on the user's token. Web applications using Windows Integrated Authentication, for example, are able to leverage the user's security context to manage access to pages and the capabilities of the application. This is more efficient than performing recursive *memberOf* enumeration, so these applications are typically written to do so. The groups used by these applications must be security groups.

If you know that an application can use distribution groups as scopes of management, don't add to the bloat of users' PACs and tokens by creating security groups. If you are unsure, experiment. Remember that you can convert groups back and forth between security-enabled groups and distribution groups.

# Consider group scope: global, domain local, and universal

If you've been using Windows for any length of time, I'm sure you've heard the best practice for managing users and groups: Put users in global groups, put global groups in domain local groups, and assign domain local groups permissions to resources. Oh yes, and in a multi-domain forest, you might put users or global groups from different domains into universal groups, which you can then nest in domain local groups or assign permissions to resources. This set of best practices is related to the following group characteristics:

**Replication**    The membership of universal groups is replicated to the global catalog. Global and domain local groups are replicated only within their domain.

**Membership**    Global groups can contain as members users and other global groups from the same domain only. Domain local groups can contain users and global groups from any domain in the forest, and from trusted domains in external forests. They can also include other domain local groups. Universal groups' membership can include users, global groups, and other universal groups from anywhere in the forest.

**Visibility**    Domain local groups can be used to manage security for resources in this same domain only. Universal groups and global groups are visible to all domains in the forest.

This is a summary only—the details get pretty gory. The point is, if you understand the factors that drive the recommended practice, you can then decide whether the best practice is necessary or even applies in your directory service.

Let's start with a simple example of a single-domain Active Directory forest. In a single domain, you can actually get by using only global groups. Assuming your domain functional level is no longer *mixed* or *interim*, which implies the existence of Windows NT 4.0 domain controllers, you can nest global groups in global groups. You can certainly assign permissions for a resource to a global group. There is no functionality that I'm aware of that is dependent on a group being of domain local scope. The reverse is not true, as Group Policy objects can be filtered only with global groups.

Why would you want to use only global groups? Token size. In the token, global groups consume only 8 bytes, whereas domain local groups consume 40 bytes. That means you could have five times more group memberships for a user before hitting the limit of the current *Max-TokenSize*.

What's the downside? Well, now that global groups can be members of other global groups, I don't really see one, particularly in a single-domain environment. As soon as the environment gets more complex, changes will have to be made. If an additional domain is added to the forest or if a trust is established with an external domain, you might need to convert one or more of your global groups to domain local scope to add users and groups from the other domain as members of your groups.

It is easy to change the scope of a group. You can do so in the Active Directory Users and Computers snap-in in the Properties dialog box for group. You can also use the Dsmod command with the *–scope { l | g | u }* switch to change a group's scope. You can convert from domain local to universal, global to universal, universal to domain local, and universal to global. Notice that you cannot convert directly from global to domain local or vice versa. However, you can convert between those two scopes by first converting to universal. For example, to convert a global group to a domain local group, you can use the following command:

```
dsmod group "DN of group" -scope u
dsmod group "DN of group" -scope l
```

I'm not suggesting that everyone reading this book should race out and change all their groups to global groups quite yet. However, in environments where *MaxTokenSize* limits are being encountered, I would certainly consider converting some groups to global, where such a change would not have an impact on the management purpose of the group.

Let me give you an example. A large, distributed organization implemented a sophisticated, role-based management approach to the delegation of administration and Active Directory. The decentralized nature of the company's administrative model and the granular delegation that was implemented produced a lot of nested groups that managed delegation. The result was very powerful, but administrators at the top of the food chain found themselves with something more than 400 group memberships and started to encounter errors related to token size. These errors only affected their secondary logon accounts—their administrative accounts—but were problematic nonetheless. Because the delegation management groups were a relatively self-contained collection, the company had the option of converting these groups to global groups instead of configuring a larger *MaxTokenSize* to the domain controllers, servers, and clients to which those administrators authenticated.

Another type of group that lends itself to being scoped as global, rather than domain local, is application groups. Application groups can be used to manage access to applications by granting Read permission to application software distribution folders. They can also be used by software distribution mechanisms such as Microsoft System Center Configuration Manager 2007 to deploy the application itself. If you make extensive use of application groups, an individual user could easily have several dozen memberships. Consider converting application groups to global groups if you start to encounter group membership limitations.

## Solution summary

Anyone who has supported a Windows environment has experience creating and managing group objects. In this solution, we explored best practices for attributes, including group name, description, and notes. We discovered how easy it is to protect a group from accidental deletion. And we learned why, particularly in environments where users belong to several hundred groups or more, best practices and conventions regarding group type and group scope should be reexamined.

# 8-2: Delegate Management of Group Membership

## Solution overview

| | |
|---|---|
| **Type of solution** | Guidance |
| **Features and tools** | The security interfaces of the Active Directory Users and Computers snap-in, Dsacls, the Managed By tab |
| **Solution summary** | There are several methods with which to delegate the Write::Members permission that enables the management of a group's membership. There are even scenarios that warrant delegating the permission to individual group objects rather than to an entire OU. |
| **Benefits** | Least-privilege delegation of group membership management and the ability to allow business owners of resources to manage access to those resources. |

## Introduction

This Solution Collection builds a framework that enables more sophisticated group management, including the creation of groups that allow users to subscribe and unsubscribe from particular capabilities, and the creation of group management tools that allow nontechnical users who manage resources to have direct control over access to those resources. Each of these solutions rely in some regard on a user's permission to modify the membership of a group. In this solution, I describe relatively straightforward methods you can use to delegate the management of a group's *member* attribute.

## Examine the *member* and *memberOf* attributes

The *member* attribute of a group is the attribute that maintains the list of each of the group's members. The attribute is a multivalued attribute, so there is one value per member. The values themselves are distinguished names. For example, if Mike Danseglio is a member of the Finance group, the Finance group's *member* attribute includes Mike's distinguished name—"cn=Mike Danseglio,ou=Contractors,ou=People,dc=contoso,dc=com"—along with the distinguished names of all other member users, computers, and groups.

When you move an object to another OU, the references to that object are updated automatically in Active Directory. When Mike is hired full time and moved to the Employees OU, the *member* attribute of the Finance group is automatically updated to reflect the change.

To display a group's members using VBScript, you can bind to the group using the LDAP provider and set an array variable to the value of the *member* attribute. You can then loop through the contents of the array using a *For Each...Next* structure. The following code shows an example:

```
set oGroup = GetObject("LDAP://cn=Finance,ou=roles,ou=groups,dc=contoso,dc=com")
aMembers = oGroup.GetEx("member")
For Each sMember in aMembers
    WScript.Echo sMember
Next
```

The *GetEx* method is, in my experience, the most effective way to extract a multivalued attribute for use in the script. If an attribute does not exist for a particular object, an error is thrown. For example, if the Finance group referred to in the preceding code does not have any members, an error will occur on the second line. The best way to work around that error is to trap it. You can use the *On Error Resume Next* statement to instruct the script processor to ignore an error and continue with the next line. It is best practice to use *On Error Resume Next* only immediately before a line that you anticipate will throw an error, and then examine the *Err* object to determine whether an error occurred. Don't forget to clear the *Err* object so that it is not misinterpreted as a different error later in the code, and use the *On Error Goto 0* statement to resume normal processing. The code shown earlier is revised here to reflect this approach:

```
set oGroup = GetObject("LDAP://cn=test,ou=groups,dc=contoso,dc=com")
On Error Resume Next
aMembers = oGroup.GetEx("member")
If Err.Number = 0 Then
    For Each sMember in aMembers
        WScript.Echo sMember
    Next
Else
    WScript.Echo "No members."
    Err.Clear
End If
On Error Goto 0
```

When you add an object as a member of a group, the *memberOf* attribute of that object is modified to reflect the change. This happens automatically, because *memberOf* is a back link attribute. Back links are discussed in Solution 7-4 on page 506. You cannot directly write to the *memberOf* attribute of a user, group, or computer. You might be thinking to yourself, "But I can open the properties of a user, computer, or group and click the Member Of tab and add the object to a group." And you'd be right—you can do that in the user interface. But what Windows is doing behind the scenes is actually changing the *member* attribute of the selected group. So the *memberOf* attribute is dynamically maintained by Windows. It is also multi-valued and contains distinguished names. The following script lists the memberships of the user Mike Danseglio:

```
set oUser = GetObject("LDAP://cn=mike danseglio,ou=new users,dc=contoso,dc=com")
On Error Resume Next
aMemberOf = oUser.GetEx("memberOf")
```

```
If Err.Number = 0 Then
    For Each sMemberOf in aMemberOf
        WScript.Echo sMemberOf
    Next
Else
    WScript.Echo "No memberships."
    Err.Clear
End If
On Error Goto 0
```

You can see the similarities between the scripts used to access the *member* and *memberOf* attributes. Later in this Solution Collection, I go into more detail about how to programmatically access and manipulate these attributes. At this point, if you understand that both attributes are multivalued and contain distinguished names but only *member* is written to, you are in great shape.

# Delegate permission to write the *member* attribute

There are several ways to assign the Write permission for the *member* attribute of groups. Many of these were detailed Solution Collection 5, "Active Directory Delegation and Administrative Lock Down." Let's apply the procedures covered in that Solution Collection specifically to the delegation of group membership management.

## Create a capability management group

If you will be delegating group membership management for a large collection of groups, or for an OU of groups, I recommend that you follow the tenets of role-based management. Create a capability management group that represents the permission you are managing. Follow the naming convention that you established for your enterprise. If you adhere to the naming standards proposed in Solution Collection 5, the prefix for Active Directory delegation groups is *AD_*.

For example, AD_Resource Access Groups_Membership might be the name for a group that you have given permission to manage membership for all groups in the Resource Access OU. You can then nest the appropriate roles into the capability management group to manage the delegation of the capability to the roles. You might make the Help Desk group a member of AD_Resource Access Groups_Membership. After you have created the capability management group, you can assign it the appropriate permission, which is Write::Member.

## Delegate using the Advanced Security Settings dialog box

The first option for delegating group membership management is to use the ACL editor user interface. Follow these steps to delegate the ability to manage membership for all groups in an OU:

1. Open the Active Directory Users and Computers snap-in.
2. Right-click the OU and choose Properties.

3. Click the Security tab.

4. Click the Advanced button.

5. In the Advanced Security Settings dialog box, click the Add button.

   If the Add button is not visible, click the Edit button, and then click the Add button.

6. In the Select dialog box, enter the name for the group to whom you want to grant permission, or click Browse to search for the group. Continuing the example from the previous section, you might select the group AD_Resource Access Groups_Membership. When you are finished, click OK. The Permission Entry dialog box appears.

7. Click the Properties tab.

8. In the Apply To drop-down list, choose Descendant Group Objects. If you are using earlier versions of the Active Directory Users and Computers snap-in, choose Group Objects.

9. In the Permissions list, select the Allow check boxes for the Read Members and Write Members permissions.

   By default, all users have the ability to Read Members, so that permission is not required. However, role-based access control is best implemented by assigning to a group all the permissions required for that group to achieve the desired capability, rather than relying on permissions assigned indirectly.

   Figure 8-2 shows the resulting Permission Entry dialog box.

10. Click OK to close each of the security dialog boxes.

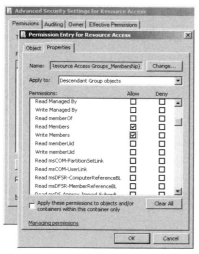

**Figure 8-2**   The Permission Entry dialog box showing the delegation of group membership management on the Groups OU

## Delegate using the Dsacls command

The Dsacls command can also be used to delegate membership management for an OU or for individual group objects. To delegate membership management for an entire OU, use the following syntax:

```
dsacls "DN of OU" /I:S /G "DOMAIN\group":rpwp;member;group
```

The group represented by *DOMAIN\group* is the group that will have permissions to make changes to group membership—for example, the AD_Resource Access Groups_Membership capability management group. It will be able to manage permissions for all groups in the OU specified by *DN of OU*.

While we're on the subject of Dsacls, let me remind you of the other common delegations related to group objects. Examine the following command:

```
dsacls "DN of OU" /I:S
    /G "DOMAIN\group":rpwp;member;group
    /G "DOMAIN\group":rpwp;cn;group
    /G "DOMAIN\group":rpwp;name;group
    /G "DOMAIN\group":rpwp;sAMAccountName;group
    /G "DOMAIN\group":rpwp;description;group
    /G "DOMAIN\group":rpwp;info;group
```

This command delegates the group represented by *DOMAIN\group* permissions to change the membership, name, description, and *info* attribute of groups in the OU specified by *DN of OU*.

## Delegate membership management for individual groups

As you know, it is best practice to manage permissions for objects as a collection. For file servers, this means applying permissions to folders rather than to individual files. In Active Directory, this means applying permissions to OUs rather than to individual objects.

However, in the case of groups, many enterprises are trying to get their information technology organization away from playing resource security middleman. Review the first scenario in "Scenarios, Pain, and Solution" on page 531, which illustrates this issue. If you want to begin to push the management of group membership to the users who have business responsibility for that membership, it is likely that you will deviate from the best practice and assign Write::Member permission on individual groups. For the example presented in the first scenario, you might grant Mike Danseglio the Write::Member permission for the AD_Engineering Program_Contribute group. Of course, if there are a large number of groups that will be assigned identical permissions, you will be best served by placing those groups in an OU. But quite often, group membership management ends up being done on a per-object basis.

> **Important**    Later in this Solution Collection, I discuss *proxying*, which allows a user to make changes to group membership without being delegated permission to do so. If you elevate your management to that level, you do not need to delegate membership management to individual groups. See Solution 8-7 on page 570 for more information.

If you want to delegate membership management for a single group, use this command:

```
dsacls "DN of group" /G "DOMAIN\group":rpwp;member;group
```

You can also use the ACL editor user interfaces—the security dialog boxes—to perform the delegation. Follow the 10-step procedure shown earlier, with two exceptions. First, in step 2, open the properties of the group rather than all of an OU. In step 8, do not change the default setting in the Apply To list—it should remain This Object And All Descendant Objects.

## Delegate individual group management with the Managed By tab

Microsoft recognized the possibility that organizations might delegate group membership management at the object level rather than at the OU level. So the Active Directory Users and Computers snap-in provides a very slick user interface to support this process.

The Managed By tab of a group object's Properties dialog box, shown in Figure 8-3, serves two purposes. First it provides contact information related to the manager of a group. In the first scenario presented in "Scenarios, Pain, and Solution," the IT organization could use this information to contact the business owner of a group to obtain approval prior to adding a user to the group.

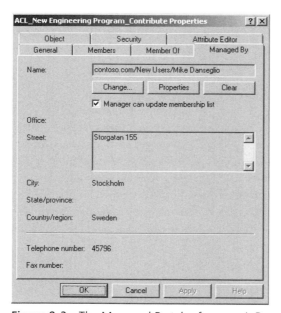

**Figure 8-3**    The Managed By tab of a group's Properties dialog box

The second purpose served by the Managed By tab is to manage the delegation of the *member* property. Note the check box shown in Figure 8-3. It is labeled Manager Can Update Membership List. When selected, the user or group shown in the Name box is given the Write::Member permission.

> **Note**   This is another of the strange and rare places where you must actually click OK to implement the change. Clicking Apply does not change the ACL on the group.

Fantastic! Microsoft even coded this interface so that when you change or clear the manager, the explicit permission assigned to that manager is automatically removed from the group's ACL. Just remember that if you change the manager, the check box is cleared by default, so you must reselect Manager Can Update Membership List. The results of the Manage By tab are as follows:

■ It is easy to associate the user who has business ownership of a group with the group itself.

■ Contact information for that user is exposed.

■ That user's ability to modify a membership of the group is managed automatically.

The Microsoft interface falls short in scenarios where a group has more than one user who is responsible for that group. Continuing the example provided by the first scenario in this Solution Collection, let's assume that the AD_Engineering Program_Contribute group is managed not only by Mike Danseglio but also by the other leaders of the program. The program leads belong to a group named Engineering Program Leads. It is not straightforward to assign Engineering Program Leads to be the manager of the AD_Engineering Program_Contribute group.

To use a group on the Managed By tab, click the Change button. The Select User, Contact, Or Group dialog box appears, shown in Figure 8-4. If you enter the name of a group and click OK, an error occurs. That's because this dialog box is not configured to accept groups as valid object types, even though "Group" is in the name of the dialog box itself. To work around this odd limitation, click the Object Types button, and then select the check box next to Groups. Click OK to close both the Object Types and Select dialog boxes. Be sure to select the Manager Can Update Membership List check box if you want to assign the Write::Member permission to the group. The other limitation of the interface is that when a group is used on the Managed By tab, no contact information is visible, as groups do not maintain contact-related attributes.

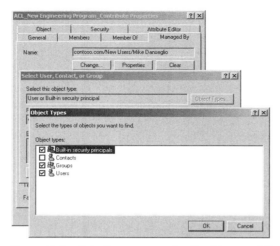

**Figure 8-4**   Selecting a group for the Managed By property

## Bridge the tool gap

After you have delegated permission to manage the membership of a group, particularly to nontechnical users, your problems are not completely solved. You must provide your users with tools they can use to add and remove members.

An obvious choice of tools is the Active Directory Users and Computers snap-in. You can make it somewhat easier for nontechnical users to manage group memberships by creating a custom Microsoft Management Console (MMC) with a task pad. Creating custom taskpads is described in detail in Solution 7-3 on page 499. To deliver a taskpad for end users who need to manage groups, follow these steps:

1.  Create one or more saved queries that enumerate the groups to which the user has been assigned on the Managed By tab. The LDAP query syntax for this type of saved query is as follows:

    ```
    (&(objectClass=group)(managedBy=cn=mike danseglio,ou=employees,
        ou=people,dc=contoso,dc=com))
    ```

    The distinguished name of the user or group for which you are querying must be specified in full. The saved query will not allow you to use a wildcard such as an asterisk.

2.  Add a task to the taskpad for the menu command *Properties*.

3.  Use the View menu to remove all extraneous information, such as the Type column, and to hide the complexity of the Active Directory Users and Computers snap-in.

4.  Save the taskpad in User mode so that the user cannot change it.

Most organizations do not relish the idea of distributing administrative tools to end users just so that they can use the Active Directory Users and Computers snap-in to manage group memberships. You are better served by creating custom tools for managing group membership. Such tools are presented later in this Solution Collection.

## Solution summary

Before a user can change the membership of the group, that user must be assigned the Write::Member permission for the group. There are several ways to perform this delegation, including using the ACL editor user interfaces in the Active Directory Users and Computers snap-in and the Dsacls command. As you begin to implement role-based management, you might find that it's useful in certain scenarios to delegate permission to change the membership of a group to the individual or team who have business responsibility for the resource managed by the group. This requires delegating the Write::Member permission on individual group objects. Microsoft has made that process somewhat easier with the Managed By tab of the group object's properties dialog box.

# 8-3: Create Subscription Groups

## Solution overview

| | |
|---|---|
| **Type of solution** | Scripts and guidance |
| **Features and tools** | Group_Subscribe.vbs, Group_Unsubscribe.vbs, Active Directory group ACLs |
| **Solution summary** | Support group management scenarios in which groups allow users to add or remove themselves. |
| **Benefits** | Increased responsiveness to user needs and reduced support burden on the IT organization. |

## Introduction

Because groups are used to manage resources such as shared folders and applications, most changes to group membership require some level of workflow. In other words, if a user wants or needs to be added to a group, someone else in the organization is usually responsible for approving that change. However, not every scenario requires a workflow or middleman. Take, for example, e-mail distribution groups. Some e-mail lists within an organization are optional—users can subscribe or unsubscribe from lists. In this solution, we look at how to implement groups that allow users to subscribe or unsubscribe—that is, to add or remove themselves as members. I call these *subscription groups*, which is not an official Microsoft term, but there is no Microsoft term for such groups.

# Examine scenarios suited to the use of subscription groups

You can use the concept of subscription groups in scenarios other than e-mail lists. In this solution, I use an example of the user-interface configuration. The user interface in Windows Vista is somewhat different than in Windows XP, and it's radically different from Windows 2000. To make the transition to Windows Vista smoother, you can use Group Policy settings to provide a more familiar Start menu and other user-interface elements. Let's assume that you have created a GPO that collects all the settings required to create a "Classic Windows" user experience. You have even named the GPO *Classic Windows*. But you don't want to force all users into Classic Windows mode. You know that some users will adapt rapidly to the new and more productive Windows Vista interface, and that some users will already be familiar with Windows Vista through their experience at home or at other organizations. So you want to make Classic Windows the default for users as you deploy Windows Vista, but you want users to be able to opt out of the configuration so that the standard Windows Vista interface is applied.

To achieve this goal, create a group to manage the application of the Classic Windows GPO. I'll call the group *GPO_Classic Windows* as an example. GPOs can be filtered only by global groups, so the group must be a global security group. Filter the GPO so that it applies only to the GPO_Classic Windows group. (Details of security group filtering are presented in Solution Collection 10, "Implementing Change, Configuration, and Policies.")

Put all users into the GPO_Classic Windows group so that they receive the Classic Windows experience when Windows Vista is deployed to their system. Then provide a way for users to remove themselves from the group when they are ready for the full Windows Vista experience. The remainder of this solution explains how to do that.

As another example, let's assume you have a software distribution framework such as Configuration Manager 2007 or the build-it-yourself framework presented in Solution Collection 9, "Improving the Deployment and Management of Applications and Configuration." You use application groups to control the deployment of and access to applications. Let's also assume you have an application with a license that allows you to deploy the application to all employees, but not all employees require the application. You want to enable employees to request and receive the application without administrative intervention. This can be achieved by implementing the application group as a subscription group. A user can simply add herself to the group, and then the software distribution framework kicks in to deploy the application to her.

With the examples of e-mail distribution lists, groups that control optional configuration settings, and subscription-based application deployment groups, let's turn our attention to the steps required to create subscription groups.

# Delegate the Add/Remove Self As Member validated write

The most important step for creating subscription groups is the proper delegation of permissions. The goal is to allow a user to add himself to or remove himself from a group. You do not want that user to be able to add or remove other users—the broader delegation of group membership management was discussed in Solution 8-2 on page 541. When you delegate the ability to manage the membership of the group, you assign the Write::Members permission. This permission allows a user to add or remove any value from the multivalued *member* attribute of the group. In this scenario, however, you want the user to add or remove only the user's own *distinguishedName* to the *member* attribute—not another user's *distinguishedName*. In other words, when the change to the *member* attribute is made, Windows needs to perform data validation to make sure the changed value is the same as the user's own *distinguishedName*.

This is achieved by assigning the Add/Remove Self As Member permission. Let's learn about the permission by applying it. To grant the Add/Remove Self As Member permission, follow these steps:

1. Open the Active Directory Users and Computers snap-in.

2. Right-click the subscription group and choose Properties.

   If you have multiple subscription groups, place them in an OU and perform the delegation on the OU instead.

3. Click the Security tab.

4. Click the Advanced button.

5. In the Advanced Security Settings dialog box, click the Add button.

   If the Add button is not visible, click the Edit button, and then click the Add button.

6. In the Select dialog box, enter the name for the group that should be able to subscribe to this group, and then click OK.

   In many scenarios, you will select Authenticated Users. By doing so, you are saying, "Anyone can join or leave this group." If the group's potential subscribers should be limited, select a specific group. For example, if you select the Finance group, you are saying, "Anyone in the Finance group can join or leave this group."

7. Click the Object tab.

8. Configure the Apply To drop-down list.

   If you are creating a single subscription group, the default is correct. Permissions will be applied to the selected subscription group and its child objects.

   If you are creating an OU of subscription groups, choose Descendant Group Objects in the Apply To drop-down list. If you are using earlier versions of the Active Directory Users and Computers snap-in, this option is labeled Group Objects.

9. In the Permissions list, select the Allow check box for the Add/Remove Self As Member permission.

Figure 8-5 shows the resulting Permission Entry dialog box.

10. Click OK to close each of the security dialog boxes.

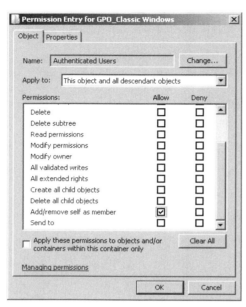

**Figure 8-5**  Delegating the Add/Remove Self As Member permission to create a subscription group

# Provide tools with which to subscribe or unsubscribe

After you have delegated permission so that users can add or remove themselves as members of a subscription group, you must provide them with a tool to do so. Although you could distribute the Active Directory Users and Computers snap-in, that's probably overkill. I recommend using simple scripts to do the job.

The following code is a generic function that adds the user who runs the script to a group specified by *sGroupDN*.

**Group_Subscribe.vbs**
```
' CONFIGURATION BLOCK - You only need to change sGROUPDN
sGroupDN = "cn=GPO_Classic Windows,ou=CCM,ou=Groups,dc=contoso,dc=com"
sUserDN = CreateObject("ADSystemInfo").UserName
If Group_AddMember("LDAP://" & sGroupDN, "LDAP://" & sUserDN) Then
    MsgBox "You have been successfully added to the group."
Else
    MsgBox "There was a problem adding you to the group."
End If
```

```
Function Group_AddMember(ByVal sGroupADsPath, ByVal sMemberADsPath)
    ' Version 071130
    Dim oGroup, oMember
    On Error Resume Next
    Set oGroup = GetObject(sGroupADsPath)
    If Err.Number <> 0 Then
        ' Handle error: could not connect to group
        Group_AddMember = False
        Err.Clear
        Exit Function
    End If
    oGroup.Add sMemberADsPath
    If Err.Number > 0 then
        ' Handle error: could not add member
        Group_AddMember = False
        Err.Clear
    Else
        Group_AddMember = True
    End If
    On Error Goto 0
End Function
```

The next script removes the current user from the group.

**Group_Unsubscribe.vbs**

```
' CONFIGURATION BLOCK - You only need to change sGROUPDN
sGroupDN = "cn=GPO_Classic Windows,ou=CCM,ou=Groups,dc=contoso,dc=com"
sUserDN = CreateObject("ADSystemInfo").UserName
If Group_RemoveMember("LDAP://" & sGroupDN, "LDAP://" & sUserDN) Then
    MsgBox "You have been successfully removed from the group."
Else
    MsgBox "There was a problem removing you from the group."
End If

Function Group_RemoveMember(ByVal sGroupADsPath, ByVal sMemberADsPath)
    ' Version 071130
    Dim oGroup, oMember
    On Error Resume Next
    Set oGroup = GetObject(sGroupADsPath)
    If Err.Number <> 0 Then
        ' Handle error: could not connect to group
        Group_RemoveMember = False
        Err.Clear
        Exit Function
    End If
    oGroup.Remove sMemberADsPath
    If Err.Number > 0 then
        ' Handle error: could not remove member
        Group_RemoveMember = False
        Err.Clear
```

```
      Else
          Group_RemoveMember = True
      End If
      On Error Goto 0
   End Function
```

You can see that the two scripts are very similar. The subscription group is specified by the variable *sGroupDN*. The current user is identified using the *UserName* property of the *ADSystemInfo* object and is assigned to the variable *sUserDN*. Both of those variables are distinguished names. The functions that add or remove group members are coded to receive the group and user not as distinguished names but as ADsPaths. So when the code calls the functions, it prefixes the user and group with "LDAP://" to create an ADsPath from the distinguished name. The *Group_AddMember* and *Group_RemoveMember* functions return *True* if successful and *False* if an error was encountered. The user is notified accordingly.

The *Group_AddMember* and *Group_RemoveMember* functions are wrappers around the *Add* and *Remove* methods of group objects. These two methods take the ADsPath of the member as an argument and manipulate the *member* attribute for you. The *Add* method returns *True* if the user ends up in the group—even if the user was already a member. It avoids errors that can occur if you directly manipulate the *member* attribute and try to add a user who already belongs to the group. Likewise, the *Remove* method returns *True* as long as the user is out of the group—even if the user was already not a member.

Now that you've seen VBScript code that allows a user to subscribe to or unsubscribe from a subscription group, you can decide how to distribute the script. You could put the script in a folder accessible on the network. I've seen simple yet effective implementations in which all subscription and subscription scripts were collected in a central shared folder, and users knew where to go to make subscription changes. You could also embed a similar script in an HTML Application (HTA). We'll build just such an HTA in the next solution. Finally, you could create a Web application with which users can join and leave groups. This approach is discussed in Solution 8-7 on page 570.

## Solution summary

Certain group management scenarios support business workflows in which users should be able to add or remove themselves from groups. I call these subscription groups. Subscription groups are created when you assign the Add/Remove Self As Member permission for the group objects. This permission allows an individual user to add or remove his or her own account from the group's *member* attribute. After that permission has been granted, you simply provide tools that allow users to add or remove themselves without needing the Active Directory Users and Computers snap-in. By implementing subscription groups for these specific scenarios, you can empower users to manage their own IT service, reduce the support burden on the IT organization, and continue to maintain least-privilege security.

# 8-4: Create an HTA for Subscription Groups

## Solution overview

| | |
|---|---|
| **Type of solution** | Tools |
| **Features and tools** | Group_Subscription.hta |
| **Solution summary** | Create an HTA that enables users to add themselves to or remove themselves from subscription groups. |
| **Benefits** | Provide users a simple way to manage their membership in subscription groups. Learn how to leverage group name and attribute standards in custom tools. |

## Introduction

The previous solution introduced the concept of subscription groups, which allow users to add or remove themselves as members. In that solution, I provided scripts that a user could double-click to subscribe to or unsubscribe from a group. In this solution, I go to the next step and create an HTML Application (HTA) that provides a graphical user interface (GUI) tool with which users can subscribe to or unsubscribe from groups: Group_Subscription.hta.

As I explain this tool, I will lay the foundation for additional tools introduced later in this Solution Collection, so I recommend that you read this solution even if you do not plan to introduce subscription groups right away.

## Use Group_Subscription.hta

In the Scripts folder of the companion media, you will find Group_Subscription.hta. The tool is designed to allow users to join and leave subscription groups. The tool is shown in Figure 8-6.

**Figure 8-6**   Group_Subscription.hta

There are several changes you need to make to the tool in your environment before it is ready to use:

■   Implement subscription groups as described in Solution 8-3 on page 549. Group_Subscription.hta is coded with the assumption that all subscription groups are contained within a single OU and its sub-OUs. I recommend that structure because it allows you to delegate the Add/Remove Self As Member permission at the OU level.

■ Populate the *description* attribute of subscription groups so that it explains the purpose of the group. Group_Subscription.hta displays the *description* attribute to the user.

■ Change the *Configuration Block* of Group_Subscription.hta to specify the location of your subscription groups OU in the variable *sGroupsOUDN*.

■ The code assumes that your naming convention uses underscores as delimiters. It assumes that groups in the subscription groups OU have prefixes, and it strips off the prefix to make the display of group names more readable. If this is not appropriate in your environment, change or delete the commented code in the *cboChoice_Create* sub-routine.

■ Test and validate the code and the tool in your lab.

When a user launches the tool, it produces a list of all groups in the subscription groups OU. When a group is selected, its description is displayed, along with an indication of whether the user is already a member of the group. The user can then click the Join Group or Leave Group button, which adds the user to or remove the user from the group, respectively.

## Understand Group_Subscription.hta

Even if you are not a strong coder, I recommend that you open Group_Subscription.hta in Notepad or in a script editor and follow along as I describe the high-level functionality of the tool.

When you open an HTA, a subroutine named *Window_OnLoad* is executed automatically if it exists. In Group_Subscription.hta, that subroutine calls the three other routines to size and position the window, identify the current user and domain, and generate a drop-down list of subscription group names.

The *cboChoice_Create* subroutine is the routine called to create the drop-down list. It configures a search of the OU specified by *sGroupsOUDN* in the *Configuration Block*, requesting the *aDSPath* and *sAMAccountName* attributes of all group objects sorted by *sAMAccountName*. The search itself is performed by the *AD_Search_RS* function, which returns the results as an ActiveX Data Object (ADO) recordset, which you can think of as a data table if you are not familiar with ADO.

The routine then loops through each record of the recordset to create an HTML drop-down list. The drop-down list displays the group name and stores the *aDSPath* of the group as the value behind the scenes, which will be helpful later in the code. To make the display as readable as possible, each group name in the recordset is stripped of any prefix. The code assumes that the underscore character is used as a delimiter between components of the group name. So before the group name is added to the drop-down list, any part of the name before the first underscore is stripped off. The resulting HTML for the drop-down list is used to replace the placeholder drop-down list in the part of the page bookmarked by the <div> tag named *divChoice*.

At this point, the HTA is fully generated and displayed to the user. When the user clicks the Group drop-down list, the list of subscription group names that was generated by *cboChoice_Create* appears. When the user selects a group from the list, the *cboChoice_OnChange* subroutine is triggered.

This subroutine first looks at the behind-the-scenes value of the entry in the drop-down list. Remember that when the drop-down list was created, the *aDSPath* attribute of the group was saved as the option value, while the *sAMAccountName* was stripped of its prefix and displayed visibly in the list. This trick allows the routine to find the *aDSPath* of the selected group without having to perform another search of Active Directory.

The routine then connects directly to the selected object in Active Directory and retrieves the *description* attribute of the group. It also performs a quick check to see whether the user is a member of the group. If the user is a member, the Leave Group button is enabled and the Join Group button is disabled. If the user is not a member, the Join Group button is enabled and the Leave Group button is disabled. The routine checks only direct membership of the group, not membership in nested groups, which is appropriate for the scenario of subscription groups in which users added and removed themselves as members.

The description and the information about whether the user is or is not a member of the group is displayed dynamically in a part of the HTML bookmarked by the *<span>* tag named *spnDetails*.

When the user clicks the Join Group or Leave Group buttons, JoinGroup or LeaveGroup subroutines are called that identify the *aDSPath* of the selected group, again by looking at the behind-the-scenes *value* attribute of the selected option in the drop-down list. The routines also identify the *aDSPath* of the current user by prefixing the *distinguishedName* of the user (which was discovered by the *Initialize* subroutine called by *Window_OnLoad*) with "LDAP://". The routines then call the same *Group_AddMember* or *Group_RemoveMember* functions introduced in the previous Solution Collection.

## Take away lessons in the value of group standards

This HTA begins to demonstrate some of the value that you can obtain by implementing standards and best practices such as those introduced in Solution 8-1 on page 533. Let's examine some of the results of our efforts:

**Groups of a specific type are collected within a single OU.**     In our example of subscription groups, all subscription groups exist within a single OU subtree. As I've mentioned in other Solution Collections, OU design should be driven by your delegation. Subscription groups share a unique delegation, the Add/Remove Itself As Member permission. This permission is most easily delegated at the subscription groups' OU so that all groups within the OU inherit the permission. By having all groups within a single OU, we are able to easily generate the drop-down list of subscription groups with simple LDAP search queries for all objects of class *group*.

**Groups of a specific type can be identified by a prefix.**    It won't always be possible to put all groups of a specific type within a single OU. When that's the case, you'll be well served by your naming convention, which uses a prefix to indicate the group type. For example, if we wanted to search Active Directory for all groups that manage resource access, and if our naming convention included the prefix *ACL_* for resource access management groups, we could use a search similar to the following:

```
sLDAP = "<LDAP://" & sGroupsOUDN & ">;" & _
        "(&(objectClass=group)(sAMAccountName=ACL_*));" & _
        "aDSPath,sAMAccountName;subtree"
```

Here, the search looks for all objects of class *group* with *sAMAccountNames* beginning with "ACL_". The Group_Subscription tool did not need to use group prefixes as a basis for the search because all subscription groups are contained within a single OU. But the Members_AccessReport.hta introduced in Solution Collection 1 used this type of search to locate resource access groups within an OU subtree.

**Group naming standards can be used behind the scenes, transparent to users.**    This HTA displays the *sAMAccountName* attribute of subscription groups in the drop-down list, but to make the user interface more friendly, group prefixes were stripped off. So group prefixes, which can be very useful behind the scenes for locating and identifying group types, do not have to be made visible to users as long as you are creating custom tools.

**Group attributes can be leveraged in creative ways.**    When a user selects a subscription group, the HTA displays the group's *description* attribute. By creating standards and disciplines for the use of particular object attributes, you open up the ability to use those attributes in custom tools. The *description* attribute isn't just useful within the details pane of the MMC. Although this particular version of the HTA does not display other group attributes, it is reasonable to consider displaying other group information, such as the *info* and *managedBy* attributes discussed earlier in this Solution Collection.

## Solution summary

Group_Subscription.hta is a GUI tool with which users can add themselves to and remove themselves from subscription groups. It also demonstrates several useful coding tricks, including the creation of a drop-down list based on an Active Directory search. Finally, it provides several examples of how, after you've implemented standards for group names and attributes, those standards can be leveraged by code and custom tools to facilitate group management and automation.

# 8-5: Create Shadow Groups

## Solution overview

| | |
|---|---|
| **Type of solution** | Scripts |
| **Features and tools** | Group membership, user and computer objects, fine-grained password policies, Group_Shadow.vbs |
| **Solution summary** | Create groups with memberships that reflect the objects in one or more OUs and that are dynamically updated. |
| **Benefits** | The ability to scope security, Group Policies, password settings objects, software deployment, and other technologies that are reliant on security groups rather than your OU structure. |

## Introduction

You've no doubt heard my message in this resource kit—management is all about applying configuration, security, and other elements to scopes of users and computers, and scopes are best managed as groups. Sometimes, you have a choice about how to scope a particular management task. Group Policy objects, for example, can be scoped using links to sites or OUs or using security group filtering. Sometimes, you don't have a choice. Permissions can be assigned only to groups, not to OUs. Windows Server 2008 fine-grained password policies are linked to groups, not to OUs.

But what happens when a technology can be scoped only by using a group, but you already have the scope defined as an OU? Let me give you an example. If you have an application that must be deployed to computers in several different business units and your business units are represented by distinct OUs, you can create a single group to scope the deployment of the application. The group would be configured with a membership that is identical to the computers in the business unit OUs. Such a group is called a *shadow group*. Ideally, the shadow group should be dynamic so that as objects are added to or removed from the OU, they are automatically added to or removed from the group. In this solution, we learn how to create dynamic shadow groups.

## Shadow groups and fine-grained password and account lockout policies

Before we dive into the technical details of creating shadow groups, let me give you one more scenario in which shadow groups are likely to play a very important role. Windows Server 2008 introduces fine-grained password and account lockout policies, which allow you to specify unique password and account lockout settings for different users in your domain. You can now ensure that administrative passwords are longer and must be changed more frequently than passwords of nonprivileged accounts. See the Windows Server 2008 Technical

Library at *http://technet.microsoft.com* for details about this fantastic new capability. Password settings objects (PSOs) that drive the configuration are applied by associating the PSO with a global security group. You do not apply PSOs to OUs.

However, I hope and expect that you have already defined a scope of administrative accounts as an OU in your Active Directory. As I discussed in Solution Collection 5, your Active Directory design should be driven by your administrative model so that it effectively manages the permissions (ACEs on ACLs) on your Active Directory objects. You should have the user accounts that are used for administration—secondary logon accounts, for example—in an OU that is separate from the accounts of normal users because there should be much tighter security for administrative accounts.

Because you cannot apply a PSO to the administrative identities' OU, you must create a shadow group with a membership that tracks the objects in the OU. You link the PSO to the shadow group and thereby apply these stricter password settings to administrative accounts. As accounts are added to or removed from the OU, the shadow group is modified accordingly.

## Understand the elements of a shadow group framework

To create a shadow group, we must first create the group object itself. Then we must develop a framework that does the following to manage the group's membership:

- Defines a query with which the shadow group membership is defined.
- Defines the base scopes of the query.
- Develops a script to manage the group's *member* attribute based on the query.
- Minimizes the impact on network replication.
- Executes the script on a regular interval, or triggers the script as a response to changes in the OU.

## Define the group membership query

You can use an LDAP query to define the desired membership of the shadow group. For the sake of simplicity and to address the most common scenarios, we'll use a query that locates all user objects within an OU and its sub-OUs. The LDAP query we need is simple:

```
(&(objectCategory=person)(objectClass=user));distinguishedName;subtree
```

The criteria of the search is "all user objects." We could get more creative about which users we want for the shadow group members. For example, we could search for specific job titles, departments, addresses, or descriptions. The attribute we need to get back is the *distinguishedName*, because this is what needs to be placed in the group's *member* attribute. The scope of the search, *subtree*, indicates the OU and all sub-OUs. Other available scopes include *base*, which searches the OU only, not its sub-OUs, and *onelevel*, which searches the base and its immediate children (subcontainers or sub-OUs).

To search for all computers in an OU and its sub-OUs, use the following LDAP query:

```
(&(objectCategory=person)(objectClass=user));distinguishedName;subtree
```

You can use the saved queries feature of the Active Directory Users and Computers snap-in, discussed in "Scenarios, Pain, and Solution" of Solution Collection 7 if you want to use a GUI tool to help build the query.

## Define the base scopes of the query

What if you want all computers from four different OUs in the shadow group? There's no way to achieve that with the LDAP query itself—we must simply call the same query several times. In the script we'll build, we'll use an array to store the distinguished names of the OUs we want to search. Examine the following code:

```
aSearchOUs = Array("ou=NYC,ou=clients,dc=contoso,dc=com", _
               "ou=SYD,ou=clients,dc=contoso,dc=com", _
               "ou=AMS,ou=clients,dc=contoso,dc=com")
```

The *aSearchOUs* variable is created as an array with three elements—the distinguished names of the New York, Sydney, and Amsterdam OUs. The underscore characters at the end of each line are line continuation characters in VBScript. So the three lines of code are executed as a single statement. I like breaking up long and complex area elements to make the code more readable.

Later in our script, we will simply loop through the array, executing the LDAP query once for each OU.

## Develop a script to manage the group's *member* attribute based on the query, while minimizing the impact on replication

The code that executes the LDAP query returns a dictionary of matching objects. Dictionaries are a form of array that can store multiple elements—perfect for storing multiple objects—and can be easily searched. The dictionary returned by the search routine is named *dTargetMembership*, and it represents the desired end state for the shadow group's *member* attribute. We could simply replace the entire *member* attribute with the content of the dictionary. For small shadow groups, that approach might be perfectly reasonable. However, if the shadow group has a large membership, replacing the entire membership of the group results in unnecessary replication if only one or a small handful of changes has been made in the OU.

It will be more efficient for the replication of the *member* attribute if we compare the existing membership of the group with the desired membership represented by *dTargetMembership*, which lists the objects returned by the search. If an object exists in *dTargetMembership* but is not in the *member* attribute, we will add it to *member*. Similarly, if an object exists in the *member* attribute but not in *dTargetMembership*, we remove it from *member*. In other words, we synchronize rather than replace the group membership. Because the *member* attribute is multivalued, only the differences need to be replicated, assuming your domain is at a Windows Server 2003 or higher functional level.

## Examine the Group_Shadow.vbs script

If you are interested in the script itself, its guts are shown here:

```
' CONFIGURATION BLOCK
sDomainDN = "dc=contoso,dc=com"
sGroupSAMAccountName = "Employees"
aSearchOUs = Array("ou=employees,ou=people,dc=contoso,dc=com")
sQuery = "(&(objectCategory=person)(objectClass=user));distinguishedName;subtree"

' Perform LDAP searches, adding to the final list stored in dTargetMembership
For Each sSearchOU In aSearchOUs
    sLDAPQuery = "<LDAP://" & sSearchOU & ">;" & sQuery
    Set dResults = AD_Search_Dictionary(sLDAPQuery)
    Call DictionaryAppend(dResults, dTargetMembership)
Next

' Locate group
sGroupADsPath = ADObject_Find_Generic(sGroupSAMAccountName, sDomainDN)
Set oGroup = GetObject(sGroupADsPath)

' Get members and store in dictionary
aMembers = oGroup.GetEx("member")
Set dCurrentMembership = ArrayToDictionary(aMembers)

' Calculate the "delta" between the current and desired state
Set dMembershipChanges = Dictionary_Transform(dCurrentMembership, dTargetMembership)

' Make the membership changes based on the transform dictionary's instructions
For Each sMember In dMembershipChanges
    If dMembershipChanges.Item(sMember) = "ADD" Then
        oGroup.Add "LDAP://" & sMember
    End If
    If dMembershipChanges.Item(sMember) = "DELETE" Then
        oGroup.Remove "LDAP://" & sMember
    End If
Next
```

Several of my standard functions are not shown, but their names should give you a feeling for what they do. The code performs the query specified by *sQuery* for each OU in the array *aSearchOUs*. As it does so, it appends the results to a dictionary object called *dTargetMembership*. Then the code finds the *member* attribute of the group specified by *sGroupSAMAccountName* and transfers its membership into a dictionary object called *dCurrentMembership*.

The magic happens when the code passes *dCurrentMembership* and *dTargetMembership* to a function called *Dictionary_Transform*. This function returns yet another dictionary object that holds the *delta*—the changes required to go from the current membership to the target membership. That dictionary object contains the *distinguishedNames* of the groups as the key and, for the item, contains either "ADD" or "DELETE." So the code loops through each instruction and makes the appropriate change to the group membership.

# Execute the script on a regular interval

Now that the script is created, you must find a way to run it regularly so that group membership is updated at the frequency required to meet your business requirements. Use the Task Scheduler to schedule the script. Be sure that the task runs with domain credentials that can read the script and change group membership. The account used for the task must also have at least the Log On As Batch Job user right.

You can create a scheduled task using the Task Scheduler console. Create a task that runs one time but is repeated indefinitely based on the interval that meets your requirements. Make sure the domain credentials have been entered and that the script will run even if the user is not logged on. Alternately, you can use the command line, which I prefer. The following command creates a task that runs the script every 15 minutes:

```
schtasks.exe /create /RU DOMAIN\Username /RP password /TN TaskName
/TR "cscript \\contoso.com\it\maintenance\group_shadow.vbs"
/sc MINUTE /mo 15
```

Type **schtasks.exe /?** at the command prompt for help with the schtasks command.

# Trigger the script based on changes to an OU

You can monitor the addition or deletion of objects in an OU and trigger the script as a response to that event. We don't have enough space in this resource kit to go into all the gory details, but let me give you a quick overview. Microsoft *incorporated* a tool called event-triggers.exe into Windows XP and Windows Server 2003. Eventtriggers allows you to execute a command based on an event appearing in the event log. Windows Server 2008 has functionality built in to the new event log system to do the same thing.

There are a couple of tricks, though. First, you'll need to decide what event to use as a trigger. The answer depends on your business requirements. Windows Server 2008 allows you to audit for more granular changes to Active Directory, so you will have a broader range of choices with Windows Server 2008. See the Windows Server 2008 technical library at *http://technet.microsoft.com* for more information about auditing Active Directory changes.

You must also consider that events are logged on a per-domain controller basis, so you have to determine whether you configure the trigger on every domain controller or whether you use the new eventing system in Windows Server 2008 to consolidate logs and run triggers from the central location. Again, the new eventing system is discussed on TechNet.

## Solution summary

There are management scenarios in Windows that require the use of security groups, the membership of which should be dynamic. In Solution Collection 5, I provided a script that updated groups for desktops an laptops. In this solution, Group_Shadow.vbs delivers a more sophisticated approach to building dynamic groups—one that places less burden on replication and enables a search across multiple distinct OUs. Although the example focused on synchronizing a group with the objects in one or more OUs, you can modify the LDAP query used to create more targeted criteria for group membership.

# 8-6: Provide Friendly Tools for Group Management

## Solution overview

| | |
|---|---|
| **Type of solution** | Tools |
| **Features and tools** | MemberOf_Report_V2.hta, My_Memberships_V2.hta, Group_Membership.hta, Group_ChangeMember.hta, Group_MyGroups.hta |
| **Solution summary** | Create tools that allow nontechnical users to manage group membership. |
| **Benefits** | Empower business owners of resources to manage the membership of groups that scope access to or use of those resources. |

## Introduction

Most organizations encounter scenarios in which some level of management capability should be allowed for a nontechnical user. A manager simply wants to know who is in a group associated with her division. A project leader needs to be able to grant access to data controlled by the project. A developer needs to deploy an update to the users of his application. These are just a few examples.

Unfortunately, Microsoft's native toolset does not provide robust group management capability to administrators, let alone to end users. But you can easily build tools that not only provide that capability but also align it more directly with the requirements of your enterprise. In this solution, I introduce several HTML Applications (HTAs) that demonstrate the approach you can take to develop group management applications without having to crack open Microsoft Visual Studio. With VBScript to access and manipulate Active Directory and HTML to make an effective user interface, you can and should extend Windows' group management tools.

# Enumerate *memberOf* and *member*

Several of these tools enumerate, or list, the effective membership of a user or the effective members of a group, including nested groups. They do this through a process called *recursion*, which means drilling down. For example, a user's *memberOf* attribute is examined, and each group to which the user belongs is then opened and the group's *memberOf* attribute is examined. The process iterates until all nested memberships have been discovered.

You will see functions that are shared across the tools: *MemberOf_Get* and *MemberOf_Enum* produce a dictionary object—a type of array—that contains the enumeration of the *memberOf* attribute of users, computers, and groups. *Member_Get* and *Member_Enum* create a dictionary that contains the recursively enumerated *member* attribute of groups.

Each tool then does something with that dictionary object to display its information in a useful way, whether reporting direct versus nested memberships, group types, or the object class of members.

Recursive enumeration is one of the most accurate ways to capture the complete membership of a user, computer, or group, but it requires that the code touch Active Directory repeatedly as it drills down the *memberOf* or *member* attributes. So it isn't the fastest script in the world, particularly in scenarios involving a large number of members or memberships.

Additionally, and importantly, the *Member_Get* function, which performs a recursive enumeration of the *member* property of a group to determine all of the group's members, will *not* show users who are assigned to the group as their primary group. Most organizations do not manage the *primaryGroupID* attribute of users or computers, which are assigned to Domain Users and Domain Computers by default. I recommend that you keep it that way—don't change primary groups. And don't nest Domain Users or Domain Computers into any of your groups. Windows, of course, adds Domain Users to the local Users group of each computer in the domain. That's fine. Let Windows do what it does with Domain Users, Domain Computers, and Domain Controllers.  Don't use those groups for any of your own management.

On the resource kit Web site, *http://www.intelliem.com/resourcekit*, I provide details about membership enumeration as it is implemented in these tools.

# Report direct, indirect, and primary group memberships

In Solution Collection 1, I introduced MemberOf_Report.hta. The code from that tool served its educational purpose. In this solution, the tool has been updated with more robust routines and has been renamed MemberOf_Report_V2.hta. As shown in Figure 8-7, MemberOf_Report_V2.hta produces a list of a user's effective group memberships, including all nested security and distribution groups and the user's primary group. It displays the groups in three categories: the user's primary group, direct memberships, and indirect memberships. Within each category, groups are shown in alphabetical order.

**Figure 8-7**    MemberOf_Report_V2.hta

The tool can be opened directly, or it can be integrated either into the Active Directory Users and Computers snap-in as a task in a taskpad or in the context menu by modifying display specifiers. Both of these methods of integrating MemberOf_Report.hta are detailed in Solution Collection 1.

# List a user's membership by group type

As we explored role-based management in Solution Collection 1, and group naming standards in both that and this Solution Collection, I've emphasized the importance of group naming standards and have recommended using prefixes in the group name to identify the type of group. My_Memberships_V2.hta adds some best practice group enumeration to the version discussed in Solution Collection 1. My_Memberships_V2.hta is shown in Figure 8-8. It enumerates a user's group memberships and then uses the prefixes of the group names to display the groups in the appropriate section of the report.

The tool can be opened directly, or it can be integrated either into the Active Directory Users and Computers snap-in as a task in a taskpad or in the context menu by modifying display specifiers. Both of these methods of integrating HTAs into the Active Directory Users and Computers snap-in are detailed in Solution 1-3.

**Figure 8-8**    My Memberships_V2.hta

# Display all members of a group

Although the first two tools enumerate the *memberOf* attribute of a user, computer, or even a group, Group_Membership.hta does the reverse. It enumerates the *member* attribute of a group, recursively analyzing nested groups. It then displays the list of members based on object class (groups, users, and computers) and whether the member belongs directly to the selected group or is an indirectly nested member. Group_Membership.hta is shown in Figure 8-9.

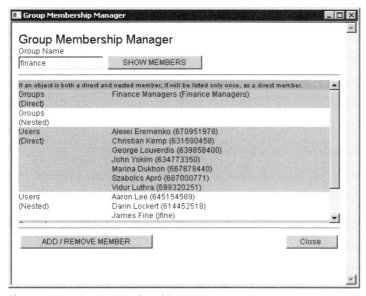

**Figure 8-9**    Group Membership Manager

The tool can be opened directly, or it can be integrated either into the Active Directory Users and Computers snap-in as a task in a taskpad or in the context menu in by modifying display specifiers. Both of these methods of integrating HTAs into the Active Directory Users and Computers snap-in are detailed in Solution 1-3.

## Add or remove group members with Group_ChangeMember.hta

If you noticed in Figure 8-9 that there is an Add/Remove Member button, you might have guessed what's next—a tool to let you change group membership. It's called Group_ChangeMember.hta, and it's shown in Figure 8-10.

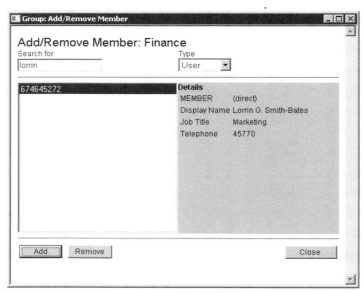

**Figure 8-10**   Group_ChangeMember.hta

Use the Search For and Type controls to locate a member that you want to add or remove. You can search for users by entering a pre–Windows 2000 logon name, first name, last name, or user principal name in the Search For box. You will see a list of matching users on the left-hand side of the tool. When you select a user, you'll see some of the user's details—including display name, job title, and telephone numbers—on the right-hand side, so you can be sure you've located the correct user before adding the user to or removing the user from the selected group.

If you are interested in scripting, the tool demonstrates several types of Active Directory searches and an approach to creating a list/details view. The HTA also includes code to add and remove group members.

This is one tool that is not meant to be opened directly. It expects to be opened using a command that includes the name of the group to be modified. You can therefore open the tool by using one of these methods:

■ Configure a task pad task that uses the pre–Windows 2000 logon name of the group as an argument.

■ Modify the display specifiers to open the HTA when a group object is selected.

■ Launch the HTA from another HTA. Pass the group name as an argument on the command line.

The first two methods were detailed in Solution 1-3, and the third was demonstrated in the Group_Membership.hta tool shown earlier.

## Give users control over the groups they manage

The HTAs described in the preceding sections demonstrate simple group management tools that are useable even by nontechnical users. The next step, I suggest, is to give users visibility to the groups they manage. Group_MyGroups.hta is a variation of Group_Membership.hta. It displays the membership of a group and provides a button that launches the Add/Remove Member functionality of Group_ChangeMember.hta.

When you open Group_MyGroups.hta, it displays the groups for which you are a manager, based on the groups' *managedBy* attribute. If you are included in a group's *managedBy* attribute, either directly as a user or indirectly through one of your own group memberships, the group is displayed in a list on the left-hand side of the tool.

The inspiration behind such a tool is the need to remove the IT organization as a middleman between the technology and the business requirements. In appropriate scenarios, you can provision role-based access to a shared folder, for example, and then delegate one or more users the ability to manage the membership of the groups that manage permissions to the resource. The groups' managers are delegated Allow::Write::Member permission for the groups, and are indicated using the *managedBy* attribute of the groups. The group managers can then use a tool like Group_MyGroups.hta to see their groups, report on the groups' membership, and add or remove members. And there's no need to deploy the Active Directory Users and Computers snap-in or to expect the group managers to learn complicated tools.

## Identify notes and next steps for group management tools

The samples provided as part of this solution should give you a good start toward creating tools that meet your business requirements. Group_MyGroups.hta demonstrates a tool that exposes a subset of Active Directory groups based on a query—in this case, on the *managedBy* attribute—and allows you to report on the membership of those groups. Group_MyGroups is actually user based, meaning that it is the user account that determines which groups are shown. Group_Membership.hta reports the membership of a single group. Both tools use a recursive process to list all the members of the selected group, including nested members.

Both tools can call Group_ChangeMember.hta to make changes to membership. Group_ChangeMember.hta demonstrates an HTA that produces a set of results from an Active Directory query and then displays details for the selected item. This list/details structure can be useful for many administrative tools.

The tools are designed to balance simplicity and functionality at the possible expense of performance. In scenarios involving a large number of members or memberships, the tools might be slow because they perform recursive analysis of the *member* or *memberOf* attribute. There are other choices that could be made to improve performance, such as showing only direct membership—the choice made by Microsoft when developing the Active Directory Users and Computers snap-in.

Like other script and tool samples in this resource kit, the tools are light on error trapping, options, and logging in order to make the important code easier to understand. Finally, the tools are just scripts—everything is written in VBScript and running on the client side. You can absolutely boost performance, scalability, manageability, and security by elevating the workflows supported by these tools into .NET applications.

## Solution summary

The Active Directory Users and Computers snap-in and other Microsoft tools are limited in their ability to report what's really going on with groups. There's no list or details view to help you see information about a group's member to know who that member really is. There's no visibility to the fully enumerated membership of a user or to the fully enumerated members of a group. And there's no easy way to provide visibility to a subset of groups that should be managed, except for the few views supported by your OU structure or saved queries. This solution provides sample tools that work around those limitations of the native toolset. They demonstrate that, with a little creativity, you can align group management with the needs of your organization.

# 8-7: Proxy Administrative Tasks to Enforce Rules and Logging

## Solution overview

| | |
|---|---|
| **Type of solution** | Scripts, tools, and guidance |
| **Features and tools** | An entire framework for proxying administrative tasks |
| **Solution summary** | Allow administrative tasks to be performed by users and down-level administrators without delegating them permissions in Active Directory. Integrate business rules and logging into administrative workflows. |
| **Benefits** | Enforce business roles, workflow, and logging. Increase consistency and compliance. Increase security. |

# Introduction

Throughout this resource kit, I've provided guidance, tools, and scripts that illustrate methods for aligning Windows technologies with your business requirements. We've talked a lot about provisioning, which means implementing rules, business logic, or workflow to achieve a result. We've provisioned shared folders in Solution Collection 2, user data stores in Solution Collection 3, and computer and user accounts in Solution Collections 6 and 7. We've examined custom tools that integrate business rules. For example, when creating a user account, you can enter the employee ID number, first name, and last name, and the tool automatically generates the common name, user logon names, and display name according to your standards. We've made it easier to follow the rules by providing tools that are actually easier to use than the native administrative tools.

But we have not *enforced* our workflows and rules. Administrators still have the option to open the Active Directory Users and Computers snap-in and create an object without following the process or logic dictated by the organization. That's because, until now, our administrators have been delegated the permission to perform the task using their credentials.

In this solution, I address that problem by introducing and implementing the concept of *proxying*. To *proxy* means to perform an action on behalf of another person. Let me give you an example. I need to create a user account. My organization expects me to follow business logic regarding the attributes that must be populated and the standards for those attributes. So my organization does not let me create a user account. Instead, it gives me a tool with which I *request* that a user account be created. A proxy service receives my request and performs the account creation on my behalf, enforcing additional business rules such as logging. The proxy service runs with credentials that can create the user.

 **Important**    A proxy executes an administrative task that was requested by a user. The proxy runs with credentials, unknown to the user, that have permission to perform the task.

The difference between proxying and using a secondary logon is that I, the administrator, do not have and do not know the credentials required to perform the task. Therefore, I cannot work around the business rules by using the Active Directory Users and Computers snap-in to make the change myself. I'm forced to use the tools, to follow the rules, and to do things correctly.

In this solution, I'll lay out the components of a proxy framework. I'll provide you with a sample that illustrates proxying, and you can customize the tools to implement a level of proxying for your organization. It will all be done with basic Windows automation technologies: VBScript, HTML Applications (HTAs), shared folders, NTFS permissions, a Microsoft Access database, and a scheduled task that acts as the proxy service. You can certainly create a more robust framework using a .NET Web application and a real Windows service, if you have the desire and the resources to elevate these tools to that level.

This is my favorite solution in this resource kit because it puts together so many pieces of Windows to achieve a framework that can have a significant impact on your ability to align Windows with your business requirements. I hope you enjoy it!

# Understand proxying

Let me guide you through the big picture of how proxying works so that as we build each piece, you have a feeling for how they all fit together. I'll use an example of creating a user account:

1. An administrator opens a custom tool to create a user account. The tool enforces standards regarding user attributes. It performs data validation and assembles all the information required to create the user account. This is called *marshalling*.

2. The tool submits a *task request* to a queue.

   The custom tool runs with a nonprivileged account—it does not have permission to perform the requested task. It simply marshals the information necessary to submit a request.

3. The proxy service identifies the new task request and executes the task. This is the *proxied execution* or *task request fulfillment* phase.

   The proxy service runs with a privileged account that can perform the tasks requested of it.

4. After execution, in the *logging* phase, the proxy service removes the task from the queue and logs the results of the task.

## Identify the security concerns

Along the way, security is obviously of the utmost concern. You don't want the proxy service to execute just any task—you want to manage the tasks it is capable of performing. And you don't want the proxy service executing an allowed task for any user—only the users who are allowed to request the task. The security model is the trickiest part.

If you are building a .NET application for proxying, you can use a Web application for steps 1 and 2. The Web application identifies the administrator using integrated Windows authentication and performs the logic necessary to determine what requests the administrator can or cannot submit. The Web application submits the request to the queue. A Web application runs with its own credentials—those of the application pool. Those credentials have permission to write to the task queue, so administrators cannot bypass the application and submit directly to the queue. So, in a way, the Web application is proxying the request submission itself. For steps 3 and 4, a Windows service monitors the queue and executes the task using the service's credentials. Because service credentials are entered directly into the Service Control Manager, there are no administrative credentials exposed.

We, however, are not building a .NET application. So we'll have to be creative. We'll make some choices, and all choices carry security implications—even the choices to build a custom tool, to delegate administration, and to proxy administrative tasks have security implications. But I propose that, in the big picture, reducing administrators' privileges in Active Directory and implementing a proxying framework—even a build-it-yourself framework—will provide security benefits that greatly outweigh the risks; and the manageability benefits will be the icing on the cake.

# Explore the components of the Proxy Framework

In the Scripts folder of the companion media, you'll find the Proxy Framework folder. Inside the folder are the components of the proxy framework. We'll start by looking at the big picture, and then we'll examine each component in detail.

## Understand the model of the Proxy Framework

The custom administrative tools are variations on the HTAs provided elsewhere in this resource kit. They've been modified so that, instead of actually performing a change directly in Active Directory, they marshal the task request and submit it to the queue.

To keep everything as simple as possible, the queue is a Microsoft Access database. The proxy service is simply a script that runs as a scheduled task. The proxy script looks in the database for unfulfilled tasks and executes them. The proxy service can be configured to allow a certain number of retries before it gives up. When a task is completed, or cannot be completed, the proxy service records the results in the Access database and closes out the task.

So that the framework can be as visible and customizable as possible, the tasks themselves are individual VBScripts. To add a new task to the framework, you simply add a VBScript that performs the task. This approach allows the proxy service itself to remain lean. It does not have to know how to perform the tasks; it simply calls the appropriate script. The script inherits the elevated credential of the proxy service.

Now let's consider the security model. Again, I've made choices to create a framework that is visible, flexible, and easy to customize. But I've tried to use standard Windows security components to ensure that the framework is reasonably secure. We'll look at each part of the process to identify the security exposures and the steps that have been taken to reduce those exposures.

The scripts that perform the tasks are an exposure. A script that is compromised and performs a task other than what it is intended to do can cause damage limited only by the delegation given to the proxy service account. Therefore, you must secure and manage the script repository. We'll set up the script repository so that only the proxy service can read scripts and only administrators of the server running the framework can modify the scripts. Therefore, to be able to add or modify a script, you must be a member of the Administrators group on the server. If that group is compromised, you probably have bigger problems than just your proxy framework. So NTFS permissions will secure the scripts to keep them from being tampered with.

The scripts are called by the proxy service in response to task requests in the queue. It is possible for a task to be entered that calls a script in another location to hijack the proxy service for malicious purposes. To reduce this exposure, the task queue includes a *command* field. The *command* field must match the name of a script in the script repository. If the *command* does not match the name of a script in the repository, it is not executed. And commands are executed only from the script repository—the service will not accept a path to a script in another location.

We need to be able to allow different administrators to submit different requests. For example, you might be allowed to create a user and create a computer through the proxy, but I might be allowed only to create computers. We need to be sure that a request isn't *spoofed*. That is, the framework must ensure I am prevented from pretending to be you and submitting a task request to create a user.

The task queue itself is an Access database. We can set permissions on the database so that only certain administrators can write tasks to it, but that doesn't allow us to be more granular. If both you and I have permission to add records to the database, we could add records of any kind—I could add a record to create a user. Access cannot track the security identification of the user who creates or modifies a record.

This is the part that's toughest to do without a .NET application. We need to know who submitted a task request and then, prior to actually performing the task, make sure that person has permission to request it. My solution requires several steps. First, we cannot let administrators write directly to the task queue in the Access database because we cannot authoritatively identify the source of the request. So we'll use a workaround. We'll create a folder on an NTFS volume. The task requests will be submitted as text files. We can identify the user who submitted the request by looking at the file's owner, and then we move the task request into the queue with that information. So the proxy service that I'm providing as an example performs that task as well—it monitors the *Requests* folder for new files and then translates the requests into entries in the database task queue. Only the proxy service has permission to write to the Access database.

By using NTFS security, we can be reasonably certain that we know the source of the request. I cannot pretend to be you. If I submit a request to create a user, my identity is the owner of the request, so the request can be rejected by the task script. And that is the final piece of the security puzzle: The task script must evaluate whether the requestor is allowed to request the task.

The *Requests* folder will receive requests as text files. So our custom administrative tools will simply create the text file in the correct folder rather than making changes directly in Active Directory. We'll secure the *Requests* folder so that only individuals who can request a proxied task have permission to add files. Additionally, we'll use NTFS permissions that prevent those individuals from changing each other's request files.

So the resulting security model is that anyone with permission to the *Requests* folder can submit a request of any kind. The proxy service monitors incoming requests and moves them into the task queue along with the identity of the requestor discovered from the request file's owner attribute. When the task is executed, that identity is passed to the task script, and the task script validates whether the requestor has permission to request the task. We're taking the identity of the requestor all the way through the model, and validating the requestor's ability to request the task at the very end of the process, before executing the task.

If our framework used a Web application as the administrative tool, the Web application running under its own credentials could validate the requestor's ability to request a task before submitting it to the queue. In that way, the queue would be trusted and any task in the queue would be executed by the proxy service.

If it sounds complicated, it is, but just a little. I think you'll find that as we explore each component in detail, it will become clearer and the elegance of the model will shine through.

> **Important**    Be certain to evaluate the Proxy Framework in a lab setting before customizing it and considering its implementation in your production network.

## Create Active Directory objects required to support the Proxy Framework

Although the proxy service is called a "service," it is actually a scheduled task running very frequently. Not as rich and robust as a Windows service, but not as crazy to develop as an IT professional, either. A scheduled task, like a service, maintains its credentials so that there is no permanent record of the credentials under which the task runs. Because it is so similar to a service, I recommend that you create a user account for the proxy service that follows your organization's guidelines for service accounts. In this documentation, I call the account SVC_Proxy. The account must be delegated sufficient permission to perform all tasks that will be proxied. Don't overdelegate it, though. Don't just put it in the Domain Admins group. Delegate with least privilege, but be sure it can successfully complete the tasks that you will ask it to perform. The proxy service user account must have the right to log on, or to log on as a batch job, for the machine on which the scheduled task will run.

Following my own guidance related to role-based management, I recommend you create the following capability management groups as domain local security groups in Active Directory:

**AD_Proxy_Requestors**    This group represents the users or administrators who have permission to submit requests to the Proxy Framework.

**AD_Proxy_Monitors**    This group has the ability to read the Access database to monitor progress, audit the task queue, and so on.

**AD_Proxy_Admins**    This group has the ability to add and modify scripts, and to modify the Access database. This is a highly privileged group—it can modify the Proxy Framework in a way that allows any task to be performed up to the delegation of the proxy service (SVC_Proxy) account itself. Therefore, members of this group should have existing delegations that are greater than that of the proxy service; otherwise, you are giving them indirect delegations greater than their existing delegations.

Group names can be changed, of course. These groups have an indirect impact on Active Directory, so you should create the groups in an OU with limited delegation to modify the groups' membership. In my sample OU structure, I create the groups in the Admins\Admin Groups\AD Delegations OU that includes all of my Active Directory delegation management groups.

## Create the shared folders required by the Proxy Framework

Place the contents of the Proxy Framework folder from the companion media on a shared folder so that it is centrally accessible. NTFS permissions should be highly restrictive. I recommend the following:

> **Important**    If you are testing these permissions, note that they are least-privilege permissions. The Administrators group of the server is not assumed to have any rights to the Proxy Framework resources. That means you'll lock yourself out unless you add your user account or a group to which you belong to the AD_Proxy_Admins group. Then log off and log on so that your user account is given the capabilities associated with administering the Proxy Framework.

**Proxy (top-level folder)**    Disable inheritance, and remove all previously inherited permissions. System::Allow::Full Control (Apply To: This Folder, Subfolders And Files) and AD_Proxy_Admins::Allow::Full Control (Apply To: This Folder, Subfolders And Files)

**Proxy\Scripts**    SVC_Proxy::Allow::Read & Execute (Apply To: This Folder, Subfolders And Files)

**Proxy\Errors and Proxy\Archives**    SVC_Proxy::Allow::Modify (Apply To: This Folder, Subfolders And Files)

**Proxy\Requests**    SVC_Proxy::Allow::Modify (Apply To: This Folder, Subfolders And Files) and AD_Proxy_Requestors::Allow::Create Files/Write Data (Apply To: This Folder Only)

**Proxy\Service**    SVC_Proxy::Allow::Modify (Apply To: This Folder, Subfolders And Files) and AD_Proxy_Monitors::Allow::Read And Execute (Apply To: This Folder, Subfolders And Files)

You've probably noticed that I am applying permissions directly to the service account rather than nesting the service account in a group. That is because there will always be only one account—the one used by the service—that requires these permissions. If I put it into a group, I'd have to worry about the delegation of that group's membership because another identity could be added to the group that would compromise the framework. For the same reason, I'm delegating only Read permission to the Scripts folder for the SVC_Proxy account. If that account is ever compromised, I can limit the exposure by preventing the account from being used to modify scripts. The compromised account could be used to add unauthorized tasks in to the queue, but those tasks could only perform actions supported by existing scripts. The most important security concern is the membership and delegation of the AD_Proxy_Admins group, as mentioned earlier.

I don't mean to scare you too much about the security risks of the framework. These kinds of concerns are fundamental and universal. Any power that can be used for good can be used for evil. It isn't often as IT professionals that we need to look at the security implications of code and frameworks. Developers have to do it every day.

You can share the folder after the NTFS permissions have been applied. Share permissions should allow connection by the AD_Proxy_Requestors, AD_Proxy_Admins, AD_Proxy_Monitors, and SVC_Proxy account. You can reduce the security surface of the framework by assigning only Change share permission to these accounts. After the share is in place, I recommend that the folder be included in your DFS namespace so that tools can refer to the folder using a logical, domain-based namespace such as \\contoso.com\IT\maintenance\proxy.

## Create scripts that perform tasks

You must add scripts to the Scripts folder for each task that can be proxied. The scripts obviously have to accept arguments that determine their behavior. I highly recommend that you use named arguments in your scripts to add clarity and manageability. As I mentioned in the discussion about the security model for this framework, the script needs to validate that the requestor does, in fact, have permission to request that specific proxied task. In my sample scripts, a */requestedBy* argument is used to send the script the requestor's identity. The script then uses business logic to determine whether the requestor is valid. If the requestor is valid, the task is executed; if not, an error message is returned.

The script must run noninteractively. No message boxes or input boxes are allowed because the script is run by the proxy service, not by an administrator. The script *can* produce output using WScript.Echo. Such output will be captured by the proxy service and added to the log entry for the task. I suggest that you trap errors in the script and echo descriptions of the errors so that if a task is not executing successfully, a member of AD_Proxy_Monitors or AD_Proxy_Admins can examine the task queue and see the output of the task script.

Examine the scripts I included in the Scripts folder of the companion media as samples to guide your development of task scripts. I am sure that the resource kit Web site, *http://www.intelliem.com/resourcekit*, will develop a repository of community-developed scripts that fit into the Proxy Framework.

## Add the Access database

The Access database, Provision.mdb, is ready to use by the sample proxy service. As long as it is in the Proxy\Service folder and is secured according to the earlier guidance, it should be ready for testing.

## Establish the proxy service

The sample proxy service script should be usable in a lab as long as the Proxy Framework folder structure is in place. The script and the database must be in the same Proxy\Service folder.

The proxy service script is designed to run as a scheduled task on a frequency that is appropriate for your business requirements. When you create the scheduled task, you assign the credentials you created earlier. As I mentioned earlier, the Proxy Service account must have the user right to log on as a batch job in order to run as a scheduled task. Configure the user right using a GPO scoped to the server. You can use the schtasks.exe command to create the scheduled task as follows, which will execute the proxy service every two minutes:

```
schtasks.exe /create /RU DOMAIN\SVC_Proxy /RP password /TN "Proxy Service"
/TR "cscript e:\proxy\service\proxy.vbs"
/SC MINUTE /mo 2
```

Because the proxy service runs on the same system as the Proxy Framework folder, use a local path when scheduling the task.

The script has two major jobs: to add new inbound requests to the queue and to execute open tasks.

**Add inbound requests to the queue**   Requests are submitted by custom administrative tools as two-line text files. The first line is the task, or *command*, to run; the second line contains the *parameters*—the arguments—to pass to the command. When Proxy.vbs runs, it looks in the *Requests* folder and processes each text file it finds to add the command and parameters to the task queue, along with the identity of the requestor. But it doesn't do that blindly. It performs a modicum of validation to ensure that the command is a valid command. It does this by passing each text file to the *ValidFile* function. The *ValidFile* function looks at the first line, the command, and checks to see that there is a script by that name in the Scripts folder. If the text file does not request a valid command, it is moved to the Errors folder. You can monitor the Errors folder to see what files are there, when they were created, and who created them (the owner of the file).

If task requests a valid command, the request file is moved to the Archives folder, and the command and the parameter line are added to the request queue in the Access database. The task request record also contains the date of the task request (identified using the *DateCreated* attribute of the request file) and the requestor (found by examining the *Owner* attribute of the file).

There's an important note here about the requestor and the file owner. As you probably know, a user who creates a file is the file's initial owner unless that user is a member of the local Administrators group. If that is the case, the Administrators group is assigned as the owner— not the individual user. That behavior prevents you from knowing exactly who created the file. There are two workarounds to this problem. The first is to modify the task scripts so that when they are told that the requestor is the Administrators group, they can make an informed decision about whether to complete the task or to throw an error.

The second approach, and the one that I have implemented in the sample framework, is not to worry about it. The whole point of a Proxy Framework is to allow *nonprivileged* accounts to make workflow-enabled changes in Active Directory. The custom administrative tools that submit the requests should not be run with credentials that are in the Administrators group of the Proxy Framework server. There's no need to run them with that level of credentials. So if the custom tools are run with standard user credentials, the ownership problem goes away.

**Process open tasks**    After adding any new requests to the queue, the Proxy.vbs script looks for open tasks that have not been fulfilled, including those that were just added. The *Status* field of the task record indicates whether or not the task is *open*. So the proxy script queries for open tasks and then attempts to run each task sequentially. It uses the *Exec* method of the *Shell* object to run the task script with cscript.exe. *Exec* returns the output of the script, and it can support timeout and termination of a task that is not responding or completing. The *Execute_Capture* function handles all of that. The *Configuration Block* includes settings that control the timeout of a task, five seconds by default, and the number of retries.

Each time that Proxy.vbs attempts to execute the task, the output of the task is added to the task record's *Notes* field. A member of the AD_Proxy_Monitors or AD_Proxy_Admins group can look at the task queue and see when the task was requested, when it was last executed, and how many times it was retried. (Zero means it was successful on the first execution and required no retries.) The *Notes* field includes any information returned by the task script.

## Submit task request files with custom administrative tools

The last step in our examination of the framework, and the first step in how the framework is used, is the submission of the task request file. Task request files are two lines: the command name, which must match the name of a task script without the .vbs extension, and parameters. The parameters can be blank, theoretically, but most tasks need to be directed with arguments.

I've provided a simple script to demonstrate the bare-bones code required to submit a task request file. The script is called Proxy_TaskSubmit.vbs. It is in the Samples folder in the Proxy Framework folder. The sample HTA provided uses the same function as Proxy_TaskSubmit.vbs to submit their requests.

The Proxy_TaskSubmit.vbs script removes a user from a group. The user and group are specified in the script's *sParameters* variable. The request that is submitted calls the group-removemember.vbs script within the Proxy\Scripts folder. That script makes sure that the requestor is allowed to make the change by examining the group's Managed By assignment. So, to test this script, you must first customize the *sRequestPath* and *sParameters* variables. You must make sure the user belongs to the group so that the proxied task can remove the user. You must configure the group's Managed By tab so that your user account, or a group to which you belong, is indicated by the group's *ManagedBy* attribute. Finally, you must make sure you are a member of the AD_Proxy_Requestors group so that you can submit the request. Do *not* perform the test as a member of the Administrators group, for reasons mentioned above.

You can follow the progress of the proxied task using these steps:

1. Open the Proxy\Requests folder so that you can watch the request file appear.

2. Run Proxy_TaskSubmit.vbs.

3. The task request text file appears in the Proxy\Requests folder.

    If the task request text file doesn't appear, one of several potential problems should be evaluated. First, you might have been very lucky with your timing, and the task request file was created just at the time the scheduled task ran the proxy service script. Check to see if the file has been moved to the Archives or Errors folder.

    You might not have permissions to submit the request. Are you a member of the AD_Proxy_Requestors group? Run *whoami /groups* at the command prompt to see if you are a member of that group. Try to manually create a new text file in the Proxy\Requests folder.

    If you can manually create a text file in the Requests folder, it is most likely that the configuration of Proxy_TaskSubmit.vbs is incorrect. That's all that the script does—create a text file.

4. When the scheduled task launches the proxy service script, the task request text file will disappear and be moved to either the Archives folder or the Errors folder.

    If the text file was moved to Archives, it was successfully transferred into the task request queue in the provisioning database. If it was moved to the Errors folder, there was something wrong with the text file itself. Open it to examine its contents. Is it corrupted somehow?

5. Open the Provisioning.mdb file with Microsoft Office Access, and open the RequestQueue table.

    If the text file was moved to Archives, the request should appear as a record in the RequestQueue table. If the record shows a status of *complete*, the task was executed. If the task record status is *error* or *open*, examine the *Notes* field to identify the cause of the problem. Review the information discussed earlier about the functionality of this sample.

Compare Group_ChangeMember_Proxy.hta to the Group_ChangeMember.hta discussed in the previous solution. You'll see that the difference is in the functions that add and remove members. Instead of performing the operation directly, a task request is submitted.

### Implement business logic and rules

The custom tools that submit task requests marshal the information required to perform the task. The output of the tool consists of the command and the parameters required by the task script. Business logic and rules can be implemented in two places: in the custom tool or in the task script. For example, when creating a user, the custom tool prompts for the user's first name and last name. The tool can derive the display name by applying a naming convention such as *LastName, FirstName*, and then pass the first, last, and display name to the task script. Alternatively, the task script can be sent only the first and last name, and the task script can then derive the display name. I generally prefer to put the logic in the task script because the user could, in theory, manually create a text file with parameters that deviate from the business rules. If the task script accepts only arguments that *should* be entered by the user and then applies all the business logic before performing the task, there's less exposure to inappropriate manipulation of the task requests. You'll see the user creation sample demonstrate that approach. The task script accepts the *FirstName* and *LastName* arguments and then derives the *displayName* attribute for the user internally. The HTA *also* derives the display name, but only for the purpose of showing the results to the user. The HTA does not pass the display name to the task script.

## Imagine what proxying can do for you

Proxying is a very useful concept because it enables you to do the following:

1. Enforce business rules for object creation, deletion, and modification. Custom tools such as Group_ChangeMember_Proxy.hta allow you to incorporate naming standards, logic, and workflow. Because users are not given direct permission to make changes in Active Directory, you can be more certain that business rules are being followed.

2. Log administrative actions with details that would not be captured by Active Directory auditing. For example, you can require administrators to enter a business justification for a particular task.

3. Protect Active Directory. In earlier solutions, I described challenges related to delegating the ability to move objects between OUs. To be able to move objects, you must be able to delete them, and you must tightly restrict who can delete objects in order to prevent accidental or intentional deletion. You can restrict administrators from deleting objects and allow them to move objects through a proxy.

4. Delegate management tasks to business owners. In the previous solution, we provided tools that allow users to manage groups more easily, but that still required them to be delegated the Write::Member permission. With proxying, you can allow users to manage groups without actually delegating permission to them.

# Delegate group management to users with increased confidence and security

We've brought our discussions of business rules and standards from Solution 8-1, the delegation of group membership management from Solution 8-2, and the creation of friendly tools in Solution 8-5 to an ultimately productive framework. With a Proxy Framework in place, you can delegate the management of group membership to the proxy service account only. Users can be given custom tools to manage group membership, and the actions they take with those tools provide an audit trail to the changes they make. Because users do not have permission to make changes directly in Active Directory, you can be confident that rules are being followed and appropriate metadata is being logged. Now you can step out of the way, in appropriate situations, and allow business owners of resources to directly manage access to those resources.

# Improving the Deployment and Management of Applications and Configuration

Every administrator has spent time supporting the installation of applications on Microsoft Windows systems. So you know what it's like to sit in front of a computer and click through the Setup Wizard of an application. You know that some applications can be automated so that they can be installed silently—in an unattended mode. And you know that there are software management applications such as Systems Management Server (SMS) and Systems Center Configuration Manager 2007 (Configuration Manager) that offer robust features such as granular targeting of applications to specific users or computers and reporting.

In this solution, I present guidance and tools that will improve your application management capabilities whether or not your enterprise uses a tool such as SMS or Configuration Manager. I also provide a framework with which you can attain the key features of software management (targeted change management and reporting) without investing in a commercial tool. Finally, I reveal a fantastic trick to automate application installation and configuration that otherwise requires you to click through a user interface.

## Scenarios, Pain, and Solution

The pain that arises from a poorly implemented (or thoroughly lacking) software management infrastructure should sound familiar to you:

■ The primary software share at Litware, Inc., is a disaster. Application installation folders and loose application installation files are strewn about as if an IT hurricane had blown through. Users and administrators alike have trouble finding the applications they need to install, and on several occasions users installed a very outdated version of an application simply because it was the first one they stumbled across when looking for the application.

■ Two and a half years ago, a team at Contoso, Ltd., worked for several weeks to create automated installation routines for a number of common applications. Since then, almost 50 percent of the applications that have been upgraded use completely new setup routines that require new setup commands. The team is in the process of altering all the scripts, packages, and references to the applications to account for the changes. The team wants to find a way to minimize the impact that application setup procedures have on the rest of its software management framework.

■ Many of the applications in use at Adventure Works are updated regularly. Applications such as Adobe Acrobat Reader, Apple QuickTime, Adobe Flash Player, Windows Media Player, and others seem to be revised every few months. Because the organization is growing so quickly and new systems are being released each week using images built by Microsoft Deployment, Adventure Works needs to be sure that the images are up to date. But keeping up with the applications' releases has become a big challenge.

■ Proseware's IT organization supports several methods for application deployment, including Group Policy Software Installation, over-the-network and CD-ROM-based manual installation, scripts used to set up applications in images, and a limited test of Configuration Manager. Any change to an application's setup command or requirements has a painful domino effect, as each of these tools has to be updated.

■ Trey Research is equipping its administrators with a number of tools based on the scripts provided in this resource kit, and it wants to provide utilities such as PSExec and Joe Richards's Active Directory utilities (*http://www.joeware.net*). These tools do not need to be installed on clients—just copied to them. The deployment team wants to find a way to manage this process and to keep administrators' systems updated with the latest version of these files.

■ Northwind Traders is trying to get a handle on the deployment of applications. The company wants to automate application deployment so that users do not have to be administrators on their computers. It also requires reporting of application installation for license reconciliation. It wants a software deployment framework in place before it deploys Microsoft Office 2007, which is, of course, a large and high-impact application. But a tool such as Configuration Manager is not within its budget for the upcoming fiscal year. The company wants to put pieces together to build a framework without a commercial tool.

■ World Wide Importers just hired a new desktop manager. She is looking through the help desk logs to identify problems that can be proactively solved. Several of the common help desk issues can be addressed by configuring Windows more effectively—for example, setting the default folder view to Details. But these changes can be made only interactively, by clicking through the Windows user interface. She wants to find a way to automate these otherwise manual tasks.

The solutions in this chapter put in place a powerful software management, packaging, configuration, and deployment framework that addresses these and other pain points. It starts in Solution 9-1 with a disciplined and well-thought-out network software distribution point. Within each application's software distribution folder, create a custom installation package that will abstract the complexities in the application's setup routine and the changes in that routine as the application is updated over time. Separate the application's installation from its configuration so that configuration can be reapplied later in the application's life cycle—for example, when a user makes unwanted changes to the configuration that need to be reset to the enterprise's custom defaults as part of troubleshooting. Leverage Group Policy Software Installation and the new Files and Registry preferences to deploy software and apply configuration. Build a framework for deployment that supports targeted installation, reporting, and optional user control over the timing of installation to minimize user impact. And automate tasks that seem to be impossible to automate using macro-like sequences of keystrokes. These components enable sophisticated application management that will complement third-party software management applications and, in many environments, enable management without those tools.

# 9-1: Providing Software Distribution Points

## Solution overview

| | |
|---|---|
| **Type of solution** | Guidance |
| **Features and tools** | NTFS folders and permissions, SMB share permissions, DFS Namespaces |
| **Solution summary** | Create a highly organized physical and DFS namespace for network software distribution points. |
| **Benefits** | Improved security and application manageability |

## Introduction

Most software management infrastructures include software distribution points. Software distribution points are shared folders on network servers that contain the files required to install applications. Software makers use various terms when referring to software distribution points: deployment points, distribution shares, administrative installations, and network installation points are just a few. In many of the organizations I've encountered, the software share is, to put it charitably, a mess.

In the solution, I recommend practices that will help you gain control and increase the manageability of your software distribution points. I also outline steps you can take to replicate software distribution points to branch offices at remote sites.

# Rationalize your software folder namespace

Let's assume that you've created a top-level folder on a file server, within which you will store distribution points for individual applications. We'll call this top level your Software folder because most organizations name this top-level folder *Software* or *Applications* or something along those lines.

A software management infrastructure begins with the disciplined management of the Software folder and the namespace you create within that folder. The most productive environments I've encountered use a namespace that is based first on vendors, second on applications, and third on versions. For example, the distribution point for Microsoft Office 2007 would be found in Software\Microsoft\Office 2007. The distribution point for Adobe Acrobat Reader 8.0 would be found in Software\Adobe\Acrobat Reader\8.0. A representative sample of a software distribution point is seen in Figure 9-1.

**Figure 9-1**    Software distribution point namespace

In the figure, some folders are fully expanded and some are not. But the figure illustrates the basic concept. The art and science of the software folder namespace is determining what, exactly, is an application and what is a version. You'll notice in Figure 9-1 that versions 7.0, 7.0.5, and 8.0 of Acrobat Reader are stored in separate folders beneath a folder for the application. On the other hand, Office 2003 and Office 2007 are stored as individual applications beneath the folder for the software maker, Microsoft. Although there is no golden rule to identifying applications or versions, I prefer to have a folder for individual applications with subfolders for versions for just about every application. Office 2003 and Office 2007 are exceptions, for me, only because they are such large and high-impact applications.

The next trick is to identify what constitutes a version. In Figure 9-1, you can see three versions of Acrobat Reader: 7.0, 7.0.5, and 8.0. Adobe released several interim versions of Acrobat Reader, including 7.0.1 and 7.0.2. But these were updates to 7.0. They could not be installed as stand-alone applications—they were upgrades to an existing 7.0 installation. Version 7.0.5, however, could be deployed on its own.

It might take some time and experimentation for you to define these upper levels of the software distribution point namespace. And you'll probably find that you need to treat some applications differently than others. Again, I recommend that, at some point in your namespace, you have a folder that represents a version of an application that is granular and can be installed on its own. I will refer to this as the *software distribution folder* for the application—the concept of a specific version will be implied.

For the software distribution folder for an application, my recommendations become a bit more concrete. Let's look inside my software distribution folder for Microsoft Office 2007, shown in Figure 9-2.

**Figure 9-2**    The software distribution folder for Microsoft Office 2007

The primary contents of a software distribution folder will be the applications' own setup files and folders. Those items will, of course, vary from application to application and vendor to vendor. The nature of Microsoft Office makes it one of the larger and more complex software distribution folders that you're likely to encounter. You'll notice a number of subfolders for individual components of Microsoft Office, as well as Office's setup program, Setup.exe.

But you'll also want to store files within the software distribution folder. You might create scripts or packages to automate the deployment of the application. There might be specific patches that must be applied to the application after deployment. You might use utilities such as the Office Customization Tool (OCT) to create files that customize or control installation. And you might collect or develop documentation that describes how to package the application.

I recommend that you centralize all the components related to the installation of an application within its software distribution folder. The problem is that you do not want to conflict with the folders provided by the software manufacturer. For example, if you used a folder called Updates to store updates to a particular application, that folder would be in conflict with the new Updates folder that has a specific purpose during installation of Microsoft Office 2007. Therefore, I suggest that you create a disciplined namespace for the components that you bring to the installation. Create folders that are prefixed with your company's name. You can see the Contoso_Setup, Contoso_Updates, and Contoso_Customization folders in Figure 9-2. You can also see two scripts, Contoso_Setup and Contoso_Configure. I discuss the purpose of these scripts later in the Solution Collection.

You can also see in Figure 9-2 one beneficial result of this approach. All files and folders that I've added to the software distribution folder are immediately visible and grouped together, alphabetically. I don't have to scan through dozens of folders or files to find what is mine and what is Microsoft's. If a new version of the application is released and I create a new software distribution folder for that version, I can easily identify and copy all the changes I made to the previous version and bring them into the new version.

The primary lesson in this section is discipline. Come up with a system and stick with it. Don't let your software share become a disorganized swamp of distribution folders. You'll see in later solutions that the discipline pays off in very big ways. For example, in Solution 9-2 on page 594, I create a script that allows you to install the current release of most applications with incredible ease. It all starts with discipline.

**Best Practices**   Create a physical namespace for software distribution folders that is disciplined and relatively consistent across applications. With an application's software distribution folder, collect all the components and customizations that you add to the application in folders prefixed with your company name so that your additions do not conflict with the vendor's own namespace.

## Manage access to software distribution folders

In later solutions, we'll discuss options for actually deploying the application stored in software distribution folders. One option is, of course, to navigate to the software distribution folder and launch the installation of the application. To maintain control over software licensing, you should restrict who has access to software distribution folders. The easiest way to do this is to grant Read And Execute permission to a security group that represents users of the application. To do this, you perform the following tasks:

- Create a security group in Active Directory that represents the application.

  Use a naming convention that indicates the purpose of the group. For example, create a group called APP_Visio to represent Microsoft Office Visio 2007. As I mention in later solutions, application groups will generally be created as global security groups.

- Assign the group Read And Execute permission to the software distribution folder.

- Use the same group to scope the deployment of the application using your software deployment tool of choice, such as SMS or Configuration Manager.

- Populate the group with the users of the application and the computer accounts representing the computers on which the application has been installed.

In Solution 9-5 on page 615, I revisit this topic in significantly more detail.

You must also consider granting permissions that enable the team that owns the application in your organization to make changes to that application's distribution folders. This entails assigning Modify permission to a security group that represents the application owners. Finally, you should configure permissions for the entire Software namespace. At the top-level Software folder, assign permissions that enable an appropriate team to fully administer the software distribution point.

> **Best Practices**    Grant Read And Execute permission to an Active Directory security group that represents users of the application and computers on which the application has been installed.

## Share the Software folder, and abstract its location with a DFS namespace

After you have applied appropriate NTFS permissions to the Software folder, you are ready to create a Server Message Block (SMB) share for that folder. Follow these practices when sharing the Software folder:

- Name the folder so that the share itself is hidden. For example, you can name the shared folder Software$.

- Configure the caching settings on the share to disable caching.

- Because the folders are sufficiently secured using NTFS permissions, set the share permissions to Everyone::Allow::Full Control.

- Optionally, enable access-based enumeration for the shared folder. By doing so, users who connect to the software share will not see folders to which they have no access.

For the sake of example, let's assume that you have created and shared a software folder on a server called SERVER11, and that the resulting SMB namespace path to the software share is \\SERVER11\software$. Now comes a simple and very important recommendation: Never, ever, use that path to access the software share or to install applications.

Why? There is no guarantee that in months or years to come the software share will remain on SERVER11. It's possible, and in fact likely, that you will move it in time. You have probably encountered software that remembers the location from which it was installed and looks to that location for installation files when updates are applied, repairs are made, or the application is uninstalled. Can you think of such software? Oh, yes: Windows XP, Microsoft Office, and, of course, many others. In addition, you might now or in the future want to distribute the software share to remote sites and branch offices.

For these reasons and others, you do not want to be tied to the server and the physical namespace of software distribution folders. Instead, you should abstract that namespace and present it in a logical, organized DFS namespace. I discuss DFS Namespaces in several Solution Collections in this resource kit. One of the most high-value uses of DFS Namespaces is to support software distribution.

Create a domain-based DFS namespace for software. For example, I created the namespace \\contoso.com\software shown in Figure 9-3. Within the DFS namespace, replicate as much of your physical namespace as is necessary to support your software management framework. You'll notice that the DFS namespace shown in Figure 9-3 closely parallels the physical namespace shown in Figure 9-1.

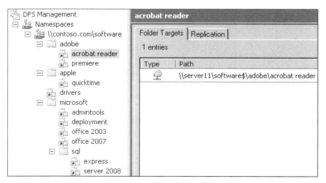

**Figure 9-3**  A DFS namespace for software management

The folders at the end of each branch of the DFS namespace link to software distribution folders for that application. For example, the folder \\contoso.com\software\adobe\acrobat reader links to \\server11\software$\adobe\acrobat reader. There are no DFS folders for the individual versions of the application. When a user navigates to \\contoso.com\software\adobe\acrobat reader, she will see the version folders, but those are being exposed by the physical namespace on the server rather than by the DFS namespace. This structure is helpful for keeping applications current on client systems, as you will see in Solution 9-2.

Using DFS Namespaces to abstract a certain portion of the software namespace enables you to more easily manage application distribution. Applications will be accessed, managed, and installed using DFS namespace paths. If one or more applications need to be moved to another server, you can do that. Simply change the target of the applications' DFS folder. Change the target of the Acrobat Reader folder to reference \\server43\software$\adobe\acrobat reader to relocate that application to SERVER43. As long as you maintain a consistent physical namespace beneath the folder that is targeted by DFS, you won't have to change any of the references to that software distribution folder. For example, if you uninstall the application, it might look for supporting files in the path from which the application was installed: \\contoso.com\software\adobe\acrobat reader. The fact that the physical storage of the software distribution folder has been moved to another server is completely transparent to the application.

> **Best Practices**    Abstract the physical and SMB namespace of your software distribution infrastructure using DFS Namespaces. Create a DFS namespace that is as deep as the application level of the physical namespace.

# Replicate software distribution folders to remote sites and branch offices

In a distributed enterprise, application management is facilitated by maintaining copies of software distribution folders on servers in remote sites and branch offices. DFS-R is the perfect tool to create replicas of software folders and to keep those folders synchronized. Solution 2-15 on page 151 explains how to configure a hub-and-spoke replication topology in which changes are made to the master copy of a resource and are replicated to read-only copies in other locations. This type of topology is ideal for maintaining software distribution folders.

In smaller organizations, it might be possible to have a single server act as the hub for the entire software distribution folder, and to replicate the entire folder to remote sites and branch offices. To achieve this, the software share in the hub has the share permission Everyone::Allow::Full Control. Of course, the effective access of users to resources within the software share are managed by NTFS permissions. The shares in the spokes restrict users to a maximum effective access of Read And Execute with the Everyone::Allow::Read share permission on the replica's shares. See Solution 2-15 for details.

However, in larger and more complex enterprises, an application likely will be used in some sites but not others. Additionally, the teams responsible for packaging, managing, and maintaining applications might be distributed across locations. In these environments, the master copy of an application's software distribution folder should be on a server that is local to the team that owns the application. The master of that application can be replicated to servers in locations that use the application. A simple diagram that illustrates this topology is shown in Figure 9-4. The shaded folders represent the master copies of the application. The unshaded folders represent replicas.

As suggested by Figure 9-4, it is not necessary to replicate the entire software folder to all servers. In this more complex model, the shared folder, the Software$ share, will be configured with the Everyone::Allow::Read permission on all servers. To give an application's owners the ability to change the software distribution folder for the application, the software distribution folder on the hub server for that application will be shared separately with a share permission giving the application owners Full Control permission. If changes need to be made to the software distribution folder, they will connect directly to the application's shared folder on the hub server.

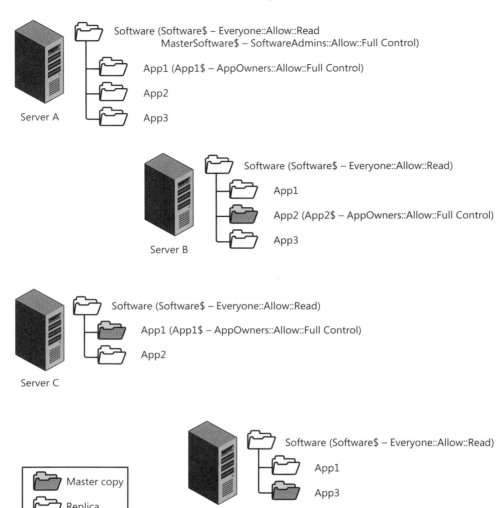

**Figure 9-4** A complex topology of replication for multiple applications using a hub-and-spoke model

Figure 9-5 illustrates the DFS namespace for a replicated topology for Adobe Acrobat Reader. Users access the software distribution folder through the path \\contoso.com\software\adobe\acrobat reader, which targets replicas on three separate servers through the Software$ shares on those servers. Owners of the application use the DFS namespace path \\contoso.com\software\adobe\acrobat reader (primary), which targets an application-specific shared folder on the hub server—for example, \\server11\adobe acrobat$. That share has Full Control share permission. The NTFS permissions on the folder ensure that only application owners can make changes.

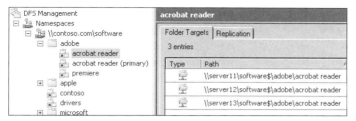

**Figure 9-5**   The DFS namespace folder for a replicated application, and the separate namespace folder that allows access by the application owners

Figure 9-4 also illustrates another recommendation: that one server (SERVER A in the figure) should host a replica of all software distribution folders so that there is one place where all software can be accessed if necessary. Consider creating a separate, top-level share on the server that provides Full Control share permission so that changes can be made to all software distribution folders on that server. For example, create a MasterSoftware$ share with Everyone::Allow::Full Control share permission to be used by application owners and administrators in addition to the Software$ share with Everyone::Allow::Read permission that is targeted by DFS namespace folders. This is illustrated in Figure 9-5.

**Best Practices**   Use DFS-R to replicate software to remote sites and branch offices. Whether your topology is simple—in which case, the entire Software folder is replicated from a hub to distributed replicas—or more complex and enmeshed, DFS-R can ensure that applications are local to the users that require them.

# Create a place for your own tools and scripts

Be sure to create a software distribution folder for your own applications, tools, and scripts. For example, I created a folder, Contoso, and put it into the DFS namespace shown in Figure 9-5. Inside it, there is a folder called Software Management that contains the tools used later in this Solution Collection, specifically SystemConfigurationDB.mdb and Software_Setup_Core.vbs.

# Solution summary

A disciplined and well-managed infrastructure for software distribution points is fundamental to the success of a software management framework. Create a physical namespace that organizes software by vendor, application, and version. Secure the namespace so that applications can be accessed only by users and computers that require them. Abstract that namespace using DFS Namespaces so that references to applications are not bound to the server-based physical or SMB Namespaces. Then, if necessary, replicate application software distribution folders to remote sites and branch offices so that users have local, high-performance access to the folders. Be sure to create a location for your custom tools and scripts.

# 9-2: New Approaches to Software Packaging

## Solution overview

| | |
|---|---|
| **Type of solution** | Guidance and scripts |
| **Features and tools** | VBScript, setup.exe, msiexec.exe |
| **Solution summary** | Create a wrapper around the many various application setup routines in your environment so that there is always one consistent, easy-to-find way to launch the installation of any one application. Separate application installation and configuration, and then link them together. |
| **Benefits** | Ability to upgrade application versions without modifying the software management framework; easier deployment and support. |

## Introduction

The primary goal of a software management infrastructure is to support the installation, repair, and removal of applications. There are numerous tools that can be used to deploy an application, with SMS and Configuration Manager being among the most obvious. Regardless of the tool you use to actually push an application to a client, you must have a way to automate that application's installation and configuration. In this solution, I introduce some methods and scripts that can greatly facilitate the automated management of applications throughout their life cycle. These tools and methodologies will be extended in later solutions to build a software management framework that provides reasonable functionality without commercial systems management tools. However, most of the tools and methodologies discussed in this solution facilitate more effective software management even with such tools.

Software deployment should be as hands-free as possible. The good news is that most commercial applications targeted for business use provide some option for automated installation. The bad news is that there is little consistency across applications—there is no magic *setup / automatically* command that will work for all applications.

So if there isn't one, why not create one? Wouldn't it be nice to be able to look for a single file— let's call it Contoso_Setup.vbs—in any application's software distribution folder and know that, just by calling that file, the application would be installed? Let's do it! We'll create a script named *Company*_Setup.vbs—Contoso_Setup.vbs, for example—that will be found in every application's software distribution folder and that you will always use to launch the installation of that application.

Not only do we make it easier to locate and launch installations, we make it easier to maintain our software management infrastructure. If we have several ways that we install an application—manually and using an automated method, for example—and if the application vendor changes the rules by which its application is installed, we need simply to change our script to reflect the application's new rules. We don't need to change the references in our software management tools or the procedures used for manual installation.

And while we're at it, think about a common business reality—you are tasked with installing *the current version* of an application. Not specifically version 3.0 or 4.0 or 5.0, but rather the version that is most recent. We'll tackle that, as well, while not preventing you from installing a specific, older version in scenarios where a dependency or other requirement locks you into a version other than the most recent.

Finally, I'll address why it is useful to pull the configuration that you apply to an application out of the application's installation package and then link them together.

## Determine how to automate the installation of an application

Packaging, in the broadest sense, entails automating the installation of an application, including the components and configurations that are unique to your environment. Your first step, therefore, is to determine how an application's installation can be automated. Because there is no single method that works for all applications, you must spend some time researching the applications in your environment to determine if and how they can be installed without intervention. Search the Web sites of your applications' vendors. I generally find the information regarding automated installation by pairing a keyword such as *silent*, *unattended*, *quiet*, or *enterprise* with a keyword such as *deploy*, *deployment*, *installation*, or *setup*.

I also recommend searching the Internet at large for tips regarding automated installation of applications. Particularly for well-known applications, you will find many resources and tips posted by other administrators supporting those applications.

As you collect information about automated setup, you'll find that many applications fall into a small handful of categories, each of which are installed similarly. The first such category is applications that you install using Windows Installer files, better known as .msi files. These applications can be set up using MSIExec. The MSIExec command supports several useful switches, described in the following list, that control the level of interactivity:

**/qn**   A completely automated and silent installation with no user interface.

**/qb**   A basic user interface, usually consisting of a simple progress bar, is shown. Error messages are also displayed.

**/qb-**   A basic user interface is shown, but modal dialog boxes, such as error messages, are suppressed.

When I deploy applications for automated installation, I have the best luck using /qb-. This switch suppresses modal dialog boxes that could interrupt the progress of an installation, but usually it provides a progress bar so that I have a visual cue that installation is underway.

You can perform an automated installation of XML Notepad—a useful editor for XML files freely available from the Microsoft Downloads site (*http://www.microsoft.com/downloads*)—using the following command:

```
msiexec.exe -i xmlnotepad.msi /qb-
```

The *-i* switch instructs MSIExec to install the application. MSIExec has other switches to specify repair or removal of an application. Type **msiexec.exe /?** in a command prompt for a list of switches.

A second category of applications are those that use a setup.exe command to launch the application's installation. You can often automate applications of this type using simple switches such as */s* for silent or */q* for quiet. You can experiment to discover what switch a particular setup.exe command supports, but you are better off researching on the vendor's site.

There are also applications that use a Setup.exe command to perform specific tasks before handing installation over to an .msi file. A common syntax for automating installation of such applications is the following:

```
setup.exe /q /v /qn /norestart
```

The */q* switch informs the part of the installation controlled by setup.exe to be quiet. This instruction usually suppresses a Welcome page of a setup wizard. When setup.exe launches the application's .msi file, it passes to msiexec.exe the switches following the */v* switch. So, in the preceding example, the */qn* and */norestart* switches are actually handed to and used by MSIExec.

More complex applications often require a Windows Installer transform file (an .mst file) to script the answers to questions that would normally be posed by the installation wizard. Office 2003, for example, requires the transform for automated installation. When a transform is used, its name must be passed to MSIExec. This process is often handled by the application's setup.exe command. For example, to launch an automated installation of Microsoft Office 2003, the following command is used:

```
Setup.exe TRANSFORMS=TransformName.mst NOUSERNAME=TRUE /qb-
```

The *NOUSERNAME=TRUE* property is unique to Office 2003. It ensures that users are prompted for their name when they first open an Office application. Without that switch, all user names within Office applications are, by default, the name of the user who installed the application. You can see that Office's setup command passes the */qb-* switch I specified to MSIExec.

Some applications are just downright nasty to install. They insist on presenting dialog boxes and other interfaces that are modal and require interaction before proceeding. For these applications, you should definitely search the Internet to locate solutions that have been developed by other administrators. You might also break down and purchase a commercial application-packaging utility. Such utilities can run a monitor during the application's installation, capture all the changes it makes, and create a new package that is capable of being deployed without interaction.

**Best Practices**    For each application, determine the specific command that enables automated, hands-free installation.

**Note**    Many applications that arrive as a single executable are in fact a compressed file, within which you'll find a standard setup.exe or .msi file. I highly recommend using WinRAR from RAR Labs (*www.rarlabs.com*) to decompress application packages. WinRAR is similar to WinZIP, but it offers additional functionality that is particularly useful for breaking apart setup packages.

## Identify the success codes produced by application installation

When processes are terminated, they typically return a code that indicates success or failure. It's important that you know the code that an application uses to signal a successful installation so that other codes—which indicate an error—can be managed appropriately. One way to determine the success code is to consult technical documentation from the vendor. A second way is to launch the automated installation from the command prompt and then, after installation is complete, type the command **echo %ERRORLEVEL%**. The ERRORLEVEL environment variable reflects the most recently completed command. The vast majority of software installation processes return either a zero or 3010 to indicate success. If you have to gamble, bet on those two codes.

## Use Software_Setup.vbs to install almost any application

After you've identified the command needed to automate the installation of an application and the codes that result from a successful installation, you're ready to use the Software_Setup.vbs script located in the Scripts folder of the companion media. This script creates the silver bullet I mentioned earlier. You will use it to create a setup package for each application—and for each application, the name of the script will be the same: *Company*_Setup.vbs.

The script wraps a layer of abstraction and logic around the unique setup process of an application so that the unique aspects of the application are managed transparently. This allows you to look for and launch *Company*_Setup.vbs in any application's folder without having to remember specific command sequences for that application.

The critical lines of the script are the *Configuration Block*, shown next, and the call to the *Install()* subroutine:

```
sWorkingDir = "%CD%"
sCommand = "%WD%\XMLNotepad.msi"
sCommandArgs = ""
sCommandType = "MSI"
sSuccessCodes = "0,3010"
sCoreFileName = "\\contoso.com\software\contoso\
    software management\Software_Setup_Core.vbs"
Call Install()
```

For most applications, you need to change only the items in the *Configuration Block*. They specify the location from which installation is launched, the command that is used, and the codes that are returned from a successful installation. Let's look at each of the variables in the *Configuration Block*:

**sWorkingDir**   Specifies the working directory. This folder acts as the root directory for the application's installation. Typically, this will be the application's software distribution folder. As you saw in Figure 9-2, this will usually be the folder in which the *Company_Setup.vbs* script is located. This is indicated by the "%CD%" token. When *sWorkingDir* is equal to %CD%, that tells the script that the working directory is the folder where the script itself is located. You'll find that this location is appropriate for most applications.

**sCommand**   Specifies the setup command. This variable indicates the executable or .msi file that drives installation. The path to the setup command must be included. However, you can use the "%CD%" or "%WD%" tokens to represent the current directory (where the script itself is located) or the working directory defined by *sWorkingDir*. In most cases, the setup command will be in the working directory, which itself will be the same as the current directory, so the syntax shown in the preceding code will be appropriate.

**sCommandArgs**   Specifies command arguments. These are the switches that you identified as necessary to drive an automated installation of the application. Specifically, these are switches that follow the setup command. If *sCommandArgs* is blank for an .msi file, the installation script uses */qb- /norestart* automatically, which is a great default for most .msi files.

**sCommandType**   Indicates the command type—EXE or MSI are supported. This indicates whether the setup command specified by *sCommand* is an executable command or an .msi file. This variable is used by the script to determine how the final setup command line is assembled. If the command type is an executable, the final setup command line consists simply of the command itself (*sCommand*) followed by its arguments (*sCommandArgs*). If the command type is an .msi file, the final command line is *msiexec.exe -i* followed by the .msi file (*sCommand*) followed by the arguments (*sCommandArgs*).

**sSuccessCodes**   Shows a comma-delimited list of the codes returned from a successful installation. When installation is complete, the script compares the code returned by the installation to the list of codes in *sSuccessCodes*. If the code matches, the installation is considered a success. If not, the installation is considered a failure.

*sCoreFileName*   Indicates the path to a centrally stored copy of Software_Setup_Core.vbs. This script is included in each execution of Software_Setup.vbs. It is discussed in more detail in the following paragraphs.

The sample *Company_Setup.vbs Configuration Block* just shown installs XML Notepad. Note that *sCommandArgs* can be left blank because the script's hard-wired defaults, */qb- /norestart*, are appropriate for most .msi files, including XML Notepad.

Copy Software_Setup.vbs, rename it **Company_Setup.vbs**, and change the *Configuration Block* for each application. Save the resulting, application-specific Company_Setup.vbs file in the application's software distribution folder.

You must also place the script Software_Setup_Core.vbs in a centrally accessible location. Configure the *sCoreFileName* variable in the *Configuration Block* to point to Software_Setup_Core.vbs. This script contains universal code that is used by each application's *Company_Setup.vbs* script. Software_Setup_Core.vbs is incorporated into the *Company_Setup.vbs* script on the fly, when the script is executed. If you are familiar with the concept of *includes*, that's what is happening. The small *Company_Setup.vbs* script for each application includes the code in Software_Setup_Core.vbs, which does the heavy lifting. It interprets the variables in the *Configuration Block* of an application's *Company_Setup.vbs* script, assembles the command line, executes it, interprets the results, and returns the success or failure code to the parent *Company_Setup.vbs* script for any further processing.

By separating the core functional code into Software_Setup_Core.vbs, I can keep the application *Company_Setup.vbs* scripts lean and mean. *Company_Setup.vbs* requires only the *Configuration Block* specific to that application and the code that locates and includes Software_Setup_Core.vbs. So an application's *Company_Setup.vbs* must manage only the details specific to that application. Separating and including the core code also allows me to make functional improvements to the core code, or to fix bugs, without having to update dozens of individual application scripts.

Although I provide several examples of ways to use these scripts in this solution, I encourage you to explore the scripts in depth if you have an understanding of VBScript, and to join in discussions about this tool on the resource kit Web site, *http://www.intelliem.com/resourcekit*.

## Separate the configuration from the application installation

Apple's QuickTime Player exemplifies a more complex challenge. It is deployed as an .msi file, so it can be automated using the command *msiexec.exe −i QuickTime.msi /qb-*. So the *Configuration Block* changes required to set up QuickTime are as follows:

```
sWorkingDir = "%CD%"
sCommand = "%WD%\QuickTime.msi"
sCommandArgs = ""
sCommandType = "MSI"
sSuccessCodes = "0,3010"
```

The script's hard-wired defaults for command arguments are */qb- /norestart*; you do not need to configure *sCommandArgs*.

When QuickTime Player installs, it adds itself to the Run key of the registry so that it launches in the system tray at logon. My users do not require QuickTime in the tray, and in fact prefer a speedy logon to waiting for applications such as QuickTime to load. So I need to remove QuickTime from the Run key after installation.

The VBScript code for removing QuickTime and iTunes from the system tray looks like this:

```
Option Explicit
' Registry key constants
Const HKEY_LOCAL_MACHINE = &H80000002

Dim sComputer, oRegistry, sKeyPath, sValueName, vValue, iReturn
sComputer = "."
Set oRegistry = GetObject("winmgmts:"_
    & "{impersonationLevel=impersonate}!\\" &_
    sComputer & "\root\default:StdRegProv")
sKeyPath = "SOFTWARE\Microsoft\Windows\CurrentVersion\Run"
sValueName = "QuickTime Task"
iReturn = oRegistry.DeleteValue(HKEY_LOCAL_MACHINE,sKeyPath,sValueName)
sValueName = "iTunesHelper"
iReturn = oRegistry.DeleteValue(HKEY_LOCAL_MACHINE,sKeyPath,sValueName)
```

This code creates a connection to the registry, dives into the Run key, and deletes the values for the QuickTime Task and iTunesHelper.

Although you could include this in the *Company*_Setup script, I highly recommend that you separate and modularize configuration such as this. If a user accidentally re-enables Quick-Time in his system tray, you should be able to revert to the standard configuration using the exact same tools you use to deploy the application. Therefore, keep installation routines separate from all configuration changes you might use for troubleshooting or resetting systems to standards. For example, you could create a script, *Company*_Configure.vbs, and enter the code just shown. That way, if a user complains that QuickTime is in the system tray, you can simply rerun the script.

Then call the configuration script from the installation script so that you continue to have a single command required to set up the application, but that command also configures the application. For example, you could add the following three new lines after the call to the *Install* subroutine in Software_Setup.vbs:

```
Call Install()
sCommand = "cscript.exe """ & sCurrDir & "\Contoso_Configure.vbs"
Call Execute_Capture()
```

This code creates a new command that executes Contoso_Configure.vbs using cscript.exe. The *Execute_Capture* subroutine is located in Software_Setup_Core.vbs.

Another way to manage configuration is to apply it with Group Policy. Using Group Policy to manage configuration achieves the same result—it applies to an application after deployment and on an ongoing basis.

> **Important** Manage the configuration of applications in a way that separates configuration from installation so that you can reapply the configuration settings if necessary later in the application's life cycle. Then call the separate configuration routine as part of the installation routine.

# Install the current version of an application

As I suggested in the introduction to this chapter, it's quite common to be tasked with installing the current version of an application, abstracted from a specific version. Think, for example, how nice it would be for users to go to an intranet site where they could install selected applications by clicking a link on a Web page. That kind of tool should deliver to users the current version of the applications. But when an application is updated and you create a software distribution folder for the new version, you must then also change the link on the intranet site to point to the new folder.

As another example, consider using a deployment tool such as Configuration Manager or Microsoft Deployment to build and maintain images of client computers. I want to ensure that the images I deploy include the latest versions of applications. But I don't want to have to reconfigure my software management framework each time I add a software distribution folder for a new version.

One solution to this problem is to use business logic to abstract the concept of "current version." Continuing our earlier example of QuickTime, consider that Apple releases new versions regularly. I simply want to ensure that I can install the most recent version. To do that, my script can scan the version subfolders in my QuickTime folder, shown in Figure 9-6, to decide which version is the most recent using a standard alphanumeric sort. It can then launch installation using the QuickTime.msi file in that folder. This is where the disciplined Software folder namespace discussed in Solution 9-2 begins to pay off!

**Figure 9-6**  A disciplined namespace allows automated identification of the most recent version.

Notice that I now have my setup script in the application folder rather than in the version folders. I can always launch this script and, no matter how many versions I have available, the script will identify the most recent and will install QuickTime from that version's software distribution folder. I've renamed this script *Company*_Setup_Current.vbs to indicate that it is a dynamic script that installs the most recent version.

Of course, I can still have *Company*_Setup.vbs script in the individual version folders if I so choose. There might be a scenario in which another application requires version 7.0 of Quick-Time and does not support newer versions. This new structure does not rule out the continued installation of specific versions—it simply enables a new and more commonly needed scenario of installing the current version.

To convert Software_Setup.vbs into a script that installs the current version, add the following new line before the *Call Install()* line:

```
sWorkingDir = FindFolder()
Call Install()
```

Doing so redefines *sWorkingDir* using the *Find_Folder()* function, which itself is located in the Software_Setup_Core.vbs script. That function looks for subfolders in the current directory in which the script is located. It looks at every folder that begins with a number and sorts them, and then returns the folder name that's last in the sort—the highest version number.

## Solution summary

In this solution, I presented the Software_Setup.vbs script, which can be modified for each application to direct the unattended installation of the application. It can even be configured to install the current version of the application, without the need to update the script each time a new version is added to the application folder. These tools allow you to create packages that automate the installation of many applications. You can turn to third-party packaging tools and software management tools such as Configuration Manager to go all the way. But even if you manage your software with a tool such as Configuration Manager, consider the benefits of abstracting the concept of "current version" so that you can add new software versions and packages while minimizing the need to change references and the configuration of your software management infrastructure. Finally, manage the configuration of your applications in such a way that configuration can be applied during installation or at any time after installation.

# 9-3: Software Management with Group Policy

## Solution overview

| | |
|---|---|
| **Type of solution** | Guidance |
| **Features and tools** | Group Policy Software Installation, Active Directory Groups |
| **Solution summary** | Deploy applications using Group Policy Software Installation. |
| **Benefits** | Reasonably robust software management with a native Windows technology |

## Introduction

Windows Group Policy Software Installation (GPSI) allows you to deploy software that is installed using Windows Installer files (.msi files). This is a perfectly reasonable way to deploy many applications, and it is in use at a number of enterprises. In this solution, I discuss the best practices for managing GPSI, including the use of application groups to control the scope of software deployment. We will use the deployment of XML Notepad, freely available from the Microsoft Downloads site, to explore the concepts and skills needed to deploy an application using Group Policy.

## Prepare an application for deployment with GPSI

Before you create a GPO to deploy an application, you must first stage the application on the network. In Solution 9-1 on page 585, I explained how to create a manageable software deployment point using a shared folder on a server and a DFS namespace to present and manage redirection to a specific application. After you have prepared the software deployment point on the network and have determined that the application can be installed using a Windows Installer file, you are ready to proceed with the configuration of the GPO.

For our example, let's assume that the XML Notepad installation files can be accessed using the DFS namespace path \\*contoso.com\software\microsoft\xml notepad*. Within that folder is the XMLNotepad.msi file.

## Configure a GPO to deploy an application

To create a GPO to deploy an application such as XML Notepad, follow these steps:

1. Open the Group Policy Management Console.
2. Expand the Forest and Domains nodes, and the node representing your domain.
3. Select the Group Policy Objects container.
4. Right-click the container and choose New.
5. In the New GPO dialog box, enter a name for the GPO.

I recommend a highly descriptive name—for example, APP_XML Notepad. Use a prefix, such as *APP_*, so that when you are viewing a sorted list of your GPOs, you can easily identify the GPOs related to application deployment.

6. Click OK.

7. Right-click the new GPO and choose Edit.

8. Navigate to Computer Configuration, Policies (visible in the new Group Policy Management Editor), Software Settings, Software Installation.

9. Right-click Software Installation and choose New, Package.

10. An Open dialog box appears. Locate the .msi file for the application.

    Be certain that you navigate to the application using the namespace that you want application deployment to use. If you have been following the best practices in the solution, you will navigate through a DFS namespace—for example, \\*contoso.com\software\microsoft\xml notepad\XML Notepad.msi*.

11. Select the .msi file and click Open.

12. In the Deploy Software dialog box, click the Advanced option button and click OK.

13. Examine the options in the *Application* Properties dialog box to determine if you need to change any of the default settings.

    Many of these settings can be configured after you have created the package, but some—such as transforms—must be specified when the package is created and cannot be changed afterward.

14. Click OK.

The resulting Group Policy setting should appear similar to the XML Notepad package shown in Figure 9-7. For more details about the creation of a GPSI package, including the settings in the package properties dialog box, consult the Group Policy help files.

**Figure 9-7**   A package to deploy XML Notepad using GPSI

You'll notice I recommend deploying software by assigning the software to the computer rather than to the user. Most software is licensed per computer, making computer-based deployment the appropriate choice. Additionally, if you deploy software by assigning it to users, the application can potentially be installed on each computer to which the users log on. It becomes difficult to manage the scope of deployment of an application when it follows the user around the enterprise. You can use the same steps to deploy an application to users, however, and there will certainly be a few scenarios for which that is appropriate.

# Scope the deployment of an application using application groups

Whether you deploy an application to computers per my recommendation or to users, you should create a way to manage the scope of deployment. For that purpose, I recommend *application groups*—security groups in Active Directory that represent the users of an application and the computers to which the application is installed. Application groups are a variation of capability management groups introduced during the discussion of role-based management in Solution Collection 1, "Role-Based Management."

Application groups are generally created as global security groups. That is because some software deployment mechanisms, including GPSI, require groups to be of global scope. The group's name should follow the naming convention established by your organization. In Solution Collection 1, I recommended that naming standards should include a prefix that indicates the purpose of the group, and I suggest *APP_* for application groups—*APP_XML Notepad*, for example. It is not a problem that our group and our GPO have the same name—in fact, I find it quite helpful.

If you are managing multiple applications, I recommend creating an organizational unit (OU) dedicated to application groups—for example, *ou=Applications,ou=Groups,dc=contoso,dc=com*. A dedicated OU can make it easy to locate the groups and, more importantly, to delegate control of who is allowed to change the membership of application groups. The idea is that when a computer and user are added to an application group, the application becomes available or is in fact automatically deployed. Therefore, group membership has a direct relationship with the management of software licenses. It is wise to assign the management of application group membership to a user or team responsible for software licensing.

When a user requests an application, you will generally add the user's computer to the application group, because it is the computer that needs to be within the scope of the software deployment mechanism. However, you can also choose to add the user to the group. In Solution 9-1, I mentioned the need to assign permissions to a software distribution folder so that the users of the application have Read And Execute permission to the folder. That way, if an application needs to be installed manually, the user can navigate to the software distribution folder and launch the appropriate setup routine. In the end, both the computer and the user generally require permission to the software destination folder.

As mentioned in Solution Collection 6, "Improving the Management and Administration of Computers," the Active Directory Users and Computers snap-in, unfortunately, is not accustomed to managing groups that include computers as members. If you open a group object, click the Members tab, and click the Add button to add a new member, you must click the Object Types button and specify that you are searching for computer objects. The button is highlighted in Figure 9-8.

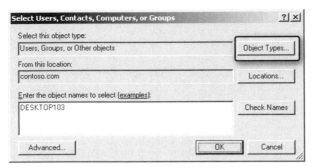

**Figure 9-8** Click the Object Types button to successfully add a computer to a group.

So, for our example of XML Notepad deployment, create a global security group in the Applications OU called APP_XML Notepad, and add the computers and users who require XML Notepad.

# Filter the software deployment GPO with the application group

You can now use the application group to manage the scope of the application's deployment. If you are using GPSI to deploy the application, simply filter the GPO so that it applies only to members of the application group. Follow these steps:

1. In the Group Policy Management console, navigate to the Group Policy Objects node and select the application deployment GPO.

   In the details pane, in the Security Filtering section, you will see that the GPO applies by default to Authenticated Users.

2. Select Authenticated Users and click Remove.

3. Click OK to confirm.

4. Click Add.

5. Enter the name of the application group—for example, **APP_XML Notepad**.

> **Important** GPOs can be scoped only with global security groups, not with domain local security groups.

6. Click OK.

The Security Filtering section of the GPO should look similar to Figure 9-9, which is shown in the next section.

# Link the GPO as high as necessary to support its scope

You have now limited the maximum scope of the applications deployment to the members of the application group—for example, *APP_XML Notepad*. And because you used the Computer Configuration version of Software Installation, the scope is further limited to computers that belong to that group. But the GPO will not yet apply in your environment because you have not linked it to a site, domain, or organizational unit.

You must link the GPO to a container that is above all the objects to which the policy should be scoped. In this case, that might mean all client computers—in which case, you could link the GPO to an OU that represents all clients, or simply link the OU to the domain itself. It is very common to see software installation GPOs link to the domain. As long as the GPO is filtered with a security group, the scope of the GPO is fully managed. One advantage of linking the GPO to the domain rather than to an OU of client computers is that you might need to deploy user-based settings for an application. If a GPO includes user-based settings and is linked to the domain, users that belong to the application group will receive the appropriate configuration.

So, continuing our example, you link the APP_XML Notepad GPO that is filtered by the APP_XML Notepad application group to the domain. To link a GPO to a domain or OU, follow these steps:

1.  In the Group Policy Management Console, right-click the domain or an OU and choose Link An Existing GPO.

2.  In the Select GPO dialog box, click the appropriate Group Policy object and click OK.

Alternately, you can drag and drop a GPO from the Group Policy Objects container to the OU or domain.

The resulting GPO Scope tab should appear similar to Figure 9-9.

Now, as systems receive their Group Policy settings, computers that are members of the application group will install the application from the software distribution folder. Because the software distribution folder resides in a DFS namespace, it will be possible to move the physical location of the application without modifying the GPO—only the target of the DFS folder for that application will need to be changed. And, if for some reason a user needs to install the application directly, the user has NTFS permissions to the software distribution folder through her membership in the application group.

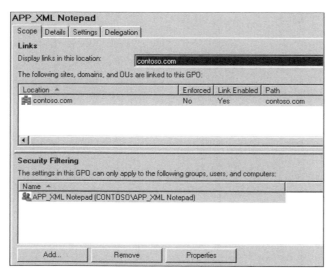

**Figure 9-9** The Links and Security Filtering properties of an application-deployment GPO

## When to use GPSI

GPSI is a valuable tool in your application deployment toolset. However, it has two major drawbacks. First, you cannot control the timing of installation, which will happen at startup if the application is deployed through Computer Configuration policy settings, or at logon if it is deployed through User Configuration settings. Second, there is no feedback mechanism to let you know whether installation was successful or not. The software deployment framework we'll create later in this Solution Collection provides an alternative that addresses those two weaknesses of GPSI. As long as you account for GPSI's limitations, you can identify the scenarios in which you can leverage GPSI to deploy applications in your enterprise.

## GPSI and Microsoft Office 2007

The three versions of Microsoft Office prior to Microsoft Office 2007 could be deployed effectively through GPSI, but Microsoft Office 2007 can't. Now, you might hear that you can use Group Policy to deploy Office 2007, and Microsoft even has documents discussing the methodology (*http://technet2.microsoft.com/Office/en-us/library/efd0ee45-9605-42d3-9798-3b698fff3e081033.mspx*). However, I can tell you from lots of testing that deploying Microsoft Office 2007 with GPSI is usually not a practical option even if it is a technical option.

Because GPSI uses .msi files with transforms (.mst files), whereas Microsoft architected Office Setup to use the Setup command with setup customization files (.msp) files to drive installation, you will find that GPSI just doesn't support the kind of functionality and customization that you need. You are forced to do all customization in the config.xml file, and even then only a few very rudimentary customizations are supported: the product key, language, and applications to install. No company name, no configuration, nothing else. And trying to configure the applications to install, using the *OptionState* element of config.xml, is painful to say the least.

The aforementioned TechNet article provides guidance if you are so inclined to self-torture. You can test GPSI installation of Microsoft Office 2007, but I expect you will find, like administrators in most organizations, it's just not fully featured enough to be useful. Instead, I suggest you explore the approach I lay out in Solution 9-5.

## Take it to the next level

Use solutions presented in Solution Collection 8, "Reimagining the Administration of Groups and Membership," to manage the application groups used to scope software deployment GPOs. Solutions such as shadow groups and subscription groups can be a powerful way to manage the users or computers to which an application is deployed.

## Solution summary

In this solution, I highlighted the best practices for managing software deployment with GPSI. Packages are created that refer to software distribution folders through the DFS namespace. They are assigned to computers to enforce licensing restrictions and to prevent applications from following users from computer to computer. GPOs are linked to high-level containers in the Active Directory structure and filtered using an application group—created as a global security group—that contains as members the computers to which the software should be deployed and the users of the application. For more details regarding GPSI, refer to the Group Policy help files and to *Windows Group Policy Resource Kit: Windows Server 2008 and Windows Vista* by Derek Melber (Microsoft Press, 2008).

# 9-4: Deploy Files and Configuration Using Group Policy Preferences

## Solution overview

| | |
|---|---|
| **Type of solution** | Guidance |
| **Features and tools** | The new Group Policy Files and Registry preferences extensions |
| **Solution summary** | When applications, tools, scripts, files, or configurations need to be copied to computers and do not require installation, you can use the new features of Group Policy to deploy the changes. |
| **Benefits** | Easier distribution of administrative tools, scripts, and configuration |

## Introduction

Throughout this resource kit, I have introduced a number of tools that can be valuable additions to your administrative toolset. In addition to the scripts and HTAs written for this resource kit, I've highlighted extremely useful utilities from Microsoft and other vendors.

Many of these tools you do not need to install per se, rather you need only copy them to a system. For example, you can copy PSExec to the system path—C:\Windows\System32, for example—of administrators' computers, and they can then immediately use it, although the first time it is launched the user will be prompted to agree to the End User License Agreement (EULA).

In this solution, I discuss options for deploying such file-based applications—how to copy files using Group Policy. To do so, I'll introduce you to a brand-new feature of Windows Server 2008 Group Policy: preferences. These Group Policy settings allow you to manage many useful administrative tasks, including copying files.

Group Policy preferences also allow you to manage registry-based configuration so easily that you'll never want to use an administrative template again. I'll show you how you can push registry changes to clients, and in the course of doing so, you'll learn how to automate the acceptance of the End User License Agreement for PSExec. I'll also demonstrate how you can delete information from the registry. As an example, we will, using Group Policy preferences, remove an application (QuickTime Player) from the Run key of the registry to prevent it from starting at each logon.

## Deploy files with Group Policy Files preferences

A significant new feature in Windows Server 2008 is Group Policy preferences. If you have followed Microsoft's progress in the field of Group Policy, you might know that several years ago it purchased a company called Desktop Standard. One of that company's products, Policy-Maker, has been incorporated into Windows Server 2008 as Group Policy preferences. The feature adds many new client-side extensions that greatly enhance your ability to manage your enterprise using Group Policy. One of those extensions is the Files preferences extension, which allows you to copy, modify, and delete files on a system.

To learn about Files preferences, let's deploy PSExec. PSExec does not need to be installed—you simply need to copy it to a folder in the system path (%PATH%), such as C:\Windows\System32. To deploy PSExec with Files preferences, follow these steps:

1.  Create a new Group Policy object. Give the GPO a descriptive name—for example, *APP_PSExec*.

    Edit the GPO using the new version of the Group Policy Management Editor (GPME). You will recognize the new version of the tool because, underneath Computer Configuration and User Configuration, you'll will see Policies and Preferences folders.

    At the time of my writing this, only the Windows Server 2008 GPME could be used. I anticipate that the new version of the GPME will be made available to, or be a part of, Windows Vista SP1.

2.  Expand Computer Configuration, Preferences, Windows Settings, and then select Files.

    Files preferences exist in both Computer Configuration and User Configuration. If you want files to follow a user and to be copied to each system that the user logs on to, use the Files preferences under User Configuration. To scope file copies to specific computers, use the Files preferences under Computer Configuration.

3. Right-click Files, and choose New and then File.

   The New File Properties dialog box appears.

4. In the Action drop-down list, select either Create or Replace.

   The Create action copies files from the source location to the destination only if the files do not already exist at the destination. The Replace action also copies files from the source to the destination, but it overwrites existing files. I recommend using the Replace action for deploying application files such as PSExec because it ensures that the destination location always contains the most recent version of the file.

5. In the Source File(s) box, enter or browse to the path of the source file, PSExec.exe.

   Be sure to enter a network path, preferably one that references a DFS namespace, so that the policy does not have a hard-wired reference to the physical location of the files.

6. In the Destination File box, enter the full path to the destination file.

7. Optionally, you can modify the attributes of the destination file.

   The resulting New File Properties dialog box should appear similar to Figure 9-10.

8. Click OK.

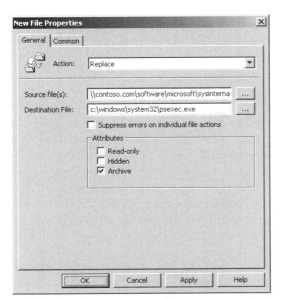

**Figure 9-10**   Using Files preferences to copy PSExec

The rest of the process is identical to the process I outlined in Solution 9-3 on page 603. Create an application group to scope the deployment of PSExec—*APP_PSExec*, for example— and then filter the GPO so that it applies only to that group and link the GPO to a high-level container such as the domain. Of course, if you are deploying multiple administrative tools along with PSExec, you can create a single GPO that copies all files required by administrators.

Amazing, huh? It's fantastic that you can manage the distribution of files and therefore file-based applications using Group Policy. What's the downside?

Well, at the time of my writing this, Microsoft has not made it clear how you will give Windows XP, Windows Server 2003, and Windows Vista clients the ability to implement Group Policy preferences. I expect that you'll be required to install the client-side extensions for Group Policy preferences on all systems. Perhaps Microsoft will make the client-side extensions available as a Windows Update or integrate the extensions into Windows Vista SP1 and Windows XP SP3. By the time you read this book, I am confident that there will be plenty of documentation on the Microsoft Web site to explain how to implement Group Policy preferences in an enterprise.

# Push registry changes using Registry preferences

In the past, if you wanted to deploy a custom registry change using Group Policy, you had to create a custom administrative template, which is not an intuitive exercise. Group Policy preferences make it significantly easier to add, remove, and update registry keys and values.

## Add a registry value

To learn how to add information to the registry, let's address the fact that the first time you run PSExec, you are prompted to agree to the license agreement. This can be problematic if you are using PSExec as part of an automated process—the EULA prompt will interrupt the process.

When you do agree to the EULA, a registry entry is made so that you are not prompted in the future. We'll use Registry preferences to deploy that registry change so that PSExec can be used immediately. Of course, by doing so, you are effectively agreeing to the license agreement as well.

To deploy a registry change with Group Policy preferences, follow these steps:

1. Create a new Group Policy object or edit an existing one using the new version of the GPME. For our example, edit the existing GPO *APP_PSExec*.

   You will recognize the new version of the tool because, underneath Computer Configuration and User Configuration, you'll see Policies and Preferences folders.

   At the time of my writing this, only the Windows Server 2008 GPME can be used. I anticipate that the new version of the GPME will be made available to, or be a part of, Windows Vista SP1.

2. Expand User Configuration, the Preferences folder, and the Windows Settings folder, and you will see the Registry node.

The Registry node under Computer Configuration manages registry entries deployed to all registry hives except for HKEY_CURRENT_USER. The reason should be obvious—when settings are applied at startup, no user is logged on interactively.

For our example—agreeing to the PSExec EULA—the change needs to be made to HKEY_CURRENT_USER, so it needs to be made in the Registry preferences under User Configuration.

3. Right-click Registry and choose New, Registry Item.

4. In the New Registry Properties dialog box, select Replace from the Action drop-down list.

   Replace will delete an existing registry value and re-create it.

5. In the Hive list, choose HKEY_CURRENT_USER.

6. In the Key Path text box, enter **Software\Sysinternals\PsExec**, and in the Value Name box, enter **EulaAccepted**.

   Better yet, click the browse button next to the Key Path text box and browse visually to select the Registry item. As you browse, you will be seeing the registry on your system, which might not have the key or value that you are trying to manage. If that's the case, simply enter the key path and value name manually.

7. The Value Type in this example should be REG_DWORD.

8. The Value Data is 1.

   The result should appear similar to Figure 9-11.

**Figure 9-11** Adding a registry value with Registry preferences

9. Click OK.

## Delete a registry value and optimize logon time

You learned in an earlier solution that I don't like the fact that QuickTime Player adds itself to the Run key of the registry, causing it to start automatically at each logon. To keep logon time optimized, I remove QuickTime Player from the Run key each time that I install the application. With Registry preferences, I can ensure that QuickTime stays out of the Run key using Group Policy and thereby improve logon time for users.

To delete a registry value using Group Policy preferences, follow these steps:

1. Create a new Group Policy object, or edit an existing one using the new version of the GPME. For example, create a GPO called *USR_StartupItems* to manage what does and does not launch at startup.

2. Expand the Preferences folder and the Windows Settings folder, and you will see the Registry node.

   For our example—removing QuickTime from the Run key—use the Computer Configuration Registry preferences so that the setting is bundled in the same part of the GPO as the application installation. However, you can also use the User Configuration Registry preferences.

3. Right-click Registry and choose New, Registry Item.

4. In the New Registry Properties dialog box, select Delete from the Action drop-down list.

5. In the Hive list, choose HKEY_LOCAL_MACHINE.

6. In the Key Path text box, enter **Software\Microsoft\Windows\CurrentVersion\Run**, and in the Value Name box, enter **QuickTime Task**.

   The result should appear similar to Figure 9-12.

7. Click OK.

You can repeat these steps to add more registry items that delete specific items from the *Run* key of the registry. I recommend that you download AutoRuns from *http://technet.microsoft.com/sysinternals* to evaluate the items that are being loaded into the *Run* key of clients in your organization, and that you use a GPO to remove the items that are unnecessary or even counterproductive.

**Figure 9-12**  Deleting a registry value with Registry preferences

## Solution summary

In this solution, we applied the new Files and Registry preferences in Group Policy to manage the deployment and configuration of applications. These and other preferences extensions enable a lot of management that was, until now, complex or impossible to control. Be sure to look at the Microsoft Web site to learn about how to deploy client-side extensions to your pre–Windows Server 2008 systems.

# 9-5: A Build-It-Yourself Software Management Infrastructure

## Solution overview

| | |
|---|---|
| **Type of solution** | A framework consisting of scripts and Windows technologies |
| **Features and tools** | Software_Deploy.vbs, startup scripts, logon scripts, Active Directory groups, delegation, DFS Namespaces |
| **Solution summary** | Build a software management framework without commercial applications that leverages native Windows technologies to provide deployment, reporting, and optional user control of the timing of application installation. Deploy Microsoft Office 2007 without third-party software management tools. |
| **Benefits** | Improved software management with no investment in commercial applications |

# Introduction

Group Policy Software Installation (GPSI), discussed in Solution 9-3, has several disadvantages. First, it supports the automated deployment of Windows Installer files only. Other applications can be published using .zap files. (Learn more at *http://technet.microsoft.com/en-us/library/Bb742421.aspx.*) However, publishing applications only makes them visible to be installed—it does not actually install the application. Second, it does not allow you or a user to control the timing of installation—applications will be installed immediately on startup if assigned to the computer, or on logon if assigned to the user. Third, GPSI does not report its success, so you have no way to know what systems have successfully installed the application and what systems need to be examined because of failures in installation.

Systems Management Server (SMS), Systems Center Configuration Manager (Configuration Manager), and tools by other vendors provide this functionality as well as other features that facilitate the management of assets and applications. But of course, those tools aren't free. In this solution, I introduce a framework that supports the more nuanced deployment of applications. It uses a combination of Group Policy startup script policies, a sophisticated application installation script, centralized logging, and a creative approach to managing change and configuration using Active Directory groups.

The application that I use as an example in the solution is Microsoft Office 2007. So the solution should also serve to facilitate the deployment of Microsoft Office 2007 in environments without SMS or Configuration Manager. But the framework will lend itself to the management of most applications and configuration.

# Identify the challenges of deploying applications such as Microsoft Office 2007

Microsoft Office 2007 deployment using GPSI is highly problematic. Because of the size of the application, the weaknesses of GPSI related to the timing and reporting of application installation become all the more salient. In addition, as I mentioned in Solution 9-3, Microsoft Office 2007 does not support Windows Installer transform files (.mst files), so customization of the installation must be made using the Config.xml file, which supports a very limited number of customizations. I recommend that GPSI deployment of Microsoft Office 2007 be attempted only in organizations that are deploying the default configuration of the application suite to a very limited number of clients.

For the rest of us, we need to find a solution that allows us to fully customize the installation of Office, to deploy the application effectively, to provide control over the timing of installation so that it does not interfere with user productivity, and to receive feedback from systems as to the success or failure of installation. There is an additional challenge with Office installation: The setup.exe command can be run only by a user who is a member of the computer's local Administrators group. This requirement is particularly problematic for enterprises that have implemented a secure desktop environment in which users log on with nonprivileged accounts. The framework developed in this solution must address all of these needs.

> **Important**   Automated installation is available only for corporate versions of Microsoft Office 2007. It is not available for retail versions of the product.

# Prepare a software distribution folder for Microsoft Office 2007

Because I am using Microsoft Office 2007 as the sample application for this solution, let me briefly outline the steps required to prepare Office for deployment. First, you must create and populate a software distribution folder. Use the following steps:

1. Create a software distribution folder for Office using the guidance provided in Solution 9-1.

2. Copy the contents of the product's media—for example, the Microsoft Office 2007 Enterprise DVD—to the software distribution folder. Keep the following considerations in mind:

   ❑ Office 2007 no longer uses the administrative installation (the */admin* switch) to create an uncompressed network distribution. Now you simply copy the product DVD to the network folder.

   ❑ If you are deploying multiple products in the Microsoft Office 2007 System—such as Microsoft Office Visio, Microsoft Office SharePoint Designer, or Microsoft Office Project—copy the contents of the media into the same folder. Microsoft Office products now share a significant amount of common code, so a number of files are identical across Office products. Therefore, if you are prompted to overwrite existing files, click No so that the file copy is faster.

   ❑ If you are deploying language packs, copy them into the same folder.

3. Obtain all security and product updates from the Microsoft Downloads site.

   Office updates are downloaded as a package that include an installer and the patch file itself.

4. Extract the patch file from the package using this command:

   *packagename* /extract:*path*

   In this command, *path* is the folder path to which the package should be extracted. If the path includes a space, surround the path with quotes.

5. Copy the patch files to the Updates folder in the software distribution folder.

   One of the exciting new features about Office installation is that updates included in this folder are applied automatically during Office setup, so the applications are fully updated before they are launched for the first time.

6. Download any add-ons that you want to install along with the Office applications.

   I recommend, for example, that you download the add-on that enables Office applications to save documents in the PDF and XPS formats.

7.  Save add-ons in a custom folder within the software distribution folder—for example, *Company*_Add-ons.

# Create a setup customization file

After you have created the network installation point for Microsoft Office 2007, you can create the file that specifies the unique configuration of the Office installation for your enterprise. This file is called a *setup customization file*. It is created using the Office Customization Tool (OCT), which is built into the setup.exe command. The setup customization file is a Windows Installer patch file (.msp), not a Windows Installer transform (.mst) as in previous versions of Office. To launch the OCT and create a setup customization file, follow these steps:

1.  From the software distribution folder, run **setup.exe /admin**.

    The OCT appears.

2.  Select the Office product that you want to customize, and then click OK.

    The OCT gives you granular control over the customization of Office. In this procedure, I focus only on the steps useful for automating setup.

3.  On the Install Location And Organization Name page, enter your company name into the Organization Name text box.

4.  Click the link to the Licensing And User Interface page.

5.  Enter your volume license key in the Product Key text box.

6.  Select the I Accept The Terms In The License Agreement check box.

7.  In the Display Level drop-down list, choose None.

8.  Click the link to the Add Installations And Run Programs page.

9.  If you want to install an add-on, such as the Save As PDF Or XPS feature, click the Add button and enter the command required to install the add-on in unattended mode. The Save As PDF Or XPS add-on uses the */quiet* switch.

10. Click the link to the Set Feature Installation States page.

11. Configure the installation state for each application.

12. Click the Save command in the File menu.

13. Browse to your custom subfolder in the Microsoft Office 2007 software distribution folder—for example, *Company*_Setup—and save the file.

You can create as many setup customization files as you require for your environment. You can, for example, have separate customization files for each department, with unique settings and application installation states. For more information about the OCT, see *http:// technet2.microsoft.com/Office/en-us/library/8faae8a0-a12c-4f7b-839c-24a66a531bb51033.mspx*.

# Launch an unattended installation of Office 2007

After you have created the network installation point and the setup customization file, you can log on to a system as a local administrator and launch the installation of Office 2007 with the following command:

```
setup.exe /adminfile path\SetupCustomizationFile.msp
```

If you have copied more than one Office System product into the software distribution folder—for example, if you have added Microsoft Office Project or SharePoint Designer—you must add the */config ProductFolder\config.xml* switch, where *ProductFolder* is the folder for the specific Office product. For example, to install Office 2007 Enterprise Edition from a distribution folder that includes other Office products, the command line is as follows:

```
setup.exe /adminfile path\SetupCustomizationFile.msp
    /config path\Enterprise.WW\config.xml
```

Notice Microsoft Office 2007 Enterprise is considered the *product*, although it consists of multiple applications such as Word, Excel, and PowerPoint. Other Office applications such as SharePoint Designer and Project are individual products.

For more information about the customization of Microsoft Office 2007, and about Office deployment, see *http://technet2.microsoft.com/Office/en-us/library/78ad4dd8-f15e-41a9-8bf1-92cfeaac47801033.mspx.*

# Identify the requirements for a build-it-yourself software management framework

We are now ready to create a framework to support the deployment of Microsoft Office 2007 and other applications. Before building any framework, I recommend that you identify requirements that you can design toward. Following are the requirements this framework must meet:

- Support for the deployment of Microsoft Office 2007 and other applications without the need for commercial software management tools

- Reporting to a central database so that the progress of deployment can be monitored and problems can be identified

- The ability to control the scope of deployment for an application so that it can be targeted to a specific set of computers

- Application installation using administrative credentials without requiring users to be local administrators on their systems

- Support for user control over the timing of installation so that users can delay an application's deployment for a certain period of time

# Customize Software_Deploy.vbs to enable application deployment

The Software_Deploy.vbs script on the companion media provides the engine to meet the first two requirements of the software management framework—remaining requirements will be addressed later in this solution. Software_Deploy.vbs will do the following:

- Run a command, such as the unattended setup of an application.
- Interpret the success or failure of the command.
- Log the results of the command to a central database.

Software_Deploy.vbs is designed to be executed as a startup script, which runs under the credentials of the System account, which is equivalent to Administrator—it should not run into any obstacles related to permissions or rights when running a command.

To use Software_Deploy.vbs, you must do the following:

- Customize the *Configuration Block*. Read all the comments in the *Configuration Block*, and make sure that they match your environment.
- Put the script in a location accessible to all the computers that will install the application. I recommend placing it in your *Company_*Setup folder in the software distribution folder for the application.
- Make sure that the computers (as well as users) have NTFS Read And Execute permission to the software distribution folder.
- Create a software management database, and place it in a centrally accessible location, where all users and computers have NTFS Write permission.
- Create a GPO with a startup script setting that points to the script.
- Scope the GPO so that it applies to the computers.

## Execute a command

The best way to learn about these steps is to explore the script's functionality. I recommend that you open the script in Notepad or in a script editor and explore each section of the script as I explain it.

Let's start with the fundamental requirement for the framework: support for application deployment. The script must be able to execute a command. It does so with the *Execute_Capture* function. *Execute_Capture* is a wrapper around the *Exec* method of the *Shell* object—a method that does, in fact, run a command. The key line of this subroutine is shown here:

```
Set oExec = WSHShell.Exec(sCommand)
```

The command specified by the variable *sCommand* is passed to the *Exec* method for execution. The command, *sCommand*, is passed to the *Execute_Capture* function as its first argument. Earlier in the script, you'll find the line that calls the function:

```
aResults = Execute_Capture(sCommand, iTimeout, True)
```

The definition of *sCommand* is in the *Configuration Block*:

```
sCommand = """\\contoso.com\software\microsoft\office 2007\setup.exe"" " & _
    "/adminfile ""\\contoso.com\software\microsoft\office 2007\" & _
    "Contoso_Setup\Contoso_Standard_Configuration.msp"""
```

This line will, of course, need to be customized for your environment. Notice that because there are spaces in the DFS namespace path, quotation marks are required. Also, because we are building a string in VBScript, where quotation marks represent the beginning or end of a string, I need to use *two quotation marks* wherever there would normally be one quotation mark in the string. You can make your life a lot easier by avoiding spaces in your paths and filenames, though you'll see in my example *sCommand* above, I don't always follow my own advice (partly so that I'd have an example of using two quotation marks).

The command is executed by the *Exec* method, which returns an error if there is a problem finding or accessing the command—for example, if there is an error in the path or filename. If the command is launched successfully, *Execute_Capture* waits for it to complete. There is, however, a timeout specified by the *iTimeout* argument passed to *Execute_Capture*. The timeout is also configured in the *Configuration Block*. If the command does not complete within the specified timeout, the *Exec* method is canceled. This is to ensure that the script does not hang indefinitely. I recommend you set the timeout (which is specified in seconds) for quite a long period (20 to 30 minutes) when deploying a large application such as Microsoft Office 2007. More importantly, you should test the script to determine the most appropriate configuration.

The *Execute_Capture* function returns an array of results, the first of which is the exit code from the command. As I mentioned earlier in this Solution Collection, processes return an exit code when they are terminated, and the code indicates success or failure of the command. Other elements in the *Execute_Capture* array include the *StdOut* and *StdErr* streams, which contain any output of the command. Most application setup routines will return output.

## Interpret the results of the command

When the code returns from the *Execute_Capture* function, it examines the array of results returned by the function to identify the exit code and streams. It then looks at the exit code. An exit code of zero indicates success, anything else denotes failure. The script creates a string, *sStatus*, that is set to either *SUCCESS* or *ERROR*, accordingly. It also creates a string, *sNotes*, that in the case of failure contains the exit code and *StdErr* stream for a description of the error.

## Log the results to a central database

These strings are then logged to a central database. The definition of the database is in the *Configuration Block*:

```
sFile = "\\contoso.com\software\microsoft\Office 2007\" & _
    "Contoso_Setup\SystemConfigurationDB.mdb"
sTable = "Log" ' Name of Access table or Excel sheet within the file
sComputerNameField = "ComputerName"
sActionField = "Action"
sStatusField = "Status"
sDateField = "Date"
sNotesField = "Notes"
```

The variable *sFile* points to the database, which must be accessible with Write permission to the computers within the scope of the deployment. By default, the database is a simple Access database file (.mdb format), although an Excel spreadsheet is also supported. Both Office 2003 and Office 2007 file types are available, but if the Office 2007 installation fails, computers won't have the correct Office 2007 database drivers, and therefore will not be able to log an error successfully. All Windows systems have Excel and Access 2003–compatible database drivers, so I highly recommend that for Microsoft Office 2007 deployment you stick with down-level Office 2003 file formats for the database.

The variable *sTable* refers to the Access table name (within the database) or Excel worksheet name (on the sheet's tab). The log-writing routine expects to log five fields: the computer name, the action that was attempted, its success or failure, the date and time, and any notes. There must be five fields (or columns) in the table (or sheet) to accept these data points. The remaining variables in the *Configuration Block* shown earlier define the names of the fields in the database.

There is a precreated database, SystemConfigurationDB.mdb, in the Scripts folder of the companion media. It will work with the *Configuration Block* just shown, as long as you change *sFile* appropriately.

After interpreting the success or failure of the command and building strings to be logged, the code calls the *Log_WriteCommandResults* subroutine to write to the log. There are several other routines from my library, each beginning with *Log_* or *ADO_*, that support the connection to the log.

## Enable debug mode

In the *Configuration Block*, the variable *bDebugMode* can be set to *TRUE* to enable debug mode. In debug mode, the script will dump a log of results to a text file, C:\Software_deploy_log.txt, on the computer on which the installation was attempted. This is particularly helpful to debug problems when the computer is having problems writing to the central log.

## Implement Software_Deploy.vbs as a startup script

Before implementing the startup script, review the following list of preparatory tasks:

- Customize the *Configuration Block*.

- Put the script in a location accessible to all the computers that will install the application. I recommend placing it in your *Company*_Setup folder in the software distribution folder for the application.

- Make sure that the computers (as well as users) have NTFS Read And Execute permission to the software distribution folder.

- Create a software management database, and place it in a centrally accessible location, where all users and computers have NTFS Write permission. You can use the sample, SystemConfigurationDB.mdb, in the companion media's Scripts folder.

The script will be deployed as a startup script. Startup scripts are executed by computers during the startup sequence. They run under System credentials, locally, which ensures that applications such as Microsoft Office 2007 that require administrative credentials will have the permissions they require to install.

The disadvantage of startup scripts is that they must be completely noninteractive and unattended—they cannot accept input or provide output to the screen. Our script is written to those requirements. Because running the script as a startup script adds one more layer of complexity, you should test the script while logged on to a client computer as a domain user who is a local administrator so that you can identify problems with the script, configuration, or permissions before you run it as a startup script. Remember you can set *bDebugMode* to *TRUE* to get more information about problems that the script is encountering.

Now you can create a GPO that executes Software_Deploy.vbs as a startup script. Follow these steps:

1. In the Group Policy Management Console, expand the Forest, Domains, and then the node for your domain.

2. Select the Group Policy Objects container.

3. Right-click Group Policy Objects and choose New.

4. Enter a name for the GPO.

    I suggest a name such as *CCM_Office 2007 Deploy*. This name represents the fact that the GPO implements change and configuration management (CCM) and is implementing a single change—the deployment of Office 2007. This GPO will not be used to manage ongoing maintenance of the application, only the deployment of it. Additionally, the name will then match the deployment group that I will discuss shortly.

5. Click OK.

6. Right-click the GPO and choose Edit.

   The Group Policy Management Editor (GPME) appears. In earlier versions of the administrative tools, the Group Policy Object Editor appears.

7. Expand Computer Configuration, Policies (visible only in new versions of the GPME), and Windows Settings, and then select Scripts (Startup/Shutdown).

8. In the details pane, right-click Startup and choose Properties.

9. Click the Add button.

10. In the Script Name text box, enter **cscript.exe**.

11. In the Script Parameters text box, enter the path to the script using a network namespace, preferably a DFS namespace—for example, \\contoso.com\software\microsoft\office 2007\contoso_setup\software_deploy.vbs. If there are spaces in the path, surround it with quotes.

12. Click OK two times to close the two dialog boxes.

> **Important**    You must also configure the script timeout settings for Group Policy startup scripts.

Group Policy startup scripts are terminated if they do not complete within a specified period of time so that a script does not hang indefinitely. By default, the timeout is 10 minutes. The installation of Microsoft Office could very well take longer than that, so I recommend you configure the startup script timeout setting according to your experience in the lab. Because you are making this change in the same GPO that deploys Microsoft Office, the setting will no longer apply after systems have deployed Office.

13. Navigate to Computer Configuration, Policies (visible only in newer versions of the GPME), Administrative Templates, System, Scripts.

14. Right-click Maximum Wait Time For Group Policy Scripts and choose Properties.

15. Select Enabled and then configure the wait time in seconds.

    Fifteen to twenty minutes (900 to 1200 seconds) should be sufficient. I highly recommend you configure the wait time to be 30 to 60 seconds longer than the timeout specified by *iTimeout* in the script's *Configuration Block*.

16. Click OK.

The startup script will not yet run on any computers. You must first scope the GPO to apply to appropriate computers. There is still a little more customization of Software_Deploy.vbs to perform. That takes us to our next discussion.

# Manage change using group membership

The next requirement of our software management framework that we tackle is this one:

- The ability to control the scope of deployment for an application so that it can be targeted to a specific set of computers

## Scope a Group Policy object to apply to a security group

To meet this requirement, scope the application deployment GPO with a security group. Follow these steps:

1. In the Active Directory Users and Computers snap-in, create a global security group.

   ❑ Remember that GPOs can be filtered only with global groups.

   ❑ Use a descriptive name that meets your organization's naming standards.

   ❑ I recommend naming the group CCM_*Application* Deploy—for example, CCM_Office 2007 Deploy. This name indicates that the purpose of the group is to manage a change—specifically, the deployment of a single application.

2. In the Group Policy Management Console, in the console tree, select your GPO in the Group Policy Objects container.

3. In the Security Filtering section in the details pane, select Authenticated Users and click Remove. Click OK to confirm this action.

4. Click Add.

5. Enter the name for your deployment group—for example, CCM_Office 2007 Deploy.

6. Click OK.

The result should look similar to Figure 9-13.

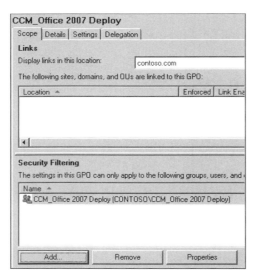

**Figure 9-13** Filtering a GPO to apply to a security group

## Implement fine-grained control over change

It is important that our script attempt to install the application only one time. If there are errors, we need to troubleshoot them. If the installation is a success, there's no need to repeat the command at each startup.

To achieve this, the Software_Deploy.vbs script is coded so that after running the first time, the script removes the computer from the CCM_Office 2007 Deploy group. This functionality prevents the script from being run more than one time. It also takes the computer out from under the scope of the GPO so that any other deployment-related configurations, such as the Maximum Wait Time For Group Policy Scripts, are also removed.

If the installation is a success, the script adds the computer to a different security group, APP_Office 2007 by default. By doing so, the script is communicating to the software management framework that the computer now has Office 2007 installed. Any further ongoing management of change related to that application is scoped using the APP_Office 2007 group. For example, you might use the Microsoft Office Group Policy administrative templates, available from the Microsoft Downloads site, to configure the settings that apply to existing installations of Office. The GPO with those settings are scoped using the APP_Office 2007 group.

If the installation is a failure, the script adds the computer to a different security group, ALERT_Office 2007 by default. This group is meant as a way to collect information about systems that have failed installation. It is in addition to the log, which will also have entries for each system that failed installation.

So a computer starts in the *staging group*, CCM_Office 2007 Deploy, that represents computers to which Office 2007 should be deployed. The GPO that executes Software_Deploy.vbs is scoped using this group. The script runs at each computer's next startup. When the script completes, it moves computers out of the staging group into either the *success group*, APP_Office 2007, or the *failure group*, ALERT_Office 2007.

Before implementing this framework, you must ensure that all three groups exist and that all computers have permissions to change the memberships of these groups. To do this, a group representing the computers must be given permission to Add/Remove Self As Member. That enables a computer (or user) to add or remove itself from a group, but not to add or remove other members. You can change the delegation on the individual groups, or you can put all the groups into an OU with this delegation.

In the Active Directory Users and Computers console, select View and then Advanced Features. Then right-click the group or OU and choose Properties. On the Security tab, click Advanced. Click Add and select a group that includes all the computers to which the application will be deployed—you can even use Authenticated Users. Click OK. In the Permission Settings dialog box, click the Object tab and choose Descendant Group objects from the drop-down list. (The option is labeled Groups in earlier versions of the Active Directory Users and Computers snap-in.) Select the Allow box for the Add/Remove Self As Member permission. Solution 8-3 on page 549 has more details about this permission.

> **Important**   Be sure to create the groups specified by the *sStagingGroup*, *sSuccessGroup*, and *sErrorGroup* variables in the *Configuration Block* of Software_Deploy.vbs. The computers need the permission to Add/Remove Self As Member. See Solution 8-3 for details about this permission.

## Link the GPO

Now you must link the GPO to an OU that is a parent to the computers requiring the application or to the domain itself. Follow these steps:

1. In the Group Policy Management console, right-click the domain or an OU and choose Link An Existing GPO.

2. In the Select GPO dialog box, select the appropriate Group Policy object and click OK.

   Alternately, you can drag and drop a GPO from the Group Policy Objects container to the OU or domain.

Now that the group, GPO, security group filter, and GPO link are in place, you can deploy the application simply by adding computers to the security group. When the computers restart, the application will be deployed.

# Deploy an application using a scheduled task

As an alternative to a Group Policy startup script as the mechanism for deploying an application using Software_Deploy.vbs, you can push a script to systems by creating a scheduled task. The schtasks.exe command allows you to do just that:

```
schtasks.exe /create /s desktop101 /tn "Deploy Office"
    /tr "cscript.exe path\Software_Deploy.vbs" /ru SYSTEM
    /sc ONCE /ST 14:14 [/v1 ]
```

This command creates a task on DESKTOP101 called "Deploy Office." (The task name specified by */tn* can be anything.) The task executes *cscript* with the path to the script. If the path to the script includes a space, you must enclose the path in quotes, but of course the entire */tr* argument is itself in quotes. Therefore, if there is a space in the path, you must enclose the path between a pair of backslash and quotation marks, as in the following example:

```
/tr "cscript.exe \"\\contoso.com\software\microsoft\office 2007\
    contoso_setup\software_deploy.vbs\""
```

The task runs as the System account at the time specified in 24-hour time by */ST*—for example, 2:14 p.m. Scheduled tasks work quite differently on Windows Vista than on previous versions of Windows. If you are running schtasks.exe on a Windows Vista machine to push the script to a Windows XP machine, you need to add the */V1* switch. You *cannot* run schtasks.exe on a Windows XP (or Windows 2003) system to create a task on a remote Windows Vista machine. Use PSEXEC, described in the next section, to push the schtasks.exe command:

```
psexec \\desktop101 schtasks.exe /create. . .
```

The result is that, at the scheduled time, the System account runs the script, just as it would if you used Group Policy startup scripts to launch the script. With just a little work, you could enumerate the members of the CCM_Office 2007 Deploy group and execute schtasks.exe on those systems.

# Give users control over the timing of installation

The final requirement of the software management framework is this one:

- Support for user control over the timing of installation so that users can delay an application's deployment for a certain period of time

I'd like to suggest two approaches, each detailed in the following sections.

### Enable users to add their computer to the staging group

Computers will install the application when they are added to the staging group—for example, CCM_Office 2007 Deploy—with which the deployment GPO is scoped. To give users the ability to control the timing of deployment, you can give users permission to add their computers to the staging group. Complete these tasks:

- Create a global security group that represents the users that you want to allow to control the installation of Office—for example, CCM_Office 2007 User Staging.

- Give that group permission to change the membership of the application staging group, CCM_Office 2007 Deploy. In other words, open the advanced security settings of the CCM_Office 2007 Deploy group and add this permission: CCM_Office 2007 User Staging::Allow::Write Members.

Add users to the user staging group, CCM_Office 2007 User Staging. Those users can now add their computer to the application staging group, CCM_Office 2007 Deploy. The obvious question is, "How?" What can you do to make it easy for the user to add his or her computer to the group without requiring the Active Directory Users and Computers snap-in?

Use a logon script. In the Scripts folder of the companion media, you'll find the script Software_User_Staging.vbs. This script prompts a user to install Microsoft Office 2007 and, if the user approves, it adds the user's computer to the CCM_Office 2007 Deploy group and restarts the machine. At that point, the application deployment GPO scoped to the CCM_Office 2007 Deploy group begins the installation of Office.

To use the script, create a GPO that configures Software_User_Staging.vbs as a logon script. Scope the GPO so that it applies to the user staging group (CCM_Office 2007 User Staging). You can use the steps described earlier for configuring and scoping script policies—just use the Logon Script policy setting under User Configuration rather than the startup script policy under Computer Configuration.

Add users to the user staging group (CCM_Office 2007 User Staging) when you want to deploy Office to them. Thereafter, at each logon, the logon script will prompt the user to install Office. When the user approves installation, the script removes the user from the user staging group so that the user will no longer be prompted.

The software deployment workflow is complete, and is entirely managed through group memberships. When a user is to receive an application, the user is added to the user staging group (CCM_Office 2007 User Staging). When the user accepts installation, the user's computer is added to the application staging group (CCM_Office 2007 Deploy). When the installation has completed, the computer is moved to either the success group (APP_Office 2007) for ongoing management or to the error group (ALERT_Office 2007) for troubleshooting.

## Deploy an application using a scheduled task

Alternately, to give the user control over the timing of the installation, you can in some way provision the application installation script as a scheduled task. The task that runs the installation must run as an administrator or as the System account. To schedule a task that runs with those credentials, you must run the schtasks.exe command with administrative credentials. So, for example, you can institute a process in which users, when ready to receive Office 2007, contact the help desk. Help desk personnel, using credentials that belong to the Administrators group on the user's system, can use schtasks.exe to schedule the command at the time requested by the user.

## Solution summary

This solution provides a framework with which to manage change and configuration using built-in Windows technologies, without requiring the use of additional software management tools. The concepts, scripts, and processes outlined in this solution can be used with minimal configuration to deploy Office 2007 in an enterprise, and they can be adapted for a wide range of system management tasks. You can also use what you learned in this solution to augment and complement the functionality of commercial grade tools such as SMS or Configuration Manager.

# 9-6: Automate Actions with *SendKeys*

## Solution overview

| | |
|---|---|
| **Type of solution** | Scripts |
| **Features and tools** | *SendKeys* and AutoIt |
| **Solution summary** | Automate installation and configuration even with applications that require interaction. Examples include toggling the visibility of the Quick Launch bar and setting the default view of all Explorer folders to Details. |
| **Benefits** | Automated configuration |

## Introduction

I expect there are at least a few applications in your environment that are brutal to install and impossible to automate. They might require interaction to click through an installation wizard, make selections, or agree to a license agreement. To deal with such demanding applications, you need to pull out the big guns: *SendKeys* and AutoIt. These are two tools that can perform macro-like automation tasks. Although they are not as robust and reliable as the silent installation options offered by an application's maker, they are exactly what is needed when an installation cannot be automated from the command line.

## Use *SendKeys* to automate an action sequence

*SendKeys* is a scripting method that literally performs key presses, just as if you typed the keys yourself. So if you know the key sequences that can perform an action, you can automate it.

When I was creating images for a 3000-machine deployment, we needed to ensure that the Quick Launch bar was visible on user desktops. I wanted the change to take effect immediately, without requiring logoff and logon, as a registry change would require. And I wanted a tool that users could double-click to enable Quick Launch if, for some reason, it vanished.

Believe it or not, this is not a simple configuration to automate, as it is stored in a binary registry entry. Of course, I know how to manually enable Quick Launch: Open the Taskbar And Start Menu Properties dialog box, and select the Show Quick Launch check box. In that Properties dialog box, pressing the Alt key reveals the shortcut keys for each option: Alt+Q toggles the Show Quick Launch check box. I then have to click OK or press Enter.

With that information, I can automate the task using *SendKeys*. First, I need to know how to open the Taskbar And Start Menu Properties dialog box within a script. A quick search of the Internet led me to several methods. The solution I selected had these lines of code, which work on both Windows Vista and Windows XP:

```
Set WSHShell = WScript.CreateObject("WScript.Shell")
WSHShell.Run "rundll32.exe shell32.dll,Options_RunDLL 1"
```

The *Run* method of the *WshShell* object ("Wscript.Shell") allows you to run commands. The argument that you send to the method is identical to what you would type in the Run command on the Start menu. So you can use the two lines of code just shown to execute any Windows shell command—anything you would do from the Run command. You just change the command inside the quotes.

If your command requires quotes, use two sets of quotation marks wherever your command requires one. For example, if you need to open the folder C:\Documents and Settings, you need to type the command **"C:\Documents and Settings"** at the Run command, surrounding the path with quotes. So you could use the following code to automate the opening of that folder:

```
Set WSHShell = WScript.CreateObject("WScript.Shell")
WSHShell.Run """C:\Documents and Settings"""
```

Notice that the Run method has its own quotes that surround my command. My command required quotes, so I replaced each quotation mark with two quotation marks. That resulted in *three* quotation marks at the beginning and end. Sounds and looks crazy, but it works.

Returning to the automation of Quick Launch bar visibility, I have opened the Taskbar And Start Menu Properties. Now I simply have to press Alt+Q and Enter using a script. This code does the trick:

```
WSHShell.SendKeys "%Q"
WSHShell.SendKeys "{ENTER}"
```

You now can see the *SendKeys* method in action. It is a method of the *WshShell* object, represented by my object reference, *WSHShell*. You can press a single key—for example, *WSHShell.SendKeys "Y"* will send the *Y* keystroke to the shell. You can also send modifiers: Ctrl is represented by the carat (^), Shift by the plus sign (+), and Alt by the percent sign (%). So the first line of code sends Alt+Q. To send special keys, you use an identifier such as *{ENTER}* or *{TAB}*. See *http://msdn2.microsoft.com/en-us/library/8c6yea83.aspx* for all the details about *SendKeys*.

There are two major tricks that are required for automating with *SendKeys*. They relate to knowing exactly where the keystrokes you send are going. How do you ensure that they are being sent to the Taskbar And Start Menu Properties, for example? As you know, Windows Explorer can sometimes take a moment to open a window. If you use the *Run* method shown earlier to open the Taskbar And Start Menu Properties, it is wise to wait a moment before executing the *SendKeys* method so that you can be sure that the desired application is open and active.

The *Sleep* method of the *WScript* object can help. *WScript.Sleep* can be used within a VBScript script to cause the script to pause for a specified number of milliseconds. This code causes the script to wait one second:

```
wscript.sleep 1000
```

The second trick that we can apply is the *AppActivate()* method of the *Shell* object. This method is equivalent to clicking a window. It makes it active and gives it focus. Thereafter, key sequences executed using the *SendKeys* method are sent to the active window. This code activates the Taskbar And Start Menu Properties dialog box after it has been opened:

```
bActivated = WSHShell.AppActivate("Taskbar and Start Menu Properties")
```

The name of the window is included as an argument for the *AppActivate()* method. The argument can be the entire name of the window or a string that is found at the beginning or end of the window title. The method returns a Boolean value—*True* or *False*—that can be used to determine whether it was successful at activating the window. The line of code just shown assigns that value to a variable, *bActivated*. So I can evaluate that variable to determine whether to continue executing the script. For more information about the *AppActivate()* method, see *http://msdn2.microsoft.com/en-us/library/wzcddbek.aspx*.

The resulting script that can attempt to automate Quick Launch visibility follows:

```
Config_QuickLaunch_Toggle_Simple.vbs
Set WSHShell = WScript.CreateObject("WScript.Shell")
WSHShell.Run "rundll32.exe shell32.dll,Options_RunDLL 1"
WScript.Sleep 1000
bActivated = WSHShell.AppActivate("Taskbar and Start Menu Properties")
if not bActivated then WScript.Quit
WScript.Sleep 500
WSHShell.SendKeys "%Q"
WScript.Sleep 500
WSHShell.SendKeys "{ENTER}"
```

The script launches the Taskbar And Start Menu Properties dialog box, pauses one second, and attempts to activate the window. If it is not successful, the scripts exits. Otherwise, the script sends the Alt+Q and Enter key sequences that toggle the visibility of the Quick Launch bar.

# Understand and customize Config_QuickLaunch_Toggle.vbs

On the companion media, you will find a script that extends the simple code just presented to automate the toggling of Quick Launch visibility. The script is named Config_QuickLaunch_Toggle.vbs. The code performs the exact same function as the shorter code shown earlier, but it modularizes the functionality so that you can more easily create your own custom action sequences to perform other automated tasks.

Examine the *ActivateWindow()* function in the script. It is a wrapper around the *AppActivate()* method that provides some additional logic. The function attempts to activate the window for a specified period of time and, optionally, causes the entire script to quit if it is unable to successfully activate the window within that time. You can use this function as a replacement for the *Shell* object's *AppActivate()* method.

The script also adds sophistication to the delays between actions. Two variables are used to configure two types of delays. The *iWait* variable is set to a delay that is required for Windows Explorer to open a window or dialog box. It is set to one second by default, but if a particular script is failing because windows are taking too long to open, you can configure a longer delay. Conversely, you can shorten the delay if the performance of the script can be improved without risking failure. The *iObserve* variable represents a delay that is not necessary for the success of the script actions, but rather slows down the actions so that they can be observed by the user executing the script. By default, *iObserve* is set to two seconds, so wherever the script pauses using *wscript.sleep iObserve*, the user has two seconds to observe the results of the actions. *iObserve* should be used only between keystrokes within a single window or dialog box tab—within a single focus. You can reduce *iObserve* to zero without affecting the functionality of the script, but the actions will happen so quickly that you might not be able to follow them. Use *iWait* to pause between major actions.

Finally, you'll see a trick I use that allows a script to run unattended or interactively. The *Popup* method of the *Shell* object produces a dialog box, similar to the *MsgBox* statement in VBScript. The difference is that the *Popup* method's second argument specifies a timeout, after which the dialog box disappears. Using the *Popup* method allows me to display a message to a user who launches the script interactively. However, if the script is running unattended, the message disappears after the specified delay and the script can continue.

# Set the default folder view to Details for all folders

I wish I had a dollar for each time a user asked, "How can I set Windows so that all folders show the Details view by default?" I'd be a wealthy man indeed. Why Microsoft opted to use the large icons view as the default, at least through Windows XP, is a mystery to me.

This is a very difficult configuration to change—I've never found a silver bullet. So I created Config_FolderView_Details.vbs in the Scripts folder of the companion media. This script runs on Windows XP and executes a long series of *SendKeys* actions that apply Details as the default view for all folders and then changes the default view for specific folders: Control Panel, My Pictures, Network Places, Network Connections, and My Computer. The script assumes that Control Panel is in Classic View and might produce an error if it is not.

I recommend incorporating this script into your image-creation scripts for Windows XP so that all Windows XP systems begin with Details as the default Windows Explorer view.

## Automate with AutoIt

The methods I've introduced in this section—*SendKeys*, *AppActivate*, and *Sleep*—can get you a long way toward automating installation and configuration tasks that otherwise require interaction. For even more complex tasks, I recommend that you examine AutoIt, a freeware scripting utility that can automate just about anything. It's available from *http://www.autoitscript.com*.

## Solution summary

When an application's installation routine refuses to be automated, you can use brute force, creating a script that uses methods such as *SendKeys* and *AppActivate* to perform macro-like sequences of actions, automatically. Although *SendKeys* is not bulletproof and it might not solve every problem, it is, along with AutoIt, a helpful tool in your installation and configuration tool chest.

Solution Collection 10

# Implementing Change, Configuration, and Policies

Change is, of course, inevitable in an organization. Today, *agility* is a corporate buzzword that implies the ability to respond to change, and to respond to change you must be able to manage change. If your organization wins a new contract that requires all users to begin using a new application immediately, you must be able to respond with an infrastructure that can deploy that application. Of course, there are a variety of alternatives: You can use Group Policy to deploy software, you can use System Center Configuration Manager or another third-party software deployment tool, or you can manually touch each machine—but the last option mentioned is hardly a shining example of managing the change.

If a new security vulnerability is revealed that requires you to make a particular registry change to all systems in your enterprise, you need to be able to push out the change rapidly. If you buy a new printer to respond to increased business, you should be able to deploy that printer automatically to appropriate users. These are just a few examples of the many regular changes that we must manage as IT professionals. We are also expected to manage corporate policies—those policies (with a small "p") that are delivered by organizational leadership as directives for human and technical behavior, and that we must implement, comply with, and audit.

Group Policy is one component of a broader framework to support the management of change and configuration. It amazes me that so many enterprises have done so little with Group Policy. I believe that part of the problem is that there is a disconnect or miscommunication regarding its role in aligning your enterprise information technology with business require-ments. In this Solution Collection, I examine Group Policy, along with several other features—including fine-grained password policies and Directory Service Changes auditing—in an effort to align these technologies to meet common business requirements for the management of change, configuration, and policy.

# Scenarios, Pain, and Solution

Group Policy and the other technologies addressed in this Solution Collection are phenome-nally useful features of Microsoft Windows and Active Directory. They allow you to centrally manage configuration, including software distribution, security, and a virtually unlimited number of individual settings that have an impact on computers and users in your enterprise. Let's preview some of the scenarios we'll address in these pages:

■ Adventure Works, a global travel organization, has two subdivisions: Luxury and Bud-get, which are the legacy of previous mergers and acquisitions. Administration within the single domain is decentralized, with Information Technology (IT) organizations in each division creating and managing Group Policy objects (GPOs) for their users and computers. Recently, the Luxury division decided to deploy an application that locks down desktops and laptops. They deployed the application using Group Policy Software Installation (GPSI), assigning the application in the User Configuration node of the GPO. During a recent company-wide meeting, users from the Luxury division traveled to the office of the Budget division and used systems in the Budget division to access their e-mail. When they logged on to the Budget division computers, the application was installed. Those computers were then locked down with settings that caused a work stoppage at the Budget division. Because the desktop support organization of the Bud-get division was unprepared to manage this application, significant resources were spent troubleshooting and removing the application from their systems.

■ The board of directors has instructed the leadership of Tailspin Toys to ensure that sys-tem security is increased, and that corporate security and IT usage policies (again with a small "p") are not just words on paper, but are enforced within the IT environment.

■ The security team at Contoso, Ltd., wants to increase the security of privileged accounts used by IT administrators and services, to reduce the vulnerability of account passwords to brute-force attack.

■ The compliance team at Trey Research has determined that, in response to its interpre-tation of new governmental regulations, membership of the Domain Admins group must be monitored, with each new or removed member identified.

■ To increase corporate agility, the IT organization of Litware, Inc., wants to establish a change control process that ensures responsiveness to a request for change and ensures a thorough and confident validation of the change prior to its widespread deployment.

■ As part of the same effort towards agility, Litware's enterprise administrators have initiated an effort to identify the risks and benefits of delegating Group Policy management to business unit administrators.

In this Solution Collection, we address Group Policy—a complex framework about which I could write a book. Luckily, two of my friends and über-gurus have already done that. So I point you to Derek Melber's *Windows Group Policy Resource Kit: Windows Server 2008 and Windows Vista* (Microsoft Press, 2008) and Jeremy Moskowitz's *Group Policy: Management, Troubleshooting and Security: For Windows Vista, Windows 2003, Windows XP and Windows 2000* (Sybex, 2007) for great information about the internals and procedures of Group Policy management. I also highly recommend both Jeremy's Web site, *http://www.gpoanswers.com*, and the site of another friend and über-guru, Darren Mar-Elia, at *http://www.gpoguy.com*. If you have the resources from these three guys in sight, you have most of what you'll need to know about Group Policy!

In this Solution Collection, I'll approach the topic assuming you are familiar with the fundamentals and functionality of Group Policy, and I'll be intentionally skimpy on step-by-step procedures, as both the Group Policy Help embedded in the Group Policy Management Console (GPMC) and the aforementioned books provide the fundamentals, procedures, and under-the-hood perspective on Group Policy. Rather than reiterate what has been said so well already, I'd like to spend the pages we have here working to deliver solutions based on what clients ask me as a consultant: to align Group Policy with business requirements, to deliver solutions with Group Policy, to introduce several new policy-related technologies, and above all to increase the manageability of their Group Policy framework .

# 10-1: Create a Change Control Workflow

## Solution overview

| | |
|---|---|
| **Type of solution** | Guidance |
| **Features and tools** | Group Policy objects, Active Directory groups |
| **Solution summary** | Understand the process of change management, beginning with the realization that a change is necessary and continuing through the design, testing, and deployment of that change. |
| **Benefits** | Build a change control framework that includes each component of the change management process. |

## Introduction

To begin our exploration of change, configuration, and policies, I'd like to step you through the change management process, from the moment that someone identifies a change is required or valuable, through the evaluation and piloting of the change, to the widespread deployment of that change. Although this Solution Collection assumes you are familiar with

Group Policy, a small handful of issues are critical to attaining an understanding of the best way to elevate the manageability of Group Policy. So, along the way, I'll touch on those issues. With an understanding of each phase of change and configuration management (CCM), you can create a change control process for your organization that outlines exactly how a change will be deployed in the enterprise.

## Identify the need for change

The seed of every action is the idea, and in the case of Group Policy, the idea is the recognition that a change is necessary or can add value and that the change should be deployed and managed in the enterprise. Change can result from the imposition of corporate policies, with a small "p"—directives from the organization's leadership. Change can result because, on analysis of your help desk logs, you recognize the opportunity to reduce costs. For example, you might realize that turning off Fast Saves in Microsoft Office PowerPoint can reduce the number of support requests related to bloated PowerPoint presentation size preventing users from sending presentations as e-mail attachments.

Change can arise from any number of sources and can be brought to your attention by any user—technical or nontechnical. The first step in change management is identifying the change that must be made.

When the need for change is identified, document the change. Explain the scenario that the change addresses. Why is it important? What is the business impact of the change? What are the risks associated with not changing, the benefits of the change, and the risk associated with implementing the change? How can the change and its effect be measured? Is there a baseline against which success can be evaluated? Who originated the change request? What are the timelines for the desired and required deployment of the change?

Finally, to what users or computers shall the change be targeted? The concept of *scope*—of identifying and managing the subset of users or computers to which a change will apply—is paramount to the discussion of change management with any technology, including Group Policy. The change identification phase should specify the objects to which change will be scoped.

## Translate the change to Group Policy settings

After you have identified that a change must be deployed or managed in your environment, you must determine how to implement the change using Group Policy. This step is usually performed by an individual or team that is expert in Group Policy. It is the most technical step, as it requires intimate familiarity with the settings already exposed by Group Policy as well as the options for extending Group Policy, such as Group Policy Preferences and custom administrative templates. A change control process should include the assignment of the change to one or more change owners, who are responsible for the evaluation, design, and testing of the change. The change owners should also determine the mechanisms with which the change will be scoped to the users or computers identified in the previous phase.

## Test the change in a lab environment

Changes and their proposed mechanisms should always be proven in an isolated lab environment prior to deployment in the production domain. Any issues that arise in testing should be documented and solved, and the resulting change should be retested.

## Communicate the change to users

While testing is being conducted, a parallel workflow can identify the users who will participate in the pilot of the change in the production environment and those who will be affected by the GPO in its final scope. Decide what, if any, information should be provided to users to help them understand, plan for, or work with the change.

## Test the change in the production environment

Evaluating a change in a lab is a critical first step because there are so many moving parts in a Group Policy infrastructure, but success in a lab hardly guarantees success in production. Few labs fully and completely emulate the production environment with its myriad applications, systems, and users. Therefore, it's equally, if not more, critical to test a change in the production environment with a limited but representative sample of systems or users.

In Solution 10-7 on page 679, I detail the process for moving a GPO from the lab to the production environment and conducting an effective and informative pilot.

## Migrate users and computers in the production environment to the scope of the change

Solution 10-7 also details how to migrate objects to the scope of the validated GPO. It's a topic big enough to warrant its own solution, and a topic that leverages other manageability techniques discussed in this Solution Collection.

## Implement more GPOs with fewer settings

As you begin to move the change into the production environment, you must choose whether to incorporate the change into an existing GPO or to create a new GPO with which to manage the change. A common question related to Group Policy is, "Should I have more GPOs with fewer settings per GPO, or fewer GPOs with more settings per GPO?" The answer is generally the former—you will be better served with a greater number of more granular GPOs than by a few "mega GPOs." The justifications for this recommendation are as follows:

- GPOs that are singular in their purpose are easier to scope to specific users or computers. A larger GPO might not be completely and perfectly applicable to all the objects within its scope.

- It is easier to manage objects that are stable. If your GPOs are granular and targeted to their purpose, they are less likely to require or receive changes over time. You can build them once and leave them in place.

- If you roll out new settings in a new GPO, and if those settings cause problems, you can easily disable the GPO's link and roll back those settings. If the settings are integrated into an existing, larger GPO, you must edit each setting individually to roll back the change.

- In a multidomain environment, granular GPOs can be duplicated more easily and with fewer errors.

- There is less load on domain controllers (DCs) because clients can continue to cache GPOs that have not changed, and only new policies must be downloaded. This also means reduced startup and logon time.

- If there are file replication problems for a Group Policy template (GPT), the potential impact of those problems is limited to the settings of that GPO. I describe GPTs later in this solution.

I recommend using multiple, granular, targeted, single-purpose GPOs—GPOs that apply one or more settings that, together, result in the desired change. The cost of using multiple GPOs in an enterprise is that more GPOs must be evaluated and processed during refresh. There are two major components of this cost: GPO download and GPO evaluation. Because GPOs are downloaded only when introduced or changed, I suggest that multiple GPOs actually *improve* the infrastructure because you are less likely to have to change those GPOs over time—instead, you'll introduce a new, small, targeted GPO to roll out new changes. The cost associated with evaluating GPOs—examining the security group filters, for example, to determine whether or not the GPO should be applied—is technically real, but practically very minor. Too many organizations get caught up in the idea that multiple GPOs will slow down startup and logon. They do slow down startup and logon, but—and it's a big "but"—it's unusual that you would actually be able to see the difference. We're talking about only a few ticks of your processor.

As your CCM infrastructure stabilizes, you can begin to consolidate GPOs with identical scopes in an effort to reduce the overall quantity of GPOs. But do so only after stabilization has begun to occur so that you are confident in both the settings and the scopes of your changes.

## Establish a GPO naming convention

Your naming standards for GPOs should indicate the purpose of the GPO. The naming standard should also indicate, where possible, the target of the GPO—the users or computers to which the GPO is scoped. I suggest that the purpose of the GPO be the first component of the name, and that the target be the second component. For example, you might have two GPOs, named Standard Configuration_Desktops and Standard Configuration_Laptops.

There's not a lot of value added by naming GPOs with a prefix such as *GPO_*. You know a GPO is a GPO because it's a GPO, right? It's not like you will look at a list of Active Directory objects and see users, computers, groups, and GPOs mixed together! I do recommend, however, using a prefix such as *GPO_* in your *group* naming convention so that you understand that the purpose for a particular group is to manage the scope of a GPO.

## Ensure a new GPO is not being applied while you are configuring its settings

A GPO is actually two pieces, the first of which is the Group Policy Container (GPC). The GPC is an object in Active Directory that replicates from the Primary Domain Controller (PDC) operations master, which is the default birthplace of all new GPOs, to other domain controllers using standard Active Directory replication. The GPC defines basic properties of a GPO, including its globally unique identifier (GUID), name, and the access control list (ACL) that determines who can read the GPO, to which objects the GPO applies, and who can change the settings of the GPO.

The other component of a GPO is the Group Policy Template (GPT). The GPT is stored in the SYSVOL of the domain controllers–. As with the GPC, the GPT starts on the PDC operations master and is replicated to other domain controllers, but with an entirely different replication mechanism (File Replication Service or DFS Replication) than the GPC.

Because the two halves of a GPO replicate using different mechanisms, problems can arise. A client might detect a new GPO in Active Directory, attempt to download the GPT, and discover that the GPT is not fully replicated to the DC's SYSVOL. Potentially worse, you might be in the middle of changing the GPO's settings and the partially configured GPT might be replicated, causing systems to apply some but not all of the desired settings. Eventually, all settings will be applied, but there could be some inconsistent and potentially undesired effects in the meantime.

Therefore I recommend that you create a new GPO in the Group Policy Objects node of the GPMC. Complete the configuration of settings, and let both the GPC and the GPT replicate to all domain controllers *before* linking the GPO to a site, domain, or organizational unit (OU). You can use either GPOTool or Replmon to verify that GPOs are in synch–that the GPC and GPT have fully replicated. Search the Microsoft Web site for details about those two tools.

Another way to accomplish the same goal is to create the GPO and link it to the site, domain, or OU, but to disable the GPO link or disable the GPO entirely. After the GPO has fully replicated, you can enable the link or the GPO.

The problem I address in this section is easy to manage when creating a new GPO, but it's more complex to manage when changing the settings of an existing GPO. Be aware of the problem: As you are changing settings, some of those settings might begin to replicate. Consider what can be done to limit any potential detrimental effects of this reality given your environment, the changes you will make, and the scope of those changes.

# Back up a GPO prior to and after changing it

If you are changing an existing GPO, you can implement a form of version control by backing up a GPO prior to making changes to its settings, and again after changing it. You can back up a GPO's settings by right-clicking on the GPO in the Group Policy Objects node of the GPMC and choosing Back Up.

The Microsoft Desktop Optimization Pack, available to Software Assurance customers for a very reasonable fee, includes Microsoft Advanced Group Policy Management, which enables Group Policy change management workflow. See *www.microsoft.com/windows/products/windowsvista/enterprise/mdop* for more information.

# Document the settings and the GPO

Windows Server 2008 enables you to add comments to a GPO and to the individual settings. Use comments to document the purpose of the GPO, the effect of each setting, and issues you learned related to the settings and their application. We finally have a bit of functionality we've wanted all along and have gotten used to not having. Use comments!

# Carefully implement the scope of a GPO

Many of the solutions in this Solution Collection relate to the proper and effective scoping of a GPO—that is, determining the objects to which settings in a GPO will or will not be applied. As part of your change management process, scope should be determined early in the process, when the need for change is identified, and the mechanisms used to scope the GPO—links to domains, sites, or OUs; security group filtering; Windows Management Instrumentation (WMI) filters; or internal filters—should be well documented for the GPO.

# Establish a change management workflow with service levels

The preceding sections stepped you through the key phases of implementing a change with a GPO. There are more details in later solutions, particularly regarding the pilot phase and scoping GPOs. I recommend that you implement a change control process to support the introduction and management of changes using Group Policy in your enterprise. Your process should address the issues raised in this Solution Collection, and it should establish expectations for service level agreements (SLAs). That is, define how long it should take for an idea—the request for change—to be received, evaluated, tested, and deployed. You should define SLAs for both standard changes and for emergency changes that are a response to critical issues, and define what constitutes a valid emergency.

# Understand the behavior of client-side Group Policy application

Now that your GPO is deployed, let's turn our attention to how the changes contained in a GPO get applied to a client. One of the most important concepts of Group Policy is that GPOs are not pushed in any way to clients. Instead, client processes, such as the Winlogon service in Windows 2000 and Windows XP, the Group Policy Client service in Windows Vista, and workhorses called *client-side extensions* (CSEs) are responsible for requesting, downloading, processing, and implementing GPOs and their settings. But the story doesn't end there. Just making a change to the registry, for example, doesn't effect a change—there must be an application or a component of Windows that pays attention to that change and makes a modification to its behavior accordingly.

When a computer joins a domain and starts up, it checks to see whether a domain controller is online, and if it is, the computer downloads all GPOs linked to its site, domain, and OUs. After the GPOs have been downloaded, filtering occurs on the client to determine which of the downloaded GPOs are or are not to be applied to the computer. When a user logs on, the process repeats, except that the GPOs downloaded are those that are linked to the user's site, domain, and OUs. Again, after GPOs have been downloaded, filtering is applied to determine which downloaded GPOs are or are not applied. This process is called *background refresh*. Every 90 to 120 minutes thereafter, the computer performs another background refresh, during which it checks to see if any GPOs have changed. If any have changed, those GPOs are downloaded and applied as directed by any filters.

The application of the settings in a GPO is managed by one or more client-side extensions. There are CSEs that specialize in the interpretation and application of each type of policy setting, including software installation, security, folder redirection, and registry settings.

There are several Group Policy application fundamentals that I'd like to be sure you understand, even though the assumption of this Solution Collection is that you are familiar with Group Policy.

## GPOs are not downloaded unless they have been changed

The process of downloading GPOs as described so far occurs only when a computer starts up for the first time after joining a domain, and when a user logs on to a system for the first time. After that, to maximize efficiency and network utilization, the client downloads only GPOs that have changed. Unchanged GPOs are processed from the local cache. The client determines whether a GPO has changed by examining the version number of the GPC in Active Directory and comparing it to the version number of the downloaded GPT.

## GPOs are not reapplied unless they have been changed

Similarly, GPOs are not reapplied, by default, unless they have changed. This behavior can be problematic and will be one of the issues addressed later in this Solution Collection. The exceptions to this rule are the settings in the Security Settings node of a GPO, which are processed by the security CSE. These settings are reapplied every 16 hours during background refresh, even if a GPO with security settings has not been changed. Later in this Solution Collection, I'll recommend enabling the reapplication of GPOs at each background refresh.

### GPOs apply even if a system is disconnected from the network

The settings in GPOs persist when a computer is disconnected from the network. Of course, the client cannot contact a domain controller to determine whether any GPOs have changed or whether any new GPOs are to be downloaded. Additionally, startup, shutdown, logon, and logoff scripts do not run unless the computer is connected to the network.

### Background refresh does not fully implement all policy changes

Background refresh results in the tangible change specified by policies that are processed by most of the CSEs. However, several CSEs do not fully implement their policies during background refresh. These include folder redirection, software installation, scripts, and disk quotas. For example, if you change a user's folder redirection target while the user is logged on, the system learns of the new target but does not change the actual target of the user's folders, to avoid corruption. When the user logs off and then logs on, the change will be completed. Such changes require one, or even two, logons or restarts for the change to complete.

## Solution summary

We examined the life of a change—identifying the change needed, evaluating and testing the change, deploying the change in a GPO, and applying the change by CSEs. I hope this discussion helped you to put the technologies and characteristics of Group Policy into a perspective that aligns with the reality of change management in your organization. Use this timeline-oriented view of change to create a change control process in your organization that defines the phases, roles, and tasks of change management, and establishes SLAs with which you can govern both standard and emergency changes.

# 10-2: Extend Role-Based Management to the Management of Change and Configuration

## Solution overview

| | |
|---|---|
| **Type of solution** | Guidance |
| **Features and tools** | Security group filtering of GPOs, role-based management |
| **Solution summary** | Use security group filtering to efficiently manage the scope of Group Policy objects—both the objects to which GPOs apply and those that are exempted from GPOs. |
| **Benefits** | Granular and manageable application of settings deployed through Group Policy |

# Introduction

Throughout this resource kit, I've encouraged you to break free from the bonds of the logical, OU-based structure of your Active Directory and to elevate your management infrastructure to one that provides a rule-driven, database-supported approach to aligning Windows technologies with your business requirements. We've used groups as the fundamental component of such an infrastructure, as they enable both the data and business logic layer of role-based management. In this solution, we'll extend the use of groups, and of role-based management, to Group Policy as we examine the use of security group filtering as a mechanism for scoping GPOs.

# Scope GPOs to security groups

As discussed in Solution Collection 5, "Active Directory Delegation and Administrative Lock Down," Active Directory design should be based, first and foremost, on the efficient management of security—on the propagation of access control lists (ACLs) to Active Directory objects using inheritance from an optimal number of OUs. The result is an Active Directory design that effectively supports the management of delegation and the administrative model of your organization.

My experience has been that, in many organizations, the scopes of administration and scopes of configuration are often quite different. In other words, the OU structure does not necessarily create the scopes of management required to deploy GPOs, so these organizations do not have the luxury of linking GPOs to lower-level OUs. There's nothing wrong with that—it's just the result of a thoughtful OU design based, first, on administrative delegation.

When you cannot create a single OU to represent a scope of users or computers without upsetting your Active Directory delegation, don't! Instead, create a global security group to represent the scope. That security group can be used to filter a GPO. For example, you might create a global security group to represent a scope of computers that act as kiosk-like systems in publically accessible areas, from which users and visitors can access the Internet. The computer accounts for these systems might be scattered across multiple OUs. A GPO linked to a higher-level OU or even to the domain itself can be filtered to apply only to the computers that are members of that group.

 **Best Practices** Most organizations find themselves better able to manage both security and configuration when they rely on security group filtering than when they try to twist their OU structure into one that supports scoping GPOs.

The following sections describe how to filter a GPO to apply to a security group.

## Create a security group with which to filter the GPO

First, create a global security group that will be used to filter the GPO.

> **Important**    Perhaps the single most important thing to remember about creating a global security group for filtering the GPO is this: Group Policy Objects can be filtered only with global security groups. You cannot use domain local security groups to filter a GPO.

Follow a strict naming convention to determine the group's name. I recommend a prefix that indicates the purpose of the group—*GPO_*—followed by the name of the GPO that will be filtered with the group, followed by another underscore and a flag as to whether the group causes the GPO to be applied or denied. For example, you might call a group that causes systems to require Internet Protocol Security (IPSec) to communicate with each other GPO_IPSec Require_Allow. Or, if you want to use a security group to provide exemption from a GPO that applies software restriction policies, you might call the group GPO_Software Restriction_Deny. Be sure to use the group's Description and Comments fields to fully describe the purpose of the group.

The resulting GPO filter group reflects what I call a capability management group. The group manages a specific capability—the application, or denial of application—of a configuration. As we saw in Solution Collection 1, "Role-Based Management," capability management groups contain role groups and, on occasion, individual users or computers. So you nest role groups into the GPO filter group. Role groups are global groups, as are GPO filter groups. So this infrastructure requires a domain that is not in an interim or mixed domain functional level—you must be at a Windows 2000 domain functional level or greater for global groups to nest into global groups. GPO filter groups are one of the few capability management groups that must be created with global scope—again, because that is what is supported by Group Policy.

## Scope a GPO to apply only to a specific security group

After you create the group, you can configure the GPO to apply to that group. Follow this simple procedure:

1. Open the GPMC.

2. Expand the domain and the Group Policy Objects container.

3. Select the GPO that you want to filter.

4. In the details pane, click the Scope tab.

5. Below Security Filtering, select the Authenticated Users group, and click Remove.

    By default, all new GPOs apply to Authenticated Users, which means all users and all computers within the scope of the GPO link—the site, domain, or OU. To restrict the application of the GPO to only your custom security group, you must remove Authenticated Users.

6.  Click Add.

7.  Select the group that you created for filtering the GPO, and click OK.

    Remember that GPOs can be filtered only by global security groups.

8.  Link the GPO to a site, domain, or OU above all users or computers that belong to the security group.

    Typically, GPOs that are filtered with security groups are linked at a high-level OU or even to the domain.

When you have completed the preceding procedure, the Scope tab of the GPO properties should look similar to Figure 10-1.

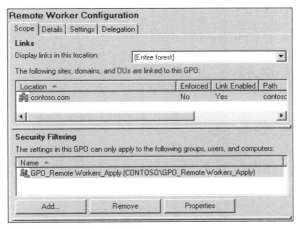

**Figure 10-1**   A GPO scoped to apply to a global security group

When you filter a GPO to a security group, you are changing the access control list (ACL) of the GPO. The Allow::Apply Group Policy permission determines whether the client applies the settings in the GPO for the computer or for the user. Using the procedure just shown, you have removed the Allow::Apply Group Policy permission that is assigned to the Authenticated Users group by default for each new GPO, and you have specified that your group be granted the Apply Group Policy permission. The Scope tab of the GPMC masks the underlying change to the ACL, but it is useful to know what is happening behind the scenes.

## Scope a GPO to exempt a specific security group

If you want a GPO to *exempt* a group—that is, *not* to apply to those users or computers—you must more directly manipulate the ACL of the GPO. Follow this procedure:

1.  Open the GPMC.

2.  Expand the domain and the Group Policy Objects container.

3.  Select the GPO that you want to filter.

4. In the details pane, click the Delegation tab.

5. Click the Advanced button.

   The Security Settings dialog box appears.

6. Click the Add button.

   If User Account Control is enabled, you might have to click Edit before the Add button becomes visible.

7. In the Enter The Object Names To Select text box, type the name of the security group that you want to exempt, and click OK.

8. In the Permissions for *group_name* list, select the Deny check box for the Apply Group Policy permission.

   The result should appear similar to Figure 10-2.

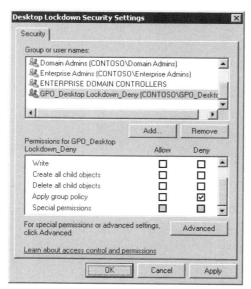

**Figure 10-2**  The Security Settings dialog box displaying a Deny::Apply Group Policy permission

9. Click OK.

Unfortunately, the GPMC interface does not give good visibility to GPO exemption. The Scope tab, shown in Figure 10-1, shows only the groups to whom you assigned the Allow::Apply Group Policy permission—it does not show the groups that you have exempted. Even the Delegation tab is not as clear as it should be—a Deny permission is shown as "Custom" in the Allowed Permissions column. For these reasons, I recommend you use a group name that clearly indicates you use it to deny a GPO's application.

Because the GPMC is built to give visibility to the groups to which a GPO is applied, and not to those to which a GPO is denied, I recommend that, whenever possible, you manage GPOs to control their application rather than the denial. But there will certainly be scenarios, such as those related to corporate security and usage policies, for which managing exemptions—that is, denial—are warranted.

## Manage exemptions from an entire GPO

The procedure just described is used to prevent a GPO from applying to a specific security group. In most of the organizations with which I've worked, there are very few GPOs that should apply to every user or computer in the enterprise. There are almost always exceptions.

I recommend that for any change that will be deployed widely within an enterprise, you pro-actively configure an exemption mechanism, whereby computers or users can be exempted from the change temporarily or permanently. The easiest way to do this is with a security group that has the Deny::Apply Group Policy permission for the GPO. As systems or users are identified that require exemption, they can be added to the group. The group then becomes a scope of management. Even if you move all objects temporarily into the exemption group, you have at least begun to manage them. You can, over time, determine whether those exemptions must be permanent or whether they can be worked around, solved, and removed from the exemption.

## Manage exemptions from some settings of a GPO

Occasionally you'll encounter a situation in which there must be exemptions from some, but not all, of the settings being configured by a GPO. In such situations, I recommend that you create a security group to contain the exempted users or computers. Then create a second GPO with all but the problematic settings of the original GPO. Scope the second GPO so that it applies only to the exemption group; and scope the original GPO so that it excludes the exemption group. I prefer this approach over trying to create a GPO that overrides the individual problematic settings. This approach has been successful and is also the solution implemented by Microsoft IT for its internal Group Policy management.

## Link group-filtered GPOs high in the structure

After you have filtered a GPO using a security group, you can scope the GPO to a container that includes all the members of the security group—typically, a high-level OU or even the domain itself. The GPO link scopes the GPO's maximum possible impact, but the security group filter effectively limits the scope. The resultant scope of the GPO is the intersection of objects scoped by the link and scoped by the security group filter.

To facilitate manageability and visibility of your GPO infrastructure, I recommend that you link GPOs that are filtered by security groups very high in your OU structure or to the domain itself. If a GPO includes only user settings, for example, you might link the GPO to the OU containing your user accounts, or to the domain. Similarly, if a GPO contains only computer settings that apply to the client systems in your organization, link that GPO to the top-level OU that contains your client computer accounts, or to the domain.

An important point to remember is that a system downloads all GPOs scoped to its site, domain, and OUs. It then processes the GPOs from the local cache. So whether you've linked these GPOs to the domain or to the top-level users and computers OUs, all the appropriate GPOs end up being downloaded by clients. For this reason, I prefer to simply link all such GPOs to the domain—my opinion is that if the GPOs are going to be downloaded anyway, why make the visibility of the GPO links more difficult than it needs to be by linking them to top-level OUs? So my recommendation is to link all GPOs that are filtered by security groups to the domain itself. As long as the GPOs are relatively static—that is, the settings are not being changed—they will be downloaded once and processed from the clients' local cache from that point forward. The impact to the client and to the network of multiple domain-linked GPOs is fairly minimal, and the benefit to manageability is real.

To give you an example of just how powerful security group filtering can be, Microsoft itself has over 900 GPOs in its production domain, almost all of which are linked to the domain and scoped to apply to security groups. So a typical computer might have only 14 GPOs that are scoped to apply to that system or user. This approach is in use at many other organizations, and it works.

# Maximize group management techniques to control GPO scoping

In Solution Collection 8, "Reimagining the Administration of Groups and Membership," I presented sophisticated, but not difficult, techniques that you can use to manage group membership. These techniques included the following:

- Subscription groups that allow users to join or leave the group on their own accord
- Shadow groups that update their membership dynamically based on an Active Directory query
- Delegated and proxied management of group membership so that resource owners can manage group membership directly

As you plan the scope of a GPO that will be filtered using a security group, determine which of these techniques might be useful to align the burden of managing the scope of the GPO with the GPO's purpose.

## Avoid using Block Inheritance to exempt objects from the scope of GPOs

Let's wrap up with one small but important recommendation that relates to one other way to exempt a subset of objects from a broadly scoped GPO. It is possible to block GPO inheritance on an organizational unit: Right-click the OU in the GPMC and choose Block Inheritance. After doing so, only the settings in enforced GPOs from the domain, site, and parent OUs will apply. Any GPOs linked directly to the OU will also apply. But nonenforced policies from above will be blocked.

A model that includes Block Inheritance is difficult to audit and manage. If an entire OU requires exemptions from some GPOs, create a shadow group (as described in Solution 8-5 on page 559) that contains the computers or users in the OU, and deny the Apply Policy permission to the shadow group. I recommend that the only time you use the Block Inheritance approach is when you need to block *all* GPOs, or so many GPOs that it becomes unwieldy to manage the Deny permissions on each GPO.

## Solution summary

When you consider that your Active Directory OU design should be based first on security and delegation, and that for almost any rule there will be exceptions, you quickly come to the conclusion that scoping GPOs using OUs will have limited application. Either the objects to which settings should be applied are not contained in a single OU, requiring you to link a GPO to multiple OUs, or there will be objects within the OU that should be exempted. These considerations—along with a broader drive to manage the enterprise with rule-driven, role-based management—lead to the recommendation that most GPOs should be scoped using security group filtering. For a GPO, create groups that manage the objects to which settings will be applied or, if necessary, the objects that will not be affected by a GPO. Filter the GPO using the group or groups you create, and link the GPO to a high-level OU or to the domain itself. Using global security groups to filter objects into and out of the scope of a GPO, you can extend your role-based management infrastructure into the management of change and configuration.

# 10-3: Implement Your Organization's Password and Account Lockout Policies

## Solution overview

| | |
|---|---|
| Type of solution | Guidance and tools |
| Features and tools | The Default Domain Policy GPO, account lockout policies, password policies, fine-grained password policies, User_ResultantPSO.hta, Password Policy Basic from Special Operations Software |
| Solution summary | Modify the settings in the Default Domain GPO to implement your organization's policies regarding passwords and account lockout, and use Windows Server 2008 fine-grained password policies to manage special accounts. |
| Benefits | Manage account-related policy settings; increase the security of privileged accounts; manage compliance. |

# Introduction

One of the first policies encountered by and modified by administrators of Windows domains is the domain's password policy. The default password policy for a Windows Server 2008 domain controller requires a minimum password length of seven characters, a maximum password age of 42 days, a password history of 24 passwords, a minimum password age of one day, and password complexity. I expect there are few organizations with password policies that align exactly with Windows' defaults. In this solution, I'll explain how to implement your enterprise's password and lockout policies by modifying the Default Domain Policy GPO. I also expect that most organizations want to increase the security of privileged accounts—accounts in the domain's Administrators group, accounts with security-sensitive Active Directory delegation, and service accounts. So in this solution I'll also show you how, in a Windows Server 2008 domain, you can implement fine-grained password policies.

# Determine the password policies that are appropriate for your organization

You might know for certain that a 42-day maximum password age or a seven-character password length with complexity is not right for your organization. You might be asking yourself, "Is Dan going to tell me exactly *what* settings to implement?" Sorry to disappoint you—the answer depends heavily on your business and its requirements. I will, however, point you to two hubs of information regarding these settings:

- *http://technet2.microsoft.com/WindowsServer/en/library/4ca0ea83-3e0b-480f-8dcc-1b9f923326c31033.mspx*

- *http://technet2.microsoft.com/WindowsServer/en/library/619e73f6-5676-412e-8341-8125f0c03a2f1033.mspx*

The pages referred to above are part of the Windows Server 2003 technical library. Although they apply perfectly well to a Windows Server 2008 domain too, keep an eye out on TechNet for any revisions of these articles for Windows Server 2008. Additionally, I'll make a couple of points that I think are particularly important about considerations that have changed in recent years. Let's look at each of the components of the Account Policies node of a Group Policy object.

## Password policy: Longer passwords are a must

If you are concerned about password security—and you should be if your business has any data that is valuable to the business or that is under external requirements for security or compliance—a six- or seven-character password just ain't enough any more. Security experts are now suggesting a 12-character minimum. I would extend that to recommend a 15-character minimum because that length makes some changes to the way the password is saved within

Active Directory, which makes the password hash that is saved in the domain's database even more resistant to attack.

A long password might seem challenging to you, and it probably will seem even more heinous to your users, who can't remember a six-character, let alone a 15-character, password. There are two major concerns you must balance in your password policy: vulnerability to password hacking and vulnerability to social engineering. The former relates to tools that can be used to reveal passwords based on password hashes, including brute-force attacks, which iteratively attempt to validate or match the hash of a password using a dictionary or random-character generator. The latter relates to figuring out a user's password based on characteristics learned about or from the user, including the dreaded "password on a sticky note underneath the keyboard or on the monitor."

There is a school of thought, to which I subscribe, that the latter is actually a much greater concern than the former. This school of thought suggests that you should implement very long passwords—perhaps 20 characters or more—but take away complexity requirements. Complexity requirements simply enforce greater variability in a password to make it more difficult to derive a password through dictionary attacks and other hacking tools. In a short password, you must have greater variability to increase the resistance to brute-force attacks. If you have an extremely long password, your variability is introduced by the number of characters in the password that must be attacked. A very long password is extremely resistant to technical hacks, even without complexity.

By removing complexity requirements, you open up the possibility for pass*phrases* rather than passwords. Passphrases can be long yet very memorable. They can even include the types of components that we've been trying, unsuccessfully, to get users to stop incorporating in their passwords: their children's names, their pets' names, the names of their favorite sports teams. So rather than a user having a complex password based on his dog's name, such as M@dd!e (my dog's name is Maddie), a passphrase could be "MaddieLovesPeanutButter." This 23-letter passphrase is highly resistant to brute-force attacks and very easy for the user to remember. Therefore, it's unlikely to need to be recorded on a sticky note under the keyboard.

The same school of thought suggests that, with appropriate analysis and auditing of logons, you can extend the maximum password age of long passwords because, again, it will take a technically unfeasible number of years to brute-force attack a long password.

The bottom line here is that you really should have passwords longer than six or seven characters. Second, as password lengths increase, you should consider going all the way to passphrases, which have both technical and social engineering benefits to the overall security of your user accounts. You must consider the integration of your Windows authentication with non-Windows technologies. For example, your Network-Attached Storage (NAS) devices might rely on Windows authentication but be unable to support a 23-character password. But do start considering password policies now—times they are a-changing!

## Lockout policies expose a denial-of-service possibility

Lockout policy settings specify the number of invalid logons that must occur in a specific timeframe to trigger lockout and, after lockout has occurred, how long the account will remain locked out before it is either unlocked automatically or unlocked by an administrator. For many years, account lockout was preached as a best practice. The idea is, of course, that if a user attempts to log on several times with an incorrect password, the account will be locked out under the assumption that it is a malicious attempt to gain access to the domain.

Let's assume you applied lockout policies that specified that a locked-out account will remain locked for 30 minutes, or perhaps remain locked indefinitely until unlocked by an administrator. A problem arises. Lockout policy affects all accounts—not just human users. So an accidental or malicious exploit could lock out accounts used by computers or by services. If I know the account you use for your domain's SQL servers, for example, I could attempt to map a drive with that account and an invalid password, and after the specified number of attempts, I would lock out your SQL Server service account.

You must therefore give serious thought about how to achieve a balance between preventing attempts to gain access to the network using a domain account and preventing denial of service by intentionally locking out an account. There's no universal equation you can use to determine the policy that's right for your enterprise. You must evaluate your threats, your data security requirements, your business model, and the variety of options at your disposal for mitigating security exposure.

As you do so, consider that auditing failed logons and monitoring event logs for failed logons can achieve the goal of catching attempts to access the network—you don't necessarily have to lock out the account in response. Similarly, very short lockout durations will generate a lockout event in the Security log that can be monitored or used to trigger an alert to administrators—you don't necessarily have to lock out an account for a long or indefinite period of time.

## Kerberos policy settings should be modified only with a deep understanding of Kerberos authentication

When domain authentication policies are discussed, usually the password requirements and lockout settings get the spotlight. But there are also the Kerberos policy settings, which determine the behavior of Kerberos authentication activities in the domain. We don't have room in this book to explain Kerberos authentication in detail, and the good news is that I've not yet, personally, run across an enterprise that had a business need to modify the Kerberos policy settings. I'm sure such companies exist—I just haven't found one yet. Don't modify these settings until you have a very thorough understanding of Kerberos authentication, and—perhaps above all other policy setting changes—be absolutely certain that you have tested the proposed changes exhaustively in a lab environment.

# Customize the default GPOs to align with your enterprise policies

There are two default GPOs in an Active Directory domain: the Default Domain Policy and the Default Domain Controllers Policy. The former is responsible for password, lockout, Kerberos, and other authentication-related policy settings; the latter is responsible for settings regarding user rights on domain controllers and auditing of Active Directory–related activities.

As you probably know, it is absolutely a best practice to manage all password and lockout policies in a single GPO rather than to have several GPOs that, together, create the resultant policies for the domain. An individual setting, such as password length, ends up applying to all accounts in the domain. It is not possible using Group Policy to have one password length for some users and another password length for other users in a single domain—but that story changes with Password Settings objects in Windows Server 2008, which will be discussed later in this solution. Because there can be only one resultant policy setting for the entire domain, it makes sense to define them only once, in a single GPO.

The question is, should you modify the Default Domain GPO, or should you create your own GPO to implement your enterprise's password and lockout policies? In the early days of Active Directory, Microsoft's documentation and consultants, such as myself, recommended against modifying the default GPOs and recommended, instead, to create custom GPOs with higher precedence and to make changes to the custom GPOs. The recommendation was based on the fact that it was extremely difficult to reset the Default Domain Policy GPO back to its default settings. That is no longer the case. Microsoft has a Knowledge Base article that describes how to recover the Default Domain GPO: Knowledge Base (KB) article 324800 for Windows Server 2003 (*http://support.microsoft.com/kb/324800/en-us*). I also expect a KB article to be published for Windows Server 2008 following the product's release. You can also follow the best practice for modifying any GPO: Back it up first.

Therefore, to make visibility, auditing, troubleshooting, and all other management-related tasks more straightforward, I recommend that you modify the Default Domain GPO, but only for password, lockout, Kerberos, and authentication-related policies. In other words, look at the categories of policy settings managed by the default GPO—which you can do by clicking the Settings tab for the GPO in the GPMC—and make changes to settings only in those categories. If you have other policy settings that you want to apply to the domain—a password-protected screen saver, for example—create a custom GPO to implement those settings, as described in Solution 10-5 on page 669.

 **Best Practices**    Make changes to Account Policies already managed by the Default Domain Policy GPO by modifying that GPO directly, rather than attempting to override the settings with a custom GPO. Just be sure to back up the GPO prior to making changes.

# Implement your password, lockout, and Kerberos policies

You should modify the Default Domain Policy GPO to reflect your organization's policies for passwords, lockout, and Kerberos authentication. First, you must back up the Default Domain Policy GPO, using these steps:

1. Open the GPMC.
2. Expand the Forests and Domains nodes, and the node for the domain you want to manage.
3. Select the Group Policy Objects container.
4. In the details pane, right-click Default Domain Policy and choose Back Up.
5. Enter the name of, or browse to select, a folder in which to store the GPO backup.
6. Optionally, enter a description—for example, **Default Out-Of-Box Default Domain Policy GPO**.
7. Click Back up.
8. When the GPO backup operation is complete, click OK.

Now you are ready to implement your custom policy settings. To do so, perform these steps:

1. Open the GPMC.
2. Expand the Forests and Domains nodes and the node for the domain you want to manage.
3. In the console tree, select the Group Policy Objects container. In the details pane, right-click the Default Domain Policy and choose Edit.

   The Group Policy Management Editor (GPME) appears.
4. Navigate to Computer Configuration \ Policies \ Windows Settings \ Security Settings \ Account Policies, and expand Account Policies.
5. Select Password Policy in the console tree.
6. Modify password policy settings to reflect your enterprise policies.
7. Select Account Lockout Policy in the console tree.
8. Modify account lockout policy settings to reflect your enterprise policies.
9. Select Kerberos Policy in the console tree.
10. Modify Kerberos policy settings to reflect your enterprise policies.
11. Close the GPME.

# Implement fine-grained password policies to protect sensitive and privileged accounts

Prior to Windows Server 2008, the domain's resultant password and lockout policy applied to every user (and computer) account in the domain. It was not possible to carve out a subset of accounts and apply a stricter or looser password or lockout policy. If you wanted to do so, you needed separate domains or third-party password management utilities.

Windows Server 2008 introduces fine-grained password policies, which enable you to specify unique password and lockout policies for groups of users and for individual user accounts. It's a fantastic addition to Active Directory, but it requires you to implement the Windows Server 2008 domain functional level.

Fine-grained password policies are not part of Group Policy.

> **Important**    Let me repeat that: Fine-grained password policies are not part of Group Policy.

However, they allow you to target specific groups of users, or individual user accounts, for exemption from the single password and account policy that you established in the Default Domain Policy GPO; and fine-grained password policies are certainly part of the same solution—implementing your enterprise's password and lockout policies. So I'm including them in this Solution Collection.

> **More Info**    The details for implementing fine-grained password policies are found at *http://technet2.microsoft.com/windowsserver2008/en/library/2199dcf7-68fd-4315-87cc-ade35f8978ea1033.mspx*.

Rather than repeat each procedure related to fine-grained password policies here, I'd like to point out the best practices and some tips, because they tend to get lost in the gory details of the documentation, which tries to describe every way you can implement the policies. Let's focus on the best way to do so.

## Create Password Settings objects for each exception policy

The best practice is to define your domain's standard policy and lockout settings using the Default Domain GPO, as described in the previous section. Then create a Password Settings object (PSO) for each exception policy. You might have unique password and lockout requirements for the following items:

- Accounts in the Domain Admins group
- The domain's Administrator account

- Accounts that have been given security-sensitive delegation, including the ability to create OUs, change permissions on OUs, or reset user account passwords

- Service accounts

You define these unique, exceptional policies using Password Settings objects. PSOs are Active Directory objects just like GPOs, users, groups, and computers. They are records in the database that is Active Directory. All PSOs exist in a single container, the Password Settings Container (PSC), just as all GPOs exist in the Group Policies Container.

A PSO defines a collection of password and account lockout policy settings. The settings defined by a PSO are identical to those defined in the Default Domain Policy GPO. Table 10-1 summarizes the policy setting attributes of a PSO and their meanings.

**Table 10-1    PSO Password and Lockout Attributes**

| Attribute name | Description |
| --- | --- |
| msDS-PasswordHistoryLength | Password history length for user accounts |
| msDS-PasswordComplexityEnabled | Password complexity status for user accounts |
| msDS-MinimumPasswordLength | Minimum password length for user accounts |
| msDS-MinimumPasswordAge | Minimum password age for user accounts |
| msDS-MaximumPasswordAge | Maximum password age for user accounts |
| msDS-PasswordReversibleEncryptionEnabled | Password reversible encryption status for user accounts |
| msDS-LockoutThreshold | Lockout threshold for lockout of user accounts |
| msDS-LockoutObservationWindow | Observation window for lockout of user accounts |
| msDS-LockoutDuration | Lockout duration for locked-out user accounts |

Each attribute shown in Table 10-1 is a required attribute. A PSO must fully define the password and lockout policy—there is no merging or inheritance of settings. As you'll see later, a user account is under the management of one and only one password policy—either the domain's, or one and only one PSO. So each PSO must fully define each attribute of the policy.

## Scope each PSO to the groups or users to whom the policies should apply

While or after creating a PSO, you scope the PSO to apply to appropriate groups or users. The surprise here is that PSOs apply to groups, not to OUs. A little bit of analysis reveals that this design decision by Microsoft provides much greater flexibility for managing password policies. Service accounts, for example, might be scattered across multiple business-unit OUs to reflect the delegation of administrative control over those accounts. You can apply a strict password policy to those accounts without having to move them to a single OU.

The best practice is, of course, to scope PSOs to groups—specifically, global security groups. Following the tenets of role-based management, I suggest creating a capability management group that manages the capability to receive a PSO. For example, create a group called PSO_Service Account Passwords, where the prefix *PSO_* indicates that the group is used to manage the application of a PSO, and the remainder of the name matches the name of the PSO scoped by the group.

> **Important**    Groups used to scope PSOs must be global security groups.

PSOs are scoped to groups using the PSO's *msDS-PSOAppliesTo* attribute. You can configure this attribute when creating the PSO or afterward. It is a multivalued attribute of distinguished names of groups or users to whom the PSO applies.

Again, best practice and role-based management suggest that a PSO should apply to one group: the capability management global group—PSO_Service Account Passwords, for example. But occasionally you might apply PSOs directly to a user object. For example, you might create a PSO for the domain's Administrator account. If that is the only account to which the PSO will apply, you can skip the group and apply the PSO directly to that user account.

One final note about scoping PSOs to groups. Don't forget the technique covered in Solution 8-5 for creating shadow groups that dynamically update their membership based on an Active Directory query. So although PSOs are applied to groups, not to OUs, you can create a group that contains the users within an OU so that a PSO can, indirectly, be applied to the users in the OU.

## Understand PSO precedence

You can imagine that it's possible for a user to belong to more than one group, to whom separate PSOs are applied. I mentioned earlier that only one PSO ends up affecting a user. Which one? The answer is found in the last attribute of a PSO—the one I've yet to mention—called *msDS-PasswordSettingsPrecedence*. This attribute takes a value greater than zero and, if an account is within the scope of more than one PSO, the greater precedence value wins. But wait! "Greater" actually means "closer to 1." The precedence value of 1 is the highest precedence. So if two PSOs are scoped to groups to which a user belongs, one with the precedence set to 10 and the other with a precedence of 20, the PSO with the precedence value of 10 applies to the user. There is no merging or inheritance of settings. The password settings that have an impact on that user's account are all those defined by the PSO with a precedence of 10.

But it's not quite that simple. If a user belongs to groups and the groups are linked to by the PSO, it works as I just described. But if a user is linked to directly by a PSO—that is, if a PSO's *msDS-PSOAppliesTo* attribute points directly to the user—none of the group PSOs apply. Only the user-linked PSO applies. It doesn't matter what precedence the group PSOs have—they're out of the running.

If by some chance two or more PSOs link directly to the user, the precedence of those PSOs determines which one wins. But group PSOs will still be out of the race, no matter what their precedence is. And I recommend that you avoid getting yourself into situations where two or more PSOs link to an individual user. That would indicate a mistake, or poor management of PSOs, to a consultant like myself.

## Use a unique precedence value for each PSO

To facilitate management of PSOs, I recommend entering a unique value for *msDS-Password-SettingsPrecedence* for each PSO you create. The value of *msDS-PasswordSettingsPrecedence* can be anything greater than zero. Remember that the value 1 is the highest precedence. Don't feel like you have to bunch up all your precedence values. Perhaps the first three PSOs you create have values 100, 500, and 1000. That gives you plenty of wiggle room for new PSOs that fall ahead of, behind, or between those three PSOs.

By the way, if two PSOs apply to a user and the PSOs both have the same precedence, the object with the smallest GUID wins. Effectively, this means that Windows makes a choice that you're not in control of. Don't get yourself into that situation. Use unique precedence values.

## View resultant PSO for a user or group

It's up to you to manage the precedence values of your PSOs, but Windows takes away the need for you to do the math to determine which PSO will apply to a user or group. For any user or group, you can look at the object's properties in the Active Directory Users and Computers snap-in. On the Attribute Editor tab that is visible when Advanced Features are enabled, you can view the *msDS-ResultantPSO* attribute, which is a calculated attribute that reveals the name of the effective PSO.

Slick! Too bad you have to dig so deep to get it. In the Scripts folder of the companion media, I've provided User_ResultantPSO.hta, which shows the resultant PSO for any user. Like other HTAs in this resource kit, you can open it directly or use it as a taskpad task or context menu command, as described in Solution Collection 1.

## Delegate the management of password policy application

Microsoft's online documentation, mentioned earlier, goes into detail about how to delegate the creation of PSOs and the application of PSOs to groups. Here's my advice: don't. Password policies are a critical element of security for your enterprise. A centralized effort should result in the creation of PSOs linked to capability management groups. Don't delegate the creation of PSOs. Don't delegate the linking of PSOs to groups.

What you can do, as appropriate, is delegate the membership of the capability management groups. For example, you might give your server administrators the ability to add service accounts to the PSO_Service Account Passwords group. By doing so, they are effectively applying the PSO to the accounts, but they are doing it indirectly, without touching the attributes of the PSO itself.

### Make it all so much easier

To summarize, you create a PSO for each unique password policy in your organization, and then you apply the PSOs to global groups or, in exceptional scenarios, to individual users. The links and precedence of PSOs are used to decide which one PSO determines the password policy that affects a specific user.

Microsoft's detailed documentation at *http://technet2.microsoft.com/windowsserver2008/en/library/2199dcf7-68fd-4315-87cc-ade35f8978ea1033.mspx* reveals one of the dirty little secrets about fine-grained password policies in Windows Server 2008: The tools that are available to manage them are lousy. You have to use ADSI Edit and the Attribute Editor tab in the Active Directory Users and Computers snap-in to create and manage PSOs by direct manipulation of the attributes. There's no pretty GUI or easy tool to manage PSOs in Windows.

Why? Beats me. This feature was nailed down very early in the development of what was then called Longhorn Server. I guess that team sent the user-interface guy over to the Server Manager tool team.

Luckily, Special Operations Software, a Swedish company, came to the rescue of administrators worldwide with a tool called Password Policy Basic. It's a free—let me repeat, *free*—tool that you really can't live without if you're managing fine-grained password policy. It takes all the crazy attribute-level PSO procedures that Microsoft expects you to perform and makes them very accessible and easy to manage. The tool is available from *www.specopssoft.com*.

 **Note**    Before you even begin to implement fine-grained password policy, make sure you have the free utility from Special Operations Software.

## Solution summary

Your enterprise's password and account lockout policies are the front line of defense against access to your domain through a compromised user account. We explored some of the big-picture issues: that passwords must be much longer but that they can be made easier for users to remember, and that account lockout policies must be designed with consideration of denial-of-service exposure. We learned how to modify the Default Domain Policy GPO to implement your standard password and lockout policy. Finally, we discovered a long-awaited enhancement to Windows Server 2008's Active Directory: fine-grained password policies.

# 10-4: Implement Your Authentication and Active Directory Auditing Policies

## Solution overview

| | |
|---|---|
| **Type of solution** | Guidance |
| **Features and tools** | Default Domain Controllers Policy GPO, auditing policy settings, system access control lists, Security log |
| **Solution summary** | Modify the Default Domain Controllers Policy GPO to reflect your business's needs for auditing of authentication and Active Directory changes. |
| **Benefits** | Optimized levels of auditing to identify problems and ensure compliance |

## Introduction

Just as the out-of-box default password policies in an Active Directory domain must be tailored to your enterprise, there is likely to be similar lack of alignment between the auditing policies of a default configuration and those required by your organization. Your enterprise's auditing needs should be driven by a determination of the security events that are of concern, based on an analysis of security exposures, and by requirements for auditing, logging, and reporting placed on your organization by external factors such as compliance regulations. In this solution, I'll explain how to implement your enterprise's auditing policies by modifying the Default Domain Controllers Policy GPO, and how to expose new levels of auditing detail using Windows Server 2008 Directory Service Changes auditing.

## Implement your auditing policies by modifying the Default Domain Controllers Policy GPO

The Default Domain Controllers Policy GPO is responsible for managing the auditing settings for domain controllers. It also configures the user rights that apply to users accessing domain controllers locally, using remote desktop or over the network. Users access DCs over the network when they open their GPTs and logon scripts.

In the previous solution, I discussed the fact that, contrary to early best practices, it is now recommended by most pundits, including myself, to configure the Default Domain Policy GPO rather than to create a custom GPO for the domain's password policies. My recommendation applies also to the Default Domain Controllers Policy GPO. Change it to reflect your organization's requirements for user rights on domain controllers and other settings already managed by the default GPO. In addition, use the Default Domain Controllers Policy GPO to configure auditing policies for Active Directory–related activities, which we'll discuss in the following paragraphs. For categories of settings not already managed by that GPO, create a custom GPO—although you should not need to configure settings other than the existing settings, particularly for dedicated domain controllers.

> **Caution**    Organizations often want more detailed auditing for domain controllers and Active Directory. Be sure that these settings are scoped to domain controllers only, by changing the Default Domain Controllers Policy GPO. I've seen several environments where high levels of auditing were applied in the Default Domain Policy GPO, which effects that auditing on every server and client computer—causing an unnecessary performance impact on those systems. Scope your policies carefully.

You should use the Default Domain Controllers Policy GPO to implement your enterprise's policies related to the auditing of authentication and Active Directory changes. Like password and lockout policies, there can be only one resultant setting that applies to all domain controllers; otherwise, auditing and logs would be chaotic. Therefore, it is best to manage auditing settings in a single GPO. Because only domain controllers are capable of auditing Active Directory activities, you should scope the settings to DCs only. The Default Domain Controllers Policy GPO contains the out-of-box default settings for domain controllers. Customize it. To edit the Default Domain Controllers Policy auditing policy settings, perform these steps:

1. Open the GPMC.

2. Expand the Forests and Domains nodes, and the node for the domain you want to manage.

3. Expand the Domain Controllers OU.

4. Right-click the Default Domain Controllers Policy and choose Edit.

   The Group Policy Management Editor (GPME) appears.

5. Navigate to Computer Configuration \ Policies \ Windows Settings \ Security Settings \ Local Policies, and expand Local Policies.

6. Select Audit Policy.

Within the Audit Policy container are settings that affect the auditing of Active Directory changes as well as other activities. Table 10-2 provides a summary of the Active Directory–related audit policies and their default settings.

Table 10-2  **Active Directory–Related Auditing Settings**

| Auditing Policy Setting | Explanation | Default Setting for Windows Server 2008 Domain Controllers |
|---|---|---|
| Audit Account Logon Events | Creates an event when a user or computer attempts to authenticate using an Active Directory account. For example, when a user logs on to any computer in the domain, an account logon event is generated. | Successful account logons are audited. |
| Audit Logon Events | Creates an event when a user logs on interactively (locally) to a computer or over the network (remotely). For example, if a workstation and a server are configured to audit logon events, the workstation audits a user logging on directly to that workstation. When the user connects to a shared folder on the server, the server logs that remote logon. When a user logs on, the domain controller records a logon event because logon scripts and policies are retrieved from the DC. | Successful logons are audited. |
| Audit Account Management | Audits events, including the creation, deletion, or modification of user, group, or computer accounts and the resetting of user passwords. | Successful account management activities are audited. |
| Audit Directory Service Access | Audits events that are specified in the system ACL (SACL), which is seen in an Active Directory object's Properties Advanced Security Settings dialog box. In addition to defining the audit policy with this setting, you must also configure auditing for the specific object or objects using the SACL of the object or objects. This policy is similar to the Audit Object Access policy used to audit files and folders, but this policy applies to Active Directory objects. | Successful directory service access events are audited, but few objects' SACLs specify audit settings. See the discussion later in this solution for more information. |
| Audit Policy Change | Audits changes to user rights assignment policies, audit policies, or trust policies. | Successful policy changes are audited. |
| Audit Privilege Use | Audits the use of a privilege or user right. See the explanatory text for this policy in the GPME. | No auditing is performed by default. |
| Audit System Events | Audits system restart, shutdown, or changes that affect the system or security log. | Successful system events are audited. |

As you can see, most major events are already audited by domain controllers, assuming that the events are successful. So the creation of a user, the resetting of a user's password, a user's logon to the domain, and retrieval of her logon scripts—all of these activities are logged. Two major categories of events are not logged: failure events and changes to specific properties of objects.

## Consider auditing failure events

You might need to implement failure auditing based on your organization's IT security policies and requirements. Auditing failed account logon events, for example, will expose malicious attempts to access the domain by repeatedly trying to log on as a domain user account without yet knowing the account's password. Auditing failed account management events can reveal someone attempting to manipulate the membership of a security-sensitive group.

## Align auditing policies, corporate policies, and reality

One of the most important tasks you must fulfill is to balance and align the auditing policy settings of Active Directory with your corporate policies and reality. Let me explain. Your corporate policy might state that all failed logons and successful changes to Active Directory users and groups must be audited. That's easy to achieve in Active Directory. But how, exactly, are you going to use that information? Verbose auditing logs are useless if you don't know how or don't have the tools to manage those logs effectively. If a tree falls in a forest and nobody is around, does it make a sound? If a failed account logon event is logged and nobody's looking, does it matter? Good luck with this task, as it is a political and business task more than a technical one.

## Audit changes to Active Directory objects

Another broad class of events that are not audited are changes to Active Directory objects or their specific properties. For example, changing the membership of a group is not audited.

To audit changes to Active Directory objects, two things must be in place. The audit policy must be enabled, and the system ACL (SACL) of an object must be configured to trigger auditing. By default, the Audit Directory Service Access policy is defined to audit successful events, but the SACLs of most Active Directory objects—groups, for example—do not specify audit settings.

One of the classes of changes that are audited by default is composed of changes to Group Policy object links. Figure 10-3 shows the Auditing Entry dialog box from my Groups OU. The entry directs the domain controller to audit new or deleted GPO links.

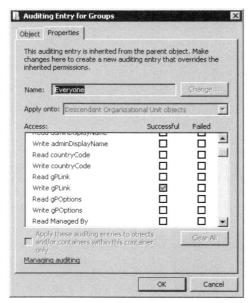

**Figure 10-3** The SACL of the Groups OU, showing that changes to Group Policy links will be audited

To access the auditing settings in the SACL of an Active Directory object, follow this procedure:

1. Open the Active Directory Users and Computers snap-in.

2. Click the View menu, and ensure that Advanced Features is selected.

3. Right-click an object and choose Properties.

   As with the management of permissions in the discretionary ACLs (DACLs) of Active Directory objects, it is a best practice to manage auditing settings in the SACLs by configuring auditing on an OU, and allowing those settings to be inherited by objects within the OU.

   Therefore, you will most often be right-clicking an OU to manage auditing settings.

4. Click the Security tab.

5. Click the Advanced button.

6. Click the Auditing tab.

   The auditing entries are summarized on the Auditing tab. To view the individual settings in each entry, continue to the next step.

7. Select an entry from the Auditing Entries list, and click the Edit button.

   The Auditing Entry dialog box appears.

You can configure audit settings similarly to the configuration of permissions. Select the object class for which auditing should be performed, and then choose the object or property-level access that you want to audit. I can't emphasize enough that you must consider the reality that more auditing means more logging, which means more data to weed through. Don't overaudit unless you are prepared to process the resulting volume of information to locate the specific events that are of concern to your enterprise.

## View audit events in the Security log

After you have enabled the Audit Directory Service Access policy setting and specified the events you want to audit using object SACLs, you can view the events that are logged by audit triggers in the Security log of the domain controller. Domain controller event logs are specific to the DC—they are not replicated. But the audit policies and SACLs of Active Directory objects are replicated. That means you must examine the security log of each domain controller to locate events.

 **Important**   You must examine the Security log of all domain controllers to locate events, because although auditing-related settings are replicated between domain controllers, the logs are not.

Windows Server 2008's event logs have been completely re-architected to allow you to consolidate and centralize specific logs or events. After the release of Windows Server 2008, the Windows Server 2008 technical library on the TechNet site (*http://technet.microsoft.com*) will have documentation about leveraging the new capabilities of the event logs. As of the writing of this solution, information about new event features can be found in the Troubleshooting \ Events and Errors \ Management Infrastructure container in the technical library.

## Leverage Directory Service Changes auditing

In Windows Server 2003 and Windows 2000 Server, you could audit directory service access, and you would be notified that an object, or the property of an object, had been changed, but you could not identify the previous and new values of the attribute that had changed.

Windows Server 2008 adds an auditing category called Directory Service Changes. The important distinction between Directory Service Changes and Directory Service Access is that with Directory Service Changes auditing, you can identify the previous and current values of a changed attribute, the previous and new location of a moved object, and changes related to the undoing the deletion of objects.

Directory Service Changes is not enabled by default in Windows Server 2008. Instead, Directory Service Access is enabled to mimic the auditing functionality of previous versions of Windows. To enable auditing of successful Directory Service Changes, open a command prompt on a domain controller and enter this command:

```
auditpol /set /subcategory:"directory service changes" /success:enable
```

You must still modify the SACL of objects to specify which attributes should be audited. Although you can use the preceding command to enable Directory Service Changes auditing in a lab and explore the events that are generated, don't implement this in a domain until you've read the documentation on TechNet, starting with the step-by-step guide found at *http://technet2.microsoft.com/windowsserver2008/en/library/a9c25483-89e2-4202-881c-ea8e02b4b2a51033.mspx*.

## Audit changes to the membership of Domain Admins

To understand the benefit of Directory Service Changes auditing, first examine Figure 10-4. This figure shows a Directory Service Access event log entry resulting from a change to the membership of the Domain Admins group. Directory Service Access events are available in both Windows Server 2008 and Windows Sever 2003. The Event ID is 4662 in Windows Server 2008. If an equivalent event is logged on a Windows Server 2003 DC, it is given Event ID 566.

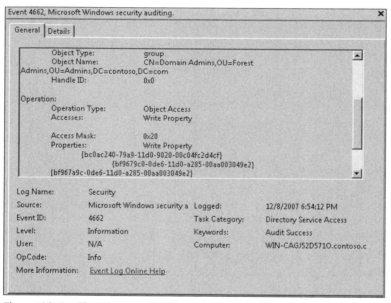

**Figure 10-4**   The Directory Service Access event for a change to the membership of Domain Admins

It's not exactly easy to identify what happened here. The group, Domain Admins, is clearly indicated, but the change is shown as a Write Property access to properties of certain GUIDs. Not very administrator friendly.

Now examine Figure 10-5, which shows the Directory Service Changes event, Event ID 5136, for the exact same action. The group, property, action, and value are all indicated. I know that Mike Fitzmaurice was added to the Domain Admins group. Higher up (but not shown in the figure) is the name of the user who made the change. The new Directory Service Changes event is much more detailed and administrator friendly.

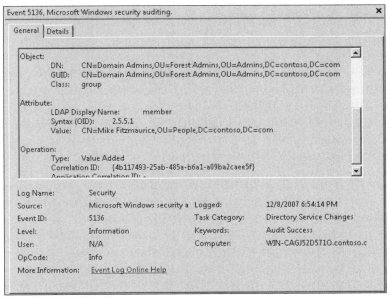

**Figure 10-5**   The Directory Service Changes event for a change to the membership of Domain Admins

## Solution summary

Most organizations require some level of auditing for authentication and the modification of certain Active Directory objects. In this solution, we examined the steps required to implement auditing of Active Directory–related activities by modifying the settings of the Default Domain Controllers Policy GPO. We also examined the new feature of Windows Server 2008, Directory Services Changes auditing, which enables you to see not only that something changed in Active Directory but also the attribute name, previous values, and new values.

# 10-5: Enforce Corporate Policies with Group Policy

## Solution overview

| | |
|---|---|
| **Type of solution** | Guidance |
| **Features and tools** | Domain-linked GPOs, security group filtering, enforced GPO links |
| **Solution summary** | Enforce corporate IT security and usage policies using enforced, domain-linked GPOs, but be prepared to manage exceptions and migration to the policies. |
| **Benefits** | Fully managed application of corporate IT security and usage policies |

# Introduction

Your organization probably—hopefully—has a document that specifies its policies regarding IT security and the usage of company computers and networks. If not, you should develop one! Assuming you have something like that in place, or at least thought out, you can begin to implement those policies within your Active Directory domain by creating domain-linked GPOs with enforced settings.

For example, many organizations require that systems have a password-protected screen saver to prevent unlocked computers from being accessed by unauthorized and unauthenticated personnel. Those policy settings would be scoped to all systems using a domain-linked GPO. There might also be corporate policies regarding the use of computers—for example, you might prohibit users from directly installing software on their systems.

In this solution, we'll discuss the steps you can take to enforce security and usage policies using Group Policy objects. If you haven't put such GPOs in place yet, don't just run out and do it, because you are likely to break some things when you do! Careful testing and thoughtful migration is required. In this solution, I'll also detail how to provide a managed migration path to the universal, or almost-universal, application of those policies.

## Translate corporate policies to security and nonsecurity settings

The first step in this exercise is to translate the corporate IT security and usage policies, which are usually documented in a human-readable form, into the specific settings required to implement those policies on Windows systems. This is a step that is so dependent upon your specific policies that I'll have to leave it to you, your expertise, and your consultants to help you make the leap.

## Create GPOs to configure settings derived from corporate policies

After you've identified the settings required to enforce your corporate policies, you are ready to create GPOs that implement them. If your security policies are cohesive and should be applied to all systems and users in the domain, you can get by with a single GPO. There might be reasons to break settings up across several GPOs, which we'll address later.

## Scope GPOs to the domain

Corporate security and usage policies must apply to all computers and users in an enterprise. That's why they're policies, right? So GPOs that implement settings related to these policies must be scoped to the entire domain. After you have created the GPO and have allowed the GPC and the GPT to replicate, link the GPO to the domain.

# Enforce corporate security and configuration policies

As you know, GPOs are applied by clients in an order commonly abbreviated as *SDOU*: site, domain, and organizational unit. Client-side extensions first apply the policies that are linked to the client's site, then the policies linked to the client's domain, and then the policies linked to the OUs in the path of the client's distinguished name. If there are conflicting policy settings, the policy setting that is closest to the user or computer object takes precedence. So, for example, if the corporate, domain-scoped GPO specifies a 10-minute screen-saver timeout, but a GPO linked to a business unit OU configures a 30-minute timeout, the users in that business unit will experience a 30-minute timeout.

The theory behind the GPO application and precedence model is that a setting that is scoped broadly—to the domain, for example—is a general rule. Settings that are scoped more narrowly, and more closely to the user or computer, are more specifically targeted and therefore should take precedence. Although this model works well for most policy and change management scenarios, it does not work well for policies that implement corporate security and IT usage policies. Those corporate-level policies that are carved in stone, and should absolutely apply to all users and computers, must take precedence.

So for GPOs that implement corporate security and IT usage policies, you must set the options of the GPO link to *enforce* the GPO. To enforce a GPO, right-click the link that scopes the GPO and select Enforced, as shown in Figure 10-6.

**Figure 10-6**  Enforcing a Group Policy object's settings

When a GPO is enforced, its settings take precedence over conflicting settings of GPOs that would otherwise have precedence. Enforced GPOs also apply to users and computers in OUs that are configured to block inheritance. So even if an OU is blocking other, higher-scoped GPOs, the enforced GPOs will be applied. These behaviors make enforced GPOs optimal for applying settings that, according to corporate policies, must be consistently applied. The only ways to exempt a user or computer from an enforced GPO are either to assign the Deny::Apply Group Policy permission to the exempt objects or to have another GPO with even higher precedence.

> **Best Practices**    Configure settings that are driven by corporate security and IT usage policies in GPOs that are linked to the domain and are enforced.

# Proactively manage exemptions

Even settings related to corporate IT security and usage policies have exceptions. For example, I ran across a client whose legal and security teams had determined that a logon message was required—that every time users log on to a system, they must be presented a message that reminds them that the system and its data are corporate assets and that using the system implies consent to abide by security and usage policies. That's a pretty common setting to enforce with Group Policy. Unfortunately, there were a couple of systems that ran a custom application that had been written ages ago by a developer who had long since departed from the company. This application required that the computer use automatic logon so that, in the event of a power outage or other restart, the application would resume automatically. The logon banner interfered with automatic logon, so those systems had to be exempted from the policy.

The key that is required to manage exemptions is a global security group to which the Deny::Apply Group Policy permission has been assigned. Objects in this group will not receive the settings that are implemented by the GPO. Creating an exemption group with this method was detailed in Solution 10-2 on page 644.

# Provide a managed migration path to policy implementation

The exemption group is also your ticket to the migration to policy enforcement. Let's assume your current environment is not subject to one or more settings that must now be applied to ensure compliance with corporate policies. If you blast that change out to your entire domain, you're likely to break something. Most corporate policies have an impact on security settings, which might have an impact on the behavior of a user, application, service, or device. Of course, you must test settings before bringing them into the production environment, but you must also account for the fact that there will always be unforeseen problems. As long as you can manage those problems, you are in great shape.

So, to migrate to the new settings, which you have created in a GPO that is filtered with an exemption group, you can add *every* user and computer to the exemption group before you enable and enforce the link. Doing so means that the GPO and its settings are let loose in your domain, but nobody is listening.

You can then begin to thoughtfully migrate users and computers *out* of the exemption group, thereby allowing them to receive the settings. If a problem is encountered, then whoops!—you put the object back into the exemption group. The exemption group becomes your management tool. It allows you to see the objects that remain to be migrated, or that must be examined for troubleshooting purposes.

To take this approach to the next level to manage the migration of a significant new GPO, consider creating three exemption groups. I'll call them GPO_PolicyName_Not Yet Applied, GPO_PolicyName_Exemptions, and GPO_PolicyName_Troubleshoot.

All objects (users and computers) begin in the Not Yet Applied group. When you move an object out of that group and the GPO is applied, if the change is successful, you're finished. If the change causes a problem, you move the object into the Troubleshoot group, which is also exempt from the GPO. That group records the objects that must be more closely examined to determine the causes of the problem. As you evaluate an object, you either remove it from the Troubleshoot group to once again receive the settings or move it to the Exemptions group, which collects objects that will, for the near term at least, continue to be exempt from the policy because the problem could not be solved.

Your goal in this approach is to empty out the Not Yet Applied and Troubleshoot groups, at which point you have migrated as fully as possible to the GPO and its settings. The Exemption group maintains, manages, and records the objects that—for whatever reason—cannot be subject to the settings. Obviously, over time, you address those problem children if possible so that the policy can be applied domain-wide and unfiltered.

## Determine whether you need more than one GPO for corporate policy implementation

Earlier in this solution, I suggested that you might be able to get away with a single GPO for the implementation of corporate IT security and usage policies. Now that we've discussed the migration path, you can see why you might need more than one GPO. If certain objects—users or computers—cannot be subject to the single GPO because a subset of its settings causes things to break, you should separate out those problematic settings. The GPO or GPOs with the problematic settings can be filtered by exemption groups, and settings that you are able to successfully apply to all domain objects can be applied in the unfiltered GPO.

In other words, you don't want to prevent all settings from applying to exempted objects just because a subset of those settings are problematic. Split up the settings so that each object can receive as many of the corporate policy settings as possible.

## Solution summary

Corporate IT security and usage policies can be implemented in an Active Directory domain by creating one or more domain-linked Group Policy objects with enforced links that will assure the organization that settings will be applied by Windows systems. Because such settings are significant and likely to cause isolated problems with applications or processes, you should create an exemption group for each GPO that allows you to specify which users or computers do not receive that GPO's settings. To migrate to an enterprise-wide GPO implementation of security and usage policies, you can begin with all users and computers in the exemption groups so that no object is actually affected by the settings. You can then perform a thoughtful migration of objects, removing them from exemption to receive settings, and returning them to exemption in the event of problems. The exemption groups provide a point of management and visibility of the migration's progress.

# 10-6: Create a Delegated Group Policy Management Hierarchy

## Solution overview

| | |
|---|---|
| Type of solution | Guidance |
| Features and tools | Group Policy delegation, starter GPOs |
| Solution summary | Delegate appropriate subsets of Group Policy management tasks. |
| Benefits | Realize the cost savings and manageability benefits of Group Policy. |

## Introduction

To this point in the Solution Collection, we have discussed GPOs linked very high in the Active Directory structure—to the domain and to the Domain Controllers OU. We used security groups to filter the effective scope of domain-linked GPOs. Linking GPOs to OUs to manage the GPOs' scope is nice because it saves a very small amount of processing over the evaluation of security group filters (GPO ACLs). But from a practical perspective—particularly in organizations with any size or complexity—OU links rarely fall out of a careful analysis as the most manageable solution for deploying policies in the enterprise.

However, some organizations choose to create a less centralized management framework for Group Policy, in which enterprise-level policies are deployed as we've discussed so far, but business units, sites, or other organizational divisions have the ability to leverage Group Policy to manage configuration. For example, I have two large clients in which the enterprise manages domain-level policies, and business units are able to create and manage GPOs scoped to their business. In this solution, we'll look at both the technical and business issues related to delegating the management of Group Policy.

Let's start by examining the technical procedures related to delegating Group Policy management. As an example, we'll assume that Contoso has a business unit that produces video games. The business unit's users and computers are within a Video Games OU. Video Games' administrators have asked for the ability to manage change using Group Policy.

## Delegate permissions to link existing GPOs to an OU

The most restrictive way to delegate GPO management is to allow individuals to link existing GPOs to an OU. Doing so allows the enterprise to maintain strict control over the number of GPOs in the environment and the settings in the GPOs, but it allows divisional administrators to pick and choose specific GPOs, as if from a menu, and apply those GPOs to their users and computers. To delegate permission to manage GPO links, follow these steps:

1. Open the Active Directory Users and Computers snap-in.

2. Right-click the OU for which you will delegate the Manage Group Policy Links permission and choose Delegate Control.

   The Delegation Of Control Wizard appears.

3. Click Next.

4. Click Add, and select the group to which you will delegate Manage Group Policy Links permission.

5. Click Next.

6. Select the Manage Group Policy links check box, as shown in Figure 10-7.

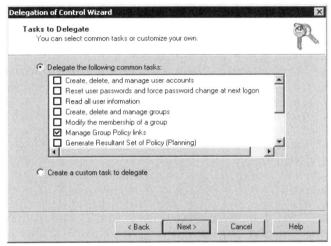

**Figure 10-7**   Delegate the Manage Group Policy Links permission.

7. Click Next.

8. Click Finish.

The delegation that is applied allows the group to manage (that is, create and delete) the linked GPOs and to manage the link options, such as whether the link is enforced. You can also use the Dsacls command, discussed in Solution 5-5 on page 391, to delegate the management of GPO Links. Use these commands:

```
dsacls "OUDN" /I:S /G "DOMAIN\group":rpwp;gpLink
dsacls "OUDN" /I:S /G "DOMAIN\group":rpwp;gPOptions
```

Keep in mind that by doing so you are delegating the abilities both to create and delete links, so the divisional administrators can delete GPOs that you've linked to the OU. If you have delegated the management of GPO links, you must ensure that enterprise policies are enforced at the domain level so that changes made in OUs do not interfere with or override those policies.

# Delegate the ability to manage an existing GPO

You can also delegate to an individual or team the ability to modify settings within an existing GPO, to manage the security of the GPO, or to delete the GPO. Tailspin Toys' administrators created a GPO and linked it to the Video Games OU. They can now delegate GPO settings management to the Video Games administrators. To delegate the ability to modify settings of an existing GPO, follow these steps:

1. Open the GPMC.

2. In the console tree, select the GPO in the Group Policy Objects container.

3. In the details pane, click the Delegation tab.

4. Click the Add button.

5. In the Select User, Computer, Or Group dialog box, enter the name of, or browse to identify, the group to which settings management will be delegated. Click OK.

   The tenets of role-based administration suggest that you create a capability management group to manage the delegation of GPO settings management. For example, you can create a group called AD_GPO_PolicyName_Settings Management.

6. In the Add Group Or User dialog box, select the authority you want to delegate to the selected group. Figure 10-8 shows an example.

7. Click OK.

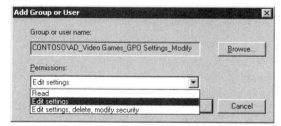

**Figure 10-8**   Delegation of management of an existing GPO

The Permissions list shown in Figure 10-8 reveals the common permissions delegated for an existing GPO. Read permission allows the specified group to open the GPO and examine its settings. By default, Authenticated Users can Read a GPO. So you need to delegate Read permission only if you've removed Authenticated Users from the GPOs ACL in order to filter the GPO to apply to a specific security group. Read permission is implied by the other two permissions.

The Edit Settings permission allows the specified group to modify the GPO's settings. This permission is called for in our example of the Tailspin Toys' Video Games division. There's no way to specify *which* settings can be changed. It's all or nothing. Sorry to be the bearer of bad news.

The Edit Settings, Delete, Modify Security permission extends the Edit Settings permission to allow the specified group to delete the GPO altogether and to modify the ACL on the GPO. The latter permission allows the group to change the security group filtering of the GPO, which, in the case of a business unit GPO, might make sense. The Video Games administrators might want to filter the GPO to apply only to engineers in the business unit, using an appropriate security group.

# Delegate permission to create GPOs

In the old days, you had to add a user to the Group Policy Creators group for the user to be allowed permission to create a GPO. Now you can click the Delegation tab of the Group Policy Objects container and add a user or group, as shown in Figure 10-9.

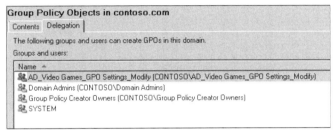

**Figure 10-9**   Delegation of GPO creation using the Group Policy Objects container in the GPMC

Is this any more dangerous than delegating the ability to modify the settings of an existing GPO? In my opinion, there is no practical difference. If an administrator is going to do something stupid or malicious, he can do it just as well within a single existing GPO to which you've delegated the right to modify settings as he can do it by creating a new GPO.

It's all a question of *scope*. If an administrator can create GPOs, she can change their settings, but those settings won't affect users or computers in the domain until that GPO is linked to an OU (or domain or site) to establish its maximum scope. So the real question is this: "To which OUs can the administrator link her new GPOs?" If she's limited to her own business unit, the maximum scope of the benefit or damage caused by the GPO is her business unit.

## Provide a baseline GPO for new GPOs

If you allow a divisional administrator to create a GPO, you might want to give that administrator a head start by providing a baseline GPO with common settings so that the administrator can tweak those existing settings rather than build a GPO from scratch. There are three ways to achieve this goal.

First, you can use the new Starter GPO functionality of Windows Server 2008. When you create a new GPO, you can base it on a starter GPO, which is a kind of template. Unfortunately, starter GPOs contain only registry policy settings—those stored in administrative templates—so I think their functionality is far too limited.

The second option is to create a kind of template GPO and back up its settings. When the divisional administrator creates her GPO, she can import those settings as a baseline.

The third, and potentially most powerful, approach is to script the creation of GPOs. Darren Mar-Elia, Group Policy MVP, has created a groundbreaking tool that scripts GPO settings. You can check the tool out at *http://www.sdmsoftware.com*. Think about it. You could create scripts that generate specific sets of policy settings. A down-level administrator could use a proxy tool, similar to the tool introduced in Solution Collection 8 to request that those settings be added to a GPO. Putting those two pieces together, you have given down-level administrators the ability to respond to the needs of their customers while maintaining tight control over the creation, modification, and management of Group Policy.

## Understand the business and technical concerns of Group Policy delegation

That leads us to an examination of the basic question: "Should our enterprise delegate the management of Group Policy or keep it centralized?" The *technical* answer is: It doesn't matter. The *political* answer is: It depends on business requirements, expertise, and trust.

Remember that, in the end, Group Policy is managing configuration. As an administrator of systems in your division, you can make changes to them. You could go to each machine and rename the Administrator account, disable or enable the firewall, and do all kinds of other things that could improve or worsen the security, performance, and functionality of your systems. You could even make changes that would prevent the successful application of enterprise-level GPOs. With Group Policy, you can do all those things in one place, centrally. So you can more easily respond to help desk calls by implementing a change that improves the user experience, and you can more easily mess things up for everyone. Your power that can be used for good can also be used for evil—Group Policy just makes your power more easily applied to your realm.

That's why, from a technical perspective, if your organization centralizes the management of GPOs and prevents you from leveraging and implementing Group Policy directly to the systems and users in your part of the enterprise, the organization is not removing your effective ability to make positive or negative changes to your environment. They're just removing one tool. Pull out a script editor and you can go back to making positive or negative changes.

To me, it's all about training, managing *scope*, and monitoring. If you've been trained to effectively implement Group Policy, if the scope of your power is effectively managed by, for example, delegating the ability to link GPOs to only your OUs, and if both you and your enterprise are monitoring Group Policy to make sure that settings are both being applied correctly and producing the intended effects, it's all good! I tend to encourage customers to push the envelope of decentralizing Group Policy management. My feeling is that, for example, the Help Desk at an organization is sitting on top of a wealth of knowledge about how the environment could be improved. If that knowledge could be channeled into changes deployed through GPOs, the cost of support would be significantly reduced. Someone other than the top-of-the-pyramid domain administrators should be able to tackle that project!

My perspective does not translate into a universal, bulletproof recommendation, however. Absolutely, there are environments in which strict, centralized control of Group Policy is critical. But I challenge you to start from a perspective that a thoughtful delegation of Group Policy management can unlock significant savings through improved configuration of user and computer settings, and then prove to me that doing so would be too dangerous for your enterprise based on its policies and requirements. Then prove to me that those effects could not be managed away using higher-level tools, such as domain-linked and enforced GPOs, monitoring, and auditing.

## Solution summary

It is technically feasible to delegate the management of Group Policy at several levels. You can allow administrators to link existing GPOs to their OUs. You can enable them to change settings within existing GPOs. And you can enable them to create a GPO, although they still will be limited by the GPO link delegation as to the maximum scope of the newly created GPO. I believe that most enterprises are leaning toward tightly controlled and centralized Group Policy management at the expense of agility and reduced support costs that could be obtained by delegating the power of Group Policy to levels of the organization that experience the pain of poor configuration. With training, scope management, monitoring, and auditing, most of these enterprises could confidently delegate Group Policy management to some extent and realize significant value from it.

# 10-7: Testing, Piloting, Validating, and Migrating Policy Settings

## Solution overview

| | |
|---|---|
| **Type of solution** | Guidance |
| **Features and tools** | Security group filtering, resultant set of policy modeling and reporting |
| **Solution summary** | Implement effective processes for testing a change in the lab, moving that change into the production environment for a limited pilot, and migrating the change to a widespread production deployment. |
| **Benefits** | Increased confidence and manageability of change; full rollback capability. |

## Introduction

In Solution 10-1 on page 637, I stepped you through the phases of change management. However, I touched only briefly on the critical phases of conducting a pilot test of a change and migrating the change to a widespread deployment. In this solution, I detail these phases, leveraging many of the scoping and other manageability techniques introduced earlier in this Solution Collection.

# Create an effective scope of management for a pilot test

After the settings and scoping mechanisms of a change have been proven in an isolated lab environment, as described in Solution 10-1, you are ready to evaluate the change in the real world of your enterprise in a pilot test. I suggest that the only way to do this properly is to apply the change to existing systems or users without segregating those objects to an artificial or separate environment. I've seen many enterprises test Group Policies in a separate OU—and often the OU is completely different from what would be considered "normal" OUs for computers or users, so objects in the OU are not subject to the same policies or other environmental influences.

So when it comes time to test the effect of a proposed change in the production environment, scope the test to a security group that includes pilot computers or users selected to create a representative sample of users and computers.

> **Best Practices**    Scope the pilot test of a change using a security group rather than a separate OU. Include a sample of users and computers in the group that is representative of the objects that will be scoped by the change in its final deployment.

# Prepare for and model the effects of the pilot test

To prepare a pilot of a proposed change, perform the tasks in the following list. Detailed, step-by-step procedures for each task can be found in the Group Policy Management Console's Help file.

1.  Create a GPO in the Group Policy Objects container of the GPMC in the production domain. Do not link it to a site, domain, or OU quite yet.

2.  Back up the settings of the GPO that was proven successful in the lab environment. Import those settings to the new GPO in the production domain.

3.  Create a global security group with which to scope the pilot of the GPO. Name the group according to your naming conventions—GPO_New Settings_Pilot, for example. Do not add members to the group yet.

4.  Filter the scope of the pilot GPO so that it is filtered to apply only to the pilot group. Remove Authenticated Users, and add the pilot group.

5.  Link the pilot GPO to the domain or to a site or OU that includes all objects that are part of the pilot group. The GPO should not actually affect any user or computer because the pilot group with which the GPO is filtered contains no members.

6.  Perform resultant set of policy (RSoP) modeling analysis using the GPMC. Evaluate the impact on potential members of the pilot by simulating the addition of those objects to the pilot group within the Group Policy Modeling Wizard, as shown in Figure 10-10.

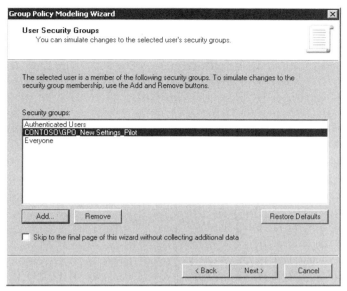

**Figure 10-10**    Simulating membership in the pilot group with the Group Policy Modeling Wizard

7. Evaluate conflicts with other GPOs.

8. Identify users that will be affected by the GPO, and determine communications and training messages that are required to help users recognize, understand, plan for, and work with the change.

## Create a rollback mechanism

You are just about ready to launch the pilot by linking the GPO to a site, domain, or OU. But before you do, consider the settings in the GPO. Many GPO settings are *managed*—that is, the setting applies if the computer or user is within the scope of the GPO, and if the computer or user is removed from the scope of the GPO, the setting automatically reverts to its previous managed or default state. Some GPO settings, however, are not managed. This means that when a computer or user is within the scope of the GPO, the change is made, but if the object is no longer within the scope of the GPO, the change remains. The effect of the change is somewhat permanent—it is often referred to as "tattooing" the change. The change must be reverted somehow, with a manual tweak to the system or with a new GPO that implements the reverse setting of the original GPO.

If the change you are piloting implements unmanaged settings, you must proactively prepare to revert the settings in the event that the change fails. I recommend that you create a GPO to counter the effects of your change so that a user or computer for whom an unmanaged change causes unintended effects can be removed from the scope of the change and added to the scope of the GPO that resets the change. I call this second GPO the *reset GPO*.

**Best Practices** When piloting a GPO that implements unmanaged changes, proactively prepare a *reset GPO* that reverts those changes to the desired state in the event that the changes cause unintended side effects.

To create a rollback mechanism, follow these steps:

1. If the GPO contains settings that are not managed policy settings—for example, if the GPO implements registry changes outside of the Policies key—create a GPO that contains settings to revert those settings back to the desired state. I will call this the *reset GPO*.

2. Create a global security group with which to scope the reset GPO. I call this the *reset group*. Name the group according to your naming conventions—GPO_New Settings Policy_Reset, for example. No users or computers should be added to this group at this point.

3. Filter the scope of the reset GPO so that it is filtered to apply only to the reset group. Remove Authenticated Users, and add the reset group.

4. Link the reset GPO to the domain or to a site or OU that includes all objects that are part of the pilot group. The reset GPO should not actually affect any user or computer because the reset group with which the GPO is filtered contains no members.

## Implement the pilot test

Now you are ready to roll out the pilot GPO. Complete these procedures:

1. Add representative computers or users, as required by the settings in the GPO, to the pilot group.

2. Optionally, force Group Policy refresh on the computers that belong to the pilot group.

3. Monitor for success or problematic behavior.

4. Analyze RSoP using the Group Policy Results functionality in the GPMC.

5. To remove the changes of the pilot GPO or to revert to desired settings in the event of unintended effects, remove the object from the pilot group, and, if necessary, add it to the reset group.

These procedures should allow you to confidently conduct a test of a new GPO.

## Migrate objects to the scope of the new GPO

There are two approaches to methodical migration of objects to the scope of the new GPO. The first is to establish a security group to which the GPO is filtered to apply, and then slowly add objects to that group. This method was described in Solution 10-2.

The second approach is to create a security group to which the GPO is denied, add all objects to that group, and then scope the GPO to apply to Authenticated Users. The result will be that the GPO applies to no user or computer because all objects are in the exemption group. You can then slowly remove objects from the exemption group, at which point the GPO will apply to those objects. Over time, you can remove all members from the exemption group and, optionally, delete the exemption group altogether. This approach was detailed in Solution 10-5.

## Solution summary

This solution leveraged many of the scoping and management techniques introduced earlier in the Solution Collection to create an effective framework for piloting, evaluating, and deploying a change with Group Policy.

# 10-8: No-Brainer Group Policy Tips

## Solution overview

| | |
|---|---|
| **Type of solution** | Tips and pointers |
| **Features and tools** | GPUpdate, SpecOps Gpupdate, WMI Remoting, administrative templates, policy preferences, WMI filters |
| **Solution summary** | There is so much more to say about using Group Policy in an enterprise—this solution provides some pointers toward your next steps. |
| **Benefits** | Use Group Policy to add value, increase security, improve manageability, and reduce support costs. |

## Introduction

As we wrap up this Solution Collection and this resource kit, I'd like to leave you with some pointers to additional Group Policy solutions that, if we had an entire book, I would love to detail for you. Use this laundry list as inspiration and guidance to your research and evaluation of next steps with Group Policy. Use the books and Web sites mentioned in the introduction to the Solution Collection for more details. Go forth and conquer, with Group Policy!

## Deploy registry changes with templates or registry preferences

A quick note about registry changes is warranted. Until recently, the best way to manage registry changes in an enterprise was using administrative templates to extend the settings that can be deployed using Group Policy. Windows Vista and Windows Server 2008 improve administrative templates, with the new XML-based, language-neutral ADMX and ADML templates. Using Windows Vista (or Windows Server 2008) to manage Group Policy also opens up the possibility of centralizing the management of templates themselves with the Central Store. See *http://www.gpoguy.com/cssu.htm* for information about the Central Store and a tool to create it.

But with the introduction of Group Policy preferences, and its registry client-side extension, the whole story changes. I believe that the preferences registry extension will make ADM, ADMX, and ADML files "old school," though ADML files are only a year old! Keep this in mind as you evaluate registry-based changes in your environment—you'll probably be better served using the new preferences functionality.

## Use loopback policy processing in merge mode

This is a recommendation that I need to squeeze in, but it's important that you research the functionality and internals of loopback Group Policy processing. There are scenarios in which you will want to apply policy settings in the User Configuration half of a GPO based on the computer to which a user is logging on. In Solution Collection 3, "Managing User Data and Settings," I specifically called out using a loopback-based GPO, scoped to laptop computers, to enable the automatic caching of redirected folders, which is a user-side policy setting. This is but one very big example.

A lot of documentation and guidance out there suggests that loopback processing should be avoided. It shouldn't be avoided. It is just one more way to scope policy settings. If you are well versed in how loopback processing works, you can leverage it as a very powerful scoping mechanism, along with the other scoping mechanisms at your disposal. In the end, it's only a question of whether the GPOs scoped to a computer or user effectively apply the settings you want applied. The key is to use loopback processing in merge mode so that you aren't replacing all user policy settings, just enhancing or modifying settings based on a computer's role. Loopback processing in replace mode is typically used only for terminal servers, kiosks, public-facing computers in conference and training rooms, and similar environments that demand more standardized user configuration. The bottom line is that there is *nothing* wrong with using loopback processing if it's used thoughtfully.

## Run GPUpdate on a remote system to push changes

You've created a new GPO or modified settings on an existing GPO, and you need to push the changes to one or more systems. How do you do it? There are several approaches.

First, you can use the script shown next, which uses WMI Remoting to run the GPUpdate command on the specified computer. Modify the switches on the GPUpdate command to meet your needs—the switches shown will do a full application of GPOs, including a logoff or reboot if required.

```
WMI Remoting of GPUpdate
strComputer = "DESKTOP101"
Set objWMIService = GetObject _
    ("winmgmts:\\" & strComputer & "\root\cimv2:Win32_Process")
errReturn = objWMIService.Create _
    ("cmd.exe /c gpupdate /force /logoff /boot", Null, Null, intProcessID)
```

Second, you can use PSExec, which can be downloaded from *http://technet.microsoft.com/ sysinternals*, using the following command syntax:

```
psexec \\computername gpupdate /force /logoff /boot
```

Third, you can download the remote Group Policy refresh tool from *http://www.gpoguy.com/ rgprefresh.htm*.

Fourth, and my personal favorite, is Specops GPUpdate, which not only updates one or more remote systems, but provides a graphical audit of the update success. You can get it at *http:// www.specopssoft.com/products/specopsgpupdate*.

# Delegate permissions to perform RSoP reporting

Use the Delegation Of Control Wizard to give your support team permissions to Generate Resultant Set of Policy (Logging) for users and client computers. RSoP is an important piece of troubleshooting a Windows environment—it needs to be in the hands of your support team.

# Scope network-related settings using sites or shadow groups

Some settings relate to network services. For example, you can configure Internet Explorer's proxy server address or the Domain Name System (DNS) suffix search order; or you can point a client to its most proximal Windows Server Update Services (WSUS) server for updates. These settings should be scoped to systems in specific parts of your network, usually based on topology. Link such GPOs to sites, or create a shadow group (as discussed in Solution 8-5) that contains objects from a location and scope the GPO using the shadow group.

# Avoid WMI filters and targeting when possible: Use shadow groups instead

There is one other scoping mechanism that we didn't have space to detail in this Solution Collection—WMI filters. WMI filters allow you to specify the objects to which a GPO applies by using WMI to query for system characteristics, such as amount of memory, free disk space, processor type, operating system version, or IP address. The problem is that WMI queries are expensive from a processing perspective, so you should use them only when the characteristic in question will change regularly. When a characteristic is likely to remain relatively static— such as the operating system version, the amount of memory, or the fact that a system is a desktop or a laptop, create a shadow group as described in Solution 8-5 and in Solution 6-4 on page 442. Populate the shadow group with systems matching that characteristic.

You could even use a self-reporting framework, such as that detailed in Solution 6-8 on page 468. With this approach, a temporary GPO is put in place with the desired WMI query, the GPO causes a startup script to run, and the startup script places the computer in a shadow group. After all computers have reported in, the WMI filter can be removed and the shadow group can be used to scope the GPO.

The bottom line here is that WMI queries are expensive. The same goes for the new WMI-based Targeting functionality of Group Policy preferences. There are a number of creative and effective ways to achieve system characteristic-based policy application using security group filtering. When you can find an alternative to a WMI query or preference target, use that alternative.

## No-brainer Group Policy settings

Clients commonly ask me, "What settings should we apply using Group Policy?" Of course, the real answer is, "It depends." However, I'd like to point you toward a couple of settings—settings that I believe are almost universally applicable. I don't have room to go into the details of each, so use this as a guide to some next-step research on your part:

- Always Wait For Network At Startup And Logon must be enabled and scoped to all Windows XP and Windows Vista clients. Without this setting, Windows XP and Windows Vista clients perform only background refreshes, meaning that a client might start up and a user might log on without receiving the latest policies from the domain. Trust me—you want this setting! Without it, your policy application is not fully managed. But feel free to see the information in Derek Melber's and Jeremy Moskowitz's books for more details.

- Policy processing. By default, most client-side extensions (CSEs) apply policy settings in a GPO only if the GPO is updated. Consider the result: You implement a change through Group Policy, the change is applied, the user modifies the configuration directly, and your setting is never reapplied. For this reason, many organizations choose to modify the policy processing behavior of CSEs so that all policy settings are reapplied at each background refresh. The settings that manage policy processing are found in Computer Configuration\ Policies\Administrative Templates\System\Group Policy. Again, refer to Derek's and Jeremy's books for details.

- Restricted groups policies. Found in the Computer Configuration \ Policies\ Windows Settings \ Security Settings folder, restricted groups policies allow you to manage the membership of local groups. Here are a few suggestions:

  - Use the Members version of the policy to ensure that Backup Operators, Account Operators, and Power Users groups are empty.

  - Use the Member Of version of the policy to add support groups to the local Administrators groups of desktops and laptops. In case you missed the change introduced with Windows XP, the Member Of version of Restricted Groups policy is nondestructive—that is, it adds the policy-specified group as a member of the target group without removing other members. Create a policy specifying the Active Directory group containing your support team—SYS_Clients_Local Admins, for example—and configure the policy to make it a member of Administrators. Scope the policy to client computer objects.

- Printer deployment policies. Starting with Windows Server 2003 SP2 and continuing with Windows Server 2008, you can deploy printers to either computers or users with Group Policy. No brainer!

- Windows Firewall management. Be sure to configure which ports need to be open to enable remote administration in your enterprise. You can open ports 135 (RPC) and 445 (SMB) using the Windows Firewall policy Allow Inbound Remote Administration Exception, which is found in Computer Configuration \ Administrative Templates \ Network \ Network Connections \ Windows Firewall \ Domain profile. Or you can configure inbound rules in the Windows Firewall with Advanced Security—there is a predefined rule called Remote Administration.

- Remote Assistance policies. Allow your support team to offer remote assistance to users and to use Windows' excellent Remote Assistance functionality.

- Script deployment. Use startup, logon, and perhaps even logoff and shutdown scripts deployed with and scoped by GPOs.

- Microsoft Office administrative template settings. The administrative templates for Office 2003 and Office 2007 can be downloaded from the Microsoft Web site. They provide the ability to manage settings that are both corporate-security related and productivity related. Be sure to integrate them into your environment if you use any Office applications.

- Disallow Fast Saves. This specific PowerPoint setting, configurable using the aforementioned Office templates, should be implemented for each version of PowerPoint in your enterprise. The unfortunate (enabled) default configuration of Fast Saves in PowerPoint results in tremendous file-size bloat and streams within the PPT file that might contain sensitive information, unbeknownst to the user. This is absolutely a no-brainer. You *must* apply this setting if you use PowerPoint and have any concern about information security.

- Folder redirection and roaming profile policy settings, as discussed in Solution Collection 3.

Group Policy preferences. New to Windows Server 2008, and downloadable for Windows XP Service Pack 3 (SP3) and Windows Vista SP1, preferences open up a treasure trove of configuration management, including drive mapping, copying files and folders, creating shortcuts, configuring Control Panel options, managing registry changes, and making tweaks to applications. The list goes on: power options, file associations, shared folders, scheduled tasks, virtual private network (VPN) and dial-up networking (DUN) connections, and hardware device disabling. And all of these preferences can be targeted with an incredible level of granularity based on an equally incredible number of criteria. Keep your eyes out for more information about Group Policy preferences coming from me and the Group Policy MVPs.

# Index

# What do you think of this book?

# We want to hear from you!

Do you have a few minutes to participate in a brief online survey?

Microsoft is interested in hearing your feedback so we can continually improve our books and learning resources for you.

To participate in our survey, please visit:

www.microsoft.com/learning/booksurvey/

...and enter this book's ISBN-10 or ISBN-13 number (located above barcode on back cover*).

As a thank-you to survey participants in the United States and Canada, each month we'll randomly select five respondents to win one of five $100 gift certificates from a leading online merchant. At the conclusion of the survey, you can enter the drawing by providing your e-mail address, which will be used for prize notification only.

Thanks in advance for your input. Your opinion counts!

\* Where to find the ISBN on back cover

ISBN-13: 000-0-0000-0000-0
ISBN-10: 0-0000-0000-0

**Example only. Each book has unique ISBN.**

No purchase necessary. Void where prohibited. Open only to residents of the 50 United States (includes District of Columbia) and Canada (void in Quebec). For official rules and entry dates see:

www.microsoft.com/learning/booksurvey/